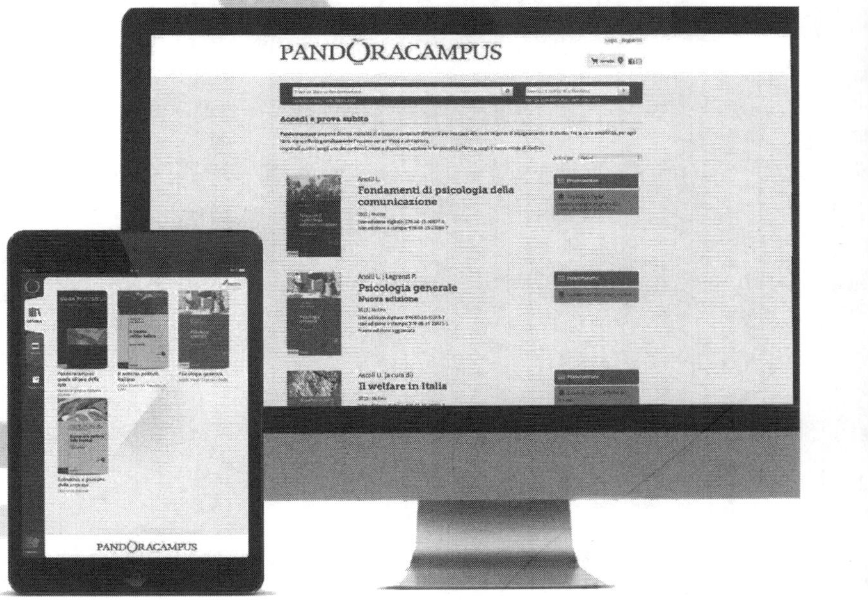
PANDORACAMPUS
Accedi e prova subito
Fondamenti di psicologia della comunicazione
Psicologia generale
Nuova edizione
Il welfare in Italia
PANDORACAMPUS

www.pandoracampus.it

> Per chi studia:

- tutto il testo e molto di più, su web e su tablet, pensato per garantire un'alta leggibilità anche agli studenti con DSA (in particolare, dislessia);
- materiali per approfondire e verificare l'apprendimento;
- contenuti attivi come link, glossari e flashcard, video, cronologie, mappe e grafici con i quali interagire;
- la possibilità di evidenziare, prendere appunti e fare ricerche;

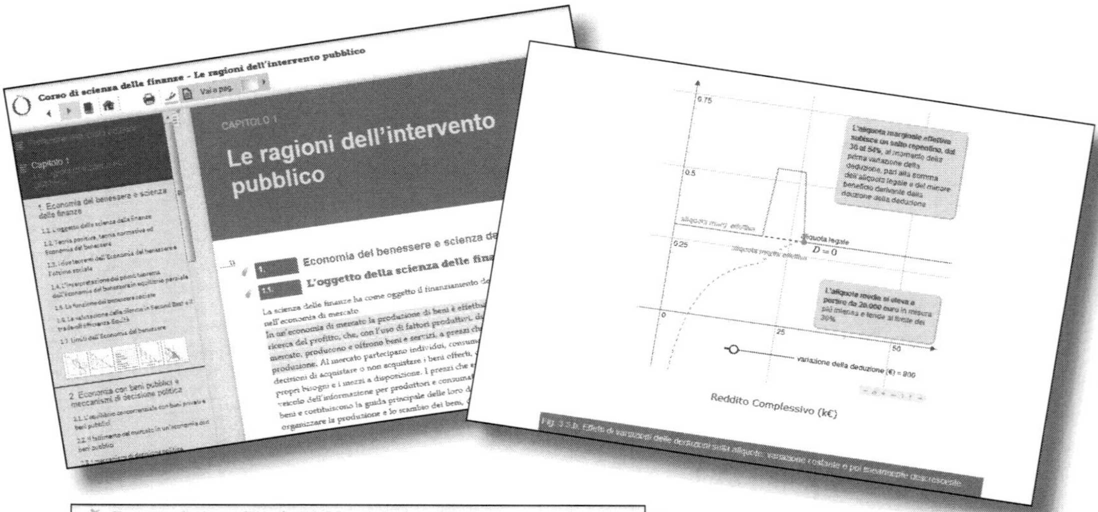

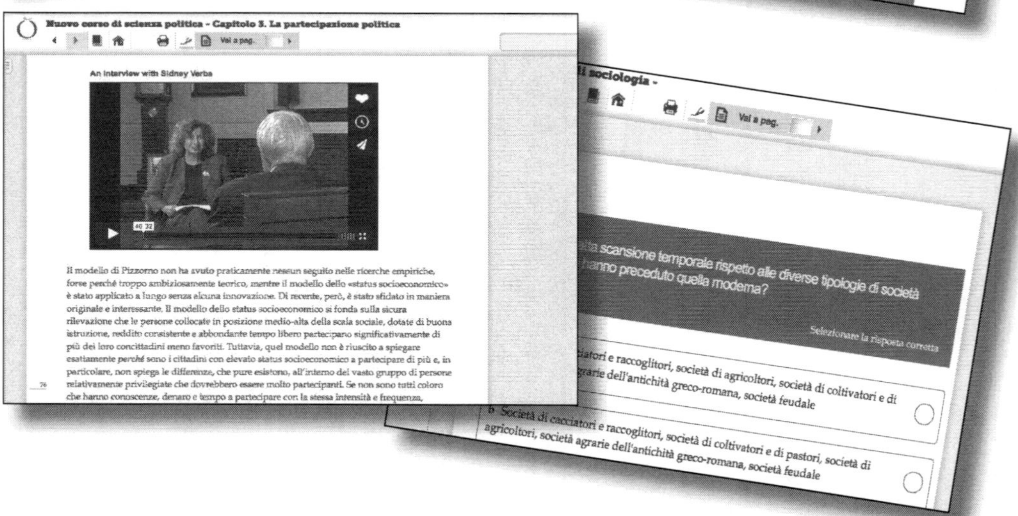

www.pandoracampus.it

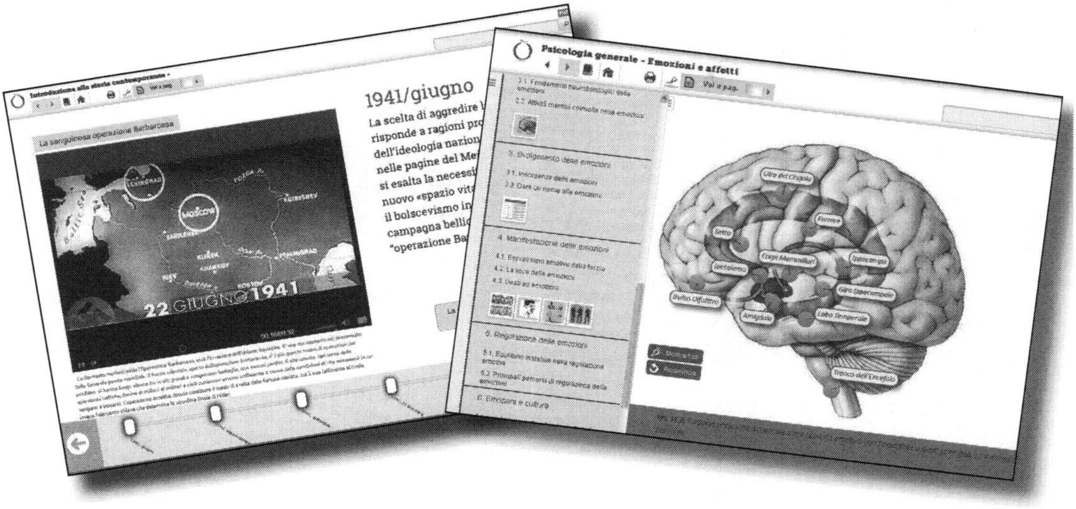

- la possibilità di confrontarsi e interagire con chi sta studiando lo stesso manuale e, quando disponibile, con un tutor a cui fare domande;
- strumenti di organizzazione dello studio per programmare l'esame e creare un calendario con gli obiettivi da raggiungere.

www.pandoracampus.it

> Per chi insegna:

- un'opzione in più da offrire agli studenti, con formule di accesso innovative e convenienti;
- materiali elaborati appositamente per la didattica;
- l'opportunità di personalizzare le proprie scelte attraverso la creazione di coursepack.

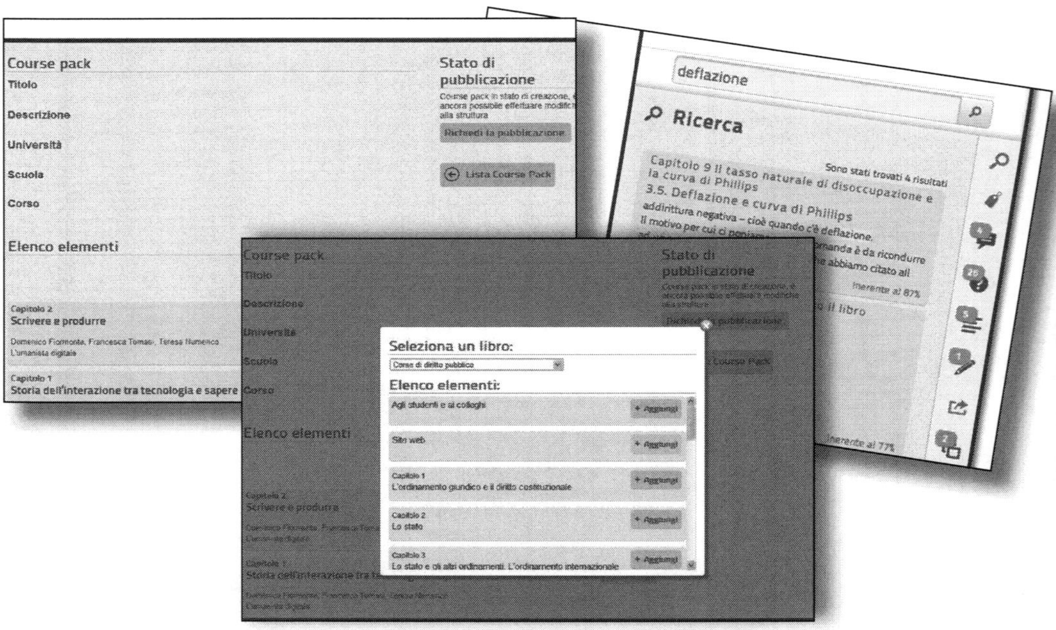

MANUALI

Law

PIETRO SIRENA

Introduction to Private Law

Third Edition

il Mulino

ISBN 978-88-15-29018-2

Copy-editing and book production: Edimill srl - www.edimill.it

Table of contents

Foreword

This book draws on my experience of teaching at Bocconi University, where I have been responsible for the course titled *Introduction to the Legal System I* (ILS) over the last two academic years.

When I moved to Bocconi in 2016, this course represented a major challenge for me for several reasons. First, it is a course of law that is taught not in a school of law, but in a school of economics. Secondly, it is addressed to Italian and foreign students on the same footing, and therefore it does not deal with Italian law as such. Even though I was not unaware of some of the unique aspects of Bocconi's international BSc programs (ie the strong interdisciplinary approach and a high level of internationalization), I must confess that I felt somewhat puzzled and unprepared to hold such classes. After all, I had until then been teaching (Italian) law to MA students in law. At Bocconi, I was asked to teach a law that was not Italian (nor of any other national jurisdiction) and to teach it to students who were not necessarily Italian and, furthermore, who were not engaged in legal studies as such. However passionate about investigating comparative law and committed to furthering the development of European law, I was undeniably used to a formalistic and nationalistic approach to (Italian) law, one centered on the exegesis of the legislature, starting with the provisions of the Italian Civil Code. I had no idea of how to set out a course of law, namely of private law, that deviated from such features, also because I could not find a suitable textbook for me and my students.

Luckily enough, I could count on some younger colleagues who, although based at other universities, were ready to support me as instructors for the six offerings of this course at Bocconi. To two of them, namely Francesco Mezzanotte and Francesco Paolo Patti, I am particularly grateful: had they not worked so hard on preparing classes, I would have been unable to carry out the task I was entrusted with. They did most of the job, I dare say, and they did so with an enthusiasm that was addictive to me. Even more importantly, they – as well as Davide Achille – allowed me to enjoy their friendship during one of the most pleasurable periods of my academic life.

Paradoxically, however, this book does not reflect or account for the ILS course as such, which mostly deals with the law of contract, of tort, and of property. After two years of teaching at Bocconi, I realized that I was not able to write a book that contains or accounts for the course I have now grown accustomed to holding. I also realized that, although possible, such a book would not serve the intended purpose of effective teaching. In fact, I understand now that a course of lectures is something less and, at the same time, something more than explaining the contents of a textbook. It is so because the scheduled hours are always fewer than what they should be, but also, and more importantly, because they are only a portion of the job, both for the teacher and for her students. Classes must be prepared, and they require considerable work before holding them, and also afterwards. The teacher must cast the overall syllabus, select and organize the topics of each class, prepare the reading list, and make the materials available in advance. Students are required to read the relevant materials beforehand and prepare for each class, engage themselves in working with their teacher and, afterwards, revise their notes and make them consistent and useful. It is a huge job requiring an incredible amount of energy and strength! And no textbook can do it in place of the teacher and her students!

Classes are effective and fruitful only if both the teacher and her students are ready to work together on the topics dealt with and to discuss them. A textbook may be of help, but only if it is used as a point both of departure and of reference; conversely, a textbook may endanger the success of classes insofar as the teacher and her students stick to it as if it were the very subject of the course.

On a different note, I am strongly convinced that studying law means, first of all, attaining a certain degree of familiarity with its long history and its cultural complexity. Law is as old as mankind, and it stands as one of the most intriguing and fascinating phenomena of human culture. It collects hopes and fears, standing as an endeavor to improve the happiness of society and to control and submit its members. Some of the most brilliant minds in history have devoted their best energies to law because they sensed it was the right way to set out a better future for society as a whole. I believe that all this cannot be ignored by students of law, even where enrolled in a different program.

For this reason, I have always feared that teaching the subjects of contract, tort, and property to my students without introducing them to the overall complexity of law could deprive them of much, if not its very essence. I desired to instruct them on each of those topics, but, at the same time, to make them also understand that, when talking of 'sham trusts' or of the difference between 'rights *in rem*' and '*in personam*', we were actually dealing with a long intellectual history, with battles between ideas, and with trains of thoughts that had been developing for many centuries and that had engaged philosophers, economists, and sociologists.

Therefore, this book does not mirror the course I teach at Bocconi, but it does serve as a prologue to it, one which was previously destined to remain silent. At the same time, I hope that this will be of use and interest not only in introducing the study of private law, but also in complementing it, so that students can perceive the cultural complexity of each issue addressed and of each legal institution dealt with.

The chapters of this book were revised and re-organized by some younger colleagues at Bocconi and by some instructors of the last ILS course, namely Davide Achille, Francesca Bartolini, Fabio Saguato, Francesco Mezzanotte, and Francesco Paolo Patti, under the coordination of the latter. They did much more than encouraging me along the way; they indeed improved the quality of my work.

Furthermore, an amazing enterprise of proofreading was organized by Luigi Buonanno. It was carried out by him and by Giacomo Delinavelli, Andrea Maria Garofalo, Cinzia Marseglia, Valentina Ricci, Enrico Maria Scavone, Elisa Valletta, and Antonio Vercellone.

The quality of English in the work was checked and decidedly improved by Fabio Saguato and Peter Liebenberg.

My gratitude towards all of these individuals is great. Errors and mistakes remain mine.

Last but not least, this book is dedicated to my wife Mirzia and to my daughter Caterina, who supported me with their immense love. I owe the best of my life to them.

Milano-Roma, 13 January 2019
Pietro Sirena

Foreword to the Second Edition

Despite the resoluteness of my intentions after the first edition of this book, I failed to attend to an overall revision of it due to a number of events that occurred in the meanwhile and that have produced a major impact on my academic life. Among them, the two that proved most demanding – and most rewarding – have been my appointment as Dean of Bocconi School of Law in November 2018 and, more recently, my election as member of the Executive Committee of the European Law Institute.

For the same reasons, I have been compelled by constraints of time and, I have to admit, of energy to stop lecturing the courses of *Introduction to the Legal Systems I*, and this most unpleasant fact has deprived me of the opportunity to challenge the book in class and to understand effectively what of it was to be amended, and how. To be sure, I had the sense of some of the deficiencies and flaws with which it was tainted – eg excesses of erudition that burdened several pages (to make no mention of errors and mistakes that mushroomed here and there). Yet an overhaul of the nature that I had envisaged embarking on would have been possible only if I had been able to assess personally its impact on students and to let them 'take the lead' in the second edition.

Nonetheless, I could at least count on the feedback from the instructors of the six ILS classes, namely (in alphabetical order): Francesca Bartolini, Francesco Mezzanotte, Federico Mottola Lucano, Francesco Paolo Patti, and Fabio Saguato. They gave me a number of suggestions as to what should be done to make the book better, though I have been able to accomplish only few of their desiderata.

The major novelties of this second edition are twofold.

First, a new chapter, ie the twelfth, has been added on legal subjects. It is a topic that is traditionally dealt with in the 'general part' of private law, and it is necessary that the book cover it as well.

Secondly, the chapter on European law, ie the eight, has been reorganized and considerably extended, this being attributable to the relevance of the matter, particularly at Bocconi School of Law.

All the other chapters have been generally revised and, sometimes, partially re-written.

I owe my gratitude to Luigi Buonanno and Francesco Paolo Patti, who contributed generously to all the above-mentioned changes of the text, and to Marco Ventoruzzo, who, notwithstanding his commitments as Head of the Department of Legal Studies 'Angelo Sraffa' at Bocconi University, found time to review my coverage of company law and offer valuable suggestions for its improvement.

A great job was done by Michael Friedman and Jocasta Godlieb, who provided a thorough linguistic revision of the text.

The dedication of the book to my wife Mirzia and to my daughter Caterina remains untouched, as does our mutual love.

Milano-Roma, 7 January 2020
Pietro Sirena

Foreword to the Third Edition

The major novelty of this third edition consists in the elimination of the former Chapter 9, 'Legal concepts and legal studies', whose content was, however, not deleted but incorporated into Chapter 7, 'Private law and its sources'. In fact, I came to the conclusion that legal scholarship and education cannot be addressed separately from the sources of private law, in which they are so deeply entrenched. If one dares to embrace realism entirely, scholarship is actually the main source of private law.

Moreover, Chapter 10, 'Rights and duties', was completely rewritten, as were a number of paragraphs in Chapters 4, 7, 8, and 11. In doing so, I was guided by Simon Whittaker (St John's College, Oxford) into the intricacies of the law 'retained' by the UK after withdrawing from the EU: without his patience and thoroughness I would have surely got lost into such a labyrinth.

Also at this juncture, Luigi Buonanno was at my side and attended generously to editing the text and proofreading. His patience was surpassed only by his enthusiasm for the work we were conducting together.

I owe a debt of gratitude to the instructors of the course *Introduction to Private Law*, headed by Francesco Paolo Patti, and namely to Francesca Bartolini, Domenico Di Micco, Fabio Saguato, Andrea Garofalo, Francesco Mezzanotte, and Federico Mottola Lucano, as well as to Davide Achille and Antonia von Appen.

Since this very academic year, Gabriele Gagliani and Hao Jiang have joined me in the teaching of *Comparative Private Law* at Bocconi University, where they instruct with this book. Their suggestions were of great avail.

The linguistic revision of the text was carefully provided by Michael Friedman.

This new edition was written during the last weeks of life of my mentor, Prof. Cesare Massimo Bianca, who introduced me into academic life and a university career. The more time passes, the more I understand that, despite all appearances, all that I have undertaken has aimed to follow his example, which remains unparalleled.

The dedication to Mirzia and Caterina is wholeheartedly renewed.

Milano-Roma, 7 January 2021 Pietro Sirena

List of abbreviations

§/§§	Article/-s of German Civil Code
ABGB	*Allgemeines Bürgerliches Gesetzbuch*
AcP	*Archiv für die civilistische Praxis*
ACQP	*Acquis* Principles
AI(s)	Artificial Intelligence(s)
ALI	American Law Institute
Am Jur 2d	*American Jurisprudence 2nd*
BA	Bachelor of Arts – Baccalaureus artium
BGB	*Bürgerliches Gesetzbuch*
BGH	*Bundesgerichtshof*
BVerfGE	*Entscheidungen des Bundesverfassungsgerichts*
cc	*Codice civile*
CESL	Common European Sales Law
CFR	Charter of Fundamental Rights of the European Union
CISG	United Nations Convention on Contracts for the International Sale of Goods
CJS	*Corpus Juris Secundum*
DB	*Der Betrieb*
DCFR	Draft Common Frame of Reference
EC	European Community
ECHR	European Convention on Human Rights
ECJ	European Court of Justice
ECSC	European Coal and Steel Community
ECtHR	European Court of Human Rights
EEC	European Economic Community
ELI	European Law Institute
EMU	Economic and Monetary Union
ERCL	European Review of Contract Law
ERPL	European Review of Private Law
EU	European Union

EURATOM	European Atomic Energy Community
FS	*Festschrift*
GG	*Grundgesetz*
HGB	*Handelsgesetzbuch*
IoT	Internet of things
IP	Intellectual property
JZ	*Juristenzeitung*
MA	Master of Arts
NGCC	*La nuova giurisprudenza civile commentata*
NJW	*Neue Juristische Wochenschrift*
OR	*Obligationenrecht*
PECL	Principles of European Contract Law
PETL	Principles of European Tort Law
PECL	Principles of European Contract Law
PICC	Principles of International Commercial Contract
PIL	Private International Law
RabelsZ	*Rabels Zeitschrift für ausländisches und internationales Privatrecht*
Riv dir civ	*Rivista di diritto civile*
Riv dir comm	*Rivista del diritto commerciale e del diritto generale delle obbligazioni*
Riv trim dir proc civ	*Rivista trimestrale di diritto e procedura civile*
Rn	*Randnummer*
Rome I Regulation	Regulation (EC) 593/2008 of the European Parliament and of the Council of 17 June 2008 on the law applicable to contractual obligations (Rome I) [2008] OJ L 177/6
Rome II Regulation	Regulation (EC) 864/2007 of the European Parliament and of the Council of 11 July 2007 on the law applicable to non-contractual obligations (Rome II) [2007] OJ L199/40
Rome III Regulation	Council Regulation (EU) No 1259/2010 of 20 December 2010 implementing enhanced cooperation in the area of the law applicable to divorce and legal separation [2010] OJ L34
SEA	Single European Act
TEU	Treaty on European Union
TFEU	Treaty on the Functioning of the European Union
UCPD	Unfair Commercial Practices Directive
UK	United Kingdom
UKSC	United Kingdom Supreme Court
UNCITRAL	United Nations Commission on International Trade Law
UNIDROIT	International Institute for the Unification of Private Law
US	United States of America
v	versus
ZeuP	*Zeitschrift für Europäisches Privatrecht*
ZGB	*Zivilgesetzbuch*

CHAPTER 1

Law and society

- **The functions of law**
- **The law of Western society and of surviving societies**
- **Law and religion**
- **Law and technology**
- **Law and language**
- **Animal law**

Law binds a society's members with the prime purpose of solving their conflicts and, secondarily, of promoting their mutual cooperation. A lawless society could not exist and, conversely, law would be devoid of any real sense outside social intercourse. Since the Enlightenment of the late eighteenth century, law has been increasingly replacing religion as a technique deployed by society to control individuals' behavior. To date, however , law seems to be about to be supplanted by technology, which is credited with being able to carry out similar tasks with lower costs and higher efficiency (code is law).
Law does not require a state or any other kind of centralized authority to develop and carry out its social functions. Therefore, 'primitive' communities, which do not feature those characteristics, are not devoid of law.
Law does not need language to develop and carry out its social functions, although it tends to be spoken and, furthermore, reduced to writing.
It is contested whether some animals live under rules that are comparable to human law.

1. THE FUNCTIONS OF LAW

Law exists because and insofar as a society does. This assumption is embodied in the traditional maxim *ubi societas, ibi* (*et*) *ius*, which means that any society is grounded on and underpinned by law (**no society without law**). In fact, the assembly of individuals in a society requires the establishment of a certain degree of self-organization, which is provided by law.

The philosophical doctrine advocated by thinkers of early modernity, starting with Thomas Hobbes (1588-1679), traces society's origin back to the exit of mankind from a 'state of nature', which was characterized by the 'war of all against all'.[1] The negotiation of a **social contract** would have marked the foundation of society, where men agreed to exchange a certain degree of their own freedom for the advantages of mutual cooperation. The very source of law was thus to be identified in the constitutional act of society itself, which implied allegiance of every citizen to the order thus established and to the authority necessary to maintain it.

If society necessarily requires a law, it also holds good that, conversely, law outside a society would constitute a mere abstraction, which were devoid of any concrete sense (**no law without society**). Robinson Crusoe, being cast-away on a desert island, might not be said to abide (or not) by law, nor to be entitled with any right whatsoever. Any possible domain of law commences when there is a mutual relation between individuals, who come together in a group. A sole individual who find herself alone and segregated from the rest of mankind would live beyond any possible law.

The reasons why law exists are therefore to be identified in its social functions.[2] First, law serves the purpose to prevent and, as the case may be, to solve conflicts among the members of a group, which are inevitably raised either by the scarcity of resources or by different views on the common good. Insofar, law is aimed at impeding the disruption of society (**negative function of law**). Secondly, law provides guidelines of behaviors deemed to be beneficial to the survival or rise of a group, thus fostering and strengthening cooperation among its members. Insofar, law is aimed at enhancing the unity of society (**positive function of law**).

Georges Gurvitch (1894-1965) drew a distinction between 'individual law' and 'social law',[3] which would correspond to different forms of sociality. 'Individual law', particularly, would be moulded on sociality by interdependence and based on distrust, whilst 'social law' would be moulded on sociality by interpenetration and based on confidence. Therefore, a law of war, conflicts, and separation would be opposed to a law of peace, mutual aid, and common tasks.

[1] In his masterpiece *Leviathan* (1651), he described the primitive state of nature of mankind as a 'warre of every one against every one': see Thomas Hobbes, *Leviathan or the Matter, Form, & Power of a Common-Wealth Ecclesiasticall and Civill* (first published 1651, John CA Gaskin ed, OUP 2008) 475. This concept is currently also known in the Latin phrase of '*bellum omnium contra omnes*', which Hobbes formulated in his previous work *De Cive* (1642). See Thomas Hobbes, *De Cive. The Latin Version* (Howard Warrender ed, Clarendon Press 1984) 148, and Id, *De Cive. The English Version* (Howard Warrender ed, Clarendon Press 1984) 148.

[2] Manfred Rehbinder, *Rechtssoziologie* (8th edn, CH Beck 2014) Rn 96-110.

[3] Georges Gurvitch, *Sociology of Law* (Kegan Paul, Trench, Trubner & Co 1947) 166ff.

Social conflicts addressed by law consist firstly in disputes, which, when arising with regard to goods claimed by many an individual, potentially engender a winner and a looser. Mechanisms devised by law in order to **settle disputes** may be constituted by mechanical procedures (eg by taking of oaths, or by ordeal, or by combat)[4] or by human decisions. When such mechanisms grow significantly over time, however, their overall output tends to be rationalized in a set of precepts or tenets, which serves to make the settlement of future disputes predictable and consistent with the previous ones. Law may thus solve not only concrete (individual) conflicts but also abstract (general) ones, thus contributing to **framework society as a whole**.

Max Weber (1864-1920) depicted the historical development of the inner rationalization of law (*Rationalisierung des Rechts*) as based on two processes: generalization (*Verallgemeinerung*) and, in a later stage, systematization (*Systematisierung*) of legal concepts. He furthermore clarified that these two processes are not only separate (generalization would not necessarily produce systematization), but they may prove even incompatible (generalization would be compatible with a substantive legal rationality, whilst systematization would impose a formal legal rationality).[5]

A **lawless society** is not actually conceivable and, even if it were, it would hardly stand as a better alternative to the loneliness of individuals acting on their own. As a matter of fact, it would be quickly upset and ruined because of the conflicts arising from the natural instincts and selfishness of its members. At best, it would be doomed to a low degree of development, due to the lack of cooperation among its members and guidance for their behavior.

A lawless society seems to have been envisaged by Karl Marx (1818-1883) and Friedrich Engels (1820-1895) in the aftermath of the revolution of the proletariat, when the overcoming of class struggles would lead people to live together in a spontaneous state of harmony and peace. This utopian vision relies upon the premise that law, as well as morality and religion, would consist in 'bourgeois prejudices, behind which lurk in ambush just as many bourgeois interests'.

2. LAW AND RELIGION

Insofar as law is purported to avert the disintegration of a society and to neutralize its inner centrifugal forces, law exhibits remarkable commonalities

[4] James Gordley, *The Jurists. A Critical History* (OUP 2013) 3.

[5] Max Weber, *On Law in Economy and Society* (first published 1921-1922, Harvard UP 1954). Weber's work was edited and translated into English by Max Rheinstein (1899-1977), who as a student of law attended his classes in München (and during the 1930s had to flee to the United States because of his Jewish roots).

with religion. According to a famous dictum by Carl Schmitt (1888-1985), 'all significant concepts of the modern state are secularized theological concepts'.[6] Not surprisingly, therefore, it happens that law and religion are entrenched, or even largely overlaid, although their connection may tend to be lost or become obsolete over time. As pointed out prominently by H. Patrick Glenn (1940-2014), each legal tradition is founded upon a **substrate of religious nature**, which moulds the shared mentality of lawyers (and laymen) and the fundamental traits of law.[7] This religious substrate may endanger dialogue between legal traditions, let alone their integration.[8]

At the historical outset of law there is often the authority of religion, since it is a god that stipulates what is good and what is evil for the community and mandates its ministers to interpret and apply its own will. Therefore, religious authorities tend to bind the behavior of individuals and to scrutinize it.

Both law and religion may be therefore understood as **techniques of societal control**.

In the West, the Enlightenment of the late eighteenth century decidedly marked a pervasive **secularization** of society and the increasing replacement of religion with the state's legislature and judicature. Since then, religion has been increasingly confined to the private sphere of individuals and lost its grip on Western politics and social life.

> For example, one of the main novelties of private law during the French revolutionary period was that marriage was turned into a civil contract and thus removed from the jurisdiction of ecclesiastical tribunals. As a further consequence, divorce was legalized in 1792 (see *infra*, ch 4, para 3.1.1).

3. THE PROCESS OF JURIDIFICATION OF WESTERN SOCIETY

The replacement of religion's social authority with a state constitutionally based on the **rule of law** (***Rechtsstaat***) commenced a large process of juridification (*Verrechtlichung*) of Western societies, purported to prevent class

[6] 'All significant concepts of the modern theory of the state are secularized theological concepts not only because of their historical development in which they were transferred from theology to the theory of the state, whereby, for example, the omnipotent god became the omnipotent lawgiver but also because of their systematic structure, the recognition of which is necessary for a sociological consideration of these concepts. The exception in jurisprudence is analogous to the miracle in theology. Only by being aware of this analogy can we appreciate the manner in which the philosophical ideas of the state developed in the last centuries'. These observations were elaborated by Schmitt in the framework of an overall doctrine of 'political theology' ('*politische Theologie*') (see *infra*, ch 3, para 2), which drew on the ancient concept of '*theologia civilis*' ('civil theology') coined by the Roman sage Marcus Terentius Varro to legitimize the Emperor's worship. See Carl Schmitt, *Political Theology: Four Chapters on the Concept of Sovereignty* (first published 1922, George Schwab tr, Chicago UP 1985, repr 2005).

[7] H Patrick Glenn, 'Tradition in Religion and Law' (2009-2010) 25 Journal of Law and Religion 503.

[8] H Patrick Glenn, *Legal Traditions of the World: Sustainable Diversity in Law* (5th edn, OUP 2010).

struggle and to avoid political conflicts based on the selfish interests of single individuals or groups.

The concept of juridification (*Verrechtlichung*) was forged by Otto Kirchheimer (1905-1965) in the late 1920s, to depict the rise of labor law as a means to overcome the conflict of interests between entrepreneurs and workers.
A critical attitude against the overall process of juridification of society was afterwards developed by other followers of the 'Frankfurter School' of social theory and philosophy, and particularly by Jürgen Habermas, who advocated for the need of counteracting the juridification of society by improving democratic practice and citizens' participation in political debate.

This process favored the intervention of the state in areas of social life which had previously been left to the freedom of single individuals and groups, thus expanding the realm of societal control upon their behavior. According to Michel Foucault (1926-1984), law has thus normalized the style of living and enforced **social stereotypes**, particularly banning preferences not in line with the patterns authorized by the force of the majority.
It must nonetheless be remarked that law still had to compete with (religion and) **other systems of private ordering** to hold a grip on such societies, which therefore gained and maintained a considerable degree of pluralistic attitude, except for single periods of totalitarianism (during some developments of the French revolution, in Germany and Italy between the 1920s and the 1940s, and so on).

In his work *Droit flexible*, Jean Carbonnier (1908-2003) remarked that many contexts of human life are devoid of law and regulated instead by other systems (religion, friendship, technology, and so on). He depicted his theory as based on the ***hypothèse du non-droit***.[9]

4. LAW AND TECHNOLOGY

To date, a further technique of societal control is rapidly gaining dominance in societies worldwide, and it tends to replace both religion and law in this context, as well as different systems of private ordering. In fact, the development of predictive and communication technologies and the possibility of mining a huge amount of data and information scattered on the Internet about the behavior and the choices or preferences of each member of a society (**big data**) make it possible to control the life of its members in a pervasive way that was not previously experienced by mankind. The advent of **digital law** based on an information society is thus going to pose a dramatic challenge to the privacy protection of individuals and organizations, as well as to the principle of equal

[9] Jean Carbonnier, *Flexible droit. Pour une sociologie du droit sans rigueur* (10th edn, LGDJ 2014) 25.

treatment. Even more, any concept of law or approach to the enforcement of legal rules experimented with until now is becoming obsolete.[10]

Smart phones, laptops and communication devices are permanently connected to the Internet and, no less importantly, the same is occurring with domestic appliances, vehicles and the like (**Internet of things**).[11] As a consequence, a growing spectrum of daily behavior and personal choices is traceable, so that all information thus collected is recorded and oft traded.

The level of detail attained by this information potentially enables the replacement of the abstractness and generality of legal rules and standards with '**granular norms**',[12] ie personalized directives which are to be moulded on the track record of relevant information and continuously communicated to everyone (though one's vehicle, one's mobile phone, and so on).[13] For example, the maximum speed limit currently set for all drivers would be replaced by a targeted determination of the maximum of speed based on the personal skills and actual physical conditions of each driver, the weather forecasts for the date when the car will be driven, and so on. These assessments imply not only a large availability of personal information, but also a certain number of assumptions which may endanger the principle of non-discrimination, insofar as they embody social stereotypes and standardized patterns of behavior (Do women drive better or worse than men? Do elderly people drive better or worse than younger individuals?).

The track record and mining of personal information on a large scale may even become determinative in adjudicating cases involving civil or criminal lability. For instance, courts are beginning to use smart machines and artificial intelligence systems to evaluate the risks of recidivism, ie the likelihood of a suspect's reoffending (**predictive justice**).[14]

[10] Alberto De Franceschi (ed), *European Contract Law and the Digital Single Market. The Implications of the Digital Revolution* (Intersentia 2016); Stefan Grundmann (ed), *European Contract Law in the Digital Age* (Intersentia 2018); Alberto De Franceschi and Reiner Schulze (eds), *Digital Revolution – New Challenges for Law* (CH Beck-Nomos 2019); Nikita Aggarwal, Horst Eidenmüller, Luca Enriques, Jennifer Payne and Kristen van Zwieten (eds), *Autonomous Systems and the Law* (CH Beck-Nomos 2019).

[11] Francesco Mezzanotte, 'Risk Allocation and Liability Regimes in the IoT' in De Franceschi and Schulze (eds) (n 10) 169 ff; Sebastian Lohsse, Reiner Schulze and Dirk Staudenmeyer (eds), *Liability for Artificial Intelligence and the Internet of Things. Münster Colloquia on EU Law and the Digital Economy IV* (Hart 2019).

[12] Ariel Porat and Lior Jacob Strahilevitz, 'Personalizing Default Rules and Disclosure with Big Data' (2014) 112 Mich L Rev 1417; Omri Ben-Shahar and Ariel Porat, 'Personalizing Negligence Law' (2016) 91 NYU L Rev 627; Omri Ben-Shahar and Ariel Porat, 'Personalizing Mandatory Rules in Contract Law' (2019) 86 U Chi L Rev 255.

[13] Anthony J Casey and Anthony Niblett, 'The Death of Rules and Standards' (2017) 92 Indiana LJ 1401.

[14] A famous (American) case is *State v Loomis*, 881 NW2d 749 (Wis 2016), cert. denied, 137 S.Ct. 2290 (2017). See the studies carried out by the EU Commission, 'On the Use of Innovative Technology in the Justice Field' and 'Digital Criminal Justice', both of 14 September 2020 <https://ec.europa.eu/info/policies/justice-and-fundamental-rights/digitalisation-justice/relevant-studies_en> accessed 18 October 2020. See also Adrien van der Branden, *Les robots à l'assaut de la justice. L'intelligence artificielle au service des justiciables* (Bruylant 2019).

On a different note, contracts concluded and governed through algorithms (**smart contracts**) are designed to implement self-performing remedies, which, for example, automatically terminate them in the event they are breached by one of the contracting parties.[15] The rules applicable to performance and termination of such contracts, as well as a large number of legal and factual assessments which have been traditionally committed to a judge (Is a breach of contract material? Is the non-performing party at fault?), are therefore governed by algorithms.[16]

Unmanned cars, which are capable of autonomous driving, must be programmed in order to take decisions which may affect the property and life not only of passengers on board but also of other people accidentally involved in their movement.[17] For example, a crash avoidance maneuver may imply a decision whether the life of passengers on board is to prevail over that of the pedestrians who are going to be hit.

The assumption that decision-making by artificial intelligence, smart systems, and the like is compliant with legal rules and standards leads to the wishful thinking that they are but neutral mechanisms to implement the application of law in a more efficient and impartial way, not biased by personal beliefs and the individual preferences of a judge or an official (**law is code**).

In so far as no room is left to discretionary interpretation by humans, however, law is withering and being replaced by mechanisms of societal control which differ from those enshrined in legal principles and rules and the reasoning developed for many centuries on their basis (**code is law**).[18] This implies a shift of decisional power from lawyers to technocrats, as well as from the humanities (or arts) to the sciences. This implies a shift as well from the analogic reasoning of law and religion to the digital functioning of machines.

5. WESTERN LAW AND THE LAW OF SURVIVING SOCIETIES

Given the tight nexus between law and society, it is not surprising that law exhibits traits which are greatly mutable throughout the world, since they

[15] Jason G Allen, 'Wrapped and Stacked: "Smart Contracts" and the Interaction of Natural and Formal Language' (2018) 14 ERCL 307; Florian Möslein, 'Smart Contracts im Zivil- und Handelsrecht' (2019) 183 Zeitschrift für das gesamte Handelsrecht und Wirtschaftsrecht 254; Riccardo De Caria, 'The Legal Meaning of Smart Contracts' (2019) 27 ERPL 731; Mateja Durovic and André Janssen, 'The Formation of Blockchain-based Smart Contracts in the Light of Contract Law' ibid 753; Eric Tjong Tijn Tai, 'Force Majeure and Excuses in Smart Contracts' ibid 787; Louis-Daniel Muka Tshibende, 'Contract Law and Smart Contracts: Property and Security Rights Issues' ibid 871; Oscar Borgogno, 'Smart Contracts are the (new) Power of the Powerless? The Stakes for Consumers' ibid 885; Martin Fries and Boris P Paal (eds), *Smart Contracts* (Mohr Siebeck 2019).

[16] Larry A DiMatteo, Michel Cannarsa and Cristina Poncibò (eds), *The Cambridge Handbook of Smart Contracts, Blockchain Technology and Digital Platforms* (CUP 2019).

[17] Francesco P Patti, 'The European Road to Autonomous Vehicles' (2019) 42 Fordham ILJ 125.

[18] Lawrence Lessig, *Code and Other Laws of Cyberspace* (Basic Books 1999).

mirror the immense variety of social and cultural forms which characterize mankind.[19]

Because of their economic, politic and cultural predominance Western societies nevertheless amounted to forge a Western paradigm of law, which tends to be identified with the law itself. The risk is thus engendered that the contingent and relative features of their laws are turned into necessary and absolute requirements of law as such, so that any societal organization not matching Western standards may be deemed to be devoid of law at all (**ethnocentrism**).[20]

> '**Anthropology of law**, or **legal anthropology**, is the field of anthropology where the focus is on the normative aspects of cultural and biological human life that are based on the law (law defining) elements of authority and sanction [...]. Thus, the anthropology of law will find itself embedded in more general themes of anthropology such as religion, customs, behaviour, and neurology'.[21]

The risk that Western law is considered as the final stage of the history of mankind is thus also engendered, where any possible instance of progress and civilization would have been brought to perfection (**traditionalism**).

> **Lewis H. Morgan** (1818-1881) assumed that the history of mankind is to be recapitulated as a progress of 'ethnical periods', running from the bottom (of savagery) through a middle status (of barbarism) up to the top (of civilization). Each of the first two periods would in turn be divided into three subperiods, corresponding to a lower, middle and upper status of savagery and, respectively, barbarism.[22]
>
> According to **Henry Sumner Maine** (1822-1888), the historical development of law is invariably structured in three consecutive stages. At its very outset, law would be dictated by a deity or a divine agency,[23] who afterwards would give way to an epoch of customary law,[24] eventually followed by one of written codes.[25]
>
> In his masterpiece about matriarchy (*Mutterrecht*),[26] which commanded a wide consensus between the end of the nineteenth century and the beginning of the twentieth century, **Johan Jakob Bachofen** (1815-1887) reinterpreted the history of mankind as a struggle between women and men about taking over control of religion and society. Particularly, after a first period of

19 Leopold J Pospíšil, *Anthropology of Law. A Comparative Theory* (Harper & Row 1971) 97ff.

20 Mark Goodale, *Anthropology and Law. A Critical Introduction* (New York UP 2017) 141-201.

21 Wolfgang Fikentscher, *Law and Anthropology* (2nd edn, CH Beck-Hart-Nomos 2016) 2.

22 Lewis H Morgan, *Ancient Society* (Henry Holt & Co 1877) 3ff.

23 Henry Sumner Maine, *Ancient Law* (first published 1861, John Murray, Albemarle Street 1930) 5. On the ancient identity of lawyers and priests, see Id, 'Religion and Law' in *Early Law and Custom* (BR Publishing 1883, repr 1985) 26.

24 Maine, *Ancient Law* (n 23) 11.

25 ibid 12.

26 Johan Jakob Bachofen, *Das Mutterrecht: Eine Untersuchung über die Gynaikokratie der alten Welt nach ihrer religiösen und rechtlichen Natur* (Krais & Hoffmann 1861). See also Id, *Urreligion und antike Symbole*, 3 vols (P Reclam 1926); Id, *Mutterrecht und Urreligion* (Kröner 1927).

communistic and polyamorous living, called Hetaerism and allegedly ruled by an early proto Aphrodite, women would have taken power, founding a society based on agriculture and the cult of an early Demeter. A transitional (Dionysian) period would have followed, after which patriarchy began to emerge and eventually triumph under the lead of Apollo, thus establishing modern civilization.

A universal process of continuous refinement of law was thus laid down, which implicitly identifies its more 'primitive' stages in far-off or ancient societies and its acme in contemporary Western societies. This value judgment is currently rejected as well as its underpinning of **historical determinism**, which was largely imbued with both Hegel's philosophy of history and Darwin's doctrine of evolutionism.[27] Furthermore, it is highly disputable whether it is possible to infer that Western societies in the previous stage of their historical development might have had the same characteristics of primitive peoples.[28] Particularly, it is contended whether law necessarily requires an institutional authority to be in charge of its enforcement and, in that case, what requirements such authority should meet. The first question has long been answered in the affirmative and the state and its officials (as courts) have been identified as the central authority that law must be enforced by.[29] However, experience shows that law is not necessarily incompatible with vengeance and other devices of self-help, provided that they may follow up on the settlement of a dispute.[30] More generally, many a (cultural) factor may trigger people's abidance by law, including psychological or even neurological issues.

To that extent, law may well be encountered in primitive tribes or indigenous peoples which do not acknowledge central authorities in charge of its enforcement.[31]

Determinative of this view were the inquiries by Bronisław Malinowski (1884-1942) in the Trobriand Islands,[32] which are generally considered as the first application of ethnographic methods in the study of law.[33]

Law of primitive communities or peoples is investigated by **legal ethnology**, which in the Anglo-American academical environment is mostly classified as a branch of **legal (or cultural) anthropology**.[34]

In the United States, a true pioneer of the discipline was E. Adamson Hoebel (1906-1993), who undertook his researches under the supervision of Karl

[27] Norbert Rouland, *Legal Anthropology* (The Athlone Press 1994) 23ff.

[28] Konrad Zweigert and Hein Kötz, *An Introduction to Comparative Law* (Tony Weir tr, 3rd edn, OUP 1998) 9.

[29] Weber (n 5).

[30] Vengeance and other devices of self-help were well established to solve disputes at ancient Roman law (see Gordley (n 4); Rouland (n 27) 73). See also *infra*, ch 2, para 1.

[31] Arthur S Diamond, *Primitive Law. Past and Present* (Methuen 1971) 157ff.

[32] Bronisław Malinowski, *Crime and custom in savage society* (Paul, Trench, Trubner & Co 1932).

[33] For a general account of his theories, see the essays collected in Mateusz Stępień (ed), *Bronislaw Malinowski's Concept of Law* (Springer 2016).

[34] For a short account of the relation between the two, see Uwe Kischel, *Comparative Law* (Andrew Hammer tr, OUP 2019) Rn 41.

N. Llewellyn (1893-1962). With his masterpiece, *The Law of Primitive Man*, Hoebel contributed decisively in raising an interest of legal realism towards non-Western legal cultures (see also *infra*, ch 7, para 4).[35]

6. MUTE LAW

At its historical outset, law oft consists in a corpus of oral traditions, which are handed down from each generation to the next. At this stage, it tends to be deeply entrenched with the customs of a community.

At a certain degree of its development, law tends to be reduced to writing and embodied in a text which makes it stable. Initially this text is often secret, subsequently it becomes accessible to a small circle of adepts, and eventually it is somehow published.

In all these forms of its consolidation and transmission, law is conveyed through linguistic signs, whether oral or written. **Law and language** are therefore strictly associated.[36]

It has however been suggested that, in the history of mankind, law may have preceded language, since legal rules can be acknowledged and followed even by people who are not able to conceptualize and convey them through language. Therefore, also human species which existed before those of *homo sapiens* and of *homo neanderthalensis* might have had their own law, which, therefore, would have been 'mute', ie conceptualized and conveyed not through language, but merely **by conduct**.[37]

According to **Rodolfo Sacco**, mute law is that which nature taught to all living beings (*quod natura omnia animalia docuit*, as natural law was defined by the Roman jurist Ulpianus). During the Bronze Age it would have been overridden by rational and spoken law, but it would never completely have ceased to operate. Spoken and unspoken sources of law would coexist in contemporary legal systems, some legal acts would be performed through words (by fax, deeds, wills, and so on) and others by mere conduct (deliveries, vending machines, and so on). Nonetheless, lawyers would be primarily interested in spoken sources and acts and would feel uneasy with mute sources and acts.[38]

[35] E Adamson Hoebel, *The Law of Primitive Man. A Study in Comparative Legal Dynamics* (Harvard UP 1954).

[36] Bernd Rüthers, Christian Fischer and Axel Birk, *Rechtstheorie mit Juristischer Methodenlehre* (10th edn, CH Beck 2018) 101ff. See also Timothy Endicott, 'Law and Language' in Jules L Coleman, Kenneth E Himma and Scott J Shapiro, *The Oxford Handbook of Jurisprudence and Philosophy of Law* (OUP 2004) 935ff.

[37] Rodolfo Sacco, *Il diritto muto. Neuroscienze, conoscenza tacita, valori condivisi* (Il Mulino 2015).

[38] Rodolfo Sacco, 'Mute Law' (1995) 45 Am J Comp L 455.

7. ANIMAL LAW

If law is explained in terms of behavior taken by members of a group, its 'human' nature may be questioned, since it is a widespread assumption that animals (or at least some species) are able to gather in organized groups and therefore to act like members thereof.

Conversely, the question is raised whether (some) animals could be considered as members of society, thus being potentially vested with rights and duties (see *infra*, ch 11, para 1).

GLOSSARY

Anthropology of law [or legal anthropology] (5): field of anthropology where the focus is on the normative aspects of cultural and biological human life that are based on the legal elements of authority and sanction, thus encompassing also issues connected to religion, customs, behavior, and neurology.

Big data (4): process whereby computers sift through enormous quantities of data to identify patterns that can predict individuals' future behavior.

Cultural anthropology (5): branch of anthropological sciences that developed in the early twentieth century in the US, although its rudimentary expressions date back to the Greek historian Herodotus, who lived in the fifth century BC. This discipline examines the diversity of ways of life and thinking in different human societies. It has become increasingly established on the basis of an accurate methodological approach, centered on the participatory observation carried out by its supporters during long stays in the field under investigation. Anthropologists, besides contributing to the achievement of a knowledge about what is common and what is different in diverging cultures, strive to refine a critical prospective in our categories of thought, which, far from being universal, are elaborated in specific cultural environments.

Digital law (4): branch of law that refers to legal requirements, legal decisions and ethics relating to the digital environment, also known as Internet law. It can be considered as the legal rights and restrictions governing technology use (see also 'Granular norms', 'Internet of things', 'Predictive justice', 'Smart contracts', and 'Unmanned cars').

Granular norms (4): personalized directives which are to be moulded on the track record of relevant information and continuously communicated to everyone.

***Hypothèse du non-droit* (3)**: situation of absence of law affecting certain contexts of human life that are devoid of legal rules and regulated instead by other systems. This absence has to be considered as a negative phenomenon, which must be distinguished from the situation of unjust law and folk law which are, on the contrary, phenomena of positive presence of the law.

Individual law (1): conception of law always subject to the safeguard of the rule of law. Such a conception, mainly situated in the area of private law, sees the discipline of relations between individuals and between groups as being based on distrust. Even when individual law seems to bring its subjects to closer positions, it does so only by estranging and dividing them at the same time (see also 'Social law').

Internet of things (IoT) (4): neologism referring to a system of intertwined devices, digital machines, people, and objects that is based on a relational connectivity. It identifies the next step towards the digitization of society in which everyday appliances will become smart, have computer-implemented intelligence of their own, and be able to communicate. The Internet of things is about attaching varying amounts of identity, interaction, and inference to objects.

Juridification [*Verrechtlichung*] (3): process through which law comes to regulate an increasing number of different activities, thus expanding the realm of human life regulated by legal decisions, with the consequence that an increasing number of conflicts between individuals are solved with reference to the law.

Legal ethnology (5): discipline aimed at analyzing and examining the life of every people without distinction, through the laws of evolution of phenomena and legal institutions. According to this branch of legal studies, the course and evolution of the history of mankind is fixed by the above-mentioned laws of evolution. Therefore, 'legal ethnology' compares the rights of peoples in different stages, retracing the line of historical progress of law and, consequently, the succession of laws which symbolizes the legal evolution. Albert Hermann Post and Joseph Köhler in Germany and Henry Sumner Maine in the UK could be considered its most prominent theorists.

Mute law (6): law taught by nature to all living beings, conceptualized and conveyed not through language but merely through conduct. The concept was forged by Rodolfo Sacco, who argued that in earlier times law was unarticulated through language or rational thinking; still today, it is often unwritten and unspoken.

Negative function of law (1): primary seeking function of law to settle conflicts between individuals who have different values, needs, or views on the common good, thus contributing also to the protection of their freedoms and rights. From this point of view, law aims to prevent the dissolution of society, as well as the relational decay of its members (see also 'Positive function of law').

Positive function of law (1): promotional role of law in order to ensure the unity of society and a guidepost for acceptable behavior among its members. In a broader sense, it contributes to assure the realization of those objectives pertaining to justice in a given social structure (see also 'Negative function of law').

Predictive justice (4): recent conception of justice seeking to use various models and instruments like smart machines and artificial intelligence systems to identify whether, for example, a suspect should be incarcerated before trial or not, or to assess the likelihood of further offences by a suspect, thus reducing unpredictability and affecting the judgment.

Rationalization of law [*Rationalisierung des Rechts*] (1): concept forged by Max Weber. According to him, in order to qualify an order as 'law', it has to be 'externally guaranteed by the probability that physical or psychological coercion will be applied by a staff or people in order to bring about compliance or avenge violation'. The regulatory framework in which this theory is developed provides for a positive concept of law, intended as the pure result of every enactment of the political legislator in accordance with a validated procedure. Toward this end, to achieve the above-mentioned equivalence between order and law, the key element is represented by the subsistence of enforcement (and not by its source of legitimacy), which boosts the likelihood of its being obeyed.

***Rechtsstaat* [Constitutional state based on the rule of law; *Stato di diritto*] (3)**: constitutional state whose governmental powers are entirely governed by law. The term was forged by German jurisprudence; it has come to be increasingly used in European scholarship with the common meaning of 'rule of law'. The final purpose of this limitation is the protection of citizens from the arbitrary exercise of powers of authority. The individuals must be free to go before Courts in order to safeguard their civil rights and liberties. Each legal system attributes to the notion of *Rechtsstaat* a different nuance of meaning which prevents theorists from providing a universally valid definition of it.

Secularization [*Verweltlichung*; *Secolarizzazione*] (2): modification and transformation of a society from a strong identification with its religious values toward nonreligious values and secular institutions. The theory of secularization assumes that the theological sphere disperses its authority in all areas of social life and governance, with the growth and development of societies' progress, which become feasible with modernization and rationalization.

Self-performing remedies (4): legal tools the occurrence of which automatically flows from the breach of the contract without the need of additional activity by the contractual parties.

Smart contracts (4): set of promises, including protocols in which the parties perform other promises. The protocols are usually implemented with programs on a computer network, or through other forms of digital electronics, thus these contracts are 'smarter' than the traditional paper-based contracts. In other words, they are computer programs that can automatically execute the terms of a contract.

Social law (1): conception of law conceiving a direct participation of its subjects as a whole; so they take part in juridical relations from time to time. Differently from individual law, the social law never entirely submits to the state (the democratic version of the latter is only one species of it). According to its theorists, social law 'represents the only form of juridical regulation which seems capable of solving some social problems while remaining diametrically opposed to the totalitarianism'. The law of peace, of mutual aid, of cooperation are typical expressions of 'social law' (see also 'Individual law').

Unmanned cars (4): vehicles that are self-driven without human involvement by using a combination of sensors, cameras, radar and artificial intelligence to travel between destinations.

BIOGRAPHIES

Edward Adamson Hoebel (Madison, 1906 – St. Paul, 1993) was a prominent American anthropologist. He primarily studied at the University of Wisconsin, where he received his BA. Then he moved to University of New York to get his MA. A few years later, he earned his PhD at Columbia University, where he attended several seminars of Karl N. Llewellyn, whose fascinating thought – which is commonly ascribed to the so-called 'legal realism' (see *infra*, ch 7, para 4) – influenced his following studies. The ideas of Llewellyn induced Hoebel to focus his analysis on the 'dispute settlement processing', a well-known approach among anthropologists. It is centered on the modalities with which disputes are settled. Hoebel has been the pupil of Franz Boas, an influential pioneer of modern anthropology, who, for this reason, is often called the 'Father of American Anthropology'. Perhaps it was Boas who recommended him to stay in contact with Llewellyn. Hoebel and Llewellyn's intellectual relationship led them to strongly develop the field of legal anthropology. They were co-authors of an important book *La Voie Cheyenne. Conflit et jurisprudence dans la science primitive du droit*, published in 1941. Hoebel taught anthropology at the University of New York, Utah, and Oxford (here as Fulbright Professor). Over the years, Hoebel focused his studies on the laws of the Northern Cheyenne, Northern Shoshone, Comanches, Puebloans, and Pakistan. In his most renowned work *Anthropology: The Study of Man*, published in 1949, he showed, through the examination of the duties and rights considered as law in nonliterate peoples, his idea aimed at expanding the prospects of the legal realist method, thus opening the latter up to non-Western tradition. He was appointed Regent's Professor of Anthropology at the University of Minnesota, being also Dean of Department for 15 years. He definitively retired in 1972.

His main works are: *The Comanches: Lords of the South Plains* (1940); *La Voie Cheyenne. Conflit et jurisprudence dans la science primitive du droit* (with Karl N Llewellyn) (1941); *Anthropology: The Study of Man* (1949); *The Cheyennes: Indians of the Great Plains* (1961).

Johann Jakob Bachofen (Basel, 1815 – Basel, 1887) was a Swiss historian and anthropologist. Author of works on culture and religion, he focused his analysis on the nature and study of history for his whole life. Bachofen went to the Universities of Basel, Berlin, and Göttingen, where he met L. Ranke and F.C. von Savigny as teachers. He dedicated himself to the study of Roman law he taught at the University of Basel (1841-1843). From 1843 to 1866, he was a justice of the Court of Appeal in his hometown.
Bachofen was particularly interested in the development of societal organizations. In *Das Mutterrecht* (1861), he proposed the theory of a matriarchal social system, ie a societal organization based on matrilineal lineages. In this work, Bachofen's approach is predominantly evolutionary. The idea of evolution is combined with the traditional general symbology. It is a question of the spiritual development of a more material reality and, thus, of the passage from an unconscious legality to a more eminently individualistic expression.
Strongly influenced by Romantic thought, of which he shared idealistic and metaphysic approach, Bachofen also saw myth and religion symbolism as a product of the historical process.
His main works are: *Versuch über Gräbersymbolik der Alten* (1859); *Das Mutterrecht* (1861); *Die Unsterblichkeitslehre der orphischen Theologie* (1867); *Die Sage von Tanaquil* (1870).

Jean Carbonnier (Libourne, 1908 – Paris, 2003) was an important French jurist, expert in civil and private law. He was a Professor of French Civil Law at the University of Poitiers from 1937 to 1955. He also taught at the Paris Law Faculty until 1976, which later became the Panthéon-Assas University. In 1964 he became the director of the sociology journal *L'Année Sociologique*, creating and heading the Laboratory for Legal Sociology (*Laboratoire de sociologie juridique*) at Panthéon-Assas University in 1968. His thought and his work have always dealt with themes of philosophy and sociology of law. In particular, he was deeply influenced by the principles of realism, Protestantism and empiricism. He interpreted legal phenomena as social facts and his acute observation of reality was always aimed at an intimate understanding of it. According to him, the law must be considered an artificial essence, which is endowed with flexibility, uncertainty and changeability. It cannot be understood in a rigorous and fixed manner but must adapt to the rapid developments in our multicultural society. Carbonnier also described the process of subjectivization of the law, which tends to be more and more precise and specific. It focuses on individuals and not on society as a whole. As a result, given the particular tendency of the legislator to legal particularism, judges are increasingly inclined to adopt an abstract approach to the single cases.
His main works are: *Droit civil* (1955); *Sociologie juridique* (1968); *Flexible droit* (first published 1969).

Michel Foucault (Poitiers, 1926 – Paris, 1984) was a French philosopher. During his university studies, he focused his attention on authors such as Saussure, Kierkegaard, Heidegger, and Lacan, although it was Nietzsche's thinking that

influenced him most. He was a professor at the faculties of Letters and Human Sciences of Clermont-Ferrand (from 1964 to 1968), Vincennes (from 1968 to 1970) and, since 1970, at the *Collège de France* of Paris. Foucault's research was increasingly oriented towards the study of the processes of normalization, and therefore of the various forms through which power has attempted, in the modern West, to control individuals and their bodies in an effort to contain all forms of deviance from the established norm. Foucault's subsequent works originated from the reflections of these courses, dedicated among other things to the medicalization of 'abnormals' and the birth of the prison system of psychiatry. He studied the development of prisons, hospitals, schools and other large societal organizations, as well as sexuality, presenting his thought as a critical history of modernity. Another topic that the French philosopher has extensively analyzed is that of self-care. This is a philosophical principle that can be traced back to the Hellenistic Greek period and the late Roman imperial age. He focused mostly on the relationship between power and knowledge and how they are used as instruments of control through societal institutions.
His main works are: *Histoire de la folie à l'âge classique* (1961); *Naissance de la clinique* (1963); *Les mots et les choses* (1966-1967); *L'archéologie du savoir* (1969); *Histoire de la sexualité* (1976).

Georges Gurvitch (Novorossiysk, 1894 – Paris, 1965) was a Russian-born, naturalized French sociologist and philosopher. He worked as Professor of Sociology and Philosophy of Law at the Universities of Tomsk, St. Petersburg, Prague, Strasbourg, and Paris. He was also the editor of *Archives de philosophie du droit et de sociologie juridique* (1931-1940), *Journal of legal and political sociology* (1942-1947), *Cahiers internationaux de sociologie* (1946) and founded the *Centre d'études sociologiques* in Paris.
According to Gurvitch, law should be seen as 'an attempt to realize in a given social environment the idea of justice' through a multilateral imperative-attributive regulation, based on a demands-values link. This regulation derives its validity from the normative facts which give a social guarantee of its effectiveness.
His idea of social law is not compatible with the legal positivism and all those philosophical constructs making law dependent on the state's will, which they acknowledge as the unique source of law. On the contrary, Gurvitch's sociology of law reflects the pluralism of concepts which links law to the living social reality.
His main works are: *L'idée du droit sociale* (1932); *Sociology of Law* (1942); *La déclarations des droits sociaux* (1944); *La vocation actuelle de la sociologie* (1950); *Determinismes sociaux et liberté humaine* (1955); *Traité de sociologie* (1958); *The Social Framework of Knowledge* (1972).

Jürgen Habermas (Düsseldorf, 1929) is a German philosopher and sociologist, influenced by the Frankfurt School. He worked as a professor at the University of Heidelberg and at the University of Frankfurt, where he is now Professor Emeritus. In 1971, he became Director of the Max Planck Institute for the Study of the Scientific-Technical World in Starnberg and worked there until 1983. His *magnum opus* is *Theorie des kommunikativen Handelns* (1981). Through his work,

he emphasized the problems of communication and the function of public opinion in contemporary society, claiming the political role of rationality as a dialogue not subject to conditions of domination. His works are mainly animated by epistemological themes inherent to the foundation of social sciences reinterpreted in the light of the linguistic shift of contemporary philosophy. Habermas pays particular attention to the analysis of industrial societies in mature capitalism and to the role of institutions in a new dialogue-emancipatory perspective in relation to the crisis of legitimacy that undermines contemporary democracies and consensus-building mechanisms. His philosophical thought has always seen him actively engaged in the criticism of the method of knowing objectively. This has led him on the path of founding a new communicative reason, which he believes can free humanity from the principle of authority.
His main works are: *Strukturwandel der Öffentlichkeit. Untersuchungen zu einer Kategorie der bürgerlichen Gesellschaft* (1962); *Erkenntnis und Interesse* (1968); *Legitimationsprobleme im Spätkapitalismus* (1972); *Theorie des kommunikativen Handelns* (vol 1: *Handlungsrationalität und gesellschaftliche Rationalisierung*; vol 2: *Zur Kritik der funktionalistischen Vernunft*) (1981).

Thomas Hobbes (Westport, 1588 – Hardwick Hall, 1679) was a British philosopher and mathematician, as well as a theorist of law. He is the author of *The Leviathan*, a famous work of political philosophy published in 1651. Hobbes was interested in political theory and also wrote about history, geometry, ethics, and economics. The description made by Hobbes about human nature as substantially competitive and selfish, exemplified by the phrases '*Bellum omnium contra omnes*' and '*Homo homini lupus*', has been echoed in the field of political anthropology. Hobbes conceived a materialistic, mechanistic system (starting from first simple elements and proceeding to subsequent compositions, in a mechanical relationship of cause and effect) that was all-encompassing. The Galilean mechanistic vision of physical reality, which had been extended from Descartes to the animal world, was welcomed by Hobbes in materialistic terms for a philosophical scientific explanation of all reality.
His philosophical reflection dwelt extensively on the concepts of 'state of nature', 'laws of nature' and 'social contract'. It states that all natural rights, except the right to life, shall be transferred to a person or an assembly they shall administer for all men, with laws allowing to enforce by might the rights of nature. The agreement that gives life to civil society (*pactum societatis*) is a pact of subjection (*pactum subiectionis*).
His main works are: *Elements of Law, Natural and Politic* (1640; but 1650); *Elementorum Philosophiae Sectio Tertia De Cive* (1642); *Of Liberty and Necessity* (1646; but 1654); *Leviathan or the Matter, Form and Power of a Common-Wealth Ecclesiasticall and Civill* (1651); *Elementorum Philosophiae Sectio Prima de Corpore* (1655); *Elementorum Philosophiae Sectio Secunda de Homine* (1658).

Otto Kirchheimer (Heilbronn, 1905 – Silver Spring, 1965) was a German jurist of Jewish origin belonging to the Frankfurt School. He studied law at the University of Bonn, where he graduated. With the rise of Adolf Hitler's regime, he

first moved to Paris and then to New York; in 1943, he obtained the American citizenship. He collaborated with the followers of the so-called Frankfurter School of social theory and philosophy. From 1955 to 1962, he was Professor of Political Science at the New School for Social Research in New York, and since 1962 at Columbia University. He also worked for the Office of Strategic Services (OSS), the forerunner of the CIA. His most prominent works are *Punishment and Social Structure* (1939), in which he analyses punishment as a social institution, arguing that modes of punishment are social phenomena shaped by economic drivers, and *Political Justice* (1961), where he argues that political justice consists in the use of judicial procedures to achieve political ends that are, in general, the elimination of the opponents through their criminalization. According to Kirchheimer, after World War I, political justice was practiced in every country, not only in totalitarian regimes (from Stalin to Hitler), but also in those states based on the rule of law. In other words, political justice is a phenomenon that could take place everywhere. He also authored *Politik und Verfassung* (1964), in which he developed the concept of *Allerweltspartei* (catch-all party) as the evolution of the modern mass parties. This concept identifies a kind of political party seeking to attract votes from different ideologies and interests and in which the original ideology and interests are put in the background.
His main works are: *Punishment and Social Structure* (with Georg Rusche) (1939); *The Government of Eastern Germany* (1950); *The Party in the Mass Society* (1958); *Political Justice* (1961); *Politik und Verfassung* (1964).

Karl Nickerson Llewellyn (Seattle, 1893 – Chicago, 1963) was one of the foremost jurists of the twentieth century, as well as one of the maximum exponents of the so-called 'legal realism'. He was deeply dissatisfied with his US high school; therefore, seizing the opportunity to leave for Germany with relatives of a family friend, he opted to enter the *Real-Gymnasium* in Mecklenburg. He lived in Germany for three years, learning the language and being mesmerized by its culture. Before coming back to the US, he spent the spring of 1911 at the University of Lausanne. Llewellyn primarily attended Yale College and, later on, Yale Law School, where he was one of Arthur Linton Corbin's pupils, a prominent scholar (especially of contract law) who taught at Yale Law School, emphasizing the need to implement the casebook method of legal studies. In those years, Llewellyn worked as editor-in-chief of the Yale Law Journal. On the advice of his friend, Hans Lachmund, who spent a semester in Paris to attend fascinating courses about sociology by Charles Gide and sociology of law by René Worms, Llewellyn decided to go to La Sorbonne University in order to study Latin, law and French. His predilection for Germany led him to support its cause when World War I broke out, trying to enlist in the army; however, as he refused to relinquish his American citizenship, he was considered not eligible for the German military. Nevertheless, he had the chance to be recruited by the 78th Prussian Infantry. He got wounded close to Ypres in November 1914, being hospitalized in a military structure in Nürtingen for about three months. After his discharging, the Iron Cross (second class) was awarded to him. He came back to Yale University in 1915, starting to focus on the academic career and

studying under the supervision of William Graham Sumner, the distinguished author of *Folkways*. He was appointed associate professor at Yale University in 1923. Columbia University offered to be part of its faculty in 1925 and he stayed there until 1951. In those years, he acquired an enormous reputation for his juridical research related to 'legal realism'. He moved to the Chicago School of Law as professor in 1951. He could be considered the principal drafter of the Uniform Commercial Code.
His main works are: *The Bramble Bush: On Our Law and Its Study* (1930); 'Some Realism about Realism – Responding to Dean Pound' (1931) 44 Harvard Law Review 1222; *La Voie Cheyenne. Conflit et jurisprudence dans la science primitive du droit* (with E Adamson Hoebel) (1941); *The Cheyenne Way: Conflict and Case Law in Primitive Jurisprudence* (1941); *The Common Law Tradition. Deciding Appeals* (1960); *Jurisprudence. Realism in Theory and Practice* (1962); *The Case Law System in America* (1989); *The Theory of Rules* (2011).

Bronisław Malinowski (Kracow, 1884 – New Heaven, 1942) was a Polish social anthropologist, naturalized as British citizen. In 1908, he received a doctorate in philosophy from Kraków's Jagiellonian University, where he focused on mathematics and the physics. In 1910, he undertook studies of social anthropology at the London School of Economics. In 1914, he began a research in the Trobriand Islands (New Guinea), which lasted until 1918. In 1927, he obtained the chair of anthropology at the University of London. At the outbreak of World War II he moved to the United States, where he taught at Yale University since 1938. His research in the Trobriand Islands was of utmost importance to anthropology, as he developed the methods of modern ethnographic research in practice, more specifically the so-called 'participant observation'. This methodology aims at gaining a close and intimate familiarity with a given group of individuals or a particular community and their practices through an intensive involvement with people in their cultural environment, usually over an extended period of time. Among the leading exponents of British functionalism, he interpreted culture and social institutions as tools to satisfy needs, which he distinguished between primary or fundamental and common to other animals (the need to feed, procreate, protect themselves), and secondary or derivatives, corresponding to the cultural rules which men must respect to see their needs adequately satisfied. For Malinowski, indeed, specific of the human species is the 'indirect' way of satisfaction of the vital imperatives. For example, the need to feed is not solved by men in the simple act of consuming alone the fruits that grow spontaneously in the forest; on the contrary, in all the phases of the nutrition process (from the research of food to its preparation, from cooking to angering) there are precise human rules. Furthermore, food is obtained through collective practices, in which the use of an artificially produced apparatus (weapons, agricultural tools, technical tools) is fundamental. The 'indirect' way is therefore a cultural way of meeting needs of natural order. But this cultural fulfilment of basic needs implies for Malinowski the onset of new cultural needs.
His main works are: *Argonauts of the Western Pacific: An account of native enterprise and adventure in the Archipelagos of Melanesian New Guinea* (1922); *Crime and Custom in Savage Society* (1926); *Sex and Repression in Savage Society* (1927);

The Sexual Life of Savages in North-Western Melanesia (1929); *A Scientific Theory of Culture and Other Essays* (1944); *The Dynamics of Culture Change: An inquiry into race relations in Africa* (1945); *Freedom & Civilization* (1947).

Karl Marx (Trier, 1818 – London, 1883) was a German philosopher, economist, historian, sociologist, political scientist, journalist and politician. Coming from a bourgeois family of Jewish origin, he studied in Bonn and then in Berlin, where he began to get involved with the Hegelian left and the circles of German radicalism. He graduated in 1841 with the dissertation *Differenz der demokritischen und epikureischen Naturphilosophie*, and in October 1842, he was called to the direction of the *Rheinische Zeitung*, to which he had already been collaborating for several months with Bruno Bauer and Max Stirner. After leaving the newspaper in March 1843, he married Jenny von Westphalen in June of that same year, with whom, after a brief stay in Kreuznach, he emigrated to Paris and founded and headed the *Deutsch-französische Jahrbücher* (together with Arnold Ruge). His thought, focused on the materialistic critique of the capitalist economy, society, politics, and culture, has exerted a prominent influence on the birth of socialist and communist ideologies from the second half of the nineteenth century onwards, giving rise to the socio-economic-political current of Marxism. He is the theorist of the materialistic conception of history and, together with Friedrich Engels, of scientific socialism. Marx is actually one of the most influential thinkers on the political, philosophical and economic levels in the history of the nineteenth century. The need to analyze the way of capitalist production on the basis of the categories he had identified led Marx to draw up *Das Kapital* in 1867.
Marx is the theorist of 'the dictatorship of the proletariat'. This is a theory that, although it had already been anticipated in the 10 points of the *Manifesto of the Communist Party*, was actually conceived by Marx and Engels for the first time in 1852 in the letter to Joseph Weydemeyer, and in 1875, in the *Critique of the Gotha Program* to refer to the social and political situation that would be established immediately after the proletarian revolution.
His main works are: *Zur Judenfrage* (1843); *Zur Kritik der Hegelschen Philosophie* (1843); *Die deutsche Ideologie* (1845); *Forderungen der Kommunistischen Partei in Deutschland* (1848); *Zur Kritik der politischen Ökonomie* (1859); *Lohn, Preis und Profit* (1865); *Das Kapital*, vol 1 (1867); *Das Kapital*, vol 2 (1885); *Das Kapital*, vol 3 (1894).

Lewis H. Morgan (Aurora, 1818 – Rochester, 1881) was an American anthropologist and social theorist. He is considered one of the founders of social anthropology and the true initiator of the anthropological study of kinship systems. He was attorney by profession and practiced law at Rochester from 1844 to 1862, while gradually developing an interest for the indigenous peoples of the USA and in particular for the Iroquois. In 1851, he published *The League of Ho-dé-no-sau-nee, or Iroquois*, considered as the first ethnographic study of a North American population. He was also an active member of the Republican party, in the ranks of which he was elected to the New York State Assembly in 1861 and in the Senate in 1869. Elected as a member of the National Academy of Sciences,

Morgan served as president of the American Association for the Advancement of Science in 1880. According to his theory of cultural evolution, advances in social organization arose primarily from changes in food production. Society progressed from a hunting-and-gathering stage (which he denoted by the term 'savagery') to a stage of settled agriculture ('barbarism') and later on to an urban society possessing a more advanced agriculture ('civilization'). This theory was developed in his work *Ancient Society, or Researches in the Lines of Human Progress from Savagery through Barbarism to Civilization* (1877) and was among the first major scientific accounts of the origin and evolution of civilization. He also proposed the idea according to which the earliest human domestic institution was not the patriarchal family but rather the matrilineal clan.
His main works are: *The League of the Ho-dé-no-sau-nee, or Iroquois* (1851); *The Laws of Descent of the Iroquois* (1856); *The Indian Journals, 1859-1862* (1959); *The American Beaver and His Works* (1868); *Systems of Consanguinity and Affinity of the Human Family* (1871); *Montezuma's Dinner* (1876); *Ancient Society, or Researches in the Lines of Human Progress from Savagery through Barbarism to Civilization* (1877).

Rodolfo Sacco (Fossano, 1923) is a most distinguished Italian scholars of comparative law. He dedicated his life to scientific research. He completed his legal studies at the University of Turin. He first taught private law at the University of Trieste (1956-1961), then he moved to the University of Pavia (1961-1971) where in addition to private law he also taught civil law and comparative law. Afterwards, he moved to the University of Turin where he taught comparative private law (1971-1988), civil law (1988-1999), the law of socialist countries, African law, and legal anthropology. He is national member of the *Accademia dei Lincei* and member of several other academies, such as the *Accademia delle Scienze di Torino*, the International Academy of Comparative Law (AIDC) and the *Accademia dei Giusprivatisti Europei*. Since 1968 he is among the editors of *Rivista di Diritto Civile*, and he is the director of *Trattato di diritto civile* and *Trattato di diritto comparato*. He is now Professor Emeritus at the University of Turin. From 1960 to 1994 he also taught at the *Faculté internationale de droit comparé* in Strasbourg. Sacco is considered the forerunner in the field of comparative law in which he elaborated the doctrine of the formants and their dissociation. In 1987 he inspired the manifesto on comparative studies known as the 'Trento Thesis'. From 1970 to 1994 he animated and successfully led the movement for the insertion of comparative law among the compulsory subjects of university studies in law. Recently, his interests have mainly shifted to legal anthropology: his research on mute law is of special interest.
His main works are: *La buona fede* (1949); *L'azione surrogatoria* (1955); *L'arricchimento ottenuto mediante fatto ingiusto* (1959); *Il contratto* (1975); *Il diritto africano* (1995); *Sistemi giuridici comparati* (1996); *Antropologia giuridica* (2007); *Introduzione al diritto comparato* (2015); *Il diritto muto* (2015).

Carl Schmitt (Plettenberg, 1888 – Plettenberg, 1985) was a German legal and political theorist, often considered to be one of the critics of liberalism and par-

liamentary democracy. After teaching at various German universities, he became professor at Humboldt University in Berlin in 1933, a post he was forced to relinquish in 1945, at the end of World War II.
Schmitt's work developed during the crisis of the nineteenth century constitutional liberalism, when rapid technological change occurred, and traditional European political order was becoming inadequate.
His thought, whose roots lie in the Catholic religion, concerned the themes of power, violence, and the implementation of law. Among the key concepts were, in their lapidary formulation, the '*Ausnahmezustand*', '*Diktatur*', '*Souveränität*' and '*Großraum*'. He coined some relevant definitions, such as '*Politische Theologie*', '*Hüter der Verfassung*', '*dilatorischer Formelkompromiss*', '*Verfassungswirklichkeit*', '*Legalität und Legitimität*'. Actively involved with National Socialism, Schmitt advocated the decisionist theory of sovereign power beyond law and emphasized the importance of the *amicus/hostis* distinction in politics.
In addition to public and international law, his works are also related to other disciplines, such as political science, sociology, historical sciences, theology and philosophy (with particular focus on the ontological aspects of law).
His main works are: *Politische Romantik* (1919); *Die Diktatur. Von den Anfängen des modernen Souveränitätsgedankens bis zum proletarischen Klassenkamps* (1921); *Politische Theologie. Vier Kapitel zur Lehre von der Souveränität* (1922); *Verfassungslehre* (1928); *Der Hüter der Verfassung* (1932); *Der Begriff des Politischen* (1932); *Legalität und Legitimität* (1932); *Land und Meer. Eine weltgeschichtliche Betrachtung* (1942); *Der Nomos der Erde im Völkerrecht der* Jus Publicum Europaeum (1950); *Donoso Cortes in gesamteuropäischer Interpretation* (1950); *Die Lage der europäischen Rechtswissenschaft* (1950); Ex captivitate salus. *Erinnerungen der Zeit 1945/47* (1950); *Theorie des Partisanen. Zwischenbemerkung zum Begriff des Politischen* (1963); *Politische Theologie II. Die Legende von der Erledigung jener Politischen Theologie* (1970); *Staat – Großraum – Nomos* (2005); *Frieden oder Pazifismus?* (2005).

Henry Sumner Maine (Kelso, 1822 – Cannes, 1888) was a British historian and jurist, considered to be one of the founders of legal anthropology and sociology. His stance, based on principles of evolutionary ideology, constituted an essential reference point for a number of social theorists.
Sumner Maine was a Professor of Civil Law at Cambridge University (1847-54) and was among the first to teach Roman law in the faculty of law. *Ancient law* (1861), his best known book, outlines the progress of legal systems, describes the primitive legal systems that Sumner Maine had studied under a lens that would allow him to look beyond the structure that appeared to the theorists of the time, and then connect these primitive systems with modern legal realities. According to him, the application of the comparative method 'to customs, ideas and motivations' was not a radical solution but a corrective to the historical limitations of the analytical concept.
Sumner Maine shows how all legal, historical, and human sciences are in close correlation with each other. One cannot understand the essence of law without knowing anthropology, just as one would not grasp the structure of custom, the

source before international law, without acquiring knowledge of Roman law. The legal system, having as its object the discipline of the behavior of individuals, can only have mankind as its point of origin the man in all its aspects.
Sumner Maine developed 'from status to contract' thesis, according to which in modern societies individual rights and obligations must be created by contracts as vehicles of freedom and individualism.
His main works are: *Ancient law* (1861); *Early History of Institutions* (1875); *Popular Government* (1885); *International Law* (1888).

Max Weber (Erfurt, 1864 – Munich, 1920) was a German sociologist and political economist, considered one of the leading figures of modern sociology. His thinking has been deeply influenced by German idealism and especially by a typical conception of neo-Kantianism, according to which reality is ontologically chaotic and ambiguous. He developed this particular issue through an evolutionary prospect in many of his prominent works.
In 1894, he got the economics chair at the University of Freiburg, then in Heidelberg in 1897. In 1903, Weber was one of the editors of *Archiv für Sozialwissenschaft und Sozialforschung*, where he published his famous essays 'Die "Objektivität" sozialwissenschaftlicher und sozialpolitischer Erkenntnis' and 'Die protestantische Ethik und der Geist des Kapitalismus' (1905) which ushered in his most original and fruitful period of work.
His main contribution in the sociological field is represented by the analysis of the relationship between religion and economics, started with the above-mentioned 'Die protestantische Ethik und der Geist des Kapitalismus', and continued with the comparative study of oriental religions collected in *Die Wirtschaftsethik der Weltreligionen* (1915-1919). His purpose was to show that social behaviors cannot be reduced only to economic causes, contrary to Marxist interpretations of that time. Weber argued that Protestantism, specifically Calvinism, influenced the creation of the spirit of capitalism, as it associates work and labor with vocation. Moreover, his theory, focusing on the 'rationalization', influenced both the sphere of economic and legal studies, representing a philosophical cornerstone for any subsequent conceptual elaboration.
His main works are: *Zur Geschichte der Handelsgesellschaften im Mittelalter* (1889); *Die römische Agrargeschichte in ihrer Bedeutung für das Staats- und Privatrecht* (1891); *Die Verhältnisse der Landarbeiter im ostelbischen Deutschland* (1892); *Wissenschaft als Beruf* (1919); *Politik als Beruf* (1919); *Gesammelte Aufsätze zur Religionssoziologie* (1920-1921); *Gesammelte Politische Schriften* (1921); *Gesammelte Aufsätze zur Wissenschaftslehre* (1924); *Gesammelte Aufsätze zur Sozial- und Wirtschaftsgeschichte* (1924); *Gesammelte Aufsätze zur Soziologie und Sozialpolitik* (1956).

CHAPTER 2

The Western legal tradition

- **The Roman origins of the Western legal tradition**
- **The Justinian compilation and its historical role**
- **The medieval renaissance of Roman law**
- **The development of continental *ius commune* and the advent of national codifications**
- **The parallel development of the English common law and equity**

The Western legal tradition is firmly based on the legacy of Roman law, transmitted over centuries through the Justinian compilation.
Roman law was organized in a highly specialized and autonomous field of rational knowledge, which jurists developed over time to govern social conflicts and to provide a shared education, culture, and mentality to officials and professionals involved in the steering of society.
The foundations of the Western legal tradition may be traced back to the renaissance of Roman law, which took place between the end of the eleventh and the beginning of the twelfth century.
In Bologna, Irnerius discovered a copy of the *Digestum* and began to comment on it and teach it along with the other books of the Justinian compilation in the universities. Glossators and Commentators carried on his work through particular techniques which saw them construe the sources of Roman law according to the needs of medieval society, thus creating a lively law in action.
In the same period, the Catholic Church was reformed and organized as a political institution, thus starting to develop a law of its own: 'Canon law' (or 'canonical law'), which, albeit to a lesser extent than civil law, was also based on Roman legal thinking.
In continental Europe, the combination of Roman law collected in the Justinian compilation and the apparatus of its 'scientific' interpretations by scholars (*communis opinio doctorum*) became the general law (*ius commune*) applicable. During the seventeenth century, the

universalism of the *ius commune* was increasingly challenged by the overwhelming complexity of the interplay between the sources of Roman law and the many strands of local law. This led to an exasperated legal particularism, which, through the rationalization and simplification of private law, favored the advent of the great civil codifications of the states of continental Europe.

In England, by contrast, it was the functioning of a royal and centralized jurisdiction that, in the late twelfth century, eventually created a 'common law' of the kingdom, which was later on flanked by 'equity' administrated by the Chancery. The rivalry between common law courts and equity courts became apparent in the sixteenth century and reached its peak in the seventeenth century, when King James I finally proclaimed that 'equity shall prevail'. The two legal bodies continued to exist in parallel until the late nineteenth century, when in most Anglo-American jurisdictions (starting with the US) their duality was terminated by the legislature (though it was disputed whether this happened only at the procedural level or also at the substantive level of the law). All attempts to codify English law failed, whereas they eventually bore some fruit in the US.

1. THE ROMAN INVENTION OF LAW

The laws of Western societies are based on Roman law.[1] By and large, Western law as such is an invention of the ancient Romans,[2] standing as the utmost expression of their national genius,[3] as philosophy was to ancient Greeks.

A certain influence of **Greek thought** on Roman law is to be acknowledged,[4] but it seems to have been rather modest.[5]

Greek thought, being highly speculative and abstract, contributed decidedly toward laying the philosophical foundations of law but less toward its establishment as a social practice gaining some autonomy from politics as such. While discussions among Greek philosophers about the conflict between the laws of the city and those of nature, or about the paradigm of democracy as a political regime, may be fundamental for Western civilization, it does not seem that they acknowledged an overall concept of law that could embrace both the legal rules applicable to citizens and the legal process.[6] What is certain is

[1] James Gordley, *The Jurists. A Critical History* (OUP 2013) 1.

[2] Aldo Schiavone, *The Invention of Law in the West* (The Belknap Press of Harvard UP 2012) 3f.

[3] Max Kaser, *Das Römische Privatrecht*, vol 1, *Das altrömische, das vorklassische und klassische Recht* (2nd edn, CH Beck 1971) 1.

[4] Franz Wieacker, 'Der römische Jurist' in Id, *Vom römischen Recht* (2nd edn, KF Koehler 1961) 128, 149.

[5] Gordley (n 1) 13ff; Jacob Giltaij, 'Greek Philosophy and Classical Roman Law: A Brief Overview' in Paul J du Plessis, Clifford Ando and Kaius Tuori (eds), *The Oxford Handbook of Roman Law and Society* (OUP 2016) 188ff.

[6] Michael Gagarin and Paul Woodruff, 'Early Greek Legal Thought' in Fred D Miller Jr and Carrie-Ann Biondi (eds), *A History of the Philosophy of Law from the Ancient Greeks to the Scholastics* (Springer 2007) 7ff.

that many city-states (πόλεις, *poleis*) issued a specific set of statutes (νόμοι, *nomoi*), but only very few of them survived the centuries.

> A recognition of ancient Greek constitutions, some of them being real and others being instead figments of imagination, is contained in Aristotle's *Politics*, where they are classified into six brackets.[7] A similar taxonomy, which has a comparative character (see *infra*, ch 3, para 3.1), is set forth in Plato's dialogue titled *Statesman*.[8]
> The two major city-states, namely Sparta and Athens, were famed for their constitutions, their being attributed to legendary legislators (Lycurgus and, respectively, Draco and Solon). A text tentatively attributed to Aristotle (or to his disciples), entitled *The Constitution of the Athenians* (or *Athenian Constitution*), is an important source of information on this set of legal rules.[9]

The **novelty of Roman law** does not exclude, however, that it could have been forged and historically developed thanks to the influence of other ancient cultures and civilizations. To the extreme, it has been fiercely claimed that Roman law was devoid of any originality, consisting instead of a patchwork of transplants from other cultures, particularly of Middle Eastern and northern African civilizations.[10] Yet even if true, it would be hard to deny that it was precisely in ancient Rome (and nowhere else) that all those items were combined into a unique mix, thus generating the peculiar phenomenon which constitutes Western law. Particularly, the establishment of a professional cadre of jurists is a distinctive feature of Roman society, one which is not be encountered in any other civilization of the antiquity (including that of the Greeks).
Law was called ***ius*** by the Romans, a term whose etymology is still obscure and largely disputed. The prevailing view surmises that its root meant 'pureness' and was underpinned by some religious stance (see *supra*, ch 1, para 2). The pureness of law must have originally consisted in a state of peace with the demons and the powers of evil, which was reached at court by casting the appropriate spell during the rite of the trial. The 'pure' party thus gained the victory over its 'impure' opponent.[11]
Accordingly, primitive trial in Roman law was much akin to a religious sacrifice, but at the same time it marked a first step towards the secularization of law and overall society (see *supra*, ch 1, para 2). As the sacrificial victim was killed by the priest because it was impure, so the condemned party was defeated because it was guilty. *Ius* (as law of men towards other men) was subsequently to depart from *fas* (as law of men towards gods).[12]

[7] Fred D Miller Jr, 'Aristotle's Philosophy of Law' in Miller Jr and Biondi (eds) (n 6) 79ff.
[8] Richard F Stalley, 'Platonic Philosophy of Law' ibid (n 6) 66ff.
[9] Gagarin and Woodruff (n 6) 15ff.
[10] Pier Giuseppe Monateri, 'Black Gaius: A Quest for the Multicultural Origins of the "Western Legal Tradition"' (2000) 51 Hastings LJ 479, following upon the general account by Martin Bernal, *Black Athena: The Afro-asiatic Roots of Classical Civilizations*, 3 vols (Rutgers UP 1987, 1991 and 2006).
[11] Kaser (n 3) para 4.
[12] About the relation of *ius* and *fas*, see Schiavone (n 2) 60f.

In neo-Latin languages, the root of *ius* proved highly productive and engendered words like *just*, *justice*, *jurisprudence*, *jurist*, *jurisdiction*, and *juridical*. Nevertheless, in the common parlance of the Middle Ages the word itself fell out of use. As meaning 'law', *ius* was replaced by the term *directum*, which meant 'the straight', or, 'the right way' (to behave oneself). In neo-Latin languages it turned into French *droit*, Spanish *derecho*, Portuguese *direito*, and Italian *diritto*; and we also find German *Recht* and English *right*. In German-speaking territories, it is only the faculty of law that is still nowadays called *Ius*, or *Iura*.
In civil law systems, the same term is used in both the objective sense of law and in the subjective sense of a right (see *infra* ch 10, para 4).

In its **earlier stages** (753 bc-451 bc), Roman law was confined to a number of fixed procedures and imbued with an extreme formalism, which however loosened through the historical development of the trial system. In fact, attention increasingly shifted from the law to be applied to the judicial proceedings as such, to the law to be applied to the facts alleged by the parties. Roman law thus gained a substantive dimension.[13]
In the **late Republic** (201 bc-27 bc), jurists (*prudentes*) became a cadre of experts learned in law, whose legal decisions (*responsa*) were at first rendered mainly on the basis of intuition and experience acquired through the administration of justice.[14] Over time, however, their decisions were increasingly discussed as being principled and rationally grounded, thus showing a high degree of reasoning.[15] The collections of the legal decisions authored by the most prominent classical jurists gradually constituted a body of specialized literature (see *infra*, ch 2, para 2), which eventually amounted to the foundations of a proper *iurisprudentia* (legal wisdom, or legal knowledge).[16]
Indeed, what characterized Roman law is that it was organized in a **highly specialized and autonomous field of rational knowledge**, which jurists developed over time to govern social conflicts and to provide a shared education, culture, and mentality to officials and professionals involved in steering society and addressing its development.[17] Although increasingly challenged by contemporary legal realism, Western law is still styled as being endowed with an inner rationality and an ideal existence,[18] which oppose its single application to empirical facts and, in so doing, raise expectations of justice.

[13] Alan Watson, *The Spirit of Roman Law* (Georgia UP 1995) 39.
[14] Fritz Schulz, *History of Roman Legal Science* (Clarendon Press 1946) 102ff.
[15] Jan D Harke, 'Legal Methods in Ancient Rome' in Karl Riesenhuber (ed), *European Legal Methodology* (Intersentia 2017) 11ff.
[16] Ulrike Babuslaux, 'Legal Writing and Legal Reasoning' in du Plessis, Ando and Tuori (eds) (n 5) 176ff.
[17] Schulz (n 14) 141ff. For a different view, see however Detlef Liebs, 'Römische Provinzialjurisprudenz'. *Aufstieg und Niedergang der römischen Welt*, vol II.15 (de Gruyter 1976) 322ff; Id, 'Jurisprudenz' in Reinhard Herzog (ed), *Handbuch der Lateinischen Literatur der Antike* (CH Beck 1997) 209ff.
[18] Ernest J Weinrib, *The Idea of Private Law* (OUP 2015).

2. CLASSICAL ROMAN LAW AND THE JUSTINIAN COMPILATION

It should be noted that Roman law as such is a rough (and possibly detrimental) abstraction.
First, Roman law cannot be depicted as a stable and full-fledged legal system, which came to light once and for ever at a certain point of history. Rather, it had been growing and changing tremendously over many centuries, during which its own content and structure underwent a deep and wide historical evolution. Therefore, what is called Roman law has never existed as such, its representing instead an unhistorical mixture of legal concepts, stances, and measures belonging to distant ages and pertaining to different contexts.

> It was especially Riccardo Orestano (1909-1988) who strongly insisted on the necessity to historicize 'Roman law' as such and to distinguish it from the 'tradition' it has initiated, thus dismissing any form of 'crypto-natural law'.[19]

Particularly, the foundation of the Western legal tradition rests on a relatively tiny span of that very long history, namely the **Roman classic law** that flourished between the end of the first century bc and the beginning of the third century ad. Conventional as dates of this kind may obviously be, its rise was marked by the creation of the Empire (27 bc), and its fall was parallel to the beginning of the 'Crisis of the Third Century of the Empire', or 'Military Anarchy' (ad 235).
Secondly, our knowledge of Roman law is necessarily partial and inaccurate, and sometimes deceptive. In fact, almost all that Roman jurists of the classical age (such as Pomponius, Ulpianus, and Paulus) wrote, ie more than two thousand books, did not survive the 'dark centuries' of the early Middle Ages, which followed the **fall of the Roman empire** in the western provinces (ad 476).

> In ad 476 Odoacer (433-493), an officer of what had remained of the Roman army, was proclaimed by the Germanic *foederati* as king of Italy (*rex Italiae*) and afterwards deposed the young Emperor Romulus Augustus (derisively nicknamed as Augustulus, ie little Augustus).
> Edward Gibbon (1737-1794) popularized this event as the fall of the 'Western Roman Empire',[20] an expression which actually does not indicate a political entity on its own, but only the Western part of the Roman Empire, which had settled its own abode in Ravenna.

[19] Riccardo Orestano, *Introduzione allo studio del diritto romano* (Il Mulino 1987) 454ff. On Orestano's work, see Paolo Grossi, 'Storia di esperienze giuridiche e tradizione romanistica (a proposito della rinnovata e definitiva "Introduzione allo studio del diritto romano" di Riccardo Orestano' [1988] Quaderni fiorentini 545ff.
[20] Edward Gibbon, *The History of the Decline and Fall of the Roman Empire*, vol 6 (first published 1788, Fred De Fau & Co 1906) Ch XXXVI, 84ff.

During the upheavals of that troubled age, most of classical culture, which the Greeks and the Romans had bequeathed to mankind, went lost, except for the works that the amanuenses of the monasteries preserved and copied for posterity. Unfortunately, parchments used as media to be written on were rare and costly, so that they were recycled many times (**palimpsests**). In fact, monks were accustomed to treating old parchments containing writings they were not interested as a convenient medium which could be used again in the drafting, or even in the binding, of other (mostly theological) texts.

The sole work of Roman we possess in its original text is **Gaius's *Institutiones***. It consists of a handbook of law written around ad 161 by a law teacher, Gaius (130-180). In 1816, Barthold Georg Niebuhr (1776-1831), an ambassador and minister plenipotentiary of the Holy See at the Prussian state, made a stop in Verona during a long journey and, while visiting the local chapter library, a famous repository of ancient manuscripts and incunabula, intuited that a ponderous volume of St. Jerome's theological works was a palimpsest, which contained an even more interesting text. It was that of Gaius's *Institutiones*, which was subsequently edited with the cooperation of some of the most prominent scholars of Roman law of the time, namely Friedrich Carl von Savigny (see *infra*, ch 4, para 3.1.2) and Gustav (Conrad von) Hugo (see *infra*, ch 4, para 3.1.2). Unfortunately, the methods used to recover the hidden text destroyed it partially. The gaps were later on filled in thanks to the other sources found in the meantime, particularly a papyrus writing coming from Egypt and published in 1933 by Vincenzo Arangio-Ruiz (1884-1964). Thus, it was possible not only to have a (nearly) complete text of Gaius's *Institutiones* but also to attain evidence that it was genuine.

What remained of Roman law and was transmitted to us is contained (almost) exclusively in a compilation assembled in Constantinople (Byzantium) during the sixth century ad at the behest of the emperor Justinian I (482-565), therefore known as the **Justinian compilation**. Actually, this vast anthology served like a kind of 'Ark of the Covenant' that worked to rescue the legacy of Roman law from the deluge of the early Middle Ages and pass it on over the centuries. In doing so, Justinian decidedly contributed in setting the foundations of the Western legal tradition.

The celebrated forty-fourth chapter of Edward Gibbon's *The Decline and Fall of the Roman Empire* commences with these significant words: 'The vain titles of the victories of Justinian are crumbled into dust; but the name of the legislator is inscribed on a fair and everlasting monument'.[21]

In fact, after acceding to the imperial throne in Constantinople (Byzantium), in ad 527, Justinian mandated a commission, chaired by Tribonianus, to draw up a collection (***Codex***) of snippets from the *constitutiones* (statutes), ie the

[21] Edward Gibbon, *The History of the Decline and Fall of the Roman Empire*, vol 7 (first published 1788, Fred De Fau & Co 1906) Ch XLIV, 301. See also Michael H Hoeflich, 'Edward Gibbon, Roman Lawyer' (1991) 39 Am J Comp L 803.

normative measures issued by the emperors from the age of Hadrian and previously already gathered in a number of similar works which had been set out over time. This task was accomplished in ad 529.

After putting the legislative acts of the political power (*leges*) into order, Justinian charged the same commission with the task of doing the same with the corpus of jurisprudence (*iura*) contained in the best opinions and writings authored by jurists during the classical age of Roman law. Thus, in ad 533, a book was edited that was called the **Digest** (***Digesta*** or, according to the Greek equivalent, ***Pandectae***), meaning a well-ordered compilation and collection of texts.

It consists of a huge collection of excerpts from about two thousand writings of the most important Roman jurists (*iuris prudentes*) of the classical age, which stands for us as the only means to become acquainted with their legal thought. Our knowledge of classical Roman law is therefore very limited in quantity, since the fragments collected in the Justinian compilation represent a shred of the overall corpus of Roman legal literature, the compilation being estimated as amounting to five per cent of Roman legal authors' literary production.[22] Secondly, and perhaps more importantly, it is quite likely that the works used for the Justinian compilation were not always genuine, several of them having underwent a process of alteration during the post-classical period.[23] Some of these modifications may have been voluntary (abridgments, simplifications, apocryphal works, and so on), some others involuntary (oversights, mechanical errors of transcription, and so on).

Furthermore, Justinian himself commanded Tribonianus and the other commissioners to modernize the fragments they were in charge of collecting and to adapt them to the new social needs, since they were taken from writings dating back to many centuries before.

These amendments made by the Justinian commissioners to the text of the collected fragments bear the traditional name of 'interpolations'.[24]

Whilst the *Codex* continued to be used after Justinian, the *Digesta* were nearly destined to disappear, or at least to be neglected during the early Middle Ages. In fact, due to its classicism and the highly sophisticated level of legal reasoning they embody, the *Digesta* contained texts that must have afterwards appeared too difficult and far removed from contemporary problems, owing to the dramatic sinking of the general level of culture, particularly in the area of law.

Remaining in use after Justinian was not the above-mentioned *Codex* of ad 529 (traditionally styled as *prius* or *vetus*), but its second edition, issued in ad

[22] Gordley (n 1) 1.

[23] Franz Wieacker, *Textstufen klassischer Juristen* (Vandenhoeck & Ruprecht 1960, repr 1975).

[24] Reinhard Zimmermann, 'Corpus Juris Civilis' in Jürgen Basedow, Klaus J Hopt, Reinhard Zimmermann and Andreas Stier (eds), *The Max Planck Encyclopedia of European Private Law*, vol 1 (OUP 2012) 416.

534 (*Codex repetitae praelectionis*). Furthermore, the Justinian compilation comprised the *Institutiones*, issued in ad 533, and the *Novellae constitutiones*. The *Institutiones* were a textbook mainly directed to teaching but binding as a source of law as well. The *Novellae* collect the *constitutiones* enacted after ad 534 and until Justinian's death.

3. THE MEDIEVAL RENAISSANCE OF ROMAN LAW

The foundation of the Western legal tradition may be traced back to the renaissance of Roman law, which took place between the end of the eleventh century and the beginning of the twelfth century.

According to Harold J. Berman (1918-2007), the outset of the Western legal tradition should be traced back to the great papal revolution which took place in the late eleventh century, when Pope Gregory VII re-founded the Catholic Church as a mundane institution based upon law (see *infra*, ch 2, para 4.1). Since then, Berman claims, the Western institutions would have grown seamlessly over time, since each generation would have willingly constructed its own work upon that of the generations before. Even the major nation revolutions (as the French of 1789 and the Russian of 1917) would be in line with the legal tradition, which they (or their leaders) still purported to overcome.[25]

At the time, a jurist called **Irnerius**, also known as Wernerius, or Guarnerius (1050?-1125?), possibly of German origin, discovered in Bologna a copy of the *Digestum* and began to comment on it and to teach it and the other books of the Justinian compilation. His comments on the fragments of the Justinian compilation, which were written between the lines of the manuscript or on the margins, thus formed a critical apparatus called *glossa*.

It is possible to draw a parallel between the medieval exegesis of the Justinian compilation and that of the Bible. During the Middle Ages, both law and Catholic religion were based on a 'sacred' book and its interpretation (see also *supra*, ch 1, para 2).
On a different note, during the Middle Ages Roman law commanded an allegiance which to some extent was not exempt from religious respect. This was reflected also in the historical figure of Justinian himself, who Dante portrayed in the *Paradiso* of his *Divina commedia*.

In a short time, young people from the four corners of Europe gathered around Irnerius, eager to listen to him and to be guided on the subtilities and profundities of Roman law. A school (*studium*) was therefore born, probably in 1088. The first university of the (Western) world was thus established:

[25] Harold J Berman, *Law and Revolution: The Formation of the Western Legal Tradition* (Harvard UP 1985); Id, *Law and Revolution*, vol 2, *The Impact of the Protestant Reformations on the Western Legal Tradition* (The Belknap Press of Harvard UP 2006).

the *alma mater studiorum*, as the **University of Bologna** still nowadays styles itself proudly.[26]

This primacy may be to some extent challenged by the medical school that around 1057 had been established in Salerno and that maintained great reputation throughout the Middle Ages.

Irnerius used to begin his lessons by reading a fragment of the Justinian compilation aloud (in fact, the term 'lesson' comes from the Latin verb *legere*, meaning 'to read'). After being read, each fragment was explained, and its meaning clarified through the discussion of pertaining cases.
Students attending Irnerius's lessons copied the texts of the *Digesta* he used (*littera bononiensis*) and, returning to their native countries, brought them home, thus contributing to its dissemination all across Europe.

Irnerius's work was carried on by his four disciples (Bulgarus, Martinus Gosia, Jacopus de Boragine, and Hugo de Porta Ravennate), who transmitted his methods to future generations of scholars, known as **Glossators**.[27] The most prominent among them were Azo (1150-1225) and his disciple Accursius (1184-1263), whose *glossa* commanded so wide a consensus as to be acknowledged as a staple text for studying and applying law all across Europe, thus amounting to a cornerstone of the Western legal tradition. This *glossa* was therefore depicted as *magna*, or *ordinaria*, or *magistralis*.
Between the thirteenth and the fourteenth century, a renewal of the Bologna technique of interpreting the Justinian compilation was accomplished by the **Commentators**,[28] who were characterized as being less stuck on the text and more inclined to interpret it on the basis of its rationale, thus adapting it more promptly to the needs of contemporary society. The most prominent among them was Bartolus de Saxoferrato (1314-1357) and his disciple Baldus de Ubaldis (1327-1400).

4. THE CONTINENTAL *IUS COMMUNE* AND THE ENGLISH COMMON LAW

4.1. *Corpus iuris civilis* and *Corpus iuris canonici*

Secular law applied across Europe was therefore centered on the Justinian compilation, which the epithet of *Corpus iuris civilis* was therefore bestowed upon, ie the 'body' of civil law.

[26] Viola Heutger and Eltjo Schrage, 'Legal History and Comparative Law' in Jan M Smits (ed), *Elgar Encyclopedia of Comparative Law* (2nd edn, Edward Elgar 2012) 505ff.
[27] Stefan Vogenauer, 'Legal Scholarship' in Jürgen Basedow, Klaus J Hopt, Reinhard Zimmermann and Andreas Stier (eds), *The Max Planck Encyclopedia of European Private Law*, vol 2 (OUP 2012) 1077.
[28] ibid.

According to the teaching methodology of the school of Bologna, the Justinian compilation was reorganized into five parts, the so-called *Libri legales*. The first three of these consisted of portions of the *Digesta*, following the order they had been allegedly rediscovered by Irnerius (*Digestum vetus, Infortiatum, Digestum novum*). The fourth tome contained the first nine books of the *Codex*. The rest of the *Codes*, the *Institutiones* and 134 of the *Novellae* – subsequently supplemented by a collection of feudal books (*Libri feudorum*),[29] which formed the so-called *decima collatio* – were gathered in the fifth and last tome.
In continental Europe, the paradigm of legal education was constituted by the *Digestum vetus* and the first nine books of the *Codex*.

The work of Glossators and Commentators (see *supra*, ch 2, para 3) was strongly characterized by an overall tendency to disregard the historical remoteness of the Justinian compilation and to interpret it pragmatically as a lively source of law in action. Therefore, Glossators and Commentators were not so much interested in ascertaining what the authors of these texts intended to say in the far past when they had been living and working, but what the texts could still contribute in addressing and solving social problems after so many centuries. The tremendous changes that had in the meanwhile occurred in society and political institutions drove Glossators and Commentators to undertake a mighty endeavor of creative interpretation and adaptation of those ancient texts, so that they could cope with a material world so different from that known to their authors. Since Glossators and Commentators had been active in Italy, their methodology became characterized as ***mos italicus*** (ie Italian usage, or Italian style).

During the sixteenth century the spread of Renaissance humanism challenged the Italian style and aimed at searching for the original purity of Roman law.[30] The texts of the Justinian compilation were subject to a critique based on a historical-philological method. Its main representatives may be identified in (Giovanni) Andrea Alciato, also known as Andreas Alciatus (1492-1550), and his disciple Jacques Cujas, *alias* Cujacius (1522-1590), as well as in Hugues Doneau, also known as Hugo Donellus (1527-1591). Since the forerunner of the method, namely Alciato, had – though Italian – taught predominantly in France, these methods flourished particularly in that country, so that they were defined as ***mos gallicus*** (ie French usage, or French style).
A continuation of the philological interests and the humanistic approach that distinguished the *mos gallicus* can be seen in the **Dutch Elegant School**, which flourished in the Netherlands during their Golden Age of the sixteenth century, particularly in the University of Leiden (founded in 1575). Among its most significant exponents are Gerard Nood (1647-1725) and Ulrich Huber (1636-1694).[31]

[29] Andreas Thier, 'Feudal Law' in *The Max Planck Encyclopedia of European Private Law*, vol 2 (n 27) 689.
[30] Klaus Lug, 'Humanism' in *The Max Planck Encyclopedia of European Private Law*, vol 2 (n 27) 835.
[31] Antonio Padoa Schioppa, *A History of Law in Europe. From the Early Middle Ages to the Twentieth Century* (CUP 2017) 286ff.

The apparatus of comments enshrined in the *glossae* grew over time, up to the point that comments were no longer written between the lines or on margins of the Justinian compilation but published as a work of their own. Rapidly, the most widespread opinions rendered by the scholars of law (***communis opinio doctorum***) became as authoritative as the Justinian compilation itself.[32] During the thirteenth and the fourteenth century, the combination of Roman law collected in the Justinian compilation and the apparatus of its doctrinal interpretation by scholars gradually became the general law (***ius commune***) that was to be applied in Italy, southern France, and the Iberian Peninsula, unless differently settled in local statutes or customs, including feudal law (*iura propria*). Eventually, the Holy Roman Empire (*Sacrum Romanum Imperium*),[33] ie the political institution that claimed since the ninth century to have inherited the domination of Christianity from the ancient Roman Empire, formally and officially adopted the *ius commune* (**reception of Roman law**).[34]

> The traditional date of the reception of Roman law in German countries is 1495, when the *Reichskammergericht*, ie the Imperial Chamber Court, was established in Frankfurt.[35] Emperor Maximilian I (1459-1519) ruled that it should make its own decision 'according to the common laws of the Empire [...] and the fair and honorable individual ordonnances, statutes and customs of the principalities, sovereignties and courts, which are brought before them', including the *glossa* by Accursius and the Commentators' opinions.
> Prior to that date, some German scholars had already argued that Roman law had even been formally adopted through an order of Emperor Lothar von Supplinburg of 1135.[36] In 1643, however, Hermann Conring (1606-1681), who was eager to pave the way for the abandonment of Roman law in favor of the native law of German peoples, demonstrated that such proto-reception (*Frühreception*) of the former was but a legend (the so-called *Lotharische Legende*).[37]

Although the *ius commune* was deemed subsidiary to the *iura propria*, this relation was reversed in the legal practice of the superior courts across Europe, which were decidedly inclined to latch onto the *ius commune* as a supreme source of law. In fact, the litigant who pled for the application of the *iura propria* was burdened by the onus of proving its existence and its content,

[32] Padoa Schioppa (n 31) 297ff; Vogenauer (n 27) 1079.
[33] Hans-Peter Haferkamp, 'Holy Roman Empire' in *The Max Planck Encyclopedia of European Private Law*, vol 1 (n 24) 835.
[34] Gebhard Rehm, 'Reception' in *The Max Planck Encyclopedia of European Private Law*, vol 2 (n 27) 1416ff.
[35] Filippo Ranieri, 'Reichskammergericht (Imperial Chamber Court)' in Jürgen Basedow, Klaus J Hopt, Reinhard Zimmermann and Andreas Stier (eds), *The Max Planck Encyclopedia of European Private Law*, vol 2 (n 27) 1435.
[36] Nils Jansen, 'Ius Commune' in *The Max Planck Encyclopedia of European Private Law*, vol 1 (n 24) 1007.
[37] Klaus Luig, 'Usus Modernus' in *The Max Planck Encyclopedia of European Private Law*, vol 2 (n 27) 1756.

otherwise the *ius commune* was to be applied (*fundata intentio*).[38] Yet in many countries local customs had long remained uncodified and, even if codified, their content could prove obscure or in any event controversial, so that the proof required to apply them was too cumbersome and the way paved to an almost general application of the *ius commune*. At any rate, legislation by a state-town or a sovereign was to be interpreted narrowly (*statuta sunt stricte interpretanda*), thus leaving much room for the application of the *ius commune*.[39]

In the first book of his *The Old Regime and the Revolution*, Alexis de Tocqueville (1805-1859) devotes chapter four to 'How Almost All of Europe Had Come to Have Identical Institutions and How These Institutions Fell into Ruin Everywhere'. In particular, in a note relating to this chapter he affirms that 'Roman Law soon ended up by entirely driving out the national law from a large part of legislation, planting its roots even on the ground where it let the national legislation subsist'.[40] The author identifies two grounds for this phenomenon: (i) the prestige enjoyed by the languages and cultures of antiquity; and (ii) the aspiration of the Holy Roman Empire to stand as the continuation of the Roman Empire (thanks to the so-called *translation imperii*). In addition to the above, the author refers to the fact that Roman law was a law of servitude and, therefore, it would have been particularly apt to uphold the absolute powers of rulers of the time.

In turn, the Catholic Church, which at least from the time of Pope Gregory VII (1173-1185) was also organized as a political institution (see *supra*, ch 2, para 3),[41] had been developing a law of its own, which was based on ancient rules (*canones*) and which was later developed through letters of the Popes that formulated decisions (*litterae decretales*). This law was called **canon law (or canonical law)** and, albeit to a lesser extent than civil law, was also based on Roman legal thought.

The main collection of canons was made right before the middle of the twelfth century and, although its real name was that of *Concordia discordantium canonum*, it became universally known as the ***Decretum Gratiani***, from the name of the bishop (or '*antivescovo*') of Chiusi – also a jurist – who drafted the work. It was therefore a private collection, which for the first time gathered a selection of the sources of canon law, accumulated over a thousand years of the Catholic Church's history.
In addition, there was the collection of pontifical *decretales* which Pope Gregory IX (1170?-1241) published in 1234 with the bull *Rex pacificus* and which had been compiled by Saint Raymond of Peñafort. According to a fortunate parallelism, this collection is to the *Decretum Gratiani* what the *Codex Iustinianeus* is to the *Digestum*.

[38] Jansen (n 36) 1008.
[39] ibid.
[40] Alexis de Tocqueville, *The Old Regime and the Revolution* (Alan S Kahan tr, François Furet and Françoise Mélonio eds, Chicago UP 1998) 258.
[41] Berman (n 25).

The *Decretum Gratiani* and the *Decretales* of Pope Gregory IX thus represented the original nucleus of a larger collection of sources of canon law, which was given the epithet of ***Corpus iuris canonici***: 'body' of canonical law. A parallel with the aforementioned *Corpus iuris civilis* was thus evidently drawn.

Civil law and canonical law, therefore, shared the same Roman roots and were sensed as the two components of a 'common law' (*ius commune*), which is the matrix of the Western legal tradition (**Roman-canon law**).[42] A full jurist of the Middle Ages was supposed to master both the civil and the canonical law, thus to be learned in both of them (*doctor utriusque iuris*).

On this historical ground, still nowadays the title of 'master of the laws' (LLM) is bestowed upon those who graduate in law, whereby the plural usage historically recalls the duality (and complementarity) of civil and canonical law.

The bulk of medieval legal education consisted of Roman law (mostly classical, or at least presumed to be so) as handed down by the Justinian compilation and interpreted by the great scholars at universities: first those of northern Italy; later on also in France and Germany, as well as the Netherlands; but also at Oxford and Cambridge (see *infra*, ch 2, para 4.2). Over time, the *Corpus iuris civilis* (and above all the *Digestum*) was the subject of great works of comment and explanation, which for centuries represented the common basis of learning and teaching law in European universities.[43]

Following the model of Bologna, numerous universities were born during the twelfth century in continental Europe, some of ecclesiastical constitution, others secular. Among the most important, those established in Paris (between 1150 and 1170), Salamanca (1218), Montpellier (1220), and Padua (1222).
In German territories, the first university was erected in Heidelberg (1386), preceded by that of Prague (1348), which, though not on a German territory, was attended by many German students.

4.2. Common law and equity

The **Norman conquest** of England, traditionally marked by the battle of Hastings (1066), was followed by the development of a new law during the reign of Henry II (1154-1189), which, although coexisting with the previous local customs of the Anglo-Saxons, ruled the whole kingdom and was therefore called the common law. By the middle of the thirteenth century, the common law amounted to a full-fledged legal system, endowed with its own specialist practitioners and its own technical language and literature.[44]

[42] Jansen (n 36) 1007.
[43] ibid 1009.
[44] John Baker, *Introduction to English Legal History* (5th edn, OUP 2019) 34.

Unlike the continental *ius commune*, the English common law was not based on a fundamental book to be interpreted by scholars and studied at universities but emerged gradually from the functioning of a system of **royal jurisdiction**, which originally aimed at maintaining 'the king's peace' and at creating an alternative to the seignorial justice rendered by feudal lords, which was often slow and unsatisfactory. Consequently, the relationship between substantive law and judicial procedure has been the reverse of what is to be found in continental Europe, where substantive law comes to the forefront and procedure follows; indeed, the common law grew 'in the interstices of procedure' (see *infra*, ch 10, para 1).[45]

In fact, if a litigant distrusted local courts or did not wish to wait for the next visit of itinerant royal justices (known as justices in eyre),[46] she could turn to the king, who, by issuing a brief memorandum (***breve* or writ**), could order that the case be heard. This jurisdiction applied first to criminal cases also involving disputes over the property of land and to other torts and only subsequently (and with some hardship) to mere civil litigation arising from private agreements.

Gradually, three central royal courts (King's Bench, Court of Common Pleas, and Exchequer) became autonomous.[47] They developed a standardized panoply of **forms of action**, which encapsulated each legal claim in a stiff procedural scheme.[48]

For each type of controversy admitted to the royal jurisdiction, a new writ was created by the **Royal Chancery**, which was a procedural formula based a peculiar factual scheme. A case could be brought to the king's judges if and only if it met the factual scheme of one specific writ. This led to a gradual loss of judicial powers of the barons, which finally led to the point that through the 1285 Westminster Statute the creation of writs was forbidden.[49]

Because of the rigid formalism of both the system of writs and some cumbersome procedures, the common law as applied by the royal courts soon came to be characterized by numerous gaps and injustices. Although for different reasons, this ultimately gave rise to the very same popular discontent that the creation of common law had intended to eliminate. This resulted in even more new appeals to the sovereign, who then had to render justice for each case individually. As it became unrealistic for the king to decide this increasing number of cases one by one, it was the Lord Chancellor and, later on, the Court of Chancery that carried out the task and developed its own jurisdiction (**equity**).[50]

The **Lord Chancellor**, usually an ecclesiastic who applied and referred to the principles of canon law and, indirectly, of Roman law, could decide *secundum conscientiam* (according to his conscience) that a case should be removed from

[45] Henry Sumner Maine, *Dissertations on Early Law and Custom* (John Murray 1883).
[46] Baker (n 44) 17ff.
[47] ibid 20ff.
[48] ibid 60ff.
[49] Uwe Kishel, *Comparative Law* (Andrew Hammer tr, OUP 2019) 276.
[50] Baker (n 44) 114ff.

the courts of common law and decided on equity; he could even reopen a case that had already been decided by those courts, and he was not bound by the precedents of common law.

In order to achieve consistency and therefore predictability in their decisions, equity courts sought to forge and, as far as possible, adhere to **maxims of equity**, which could more or less provide guidance for subsequent rulings (eg 'Equity regards as done what ought to be done', 'Equity will not suffer a wrong to be without a remedy', 'Equity aids the vigilant not the indolent', etc.) (see also *infra*, ch 6, para 3).

From its origins in the twelfth century, equity had increasingly expanded to the point of standing as an alternative and competing system to common law, despite the assertion that *aequitas sequitur legem* (equity follows the law). This resulted in a strong reaction by common law courts, which were concerned about possibly losing a significant portion of their powers.[51] The Lord Chancellors had to defend their role as moderators of the rigor of the common law, particularly Thomas More (1477-1535), who was, among other things, sentenced to death for not recognizing the Anglican religious reform, and Francis Bacon (1561-1626).[52]

In the seventeenth century, the conflict fully entered the realm of the political as, during the civil war of 1649 and the revolution of 1688, common law courts had taken sides with Parliament, whereas equity, as exercised by the Lord Chancellor, constituted a typical emanation of the king's powers, and therefore it was difficult to control from a democratic point of view. In an attempt to mark a line between the two jurisdictions, a harsh debate took place between the Lord Chancellor, Thomas Edgerton, first Earl of Ellesmere (1540-1617), and Sir Edward Coke (1522-1634),[53] and it was ended by the decision of King James I, according to which '**equity shall prevail**'.

However, this decision foretold radical changes to equity. In fact, it no longer sought to pursue the justice of the single case at hand but transformed itself into a proper legal system,[54] which went on growing separately from the common law, with each system being administered by a judicial hierarchy of courts on its own. It was only in the late nineteenth century that in most Anglo-American jurisdictions (starting with the US) this dual system was terminated by the legislature (see *infra*, ch 4, para 4).

The great success of the king's jurisdiction drove the English system of common law to develop in parallel to continental civil law. According to a famous analysis, 'while the other nations of Western Europe were beginning to adopt as their own the ultimate results of Roman legal history, England was unconsciously reproducing that history; it was developing a formular system

[51] ibid 116ff.
[52] Padoa Schioppa (n 31) 389.
[53] ibid 390ff.
[54] Martin Illmer, 'Equity' in *The Max Planck Encyclopedia of European Private Law*, vol 1 (n 24) 528, 531.

which in the ages that were coming would be the strongest bulwark against Romanism and severe [...] English law from all her sisters'.[55]
Common law barristers were in fact trained at the Inns of Court in London (see *infra*, ch 7, para 4) rather than receiving degrees in canon or civil law at the Universities of Oxford or Cambridge.[56]

> The study of Roman law was brought to England in 1149 by the Lombard Roger Vacarius (1120-1200), prior to the establishment of the Universities of Oxford (1167) and Cambridge (1209), where canon law was taught as well.
> However, the teaching of canon law was suppressed by King Henry VIII in 1535, due to the Anglican religious reform and the schism with the Catholic Church.[57] From that time, therefore, the study of Roman law remained the only legal science admitted at English universities.
> Despite the fact that several universities had been founded in Scotland (St. Andrews in 1412, Glasgow in 1451, and Edinburgh in 1556), until the middle of the nineteenth century most Scottish students used to move to the continent for their legal studies, especially to the University of Leiden.[58]

Yet, it must be pointed out that some application of Roman law regularly took place also in England, particularly for subject matters that fell under the competence of ecclesiastical courts and the Court of Admiralty (see *infra*, ch 4, para 1). Even more importantly, common law itself (not to mention equity) was by no means immune from the influence of the civilian tradition, whose legal doctrines and institutions were rather continuously imported to England (see *infra*, ch 4, para 1).

5. THE ADVENT OF NATIONAL LAW (*IUS PATRIUM*) AND THE IDEAL OF ITS CODIFICATION

During the seventeenth century, the universalism of the *ius commune* was increasingly challenged by the growing complexity of the interplay between the sources of Roman law (including the medieval *glossae* embodying the *opinio doctorum*) and the many strands of local law (city statutes, feudal norms, local and regional customs, and so on) (see *supra*, ch 2, para 4.1). This development engendered a tremendous lack of legal certainty, which was reflected in the unpredictability of the decisions by the superior courts; an extreme **legal particularism** was widespread, since in each town a different law was to be applied.

[55] Sir Frederick Pollock and Frederic W Maitland, *The History of English Law before the Time of Edward I*, vol 2 (2nd edn, CUP 1898) 558.
[56] Baker (n 44) 34.
[57] ibid 141.
[58] Padoa Schioppa (n 31) 400.

With regard to the French territory in the seventeenth century, Voltaire (1694-1778) describes the situation of the law in stating that: 'In addition to these forty thousand laws, of which we always quote some random, there are five hundred and forty different customs in France, if we count all the provinces and even villages which are exempt from the principal jurisdiction of the kingdom. A man who should travel through France in a post chaise changes the law he is governed by more than he changes horses as has already been said, and a lawyer who will be very learned in his city will be an ignorant man in the neighboring city'.[59]

A cure to these shortcomings of the medieval *ius commune* was acknowledged in the advent of a national law, which could replace the abstract universalism of Roman-canon law, what for its part was also challenged by the political crisis of the Holy Roman Empire.[60]
It was initially in **France** where the urge for forging a national law was advocated and endorsed by the royal power, also due to the aim of King Louis XIV to attain a strong political unity of the country.

In opposition to Roman law and drawing on the customary local law rooted and applied in the northern part of the kingdom (*pays de droit coutumier*) (see *infra*, ch 4, para 3.1.1), Charles Dumoulin, also known as Molinaeus (1500-1566), and Yves Coquille (1523-1603) coined and elaborated on the concept of a *droit commun français*. Through the 1679 edict of Saint-Germain-en-Laye (1679), King Louis XIV eventually introduced university teaching and the professorships of '*droit français contenu dans les ordonnances et dans les coutumes*'.

The tendency towards a nationalization of private law was combined with that towards its rationalization and simplification that was clearly affirmed by the great representatives of **natural law** around the seventeenth century (see *infra*, ch 5, para 2),[61] authors who also brought up instances of social and legal reformism linked to the affirmation of the rights to freedom of all men.[62]

The initiators of 'early' natural law may be identified in Hugo Grotius (1583-1645) and Johannes Althusius (1563-1638).
One of the most prominent representatives of this doctrine was Samuel von

[59] Voltaire, Œuvres complets, tome 15 (Société littéraire 1785) 437: '*Outre ces quarante mille lois, dont on cite toujours quelqu'une au hasard, nous avons cinq cent quarante coutumes différentes, en comptant les petites villes et même quelques bourgs, qui dérogent aux usages de la juridiction principale; de sorte qu'un homme qui court la poste, en France, change de lois plus souvent qu'il ne change de chevaux, comme on l'a déjà dit, et qu'un avocat qui sera très savant dans sa ville ne sera qu'un ignorant dans la ville voisine*'.
[60] Padoa Schioppa (n 31) 368ff.
[61] Vogenauer (n 27) 1078.
[62] Johannes Liebrecht, 'Natural Law' in *The Max Planck Encyclopedia of European Private Law*, vol 2 (n 27) 1189.

Pufendorf (1632-1694),[63] whose main work, *De iure naturae et gentium*, was published in 1672.
'Late' natural law was dominated by Christian Wolff (1679-1754), who applied to law the 'geometrical method' (*ordo geometricus*) that Baruch Spinoza (1632-1677) had laid down for ethics (see *infra*, ch 5, para 2).[64] Wolff built his system of legal concepts consistently on syllogistic deductions, all of which were to be derived from the highest principles of natural law.[65] The name of Daniel Nettelbladt (1719-1791) may be mentioned as well.

The tenets of natural law, which gained a vast consensus in the countries of Protestant religion, favored the flourishing of a legal science that was purported to 'purge' the Roman-canon law of the Middle Ages, thus transforming it into a modern law. This new jurisprudence, which was later to be referred to as ***usus modernus (or hodiernus) pandectarum***,[66] claimed the abandonment of all rules of the medieval *ius commune* that had in the meantime become obsolescent, as well as for a merger of this body of rules with the indigenous law of the German countries.

One of the earliest works that inaugurated the *usus modernus* was the *Introduction to Dutch Jurisprudence* (*Inleidinge tot de Hollandsche reechtsgelerdheid*) by Hugo Grotius (1583-1645).
A text that over centuries constituted a genuine work of reference for academic studies and also for the law in action was found in the *Institutiones* of Arnold Vinnen, or Vinnius (1588-1657). His success was one of the factors leading the University of Leiden to create the first chair of *ius hodiernum*, in 1688, which was held by Johan Voet (1647-1713).
The expression of *usus modernus pandectarum*, however, appeared rather late and spread only following the homonymous work by Samuel Stryck (1640-1710), which was published in 1690.
Subsequently, the works of Adam Struve (1619-1692) and, above all, of Johan Gottlieb Heinecke, or Heineccius (1681-1741), who was also a natural law scholar, were affirmed.

The eighteenth-century Enlightenment, that was strongly imbued with the doctrines of 'late' natural law,[67] strongly advocated for a **codification of national laws**, based on the tenets of equal treatment of men, rationality of legislation, and due process.[68] The first endeavors of codifying private law happened to be performed in some German states, where political regimes of enlightened absolutism were deeply imbued with an altruistic paternalism.

[63] Samuel Pufendorf, *De iure naturae et gentium libri octo. Cum integris commentariis virorum clarissimorum Jo. Nicolai Hertii, atque Joannis Barbeyraci* (ex officina Knochiana 1744).
[64] Liebrecht (n 62) 1191.
[65] ibid.
[66] Klaus Luig, 'Usus Modernus' in *The Max Planck Encyclopedia of European Private Law*, vol 2 (n 27) 1755; Vogenauer (n 27) 1078.
[67] Liebrecht (n 62) 1191.
[68] Jean P Schmidt, 'Codification' in *The Max Planck Encyclopedia of European Private Law*, vol 1 (n 24) 222.

In **Bavaria**, Duke Maximilian Joseph III ordained that many codes be drawn up and issued, particularly that of private law in 1756. The *Codex maximilianeus bavaricus civilis* was essentially molded on the *usus modernus pandectarum*.[69]
The elaboration of the *Allgemeines Landrecht für die Preussischen Staaten* (ALR) of 1794,[70] which was adopted by **Prussia**, ruled by Frederick the Great (Friedrich II), is largely attributable to one of the great exponents of the natural law school, namely Christian Thomasius (1655-1728) (see *supra* in this para). The ALR remained in force even when, thanks to the political and military skill of Otto von Bismarck (1815-1898), Prussia was to unify all the single German territories into the German Empire (*Deutsches Reich*).
Later on, the Austrian ***Allgemeines Bürgerliches Gesetzbuch*** (ABGB) of 1811 came to the fore,[71] based on Kant's legal and philosophical thought.[72] It was preceded by the Martini project of 1794 and the *Westgalizisches Gesetzbuch* of 1797. A deep influence on these legislative achievements was exerted by the works of Christian Wolff (1670-1754) (see *supra* in this para).

Codification of private law (as well as of other areas of law, above all criminal law) rapidly took root on the European continent (see *infra*, ch 4, para 3.1) and culminated first with the *Code civil des Français* (subsequently also named the *Code Napoléon*) (see *infra*, ch 4, para 3.1.1) and then later with the *Bürgerliches Gesetzbuch* (BGB) (see *infra*, ch 4, para 3.1.2).
Both were expressions of an **authoritarian political regime** and the foundation (or re-foundation) of a **strong national state**. For France, it was the Revolution of 1789 first and later on the apotheosis of Napoleon. For Germany, it was the foundation of the German Empire (*Deutsches Reich*), whereby Prussia could unify all the German territories under a unique political regime.
A similar phenomenon occurred in Italy, where the first Civil Code (1865) accompanied the achievement of national unity (proclaimed in 1870); by contrast, the second (1942) was pursued by the fascist regime of the time (see *infra*, ch 4, para 3.1.3).
With regard to common law jurisdictions, it was only towards the mid-eighteenth century that **English law** began to be studied in a scientific way and taught at universities.

In 1753, the English common law was for the first time lectured on at a university, particularly by William Blackstone (1723-1780) at Oxford. Thanks to the legacy of Charles Viner, in 1758, the first professorship of common law was created in Oxford, inaugurated by Blackstone himself. The Vinerian Professorship of English Law currently still exists.

69 Konrad Zweigert and Hein Kötz, *An Introduction to Comparative Law* (Tony Weir tr, 3rd edn, OUP 1998) 137.
70 Phillip Hellwege, 'Allgemeines Landrecht für die Preußischen Staaten (ALR)' in *The Max Planck Encyclopedia of European Private Law*, vol 1 (n 24) 56.
71 Walter Doralt, 'Allgemeines Bürgerliches Gesetzbuch (ABGB)' in *The Max Planck Encyclopedia of European Private Law*, vol 1 (n 24) 45.
72 Padoa Schioppa (n 31) 488ff.

Cambridge created its first chair in English Law in 1800, and later on, in 1826, John Austin (see *infra*, ch 5, para 3; ch 6, para 1.1) was elected as Professor of English Law at University College London.
Still in 1883, to mark his appointment as Vinerian Professor at the University of Oxford, Albert Venn Dicey (see *infra*, ch 7, para 1) nevertheless delivered an inaugural lecture titled 'Can English Law be Taught at the Universities?',[73] where the final question mark is telling of how fragile the academic reputation of national jurisdictions still was.

Starting with Jeremy Bentham (1748-1832) (see *infra*, ch 7, para 3.2), several attempts were carried out to codify common law; whereas they may have remained completely unsuccessful in the UK, they bore instead some fruit in the US (see *infra*, ch 7, para 3.2).

[73] Albert V Dicey, *Can English Law be Taught at the Universities? An inaugural lecture delivered at All Souls College, Oxford, 21 April 1883* (MacMillan & Co 1883). On Dicey's influence on Anglo-American legal education, see also David Sugarman, 'Making Respected Gentlemen out of Law Professors. A Commentary on Albert Venn Dicey, Can English Law be Taught at the Universities?' in *Themenportal Europäische Geschichte* (2013) <www.europa.clio-online.de/essay/id/artikel-3725> accessed 21 December 2018.

GLOSSARY

***Alma mater studiorum* ('nourishing mother of studies') (3)**: the University of Bologna, traditionally considered the most ancient university in the Western world. It was founded in 1088 as a *Studium*, ie a laical association of students, who financed their teachers with donations (known as '*collectae*'). The first subject matter taught was that of Roman law, initiated by Irnerius. From the fourteenth century, the range of teachings offered was broadened: Greek, Hebrew, astronomy, arithmetic, logic, medicine, philosophy, rhetoric, grammar, and theology.

Battle of Hastings (4.2): battle between the Norman-French army of William, Duke of Normandy, and an English army under the Anglo-Saxon King Harold Godwinson, signaling the beginning of the Norman conquest of England. It took place in Hastings on 14 October 1066, close to the present-day town of Battle.

Canon law (or canonical law) (4.1): law developed and applied by the Catholic Church (and other Christian churches). Rooted into the Roman tradition, it was initially based on decisions taken by the church councils (*canones*) and later developed through letters of the Popes that formulated decisions (*litterae decretales*).

Civil law (4.1): family of legal systems typical of continental Europe (and nowadays spread in many countries in the world, such as Turkey, Egypt, Russia, and most Latin-American countries) which finds its roots in Roman law as well as in the political and scholarly tradition arising therefrom (especially codification, natural law, and legal positivism). The most important feature of civil law is that the main principles of the law are laid down into a compilation of statutory provisions which serves as the main source of the legal system (the code). Thus, as opposed to common law (see *ad vocem*), civil law holds case-law secondary and subordinate to statutory law, which is often conceptualized with a great degree of abstraction.

Commentators (3): scholars of the so-called 'School of Commentators', active in Europe between the fourteenth and the fifteenth century, especially among France and Italy. The Commentators replaced the *glossa* with the *commentum*, a more flexible approach to the interpretation of Roman law based on the *ratio* (rationale) of legal rules, thereby promoting the coordination between *ius civile* and local customary laws.

Common law (4.2): family of legal systems typical of Anglo-American countries (namely the UK, the US, and those countries that are members of the Commonwealth). Common law finds its roots in England at the beginning of the eleventhcentury and, together with the civil law (see *ad vocem*), is one of the two legal systems that form part of the Western legal tradition. The distinctive trait of common law is generally identified in the binding nature of judicial precedents and, thus, in the primacy of the judiciary in the production of legal rules. In a broader sense, the term common law also refers to jurisdictions in which a common law legal system prevails (eg the US is a common law jurisdiction).

***Communis opinio doctorum* (4.1)**: established opinion of the jurists in the scholarly interpretation of the *Corpus iuris civilis* and the *Corpus iuris canonici*. In the legal order existing in late medieval Europe and the first centuries of the modern age (roughly the sixteenth-eighteenth century), the *communis opinio doctorum* prevailed over the so-called 'opinions', which were less considered by scholarship; therefore, once stable and unchallenged, it assumed the same relevance as the previous ruling of judges, binding the latter in relation to the outcome of their decisions.

***Corpus iuris canonici* (4.1)**: multi-part collection of canon law and its sources, published in ad 1582. It is structured in six parts overall, which date back to different periods of time: the *Decretum Gratiani* (see *ad vocem*), the *Liber Extra* (or *decretales*) issued by Pope Gregory IX in 1234, the *Liber Sextus* issued by Pope Boniface VIII in 1298, the *Clementinae* (promulgated by Pope Clement V), the *Extravagantes Johannis* XXI (1317), and the *Extravagantes communes*.

Its first full publication, dating back to ad 1500, was edited by Jean Chappuis.

Decretum Gratiani **(or** ***Concordia discordantium canonum*****, or** ***Concordantia discordantium canonum*****) (4.1)**: first private collection of canon law, drafted by the Camaldolese monk Gratian (or Gratianus), who – from the monastery of San Felice and Naborre in Bologna where he lived – gathered the prominent decisions of the councils on legal matters, separating them from theology. It is thought to have been compiled by its author between ad 1140 and ad 1142. The work, whose official title is *Concordia discordantium canonum*, is divided into three parts. It represented a part of the *Corpus iuris canonici* (see *ad vocem*).

Digest (*Digesta*, or *Pandectae*) (2): collection of fifty books that is constituted by slivers of Roman jurists' works about law and justice. It was ordered in ad 533 by Justinian I, who assigned to Tribonian the role of concretely implementing it. The work is one of the four pillars of the *Corpus iuris civilis*.

Fall of the Roman Empire (2): conclusive decline of the Western Roman Empire. This event traditionally dates back to ad 476. From a strictly political-military prospect, the Western Roman Empire fell completely after being invaded by various non-Roman peoples in the fifth century and then deprived of its peninsular core by the Germanic troops of Odoacre, which were in revolt (ad 476). Both the historicity and the exact dates of such events remain uncertain. Some historians reject our talking about the 'fall of the Empire'. Opinions even differ as to whether this fall was the result of a single event or of a long and gradual process.

Gaius's *Institutiones* (2): didactic work, structured in four books, which was written by the jurist and law teacher Gaius around ad 161 (but the exact date is uncertain). It is the only work of classical Roman jurisprudence we have directly received to date, without the use of compilations that could alter its specific meaning. The four books of *Institutiones* are called commentaries. The entire subject is divided into three parts: *personae* (first commentary), *res* (second and third commentaries) and *actiones* (fourth commentary).

Glossators (3): jurists and scholars of the so-called 'School of Bologna', which was operative between the eleventh and the twelfth-century. The word '*glossator*' stems from the custom of such jurists to annotate the legal text analyzed (in particular, the *Corpus iuris civilis*). The annotation was entitled *glossa*, which indicated the clarification given by professors to the semantic of legal work.

Ius commune **(4.1)**: Roman law collected in the Justinian compilation and the apparatus of the 'scientific' interpretations given by scholars. Between the eleventh and the nineteenth centuries, the *ius commune* was the general law applicable in Western Europe, except when local or particular laws were available.

Justinian compilation (or *Corpus iuris civilis*) (2): multi-part work of Roman law commissioned by Byzantine Emperor Justinian I in the sixth century. It is the concrete result of a project aimed at collecting all the previous legislative and jurisprudential traditions. Therefore, the general objective was a holistic reorganization of both judicial practice and the study of law. The work is divided into four parts: *Codex*, *Digesta* (*Pandectae*) (see *ad vocem*), *Institutiones*, and *Novellae* (the latter being subsequently added to the collection). In the eleventh century, this compilation became known as the *Corpus iuris civilis*.

Nomoi **and** ***poleis*** **(1)**: the *poleis* were the city-states of ancient Greece. The *nomoi* were their laws, which were not perceived as specific legal provisions (although technically they were), but as the embodiment of deep and immutable principles. The legislator of an individual *polis* was thus the interpreter of this submerged world of immanent rules.

Reception of Roman law (in German countries) (4.1): process of the reception of the Roman legal tradition into Germanic countries. The traditional date of this event is generally traced back to 1495 when Maximilian I, Emperor of the *Sacrum Romanum Imperium*, established the *Reichskammergericht* in Frankfurt, ie the Imperial Chamber Court, ruling that it should make its own decisions 'according to the *ius commune*'.

Roman law (1): ancient legal system of Rome and a fundamental cornerstone for the current civil law. The Roman legal order includes a thousand years of prominent social and juridical developments, which include the Twelve

Tables (449 bc) and the *Corpus iuris civilis* (ad 529), the latter compiled under Justinian I by a commission of jurists. Romans called the concept of law *ius*, meaning pureness and, according to the prevailing opinion, were influenced by a religious stance. For this reason, *ius* and *fas* shared the same content for a long period, but, over time, and with the progressive secularization of society, the former was conceived as law of men towards other men, thus conceptually detaching itself from the latter, which was taken to mean law of men towards gods.

Royal Chancery (4.2): secretariat of the monarch of England, which, headed by the Chancellor, began hearing lawsuits during the fourteenth century. The decisions taken by the Chancery were based on fairness and conscience rather than on strict common law forms of action.

***Usus modernus (or hodiernus) pandectarum* (5)**: strand of legal studies flourished between the end of the eighteenth century and all the nineteenth century that advocated 'purging' the Roman law of the Middle Ages and merging it with the indigenous laws of the German countries. One of the main initiators of this cultural movement was Hugo Grotius (1583-1645); the *Institutiones* by Arnold Vinnen, or Vinnius (1588-1657) became a reference textbook for studying law throughout Europe.

BIOGRAPHIES

Accursius (Bagnolo or Impruneta, 1184 – Bologna, 1263) was an Italian jurist and glossator, a pupil of Azo and Jacobus Balduinus. According to some historians, he is the most important exponent of the Bologna School of Law. In his lifetime, he worked tirelessly to revise the systems of *glossae* of his colleagues and predecessors, showing an uncommon scientific stature, foresight, and legal sensitivity. His most famous work is titled *Glossa perpetua* (also known as *Magna Glossa*, or *Glossa glossarum*) and was an overall commentary to *Corpus iuris civilis*. He collected the great legal experience of the School. Every *glossa* was labelled with the name of its real author (about 97,000 *glossae*). The work acquired a great reputation, and its study was required in many of the current European countries where Roman law coincided with the *ius commune*. For over six centuries the work has imposed itself as the unofficial interpretation of the complex civil law; it was the only one capable of certifying its contents, which had to be disseminated for the purpose of educational reasons and for the exercise of jurisdiction. It embodied the instrument of the *ius commune*, created and developed in the School of Bologna, and spread through the method of its legal experts. Many scholars hold the *Magna Glossa* as an admirable synthesis of the meticulous work carried out in the Italian schools of the eleventh and twelfth centuries; moreover, they exalt the author's ability to critically examine a boundless work, being able to coordinate it in a unitary text. The School of Glossators started to decline after the publication of this extraordinary work.

Vincenzo Arangio Ruiz (Naples, 1884 – Rome, 1964) was an Italian jurist and politician. From an early age, he had a particular propensity for classical philology, and this created strong indecision in his mind when he had to face the choice about which university studies to undertake. Under his father's guide, he opted for the School of Law of Modena and, later on, decided to cultivate Roman law studies, which were strictly intertwined with his original inclinations. He moved to Naples to follow Carlo Fadda, a Roman law teacher. The name of his degree thesis is *La successione testamentaria secondo i papiri greco-egizii* (1906). The following year, Arangio Ruiz was appointed as lecturer at Camerino University, where he also taught history of Roman law. After teaching in Naples, Macerata, Perugia, Cagliari, and Messina, he became professor at the latter university in 1914. Later, he moved back to Naples.

Also because of unfavorable political conditions, he suspended his teaching activity from 1929 to 1940 to go to the University of Cairo to teach Roman law. He was appointed as Emeritus Professor at Rome University in 1954.

The author was always one of the Italian intellectuals who most opposed Fascism since its inception. He was a signatory of the *Manifesto degli intellettuali antifascisti* (so-called 'Manifesto Croce'), also contributing with articles in the political press in the fight against the nascent dictatorship. The scientific investigation of Arangio Ruiz cannot be traced back to a specific methodological school. Although in contact with important scholars, his scientific works are characterized by his own method without external influences. He was able to combine the study of Roman law with other legal experiences of classical antiquity. This is, at least in part, due to his aforementioned immense passion for philological research, which has inspired his juridical exegesis.

His main works are: *La successione testamentaria secondo i papiri greco-egizii* (1906); *Rariora. Studio di diritto romano* (1946); *Storia del diritto romano* (7th edn, 1984); *Scritti politici* (1985).

Azo (Bologna, 1150? – Bologna, 1225?) was a medieval jurist of the Bologna School of Law. His real name is uncertain. He taught as professor in Bologna for about thirty years. Azo was the pupil of Joannes Bassianus, one of the most important scholars and glossators of that School. He decided to write systematic summaries, which were named '*summae*', another kind of literary genre – based on a systematic analysis of the entire work in a rapid and simple way – that can be distinguished from '*glossa*' and '*lectura*'.

The most relevant work of Azo is the *Summa codicis*, which had a remarkable success and may be considered the cornerstone for the subsequent studies of an entire generation of medieval jurists. Knowledge of this work represented a sort of a prerequisite for being admitted to a school of law. Later on, this work was integrated by Hugolinus de Presbyteris, Odofredus, and Guidus de Suzzara with some additions. Particularly, the aforementioned work represented the cornerstone of the corresponding canonical *Summa* of Henricus de Segusio (known as the Hostiensis).

Another prominent work of Azo is the *Lectura Azonis*, which consists of some lectures about the *Corpus iuris civilis*, collected by his student, Alexander de Sancto Egidio. For a long time this work was not studied by anyone, until 1557, when the jurist Antoine Lo Conte found a manuscript of it in a stable in Orléans. It was published in Paris twenty years later, and then other reprints of the same work followed.

It has also to be noted that the intellectual contribution of Azo with regard to the *glossa* literature genre was extraordinary. He wrote *glossae* of the entire text

of *Corpus iuris civilis*, allowing his pupil, Accursio, to develop the work already done by him.
Among his pupils, Jacobus Baldovinus, Roffredus Beneventanus, Martinus de Fano, Jacobus de Ardizone, Johannes Teutonicus, and Bernardus Dorna must be remembered.

Baldus de Ubaldis (Perugia, 1327 – Pavia, 1400) was an Italian jurist. He was a pupil of Bartolus de Saxoferrato and one of his most brilliant students. He became *doctor iuris*, at the very young age of seventeen and, after that, he started teaching law. Baldus soon became very popular and was acknowledged as one of the most important jurists of his time. He was thus offered chairs in all the most prestigious universities in Italy. He began his career in Bologna, and around 1350 he moved to teach in Perugia. In 1356, he left Perugia to serve as professor at the University of Pisa. After Pisa, Baldus moved to Florence, where he gained such a great fame that he was conferred honorary citizenship. After another brief period of teaching in Perugia, Baldus was appointed for the chair of *ius civile* at the University of Padua. He then moved again to Florence and finally to Pavia, where he died in 1400.
Together with his mentor Bartolus, Baldus is generally considered as the greatest jurisconsult of the fourteenth century. The work of Bartolus and Baldus indeed represents the highest expression of the 'School of Commentators'. The writings of Baldus were strongly influenced by the new social and economic needs emerging at the time, which required the exploration of innovative legal issues and institutions. That is why the studies carried out by Baldus are characterized by a strong practical approach. Such an approach finds its roots in the activity Baldus undertook as a legal consultant, which resulted in thousands of legal opinions (*consilia*) that represented a reference for lawyers for many years.
His work mainly focused on civil and canon law: Baldus wrote important commentaries to several parts of the *Corpus iuris civilis* as well as a *lectura* of the *Decretales* of Gregory IX. He also wrote treatises on several topics, such as the *Summula Respiciens Facta Mercatorum*, a book on selected topics of commercial law, and the *De Commemoratione Famosissimorum*, a history of legal thoughts up until his time.

Bartolus de Saxoferrato (Sassoferrato, 1313 – Perugia, 1357) was an Italian jurist and the most important exponent of the school of commentators. Bartolus was a pupil of Cinus de Pistorio, a famous legal scholar at the time. He carried out his studies in Perugia and Bologna, and then he became professor in Pisa and Perugia. Bartolus, however, was not only a scholar; he also practiced law and held important public offices during his life. Among these, in 1335, Emperor Charles IV appointed Bartolus as his adviser (*consiliarius*). The scientific work of Bartolus, which mostly focused on the interactions between *ius commune* and *iura propria*, is acknowledged as very creative, sophisticated, and vast. It covered many areas of law, including private, criminal, public, procedural, and international law, and it was mostly carried out in the form of comments on the *corpus iuris*. The legacy of Bartolus, however, is not only due to his scientific writing. In fact, he also wrote hundreds of legal opinion (*consilia*), which became very popular and, for many years, have been cited to solve similar cases. The authority of Bartolus was great: after his death, many Italian universities established chairs named after him (*cathedrae Bartoli*), and the *opinio Bartoli* became a standing reference for judges both in Italy and elsewhere. In Spain and Portugal, for example, respectively in 1427 and 1446, two statutes were passed establishing that, in the case of doubt in the interpretation and application of a legal rule, the opinion upheld in the works by Bartolus should prevail.

While the main work of Bartolus is generally considered his *commenta* at the *Corpus iuris civilis*, his writings in public law (eg *De represaliis*, *De Guelphis and the Gebellinis*, *De Tyrannia*, *De Regimine Civitatis*) also had a major impact on the development of the political thought that emerged in the following centuries.

William Blackstone (London, 1723 – Wallingford, 1780) was a British jurist, judge, and Tory politician.

He completed a Bachelor of Civil Law degree in Pembroke College, Oxford, then was made a Fellow of All Souls College, Oxford, and finally admitted to Middle Temple, where he was called to the bar in 1746. He began his career as a barrister, but quickly switched to an academic career, becoming highly involved in the university administration; he definitively abandoned his practice as a barrister and, on advice of William Murray, began to give lectures in English Law, which led to the publication of *An Analysis of the Laws of England* (1756); this work was used to preface his later works.

In 1758, Blackstone was confirmed as the first Vinerian Professor of English Law. Thanks to his success as a lecturer, he returned to the bar and was elected as Tory member of Parliament in 1761, and re-elected in 1768; moreover, after repeated failures, he was also appointed Justice of the Court of King's Bench in 1770, and maintained this position until his death in 1780.

Blackstone's main work is *Commentaries on the Laws of England* (1765), which offers a complete overview of English law and has influenced several British and American scholars, besides being frequently cited in Supreme Court decisions.

His other leading works are: *An Analysis of the Laws of England* (1756); *A Discourse on the Study of the Law* (1758); *A Treatise on the Law of Descents in Fee Simple* (1759).

Alberico Gentili (San Ginesio, 1552 – London, 1608) was an Italian lawyer and jurist who served as professor at the University of Oxford for twenty-one years.

Gentili graduated in law from the University of Perugia. After graduation, he served as *podestà* (major) of the Italian city of Ascoli for three years, and then he returned to his home-town (the small village of San Ginesio) to practice as a lawyer. In 1579, he moved to Germany and the year after to London, where he lived for the rest of his life. In England, Alberico Gentili soon affirmed himself as an important legal scholar and practitioner and was appointed as legal consultant of the Crown. In 1587, he was assigned the chair of Regius Professor of Civil Law at the University of Oxford: this was the first chair in civil law established in an English university. At the same time, Alberico Gentili became the first non-English

Regius Professor of the country. Alberico Gentili is traditionally acknowledged as the father of the modern conceptualization of public international law, alongside Francisco de Vitoria and Hugo Grotius. His main studies analyze several aspects of international relations, such as diplomatic law and the law of war. His most important book, published in 1598, is indeed titled '*De Iure Belli*' (*The Law of War*). The legacy of Alberico Gentili includes more than twenty-four books.
His main works are: *De Iuris Interpretibus Dialogi Sex* (1582); *De Legationibus Libri Tres* (1585); *De Armis Romanis* (1590-1599); *Hispanicae Advocationis Libri Duo* (1613).

Edward Gibbon (Purtney, 1737 – London, 1794) was a historian, writer, and member of Britain's Parliament for the Whigs. His childhood was not easy because of his poor health. He had to interrupt his studies several times in order to cure himself; nevertheless, from an early age he developed a great love for reading, particularly Greek and Latin texts. He studied at Westminster, Cambridge, Oxford, and Lausanne. His most important and famous work, *The History of the Decline and Fall of the Roman Empire*, published in six volumes from 1776 to 1788, stands out for the quality and irony of its prose, and for its criticism of religious confessions.
Gibbon offers a precise explanation for the fall of the Roman Empire. Most of his ideas were taken from the few documents available, coinciding with those of the few Roman scholars of the fourth and fifth centuries. According to Gibbon, the Roman Empire fell under barbarian invasions because of the loss of civic sense by his subjects. They had become weak, giving the task of defending the borders of the empire to barbaric mercenaries who became so numerous and integrated into the fabric of society as to be able to destroy the empire. Gibbon argued that Christianity had created the certainty that a better life would exist after death. This idea had led the Roman citizens to an indifference about earthly life, which weakened their desire to sacrifice themselves for the Empire.
His main works are: *Essai sur l'étude de la litérature* (1759); *Critical Observations on the Sixth Book of [Vergil's] 'The Aeneid'* (1770); *The History of the Decline and Fall of the Roman Empire* (1776-1778); *Miscellaneous Works* (1814).

Gustav Conrad von Hugo (Lörrach, 1764 – Göttingen, 1844) was a German jurist. He represents one of the founders of the Historical School of Law, which was based on the conception of law as an outcome of popular consciousness. Such a juridical doctrine was contrary to the work of codification realized in those years in France. Von Hugo argued that the law, even before being a written legal norm, is rooted in the popular soul as a custom and a *modus agendi*.
The task of the jurist is to allow the emergence of the conscience of each given society from the law and to erect it as a system through the scientific elaboration of the law itself. Von Hugo was able to revive the system of sources of law and, with his philosophical inclination, gave a considerable boost to the overall arrangement of the various areas of law itself.
He followed the institutional system that dates back to classic Gaius and analyzed his law of obligations in a particularly critical way.

His most significant work is *Lehrbuch eines zivilistischen Kursus* (1792-1821), published in seven volumes. It has to be noted that von Hugo paid attention to the issue of natural law within this relevant work. Indeed, the second volume is titled *Naturrecht als einer Philosophie des positiven Rechts, besonders des Privatrechts* and, to date, the work is interpreted as a conceptual continuation of Kantian jurisprudence.
His other main works are: *Commentatio de fundamento successionis ab intestato ex jure Romano antiquo et novo* (1785); *Institutionen des heutigen Römischen Rechts* (1789); *Lehrbuch über Chrestomathie des klassischen Pandektenrechts* (1790); *Lehrbuch eines zivilistischen Kursus* (1792-1821); *Zivilistisches Magazin*, 6 vols (1790-1837); *Beiträge zur zivilistischen Bücherkenntnis der letzten 40 Jahre*, 3 vols (1828-1844).

Irnerius (Bologna, 1050? – Bologna, 1125?) was a jurist, academic, and medieval Italian glossator who founded the Bologna School of Law. He helped to recover Justinian texts and, for this reason, was nicknamed *lucerna iuris.* Very little is known about Irnerius's life. As regards his date of birth, competing views place it between 1050 and 1060. What is certain is that he took part in many *placita* (judicial assemblies) with the court of Henry V; from 1112 to 1113 as a *causidicus*, and from 1116 to 1118 as a *iudex.*
After a copy of Justinian's *Digestum* was discovered in Bologna, around 1070, Irnerius dedicated himself to studying them, at the urging of Countess Mathilda of Tuscany, who needed to solve an inheritance quarrel with the Emperor. At that time, Irnerius was probably a clerk attached to her chancellery.
Irnerius had at his disposal only the first twenty-four books of a total of fifty that made up the *Digestum*, which, for this reason, he called *vetus*. Subsequently, he found book numbers thirty-nine to fifty, and they were named *Digestum novum* by him. After further research, he also succeeded in finding the central part that he titled *Digestum infortiatum*. Therefore, the so-called *libri legales* of the Bolognese tradition total five: *Digestum vetus*, *Digestum infortiatum*, *Digestum novum*, *Codex* (which includes the first nine books), and *Volumen* (which contains *Institutiones*, the last three books of *Codex*, 134 *Novellae* divided into nine collations, some successive imperial constitutions, and *Libri feudorum*).
After Irnerius focused his efforts in the study of the Justinian Compilation, he taught it at the School called *Scola Glossatorum*, taking the name from the gloss, ie the interlinear or marginal explanation of a word or wording in a text.
Before Irnerius, Roman law had already been taught in Bologna by Pepus and others. However, Irnerius' teaching method of Roman law was based on the interpretation of individual legal terms and the linking up of legal concepts contained in Justinian's texts, following rigorous principles. For the first time law became a scientific discipline, not merely a liberal art.
Irnerius was succeeded by his pupils, called 'the Four Doctors of Bologna': Bulgarus, Martinus Gosia, Jacopus de Boragine, and Hugo de Porta Ravennate. The work of Irnerius and the Glossators was then collected and synthesized by Accursius in the *Glossa Ordinaria*, or *Accursiana*, in 1260.

Justinian I (Tauresium, 482 – Constantinople, 565) was the Eastern Roman Emperor from 527 to his death. He is also known as Justinian the Great (or Saint Justinian the Great in the Eastern Orthodox Church). He may be considered as one of the most prominent emperors of late antiquity and the medieval ages. Most historians affirm that the period of his government coincided with a great prosperity of the Eastern Roman Empire. The positive effects of this were felt in the economic, military, and civil sectors, although some have criticized the political strategy undertaken under that domination.
One of the most astonishing feats of Justinian's domination was represented by the recovery of enormous stretches of land around the western Mediterranean basin, which had escaped imperial control in the fifth century. Justinian I, as a Roman Christian emperor, considered it his divine duty to bring the Roman Empire back to its ancient borders. It should be noted that he never actively participated in military operations.
He was convinced that the existence of the common good should be entrusted to arms and to the law and, for this reason, he paid particular attention to legislation, by having a virtual monument to its perpetual memory drawn up. This is the renowned *Corpus iuris civilis*, in which Roman law was codified. It consists of the *Codex Iustinianeus*, the *Digesta* or *Pandectae*, the *Institutiones*, and the *Novellae*, and it was overseen by Tribonian. It represented the effort to unify and to strengthen the empire.
Justinian I gained lasting fame for such a legal revolution, which organized Roman law into an organic form and scheme that remains as the basis of the law of several nations today. According to some historical theories, his revolution of law allowed him to obscure some strongly negative aspects of his domination (eg the protection he gave the Blue faction from punishment). Justinian I had always had an enthusiastic interest in theological issues, and this led him to actively participate in debates on Christian doctrine. He became even more devoted to religion during the later years of his life. He died on 14 November 565, and his nephew Justin II, the son of his sister Vigilantia, succeeded him.

Riccardo Orestano (Palermo, 1909 – Rome, 1988) was an Italian scholar of Roman law. He chose to study law after listening to the prolusion of Salvatore Riccobono, a distinguished Roman scholar, with whom he graduated in 1932. The topic of his graduation thesis was *cognitio extra ordinem*. During his studies, he analyzed the changes in the regime that had taken place under Augustan domination. The so-called *auctoritas* – composed of prestige and military force – appeared to him as a *de facto* power, not strictly framed within legal schemes. Moreover, he devoted great attention to the history of legal ideas.
He decided to detach himself from the ideas of fascism in 1938, after the enactment of the anti-Semitic laws. These were the denial of law. Therefore, he was actively involved in opposition to the totalitarian regime of those years.
After World War II, Orestano joined the historiographic research with studies of greater theoretical commitment. The aim was an analysis that went beyond the legal institutions to arrive at a survey of institutions, which include empirical values and situations. The influence of Giuseppe Capograssi's thought was relevant to the theories developed by the author.

Roman law seemed pluralistic and malleable to him: not a stable order, but a set of legal situations that can be understood only by retracing the contexts in which they occurred. Orestano applied the same method to the fundamental concepts of modern science.
With Gino Gorla, Massimo Severo Giannini, and Mario Nigro, Orestano was the promoter of a new approach to law in an anti-formalist sense.
His main works are: *La struttura giuridica del matrimonio romano* (1951); *L'appello civile in diritto romano* (2nd edn, 1953); *Introduzione allo studio storico del diritto romano* (2nd edn, 1961); *I fatti di normazione nell'esperienza romana arcaica* (1967); *Il problema delle persone giuridiche in diritto romano* (1968); *Introduzione allo studio del diritto romano* (1987).

Samuel Pufendorf (Zwönitz, 1632 – Berlin, 1694) was a German jurist, economist, historian, and philosopher. Despite initially being forced to study theology at the University of Leipzig, he left it in order to specialize in the study of public law. To this end, he moved to the University of Jena, where he first approached the works of Hugo Grotius, Thomas Hobbes, and René Descartes, which had a deep impact on his career as an author. He criticized the political organization of the Holy Roman Empire and, for this reason, he faced the opposition of the Elector of Palatinate and was eventually expelled from the University of Heidelberg, where he held the first teaching position in natural rights in Europe in 1661; he had no choice but to emigrate to Sweden, where he continued his long academic profession. Indeed, Pufendorf's studies and works paid special attention to the above-noted authors' theories on natural law, something that was mainly reflected in his well-known work *De iure naturae et gentium*, published in 1672. However, his further contribution to the traditional thesis is also remarkable, eg his belief that the state of nature – identified by Hobbes as demonstrating a condition of conflict – is, instead, a peaceful state. Nevertheless, such a natural condition needs to be preserved by the development of a discipline to which individuals are to 'submit'.
Furthermore, one of his most innovative thoughts was the idea that international law should be applied to every nation, regardless of the nation's own religion, since each is comprised of individuals who are all part of humanity.
His main works are: *Elementorum iurisprudentiae universalis libri duo* (1660); *De obligatione adversus patriam* (1663); *De rebus gestis Philippi Augustae* (1663); *De statu imperii germanici liber unus* (1667); *De jure naturae et gentium* (1672); *De officio hominis et civis juxta legem naturalem libri duo* (1673); *Einleitung zu der Historie der vornehmsten Reiche und Staaten, so itziger Zeit in Europa sich befinden* (1684); *De rebus a Carolo Gustavo Sueciae rege gestis commentariorum libri septem* (1679); *De rebus gestis Friderici Wilhelmi Magni* (1733).

Christian Thomasius (Leipzig, 1655 – Halle, 1728) was a German philosopher and jurist of the Early Enlightenment. Thanks to his reformist spirit, he strongly innovated all the branches of law. Born into a family of a long legal tradition, Thomasius was educated by his father, Jacob Thomasius, and influenced by Grotius's and Pufendorf's political philosophy. He received his law degree in

1679 and then embraced an academic career. He was renowned for having been among the first to lecture in German rather than in the customary Latin in 1687. One year later, in 1688, he founded the first scientific journal (*Monatsgespräche*) in the German language. In 1690, Thomasius was banned from teaching and writing because of a number of academic controversies and disciplinary measures. Therefore, he was forced to leave Leipzig and flee to Berlin, where Elector Frederick III of Prussia offered him asylum and let him teach in the nearby city of Halle. He helped found the University of Halle (1694), where he spent the most fruitful period of his life. In Halle, he was dean and rector of the university.
In *Fundamenta iuris naturae ac gentium* (1705), his *magnum opus*, Thomasius delineated the autonomy of law from morality and politics. He linked the concepts of law, morality, and politics to the principles of *iustum*, *honestum* and *decorum* respectively. In particular, in distinguishing law and morality, he argued that while the latter refers to the individual conscience, since it tends to achieve inner peace, law regulates relationships with others, thus aiming at attaining external peace. The state is the body that may establish law by means of force, whereas it cannot do anything regarding morality, which dominates the subjective scope.
In the criminal field, Thomasius was one of the first to combat witchcraft trials, the use of harsh penalties, and torture.
His main works are: *Institutiones iurisprudentiae divinae* (1688); *De iure principis circa adiaphora* (1695); *An haeresis sit crimen* (1697); *De crimine magiae* (1701); *Fundamenta iuris naturae ac gentium* (1705); *De tortura e foris christianorum proscribenda* (1705); *Cautelae circa praecognita iurisprudentiae ecclesiasticae* (1712); *De originibus processus inquisitorii contra sagas* (1712); *An poenae viventium eos infamantes sint absurdae et abrogandae?* (1723).

Voltaire (Pseudonym for François-Marie Arouet) (Paris, 1694 – Paris, 1778) is one of the most important intellectuals of the Enlightenment. Born from a rich bourgeois family, Voltaire was educated in a Jesuit college, where he became familiar with ancient Greek, Latin, and the most important European languages. Although his father wanted Voltaire to become a lawyer, he was more interested in becoming a writer, and, since his youth, he started writing poetry and voicing mild criticism of the church and the state. In 1726, because of a scuffle with a French nobleman, Voltaire was exiled in England, where he spent three years. During this period, he was strongly influenced by British writers (such as Shakespeare) and scientists (especially by Sir Isaac Newton) and was fascinated by the English political system, which, contrary to France, was not an absolute monarchy but a constitutional one. Voltaire was also particularly impressed by the Scottish Enlightenment thinkers, such as Adam Smith and David Hume. In 1728, Voltaire returned to Paris, and between 1755 and 1788, he left France again to live in Prussia and, then, Switzerland. In 1778, he returned again to Paris, where he died the same year. Strongly anticlerical, at the cornerstone of the philosophy of Voltaire is skepticism, rationalism, and, politically, the fight against material inequalities and injustice. Although Voltaire had much in common with fellow French Enlightenment writer Jean-Jacques Rousseau, the two often disagreed and had a thorny relationship. Considered as the founder of

modern rationalism, the teachings of Voltaire had a major impact on subsequent philosophers as well as on the political arena. Indeed, his ideas, together with the ones of other important authors of the Enlightenment, inspired both the French and the American revolution as well as the work of very influential thinkers such as Beccaria, Marx, and Nietzsche. The work of Voltaire is very vast and covers several styles and disciplines.
His main works are: *Letters Concerning the English Nation* (1793); *Traité sur la tolérance* (1763); *Essai sur les mœurs et l'esprit des nations* (1756); *Œdipe* (1718); *Brutus* (1730).

Christian Wolff (Wrocław, 1679 – Halle, 1754) was a German philosopher and jurist. He is considered the most important philosopher of the period running from the death of Leibniz to the works of Immanuel Kant. The studies of Wolff represent the peak of Enlightenment rationality in Germany. Indeed, his methodology strongly relies on mathematics as well as on demonstrative-deductive reasoning. The thinking of Wolff, which was strongly influenced by that of Liebnitz, was systematized in a single *oeuvre* which basically covers almost every scholarly subject of his time. According to Wolff, philosophy is the science of the possible. Since the possible is only that which can be thought of in a rational way, philosophy needs to rely on strict logic and syllogisms. Wolff established German as a scholarly language (although he wrote also in Latin, to be read internationally), and he was the founding father of economics and public administration as academic disciplines. Wolff and his school also elaborated on some of the pivotal concepts of modern legal reasoning, such as the notion of subjective rights.
His main works are: *Philosophia Universalis* (1738); *Jus Naturae Methodo Scientifico Pertractatum* (1740-49); *Institutiones Iuris Naturae et Gentium* (1750).

CHAPTER 3

National and international law

- **Statism and nationalism of contemporary Western laws**
- **The split of national and international law**
- **Comparative law: its concept, history, and methodology**
- **Private international law**
- **Uniform law: the CISG**

In opposition to the medieval *ius commune*, which was not the expression of a central authority, national states established their own sovereignty by enacting their own laws. It was thus created a split between domestic law and international law, in which domestic law applies to the State's citizens within its territory, whereas (public) international law governs the relations between states, or between citizens of different states, and is therefore produced through inter-state agreements.

The aim of comparative law is that of 'measuring' similarities and differences between different legal systems. A structuralist methodology of comparative law tends to be opposed to a functionalistic methodology, which, in turn, is either synchronically or diachronically applied. Both methods are predominantly committed to a 'micro-comparison' of single institutes or doctrines, whereas a 'macro-comparison' focuses on the constitutional and institutional features of the different legal systems.

The aim of private international law is that of addressing conflicts of laws arising between different jurisdictions and selecting which of the conflicting laws is applicable to inter-state cases. Each state issues its own private international law, whose rules concern procedural as well as substantial aspects. Yet, private international law may be brought into uniformity through international conventions, as well as, for the Member States of the EU, through regulations of the latter.

Convergence among legal systems is achieved through tools of uniform law, such as the Vienna Convention on the international sale of goods (CIGS), which are the outcome of extensive comparative studies and accommodate the states' will to facilitate exchanges across national borders. To that end, model laws may be beneficial as well.

1. STATISM AND NATIONALISM OF CONTEMPORARY WESTERN LAWS

The historical development of the Western legal tradition came to address and conceptualize (private) law as set out by nation states, each of which exercises sovereign powers first to enact, then to apply its own law. To put it differently, contemporary Western laws tend to be stamped by the stigma of statism and nationalism, which in the last two centuries have been embodied in the codifications of (private) law (see *infra*, ch 4, para 3.1).

> Paolo Grossi has clearly expressed criticism of '**legal absolutism**', which triumphed after the age of the Enlightenment and the rise of the Jacobean ideal of legislation as the 'will of the nation'. The medieval understanding of law, based on scholarly endeavors by jurists, was thus subverted and replaced by allegiance to the sovereign's will.

From the viewpoint of both laymen and jurists it is now accepted that, since each state creates its own law, any discourse about law is possible only if it refers to a national law, ie a law engendered by a state. This view is challenged by international law, whose status as 'proper law' is sometimes subject to debate (see *infra*, ch 3, para 2).[1]

To a large extent, law thus becomes the outcome of a political decision taken by a sovereign entity, be it an absolute monarch or a democratic parliament (see *infra*, ch 5, para 3). This conception of law has largely been conveyed through the doctrine of **legal positivism** (see *infra*, ch 5, para 1), which may be said to embody the current conceptualization of Western legal systems.

As a consequence, any scientific or didactic account of law would tend to address a national law. Studying Italian law would mean ascertaining the legislation adopted by the Italian state while creating its own law, and the same would apply to German law, French law, etc. This stance led to an **overwhelming nationalism of legal education**, which is nowadays the worst threat to the future of law and of legal knowledge. In fact, the future of law (seeking justice as such), as well as of legal knowledge (seeking truth as such), is severely limited by placing it within any geo-political boundaries.

However, the concept of (private) law as national and state-made is relatively novel, since it only became established about two centuries ago. As such, it is quite revolutionary and marks a tremendous upheaval of the Western legal tradition.

Until the end of the nineteenth century, European law developed based on scholarly and judicial re-interpretation of a corpus of writings by Roman lawyers who had lived in antiquity. This analysis, conducted by more modern judicial scholars, strove to rationalize and adapt these writings to the new features of contemporary society. As a consequence, a proper common law (***ius***

[1] Herbert LA Hart, *The Concept of Law* (3rd edn, Clarendon Press 2012) 213ff.

commune) of Europe was established and went on flourishing for centuries (see *supra*, ch 2, paras 3-4).
Even though the Holy Roman Empire tended to consider the medieval *ius commune* as its own, it would appear that such law was not issued by the Emperor and, despite some ambiguities in legal historiography,[2] could not be depicted as the territorial legal system of the Empire (see *supra*, ch 2, para 4.1).

The merit of depicting the medieval *ius commune* as 'a spiritual undertaking' ('*un fatto spirituale*') may be ascribed to Francesco Calasso (1904-1965).[3] More recently Paolo Grossi has embarked upon a sharp criticism of any understanding of medieval law of Europe as enacted through the exercise of a sovereign legislative power.[4]

In fact, the geographical domain of medieval *ius commune* stretched much further than the territories encompassed within the borders of the Holy Roman Empire, given that it also reached some French *pays de droit écrit* (or *de droit savant*). Furthermore, the application of medieval *ius commune* was based on the premise that Roman law was to be understood not as state law, but either as customary law, or as *ratio scripta*, ie a repository of patterns of legal reasoning not bound to historical or national circumstance (see *supra*, ch 2, paras 3-4).

2. THE ESTABLISHMENT OF THE WESTPHALIAN PARADIGM: THE SPLIT OF NATIONAL AND INTERNATIONAL LAW

The Holy Roman Empire and the Roman Church were not definable as states in a modern sense,[5] first of all because they claimed to be universal institutions, whose powers were not confined within a closed territory. They constituted the *Res publica gentium christianarum*, which was deemed to embrace all mankind and to rule all over the world.

To put it as Frederic William Maitland (1850-1906) did, 'the imperial mother and her papal daughter were fairly good friends'.

[2] Giuseppe Ermini, *Guida bibliografica per lo studio del diritto comune pontificio* (L Cappelli 1934); Id, 'Genesi ed evoluzione storica, elementi costitutivi' in Id, *Corso di diritto comune* (Giuffrè 1943). See also Danilo Segoloni (ed), *Il diritto comune e la tradizione giuridica europea. Atti del convegno di studi in onore di Giuseppe Ermini, Perugia 30-31 ottobre 1976* (Libreria Universitaria Editrice 1980).
[3] See Francesco Calasso, 'Il diritto comune come fatto spirituale' in Id, *Introduzione al diritto comune* (Giuffrè 1951) 137ff.
[4] Paolo Grossi, *L'ordine giuridico medievale* (Laterza 1995) 228ff.
[5] For the Holy Roman Empire, see Hans-Peter Haferkamp, 'Holy Roman Empire' in Jürgen Basedow, Klaus J Hopt, Reinhard Zimmermann and Andreas Stier (eds), *The Max Planck Encyclopedia of European Private Law*, vol 1 (OUP 2012) 835.

Therefore, the medieval *ius commune* had no territorial basis at all, nor was it attached to the powers of a sovereign state. To a man of the Middle Ages, a discourse about German or French law must have sounded as out of place as speaking today of German or French theology, or Dutch or Greek medicine, and so on.
Yet, the institutional paradigm of the Empire gradually fell to pieces after the **Peace of Westphalia**, which, in 1648, put an end to the wars of religion which had been inflaming Europe for thirty years. The means to eradicate civil conflicts was found in the emergence of nation states, which replaced the universality of the Empire, and it was thus given a protective shield in the principle *cuius regio, eius et religio*. The religion adopted by the sovereign would have to be worshiped by its liegemen as well, whether or not they believed in it.
The idea of nation states as a cure for civil conflicts of religion was proposed by a French political philosopher, Jean Bodin (1529-1596), in his *Six livres de la République* (1576), where the concept of **state sovereignty** is widely expounded.

> Passionately and imaginatively, this view was later advocated by Thomas Hobbes (see also *supra*, ch 1, para 1) through the rabbinical metaphor of the **Leviathan**, which gave the title to his masterpiece of political philosophy (1651). The state is seen there as an 'infernal' machinery of decision-making procedures, which replaces the guidance of an absolute truth (of God), of an absolute justice (of law), and so on, with a convention among the citizens.

The abandonment of truth was the price citizens paid for peace. In other words, law was no longer hinged on the rationality of legal reasoning but on the state's political will and sovereign power (see also *supra* ch 2, para 5; *infra*, ch 5, para 3). The truth, pure and rational, was no longer paramount for the law, replaced instead with the sovereign's will (*stat pro ratione voluntas*). On the other hand, **wars ceased to be just or unjust** by nature or according to the goals they pursued, or because they were aimed at making the allegedly true religion triumph over the heretics and the infidels. Wars thus became a competition or a negotiation between nation states, and this negotiation was governed by rules that imposed their mutual legitimacy and their mutual respect (see also *infra*, ch 5, para 4).

> During the sixteenth century, the dilemma of defining when a war can be considered 'just' had been the subject of a vast elaboration of political philosophy, which laid the foundations of international law in a modern sense.
> The forerunner of this speculation was a Roman Catholic theologian, Francisco de Vitoria (1483-1546), who was the founder of the school of Salamanca's classical thinking, which was deeply imbued with a concept of natural law based on liberty (Second Scholasticism).[6]

[6] Andreas Thier, 'Scholastic Jurisprudence' in Jürgen Basedow, Klaus J Hopt, Reinhard Zimmermann and Andreas Stier (eds), *The Max Planck Encyclopedia of European Private Law*, vol 2 (OUP 2012) 1532.

The birth of international law as an autonomous discipline is generally recognized in the *De iure belli* by Alberico Gentili (1552-1608). However, the work that had far greater resonance was certainly *De iure belli ac pacis* by Hugo Grotius, or Huig de Groot (1583-1645).
Francisco de Vitoria, Alberico Gentili, and Hugo Grotius can therefore be considered as the forerunners of international law.

This assumption led to the establishment of the **Westphalian paradigm**, characterized by a strict separation between domestic law and international law. As regards domestic law, the state's sovereignty entitles it to bind its own citizens by enacting legal rules. Law became a product of nation states and, therefore, each of them is hinged on an autonomous system of its sources. Legal nationalism paved the way for the major codifications of private law of the nineteenth century (see *supra*, ch 2, para 5).
As regards international law, the state's sovereignty can be voluntarily self-limited by means of agreements with other states. Subsequently, each contracting state has a duty to enforce the international agreements it has entered into, by changing its domestic law accordingly.
The ancient *ius gentium*, the body of customary rules acknowledged by Romans as applicable to non-citizens, was thus replaced by a ***ius publicum europaeum***, a body of rules negotiated by the states, with the aim of binding the contracting states themselves, but not their citizens.

In the political-theological reflection of Carl Schmitt (see *supra*, ch 1, para 2) World War I caused the abandonment of the *ius publicum europaeum*, since the development of technology and the unlimited power that it makes available to mankind excludes the possibility that any war can be dominated and controlled by legal rules. The ancient wars of religion are now revolutionary wars,[7] namely absolute wars, aimed at the annihilation of the enemy.

Customary law is set apart both at the national and at the international level, although it does not disappear completely but operates in the interstices of law laid down by nation states (for example to interpret it, or to fill its gaps) (see also *infra*, ch 7, paras 3.1-3.2).

Article 38 of the Statute of the International Court of Justice stipulates that international law consists of: 1. international conventions; 2. international custom, as evidence of a general practice accepted as law; 3. the general principles of law recognized by civilized nations, whose mapping was famously undertaken by Rudolph B. Schlesinger (1909-1996).[8]

[7] Carl Schmitt, *Der Nomos der Erde im Völkerrecht des* Jus Publicum Europaeum (5th edn, Duncker & Humblot 2011).
[8] Rudolph B Schlesinger, 'On the General Principles of Law Recognized by Civilized Nations in America' (1957) 51 Am J Int Law 734.

3. COMPARATIVE LAW

3.1. Concept and historical development

The existence of a plurality of legal systems itself constitutes the reason for their comparison. This comparison aims to 'measure' similarities and differences between legal systems. In this regard, one can speak about **comparative law**, although this term may generate the false impression that what is dealt with is a legal system in itself, or a part of it. However, the term 'comparative law' is substantially and qualitatively distinct from that of **foreign law**. Notably, the latter refers to a proper legal system in force in a state other than that being used as the reference, whereas the former constitutes a mere theoretical or conceptual abstraction, which is solely the result of an intellectual and cultural operation of comparison between a national legal system and another (or even more than one).

For example, a German observer may qualify French law as 'foreign', whilst it will obviously not be such for a French person. Differently, 'comparative law' is not the law of either a French or a German national but the intellectual and cultural operation of comparing the two legal systems, to 'measure' how they resemble each other and in how they diverge.

Accordingly, it is appropriate to say that comparative law identifies a method of legal science, which may be embodied in the study and teaching of each national law or be developed on its own as an autonomous field of knowledge.[9]
The historical heralding of comparative law goes back to Greek literature of political philosophy, where some great thinkers of the classical period (among them Plato and Aristotle) discussed the rights in force in the various *poleis*, thus comparing them (see *supra*, ch 2, para 1).[10]
It is obvious that, at the time of the European *ius commune* (see *supra*, ch 2, paras 3-4) given the trend in universalism that characterized it, no particular interest was developed in comparative law, except in specific contexts where it coexisted with some local, particularly rooted, legal systems (as in France). By contrast, the progressive rise of the *ius patrium* (see *supra*, ch 2, para 5) explains why comparative law assumed new importance.

A specific case occurred in **Germany** where, due to Napoleon's military conquests, the French code that had been enacted in the meantime (see *infra*, ch 4, para 3.1.1) became effective in the Rhineland and was substantially implemented in the *Landrecht für das Großherzogthum Baden* of 1809. Therefore, law students at the famous university of Heidelberg, which is located in Baden, had to study French law. This led two of its professors, namely Karl Salomo Zachariä (von Lingenthal) (1769-1843) and Carl Joseph Anton Mittermaier (1787-1867), to

[9] Konrad Zweigert and Hein Kötz, *An Introduction to Comparative Law* (Tony Weir tr, 3rd edn, OUP 1998) 74.
[10] ibid 49.

found a journal for the review of comparative law in 1829, the *Zeitschrift für Rechtswissenschaft und Gesetzgebung des Auslandes*, which may historically be considered as the first-ever on the subject.

For similar reasons, Zachariä wrote and published a French private law manual in German for his students, namely the *Handbuch des Französischen Zivilrechts* (the first edition of which dates back to 1808 but was then republished until the fourth edition in 1837), which had a peculiar fate. Translated into French by Charles Aubry and Charles Frédéric Rau (the first edition was published between 1839 and 1844), it was then republished in several editions (more recently edited by Carl Crome) and became an influential text on the development of French law, which was influenced by the German categories Zachariä had unknowingly used.

The great comparative tradition of the University of Heidelberg is still attested by the vitality of its prestigious *Institut für ausländisches und internationales Privat- und Wirtschaftsrecht*.

Furthermore, significant comparative analysis preceded the unification of commercial law that initially occurred in Prussia (see *infra*, ch 7, para 2). From 1871, once the *Deutsches Reich* was established, the unification of different legal systems extended to private law (see *infra*, ch 4, para 3.1.2), law of civil procedure, law of bankruptcy, law of judicature (court system), and criminal law.[11]

In **France**, in 1834 Jean Jacques Gaspard Foelix (1791-1853) founded the *Revue étrangère de législation de France*, whose title, perhaps not particularly appropriate, was changed several times, until publication ceased in 1850.[12] At that same time, the first chairs of comparative law were created at several French Universities. In 1869, the prestigious *Société de législation comparée* (which still exists) was established, and started publishing the *Revue internationale de droit comparé* (also still active).

In **England**, in 1869 Henry Sumner Maine was appointed to the Oxford Chair of Historical and Comparative Jurisprudence.

From a scholarly perspective, a decisive role was played by the Italian lawyer **Emerico Amari** (1810-1870), who can therefore be considered as the true founder of comparative law in the modern sense.[13] His *Critica e storia di una scienza delle legislazioni comparate* (1857) found great resonance not only in Italy, but also in the rest of Europe.

However, the historical birth of comparative law, from which it has acquired its current physiognomy and has also begun to develop its own methodological awareness, is usually identified in the ***Congrès international de droit comparé***,[14] which, under the auspices of the *Société de législation comparée*, was held in Paris from 31 July to 4 August 1900 during the great World Exhibition celebrating the triumph of the progressive and positivist spirit of the *belle époque*.

11 ibid 16.

12 ibid 55.

13 Erik Jayme, *Rechtsvergleichung – Ideengeschichte und Grundlagen von Emerico Amari zur Postmoderne. Vorträge – Aufsätze – Rezensionen* (Müller 2000) 20.

14 Société de législation comparée (ed), *Congrès International de Droit comparé. Tenu à Paris du 31 juillet au 4 août 1900. Procès-verbaux des séances et documents*, 2 vols (LGDJ 1905).

The authors of this conference were Édouard Lambert (1866-1947) and Raymond Saleilles (1855-1912),[15] who particularly contributed to the methodology of comparative law as a science.[16] In 1921, Lambert founded the first French institute of comparative law at the University of Lyon.[17]

One of the main fathers of comparative law was **Ernst Rabel** (1874-1955), who clearly defined the scope and the methods of this field of knowledge and laid the foundations for its further development in Europe.[18] Rabel was a member of the mixed Italian-German court of arbitration that was charged with the application of the treaty of Versailles at the end of World War I. Specifically, regarding the interpretation of article X of the Treaty, which regulated the pre-war legal relationships between nationals of combatant states, Rabel confronted the issue that national laws may differently qualify the same legal institution, so that, when they collide, the application of international private law proves troublesome. He came to the conclusion that, contrary to a widespread assumption at the time, such qualification should not be based on the national law of the court adjudicating the case (*lex fori*) but on a comparative assessment (see *infra*, ch 3, para 5).[19]

Thanks to the work of Rabel, in 1926 Kaiser-Wilhelm-Gesellschaft founded the Kaiser-Wilhelm Institute of Foreign and International Private Law in Berlin, which later on moved to Hamburg and became the current ***Max-Planck-Institut für ausländisches und internationales Privatrecht***.
Once again at Rabel's instigation, notwithstanding the war, in 1916, an Institute for Comparative Law was founded at the University of Munich and was followed by many others, including that of Heidelberg which has already been mentioned.
In **Italy**, it was at Bocconi University, in 1924, that the first *Istituto di diritto commerciale comparato* was established, upon the initiative of Mario Rotondi (1900-1984).
The path was subsequently followed by the *Istituto di studi legislativi*, which Salvatore Galgano (1887-1965) created at Rome University La Sapienza in 1927.

3.2. Aims and methods

As regards the methods of comparative law, firstly it must be stated that the mere recognition or display of one or more foreign legal systems may

[15] For a critical reply to their train of thought, see François Gény, *Méthode d'interpretation et sources en droit privé positif*, vol 1 (LGDJ 1919) 267ff.
[16] Raymond Saleilles, 'Conception et objet de la science du droit comparé' in Société de législation comparée (ed), *Congrès International de Droit comparé*, vol 1 (n 14) 179ff. About Saleilles' view on comparative law, see Henri Capitant, 'Conception, méthode et fonction du droit comparé après R. Saleilles' in *L'œuvre juridique de Raymond Saleilles* (A Rousseau 1914) 110ff.
[17] Marc Ancel, 'Les Grandes Étapes de la recherche comparative au XX siècle' in *Studi in memoria di Andrea Torrente* (Giuffrè 1968) 25ff.
[18] Ernst Rabel, *Aufgabe und Notwendigkeit der Rechtsvergleichung* (Hueber 1925).
[19] Zweigert and Kötz (n 9) 59ff.

constitute a preliminary effort but does not in itself accomplish any legal comparative analysis.[20]

To this end, it is necessary to proceed with a 'measurement' (appraisal) of the **similarities and differences** between the laws considered, although it is not necessary to express a value judgment about what system should be considered as 'the best'.[21]

Historically, the modern affirmation of comparative law was motivated by the intent to create a *droit commun de l'humanité*.[22] Although they have not in themselves been contested as illegitimate, aspirations of this kind have been derided as manifestations of a utopian and good-natured spirit.[23] It has instead been affirmed that, as can also be said of any other science, the primary and inalienable task of comparative law is to gain knowledge on a specific subject matter.[24]

> The manifesto of the *Circolo di Trento*, which gathered a number of Italian comparatists around Rodolfo Sacco, begins with the following thesis: 'Comparative law, understood as a science, necessarily aims at a better understanding of legal data. Further tasks, such as the improvement of law or its interpretation, are worthy of the greatest consideration but, nevertheless, are only secondary ends of comparative legal research'.[25]

From a practical point of view, however, some advantages are to be highlighted, which can also be seen as **indirect benefits of comparative law**. In particular, comparative law may serve: 1) as an aid to the legislator; 2) as a tool of construction of national or international law; 3) as a subject to be taught and studied at universities; 4) as an incentive and a guide to uniform existing laws; 5) as a driver of a European law as such.[26]

A core issue of the comparative law method has been the quest for a criterion by which to measure similarities and differences between the legal systems under scrutiny. In fact, such a comparison is possible only if it takes place on the basis of a common denominator between the legal systems under consideration, which may validly constitute the criterion of their comparison (***tertium comparationis***).[27]

According to certain legal scholars, comparative law is easier with regard to the areas of private law which are more 'apolitical', such as contracts and

[20] ibid 6.

[21] See Zweigert and Kötz (n 9) 46f; Mathias Siems, *Comparative Law* (2nd edn, CUP 2018) 27ff, who explains why in comparative analysis one has to be careful in expressing critical policy evaluation.

[22] Édouard Lambert, 'Conception générale et définition de la science du droit comparé' in Société de législation comparée (ed), vol 1 (n 14) 26.

[23] Rodolfo Sacco, 'Legal Formants: A Dynamic Approach To Comparative Law' (1991) 39 Am J Comp L 343.

[24] Zweigert and Kötz (n 9) 3 and 15.

[25] See also Rodolfo Sacco and Piercarlo Rossi, *Introduzione al diritto comparato* (6th edn, Utet 2015) 3ff.

[26] Zweigert and Kötz (n 9) 16.

[27] Uwe Kischel, *Comparative Law* (Andrew Hammer tr, OUP 2019) 4.

obligations, whereas family and succession laws present a greater degree of inhomogeneity among them.[28] Similar considerations may apply to some areas of constitutional law.[29]

However, it has been shown that succession law also lends itself to comparison.[30] On the other hand, as regards family law, it is sufficient to note that, in recent times, it has been possible to compile a complete collection of principles that bring together and formalize the common European law in this area (see *infra*, ch 8, paras 2.1 and 2.3), so that even in this area of private law, comparison is certainly possible.[31]

Overall, it is worth pointing out that comparative law is generally characterized by an **anti-dogmatic, or even anti-conceptual, approach**. In its most reasonable and intrinsically useful form, comparative analysis mistrusts native jurists, who are implicitly 'accused' of not being the best judges with regard to their own national legal system, due to a significant level of conditioning and biases of various kinds to put it in picturesque terms, 'in their explorations on foreign territory comparatists may come upon natives lying in wait with spears'[32].

In this regard, there is an analogy between comparative law and the Freudian discovery of the unconscious, or the Marxian dialectical laws of capitalism, or even the Nietzschean death of God and nihilism. In all these philosophical theories, the basic concepts can be expressed in terms of a demystification and 'awareness' of a further truth that is veiled or unknown, mainly to those who are directly involved and conditioned by it.

On a methodological level, two approaches to comparative law can be identified, which are variously intertwined, and both can be traced back to endeavors undertaken in Germany by the Max Planck Society.

The first of them can be defined as **functionalist approach**. It was paradigmatically exposed and, above all, fully applied, in the famous handbook by Konrad Zweigert (1911-1996) and Hein Kötz.[33] Along their dictum, '[i]ncomparables cannot be usefully compared and in law the only things which are comparable are those which fulfil the same function'.[34] It means

[28] Zweigert and Kötz (n 9) 39ff; Siems (n 21) 33ff.
[29] Siems (n 21) 35.
[30] Reinhard Zimmermann, 'Kulturelle Prägung des Erbrechts?' [2016] JZ 321, 323ff. See in particular the comparative analysis carried out in Kenneth GC Reid, Marius de Waal and Reinhard Zimmermann (eds), *Comparative Succession Law*, vol 1, *Testamentary Formalities* (OUP 2011); Id, *Comparative Succession Law*, vol 2, *Intestate Succession* (OUP 2015); Id, *Comparative Succession Law*, vol 3, *Mandatory Family Protection* (OUP 2020).
[31] Dieter Martiny, 'Is Unification of Family Law Feasible Or Even Desirable?' in Arthur Hartkamp, Martijn Hesselink, Ewoud Hondius, Chantal Mak and Edgar du Perron (eds), *Towards a European Civil Code* (4th edn, Wolters Kluwer and Ars Aequi Libri 2011) 429.
[32] Zweigert and Kötz (n 9) 36, who thus quoted an observation of Ernst Rabel.
[33] ibid 34ff.
[34] Zweigert and Kötz (n 9) 34. More recently, see Hein Kötz, 'Comparative Law: A Veteran's View' in Katharina Boele-Woelki and Diego P Fernàndez Arroyo (eds), *The Past, Present and Future of Comparative Law* (Springer 2018) 25, 27: 'The principle of "functionality" means that in law the only things which are comparable are those which fulfil the same function. Solutions in different jurisdictions must therefore be cut loose from their conceptual context and stripped of their national doctrinal structures'.

that the *tertium comparationis* should be determined by the function on which practical problems are resolved, independently of the conceptual or dogmatic structure of such solutions.

The second address can be defined as **historical-comparatist approach** and may be summarized through the formula coined by Gino Gorla (1906-1992): 'comparison involves history'.[35]

This method, which refers the *tertium comparationis* back to the common Roman heritage of the comparable legal systems,[36] has been most notably adopted and developed by Reinhard Zimmermann. His masterpiece, *The Law of Obligations*, is an overall exposition of the historical development of the civilian tradition up to its codification in continental Europe.[37] This achievement is rooted in the great works of German historians of European law such as Helmut Coing (1912-2000), Franz Wieacker (1908-1994), and formerly Paul Koschaker (1879-1951).[38]

According to Alan Watson (1933-2018), Western legal systems as a whole is the result of an overall 'legal transplant' of Roman law. Therefore, a real juridical comparison would be impossible if not done in terms of a history of law (or of its tradition).

On the other hand, the method developed by Rodolfo Sacco, which focuses on the theory of **dissociation of legal formants**, can be qualified as 'struc-

[35] Gino Gorla, 'Diritto comparato', *Enciclopedia del diritto*, vol 12 (Giuffrè 1964) 930, fn 5. He thus inverted the statement by Frederic William Maitland, according to which 'history involves comparison'; see Frederic W Maitland, 'Why the History of English Law is not Written' in Herbert AL Fischer (ed), *The Collected Papers of Frederic William Maitland*, vol 1 (CUP 1911) 488.

[36] Gino Gorla, *Diritto comparato e diritto comune europeo* (Giuffrè 1981) 4.

[37] Reinhard Zimmermann, *The Law of Obligations. Roman Foundations of the Civilian Tradition* (OUP 1996). For a discussion of Zimmermann's methodology, see Carlo Augusto Cannata, 'Usus hodiernus pandectarum, common law, diritto romano olandese e diritto comune europeo' in Id, *Scritti scelti di diritto romano*, vol 1 (Giappichelli 2011) 565ff; Id, 'Usus modernus pandectarum e diritto europeo' ibid 443; Luigi Garofalo, *Giurisprudenza romana e diritto privato europeo* (Cedam 2008) 45ff.

[38] Helmut Coing, '*Europäisierung der Rechtswissenschaft*' [1990] NJW 937; Id, *Europäisches Privatrecht*, 2 vols (CH Beck 1985, 1989); Id, 'European Common Law: Historical Foundations' in Mauro Cappelletti (ed), *New Perspectives for a Common Law of Europe* (Publications of the European University Institute 1978) 31ff; Id, 'Ius commune, nationale Kodifikation und internationale Abkommen: Drei historische Formen der Rechtsvereinheitlichung' in *Le nuove frontiere del diritto e il problema dell'unificazione. Atti del congresso internazionale organizzato dalla Facoltà di giurisprudenza dell'Università di Bari, 2-6 aprile 1975*, vol 1 (Giuffrè 1979) 171; Paul Koschaker, *Europa und das Römische Recht* (4th edn, CH Beck 1966); Franz Wieacker, 'Konstituenten der okzidentalen Rechtskultur' in Okko Behrends, Malte Diesselhorst and Wulf Eckart Voss (eds), *Römisches Recht in der europäischen Tradition. Symposion aus Anlass des 75. Geburtstages von Franz Wieacker* (Gremer 1985) 355ff; Franz Wieacker, *Vom Römischen Recht* (2nd edn, KF Koehler 1961). For a different view on the relationship between Roman and European law, see among others Pio Caroni, *Die Einsamkeit des Rechtshistorikers. Notizen zu einem problematischen Lehrfach* (Helbing und Lichtenhahn 2005); Paolo Grossi, '*Unità giuridica europea: un Medioevo prossimo futuro?*' [2002] *Quaderni fiorentini* 42; Id, '*Modelli storici e progetti attuali nella formazione di un futuro diritto europeo*' [1996] Riv dir civ I 281; Id, 'Storia di esperienze giuridiche e tradizione romanistica (a proposito della rinnovata e definitiva "Introduzione allo studio del diritto romano" di Riccardo Orestano)' [1988] *Quaderni fiorentini* 545. For some critical remarks, see also Hugh Collins, *The European Civil Code. The Way Forward* (CUP 2008) 149ff.

turalist'.[39] According to this conception of comparative law, there could be a 'disharmony' between the three components that form the legal matrix, ie the legislature, the judiciary (judge-made-law) and scholars' opinion. In particular, it is possible that a legislative text does not correspond to the operational rule applied by jurisprudence, because, for example, judges interpret it from the perspective of Roman law or foreign law. It is also possible that a scholar may give an inaccurate or unfaithful representation of her own national law.[40]

The dissociation of legal formants may illuminate the fate of **legal transplants**,[41] that occur when, due to a wide range of possible reasons, a piece of legislation of one country was implemented more or less uncritically in another. Inflexibilities or 'ground-in' assumptions by legal scholarship and the judge-made law of the recipient country, may in fact cause a rejection crisis in that country, thus frustrating their purpose and degenerating into real **legal irritants**.[42]

All the methods that have been described and examined thus far have a **micro-comparison** focus, namely a comparison between the legal systems based on the operational solutions that they give to the individual practical problems that must be addressed and resolved by the law. An opposite methodology is centred on **macro-comparison**, which compares national laws on the basis of their different constitutional and institutional features, if not on the basis of the legal mentality that animates the jurists who belong to it.[43]

> In his masterpiece *De l'esprit des lois* (1748), the Baron de Montesquieu, facing the problem of how to compare two different national laws, observed that 'to determine which of those systems is most agreeable to reason, we must take them each as a whole and compare them in their entirety'.[44]

A staple of macro-comparison is constituted by the classification of national laws and above all by gathering them into **families**, ie groups of national laws that are connected by a number of characterizing features.[45]

[39] Sacco and Rossi (n 25) 55ff. For a recent critical assessment of Sacco's theory, see Kischel (n 27) 115ff. On this regard cf also the observations by Francesco P Patti, 'Review of Rodolfo Sacco/Piercarlo Rossi: *Einführung in die Rechtsvergleichung*, 3. Aufl., Baden-Baden, Nomos, 2017' [2018] ZEuP 975.

[40] Sacco (n 23) 369.

[41] Ralf Michaels, 'Legal Culture' in *The Max Planck Encyclopedia of European Private Law*, vol 2 (n 6) 1060; Jörg Fedtke, 'Legal transplants' in Jan M Smits (ed), *Elgar Encyclopedia of Comparative Law* (2nd edn, Edward Elgar 2012) 550ff.

[42] Gunther Teubner, 'Legal Irritants: Good Faith in British Law or How Unifying Law Ends up in New Divergences' (1998) 61 MLR 11.

[43] Max Rheinstein, 'Legal systems: Comparative law and legal systems' in *International Encyclopedia of the Social Sciences* (1968) 204; Zweigert and Kötz (n 9) 4ff; Kischel (n 27) 2 and 8.

[44] Charles de Secondat de Montesquieu, *De l'esprit des lois* (Éditions Gallimard 1748), Book XXIX, Ch 11 'De quelle manière deux lois diverses peuvent être comparées'.

[45] Sacco and Rossi (n 25) 105ff; Jaakko Husa, 'Legal families' in *Elgar Encyclopedia of Comparative Law* (n 41) 491ff; Hein Kötz, 'Legal Families' in *The Max Planck Encyclopedia of European Private Law*, vol 2 (n 6) 1063.

The idea of classifying national legal systems in families seems to have been formulated for the first time by Gottfried Wilhelm von Leibniz (1646-1716) in his work *Nova Methodus Discendae Docendaeque Iurisprudentiae* of 1667. In the modern era, one of the first attempts in this sense was made by Adhémar Esmein (1848-1913) on the occasion of the famous, and already previously mentioned comparative convention of 1900.[46] During the twentieth century, the work of René David (1906-1990), especially *Les grands systèmes de droit contemporains*, greatly influenced the proposed theory of families of legal systems and its application.[47]

The identification of certain characteristic elements, which reflect the style of each national law and make them immediately recognizable,[48] is rather controversial.[49] Actually, even the recognition and classification of these legal families can vary from one author to the other.
A major distinction is that between **civil law and common law jurisdictions** (see *supra*, ch 2, para 4.2; *infra*, ch 4, paras 2-4); furthermore, some **mixed jurisdictions** seem to occupy an intermediate position. Within civil law jurisdictions, a sub-division is sometimes made between **Roman laws** (France, Italy, Spain, Portugal and their former colonies) and **Germanic laws** (Germany, Austria, Switzerland). Furthermore, the **Nordic laws** (Scandinavian and Baltic countries) are sometimes considered as having peculiar traits, which make them a group on their own.[50]

4. PRIVATE INTERNATIONAL LAW

The existence of a plurality of autonomous jurisdictions itself brings with the possibility of a **conflict of laws**, when the same set of facts connects with more than one national law.
Suppose a contract has been concluded between a French and a German party and that neither of them performs. If the German party intends to sue the other, it is quite possible that the claimant will bring the case to a German court (ie in the claimant's own country) and ask for German law to be applied. Conversely, however, the other party may object and attempt to bring the case before a French court (ie of the defendant's own country) and have French law applied. A potential conflict of jurisdictions thus arises, which involves both the procedural dimension (ie the forum, the proceedings of the trial, etc.) and the substantial dimension of law (ie the legal provisions applicable regarding

46 Adhémar Esmein, 'Le Droit comparé et l'enseignement du Droit' in Société de législation comparée (ed), vol 1 (n 14) 445ff.
47 René David, Camille Jauffret-Spinosi and Marie Goré, *Les grands systèmes de droit contemporains* (12th edn, Dalloz 2002) 671.
48 Zweigert and Kötz (n 9) 67ff.
49 For an innovative view on the topic, see Ugo Mattei, 'Three Patterns of Law: Taxonomy and Change in the World's Legal Systems' (1997) 45 Am J Comp L 5.
50 Anneken Kari Sperr, 'Scandinavia, Harmonization of Law' in *The Max Planck Encyclopedia of European Private Law*, vol 2 (n 6) 1483.

breach of contract, damages, etc.). The first court petitioned therefore has to take a decision whether or not it is competent for the case and, provided that it is, which national law is to be applied. If, to take our example, the contract was signed in Italy and furthermore its subject matter consists of a parcel of land which is found in the UK, the possibilities of conflict between national laws multiply. A selection between the conflicting laws is therefore necessary. A **choice of law** must be then accomplished. Therefore, each jurisdiction must provide for rules purported and designed to carry out this very specific function, to make a choice between conflicting national laws (**conflict rules**). These are secondary rules (see *infra*, ch 6, para 2.1), because they do not set forth the procedural and substantive solutions to be applied in a case, but simply sort out which of the several legal systems involved is competent to rule it. The choice is made on the basis of a **connecting factor** among those at stake, that is declared by conflict rules as prevailing upon the others (for example in the situation mentioned above, if the applicable conflict rules resolve the conflict of laws on the basis of the national territory in which a plot of land is found, then the law of the United Kingdom will apply to the case).[51] It is also possible that different elements of the same case are connected to different national laws (***dépeçage***), thus bringing these laws into co-existence (in our example, the capacity of the contracting parties might be governed by their national laws, whilst the contract itself could be governed by another).

All rules of this sort are contained in a branch of the law which is traditionally called **private international law**. Despite the terminology, private international law is not international as to its sources, with each legal system providing its own; it is however international in its content, dealing with cross-border cases.

From a historical viewpoint, the necessity of private international law arose long before the creation of national laws and was specifically addressed in France during the sixteenth century, where a high number of customary laws, some of them being broader (*coutumes générales*) and some more local (*coutumes locales*), overlapped and thus raised complex questions with regard to conflicts.[52] Charles Dumoulin, or Molinaeus (1500-1566), and, even more so, Bertrand d'Argentré (1519-1590) are to be counted among the scholars who contributed the most to developing the coordination of different French customary laws.

The first written arrangement of private international law is found in the *disposizioni preliminari* (preliminary provisions), which were set out in the preface of Italian *Codice civile* of 1865. They were largely due to the work of Pasquale Stanislao Mancini (1817-1888).[53]

The term 'private international law' was coined by the US-American judge and

[51] Kurt Siehr, 'Connecting Factors (PIL)' in *The Max Planck Encyclopedia of European Private Law*, vol 1 (n 5) 356.

[52] Zweigert and Kötz (n 9) 77.

[53] ibid 104ff; Padoa Schioppa, *A History of Law in Europe. From the Early Middle Ages to the Twentieth Century* (CUP 2017) 509-510; Yuko Nishitani, 'Mancini, Pasquale Stanislao' in Jürgen Basedow, Giesela Rühl, Franco Ferrari and Pedro de Miguel Asensio (eds), *Encyclopedia of Private International Law*, vol 2 (Edward Elgar 2017) 1194.

scholar Joseph Story (1779-1845) in his *Commentaries on the Conflict of Laws* (1834) (see also *infra*, ch 7, para 4).[54]

Private international law may, in turn, be subdivided into a procedural part (which court is competent to hear the case and which law governs the proceedings brought before the court) and a substantial part (which law rules the rights and duties of the parties and decides how the case is to be adjudicated). In fact, it is very possible that a national court decides that while it has competence to hear the case, the substantive law to be applied is not that of the forum (***lex fori***), but that of another country (***renvoi***)[55] (returning to our example above, conflict rules might recognize the jurisdiction of the court first petitioned by one of the party, either the German or the French, that for said reason, however, will have to apply the substantive law of the UK to adjudicate the case).
Since private international law depends on individual national law, the question of conflicts between national rules of conflict paradoxically arises. Just as national laws may conflict on a contract or tort, etc., they may be conflicting as well as to their private international law.
This explains the tendency to uniform private international law by means of treaties between nations. In this regard, international bodies such as the Hague Conference on Private International Law have played an important role by elaborating the **Principles of Choice of Law in International Commercial Contracts** in 2015.
Since the 1990s, the private international law of the Member States of the EU has been mostly unified through regulations of the latter, regarding both its procedural and substantial dimensions. Therefore, it may be said that all Member States now apply the same rules of private international law (see *infra*, ch 8, para 1.5.2).

5. UNIFORM LAW

Uniform law comes into existence when many states intend to have identical rules in their own legal systems and, at that end, each of them enacts the same legislative provisions.[56]
Uniform legislation, however, does not necessarily result in uniform law, since the interpretation and application of the former have to be carried out by national judicatures. Therefore, if they adopt the criteria of interpretation provided by their own legal systems, which may obviously be divergent, then

[54] Joseph Story, *Commentaries on the Conflict of Laws, Foreign and Domestic: In Regard to Contracts, Rights, and Remedies, and Especially in Regard to Marriages, Divorces, Wills, Successions, and Judgments* (Hillard 1834) 9.
[55] Kurt Siehr, 'Renvoi' in *The Max Planck Encyclopedia of European Private Law*, vol 2 (n 6) 1449.
[56] Franco Ferrari 'Uniform Law' ibid 1732.

the risk is apparent that the outcomes are divergent as well, thus frustrating the aim of uniformity of law. As historically suggested by the studies conducted by Ernst Rabel on the subject (see *supra*, ch 3, para 3.1), the goal of uniformity of law may be achieved solely if uniform legislation is interpreted on the basis of a comparative analysis of the legal systems involved.[57]

This is the reason why article 7(1) CISG (see *infra* in this para) sets forth that: 'In the interpretation of this Convention, regard is to be had to its international character and to the need to promote uniformity in its application and the observance of good faith in international trade'.
General rules for interpretation of international treaties of rules are set out in sections 31-33 of the 1969 Vienna Convention on the Law of Treatises.[58]

Since the end of the nineteenth century, international standardisation has progressed in many areas of private law, especially in the field of commercial law, trade and labor law, intellectual and industrial property law.
The **instruments (or sources) of uniform law** are either: 1. International conventions, that oblige states applying them to change their own legal systems accordingly; 2. Model laws, that, although not binding, command a wide consensus and, therefore, are voluntarily mirrored by national legislators. The content and wording of both instruments are often drawn up by international agencies or scientific societies that conduct preliminary studies of comparative law.[59]
Two of the most important are the *Institut international pour l'unification du droit privé* (**UNIDROIT**),[60] established in 1926 by the League of Nations and re-established in 1940 on the basis of a multilateral agreement, and the United Nations Commission on International Trade Law (**UNCITRAL**), established in 1966 by the United Nations Organization.

The establishment of the UNIDROIT was due to the Italian Vittorio Scialoja and the institute is still based in Rome. Since its inception, 63 states have become members.
Its aims include:
– 'Preparing or promoting the adoption of new international conventions, model laws and uniform laws and promoting the codification and wider acceptance of international trade terms, provisions, customs and practices, in collaboration, where appropriate, with the organizations operating in this field';[61]
– 'Promoting ways and means of ensuring a uniform interpretation and application of international conventions and uniform laws in the field of the law of international trade'.[62]

[57] Ralf Michaels, 'Legal Culture' ibid 1060.
[58] Jan Asmus Bischoff, 'Interpretation of International Uniform Law' ibid 982.
[59] Zweigert and Kötz (n 9) 51.
[60] Herbert Kronke, 'UNIDROIT' in *The Max Planck Encyclopedia of European Private Law*, vol 2 (n 6) 1723.
[61] General Assembly resolution 2205 (XXI), sII, para 8 (c).
[62] General Assembly resolution 2205 (XXI), sII, para 8 (d).

One of the most successful instances of uniform law is that of the **United Nations Convention on the International Sale of Goods** (CISG) of 1980, also known as the Vienna Convention on sales.[63] It applies automatically to most international contracts of sale of goods between businesses (art. 1 CISG), unless excluded by the contracting parties (art. 6 CISG).

The CISG replaced two previous treaties concluded in 1964: the Convention on Uniform law on the formation of contracts for the International Sales of Goods (ULF) and the Convention on Uniform law on the International Sale of Goods (ULIS). The content of the CISG largely drew on the comparative law studies contained in the two volumes of *Das Recht des Warenkaufs* by Ernst Rabel,[64] who had personally contributed to the drafting of the ULF and ULIS (see also *supra*, ch 3, para 3.1).

In the US, the push for a uniform commercial law resulted in the adoption of the **Uniform Commercial Code** (UCC) in 1952 (see *infra*, ch 7, para 2.2),[65] on the basis of a major contribution from the American Law Institute (ALI).

The main drafter of the UCC was Karl N. Llewellyn, one of the leading pioneers of the legal realism that developed in the American legal tradition in the first half of the twentieth century (see *infra*, ch 7, para 4).

The UCC provides an optional model of legislation that is drafted using the restatement technique; namely, it is not binding upon individual states, which are free to adopt it and incorporate it into their jurisdiction. Despite its optional character, slightly amended, it was adopted (or partly adopted) across all of fifty states, as well as the main American territories (eg Puerto Rico).

ALI's **Restatements of Law** are uniform law models based on case law of the individual states. Some of them have been published in a third edition (those on unfair competition and tort). Others remain at the second edition (as the one on contracts). Work on a fourth edition is underway, but currently none of the planned volumes have been published.[66]

[63] For an article-by-article commentary, see Peter Mankowski, *Commercial Law* (Nomos 2019) 9ff.
[64] Ernst Rabel, *Das Recht des Warenkaufs. Eine rechtsvergleichende Darstellung*, vol 1 (Mohr Siebeck 1936) and vol 2 (Mohr Siebeck 1958). See also Peter Huber, 'Comparative Sales Law' in Mathias Reimann and Reinhard Zimmermann (ed), *The Oxford Handbook of Comparative Law* (2nd edn, OUP 2019) 938ff.
[65] Arthur T von Mehren and Peter L Murray, *Law in the United States* (2nd ed, CUP 2007) 18f.
[66] ibid 20ff.

GLOSSARY

American Law Institute (ALI) (5): US private organization, established in 1923, that brings together judges, practitioners, and scholars of law. Its aim is to promote the clarification and simplification of US common law and its adaptation to changing social needs. It is headquartered in Philadelphia, Pennsylvania.

Choice of law [*Choix de la loi applicable*; *Rechtswahl*; *Scelta della legge applicabile*] (4): stipulated according to the rules of private international law (see *ad vocem*) that solve the conflict between a plurality of autonomous jurisdictions when a set of facts deals with more than one national law.

Circolo di Trento (3.2): group of scholars that drew up a cultural manifesto (known as 'Tesi di Trento') on the task of comparative law and its research method. It is led by Rodolfo Sacco and gathers a number of the most influential scholars of comparative law in Italy, such as Paolo Cendon, Pier Giuseppe Monateri, Ugo Mattei, Gianmaria Ajani.

Comparative law [*Droit comparé*; *Rechtsvergleichung*; *Diritto comparato*] (3.1): discipline which aims at comparing various legal systems in order to 'measure' similarities and differences. It is thus a theoretical abstraction, merely being the result of an intellectual and cultural comparison between two (or more) legal systems, and it is not part of a legal system itself.

Connecting factor [*Facteur ou catégorie de rattachement*; *Anknüpfungsfaktor*; *Criterio di collegamento*] (4): in PIL, the criterion chosen by a conflict rule to sort out the prevailing jurisdiction that has to rule a case.

Families of laws (3.2): groups of national legal frameworks connected by a number of historical and judicial characterizing features, which reflect the style of each national law and make them immediately recognizable. Civil law and common law are two of the main families used to classify legal systems.

***Ius publicum europaeum* (2)**: body of rules negotiated by the states, with the aim of binding the contracting states themselves, but not their citizens. This set of rules replaced the ancient *ius gentium*.

Legal absolutism (1): doctrine which reflects the idea that law, especially private law, is set out by nation states, each of them exercising powers to enact and apply national law. The idea behind legal absolutism is therefore the sovereignty of each state over its own boundaries.

Legal transplant [*Greffe juridique*; *Rechtsübertragung*; *Trapianto giuridico*] (3.2): legislative tool by which a piece of law from one country is implemented more or less uncritically in another country, with the purpose of reducing inhomogeneity of the legal systems and encouraging their convergence.

***Lex fori* (4)**: rule of private international law, according to which, in case of a conflict between national laws, the one that must be applied is the national law of the court adjudicating the case.

Macro-comparison (3.2): method of comparison between national laws on the basis of the different constitutional and institutional features, as well as on the basis of the legal mentality that animates the jurists who belong to it.

Max Planck Institute for Comparative and International Private Law (3.1): legal research institute, which focuses on comparative and international private law, founded in 1949, formerly known as the Kaiser Wilhelm Institute for Foreign and International Private Law, founded in 1926. It has been based in Hamburg since 1956 and it is operated by the Max Planck Society for the Advancement of Science.

Micro-comparison (3.2): method of comparison between the legal systems based on the operational solutions that they give to the individual practical problems that must be addressed and solved by the law.

Peace of Westphalia (2): series of peace treaties signed in 1648 in the Westphalian cities of Osnabrück and Münster. These treaties put an end to the wars of religion which had been inflaming Europe for thirty years and mark the symbolic beginning of the modern international system, based on the concept of Westphalian sovereignty.

Political theology [*Politische Theologie*] (2): train of thought aimed at examining and describing religious stances in relation to issues of political principle, economics or society. The cornerstone of political theology is founded on philosophical inquiry regarding the opportunity to totally separate the secular and theological spheres. Carl Schmitt was one of its most prominent theorists and he paid particular attention to this notion; he used it to identify religious concepts which assume a relevant political value through their secularization. In Schmitt's view, a functioning legal order without sovereignty is inconceivable. The only possibility to make the law effective is to furnish it with an authority that establishes the most fitting way to apply general legal rules to concrete cases and how to deal with problems of controversial interpretation or under-determination.

Private international law [*Droit international privé*; *Internationales Privatrecht*; *Diritto internazionale privato*] (4): body of domestic rules and principles designed to help to select between conflicting national laws. It may be subdivided into a procedural part that aims to determine which court is competent to hear the case and which law rules the proceedings in front of it, and a substantial part that aims to establish which law rules the rights and duties of the parties and decides how the case is to be adjudicated.

(Law of) Scandinavian countries (3.2): law of the five Nordic countries, namely Denmark, Finland, Iceland, Norway, and Sweden. Historically, Scandinavian peoples had no written but customary laws, which, between the eleventh and thirteenth centuries, were reduced to writing. Each of these Nordic countries thus developed its own legal system, but in 1872 they organized a legislative cooperation and obtained a uniform legislation especially in the areas of contracts and commerce, as well as those concerned with family, nationality, and extradition.

State sovereignty (2): absolute and perpetual power of a Republic, as Jean Bodin claimed. It was conceived as a means of eradicating civil and religious conflicts, since states were recognised as the absolute power within their territory. This conception of sovereignty ranks between a Machiavellian and a Protestant point of view.

***Tertium comparationis* [*Drittes beim Vergleich*] (3.2)**: feature that two frames of reference have in common. In comparative law, it is the criterion used to measure similarities and differences between the legal systems under scrutiny, which may validly constitute a common denominator between them.

UNCITRAL (5): namely the United Nations Commission on International Trade Law, is the legal body established by the United Nations in 1966 that prepares and upholds the adoption of homogeneous legislative instruments in the field of international trade, in order to modernize the related national legislations.

UNIDROIT (5): namely the *Institut international pour l'unification du droit privé*, is an independent intergovernmental organization established by the League of Nations in 1926 and based in Rome that searches for the best methods to coordinate and modernize private and commercial national laws by applying harmonized principles and rules.

Vienna Convention on the International Sale of Goods (CISG) [*UN-Kaufrecht*] (5): signed in Vienna in 1980, it embodies the greatest milestone achieved by UNCITRAL. The treaty intends to promote international trade by removing obstacles to the choice of law and by providing a uniform and harmonized regime for contracts for the international sale of goods.

Westphalian paradigm (2): strict separation between domestic and international law, which followed up on the establishment of national states' sovereignty. It became paramount after the peace of Westphalia, which in 1648 put an end to the Thirty Years' War and broke the universalism of the Holy Roman Empire.

BIOGRAPHIES

Emerico Amari (Palermo, 1810 – Palermo, 1870) was an Italian legal theorist, a precursor of comparative law, and one of the protagonists of the liberal political movement during the *Risorgimento*. Besides law, Amari was also interested in

philosophy, history, and economics: his philosophical beliefs were inspired by a tempered empiricism, whereas his economic thoughts were oriented to a strong liberalism, hostile to any kind of customs barriers.
In 1841, he became Professor of Criminal Law at the University of Palermo, where he gave a lecture against the death penalty. Following his liberal ideas, Amari was an active member of Palermo's revolutionary committee and was then appointed deputy of the cities of Palermo and Salemi. He also worked on the draft of a new Sicilian Constitution. During his exile in Genoa, Amari became Professor of Constitutional Law, and, in 1859, he was appointed Professor of Philosophy of History at the *Istituto di Studi Superiori* in Florence. He was appointed deputy of the first Parliament of the Italian Reign, but resigned the following year due to family issues.
His main works are: *Critica di una scienza delle legislazioni comparate* (1857); *Difetti e riforme delle statistiche dei delitti e delle pene* (1839-1840); *Dell'uso di talune dottrine nei giudizi penali e dell'amministrazione della giustizia* (1840); *Del concetto generale e dei sommi principi della filosofia della storia* (1860).

Jean Bodin (Angers, 1529 – Laon, 1596) was a French jurist, economist and political philosopher, best known for his theory of sovereignty. He was educated in the Carmelite monastery of Angers, where he became a novice friar, but obtained release from his vows in 1549 and went to Paris; there, he studied at the University but also at the *Collège des Quatre Langues*. Later he studied Roman law at the University of Toulouse, where he also presumably taught comparative jurisprudence. He left Toulouse in 1560 and, in 1561, he was licensed as an attorney of the Parliament of Paris.
Bodin's education was influenced by an orthodox Scholastic approach, as well as Ramist philosophy, and by his Catholic beliefs, although he assumed a position about freedom of religion which was very tolerant for the time.
He was a prolific writer, ranging over history, economics, politics, natural philosophy, and also demonology. In his most famous publication, *Les six livres de la République* (*The Six Books of the Republic*, 1576), Bodin gave a definition of sovereignty, being intended as the absolute and perpetual power of a Republic; in the author's view, the sovereignty belonging to a governor, ie the Prince, made the latter accountable only to God. This conception of sovereignty lies between a Machiavellian point of view, which grants a governor the right to act for the benefit of his state without moral consideration, and a Protestant one, which advocates a popular government, or at least an elective monarchy.
Besides the *Six livres*, his main works are: *Oratio de instituenda in republica juventute ad senatum populumque Tolosatem* (1559); *Receuil de tout ce qui s'est négotié en la compagnie du Tiers Estat de France* (1577); *De la démonomanie des sorciers* (1580); *Sapientiae moralis epitome* (1588).

Francesco Calasso (Lecce, 1904 – Rome, 1965) was an Italian lawyer and academician, considered one of the most important scholars of *ius commune* and legal historiography. After graduating from the University La Sapienza of Rome, he became a teaching assistant and, after a period of study in Munich, he became a

Professor of History of Italian Law at the University of Urbino. Before and during World War II, he taught at several universities (of Catania, of Modena, of Pisa and of Florence), but in 1944, he was arrested and was convicted for twenty days together with other anti-fascists. After the war, Calasso returned to his academic career at University La Sapienza of Rome, where he first taught and then became the Dean of its School of Law in 1955, until his death in 1965. Calasso edited the *Rivista italiana per le scienze giuridiche* with Filippo Vassalli and Pietro de Francisci; he also planned and edited the *Enciclopedia del diritto* and, in 1957, he founded the review *Annali di storia del diritto*; he also was a member of the Accademia Nazionale dei Lincei and in 1954 he won the *Premio dei Lincei*.
His main works are: *Storia e sistema delle fonti del diritto comune* (1938); *Problema storico del diritto comune* (1939); *I glossatori e la teoria della sovranità* (1945); *Il negozio giuridico* (1957).

Helmut Coing (Celle, 1912 – Kronberg im Taunus, 2000) was a German jurist, historian and philosopher. He studied law in Kiel, Munich, Göttingen and Lille and obtained his doctorate from the University of Göttingen in 1935. In 1940, he was appointed Associate Professor in Frankfurt after completing his post-doctoral education. Following the dramatic years of World War II, he investigated the nature and the substance of the legal system, especially in two essays: *Die obersten Grundsätze des Rechts* (1947) and *Grundzüge der Rechtsphilosophie* (1950). Furthermore, his research mainly focused on the connection between law and the existing economic order. In 1955, he became Rector of the Frankfurt University. During his life, Coing was deeply engaged in the growth of the early German Federal Republic and supported the expansion of the German university system. In 1964, he founded the Max Planck Institute for European Legal History and, from 1978 to 1984, was Vice-President of the Max Planck Society for the Promotion of Research.
His main works are: *Europäisches Privatrecht* (1985); *Grundzüge der Rechtsphilosophie* (1985); *Die juristischen Auslegungsmethoden und die Lehren der allgemeinen Hermeneutik* (1959); *Epochen der Rechtsgeschichte in Deutschland* (1967).

René David (Jura, 12 January 1906 – Le Tholonet, 26 May 1990) was a French jurist and professor who is remembered for being one of the most prominent scholars in the field of comparative law during the second half of the twentieth century. Indeed, his works have been translated into numerous different languages and distributed throughout the world. David experienced the upheavals of World War II, during which he served the French army. Afterwards, he became Professor of Comparative Law at the University of Paris, and taught at the University of Aix-en-Provence from 1968 to 1976. During his career, he lectured in very prestigious universities, such as the University of Cambridge and Colombia University. Landmark projects he participated in include the UNIDROIT (International Institute for the Unification of Private Law) and the UNCITRAL (United Nations Commission on International Trade Law), being also the leader of the French delegation.
David is best known for his contributions to the field of comparative law. He suggested aggregating the different legal systems into families on the basis of

specific common denominators and ideologies shared by their members. Furthermore, he was one of the main advocates of the dichotomy between civil law and common law legal systems.
His main works are: *La protection des minorités dans les sociétés par actions* (1929); *Traité élémentaire de droit civil comparé : introduction à l'étude des droits étrangers et à la méthode comparative* (1950); *French Law* (1955); *The French Legal System: An introduction to civil law systems* (1958); *Cours de droit civil comparé* (1962); *Les grands systèmes de droit contemporains* (1964); *Major Legal Systems in the World Today* (1968); *International Encyclopedia of Comparative Law* (1975); *English Law and French Law: A comparison in substance* (1980); *Le droit comparé : droits d'hier, droits de demain* (1982).

Charles Dumoulin, also known as **Carolus Molinaeus** (Paris, 1500 – Paris, 1566) was a French lawyer and a jurist. Famous for the contributions to the formation of French civil law, and for the scholarly criticism of the texts of canon law, he distinguished himself by his forceful participation in the religious struggle of his country. He was born into a noble family. After becoming a Calvinist and being persecuted for his opinions, he decided to move to Germany where he became a professor of law. He taught at the University of Dole in the Franche-Comté in 1555 and 1556, in Besançon and Strasbourg and only moved back to Paris in 1557, but his troubles were not over.
In 1564, he published *Conseil sur le fait du concile de Trente*, in which he intended to prove the council was invalid. This provoked anger from both Catholics and Calvinists, and he was imprisoned by order of the parliament and regained his liberty only on the condition to not write anything without the permission of the king. He died two years after this ill-fated publication, in 1566.
As a scholar of Roman law, he published the opera *Extricatio labyrinthi dividui et individui*, in which Dumoulin developed and explained the theory of the divisible and indivisible obligations subsequently accepted by the *Code civil* (articles 1217-1233) and the *Lectiones Dolanae* concerning the problem of subrogation.
The originality of Dumoulin's work was above all related to his writings of French customary law. His commentary on the customs of Paris is famous and was considered a point of reference for feudal law.
He made an important contribution to the study of usury, publishing treatises on usury (1546) in which Dumoulin, not believing the usury was forbidden by divine law, argued that interest rates on loans should be regulated by the government. Despite being condemned by the Church, those treaties met with international success.
His main works are: *De Feudis* (1539); *Tractatus Commerciorum et Usurarum Redituumque Pecunia Constitutorum et Monetarum* (1546).

Adhémar Esmein (Trouverac, 1848 – Paris, 1913) was a French jurist who specialized in civil law and canon law. After becoming Doctor of Law in 1878, he taught for a brief period of time at Douai and later became Professor of Legal History and Constitutional Law at the University of Paris. During his career, he published numerous works on history of French law, Roman law, and canon law, which he taught at the *École pratique des hautes études* (EPHE).

Beyond these legal fields, French public law and French constitutional law represented the *fil rouge* of his entire life and career.
His main works are: *Histoire de la procédure criminelle en France et spécialement de la procédure inquisitoire depuis le XIIIe siècle jusqu'à nos jours* (1882); *Le mariage en droit canonique* (1891); *Cours élémentaire d'histoire du droit français à l'usage des étudiants de première année* (1892); *Éléments de droit constitutionnel* (1896); *Précis élémentaire de l'histoire du droit français de 1789 à 1814. Révolution, Consulat et Empire* (1908); *Éléments de droit constitutionnel français et comparé* (1909).

Gino Gorla (Crema 1906 – Rome 1992) was an Italian jurist, professor, and lawyer. Despite Gorla first enrolling at the University of Pavia, he completed his legal studies at the University Statale of Milan, from which he graduated in 1928 with the civil law dissertation *Il concetto generale dell'accessione nel diritto civile italiano.*
His studies focused on the contract and, throughout the years, the British legal system. Therefore, the comparative approach played a central role in Gorla's researches and works. According to his view, comparative studies are not a mere pursuit of knowledge but rather a chance to embrace European history and evolution. In this light, one of his last interests was the challenge of the harmonization process of the EU Member States' legal frameworks.
His main works are: *La riproduzione del negozio giuridico* (1933); *Del rischio e pericolo nelle obbligazioni* (1934); *L'ipoteca e il pegno* (1935); *L'atto di disposizione dei diritti* (1936); *L'assegnazione giudiziale di crediti* (1936); *La compravendita e la permuta* (1937); *L'interpretazione del diritto* (1941); *La società secondo il nuovo codice* (1942); *Il contratto, problemi fondamentali trattati con il metodo comparativo e casistico* (1954-1955); *Diritto comparato e diritto comune europeo* (1981).

Paolo Grossi (Florence, 1933) is an Italian jurist, historian, and former judge of the Italian Constitutional Court, of which he was the President from 2016 until 2018. He was Professor of History of Medieval and Modern Law at the University of Florence, from which he also graduated in 1955, discussing a dissertation on the legal system of Benedictine abbeys during the Middle Ages. Besides Florence, he also taught at the University of Siena, University of Macerata as well as at the University Suor Orsola Benincasa in Naples.
In 1971, Grossi founded the Studies Center for History of the Modern Legal Thinking and the international review *Quaderni fiorentini*: based on his academic contribution, a new generation of historians of law took root at international level.
His main works are: *Le situazioni reali nell'esperienza giuridica medievale* (1968); *La proprietà nel sistema privatistico della Seconda Scolastica* (1973); *Stile fiorentino. Gli studi giuridici nella Firenze italiana, 1859-1950* (1986); *Assolutismo giuridico e proprietà collettive* (1990); *Il diritto tra potere e ordinamento* (2005); *Ritorno al diritto* (2015); *L'invenzione del diritto* (2017); *Una Costituzione da vivere* (2018).

Hugo Grotius, or **Huig de Groot** (Delft, 1583 – Rostock, 1645) was a Dutch ju-

rist, philosopher, theologist, and philologist, commonly recognized as one of the founders of international law. He took a law degree and became a lawyer, but his studies focused also on humanism and theology; he also actively joined his country's religious-political conflicts and was sentenced to life for taking sides in favour of Arminianism. He fled a life sentence and escaped to France, where he published one of his most important works, *De iure belli ac pacis* (1625). In 1634, Grotius was given the opportunity to serve as Sweden's ambassador to France by Gustav II Adolf. Deemed to be the father of modern natural law, he was a Christian humanist, inspired by the Erasmian tradition. Grotius sought a rational pattern that constituted the essence of a theological system or of a system of legal norms, supporting the other non-substantial components of those systems. He promoted an idea of universal justice, ie the existence of a certain number of valid norms, recognized as general principles inherent specifically to human beings. The criteria that Grotius adopted to determine whether a norm stems from natural law were *a priori* and *a posteriori*: the former consists of relating the norm to the rational and social nature of human beings; the latter is about assessing whether the norm is considered fair by the most civilized populations.
His main works are: *De Indis* (ca. 1604); *Mare liberum* (1609); *De imperio summarum potestatum circa sacra* (ca. 1614 but 1647); *De Iure Belli ac Pacis* (1625); *De veritate religionis Christianae* (1627); *Inleydinge tot de Hollantsche rechtsgeleertheit* (1631); *De origine gentium Americanarum dissertatio* (1642); *De imperio summarum potestatum circa sacra* (1647).

Paul Koschaker (Klagenfurt, 1879 – Basel, 1951) was a German jurist and Professor of Roman law and civil law, which he lectured in numerous European universities such as those of Berlin, Prague, Leipzig, Innsbruck, and Frankfurt. Before completing his doctoral studies in 1903, Koschaker studied mathematics at the University of Graz. Afterwards, during his stay at the University of Leipzig, Ludwig Mitteis directed his studies to Roman law which shaped his interest for his subsequent comparative law focus.
The difficult historical period of the Nazi regime deeply affected his perception of the law and, consequently, his works. Indeed, during the early post-World War II period, he acknowledged the need for a real European unification. However, a new community required a common legal culture, which he found in the historical reconstruction of the Roman law. This theory represented the cornerstone of Koschaker's masterpiece, *Europa und das römische Recht*, first published in 1947, by which he promoted the development of a *ius commune europaeum*.
His main works are: *Translatio iudicii* (1905); *Babylonisch-assyrisches Bürgschaftsrecht* (1911); *Rechtsvergleichende Studien zur Gesetzgebung Hammurapis* (1917); *Die Krise des Römischen Rechts und die Romanistische Rechtswissenschaft* (1938); *Europa und das römische Recht* (1947).

Hein Kötz (Pila, 1935) is one of the most eminent contemporary jurists and professors, especially known for his publications that have considerably contributed to the legal fields of contract and commercial law.
Shortly after he completed his doctoral studies in 1962 at the University of Ham-

burg, he obtained a Master in Comparative Law at the University of Michigan, which played a significant role in shaping his interest in legal comparison. From 1971 to 1978, Kötz engaged in the academic profession at the University of Konstanz. Afterwards, in 1978, he was named director of the Max Planck Institute for Comparative and International Private Law in Hamburg, where he was also assigned a chair at the University.
His reputation has been further confirmed by the awards he received, such as the honorary doctorate from the Faculty of Law of the Uppsala University, which he was granted in 1995.
His masterpiece, *European Contract Law* (first edition 1996), represented a significant contribution to the study of the harmonization process of the European state's contract rules. Furthermore, the recent second edition of 2017 also takes into account the recent developments of national contract laws, such as the changes to the French Civil Code, and paints a comprehensive portrait of the most recent aspects dealing with this legal branch.
His main works are: *Sozialer Wandel im Unfallrecht* (1976); *Handels- und Gesellschaftsrecht mit Leitsätzen aus der höchstrichterlichen Rechtsprechung* (1979); *German Private and Commercial Law: An Introduction* (1982); *Rights of Third Parties. Third Party Beneficiaries and Assignment*, in *International Encyclopedia of Comparative Law* (1992).

Edouard Lambert (Mayenne, 1866 – Lyon, 1947) was a French jurist and historian of law. He began his academic career in 1896 in Lyon, where he focused on the history of law but also on comparative law. In 1906-1907, he was the head of the *Ecole khédiviale de droit* in Cairo, where he advocated Muslim law in opposition to common law; when he returned to France with several Egyptian law students, he founded the Oriental Legal Seminar; he also actively contributed to the draft of the Egyptian Civil Code.
Distinctly interested in legal comparison, he created the first Comparative law institute in France in 1921; his studies mainly focused on American law and Soviet law. Some authors claim that Lambert strongly influenced American law, thanks to his interest in judicial constitutional review, as well as the American teaching method. However, he was relatively forgotten in legal history, especially due to the conflicts between Parisian and Lyonnais scholars, the former often having discredited the latter.
In Lambert's view, the aim of comparative law is to discover common elements of different countries' legal traditions, by analyzing the so-called living legislation, ie the law and principles applied and cited by judges.
His main works are: *De l'exhérédation et des legs au profit d'héritiers présomptifs. Le droit de succession en France, son fondement, sa nature* (1895); *Etude de droit commun législatif, la fonction du droit civil comparé* (1903); *Le gouvernement des juges et la lutte contre la législation sociale aux États-Unis. L'expérience américaine du contrôle judiciaire de la constitutionnalité des lois* (1921); *The case Method in Canada and the Possibilities of its Adaptation to the Civil Law* (1929); *La place de l'économie industrielle soviétique dans l'économie mondiale* (1936); *Common law et droit civil. Leurs branches Américaines. L'étude comparative de ces branches* (1941).

Gottfried Wilhelm von Leibniz (Leipzig, 1646 – Hannover, 1716) was an eminent German mathematician, philosopher, scientist, and jurist. Thanks to his father's library, Leibniz accessed a wide range of philosophical and teleological works from his young age, which also allowed him to study the Latin language. In 1662, at the tender age of 15, he completed his bachelor's degree in philosophy. Two years later, he published his dissertation *Specimen Quaestionum Philosophicarum ex Jure collectarum* (*An Essay of Collected Philosophical Problems of Law*) by which he outlined the close relationship between philosophy and law. In 1666, Leibniz obtained the Doctorate in Law and published his work *De Arte Combinatoria* (*On the Art of Combination*), in which he developed the theory that every discovery is based on the conjunction of different elements, for example, numbers, words, sounds, colors. Leibniz is sometimes considered a precursor of the European Union since he believed in the possibility of building a confederation among European nations, governed by its own council with a representative mandate of the Member States. Mathematical studies always played a central role in his life. Indeed, one of his most remarkable successes was the elaboration of differential and integral calculus independently from the contemporaneous Isaac Newton's theories as well as the improvement of the binary number system, which is the cornerstone of today's digital devices. Alongside his mathematical studies, he also focused his attention on the philosophical field by being, with René Descartes and Baruch Spinoza, one of the most prominent advocates of rationalist thought. Leibniz was a true polymath scientist and his works have inspired a very heterogeneous range of fields such as computer science, biology, medicine, philology, history, theology, and even linguistics, since he wrote in different languages, especially in Latin, German, and French.
His main works are: *De Arte Combinatoria* (1666); *Dialogus de connexione inter res et verba* (1667); *Confessio philosophi* (1673); *Meditatio de cognitione, veritate et ideis* (1684); *Generales inquisitiones de analysis notionum et veritatum* (1686); *Scriptores rerum Brunsvicensium* (1707-1710); *Principes de la nature et de la Grâce fondés en raison* (1714); *Monadologie* (1714).

Frederic William Maitland (London, 1850 – London, 1906) was a British historian and lawyer, deemed the most relevant modern scholar of legal history. He entered Eton College in Windsor in 1863, in 1869 he enrolled at Trinity College, where he took his degree and won the Whewell Scholarship in International Law. Afterwards, Maitland joined Lincoln's Inn as a student, he was called to the bar there in 1876, and became an equity lawyer and conveyancer. He first became reader in English Law at Cambridge (1884), then founded the Selden Society (1887), a registered charity concerned with the study of English legal history, and finally became Downing Professor of the Laws of England at Downing College, a constituent college of the University of Cambridge, in 1888.
Maitland's historical method was distinguished by his accurate and sensitive use of historical sources, and by his determinedly historical perspective: his teaching urged scholars to consider and seek to understand the history of law on its own terms, rather than to investigate the past mostly by reference to the needs of the present. His academic contributions were and are held in high regard. He died

in 1906; The Downing College's Maitland Historical Society is titled in his name. His main works are: *Pleas of the Crown for the County of Gloucester before the Abbot of Reading and his Fellows Justices Itinerant* (self-published, 1884); *History of English Law before the Time of Edward I* (1895); *Roman Canon Law in the Church of England* (1898); *English Law and the Renaissance: The Rede Lecture for 1901* (1901); *Life and Letters of Leslie Stephen* (1906).

Pasquale Stanislao Mancini (Castel Caronia, 1817 – Naples, 1888) was an Italian jurist, professor, and statesman, who actively participated in the Italian unification and contributed to the evolution of the national legal system.
Mancini did not attend university but obtained a law degree through a special exception in 1844. Later, he started teaching in Naples, where he was also deputy of the Neapolitan Parliament between 1848 and 1849. He played an important role in the promotion of democracy and the unification of Italy until he was forced to leave the region by the Bourbon government. Mancini then moved to Turin, where he started teaching at the university, he pursued his efforts for the unity of the nation.
After the fall of the Bourbons, he was appointed Minister of Public Instruction. Subsequently, he mainly focused on the study of International law and arbitration and, between 1876 and 1878, he was also Minister of Justice and persuaded the Chamber to introduce limitations on capital punishment.
Mancini's main contribution to the field of international law consists of the elaboration of the concept of nationality that, in his view, was the real cornerstone of a new *ius gentium*. The most pioneering aspect of his approach was the assignment of a new value to nationality, by putting the individual at the centre of International law in a period when the state was the only subject considered as the main character of this legal field.
His main works are: *Della nazionalità come fondamento del diritto delle genti* (1851); *Commentario del Codice di procedura civile per gli Stati sardi, con la comparazione degli altri Codici italiani, e delle principali legislazioni straniere* (1855-1859); *Diritto internazionale. Prelezioni con un saggio sul Machiavelli* (1873); *Fondamenti della filosofia del diritto e singolarmente del diritto di punire. Lettere di T. Mamiani e di P.S. Mancini* (1875); *Discorsi parlamentari* (1893-1897).

Ernst Rabel (Vienna, 1874 – Zurich, 1955) was an Austrian-born, American scholar of Roman Law, German private law, and comparative law.
After graduating and receiving his PhD from the University of Vienna, he initially entered legal practice with his father, but soon followed his mentor Ludwig Mitteis to Leipzig and continued his studies there. He began actively teaching at the Leipzig University as a junior faculty member, and then was appointed Professor of Roman Law and German Private Law in 1904. Afterwards, he moved to and lectured in Basel, Kiel, Munich, where he re-oriented his academic interests towards comparative law. He was also a member of the mixed Italian-German court of Arbitration, which was charged with the application of the treaty of Versailles at the end of World War I.
In 1926, he was appointed Director of the Kaiser Wilhelm Institute for Foreign

and International Private Law, which became the Max Planck Institute for Comparative and International Private Law in the post-war period.
His main works are: *Grundzüge des Römischen Privatrechts* (1913); *Das Recht des Warenkaufs. Eine rechtsvergleichende Darstellung*, vol 1 (1936) and vol 2 (1967); *The Conflict of Laws: A comparative study* (1945-1954); *The Private Laws of Western Civilization* (1949-1950).

Mario Rotondi (Gorla Minore 1900 – Milan 1984) was an Italian jurist, lawyer, and professor, who was especially devoted to the study and research of commercial law and comparative law. In 1922 Rotondi graduated from the University of Pavia, where he was immediately noticed for his remarkable judicial abilities. Indeed, in 1926, he was appointed as Professor of Commercial Law in Pavia, a chair that he left after his decision oppose the fascist regime and he moved to Milan, where he began teaching at the Cattolica University.
He was reinstated at the University of Pavia in 1946, where he lectured until 1964, when he was assigned the chair of Private Law at the University Statale of Milan. Meanwhile, he was also professor at Bocconi University of Milan, where he had previously founded the Angelo Sraffa Institute of Commercial, Industrial, and Labor Law, which he directed until 1970.
His main works are: *L'abuso di diritto* (1923); *L'azione d'arricchimento* (1924); *Trattato di diritto dell'industria* (1929-1941); *Istituzioni di diritto privato* (1939); *Diritto industriale* (1942).

Raymond Saleilles (Beaune, 1855 – Paris, 1912) was a French jurist and one of the most eminent scholars of private law, as well as the founder of the modern French school of comparative law. Not only did Saleilles have a strong knowledge of legal subjects, but also of philosophy, sociology, history, and economics. He taught History of Law at the University of Grenoble and at the University of Dijon, where he also taught Constitutional Law and directed the *Revue bourguignonne*; in 1895 he moved to Paris to teach Civil Law, Comparative Criminal Legislation and Comparative Law. He founded the *Société d'études législatives* in 1902.
Saleilles's most important academic contribution was in the field of comparative law: he especially focused his studies on German legal doctrine and on the German Civil Code of 1900; nonetheless, his works ranged over Roman law, history of law, social, criminal, and political issues. In the field of tort law, he is one of the creators of the theory of risk, which led to a more efficient protection of work accidents.
His interpretative method of law was based on the texts of laws, but included the research of all possible solutions to a case, although not literally suitable to the existing legal provisions: a famous quotation of his was '*Au delà du code civil, mais par le code civil*' ('Beyond the Civil Code, but by means of the Civil Code').
His main works are: *Les accidents de travail et la responsabilité civile* (1897); *L'individualisation de la peine* (1898); *De la déclaration de volonté dans le code civil allemand* (1901); *Le* piae causae *dans le droit de Justinien* (1907); *De la personnalité juridique. Histoire et théories* (1910).

Joseph Story (Marblehead, 1779 – Cambridge, 1845) was one of the most influential American lawyers and jurists, especially in the field of private international law since he contributed to its development in the US as well as in the rest of the world. Graduated from Harvard University, Story became an eminent member of the Jeffersonian Republican Party and at the age of only 32 he was appointed member of the Supreme Court of the US. He is most remembered for his *Commentaries on the Constitution of the United States* (1833), which is still considered a milestone of American jurisprudence, and for the *Commentary on the Conflict of Laws, Foreign and Domestic* (1834), a legal classic that investigates the sources of the Anglo-American and continental law, and that is a landmark for the comparative approach to different legal jurisdictions. According to historians, Story's works reshaped the American law from a conservative perspective, with a special focus on the protection of property rights.
His main works are: *Commentaries on the Law of Bailments* (1832); *Commentaries on the Constitution of the United States* (1833); *Commentary on the Conflict of Laws, Foreign and Domestic* (1834); *Commentaries on Equity Jurisprudence* (1836-1837). Moreover, his *Commentaries on the Conflict of Laws* (1834) are a significant part of international private law doctrine.

Franz Wieacker (Stargard, 1908 – Göttingen, 1994) was a legal historian and one of the most eminent jurists during the post-World War II period. After completing his legal studies between the cities of Tübingen, Munich, and Göttingen, he obtained his doctoral degree from the University of Freiburg in 1930. In 1937, he was appointed Associate Professor at the University of Leipzig and, after serving in the military forces during World War II and few months of imprisonment, he started teaching Roman Law and Civil Law at the University of Freiburg. Later, in 1953, he took over the chair in Göttingen, from which he retired in 1973.
In one of his most famous works, *Privatrechtsgeschichte der Neuzeit* (1952), he investigated the development of legal thinking in Europe, starting from the High Middle Ages down to the contemporary time. One of the most remarkable aspects of this work is how he argued that the beliefs of lawyers evolve and change in parallel with their contemporary philosophical orientations, therefore outlining a close relationship between legal thought and historical conditions.
His main works are: Societas, *Hausgemeinschaft und Erwerbsgesellschaft des Römischen Rechts* (1936); *Privatrechtsgeschichte der Neuzeit* (1952); *Textstufen klassischer Juristen* (1960); *Recht und Gesellschaft in der Spätantike* (1964); *Zur Theorie der Juristischen Person des Privatrechts* (1973); *Römische Rechtsgeschichte* (1988).

Karl Salomo Zachariä (von Lingenthal) (Meissen, 1769 – Heidelberg, 1843) was a German jurist and professor of canon law and feudal law. Besides law, he studied philosophy, history, and mathematics at the University of Leipzig; he continued his legal studies at the University of Wittenberg, where he also worked as a tutor to one of the counts of Lippe. In 1794 he became *Privatdozent*, in 1798 extraordinary professor and in 1802 ordinary professor. From that time on, he focused on his academic career, making several, very valuable, contributions to the field of jurisprudence. He settled and taught in Heidelberg from 1807 until

his death, in 1843. In 1820, he took his seat in the upper house of the parliament of Baden, newly constituted, as representative of his university.
Zachariä had very conservative beliefs, strongly opposed to the democratic spirit that governed the second chamber; his fundamental theory was that the state has its origin in the consciousness of a legal duty, not in a contract (as Rousseau and Kant had stated). His writings are various and cover several fields, such as philosophy, history, Roman, Canon, German, French, and English law. The first book of much consequence which he published was *Die Einheit des Staats und der Kirche mit Rücksicht auf die Deutsche Reichsverfassung* (1797), a work on the relationship between church and state, with special reference to the constitution of the German Empire.
His main works are: *Versuch einer allgemeinen Hermeneutik des Rechts* (1805); *Die Wissenschaft der Gesetzgebung* (1806); *Handbuch des Französischen Civilrechts* (1808); *Vierzig Bücher vom Staate* (1839-1842).

Reinhard Zimmermann (Hamburg, 1952) is a German jurist and one of the directors of the Max Planck Institute for Comparative and International Private Law. After concluding his studies at the University of Hamburg, he became research assistant in Cologne before taking over the chair of Roman Law and Comparative Law at the University of Cape Town in 1981. During his stay, he wrote *The Law of Obligations: Roman Foundations of the Civilian Tradition* (1990), which is considered one of the most prominent works of comparative law of the twentieth century. In 1988, he taught Roman Law, Comparative Legal History, and Private Law at the University of Regensburg, where he was also appointed Dean of his faculty. Afterwards, in 1996 he received the Leibniz Prize of the German Research Foundation. In 2002, he was appointed Managing Director at the Max Planck Institute for Comparative and International Private Law in Hamburg and, in 2008, he started teaching Legal History at the Bucerius Law School of Hamburg. Today, he is an ordinary member of the Academy of Arts and Sciences of Göttingen and corresponding member of the Bavarian Academy of Arts and Sciences, the Royal Dutch Academy of Arts and Sciences, the Austrian Academy of Sciences, and the *Accademia delle Scienze di Torino*.
The law of obligations from a historical and comparative perspective and the relationship between the two families of common law and civil law are the main areas of his interest, with a special focus on the process of harmonization of European private law.
His main works are: *The Law of Obligations: Roman Foundations of the Civilian Tradition* (1990); *Roman Law, Contemporary Law, European Law* (2001); *Comparative Foundations of a European Law of Set-Off and Prescription* (2002); *The new German Law of Obligations* (2005).

Konrad Zweigert (Poznan 1911 – Wedel 1996) was one of the most distinguished jurists and law professors of the twentieth century.
Born in a family of lawyers, Zweigert inherited the same love for legal studies, which he completed between the Universities of Grenoble, Göttingen, and Berlin. Beyond legal practice, in 1948 he began teaching at the University of Tübingen,

where he remained until 1956, when he moved to the University of Hamburg. Afterwards, Zweigert was named director of the Max Planck Institute for Comparative and International Private Law, a position he retained until 1979.
The honorary doctorates he was assigned by the Universities of Uppsala, Paris II, and Southampton reflected the eminent reputation he gained in his life.
Among his most remembered works, he was co-author, in conjunction with Hein Kötz, of the work *Einführung in die Rechtsvergleichung* (1969), which assessed the core features of comparative law with special attention for the main legal families that classify the legal systems worldwide.
His main works are: *Die Haftung für gefährliche Anlagen in den EWG-Ländern sowie in England und den Vereinigten Staaten von Amerika* (1966); *Sources of International Uniform Law* (1971); *Einführung in die Rechtsvergleichung auf dem Gebiete des Privatrechts* (1996).

CHAPTER 4

Civil law and common law jurisdictions

- **The legacy of Roman law in Europe**
- **The division between civil law and common law traditions**
- **The national codifications of private law between nineteenth and twentieth century**
- **The mixed jurisdictions**

Legal systems in continental Europe rest upon Roman Law and have been influenced by the medieval and pre-modern *ius commune*. The common law was initially cultivated in England, being originally born as autochthonous. Later, it flourished through its application in the former colonies of England; however, it has never been isolated from the continental legal culture. Moreover, a high degree of compatibility (and to some extent even uniformity) between English law and other European national legal systems has been achieved by EU law, as well as by the judiciary of the ECHR and on the basis of the Human Rights Act 1998.

Following the entry into force of the *Code civil* (1806), French legal culture was pervaded by positivism and nationalism, a trend that was reflected by the predominant exegetical interpretation approach (*école de l'exegèse*). It was only at the beginning of the twentieth century that the exegetical attitude of the doctrine was increasingly mitigated by a new method boosting sociology and legal comparison and promoting the creative role of jurisprudence.

Former Latin-American colonies of European countries, after gaining their independence, evolved their civil codes, which had principally relied on the French model, or even revised the entire structure completely, thereby bestowing a distinctive character to their respective legal systems.

The codification process of the German *Bürgerliches Gesetzbuch* (1874-1896) was shaped by the dogmatism of the Pandectistic School, which drew on the concept of 'contemporary Roman law' advocated for by Friedrich Carl von Savigny. The particularly distinctive

feature of the BGB is its 'General Part', referring to a system of abstract legal concepts and definitions in the first book.
The Italian *Codice Civile* took up ideas from both the French and German Civil Codes and endured through the political era of fascism. Despite the last circumstance, it wholly embodies the liberal culture of its drafters, thus consistently rejecting the authoritarian or nationalistic culture of the political regime. It was historically the first code to comprise both civil law in a strict sense and commercial law, thus amounting to a unique code of private law as such.
Unlike civil law, common law is traditionally not molded by statutory law but formed by case law (precedents). However, recent developments have attributed an increasing importance to statutory law. The original dualism between common law and equity, which mirrored two autonomous judicial hierarchies, was overcome towards the end of the nineteenth century, thereby ending a period of considerable complication in the overlapping applicability of the two systems.
Where political and sociological influences have intermingled in the past, jurisdictions often evolved into a combination of both, including common and civil law features, eg on Malta, Cyprus, or in Israel (so-called mixed jurisdictions).

1. THE LEGACY OF ROMAN LAW IN EUROPE

The legacy of Roman law is generally acknowledged in continental European countries (and their former colonies), to the extent that they may be depicted as having a **contemporary Roman law**. Although it looks like a slight exaggeration, a notable source wrote that 'a law student of the time of Justinian, transported to the twentieth century, would find little to wonder at in the civil codes of modern Europe'.[1]
The jurisdictions of continental Europe can be all included in the family of **civil law** (see *supra*, ch 3, para 3.2; *infra*, ch 4, para 3), which is characterized as resting upon the medieval and pre-modern *ius commune* molded by Roman-canon law (see *supra*, ch 2, para 4.1). This became embedded into the civilian tradition, which formed the basis of the legal unity of (most of) Western Europe from the Middle Ages to the French Revolution.
On the contrary, England developed a genuinely autochthonous law, called **common law** (see *supra*, ch 2, para 4.2),[2] which was later on brought to its former colonies (subsequently, members of the Commonwealth); therefore, despite showing a certain number of unique features,[3] all these legal systems

[1] William Ewald, 'The Jurisprudential Approach to Comparative Law: A Field Guide to "Rats"' (1998) 46 Am J Comp L 701, 703.
[2] Stefan Vogenauer, 'Common Law' in *The Max Planck Encyclopedia of European Private Law*, vol 1 (OUP 2012) 265ff.
[3] Uwe Kischel, *Comparative Law* (Andrew Hammer tr, OUP 2019) 360ff.

share an extensive bulk of commonalities and can be included in one family (see *supra*, ch 3, para 3.2; *infra*, ch 4, para 4).
Despite the undeniable originality of common law (see *supra*, ch 2, para 4.2), however, English law has never been fully cut off from continental legal culture and the imprint of Roman law is clearly visible throughout its overall historical development.[4]

> 'Since the twelfth century the Civil Law has penetrated England and, in spite of the fact that it has been driven out, it has never entirely disappeared from English law. Roman thought, which could ultimately be identified with continental thought, was not excluded, however independent English law may be'.[5]
> The incorporation of Roman law into England began with **Ranulf de Glanvill** (1112-1190), who served as Chief Justiciar of England under King Henry II (1154-1189). He is thought to have authored a famous treatise on the law applied by the king's court, *Tractatus de legibus et consuetudinis regni Angliae*;[6] this work appeared only in the thirteenth century, and in some versions bears the name of **Henry of Bracton** (1210-1268).[7]

Elements of Roman-canon law were present in the law applied by many English courts where **civil lawyers** were practicing. They were educated in Roman and canon law at the universities of Oxford and Cambridge and, since the sixteenth century, trained in the Doctor's Common (or College of Civilians), an association parallel to the Inns of Court of the common lawyers (see *infra*, ch 7, para 4).[8]

> Until 1731, except for an interval in the 1650s, the official language of the common law courts was Latin, as well as that of the writers who commentated upon them. The traditional language of English law still includes many Latin terms: *habeas corpus*, *certiorari*, *dicta*, *nisi prius*, etc. At an unknown date, but definitely before 1250, French, the language of the Norman conquerors, began to be used in the King's courts. Still nowadays, when of course English is used, some 'legal French' has survived in common law parlance (for example, plaintiff, defendant, manor, felony).[9]

Up to the time of the Reformation of Henry VIII, ecclesiastical courts were responsible for important matters like marriage and succession law but also defamation and breach of contract (*laesio fidei*).[10] They applied **canon law** (see *supra*, ch 2, para 4.1),[11] which deeply affected the historical development of the

[4] Reinhard Zimmermann, 'Europa und das römische Recht' [2002] AcP 202, 243; David Ibbetson, *Common Law and Ius Commune* (Selden Society 2001).
[5] Fritz Pringsheim, 'The Inner Relationship Between English and Roman Law' [1935] CLJ 347, 349.
[6] John Baker, *Introduction to English Legal History* (5th edn, OUP 2019) 17, 185ff.
[7] ibid 185ff.
[8] Antonio Padoa Schioppa, *A History of Law in Europe: From the Early Middle Ages to the Twentieth Century* (CUP 2017) 390.
[9] John H Baker, 'The Three Languages of the Common Law' [1998] McGill LJ 5.
[10] Reinhard Zimmermann, *The Law of Obligations: Roman Foundations of the Civilian Tradition* (2nd edn, Juta & Co, CH Beck-Kluwer 1992) 542.
[11] Baker, *Introduction to English Legal History* (n 6) 135ff.

equity system as well, also due to the fact that up to the middle of the sixteenth century the **Lord Chancellors** were clergymen (see *supra*, ch 2, para 4.2).[12] Furthermore, the **Court of Admiralty** applied Roman law in maritime disputes, as well as, at least during one stage of its history, in all commercial contracts.[13]

> For instance, the Court of Admiralty applied the principles of Roman *negotiorum gestio* to adjudicate cases of salvage, as well as the connected *lex Rhodia de iactu*.[14]

Since the eighteenth century, commercial law was modernized in England through the import of doctrines and legal institutions which had been developing on the continent (see *infra*, ch 7, para 2). William Murray (1705-1793), first Earl of Mansfield, played a major role in this process while serving as Chief Justice of the King's Bench.[15]

> One of the most ambitious purposes of **Lord Mansfield** was to get English law aligned with the Roman principle of good faith (see *infra*, ch 6, para 3; ch 7, para 2).[16] He applied this doctrine to insurance contracts, which he deemed as based on the utmost good faith (*uberrimae fidei*), '[i]nsurance is a contract upon speculation [...]. The special facts, upon which the contingent chance is to be computed, lie most commonly in the knowledge of the insured only: the under-writer trusts to his representation, and proceeds upon confidence that he does not keep back any circumstances in his knowledge, to mislead the under-writer into a belief that the circumstance does not exist [...]. Good faith forbids either party by concealing what he privately knows, to draw the other into a bargain, from his ignorance of that fact, and his believing the contrary'.[17]

Actually, even legal institutions which are deemed as quintessentially English, like trust or the doctrine of consideration in contract law, initially developed as offshoots of continental legal science.[18]

2. THE DIVISION BETWEEN CIVIL LAW AND COMMON LAW TRADITIONS

A further analysis of the history of English common law, aside from certain shared aspects of history, confirms that while its separation from civil law is undeniable, it is smaller than was thought in the past.[19]

[12] Zimmermann 'Europa und das römische Recht' (n 2) 304ff.
[13] Padoa Schioppa (n 8) 390.
[14] Pietro Sirena, *La gestione di affari altrui. Ingerenze altruistiche, ingerenze egoistiche e restituzione del profitto* (Giappichelli 1999) 281ff.
[15] Padoa Schioppa (n 8) 396ff.
[16] See Martin J Schermaier, 'Bona Fides in Roman Contract Law' in Reinhard Zimmermann and Simon Whittaker (eds), *Good Faith in European Contract Law* (CUP 2000) 63.
[17] *Carter v Boehm* (1766) 97 ER 1162, 1164.
[18] Zimmermann, *The Law of Obligations: Roman Foundations of the Civilian Tradition* (n 10) 506, 913.
[19] Johannes Liebrecht, 'Legal History' in Jürgen Basedow, Klaus J Hopt, Reinhard Zim-

As already mentioned, the **dialogue between jurists** and the **circulation of ideas** between civil law and common law have been remarkable over the course of their respective historical evolution, as has the influence undoubtedly exercised over them by Roman law, albeit in a differentiated manner.[20] It is also to be noted that over the course of the past two centuries, English common law has been characterized by an increasingly intense theoretical and conceptual elaboration, so that its traditional empiricism and casuistic approach have been mitigated, making it more similar to civil law.[21] English legal scholars have seen their importance significantly increase and adopted a comparative approach when it was deemed useful, **importing legal categories and practical solutions** from the civil law.

> An example of how the two legal traditions have moved towards one another thanks to the influence of Roman law and comparative methodology can be seen in the works of Peter Birks (1941-2004) on unjust enrichment.[22]

Moreover, one must also bear in mind that, although now terminated (see *infra*, ch 8, para 1), the participation of the UK in the **European Union** has profoundly affected English law: EEC/EC/EU founding Treaties, directives and regulations, as well as the case law of the ECJ have, in fact, made its contents more similar to those of civil law, particularly in some crucial areas of private law (like contract law). Even in the aftermath of the UK's withdrawal from the EU, this patrimony of European legislation and judicature has been 'retained' in the UK's legal system, becoming domestic law (see *infra*, ch 8, para 1).
This is also a reason for the significant increase in the influence of **statutory law** in comparison with traditional case law,[23] which still continues to prevail and to be a distinctive element of common law (see *infra*, ch 7, para 3.2).[24] Somehow similarly, albeit to a lesser extent, the ECHR forced English law to attain a further degree of compatibility, if not of uniformity, with the other national legal systems of Europe. In fact, section 3(1) of **Human Rights Act 1998** stipulates that: 'So far as it is possible, primary legislation and subordinate legislation must be read and given effect in a way which is compatible with the Convention rights'.

mermann and Andreas Stier (eds), *The Max Planck Encyclopedia of European Private Law*, vol 1 (n 2) 1065.

[20] Zimmermann, 'Europa und das römische Recht' (n 4) 255ff; Id, 'Der europäische Charakter des englischen Rechts' [1993] ZEuP 4ff.

[21] Vogenauer (n 2) 265, 267.

[22] Peter Birks, *Unjust Enrichment* (2nd edn, OUP 2005). For an account of Birks' works and of his influence on English law, see Andrew Burrows and Lord Rodger of Earlsferry (eds), *Mapping the Law: Essays in Memory of Peter Birks* (OUP 2006).

[23] See Andrew Burrows, 'The Relationship between Common Law and Statute in the Law of Obligations' (2012) 128 LQR 232.

[24] See Jack Beatson, 'Has the Common Law a Future?' (1997) 56 CLJ 291.

Based on this, has been therefore remarked that the distinction between civil law and common law ought now to have been superseded.[25] This conclusion may still appear to be excessive, however, it is probably less unrealistic than one might think, considering that the divergences between the two legal traditions are ultimately no greater than some of those which can be found within the family of civil law jurisdictions. Ultimately, it has been depicted as a difference in style of reasoning, which should be deemed to be not substantial.[26]

3. CIVIL LAW JURISDICTIONS

As already pointed out, the civil law family encompasses the jurisdictions of continental Europe. It also includes the jurisdictions of the former Spanish, Portuguese, French, and Dutch colonies, for example, in Latin America.

One of the key features of civil law jurisdictions is that they have fully implemented the **doctrine of separation of powers**, the origins and genesis of which are generally traced to the French Enlightenment political philosopher Baron de Montesquieu (1689-1755). In his masterpiece, *De l'esprit des lois* (1748), he clearly advocated a division of political power into three lines; namely, a legislature (entrusted to the Parliament), an executive (entrusted to the government and the rest of the administration), and a judiciary (entrusted to courts). According to this doctrine, which is also known as the ***trias politica* principle**, courts are supposed to be 'only the mouth that pronounces the words of the law, inanimate beings that are not able to modify either its force or its rigor', as Montesquieu himself wrote. Legislative power is in the hands of the Parliament, which is the only state organ holding the power to adopt new legal rules or to change or repeal the existing ones.

Consequently, civil law jurisdictions are usually characterized by the **prevalence of statutory law** as a source of law, namely for the central role attributed to the civil code as the systematic foundation of private law.[27] Legal scholars have traditionally served as a guide in interpreting statutes, thus significantly influencing case law (see *infra*, ch 7, para 3.1).

The forerunner of all contemporary **civil codes** is that of France, the *Code civil des Français*, enacted in 1804 on the order of Napoleon in 1806, and, after he styled himself as Emperor, re-named as *Code Napoléon* (see *infra*, ch 4, para 3.1.1).

[25] James Gordley, 'Common Law und Civil Law: Eine überholte Unterscheidung' [1993] ZEuP 498; Zimmermann, 'Der europäische Charakter des englischen Rechts' (n 20) 4; Geoffrey Samuel, 'System und Systemdenken – Zu den Unterschieden zwischen kontinentaleuropäischem Recht und Common Law' [1995] ZEuP 375.

[26] Colm Peter Mc Grath and Helmut Koziol, 'Is Style of Reasoning a Fundamental Difference Between the Common Law and the Civil Law?' (2014) 78 RabelsZ 709 (focusing particularly on punitive, or exemplary, damages and alternative causation in tort law). For a different view, cf Michael L Wells, 'A Common Lawyer's Perspective on the European Perspective on Punitive Damages' (2010) 70 Louisiana L Rev 557.

[27] Ugo Petronio, *La lotta per la codificazione* (Giappichelli 2002).

The **enactment of the French Civil Code** was a historical event of extraordinary importance, because it paved the way for a wave of major national codifications, which sentenced the *ius commune* to death, by definitively replacing it.

In fact, as the other main nations of continental Europe gradually came to establish themselves as many single states, generally through a process of unification of several smaller political entities which pre-existed at a regional level, they mostly followed the French example and enacted their own civil codes. Instead of a universal law, based on an inner rationality and developed through the conjunction between the sources of Roman law and the legal wisdom of legal commentators, the above-mentioned *ius commune*, there was from then on a French, a German, an Italian law, and so on, each of them being based on the sovereignty of a single, nation state and enacted through a political decision of its own Parliament.

In specific contexts, albeit inevitably quite limited or peculiar from a historical point of view, the application of a pure *ius commune* is still to be found, such as in the case of the **Republic of San Marino**.

A significant phenomenon is the fact that **Roman-Dutch law** has survived in certain former Dutch colonies, despite the fact that in the Netherlands itself it was replaced in 1809 by the *Code Napoléon* (and subsequently by a national civil code). Roman-Dutch law refers to the *usus modernus pandectarum* specifically developed by the great Dutch jurists starting from the sixteenth century.[28] Such law is still applied in South Africa as well (see *infra*, ch 4, para 5).[29]

Even outside Europe, civil codes soon became the identity charters of nation states, generally accompanying their establishment. Particularly, as soon as **Latin-American colonies of European countries** one by one attained their independence from their respective homelands, thus becoming independent states, they each enacted civil codes; most of these pieces of legislation are closely based on the French model,[30] but in the last decades they have been intensively reformed or even replaced in most countries of Latin America, thus earning an increasingly original character.

[28] Reinhard Zimmermann, 'Roman-Dutch Law' in Jürgen Basedow, Klaus J Hopt, Reinhard Zimmermann and Andreas Stier (eds), *The Max Planck Encyclopedia of European Private Law*, vol 2 (OUP 2012) 1483.

[29] Jacques E du Plessis, 'South Africa' in Jan M Smits (ed), *Elgar Encyclopedia of Comparative Law* (2nd edn, Elgar 2012) 814.

[30] Jan Kleinheisterkamp, 'Latin America, Influence of European Private Law' in *The Max Planck Encyclopedia of European Private Law*, vol 1 (n 2) 1032.

3.1. National codifications of private law between nineteenth and twentieth centuries

3.1.1. The *Code civil des Français* (or *Code Napoléon*)

The doctrinal acknowledgment of a *droit commun français* dates back to the sixteenth century (see *supra*, ch 2, para 5) and gained further ground thanks to the legislative activism of Louis XIV, the *Roi Soleil* (1638-1715). Towards the end of the eighteenth century, the ideal of a national law was decidedly embraced by the French Revolution, thus leading to a turn in the legal history of Europe, whereby the medieval *ius commune* was dismissed and replaced with a national law.

The first purpose of this change was of a political nature, aimed at overcoming the feudal law identified as the juridical counterpart of the *ancien régime* which had been disrupted by the revolution. Instead of the mess of local and regional laws binding people, **Enlightenment** thought had affirmed the ideal of a unique law, intelligible to all men, easily accessible and clearly understandable. Furthermore, the idea was to depart from the Catholic religion and to enact a secular law, stipulated and administrated by the state. This secularization of private law was particularly important with regard to marriage, which was turned into a civil contract, giving authority to the state for the first time instead of the Church; this move paved the way for permitting divorce (which was contrary to the Catholic religion) (see also *supra*, ch 1, para 2).

Secondly, they were seeking unification of the country in terms of its law. The division into two different areas saw the application of the Roman *ius commune* (***pays de droit écrit, or de droit savant***) in the southern regions of France, starting with the reign of Philipp the Fair, or *Philippe le Bel* (1268-1314), and the Frankish-Burgundian customs alone (*coutumes*) in force in central and northern parts of the country (***pays de droit coutumier***).[31]

> **Roman law** was not acknowledged as issued though the Justinian compilation (also because the Holy Roman Empire was keen to vindicate it as a source of its own law) but as customary law. The study of Roman law flourished at the universities of Montpellier (established in 1289) and of Toulouse (established in 1229 and becoming in 1233 the first *Studium generale*). The Montpellier school of law was founded by Placentinus (1130-1192), who belonged to the Bologna school of law. He went to Montpellier in 1160 and taught there during two different periods.
>
> In 1454, Charles VII ordered that customs be collected and committed to paper, an undertaking that required much time and effort and was not completed before the end of the eighteenth century. The *droit coutumier* was thus collected

[31] For the historical reasons of this division, see Konrad Zweigert and Hein Kötz, *An Introduction to Comparative Law* (Tony Weir tr, 3rd edn, OUP 1998) 75ff.

> and published through **royal *ordonnances*,**[32] which however did not change their customary nature. To some extent they were deemed even to limit the king's legislative power, resting on an immemorial and uninterrupted tradition.[33]
> The overlapping of ***coutumes générales*** and ***coutumes locales*** often engendered conflicts and uncertainties as far as their scope of application was concerned. After its publication in 1570, a greater authority was gradually acceded to the *Coutume de Paris*, applied by the Paris parliament. In case of further doubts or gaps, reference was made to Roman law as a corpus of legal wisdom (*ratio scripta*), accessible to better understand the rationale of customary rules or even used as a last resort to fill in the gaps of the *coutumes*.
> The greatest commentator on the *coutumes* was **Charles Dumoulis**, or ***Molinaeus*** (1500-1566) (see also *supra*, ch 3, para 4), who published a renowned *Revision de la Coutume de Paris* (first edition of 1539). The commentaries by Yves Coquille (1523-1603) were also influential.

In order to overcome all the intricacies and uncertainties arising from medieval law, the advent of the **French Revolution** pleaded for the adoption of a codification of private law, which had already been advocated by natural lawyers and, later on, was strongly supported by eighteenth century legal Enlightenment.[34]
Starting from 1793, many attempts were made to draft a code, to lay down the revolutionary law (*droit intermédiarie*), but all of them failed. It was Napoleon who achieved this goal after taking up full powers. He issued five codifications, the most important being that of civil law.
The *Code civil des Français* entered into force on 21 March 1804 and in 1806 was also officially styled as ***Code Napoléon***.

> In his St. Helen's Memoirs, Napoleon (allegedly) wrote: 'My true glory is not having won forty battles; Waterloo will blot out the memory of those victories. But nothing can blot out my Civil Code. That will live eternally'.[35]

Although preceded by other civil codifications in Europe, particularly in German territories (see *supra*, ch 2, para 5), the *Code civil* stands as the prototype of all civil codifications.
The *Code* was drafted by a commission composed of only four members, who, in only four months, were able to draw up the overall structure of the *Code*. Napoleon himself, although being a layman, is attributed a meaningful role in the drafting of (parts of) the *Code*.

[32] Gebhard Rehm, 'Ordonnances' in *The Max Planck Encyclopedia of European Private Law*, vol 2 (n 28) 1226.
[33] Mario Caravale, *Ordinamenti giuridici dell'Europa medievale* (Il Mulino 1994) 609ff; Id, *Alle origini del diritto europeo. Ius commune, droit commun, common law nella dottrina giuridica della prima età moderna* (Monduzzi 2005) 156ff.
[34] Padoa Schioppa (n 8) 358.
[35] As quoted in Charles Sumner Lobingier, 'Napoleon and His Code' [1918] HLR 437: *'Ma vraie gloire n'est pas d'avoir gagné quarante batailles; Waterloo effacera le souvenir de tant de victoires; ce que rien n'effacera, ce qui vivra éternellement, c'est mon Code civil'*.

Jean-Étienne-Marie Portalis (1746-1806) was the most prominent member of the commission. He authored a famous *Discours préliminaire au projet de code civil*, where the core principles of the Civil Code are exposed.

The French code represented a fortuitous blend of the pre-existing *droit écrit* and *droit coutumier*.[36] As to succession and family law, the *code* largely rested on customary law, whereas the law of contracts and of wills, as well as the system of dowries as a contractual law regime, was based on Roman law.[37]

For customary law, the drafters of the *Code* mainly drew on the writings of François Bourjon (16?-1751).
For the law of contracts and obligations, they largely resorted to Roman law, as rationalized and exposed by Robert Joseph Pothier (1699-1772) and, to a minor extent, by Jean Domat (1625-1696), who had read Roman law through the lens of seventeenth century natural law.

The **basic ideas of the *Code*** were to: (i) make the law accessible to all citizens; (ii) break the particularism which had characterized the feudal regimes; (iii) uphold the principle of equal treatment; and (iv) apply the law irrespective of the social class or group to which a citizen happened to belong.
Despite its historical roots, the Code was less revolutionary than expected and was characterized by a fair equilibrium between legal tradition and an alignment with the new values of **freedom of contract** and **protection of private ownership**.[38]
As well as being one of the paramount characteristics of the national esprit, the French Civil Code is renowned for its **clarity and rationality**, as well as for the **elegance of its language**.[39]

In his correspondence with Honoré de Balzac, the famous French novelist Stendhal (whose real name was Henri Beyle) in 1840 stated that 'in writing the *Chartreuse*, to acquire the tone, every morning I read two or three pages of the Civil Code, so it would be natural'.[40]

After the enactment of the *Code*, French legal culture was imbued with positivism and nationalism. These aspects were clearly reflected in the strictly exegetical method that jurists adopted to interpret the norms of the Code civil (école de l'*éxegèse*).[41]

The name école de l'éxegèse was coined by Julien Bonnecase (1878-1950).

[36] Zweigert and Kötz (n 31) 75.
[37] Zweigert and Kötz (n 31) 88; Gebhard Rehm, 'Code civil' in *The Max Planck Encyclopedia of European Private Law*, vol 1 (n 2) 203.
[38] Rehm, 'Code civil' (n 37) 203.
[39] Rodolfo Sacco and Piercarlo Rossi, *Introduzione al diritto comparato* (6th edn, UTET Giuridica 2015) 196ff.
[40] Letter from Stendhal to Honoré de Balzac (30 October 1840): '*En composant la Chartreuse, pour prendre le tone je lisais chaque matin deux ou trois pages du Code civil, afin d'être toujours naturel*'.
[41] Sacco and Rossi (n 39) 198ff.

A famous sentence (perhaps falsely) ascribed to the Jean-Joseph Bugnet (1794-1866) gives a telling account of the exegetical attitude of French scholarship in the face of the newly enacted civil code: 'I am not aware of private law: I only teach the Code Napoleon' (*'Je ne connais pas le droit civil: je n'enseigne que le Code Napoléon'*).
However, Jean-Étienne-Marie Portalis (see *supra*, in this para), during the discussion of the *Titre préliminaire* of the *Code civil* in the session of the Conseil d'État of 14 *thermidor* an IX, said: 'Few cases are likely to be decided by a precise text; it is according to the general principles, to the doctrine, to the science of law, that we have always pronounced on most disputes. The *Code civil* does not disregard all this knowledge; on the contrary, it implies it'.[42]

It was only around the beginning of the twentieth century that jurists attempted to promote a radical renovation of French legal culture, done by loosening the grip of exegetical positivism in which it had been tightly bound. This objective was pursued through renewed methods based on sociology and legal comparison, as well as through greater attention to the creative role of jurisprudence.

François Gény (1861-1959) advocated the legitimacy of a more '*libre recherche scientifique*', to which resort was to be had when the positive law was defective.[43] He was also a notable supporter of natural law.
An important contribution to the renewal of French legal culture was made by Raymond Saleilles (1855-1912) (see *supra*, ch 3, para 3.1), who actively promoted the diffusion and enhancement of comparative law in France, together with jurists such as René Demogue (1872-1938) and Édouard Lambert (1866-1947) (see *supra*, ch 3, para 3.1).
Marcel Planiol (1853-1931) was the author of a famous *Traité elementaire de droit civil*, whose first edition was published between 1899 and 1901. In that work, he referred above all to the *droit vivant* (law in action), searching for it through an analysis of jurisprudence and through legal comparison. The subsequent editions of the *Traité* were co-edited by Georges Ripert (see *infra*, ch 7, para 1).

The occasion of **the Code's bicentenary**, in 2004, also marked the completion of a vast program of reforms of its main sections. It culminated in the reform of the law of contract and of the general law of obligations of 2016;[44] which entered into force on 1 October 2016 and was (slightly)

[42] 'Peu de causes sont susceptibles d'être decidées par un texte précis ; c'est par les principes généraux, par la doctrine, par la science du droit qu'on a toujours prononcé sur la plupart des contestations. Le Code civil ne dispense pas de ces connaissances ; au contraire il les suppose'.
[43] Sacco and Rossi (n 39) 203ff.
[44] *Ordonnance n° 2016-131 du 10 février 2016 portant réforme du droit des contrats, du régime général et de la preuve des obligations.* See John Cartwright and Simon Whittaker (eds), *The Code Napoléon Rewritten. French Contract Law after the 2016 Reform* (Hart 2017), a version of which is also available in French: John Cartwright, Bénédicte Fauvarque-Cosson and Simon Whittaker (eds), *La réécriture du Code Civil. Le droit français des contrats après la réforme de 2016* (LGDJ 2018); Javier Lete, Eric Savaux, Rose-Noëlle

amended in 2018.[45] The amendments served mostly to crystallize a number of the 'great judgments' (*grands arrêts*) passed by the *Cour de Cassation* to supplement the provisions of the *Code civil*, which were grossly incomplete on a number of subjects (like formation of contract). Furthermore, some provisions drawing on the new trends of European contract law were thus introduced into the *Code civil*.[46] Currently, a reform of the law of civil liability is underway: in March 2017, an *Avant-projet* was published by the French Ministry of Justice.[47]

3.1.2. The German *Bürgerliches Gesetzbuch* (BGB)

The enactment of the French *Code civil* stirred a vast debate in Germany as whether to seize the opportunity to accomplish a similar achievement.
In 1814 a famous controversy saw two great jurists of the time taking opposing sides. **Anton Friedrich Justus Thibaut** (1772-1840), professor at the university of Heidelberg, advocated for immediately drafting a German Code. **Friedrich Carl von Savigny** (1779-1861) on the other hand, although not against the idea in principle, argued to first develop a stable corpus of doctrines and concepts and only afterwards to set them out in a comprehensive codification.

> Thibaut's side was taken by a man who had historically served as the great cultural enemy and rival of von Savigny in the same Berlin University, namely the great philosopher Georg Wilhelm Friedrich Hegel (1770-1831). In his *Elements of the Philosophy of Right* (1829), which significantly carry the subtitle *Or Natural Law and Political Science in Outline*, Hegel wrote that denying a civilized nation, or the legal profession within it, the ability to draw up a legal

Schütz and Hélène Boucard (eds), *La recodification du droit des obligations en France et en Espagne* (LGDJ 2016); Florian Bien and Jean-Sébastien Borghetti (eds), *Die Reform des französischen Vertragsrecht. Ein Schritt zu mehr europäischer Konvergenz?* (Mohr Siebeck 2018); Sophie Stijns and Sanne Jansen (eds), *The French Contract Law Reform: A Source of Inspiration?* (Intersentia 2016).

[45] Pursuant to article 38(2) of the French Constitutional Charter, the 2016 *ordonnance* was ratified with modifications through the *Loi n° 2018-287 du 20 avril 2018* (see Olivier Deshayes, Thomas Genicon and Yves-Marie Laithier, *Ratification de l'ordonnance portant réforme du droit des contrats, du régime général et de la preuve des obligations*, in *La Semaine Juridique – Edition Général* n° 18, 30 avril 2018, 885). Several issues of intertemporal law were thus raised (see Jérémy Heymann, 'La réforme du droit français des contrats envisagée d'un point de vue spatio-temporel. Brèves remarques conflictualistes' in François Barrière (ed), *La réforme du droit des contrats. Incidences sur la vie des affaires, Acte du colloque tenu le 24 mars 2017 à l'Université de Lyon 2* (LexisNexis 2017) 5).

[46] For a commentary, see Olivier Deshayes, Thomas Genicon and Yves-Marie Laithier (eds), *Réforme du droit des contracts, du régime général et de la preuve des obligations* (2nd edn, LexisNexis 2018).

[47] http://www.justice.gouv.fr/publication/Projet_de_reforme_de_la_responsabilite_civile_13032017.pdf. See Jean-Sébastien Borghetti and Simon Whittaker (eds), *French Liability in Comparative Perspective* (Hart 2019).

> code would be among the greatest insults one could offer to either.[48] It was a clear attack against von Savigny's contention.

The German Confederation (*Deutscher Bund*) built up after the Restoration (1815) provided for a certain degree of codification of commercial law, both through the legislature and the judiciary (see *infra*, ch 7, para 2). The re-establishment of the German Empire (*Deutsches Reich*) in 1871, which marked the attainment of German national unity, laid down the basis of a unified civil law, although it was only some years later that it was entrusted with full legislative competence for all matters of private law.[49]
From this foundation, in 1874 a commission was charged with the task of drawing up a German Civil Code. The most prominent members of it were **Gottlieb Planck** (1824-1910) and **Bernhard Windscheid** (1817-1892), who is usually credited as having exercised a major influence on the commission's work.

> The first project (*Erster Entwurf*) did not meet with much success, as it was deemed too technical, complex, and abstract, and led to calls for a 'popular law'.[50]
> The critique was led by Otto von Gierke (1841-1921), who famously demanded that (at least) 'a drop of socialist oil' be added to the draft.[51]
> It was thus necessary to appoint another commission, which drafted a second project (*Zweiter Entwurf*), published in 1895 with the preparatory works (*Protokolle*).

The German Parliament (*Reichstag*) enacted the code in 1896, with the only vote against made by the Social Democrats.[52] The code entered into force on 1 January 1900.
In contrast to the French code, the German BGB paid **no heed to local customs, nor to any German law**, but rested completely on Roman law. In this respect, the influence of the Historical School (*Historische Rechtsschule*), led by von Savigny, proved decisive (see *infra*, ch 9, para 1),[53] in that it assumed

[48] Georg Wilhelm Friedrich Hegel, *Elements of the Philosophy of Right* (first published 1829, CUP 1991) § 211: 'No greater insult could be offered to a civilized people or to its lawyers than to deny them the ability to codify their law; for such ability cannot be that of constructing a legal system with a novel content, but only that of apprehending, ie grasping in thought, the content of existing laws in its determinate universality and then applying them to particular cases' ('Einer gebildeten Nation oder dem juristischen Standen in derselben die Fähigkeit abzusprechen, ein Gesetzbuch zu Machen – da es nicht darum zu tun sein kann, ein System ihrem Inhalte nach neuer Gesetze zu machen, sondern den vorhandenen gesetzlichen Inhalt in seiner bestimmten Allgemeinheiten zu erkennen, d.h. ihn denkend zu fassen, – mit Hinzufügung der Aufwendung aufs *Besondere wäre* – einer der größten Schimpfe, der einer Nation oder jenem Stande angetan werden könnte').
[49] Hans P Haferkamp, 'Bürgerliches Gesetzbuch (BGB)' in *The Max Planck Encyclopedia of European Private Law*, vol 1 (n 2) 120.
[50] ibid 121.
[51] ibid.
[52] Zweigert and Kötz (n 31) 142.
[53] Thomas Rüfner, 'Historical School' in *The Max Planck Encyclopedia of European Private Law*, vol 1 (n 2) 832f.

that the 'popular mentality' (*Volksgeist*) of the German people was enshrined in the Justinian compilation, ie (allegedly) classical Roman law. It thus carved out the concept of a **contemporary Roman law** (*heutiges Römisches Recht*), also fathered by Gustav (Conrad von) Hugo (see *supra*, ch 2, para 2).
The history and evolution of Roman law were characterized by its tendency towards a growing conceptualism and formalism, which reached its peak with the **German 'Pandectistic school' (*Pandektenlehre*)** of the late nineteenth century. It elaborated the theoretical and methodological basis of juridical studies that are still prevalent in civil law systems and that can be described as 'dogmatic'.
The starting point of this scientific program was provided by the great cultural enterprise of **Friedrich Carl von Savigny** (1779-1861), who worked on the creation of a system of contemporary Roman law (*System des heutigen römischen Rechts*). He was the founder of the **Historical School of Jurisprudence**, a movement characterized by two methodological aspects of equal importance – namely, the historical and the systematic approach to the knowledge of law. Focusing only on the second of these two aspects, von Savigny's epigones disregarded any historicist consideration concerning the available sources of Roman law and instead proved to be exclusively concerned with the goal of erecting an organic and coherent conceptual system. In this effort, they mainly sought to present the law and its study as a proper science (***scientia iuris***),[54] comparable to those sciences of nature that had in the meantime conquered the limelight of Western thought.

> The most significant member of this thread is generally considered to be Georg Friedrich Puchta (1798-1846), who was a disciple of von Savigny and, at the same time, a follower of one of his fiercest adversaries, Hegel (see *supra* in this para). Puchta analyzed legal concepts as a closed system, where mere formalistic and logical deductions enabling one to 'calculate' the legal response were triggered by any case.
> Largely used and influential were also the Pandectistic works by Karl Adoph von Vangerow (1808-1870), Heinrich Dernburg (1829-1907), Ernst Immanuel Bekker (1827-1916), and above all Bernhard Windscheid (1817-1892) (see *supra* in this para).

The **organicist conception of the law** advocated by the Historical School of Jurisprudence suggested a systematic classification of the contents of Roman law through their conceptual formalization in juridical institutions. If the system that the Pandectists strove to achieve can be compared to a human body, the various juridical institutions can be compared to the single organs that, within that body, coherently contribute to keeping it alive and allowing it to properly perform its functions.
Each **juridical institution** represents the synthesis of all the legal contents necessary to carry out a specific regulatory function, and each institution is characterized by a relationship of complementarity and interaction with the

[54] Paolo Cappellini, *Systema Iuris*, 2 vols (Giuffrè 1984-1985).

other institutions, since each of them is equally indispensable for the overall functioning of the system. The peculiarity of the Pandectistic school is that of having conceived juridical institutions as ideal realities, thus enabling a jurist to deductively infer – from abstract concepts – solutions and rules for unregulated cases. In this sense, borrowing a word from theology, legal scholarship still speaks of 'dogmas' and '**legal dogmatics**'.
The structure of the BGB was laid out along the so-called ***Pandektensystem***,[55] which is based upon the division of subject matters into obligations, property, family law, and succession.[56] The truly distinctive feature of the BGB, however, must be acknowledged in its **General Part** (*Allgemeiner Teil*),[57] which is the first book of the code, and sets forth all definitions and general rules to be detailed and supplemented in the subsequent provisions.[58]

The foundation of the '*Pandektensystem*' is attributed to Georg Arnold Heise (1778-1851), who laid it out in his *Grundriß eines Systems des gemeinen Civilrechts zum Behuf von Pandekten-Vorlesungen* (1807).

A recognized characteristic of the BGB lies in its development of a **huge system of abstract concepts**, that does not mirror legal practice, but rather reflects the conceptual structure built up by scholars and professors of law. In fact, German scholarship developed on the BGB is famous worldwide for its technical sophistication and systematic rigor in forging and using conceptual categories. The growing influence of dogmatism during the nineteenth century provoked a strong reaction among several exponents of the Pandectistic scholarship, guided by one of its greatest figures, **Rudolf von Jhering** (1818-1892).

In a satiric booklet first published in 1884, von Jhering played the role of 'the lame devil, who raised the roofs of the town and showed the secrets of the households to his *protégé*':[59] the households which he thus exposed to the curiosity of the reader were the studios where the scholars of civil law, including von Jhering himself, used to spend their nights at the light of a tiny lamp illuminating the sources of Roman law, thus tirelessly erecting the system of private law ('*die civilistische Konstruktion*').[60] In order to depict this line of legal thought, which entailed the entire scholarship of the preceding fifty years, von Jhering forged the neologism of 'conceptual jurisprudence' (***Begriffsjurisprudenz***).[61]

[55] Haferkamp (n 49) 122.
[56] Jan P Schmidt, 'Pandektensystem' in *The Max Planck Encyclopedia of European Private Law*, vol 2 (n 28) 1239.
[57] Zimmermann, *The Law of Obligations: Roman Foundations of the Civilian Tradition* (n 6) 10ff, 29ff.
[58] Jan P Schmidt, 'General Part' in *The Max Planck Encyclopedia of European Private Law*, vol 1 (n 2) 774. For a general account of the contents of BGB's *Allgemeiner Teil*, see Manfred Wolf and Jörg Neuner, *Allgemeiner Teil des Bürgerlichen Rechts* (11th edn, CH Beck 2016); Dieter Medicus and Jens Petersen, *Allgemeiner Teil des BGB* (11th edn, CF Müller 2016).
[59] Rudolf von Jhering, *Scherz und Ernst in der Jurisprudenz* (13th edn, Wissenschaftliche Buchgesellschaft 1924) 6.
[60] ibid 7.
[61] ibid 339.

After his work, in the subsequent literature dedicated to the methodology of civil law, this term carried a decidedly negative connotation.[62] Ironically, von Jhering claimed to be unaware of just who had originated this strand: 'As for what is known to me, this construction itself was reconstructed and given its own direction, and it was even undertaken to create a higher level of jurisprudence, which was then given the name of "higher jurisprudence"'.[63]

The polemic by von Jhering paved the way for new tendencies in legal studies. This paradigmatic turn was expected to have a direct impact on the methodology of filling legal gaps, which posed the question of how legal responses to tangible cases were to be construed.

A decisive step forward was taken by Philipp Heck (1858-1943), who intended to forge a 'teleological jurisprudence' (***Interessenjurisprudenz***), based on the assessment of the interests involved in the case and confronting the 'formalistic jurisprudence' (*Begriffsjurisprudenz*) that von Jhering had already derided.[64] This methodology was adopted by the members of the 'Tübinger school'. Adopting an even more radical approach, Eugen Ehrlich (1865-1922) proposed to rid judges of the bond of fidelity to written legislative texts and to allow them to proceed with a free search for law (**freie Rechtsfindung**), thereby advocating a strong contribution of sociological studies in the legal discourse.

During the twentieth century, large parts of the BGB were completely revised; for example, the family law enshrined in its fourth book was completely re-written. The most important and far-reaching of these reforms, however, is known as '**modernization of the law of obligations**' (*Schuldrechtsmodernisierung*) of 2001.[65] Entering into force on 1 January 2002, it not only cured some of the shortcomings of the old provisions of the BGB on obligations, but went as far as incorporating European private law (see *infra*, ch 8, para 1.5.2) that had been previously implemented in special statutes.

[62] Franz Wieacker, *A History of Private Law in Europe* (Tony Weir trs, Clarendon Press 2016) 376f; Ralf Seinecke, 'Methode und Zivilrecht beim "Begriffsjuristen" Jherings (1818-1892)' in Joachim Rückert and Ralf Seinecke (eds), *Methodik des Zivilrechts – von Savigny bis Teubner* (3rd edn, Nomos 2017) paras 352ff.

[63] Cf Rudolf von Jhering, *Geist des römischen Rechts auf den verschiedenen Stufen seiner Entwicklung*, 1/2 (Breitkopf und Härtel 1852) 285 ('nur so viel ist mir bekannt, daß einer sogar dies Konstruieren selbst wieder konstruiert und eine eigene Anweisung dazu gegeben, ja sogar zur Vornahme dieser Arbeit ein höheres Stockwerk der Jurisprudenz angelegt hat, welches danach den Namen der "höhern Jurisprudenz" erhalten hat'); and Id, 'Unsere Aufgabe' in Id and Carl Friedrich von Gerber (eds), *Jahrbücher für die Dogmatik des heutigen römischen und deutschen Privatrechts*, 1 (Maute 1857) 1ff.

[64] Philipp Heck, 'Gesetzesauslegung und Interessenjurisprudenz' (1914) AcP 1ff; Id, *Das Problem der Gewinnung* (2nd edn, Mohr Siebeck 1932); Id, *Begriffsbildung und Interessenjurisprudenz* (Mohr Siebeck 1932); Id, 'Die Interessenjurisprudenz und ihre neuen Gegner' (1936) AcP 129ff.

[65] For the overall *travaux préparatoires*, see Claus-Wilhelm Canaris (ed), *Shuldrechtsmodernisierung 2002* (CH Beck 2002).

3.1.3. The Italian *Codice civile* of 1942

After achieving national unity in 1861 thanks to the political activities of the Piedmontese prime minister, count Camillo Benso di Cavour, the cultural activism of Giuseppe Mazzini, and the military action of Giuseppe Garibaldi, a wide process of administrative and legal unification of the newly founded Kingdom of Italy was initiated. It was not a difficult task as far as private law was concerned, in light of the substantial homogeneity of the below-mentioned pre-unification codes.

After the Restoration sanctioned by the Congress of Vienna (1814-1815), the Italian territory had found itself once again divided into several small states, where the *Code Napoléon* was abrogated (only partially in the Principality of Lucca).[66]
Four such states, namely the Kingdom of Sardinia (which also included Piedmont, Savoy, Sardinia, Nice, and Genoa), the Duchy of Parma and Piacenza, the Duchy of Modena and Reggio Emilia, and the Kingdom of the Two Sicilies, enacted their own civil codes, which took the French Civil Code as a model, although amending and often improving it.
In the Kingdom of Lombardy-Venetia, under Austrian domination, the *Allgemeines Bürgerliches Gesetzbuch* (ABGB) of 1811 was introduced on 1 January 1816. By contrast, the State of the Church was left without a proper civil code.

In 1865, the **first Italian Civil Code** (***Codice civile***) was then enacted, which entered into force on 1 January 1866. It was mostly based on an Italian translation of the French *Code civil.*
In 1923, **Vittorio Scialoja** (1856-1933) was entrusted by the government to chair a commission for the reform of the Civil Code. The task was then continued and to a large extent completed by **Filippo Vassalli** (1885-1955), to whom is owed the general linguistic and conceptual review of the norms which were being drafted.
Between 1938 and 1942, the six books of which the code is made of were progressively enacted, and the code came into force in its entirety on 21 April 1942. After the fall of the Fascist regime and the dismantling of the corporatist system (1943-1944), however, it was debated whether the Civil Code would have to be comprehensively abrogated.

One of the most prominent authors who expressed himself in this direction was Lorenzo Mossa (1886-1957), Professor of Commercial Law at the University of Pisa, who came to define the Civil Code as 'codice dei fascisti' (a Fascist code).[67]

[66] Sacco and Rossi (n 39) 221ff.
[67] Lorenzo Mossa, 'Per il diritto dell'Italia' [1945] Riv dir comm I 1, 3.

The outcome of this discussion was an answer in the negative, taking into account that, despite some lexical or superficial elements, the code was the expression of the **liberal culture of its drafters**, not of the authoritarian or nationalistic culture of the political regime which had requested it.[68]

From the point of view of its contents, the Italian Civil Code can be considered a sort of compromise between the German and the French model, combining the advantages of the two.

It is also known for having eliminated the distinction between commercial and civil law (**unification of private law**) (see *infra*, ch 7, para 2).

4. COMMON LAW JURISDICTIONS

The tenets of the French Revolution could not gain ground in England, which therefore never implemented the doctrine of separation of powers.

> The historical reason for failing to take on Enlightenment doctrines in England may be that the democratization of politics had already been achieved there through the long civil war which led Oliver Cromwell to power (1642-1651), and the so-called Glorious (or Bloodless) Revolution (1688-1689).

As a result, common law jurisdictions have been traditionally based upon cases decided by the courts (**precedents**), whereas legislative measures (**statutes**) passed by the Parliament played a minor role until recent times. Intuitively, therefore, both common law and the Constitution of the United Kingdom are not codified.

The homeland of common law is **England**,[69] which, since the time of King Henry VIII, has constituted a single legal system with that of **Wales**.[70] In the context of the United Kingdom, the common law is also applied in **Northern Ireland**.[71]

> Although dependencies of the British crown, the Channel Islands (ie the Bailiwick of Jersey and that of Guernsey) are still ruled by Normand customary law (see *infra*, ch 4, para 5).[72]

Despite forming the UK with England in 1707, **Scotland** has a jurisdiction substantially anchored to the continental *ius civile*,[73] also due to its Catholic heritage.[74]

[68] Sacco and Rossi (n 39) 228ff.
[69] Vogenauer (n 2) 265ff.
[70] For a historical background, see Baker, *Introduction to English Legal History* (n 6) 35f.
[71] ibid 36ff.
[72] Kischel (n 3) 243, fn 3. For a historical background, see Baker, *Introduction to English Legal History* (n 6) 38f.
[73] David L Carey Miller and Reinhard Zimmermann (eds), *The Civilian Tradition and Scots Law: Aberdeen quincentenary essays* (Duncker & Humblot 1997). For a historical background, see Baker, *Introduction to English Legal History* (n 6) 40ff.
[74] Reinhard Zimmermann and John MacLeod, 'Scottish Private Law' in *The Max Planck*

The civil connotation of Scottish law is partly due to the work of Sir James Dalrymple (1619-1695), first Viscount of Stair.[75]

Scottish law is nonetheless considered a mixed jurisdiction (see *infra*, ch 4, para 5), built on the *ius civile* but with a strong and evident influence of English common law.
Similar considerations can be made for **Louisiana** with respect to the US and for the province of **Quebec** with respect to Canada. Both jurisdictions are former French colonies that have maintained a codified legal system based on the Civil Law.

In Louisiana, the Civil Code has been in force since 1825, and it has been amended several times over the years.
The Civil Code of Quebec (or *Code civil du Québec*) entered into force on 1 January 1994. It replaced the Civil Code of Lower Canada (*Code civil du Bas-Canada*), which had been enacted in 1865.

In general, both the **US** and **Canada** are common law jurisdictions,[76] as are **Australia**,[77] **New Zealand**, and the **other former British colonies or countries formerly mandated by England** (including some Asian, Caribbean, and African territories).
Thus, despite showing a certain number of unique aspects,[78] the legal systems of all these countries share an extensive bulk of commonalities. What we refer to as common law is the merger or at least a juxtaposition of two different components, namely common law *stricto sensu* and equity (see *supra*, ch 2, para 4.2). Their distinction was historically due to and reflected in two judicial hierarchies, each of them being autonomous from the other. Over time, such dualism proved increasingly untenable from the point of view of the judiciary and the rules of civil procedure. Indeed, the co-existence of two judicial hierarchies, sometimes running parallel and other times overlapping, caused more and more considerable complications for the functioning of common law legal systems.[79]
In the **US**, towards the mid-1800s the legislature began increasingly to enact law reform that had been previously promoted by equity courts; the latter thus became a useless complication. Eventually, the New York Constitution of 1846 abolished the court of chancery, flanked by the New York Code of

Encyclopedia of European Private Law, vol 2 (n 28) 1532ff; Hector L MacQueen, 'Scots Law' in *Elgar Encyclopedia of Comparative Law* (n 29) 789.
75 Klaus Luig, 'Institutional Textbooks' in *The Max Planck Encyclopedia of European Private Law*, vol 1 (n 2) 912.
76 Ralf Michaels, 'American Law (United States)' in *Elgar Encyclopedia of Comparative Law* (n 29) 75; Michael Deturbide and Elisabeth J Hughes, 'Canada' ibid 132.
77 Martin Vranken, 'Australia' ibid 120.
78 Kischel (n 3) 360ff.
79 Baker, *Introduction to English Legal History* (n 6) 122ff.

Civil Procedure of 1848 (see *infra*, ch 7, para 3.2), which merged law and equity.[80] Subsequently, most of the other American states did the same.
The US model was later followed by the **UK**, where the dualism between the two jurisdictions was overcome through the Judicatures Acts of 1873-1875, although it is still disputed whether this only occurred from a procedural point of view, or whether a true merger of substantial law occurred.[81]
Common law jurisdictions, notably the English, are traditionally characterized by the **precedence of judge-made law over statutes**, although this point looks like becoming less paramount over time (see *infra*, ch 7, para 3.2). Judge-made law is typically expressed through the rule of *stare decisis*, which is not recognized in civil law jurisdictions (see *infra*, ch 7, para 3.2).

In modern times, the first systematic exposition of the common law is to be found in the *Commentaries on the Laws on England* by William Blackstone (see *supra*, ch 2, para 5), whereby he affirmed the 'superior reasonableness' of common law over civil law.[82] Such statement contributes to explaining the fortune his works had in the Anglo-American world.[83]

5. MIXED JURISDICTIONS

Mixed jurisdictions are first found in those local contexts where, for historical and political reasons, a splinter of civil law coexists within a wider state context which is dominated by common law.[84]
This is the case of **Scotland**, in Europe (see *supra*, ch 4, para 5); and of **Louisiana** and **Quebec** in the US and Canada, respectively (see *supra*, ch 4, para 5).

The **Channel Islands** (see *supra*, ch 4, para 5) are a different case but are nonetheless included in the mixed jurisdictions.[85]

A somehow similar phenomenon is to be found in those countries that were, albeit temporarily, under the administration of the UK, like **Cyprus**.[86]

[80] Arthur T von Mehren and Peter L Murray, *Law in the United States* (2nd ed, CUP 2007) 4.
[81] Stephen Waddams, 'Equity in English Contract Law: The Impact of the Judicatures Act 1873-75' (2012) 33 J Legal Hist 185.
[82] Padoa Schioppa (n 8) 399.
[83] ibid.
[84] Vernon V Palmer, 'Mixed Jurisdictions' in *Elgar Encyclopedia of Comparative Law* (n 29) 590.
[85] Reinhard Zimmermann, 'Mixed Legal Systems' in *The Max Planck Encyclopedia of European Private Law*, vol 2 (n 28) 1180, 1182.
[86] ibid 1182.

This is the case of **Malta**, where the backbone of the legal system is a codified system under Italian influence,[87] to which a strong common law component was added by the English starting from the nineteenth century.
This is also the case, albeit with some differences, for **Israel**, which has built a legal system of its own starting in 1948.[88] This system, although mainly developed on civil law principles, has also been strongly influenced by the legislation enacted during the British mandate for the administration of Palestine.

> The founder of Israeli law was the Italian Guido (Gad) Tedeschi (1907-1992), who contributed to the birth of the law faculty of the Hebrew University of Jerusalem. He inspired and partially drafted a series of general laws (on contract, unjust enrichment, etc.), which have in fact carried out a progressive codification of Israeli law. A project of civil code has been under consideration before the Knesset for a number of years, which was mainly drafted by one of Tedeschi's disciples, namely Aharon Barak, who served for many years as the President of the Israeli Supreme Court.[89]

A peculiar case is **South Africa** and the other countries where Dutch-Roman law is applied (see *supra*, ch 4, para 3).

[87] ibid.
[88] Gabriela Shalev, 'Israel' in *Elgar Encyclopedia of Comparative Law* (n 29) 449.
[89] For an English translation of the project of civil code for Israel, see Kurt Siehr and Reinhard Zimmermann (eds), *The Draft Civil Code for Israel in comparative perspective* (Mohr Siebeck 2008); for a review of the Project of Civil Code for Israel, see Alfredo Mordechai Rabello and Pablo Lerner, 'The (Re) Codification of Israeli Private Law: Support for, and Criticism of, the Israeli Draft Civil Law Code' (2011) 59 Am J Comp L 763.

GLOSSARY

***Allgemeines Bürgerliches Gesetzbuch* (ABGB) (3.1.3)**: civil code adopted in Austria in 1811, in the framework of the codification of national laws performed in that period by German countries and promoted by political regimes of enlightened absolutism governing such countries. The ABGB, although many times amended, is still in force. It originated from the ideas of the Enlightenment and natural rights. It principally postulates the equality and freedom of the individual, without completely abolishing the old feudalist order of the estates.

***Bürgerliches Gesetzbuch* (BGB) (3.1.2)**: civil code drafted in Germany between 1880 and 1896 and entered into force on 1 January 1900, repealing the private law of previous pre-unitarian states of Germany (*Landrecht*). Together with the *Code Napoléon* (see *ad vocem*), the BGB is the code that had the greatest impact on subsequent codification endeavors and, in general, on the European legal culture. The elaboration of the BGB was very much influenced by the so called *Begriffsjurisprudenz* (jurisprudence of concepts), the first subschool of legal positivism which relied on a strict methodology of conceptualization and abstraction of legal principles. The BGB is divided into five books: i) general principles; ii) obligations; iii) property; iv) family law; and v) successions.

Civil code (3): organic and systematic body of statutory provisions, representing the main source of law in the civil law systems in relation to private affairs and matters falling under the realm of private law.

Civil Code of Quebec (*Code civil du Québec*) (5): code in force in the province of Quebec, Canada. It entered into force on 1 January 1994 and replaced the Civil Code of Lower Canada (*Code civil du Bas-Canada*), which had been enacted in 1865.

***Code civil des Français* (or *Code Napoléon*) (3.1.1)**: code developed in France during the French Revolution, enacted in 1804, and entered into force in 1806. Although many times amended, it is still in force. The Code sought to unify the whole system of private law and, through this, affirmed the principles of the revolution. Its technical and conceptual framework is strongly rooted in the *ius commune*, although its drafting was also influenced by the *coutumes*, namely rules and principles of French customary law. According to the Roman tradition, the Code was originally divided into three parts: i) persons; ii) property; and iii) acquisition of property.

Court of Admiralty (1): court exercising jurisdiction over all maritime contracts, torts, injuries, and offenses, relating to maritime law and events on the high seas. Historically admiralty courts were separate courts. In modern times official jurisdiction for admiralty law generally falls under part of the regular court system, usually a federal or superior level court.

***Coutume de Paris* (3.1.1)**: regional civil law, more precisely a written collection of the customs of the city of Paris. After its publication in 1570, it was applied in Paris and the surrounding region, while later on, it found application also in French overseas colonies like New France. It contained provisions concerning family and inheritance, property, and debt recovery.

Doctor's Common (or College of Civilians) (1): society of lawyers studying and practicing civil law in London. Its name derives from the civilians gathering together as in other colleges. Like the Inns of Court of the common lawyers, the society had buildings with rooms where its members lived and worked and a large library. Court proceedings of the civil law courts were also held in Doctors' Commons. According to some accounts, the society of Doctors' Commons was created by Richard Blodwell, Dean of the Arches in 1511, but others say it existed already in the fifteenth century. The society's buildings, acquired in 1567, were originally situated near St. Paul's Cathedral at Paternoster Row, and later nearby in Knightrider Street where it remained until the buildings were sold in 1865.

Founding Treaties (2): binding agreements between EU Member States. They set out EU objectives, rules for EU institutions, how decisions are made, and the relationship between the EU and the Member States. Treaties are amended to make the EU more efficient and transparent, to prepare for new member countries and to introduce new areas of cooperation – such as the single currency. Under the treaties, EU institutions can adopt legislation, which the member countries then implement (see *infra*, ch 8).

Italian Civil Code (*Codice civile*) (3.1.3): enacted by Royal decree 262 of 16 March 1942, it was created before the current Italian Constitution and amended in the postwar period. The 1942 Civil Code replaced an earlier civil code which had been in force since 1865, mostly based on an Italian translation of the *Code Napoléon*. The Code is divided into preliminary provisions (16 provisions on sources of law and their interpretation) and six books: book 1 – family law, marriage, adoption; book 2 – inheritance law, testament; book 3 – property: movable items, real estate, property rights and limits; book 4 – bonds contracts, torts, and unjustified enrichment; book 5 – commerce law and labor law; book 6 – liability, transcription, credit law, rules of evidence.

Law French (1): archaic language originally based on Old Norman and Anglo-Norman, but increasingly influenced by Parisian French and later, English. It was used in England in judicial proceedings, pleadings, and lawbooks from the Norman Conquest to the seventeenth century. Although Law French as a narrative legal language is obsolete, some lawyers and judges in common law jurisdictions continue to use many individual Law French terms. The earliest documents in which French (ie Anglo-Norman) is used for discourse on English law date from the third quarter of the thirteenth century and include two particular documents: the first is *The Provisions of Oxford* (1258), a set of terms of oath sworn by the 24 magnates appointed to correct abuses in the administration of King Henry III, together with summaries of their rulings. The second is *The Casus Placitorum* (1250-1270?), a collection of legal maxims, rules, and short narratives of cases.

Louisiana (5): state situated in the Deep South region of the southeastern US. Being a former French colony, it has maintained a codified legal system based on the civil law.

***Pays de droit coutumier* (3.1.1)**: central and northern regions of the Kingdom of France where, before the French revolution, customs (*coutumes*) were primarily applied, while the Roman *ius commune* had only a subsidiary role to play in the case where customs were not sufficient to solve the dispute.

***Pays de droit écrit* (or *de droit savant*) (3.1.1)**: southern regions of the Kingdom of France where, before the French revolution, the Roman *ius commune* was primarily applied. Roman law was acknowledged as customary law and its study flourished at some universities in this part of France like the universities of Montpellier and Toulouse.

Roman-Dutch law (3): uncodified civil-law system developed by Dutch jurists starting from the sixteenth century, produced by the fusion of early modern Dutch law, chiefly of Germanic origin, and Roman law. Roman-Dutch law is still applied in South Africa and in other former Dutch colonies, while in the Netherlands itself it was replaced in 1809 by the *Code Napoléon* and subsequently by a national civil code.

Unification of private law (3.1.3): one of the main innovations achieved by the Italian 1942 Civil Code (see *ad vocem*). The latter suppressed the distinction between commercial and civil law, extending rules that were up to that moment exclusive of commercial transactions to all private relationships. Historically, in fact, commercial rules found their systematization in separate sources of law, like commercial codes. In this way, all private economic activity is regulated by a single normative text.

BIOGRAPHIES

Aharon Barak (Kaunas, 1936) is an Israeli jurist that contributed relevantly to the experience and development of Israeli law. He was President of the Supreme Court of Israel from 1995 to 2006. He served also as a Justice of the Supreme Court of Israel (1978-1995) and as the Attorney General of Israel (1975-1978). Barak completed his legal studies at Harvard University. In 1968, he was appointed as a professor at the Hebrew University of Jerusalem, and in 1974, he became the Dean of its Law Faculty. In 1975, he was awarded the Israel Prize for legal research. After his retirement from the Supreme Court, Barak joined the staff of the Interdisciplinary Center in Herzliya, where he teaches in the master's degree program for Commercial Law. He also gives lectures in the Bachelor of Laws program. In addition, he continues to lecture at both the Yale Law School and the University of Alabama in the US, as well as the University of Toronto Faculty of Law. Alongside his service in the Supreme Court, Barak also worked as the head of a committee which, for about twenty years, drafted the Israeli Civil Code, with the aim of putting together the main civil law statutes in Israeli law under a single comprehensive legal framework. Barak's legal philosophy is based on the belief that 'the world is filled with law'. This idea considers law as an all-encompassing framework of human affairs from which no action can ever be immune: whatever the law does not prohibit, it permits; either way, the law always has its say, on everything.
His main works are: *Judicial Discretion* (1989); *Purposive Interpretation in Law* (2005); *The Judge in a Democracy* (2006).

Peter Brian Herrenden Birks (Green Hedges, Westmeston, 1941-2004), the Regius Professor of Civil Law at the University of Oxford, was a prolific, brilliant academic lawyer and one of the most creative and fertile minds of the English private law.
Birks went to the Chislehurst and Sidcup Grammar School and was accepted to the Trinity College, Oxford. Subsequently he attended a Master of Laws at the University College London. In 1995, he was appointed honorary Queen's counsel and foreign member of the Royal Netherlands Academy of Arts and Sciences in 2001. He was appointed President of the Society of Legal Scholars in 2002-2003. He taught in Europe and throughout the Commonwealth and he lectured prodigiously.
A passionate and inspirational teacher, Birks also distinguished himself as being the first general editor of *English Private Law*, a book which, reflecting Birks' thought and his passionate belief in the value of Roman law as a means of introducing students to legal concepts, categorization, and order, tried to synthesize and rationalize the English private law in a system. Paradigmatically, Birks observed that 'there is no body of knowledgeable data which can subsist as a jumble of mismatched categories. The search for order is indistinguishable from the search for knowledge'.
Birks was also considered as a key figure in the extraordinary development of the law of restitution in the last 45 years and his thought influenced the decision of the judges in *Woolwich Building Society v Inland Revenue* case, adjudicated

in 1991. Following that case, citizens were entitled for the first time to recover taxes unduly paid, if the tax authorities were not entitled to them.
His main works are: *An Introduction to the Law of Restitution* (1988); *English Private Law* (2000); *Unjust Enrichment* (2004).

James Dalrymple (Ayrshire, 1619 – Edinburgh, 1695) first Viscount of Stair, was a Scottish lawyer and statesman. He was a professor ('regent') at the University of Glasgow (1641) and after nearly seven years' service, he resigned his regency and moved to Edinburgh where he was admitted to the bar in 1648. He played a political role during the tumultuous years of the mid-seventeenth century. He went to The Hague (1649) and Breda (1650) in order to negotiate the agreement between Charles II and the Scottish Covenanters. In 1657, Stair was appointed as one of the Commissioners for the Administration of Justice in Scotland, on the recommendation of George Monk. His appointment to the bench was confirmed by Oliver Cromwell. Soon after the Restoration, Stair went to London where he was received with favor by Charles II. In 1671, he was appointed Lord President of the Court of Session, and in 1674, he became a Privy Councilor. In 1681, he fell out of royal favor after Parliament enacted the Test Act that prescribed an oath of allegiance to the Anglican church for all public officials. Indeed, he had refused such a prescription. He was therefore removed as a member of the judiciary, and he retired to his wife's estate in Galloway, after publishing his main work in 1681, *The Institutions of the Law of Scotland*. Through this, he fundamentally contributed to the systematization of Scottish law on the basis of Roman law. After a period spent in Holland, he returned to London in 1688 along with William III.
His main works are: *The Institutions of the Law of Scotland* (1681); *Physiologia Nova Experimentalis* (1686); *Vindication of the Divine Perfections* (1695).

Jean Domat (Clermont-Ferrand, 1625 – Paris, 1696), born at Clermont in Auvergne, was a French jurist, a philosopher, a writer and the king's lawyer in Paris. After studying the *humaniora* in Paris, he met and forged a powerful friendship with Pascal, to such an extent that on Pascal's death he was entrusted with the latter's private papers. Domat went on to attend the University of Bourges, obtaining a degree in law, under the supervision of Edmond Mérille. Called to the Court of Louis XIV, in Versailles, the sovereign granted him a pension equal to two thousand livres, which allowed him, starting from 1681, to devote himself exclusively to juridical studies.
Domat is considered by most of historiography to be the greatest French civilian of the eighteenth century. He reorganized the national law using the model of classical Roman law, not through the philological method adopted in the sixteenth century, but through a research characterized by a spirit of rigorous arrangement. In his work, Domat adopted a method that tried to transform the seemingly random historical sources of law into a rational system of rules. However, as a supporter of a cartesian juridical order, Domat endeavored to found all law upon ethical or religious principles, his motto being *'L'homme est fait par Dieu et pour Dieu'* ('Man was made by God and for God'). Therefore, he attempted to establish a system of French law on the basis of moral principles and he presented

the contents of the *Corpus iuris civilis* in the form of a new system of natural law. After the work of Robert Joseph Pothier, Domat's work is regarded as the second most important influence on the Civil Code of Lower Canada.
His main works are: *Les loix civiles dans leur ordre naturel : le droit public, et legum delectus* (1625-1696); *Le droit public* (1697).

Georg Wilhelm Friedrich Hegel (Stuttgart, 1770 – Berlin, 1831) was a German philosopher, considered the most significant representative of German idealism. Born on 27 August 1770 in Stuttgart, capital of the Duchy of Württemberg in southwestern Germany, Hegel went to German School at the age of three. Two years later, he attended the Latin School and he already knew the first declension, having been taught it by his mother. During his adolescence he read voraciously, following up the authors as Friedrich Gottlieb Klopstock and Enlightenment's writers like Christian Garve and Gotthold Ephraim Lessing.
In 1776, he attended the famous Stuttgart's gymnasium where Hegel concluded his studies with his *Abiturrede* ('graduation speech') entitled *The abortive state of art and scholarship in Turkey* (*Der verkümmerte Zustand der Künste und Wissenschaften unter den Türken*).
After completing his studies in his city, he entered the *Stift* of Tübingen in 1788, a sort of Protestant seminary, where he had as comrades Schelling and Hölderlin, with whom he would share the enthusiasm for the French Revolution.
He is the author of one of the most profound and complex lines of thought in the Western tradition; his philosophical reflection was born within the German cultural environment of the early nineteenth century, dominated by Kantian philosophy and its idealistic developments.
Hegel's philosophy marks a decisive turning point in the history of philosophy: on the one hand, many of the classical problems of modern philosophy will be reformulated and problematized differently, such as the relationship between mind and nature, subject-object or the themes related to law, morality, the state (in the practical and moral sphere); on the other hand, new problems are introduced, such as dialectics, the distinction between ethics and morality, between intellect and reason, etc.
His main works are: *Phänomenologie des Geistes* (1807); *Wissenschaft der Logik* (1812-1816); *Grundlinien der Philosophie des Rechts* (1820); *Enziklopädie der philosophischen Wissenschaften* (1830); *Vorlesungen über die Geschichte der Philosophie* (1831); *Vorlesungen über die Philosophie der Religion* (1832); *Vorlesungen über die Philosophie der Geschichte* (1837).

William Murray, first Earl of Mansfield (Scone, Perthshire, 1705 – London, 1793), born to Scottish nobility, was a British politician, a barrister, and a judge, who distinguished himself as having achieved the reform of English law. At the age of 13 years, William Murray went to London to take up a place at Westminster School but before it he studied in Perth, Scotland. In May 1723, he moved to Oxford to attend Christ Church, where he graduated four years later. After returning to London, the Lincoln's Inn called him to the Bar on 23 November 1730 and he quickly became a brilliant barrister. Beginning with his election as

a Member of Parliament for Boroughbridge and his appointment as a Solicitor General, in 1742, William Murray began his political career.
Known for his 'great powers of eloquence' and considered as 'beyond comparison the best speaker' in the House of Commons, during the absence of a strong Attorney General, he became the chief spokesman for the government in the House of Commons.
As a Lord Chief Justice, Lord Mansfield modernized both English law and the English courts system and valued the concept of equity that all courts should apply, through the reformation of the system by which the judgment had to be carried out to safeguarding the parties and the reduction of the time and expense for the parties. He gave the most important contributions to common, merchant and commercial law. He spent a lot of time bringing the law of England on par with that of other countries, especially in cases such as *Pillans & Rose v Van Mierop & Hopkins* [1765] 3 Burr 1663, and *Carter v Boehm* [1766] 3 Burr 1905. For this last work, he was considered by a judge as 'the founder of the commercial law of this country'.
Among the most important contributions, it is particularly relevant his judgment in *Somersett's Case* (1772) 98 ER 499 concerning the legality of keeping slaves in England; *Pillans & Rose v Van Mierop & Hopkins* (1765) 3 Burr 1663, 97 ER 1035, where Mansfield tried to challenge the doctrine about the concept of consideration in common law.

Marcel Planiol (Nantes, 1853 – Paris, 1931) was a French jurist and is seen as an innovator in his country for replacing the systematic approach with the exegetical method in the study of civil law. His *Traité élémentaire de droit civil* (1899) is considered one of the leading works examining French scholarship and case law.
Planiol studied at the Faculty of Law of Paris, where he graduated with a thesis on Roman law entitled: *Des bénéfices accordés aux héritiers. Droit Français: Du bénéfice d'inventaire.*
From an early age, he showed great interest in the history of law and published a number of works, especially in Brittany.
In 1880 he obtained the *agrégation* and began to teach civil law, Roman law, and tax law at the University of Grenoble. He also taught at the University of Rennes and then at the Sorbonne University in Paris. In 1899, Planiol published the *Traité élémentaire de droit civil*, a work primarily intended for his students and accordingly divided into three volumes corresponding to the respective civil law courses taught during the three years of undergraduate law school. Although it was originally conceived as an institutional work, the *Traité élémentaire* is deemed to be one of the most outstanding contributions to French juridical science. It deals with fault, obligation, and civil liability with a view to a moral perspective, thus abandoning the structured progression of arguments proposed by the French Civil Code in order to envisage a (diverging) systematization related to the subjects. Overall, the entire work appears to be pervaded by a particular emphasis valorizing natural law, which permeates the study of each subject. Moreover, in the title of the work there lurks a precise choice of its author. He significantly decided to mention the adjective *élémentaire* for a specific reason. His proposal

is to resort to the principles, to the so-called *éléments* of civil law, which were allegedly hidden by the *Code civil*: the concept of origin as a principle should be intended as *élémentaire* in this regard.
His ideas, developed through the above-mentioned method, had already been partly discussed in some entries in *Encyclopédie Berthelot*, which, together with the *Encyclopédie Larousse*, constitutes one of the two great encyclopedias of the nineteenth century. From the various entries that Planiol wrote in the above-mentioned work, the foundations of the civil law system that he later supported in his *Traité élémentaire* clearly emerge. The conceptual perspective is mainly based on fault as the point of analysis of legal norms. This scientific approach distinctly evokes the subjective system envisaged by Rudold von Jhering.
At the end of Planiol's university career, Georges Ripert became his collaborator, participating in the numerous revisions of his treatise.
His main works are: *Droit romain : Des bénéfices accordés aux héritiers. Droit français : Du bénéfice d'inventaire* (1879); *Une donation immobilière non transcrite est-elle opposable aux héritiers du donateur*, in *Revue critique de législation et de jurisprudence* (1880); *Traité pratique de droit civil français* (first published 1899-1901).

Jean-Étienne-Marie Portalis (Le Beausset, 1746 – Paris, 1807), was a French lawyer and a politician born to a France bourgeois family, at Le Beausset, currently in the Var *département* of Provence and 'one of the protagonists of the editing of the great codification wanted by Napoleon', which was the basis of the French legal system. He attended the University of Aix and published, as a student, his first two works, *Observations sur Émile* (on Jean-Jacques Rousseau's *Emile: Or, On Education*) in 1763 and *Des Préjugés* in 1764.
Before becoming a lawyer at the Parliament of Aix-en-Provence in 1765 and achieving an excellent reputation, in 1770 Portalis was commissioned by Étienne François de Choiseul to draw up the Decree authorizing the marriage of Protestants. He was also one of the four administrators of Provence.
After the proclamation of the First Republic as a result of the Revolution, in 1793 Portalis went to Paris. In 1800, as an expert of the *droit écrit* from the Roman model of the Midi (south) of France, he, together with the other three jurists (defined familiarly *artisans*) François Denis Tronchet, Félix Julien Jean Bigot de Préameneu and Jaques Maleville, was given the task by Napoleon of drawing up the Civil Code, which was promulgated on 21 March. Influenced by Kant and by the juridical science of the Germanic area, Portalis devoted himself in particular to the work of writing the preliminary book of the Code, writing several of the most important articles of the code, notably those on succession to property and marriage, and permeating the code with the ideals of Roman law.
His main works are: *Discours préliminaire du premier projet de Code civil* (1799); *De l'usage et de l'abus de l'esprit philosophique durant le XVIIIe siècle* (1820); *Écrits et discours juridiques et politiques* (1988).

Robert Joseph Pothier (Orléans, 1699 – Orléans 1772), born and died in Orléans, France, was a French jurist, with a very high concept of the social function of law to the point of identifying it with morality.

After studying law, in 1720 he was appointed as a magistrate of the court of Orléans, like his father and his grandfather, and from 1749 he was made professor of law at the University of Orléans. He held office for half a century, paying particular attention to the texts of Justinian, with the ambition of coordinating and presenting in a logical order the maxims of Roman law. His text *Pandectae Justinianeae in novum ordinem digestae* (published between 1748 and 1752) is considered a classic of Roman law studies. In his *Traité des obligations*, which in turn contains the *Traité du contrat d'assurance*, the *Traité du contrat de change* and the *Traité des contrats aléatoires*, Pothier developed a theory of civil law founded on moral law.

Based on Christian morality, he declared himself clearly opposed to the method of interrogating of that period, which consisted of tortures of gradually increasing intensity.

His entire scientific production – also known as the Treaty of Pothier – is still of extreme interest to the modern jurist, as it was used intensively by the commission to which Napoleon entrusted the task of drafting the *Code civil*. He is considered one of the founders of modern French law.

His main works are: *Coutume d'Orléans* (1740); *Pandectae Justinianeae in novum ordinem digestae* (1748-1752); *Traité des obligations* (1761); *Traité du contrat de vente, selon les règles tant du for de la conscience que du for extérieur* (1762); *Traité des Retraits, pour servir d'Appendice au Traité du Contrat de Vente* (1762); *Traité du contrat de louage et Traité des cheptels selon les règles, tant du for de la conscience que du for extérieur* (1764-1778); *Traités sur différentes matières du droit civil* (1781); *Traité des personnes et des choses* (1825).

Friedrich Carl von Savigny (Frankfurt am Maine, 1779 – Berlin, 1861) was a jurist, philosopher, and German politician. He is considered the founder of the Historical School (with Gustav Conrad von Hugo) and a precursor of the German Pandectistic School. Von Savigny studied at Marburg University under the guidance of Anton Bauer and Philipp Friedrich Weiss. He graduated in 1800 with a thesis in Criminal Law, *De concursu delictorum formali*. The following year von Savigny started his brilliant academic career. He became famous with the publication of his first treatise *Das Recht des Besitzes* (1803), which may be considered the cornerstone for theoretical studies on law in the nineteenth century. In 1816, he led the work of recovering the so-called 'authentic Gaius' with other prominent jurists of the time such as Barthold Georg Niebuhr (discoverer of the text) and Gustav Conrad von Hugo. The Historical School influenced the doctrinal elaboration of law, to represent a code of which permeates everyday life as opposed to positivist law. The school of von Savigny was inspired by historicism and assigned to the jurist the role of interpreting and reconstructing the spirit of the people. To this end, it was argued that an itemized intervention of the legislator does not represent a specific need. According to von Savigny, it was absolutely premature to rely on the crystallization of law into codes. For this reason, he had a robust debate with Anton Friedrich Justus Thibaut, who was a strenuous advocate of the necessity of a codification. Savigny radically criticized both natural law and the Enlightenment. To him, both were founded on the wrong prejudice of being able to establish a valid legal pattern of behavior, as a rational product conforming to the mind and intellect. On the contrary, the historicism elaborated by Savigny considered that the past could not be devalued, let alone denied. It was the fundamental substrate from which to move forward. History may not be ignored as there is a clear and evident link between past, present, and future. His main works are: *Das Recht des Besitzes* (1803); *Vom Beruf unserer Zeit für Gesetzgebung und Rechtswissenschaft* (1814); *Geschichte des römischen Rechts im Mittelalter* (1815, 1831); *System des heutigen römischen Rechts* (1840-1849); *Vermischte Schriften* (1850); *Obligationenrecht* (1853).

Vittorio Scialoja (Turin, 1856 – Rome, 1933) was an Italian jurist and politician. He was one of the leading exponents of Italian legal culture, and contributed to raising its scientific level, also thanks to the dissemination and translation of methodologies and research appearing in Germany. He was Professor of Roman Law at the University of Camerino (1879), Siena (1881), Rome (1884-1931). He was national member (1918) and president (1926-1932 and July-November 1933) of the *Accademia dei Lincei*. He was also the founder and perpetual secretary of the Institute of Roman Law, promoter and president of the International Institute for the Unification of Private Law. Alongside his study and teaching of law, he had considerable commitments in public life: a senator since 1904, he was Minister of Justice (1909-1910), Minister of War Propaganda (1916-1917) and Minister of Foreign Affairs (1919-1920), Italian delegate to the Paris Peace Conference (1919) and to the League of Nations (from 1921 to 1932), and in 1927 he was appointed Minister of State. Together with Filippo Serafini, Ilario Alibrandi, Carlo Fadda, and Contardo Ferrini, he began an impressive revision of the study of Roman law which was intended to bring a general renewal of the Italian legal science. Many of his studies determined new orientations in the fields of exegesis, history, and dogmatics.
His main works are: *I problemi dello Stato italiano dopo la guerra* (1918); *Discorsi alla Società delle Nazioni* (1932); *Studi giuridici e Scritti e discorsi politici* (1932-1936).

Guido (Gad) Tedeschi (Rovigo, 1907 – Jerusalem, 1992) was an Italian jurist, naturalized Israeli. He was born in Italy and completed his legal studies at the University La Sapienza of Rome. He was a law professor at the Universities of Cagliari, Perugia and, in 1935, of Siena, practicing at the same time as a lawyer. During his activity at the University of Siena, he achieved relevant academic exposure, earning appreciation from students and colleagues. During this period, he contributed to the works for a new Italian Civil Code. He emigrated to the British Mandate of Palestine in 1939, after the promulgation of the infamous Italian racial laws of 1938. He contributed to the birth of the law faculty of the Hebrew University of Jerusalem, where he started working as a professor in 1947. He inspired and partially drafted a series of general laws, for example on contract and on unjust enrichment, which have in fact carried out a progressive codification of Israeli law. For these reasons, he is considered to be the father of civil law in the new state of Israel. In 1953, in order to continue his activity as a teacher and researcher, Tedeschi also renounced the appointment as a member

of the Supreme Court of Israel. In 1954, Tedeschi was awarded the Israel Prize for jurisprudence.
His main works are: *Negozi giuridici incompatibili* (1929); *La divisione d'ascendente* (1936); *La filiazione* (2nd edn, 1951); *Il regime patrimoniale della famiglia* (3rd edn, 1956); *Studies in Israel Legislative Problems* (1966).

Anton Friedrich Justus Thibaut (Hameln, 1772 – Heidelberg, 1840) was the son of an officer in the Hanoverian army, of French Huguenout descent and was born in Hanover.
He was a keen philosopher, jurist, and musician, who had a great influence on the philosophical doctrine in the study of the different juridical disciplines.
After studying in Hameln and Hanover, Thibaut, as a student of jurisprudence, attended the University of Göttingen. From there he went to Königsberg and studied under Immanuel Kant, and afterwards to the University of Kiel, where he was a fellow student of Niebuhr, and achieved the degree of doctor of laws. In 1798, he was appointed extraordinary Professor of Civil Law and he taught at the Universities of Kiel, Jena, and Heidelberg.
In 1802, he was called to Jena, and during the three years that he spent here Thibaut wrote, in Friedrich Schiller's summer-house, his chief work, *System des Pandektenrechts* (1803), published into many editions. This book is famous because it is the first complete modern compendium of the subject, distinguished alike by its accurate sources and by the freedom and unpedantic manner in which the subject is handled. It is, in effect, a codification of the Roman law as it was then in Germany, modified by canon law and the practice of the courts into a comprehensive system of law.
His main works are: *System des Pandektenrechts* (1803); *Über die Notwendigkeit eines allgemeinen bürgerlichen Rechts in Deutschland* (1814); *Über Reinheit der Tonkunst* (1824).

Alexis de Tocqueville (Paris, 1805 – Cannes, 1859) was a French politician and historian. He is considered one of the major exponents of nineteenth-century liberalism. Tocqueville was a classical liberal who advocated parliamentary government, but he was skeptical of the extremes of democracy. He was appointed judge in 1827 at the court of Versailles. However, after his journey to the United States in 1831, made in order to examine prisons and penitentiaries, he decided to resign from his office. The result of his tour was the successful *De la démocratie en Amérique* (1835), awarded by the *Académie française* (1836) and today considered as an early work of sociology. Its second volume was published in 1840. His work was not just a study of American democracy and society, since it represents more a reflection in general terms on the destiny of the democratic western society. He was active in the political environment too. He served as deputy of the Manche department, being elected in 1839, 1842 and 1846. After the fall of the July Monarchy (1830-1848) during the February 1848 Revolution, Tocqueville was elected as a member of the Constituent Assembly of 1848, where he became a member of the Commission charged with the drafting of the new Constitution of the Second Republic (1848-1851). He retired from political life after Louis

Napoléon Bonaparte's 2 December 1851 coup and thereafter he began to work on *The Old Regime and the Revolution*, published in 1856. The latter work was conceived as being the first volume of a bigger one, whose title should have been *La Révolution*, that was never completed.
His main works are: *Du système pénitentiaire aux Etats-Unis et de son application en France* (1833); *De la démocratie en Amérique* (1835 and 1840); *L'Ancien Régime et la Révolution* (1856).

Filippo Vassalli (Rome, 1885 – Rome 1955) was an Italian jurist, mainly known for the role played in the drafting of the 1942 Italian Civil Code. He was Professor of Roman Law at the Universities of Camerino, Perugia, Cagliari, and then of Civil Law at those of Genoa and (since 1930) Rome. From 1944 to 1955 he was Dean of the Faculty of Law at the University La Sapienza of Rome. After giving original contributions in the field of Roman law, he extended his focus of studies to private and public law, becoming a prominent scholar even in relation to these fields. During the interwar period, he participated actively in the work of various commissions on legislative studies. In particular, Vassalli is to be considered among the main authors of the Civil Code that came into force in 1942. From 1928 to 1942, indeed, he coordinated the preparatory work for the Italian Civil Code of 1942, which is still largely in force. After the birth of the Italian Republic, he remained an important and critical voice, ready not only to advocate certain legislative choices made through the codification, but also to re-propose to future generations his forward-looking aspiration to a civil law and doctrine not bounded within national state borders. He founded and directed until his death an influential *Trattato di diritto civile italiano* (1937, onwards).
His main works are: *Concetto e natura del fisco* (1908); *Miscellanea critica di diritto romano* (1913-1918); *Lezioni di diritto matrimoniale* (1932); *Osservazioni di uomini di legge in Inghilterra* (1946); *Motivi e caratteri della codificazione civile* (1947); *La decadenza dei senatori dalla carica. Una pagina di diritto costituzionale e di diritto giudiziario* (1949); *Studi giuridici* (1959).

Bernhard Windscheid (Düsseldorf, 1817 – Leipzig, 1892) was a German jurist and a member of the Pandectistic school of law. After attending the Universities of Bonn and Berlin, where he studied law, Windscheid got his doctorate on 22 December 1838. Appointed extraordinary Professor of Roman Law and French Civil Law in Bonn (1847), he spent the same year in Basel as an ordinary professor and then in Greifswald (1852), Munich (1857), Heidelberg (1871), Leipzig (1874), where he taught until his death.
He wrote an essay on the concept of a legal action, which sparked a lively debate with Theodor Muther. Windscheid drew up the modern German law concept of *Anspruch*, distinguishing it from the Roman law concept of *actio*.
He was a very authoritative member of the commission responsible for the draft of the Civil Code for the Germanic Empire. His main work, of which the others can be considered as preparations or developments, is the *Lehrbuch des Pandektenrechts* (1862-1870), which was the main source of inspiration for the German Civil Code.

Masterful for his depth of thought and vastness of doctrine, this work hugely influenced not only German research and legislation but also abroad, and especially in Italy, where it formed the basis for the reawakening of Roman research and scholarly activity. Windscheid took part in the commission in charge of the drafting of the German Civil Code between 1873 and 1883.
His main works are: *Zur Lehre des* Code Napoléon *von der Ungültigkeit der Rechtsgeschäfte* (1847); *Die Lehre des römischen Rechts von der Voraussetzung* (1850); *Die* actio *des römischen Civilrechts vom Standpunkte des heutigen Rechts* (1856); *Zwei Fragen aus der Lehre von der Verpflichtung wegen ungerechtfertigter Bereicherung* (1878).

CHAPTER 5

Law and justice

- **Natural law and positive law (or legal positivism)**
- **The dilemma of unjust law**
- **The renaissance of natural law after World War II**

The justification of law is traditionally swinging between two extreme views. According to the doctrines of natural law, the law must be abided by because it rests on the precepts of justice (*ius quia iustum*). According to positive law doctrine (or legal positivism), the law must be abided by because it is imposed by a legitimate authority and backed up with sanctions (*ius quia iussum*). A classical bone of contention between the two views is the issue of 'unjust law', whether or not it is still law and how citizens and officials should deal with it.

Natural law doctrine flourished in antiquity and was later on based on the Christian concept of natural order (*ordo naturalis*), particularly as formulated by St. Thomas Aquinas. The 'strong' version of this doctrine claims that 'unjust law is no law at all', whereas the 'weak' version contents itself with pointing out that unjust law is defective and should be amended by the legislature.

The way to legal positivism was paved by the experimental method of natural sciences, as well as by the tenets of Darwinism. Legal positivism claims that the law 'as it is' does not necessarily meet the requirements of ethics, or of justice (the law 'as it ought to be'), thus engendering a 'pure theory of law'.

Hart's theory of a 'minimum content of natural law' strikes a balance between the two extremes of the pendulum and may be described as a 'mild' or 'weak' version of legal positivism. On the one side, this view underwent a close scrutiny by Ronald Dworkin, who accused it of being incapable of accounting for the adjudication of 'hard cases', where no black-letter rule is provided for and, therefore, principles based on the shared practices of a certain community of lawyers are paramount. On the other side, and in reply

to Dworkin, Hart's theory was challenged by Joseph Raz, who advocated for a 'strong' version of legal positivism, exalting the absolute sovereignty of the state.
After World War II, a revival of natural law doctrine took place, which culminated in the 'Radbruch formula'. It holds that, where the law is unbearable for mankind in any sense, it must not be applied. This doctrine constituted the legal basis for the Nuremberg trials against the criminals of the German National Socialist Party, who committed crimes against mankind (particularly with regard to the deportation and extermination of European Jews).

1. TWO (INCOMPATIBLE?) VIEWS OF LAW

At the very outset of his masterpiece, *The Concept of Law*, **Herbert L.A. Hart** (1907-1992) openly stated that: '*Few questions concerning human society have been asked with such persistence and answered by serious thinkers in so many diverse, strange, and even paradoxical ways as the question* "What is law?"'.[1]
Innumerable as they may be, however, the answers given during the course of history to the crucial question about the concept of law may be gathered into two main groups.[2] The first group is based on the ancient sense of law embodied in the concept of **natural law**,[3] the second, on the modern ideas of **positive law (or legal positivism)**.[4]
In a nutshell, the issue of the distinction between natural law and positive law was raised by Socrate's question to Euthyphro in Plato's dialogue: 'Is the pious (τὸ ὅσιον) loved by the gods because it is pious, or it is pious because it is loved?' (**Euthyphro dilemma**).[5] To explain the meaning of his question differently, one might ask whether the law as such must be abided by because it is just *per se* (*ius quia iustum*), or because it has been imposed or enforced by some authority entitled to do so (*ius quia iussum*) (see *infra*, ch 5, para 4). In the first case, reference is made to natural law, in the second, to positive law (or legal positivism).
These two stances are opposed to each other and constitute a major alternative. However, a wide spectrum of intermediate positions, which are subtly nuanced and differentiated, extends between the two extremes

[1] Herbert LA Hart, *The Concept of Law* (3rd edn, with an introduction by Leslie Green, OUP 2012) 1.
[2] Jes Bjarup, 'Continental Perspectives on Natural Law Theory and Legal Positivism' in Martin P Golding and William A Edmundson (eds), *The Blackwell Guide to Philosophy of Law and Legal Theory* (Blackwell 2005) 287ff; Guy Haarscher, 'Some Contemporary Trends in Continental Philosophy of Law' ibid 300ff.
[3] Mark C Murphy, 'Natural Law Theory' in Martin P Golding and William A Edmundson (eds) (n 2) 15ff.
[4] Brian H Bix, 'Legal Positivism' in Martin P Golding and William A Edmundson (eds) (n 2) 29ff.
[5] Plato, *Euthyphro* (Cathal Woods and Ryan Pack trs) para 10a, 8 <https://papers.ssrn.com/sol3/papers.cfm?abstract_id=1023143&download=yes> accessed 26 December 2018.

of the pendulum. Actually, both 'natural law' and 'positive law' may be, and as a matter of fact have been, understood in many different ways, to the point that some of the numerous versions of legal positivism may be regarded as supporting or, to some extent, including a form of legal naturalism as well.

2. NATURAL LAW AND HUMAN REASON

The classic doctrine of natural law was fathered by **St. Thomas Aquinas** (1225-1274),[6] who revisited the Aristotelian ethic consistently with Christian precepts. In his *Summa Theologiae*, St. Thomas addressed a series of 'disputes' (*quaestiones*) regarding law,[7] which he defined as 'nothing else than an ordinance of reason for the common good, made by him who has care of the community, and promulgated'.[8]
That way, law was perceived and understood as the mirror of the **natural order** (*ordo naturalis*) containing all beings and things. This order was deemed to be based on reason and mirrored not only in human law but also in divine law (although the latter was largely considered not to be accessible by mankind). Nevertheless, according to this theory, the law had to be promulgated, not only because of the fact that the vague requirements of natural law demanded it be laid down at times, but also because this was necessary in order to justify compliance with the law. In fact, as men are 'rational beings', they are amenable to abiding by and applying the law solely if they have previously been aware of and understood it.[9]
During the seventeenth century, natural law was secularized and reinterpreted not only in the light of the tenets of **Cartesianism** but also of the epistemological model of natural science. Consequently, the 'geometric model' (*ordo geometricus*), which Baruch Spinoza (1632-1677) had already applied to ethics,[10] was followed with regard to law.
Moving from the Second Scholastic, or School of Salamanca,[11] which had provided a fundamental advancement in both theological and legal thinking, natural law authors contributed to the progressive establishment of the rights to freedom for all men that led to the great religious, political, and philosophical developments of the modern age.

[6] Anthony J Lisska, 'The Philosophy of Law of Thomas Aquinas' in Fred D Miller Jr and Carrie-Ann Biondi (eds), *A History of the Philosophy of Law from the Ancient Greeks to the Scholastics* (Springer 2007) 285ff.
[7] This is what commentators have commonly addressed as St. Thomas's *Treatise on Law*.
[8] St. Thomas Aquinas, *Summa Theologica* (Cosimo Classic 2007) pt I – II Q 90 Art 4, 995.
[9] Mark C Murphy, 'Natural Law Theory' in Martin P Golding and William A Edmundson (eds) (n 2) 15ff.
[10] Benedict de Spinoza, *Ethica Ordine Geometrico Demonstrata* in Id, *Opera Posthuma* (Jan Rieuwertsz 1677).
[11] Andreas Their, 'Scholastic Jurisprudence' in Jürgen Basedow, Klaus J Hopt, Reinhard Zimmermann and Andreas Stier (eds), *The Max Planck Encyclopedia of European Private Law*, vol 2 (OUP 2012) 1532.

In the doctrine of natural law, '**unfair law is no law at all**' (*lex iniusta non est lex*) and therefore it cannot be legally enforced. In this sense, justice is interpreted as the paradigm by which the law should be defined and therefore, where this criterion is not met, no law can be deemed to exist.

This version of natural law can be defined as 'strong', making justice or injustice a defining criterion of what the law is. In other words, where such criterion is not satisfied, no law is acknowledged. Robert Alexy compares this 'strong' definition of natural law to a **'weak' definition**, under which justice is only a criterion of qualification, meaning that even when such criterion is not satisfied, one can still talk about law, as long as it is held to be defective and, therefore, with a negative connotation.[12]

In the twentieth century, a 'weak' theory of natural law was strongly advocated by **John Finnis**, who states that unreasonable laws are laws only in a secondary, derivative, and incomplete sense.[13]

As an incorrect map is still a map, unjust law is still law. Though, as an incorrect map is not able to guide someone to the desired spot, so unjust law is unfit to serve its own purposes.

3. POSITIVE LAW AND POLITICAL MIGHT

Between the sixteenth and the seventeenth century, the ancient sense of nature was increasingly questioned by science and eventually dismissed. The **rise of a new rationalism**, which had been completely unknown in antiquity, inaugurated modern thinking.

Paramount to this paradigmatic change was the adoption of the **experimental method by the natural sciences**. The view of a teleological, natural order of everything (*kosmos*), including men, was swept away and replaced by the understanding of nature as dominated by chance and coincidence (*chaos*).

Instead of following an intelligent design, where each being and thing was put in its proper (ie fair) place, the natural environment was now unveiled by science as an empty space, where matter was being transformed by random clashes of atoms and life evolved by natural selection (**Darwinism**). Therefore, deprived of any inner rationality, nature could not establish any requirement of justice, which were therefore totally abandoned to the hands of men, to their forces and decisions.

Under this understanding, law does not exist as such, but only as it is enacted through the legislature and the judicature, which deliberately create it. Law is what the legislature and the judicature stipulate it shall be. According to the harsh dictum by **Thomas Hobbes** (see *supra*, ch 1, para 1), '*auctoritas, non veritas, facit legem*' ('it is the power, not the truth, that

[12] Mark C Murphy, 'Defect and Deviance in Natural Law Jurisprudence' in Matthias Klatt (ed), *Institutionalized reason. The jurisprudence of Robert Alexy* (OUP 2012) 48.

[13] John Finnis, *Natural Law and Natural Rights* (OUP 1980) 14.

dictates the law'). In one single word, law, thus, becomes 'positive' (see also *supra*, ch 3, para 1). The advent of the Westphalian paradigm created the institutional cadre that was needed by this **new understanding of law** (see *supra*, ch 3, para 2), which inevitably implied statism and, to some extent, nationalism.

> In 1854, Bernhard Windscheid (see *supra*, ch 4, para 3.1.2) notably affirmed that 'the dream of natural law had faded',[14] although he himself, after a few decades, then confessed that he still believed it to be possible.

It is undeniable that, during the nineteenth century, legal positivism has gradually overcome legal naturalism, thus becoming the mainstream discourse about law and embodying the current mentality of jurists.

In the history of ideas, critics of natural law would argue that one cannot derive from what is (ie nature) what ought to be (ie law); this has come to be known in the history of Western thought as the '**naturalistic fallacy**', which was then differently articulated in the continental European tradition and in the Anglo-American tradition.

In the continental European tradition, it was **Immanuel Kant** (1724-1804) who clearly introduced the distinction between what the law is and what the law ought to be. In particular, in his *The Metaphysics of Morals* (1797), Kant emphasized that jurists can only deal with positive law, ie **the law as it is** (*quod sit iuris*), and that their books and theories are of value only to the extent that they correspond to the laws in force. Since legal science is bound by positive law, as such it would be 'like the wooden head in Phoedrus's fable, a mere empirical doctrine of rights', which 'is a head that may be beautiful but unfortunately it has no brain'.[15]

Moving from this approach, which had already taken root, **Julius von Kirchmann** (1802-1884) highlighted the problem of the worthlessness of legal science. In distraught and borderline disgusted terms, he had to note that: 'The jurists are "worms", who live only from rotten wood; they stay apart from what is sound, nesting and weaving solely in what is sick. Insofar science draws on a contingent subject, it condemns itself to contingency; three amending words of the legislature and entire libraries become rubbish'.[16]

According to Kant, it would be up to the philosophers to deal with natural law, ie **the law as it should be** (*quod sit ius*), thus developing a doctrine of rights grounded on practical reason, ie on justice.

[14] Bernhard Windscheid, *Gesammelte Reden und Abhandlungen* (Paul Ortmann ed, Duncker & Humblot 1904) 9, 105: *'Der Traum des Naturrechts ist ausgeträumt'*.

[15] Immanuel Kant, *The Metaphysics of Moral* (first published 1797, Mary Gregor tr and ed with an Introduction by Roger Sullivan, CUP 1996) para 6:230.

[16] Julius H von Kirchmann, *Die Wertlosigkeit der Jurisprudenz als Wissenschaft* (Julius Spinger 1848): *'Die Juristen sind, Würmer', die nur vom faulen Holz leben; von dem gesunden sich abwendend, ist es nur das Kranke, in dem sie nisten und weben. Indem die Wissenschaft das Zufällige zu ihrem Gegenstand macht, wird sie selbst zur Zufälligkeit; drei berichtigende Worte des Gesetzgebers, und ganze Bibliotheken werden zu Makulatur'*.

The Kantian approach, which implies a rigid separation between the law and philosophy (and therefore also from morality and ethics), clearly constituted a cultural foundation for the work of the scholar who can be considered the true father of European legal positivism, namely **Hans Kelsen** (1881-1973). As expounded in his masterpiece, '*Pure Theory of Law*' (*Reine Rechtslehre*), the first edition of which was published in 1933, Kelsen's theory is premised upon the basic assumption that the law resides in legal rules, or norms, which are completely autonomous from religion, morality, and so on. In this sense, this theory is qualified as 'pure'.

If in the **continental European tradition** juridical positivism is strongly characterized by rationalism and by the formalism of Kantian philosophy, in the Anglo-American tradition it is instead based on the articulation of the 'is-ought problem' posed by David Hume (1711-1776).

> 'In every system of morality, which I have hitherto met with, I have always remark'd, that the author proceeds for some time in the ordinary way of reasoning, and establishes the being of a God, or makes observations concerning human affairs; when of a sudden I am surpriz'd to find, that instead of the usual copulations of propositions, *is*, and *is not*, I meet with no proposition that is not connected with an *ought*, or an *ought not*. This change is imperceptible; but is, however, of the last consequence. For as this *ought*, or *ought not*, expresses some new relation or affirmation, 'tis necessary that it shou'd be observ'd and explain'd; and at the same time that a reason should be given, for what seems altogether inconceivable, how this new relation can be a deduction from others, which are entirely different from it. But as authors do not commonly use this precaution, I shall presume to recommend it to the readers; and am persuaded, that this small attention wou'd subvert all the vulgar systems of morality, and let us see, that the distinction of vice and virtue is not founded merely on the relations of objects, nor is perceiv'd by reason'.[17]

The **Anglo-American approach** to legal positivism has been characterized from the outset by its empirical and utilitarian terms. Positive law is that which is likely to be experienced in fact and natural law is determined by the pursuit of happiness and the well-being of society.[18]

In particular, it was the radical criticism of the position of William Blackstone (see *supra*, ch 2, para 5) which paved the way for the English road to juridical positivism; Blackstone in his *Commentaries* had stated that human laws were invalid if they were contrary to the law of God, since the latter is superior in their obligation to any other law.

The critique of Blackstone's statement is clearly found in the works of **Jeremy Bentham** (1748-1832), who thus challenged tremendously the legitimacy of the anarchist's claim not to abide by any law which does not conform to their

[17] David Hume, *A Treatise of Human Nature*, vol III, pt I, sec I (first published 1739, L A Selby-Bigge ed, Clarendon Press 1896) 469ff.

[18] Bjarup (n 2) 288.

radical principles.[19] By contrast, the foundations of the *Rechtsstaat*, which are passionately defended by Bentham, allow individuals 'to censure freely' the law, but at the same time oblige them 'to obey [it] punctually'.[20]

Moving from the same assumption, **John Austin** (1790-1859) could clearly affirm that: 'a law, which actually exists, is a law, though we happen to dislike it, or though it varies from the text, by which we regulate our approbation and disapprobation' (**imperativism**).[21]

During the twentieth century, the merit of returning to the doctrine of legal positivism is certainly attributable to **Herbert L.A. Hart** (1907-1992). Hart purged the residues of subjectivism that characterized the version as rendered by Austin and reformulated it in terms that are still widely accepted in English legal culture (see *infra*, ch 6, para 1.1). The version of legal positivism given by Hart, which was enshrined in his masterpiece *The Concept of Law*, certainly owes its origins to that of Kelsen, but is also characterized by the incorporation of some elements compatible with natural law.

In particular, Hart asserts the existence of a '**minimum content of natural law**', noting that, without such content, laws 'could not forward the minimum purpose of survival which men have in associating with each other'.[22] Reference is made, by way of example, to the rules providing for the restriction 'of violence in killing or inflicting bodily harm'.[23] Furthermore, Hart asserts that moral practices can help to identify the rule of recognition that constitutes the foundation of any legal system (see *infra*, ch 6, para 2.1).[24]

For this reason, the version of legal positivism that has been proposed by Hart can be qualified as '**mild**', or '**inclusive**'. The delicate balance characterizing it carries the risk that one of its elements might be frustrated to the extent that the whole becomes subject to a unilateral fracture, in one direction or in another. This risk was fatally exposed by the works of two of Hart's most significant disciples.

On the one hand, a strong version of legal positivism, which exalts the authority of the state and rejects any form of 'compromise' between law and morality, was put forward by **Joseph Raz**.

On the other hand, **Ronald Dworkin** (1931-2013) has subjected Hart's teachings to close scrutiny from a point of view similar to that of natural law.

[19] Jeremy Bentham, 'Anarchical Fallacies; Being an examination of the Declaration of Rights issued during the French Revolution' in *The Works of Jeremy Bentham*, vol 2 (John Bowring ed, William Tait 1843) 489, 511ff.

[20] Jeremy Bentham, 'A Fragment on Government' in *The Works of Jeremy Bentham*, vol 1 (John Bowring ed, William Tait 1843) 221, 230.

[21] John Austin, *The Province of Jurisprudence Determined* (first published 1832, CUP 1994) 157.

[22] Hart (n 1) 193.

[23] ibid 194.

[24] ibid 94ff.

Hart responded to Dworkin's criticism in a long postscript to the second edition of his *The Concept of Law*. This postscript was published posthumously in 1994.[25]

In particular, Dworkin emphasized the importance of the law being examined and represented in relation to the internal viewpoint of the members of the groups who accept and use its rules, a point which had already been clearly made by Hart.[26] Dworkin thus contrasted it with the claim of legal positivism that a proper account of law might be given through a merely descriptive and not evaluative theory (like the one developed by Hart). Instead, he advocated for an **'interpretive' and partly evaluative theory of law**, which can be actively involved in putting the law in its best light and in promoting the best possible legal response to '**hard cases**', ie cases which are not yet covered by settled law and, therefore, raise contention between different theoretical camps (see *infra*, ch 6, para 3; ch 7, para 3.2).
In order to carry out this task, jurisprudence should start not (so much) from **rules**, but from **principles** (see *infra*, ch 6, para 3), representing requirements of justice or fairness, which stand as the best framework and justification for legal practices and paradigms of law, commanding lawyers' general consensus in a given legal system. According to Dworkin's view, principles are the best depiction of **a 'preinterpretive' basis**, which is constituted by settled legal practices or paradigms of law that are shared by a given community.[27]

For example, Dworkin took into consideration the case of abortion, which inevitably raises political and juridical conflicts. Any legal decision about abortion only makes sense if it takes as starting point either the principle of the fetus' fundamental right to life (where this principle commands lawyers' consensus in that community of law) or that of the mother's privacy (where this second principle commands such consensus). For example, a statute allowing abortion for two thirds of the fetus (unworkable), or a statute allowing abortion only for mothers with blue eyes (inefficient) would not make any sense.

Legal positivism fails to account for principles because of (at least) two reasons. First, principles are (the soundest) part of the law, but they might not be acknowledged by a '**basic rule**', or '**rule of recognition**' (see *infra*, ch 6, para 2.1), since they precede any such rule. They can only be identified and recognized if one starts from the assumption of the '**law as integrity**'.[28]
Since the judge has to issue **the 'right' decision**,[29] especially when solving 'hard cases' that might lead to conflicting legal solutions, she is called to perform a demanding task, which Dworkin compared to those assigned to Hercules by Greek mythology,[30] namely that of distilling the principles and the history

[25] ibid 238ff.
[26] ibid 89ff.
[27] Ronald M Dworkin, *Law's Empire* (Harvard UP 1986) 65ff.
[28] ibid 176ff.
[29] Ronald M Dworkin, *Taking Rights Seriously* (Harvard UP 1977) 81ff.
[30] Dworkin, *Taking Rights Seriously* (n 29) 105ff; Id, *Law's Empire* (n 27) 239ff.

of the interpretive community to which she belongs into her decision, thus putting the law in its best light.[31]

Thus, a strongly **holistic conception** of the legal system is affirmed, which allows the interpreter to seek the solution to practical problems not in the individual rules considered in isolation but rather in the organic culture of the legal juridical phenomenon.

The decision for each individual case is 'just' only if, and insofar as, it is taken by the judge (or more generally by the interpreter) by bringing together the matrix of principles and history that constitute the organizational fabric of a society. In this sense, jurisprudence ceases not only to be non-judgmental but also to be general (in the sense of universal), since it constitutes instead the general part of each specific legal order, thus operating as **a 'silent prologue to any decision at law'**.[32]

Second, unlike rules, principles are not characterized by an **'all-or-nothing' application**, which is required in every instance of conflict. Any conflict of rules must be solved in favor of one of them, otherwise the consistency of the legal system is affected. Conflicts of principles however leave the principles themselves untouched because, although conflicting, each principle may play a (major or minor) role in finding the best possible answer by law to a relevant case.

In his passionate reply to Dworkin's criticism, Hart claims that differences between 'rules' and 'principles' are just a matter of appreciation, holding that both may be understood as (narrower or broader) norms in the sense advocated by legal positivism.[33]

4. THE DILEMMA OF UNJUST LAW

A classic bone of contention between legal naturalism and legal positivism comes from the issue of 'unjust law' and the attitude that citizens and officials should have towards it.

It is a classical dilemma addressed in ancient Greek philosophy, above all in Sophocles' tragedy about **Antigone**.

> Creon, the new king of Thebes, ordered that, for political reasons, the corpse of Polyneices, Antigone's brother, must not be buried. In the name of the laws of nature, however, Antigone dared to oppose the political power of the head of the city (*polis*) and accomplished what Creon had forbidden.

Due in part to the attention paid by **Georg Wilhelm Friedrich Hegel** (see *supra*, ch 4, para 3.1.2) in his *Phänomenologie des Geistes* (1807),[34] Antigone

31 Dworkin, *Law's Empire* (n 27) 225ff, 255.
32 ibid 90.
33 Hart (n 1) 238ff.
34 Georg WF Hegel, *Phenomenology of Spirit* (Arnold V Miller tr, Clarendon 1977) 268ff, paras 450ff.

has become a symbol of natural law and of its possible opposition to the men's laws.

> One of the most famous Italian scholars of commercial law of the 1950s, namely **Tullio Ascarelli** (1903-1959), put Antigone on a par with Portia, the Shakespeare's feminine protagonist from *The Merchant of Venice*, who stands as a symbol of the subtleties of legal argumentation based on positive law.[35]

If one thinks the law is such insofar as it is fair (***ius quia iustum***), it can be concluded that unjust law is not law and therefore cannot (and should not) be respected and applied. The question then arises as to who can decide when the law is unjust, and based on which criteria, and what happens when a conflict arises between those who believe it to be unjust and those who disagree according to perhaps different religious or philosophical concepts.

If, on the other hand, one thinks that the law is such because it is imposed or ordered by some authority that has the power to do so (***ius quia iussum***), one comes to the conclusion that it can (and perhaps also should) be respected and applied however unfair its content may be. This raises the problem of coordinating the imposition of orders or commands that may have repugnant content from a humanitarian point of view.

It is evident that the doctrine of legal positivism can easily attract the criticism of condescending to unjust laws, since from its point of view it must be considered as formally in force irrespective of its actual content. However, it should be noted that this accusation is not founded, at least from a moral perspective.

In fact, precisely the **distinction between 'the law as it is' and 'the law as it should be'** has enabled the best expressions of legal positivism to subject the positive law to criticism based on its irrationality or on its inability to ensure the well-being and happiness of men. In this sense, Hart has claimed that it is legal positivism itself that could be able to denounce unjust law and to promote its reform. One can, for example, consider that Bentham took a clear stand against slavery, as it caused suffering to unarmed humans.[36]

Ultimately, legal positivism is even compatible with **civil disobedience**, given that the separation between law and morality might lead to the conclusion that it is morally justified to refuse to apply and to respect unjust law, despite it being the law. If Kant's assertion in general terms that a revolt against the legislator is wrong because it contradicts a categorical imperative (obey the authority who has power over you),[37] it is also true that he justified civil dis-

[35] Tullio Ascarelli, 'Antigone e Porzia' [1955] Rivista internazionale di filosofia del diritto 756ff.

[36] Jeremy Bentham, 'An Introduction to the Principles of Morals and Legislation' in *The Works of Jeremy Bentham*, vol 2 (n 19) 132.

[37] Kant (n 15) para 6:371.

obedience for the case 'when human beings command something which is evil in itself (directly opposed to the ethical law)'.[38] In such a case, he concluded, 'we may not, and ought not, obey them'.

On the other hand, it is evident that the **doctrine of natural law** can be read as the expression of rational criticism of public power, essentially founded on the assumptions of justice in society and of human freedom.

> During the twentieth century, **Leo Strauss** (1899-1973) was the main instigator of the revival of ancient natural law as a necessary balancing of the secularization of politics and the law, and therefore as a brake on their nihilistic degeneration, thus making it an essential component of political liberalism.[39]

Despite the traditional Catholic view that natural law is eternal and immutable, it cannot be questioned that its content may change throughout history. Hence, it is striking that Aristotle argued that **slavery** conforms to natural law (see *infra*, ch 11, para 1).

> 'Those who are different [from other men] as the soul from the body or man from beast – and they are in this state if their work is the use of the body, and if this is the best that can come from them – are slaves by nature. For them, it is better to be ruled in accordance with this sort of rule, if such is the case for the other things mentioned'.[40]

Moreover, the invitation to overcome the formalistic legality that is established by positive law has sometimes served to pave the way for political decision-making, thus legitimizing the role of a single man or political party as direct interpreters of the will of the people.

> During the dark times of the Weimar Republic in Germany, Carl Schmitt (1888-1895) (see *supra*, ch 1, para 1) opposed the substantial **legitimacy** (*Legitimität*), constituted by the people's plebiscitary will, to the formal **legality** (*Legalität*) of the parliament, based on mere procedural regularity and neutrality with respect to the opposed interests at stake.[41] This harsh critique of political liberalism and of the rule of law which constituted its institutional manifestation, was in

[38] Immanuel Kant, *Religion within the Boundaries of Mere Reason and other writing* (first published 1793, Allen Wood and George Di Giovanni trs and eds with an Introduction by Robert Merrihew Adams, CUP 1998) para 6:100.

[39] Leo Strauss, Natural Right and History (first published 1950, Chicago UP 1971). See Ryan Balot, 'Leo Strauss, Natural Right and History' in Jakob T Levy (ed), *The Oxford Handbook of Classics in Contemporary Political Theory* (OUP 2015) online.

[40] Aristotle, *Politics* (tr and with an Introduction, Notes, and Glossary by Carnes Lord, Chicago UP 1984) para 1254b, 16ff. See Wayne Ambler, 'Aristotle on Nature and Politics: The Case of Slavery' (1987) 15 Political Theory 390; Jill Frank, 'Citizens, Slaves, and Foreigners: Aristotle on Human Nature' (2004) 98 Am Pol Sc Rev 91; Malcolm Heath, 'Aristotle on Natural Slavery' (2008) 53 Phronesis 243; Pierre Pellegrin, 'Natural Slavery' in Marguerite Deslauriers and Pierre Destrée (eds), *The Cambridge Companion on Aristotle's Politics* (CUP 2013) 92.

[41] Carl Schmitt, *Legality and Legitimacy* (first published 1932, Jeffrey Seitzer tr and ed with an Introduction by John P McCormick, Duke UP 2004).

line with the dictatorial developments of the authoritarian regimes that were being established in Europe.

5. THE RENAISSANCE OF NATURAL LAW AFTER WORLD WAR II

After World War II, it became quite evident in continental Europe that legal positivism had proven impotent to prevent authoritarian regimes from taking over civil societies and from causing the death of millions of victims: not only did soldiers die on the battlefield but also innocent civilians, deliberately annihilated 'in accordance' with laws issued by legitimate authorities.
According to the much-cited dictum of one of the major German thinkers of the twentieth century, **Theodor Adorno** (1903-1969), 'to write poetry after Auschwitz is barbaric'.[42] In a similar way, legal science was compelled to face the 'unbearable' thought of a total defeat of law and, therefore, of the impossibility of a continuation of the previous rule of law after the Holocaust (*Sho'a*).
Shortly afterwards, the problem of unjust law was evident again in the United States with particular reference to the issue of racial discrimination against black people and became the subject matter of the passionate letter dated 16 April 1963 that **Martin Luther King Jr** wrote from Birmingham jail.

> In the letter, he wrote that: 'One has not only a legal but a moral responsibility to obey just laws. Conversely, one has a moral responsibility to disobey unjust laws. I would agree with St. Augustine that "an unjust law is no law at all"'.[43]

Thus, legal science was faced with a dramatic urgency to radically change its paradigms.
The question of the citizens' bearing towards unjust law was expressly addressed by a German philosopher of law, **Gustav Radbruch** (1878-1949), who, in 1946, made an attempt to hold legal positivism good, but nonetheless to draw a line beyond which obedience of the law had to be dismissed. These reflections led to the so-called **Radbruch formula**:

> The conflict between justice and the reliability of the law should be solved in favor of the positive law, law enacted by proper authority and power, even in cases where it is unjust in terms of content and purpose, except for cases where the discrepancy between the positive law and justice reaches a level so

[42] Theodor W Adorno, 'Cultural Critique and Society' in Id, *Prisms* (first published 1955, Samuel and Shierry Weber trs, MIT Press 1981, reprint 1983) 33: '*Nach Auschwitz ein Gedicht zu schreiben, ist barbarisch, und das frißt auch die Erkenntnis an, die ausspricht, warum es unmöglich ward, heute Gedichte zu schreiben*'.
[43] Martin Luther King, *Letter from Birmingham Jail* (August 1963) <https://web.cn.edu/kwheeler/documents/Letter_Birmingham_Jail.pdf> accessed 26 December 2018.

> unbearable that the statute has to make way for justice because it has to be considered "erroneous law". It is impossible to draw a sharper line of demarcation between cases of legal injustice and statutes that are applicable despite their erroneous content; however, another line of demarcation can be drawn with rigidity: Where justice is not even strived for, where equality, which is the core of justice, is renounced in the process of legislation, there a statute is not just "erroneous law", in fact is not of legal nature at all. That is because law, also positive law, cannot be defined otherwise as a rule, that is precisely intended to serve justice.[44]

Radbruch's formula goes so far as to argue that, if it departs from justice in an intolerable way (**test of unbearableness**, *Unerträglichkeitsthese*), positive law is no longer to be considered as law and therefore it cannot and must not be applied or complied with.[45] This result amounted to the legal basis that allowed the **Nuremberg trials** to obtain criminal convictions for those who had become complicit in the acts committed by the Nazi Party,[46] in particular as regards the so-called 'final solution' that led to the deportation and extermination of European Jews.[47] More recently, the Radbruch formula was resorted to in **German 'border guard cases'**, involving East German soldiers who were charged with homicide because they had killed fugitives or other trespassers on the border between former East Germany (*Deutsche Demokratische Republik*, DDR), or East Berlin, and West Germany (*Bundesrepublik Deutschland*).[48]

> Charged with homicide after the reunification of Germany (*Wiedervereinigung*) of 3 October 1990, these soldiers claimed to have acted according to the instructions they received from their superiors (who were similarly brought to trial). Nevertheless, they were found guilty and sentenced to prison terms by German courts of first instance, as well as by the German federal court (*Bundesgerichtshof*),[49] on the grounds of both the Universal Declaration of Human Rights and the Radbruch formula.

[44] Gustav Radbruch, *Gesetzliches Unrecht und übergesetzliches Recht* (first published 1946, Nomos 2002) 5: '*Der Konflikt zwischen der Gerechtigkeit und der Rechtssicherheit dürfte dahin zu lösen sein, daß das positive, durch Satzung und Macht gesicherte Recht auch dann den Vorrang hat, wenn es inhaltlich ungerecht und unzweckmäßig ist, es sei denn, daß der Widerspruch des positiven Gesetzes zur Gerechtigkeit ein so unerträgliches Maß erreicht, daß das Gesetz als „unrichtiges Recht" der Gerechtigkeit zu weichen hat. Es ist unmöglich, eine schärfere Linie zu ziehen zwischen den Fällen des gesetzlichen Unrechts und den trotz unrichtigen Inhalts dennoch geltenden Gesetzen; eine andere Grenzziehung aber kann mit aller Schärfe vorgenommen werden: wo Gerechtigkeit nicht einmal erstrebt wird, wo die Gleichheit, die den Kern der Gerechtigkeit ausmacht, bei der Setzung positiven Rechts bewußt verleugnet wurde, da ist das Gesetz nicht etwa nur „unrichtiges" Recht, vielmehr entbehrt es überhaupt der Rechtsnatur. Denn man kann Recht, auch positives Recht, gar nicht anders definieren als eine Ordnung und Satzung, die ihrem Sinne nach bestimmt ist, der Gerechtigkeit zu dienen*'.

[45] Brian Bix, 'Radbruch's Formula and Conceptual Analysis' (2011) 56 Am J Juris 45.

[46] BGH 29 January 1952, BGHSt 2, 234.

[47] See also Hannah Arendt, *Eichmann in Jerusalem: A Report on the Banality of Evil* (first published 1963, Viking Press).

[48] Rudolf Geiger, 'The German Border Guard Cases and International Human Rights' (1998) 9 EJIL 540.

[49] BGH NJW 1994, 2708ff; BGH NJW 1995, 2728ff.

Although an extreme example of the realm of intolerable injustice, in the above-mentioned cases a strong version of natural law is embraced, whereby natural law prevails over positive law. This solution was openly criticized by Herbert L.A. Hart in a paper of 1958,[50] which sparked a lively polemical debate with **Lon L. Fuller** (1902-1978).[51]

In continental Europe, however, the major input to a critical revision of legal positivism came from the wave of constitutional charters which were gradually adopted after World War II. In fact, these documents not only provided for protection of human rights but also for standards of substantive justice, thus incorporating typical issues of 'natural law' and making them coexist with 'positive law'.[52]

A provision contained in the German Constitutional Charter (*Grundgesetz*) adopted in 1949, is particularly remarkable in this respect, as it mentions *Gesetz* (legal provisions) and *Recht* (law) side by side, thus implying that, although normally coinciding, they are not one single concept. Particularly, article 20(3) GG provides that: 'The legislature is bound by the constitutional order, the executive and the judicature are (bound) by legal provisions and law' ('*Die Gesetzgebung ist an die verfassungsmäßige Ordnung, die vollziehende Gewalt und die Rechtsprechung sind an Gesetz und Recht gebunden*').[53] This proposition recalls the formula *iura et leges*, stemming from the Roman law.

[50] Herbert LA Hart, 'Positivism and the Separation of Law and Morals' (1958) 71 Harvard L Rev 593. See Besik Loladze, 'Herbert Hart's Critique of Radbruch's Formula' (2014) 21 Const L Rev 21.

[51] Lon L Fuller, 'Positivism and Fidelity to Law-A Reply to Professor Hart' (1958) 71 Harvard L Rev 630.

[52] Brian Bix, 'Robert Alexy, Radbruch's Formula and the Nature of Legal Theory' (2006) 37 Rechtstheorie 139.

[53] Lena Foljanty, *Recht oder Gesetz. Juristische Identität und Autorität in den Naturrechtsdebatten der Nachkriegszeit* (Mohr Siebeck 2013). See also Manfred Wolf and Jörg Neuner, *Allgemeiner Teil des Bürgerlichen Rechts* (11th edn, CH Beck 2016) § 1 para 4.

GLOSSARY

Hard cases (3): novel cases, not yet covered by settled law, raising contention among different stances. They imply some creative interpretation of law by courts.

Imperativism (3): a theory of law, according to which legal rules are conceived as commands to behave in a certain way issued by a sovereign, ie the one who has the power to inflict sanction on those who disobey. The most important example of imperativism is the theory of law elaborated by John Austin during the nineteenth century. Austin's imperativism is positivistic and statist, since it alleges that law is the set of norms established by the state.

Is-ought problem (3): theory, developed by David Hume, according to which a clear distinction should be made between the propositions 'is'/'is not', on one side, and, on the other, 'ought'/'ought not', in order to separate the descriptive propositions from the prescriptive ones and to avoid the wrongful conversion of a description into a rule.

Legal positivism (or positive law) (1): doctrine according to which law does not consist of inherent and divine rights but rather of positive norms, and emanates from the state (or another legitimate authority). As opposed to naturalistic thought, legal positivism confers a central role to the legislative creation of the rules, since, according to this theory, law depends on human normative production and enforcement.

Natural law (1): doctrine assuming that law is an intrinsic part of human nature and, therefore, exists despite its positive recognition and enforcement. Naturalists therefore believe that natural law exists independently from men's will: it only depends on the knowledge of nature and, consequently, it does not rely on human normative production. Consequently, natural law is deemed universal and independent from the state (or another legitimate authority). Starting from this classical theory, numerous and different versions of it have been developed throughout history.

Rules (3): norms governing actions, procedures, etc. They are characterized by an 'all-or-nothing' application, therefore conflicts of rules must be solved in favor of one of them.

Rule of recognition (3): according to H.L.A. Hart, one of the secondary rules, together with the rule of change and the rule of adjudication. A rule of recognition exists in every legal system and provides a test for validity of any other rule. It is a social rule, in a double sense: because it is related to social facts and because it arises out of a common acceptance by the members of the group. For this last reason, it is also an ultimate rule: its existence does not emanate from another rule but from a social practice.

BIOGRAPHIES

Theodor Wiesengrund Adorno (Frankfurt am Main, 1903 – Visp, 1969) was a German philosopher, sociologist, psychologist, and composer, known for his critical theory of society.

From a very early age, he studied philosophy and music and obtained a degree in philosophy in 1924. In 1930 he started to cooperate with the *Institut für Sozialforschung* and in 1931 he was appointed Professor of Philosophy at the University of Frankfurt. He had to flee from Germany due to racial prosecution, and settled in Geneva and Paris, where he recreated again the *Institut für Sozialforschung* with Horkheimer, and became its co-director in 1936. After teaching at the University of Oxford from 1935 to 1937, he moved to the US and pursued his musical, philosophical, and sociological studies. He returned to Germany only 12 years later, in 1950, and recreated again the *Institut für Sozialforschung*, together with Max Horkheimer, in Frankfurt.

Adorno's thoughts have mainly been influenced by Hegel, Marx, Husserl, and Freud; he was particularly interested in Marxist dialectic, but often used research methods that were more inspired by Freud's psychoanalysis (for example in his work *The Authoritarian Personality*, where authoritarianism, racism, and fascism are explained through a sociological and psychological method). Adorno also assumed a critical position towards modern science, enlightenment, natural law, and formalities of contemporary reasoning.
His main works are: *Die Dialektik der Aufklärung* (1947); *The Authoritarian Personality* (1950); *Soziologische Exkurse* (1956); *Drei Studien zu Hegel* (1963); *Negative Dialektik* (1966).

Robert Alexy (Oldenburg, 1945) is a German jurist and legal philosopher. After graduating from the University of Göttingen, where he studied law and philosophy, Alexy obtained a PhD and became professor at the University of Kiel. Here he devoted himself to research activities, which led to the development of an influential school of legal thought. Indeed, he is predominantly well-known for giving special relevance to the real essence of legal concepts, which cannot ignore the point of view of those who should actually apply them. Therefore, in Alexy's opinion, judicial experience is at the center of the philosophical definition of the law.
His main works are: *Theorie der juristischen Argumentation. Die Theorie des rationalen Diskurses als Theorie der juristischen Begründung* (1978); *Theorie der Grundrechte* (1985); *Begriff und Geltung des Rechts* (1992); *Mauerschützen* (1993); *Recht, Vernunft, Diskurs* (1995); *Elemente einer juristischen Begründungslehre* (2003).

Thomas Aquinas (Roccasecca, 1225 – Fossanova Abbey, 1274) was an Italian Dominican friar who is remembered as one of the most influential philosophers and theologians of the medieval Scholasticism. Born into a powerful aristocratic family, during his early life Aquinas studied theology in Naples, where he secretly joined the order of Dominican monks. Despite his family strongly opposing his decision and imprisoning him for years, Aquinas did not betray his values and, once released, continued his studies in Naples. Afterwards, he lectured in theology at the University of Paris, where he also obtained the doctorate in theology giving evidence, once again, of his unique and brilliant nature.
Thomas Aquinas believed in the possibility of finding a point of connection between human senses and the mind, between two fields that until that moment, and according to the Averroes' *Theory of the Double Truth*, were considered as polar opposites, ie theology and philosophy. Indeed, such a standpoint was revolutionary and turned the persuasion of the time upside down by assessing the compatibility of faith and reason as both coming from God and their natural essence as being complements of the other.
His main works are: *De ente et essentia* (1252-1256); *Scriptum super Sententiis* (1252-1256); *Quaestiones disputatae de Veritate* (1256-1259); *Summa contra Gentiles* (1261-1263); *Officium Corporis Christi* (1264); *Quaestiones disputatae De potentia Dei* (1259-1268); *De unitate intellectus contra Averroistas* (1270); *Sententia super Librum De caelo et mundo* (1272); *Summa Theologiae* (1265-1274).

Tullio Ascarelli (Rome, 1903 – Rome, 1959) was an Italian jurist and academician who had Jewish origins. He took the oath to be faithful to fascism in 1931, but fled to Brazil in 1941, due to racial laws.
His major interests ranged over private law and legal science's methodological issues. He was Professor of Commercial law at the Universities of Ferrara, Cagliari, Venice, Catania, São Paulo, Bologna, and Rome.
His main works are: *La moneta. Considerazioni di diritto privato* (1928); *Appunti di diritto commerciale* (1931); *Consorzi volontari tra imprenditori* (1937); *Panorama do direito comercial* (1947), *Ensaios e pareceres* (1952); *Studi giuridici sulla moneta* (1952); *Studi in tema di società* (1952); *Lezioni di diritto commerciale* (1955); *Iniciación al estudio del derecho mercantíl* (1964); *Problemas das sociedades anônimas e direito comparado* (1969).

John Austin (Creeting St. Mary, 1790 – Weybridge, 1859) was a British jurist and philosopher. Born in 1790, at the age of sixteen he enlisted in the army, before training in law at Inner Temple in London. From 1818, for about seven years, he worked as a lawyer without great success. In 1826 he was called to the chair of Jurisprudence at the University of London, founded on Bentham's encouragement. After two years of preparation spent in Heidelberg and Bonn, he returned to England in 1828 and began his lessons, which, however, were not appreciated by the students. In 1832 he published a summary of his lectures, entitled *The Province of Jurisprudence Determined*, but that same year he left the chair. There followed a number of other job disappointments, interspersed with a period dedicated to the work on a legal reform for the island of Malta. Austin died in 1859. His fame was largely posthumous, and was due to a new edition of his book, edited by his widow and first published in 1861, and to a further collection of lectures, also edited by his widow and first published in 1863, entitled *Lectures on Jurisprudence; or the Philosophy of Positive Law*. In Austin's conception, law must be clearly separated from morality and is a form of order: more precisely, it is the expression of a will to impose a behavior, accompanied by the threat of a sanction. The legal orders are, according to Austin, the ones that are general and come from the sovereign. These strongly positivistic theses influenced the Anglo-Saxon doctrine and made Austin the founder of 'Analytical Jurisprudence'.
His main works are: *The Province of Jurisprudence Determined* (1832); *Lectures on Jurisprudence; or the Philosophy of Positive Law* (1863).

Jeremy Bentham (London, 1748 – London, 1832) was an English philosopher, jurist, and social reformer, considered as the founder of utilitarianism. He was born to a wealthy Tory family and, from a young age, displayed a remarkable academic precociousness. Bentham was educated at Westminster, Queens College, and Oxford and completed his master's degree in 1766, at the age of eighteen. Although he was trained as a lawyer, Bentham never practiced law. Rather he became a lifelong critic of the English legal system, which he tried to codify, though his efforts never led to an actual codification. Bentham was a very harsh critic of the doctrine of natural law. Contrary to Rousseau, he did not think that the origin of the law can be explained through a mythological 'social

pact' (which he claimed as being nothing more than 'nonsense upon stilts'), but rather through the advantages that law can bring to each individual living in a society. The fundamental axiom of the philosophy of Bentham is the principle according to which 'it is the greatest happiness of the greatest number which is the measure of right or wrong'. Applying this axiom, he assessed English law and legislation and started a great advocacy upholding individual and economic freedoms, the separation of church and state, the freedom of expression, equal rights for women as well as the abolition of both slavery and the death penalty. Bentham is generally considered among the most important thinkers of the eighteenth century and his work had a major impact in the development of primary political doctrines, welfarism above all.
His main works are: *A Fragment on Government* (1776); *An Introduction to the Principles of Morals and Legislation* (1789); *Essays on Political Tactics* (1791); *Panopticon* (1791).

Ronald Myles Dworkin (Worcester, 1931 – London, 2013) was an American philosopher and jurist.
After his graduation from Harvard University, he studied in Oxford (where he knew H.L.A. Hart) and then he attended Harvard Law School. Then he worked as a law clerk and as a lawyer and he finally started to teach at Yale Law School. In 1969 he succeeded Hart in the chair of Jurisprudence at Oxford. Later he was Professor at University College London, at New York School of Law, at New York University.
In Dworkin's conception, law is not only made up of rules but also of principles, which represent the moral and legal foundations of the system.
His thesis contrasts above all with the positivism exposed by Hart in his book *The Concept of Law*. For Dworkin, law is the result of a constructive interpretation and a separation between law and morals is not possible, while it should be accepted that a 'right' answer exists for every difficult case (even if this requires a Herculean effort that remains only ideal, never being able to translate into practice).
Politically, Dworkin was inclined to ethical liberalism: according to him, in order to be fair the legal system must guarantee the fundamental rights of its members.
His main works are: *Taking Rights Seriously* (1977); *A Matter of Principle* (1985); *Law's Empire* (1986); *Sovereign Virtue: The Theory and Practice of Equality* (2000); *Justice in Robes* (2006); *Justice for Hedgehogs* (2011); *Religion Without God* (2013).

John Finnis (Adelaide, 1940) is an Australian jurist and legal philosopher, generally known as the author of *Natural Law and Natural Rights*, first published in 1980, a remarkable contribution to the philosophy of law. In 1961, Finnis obtained his LL.B. from the Adelaide University and lectured Law and Legal Philosophy at the University of Oxford until 2010. He was Associate Professor in law at the Californian Berkeley University, Professor at the University of Malawi and is now Professor at the Notre Dame Law School. Political, moral, and legal theory, as well as constitutional law, are the main areas of his interest. Indeed, Finnis was

appointed counselor to Australian governments in constitutional issues, with a special focus on the relations with the UK.
His main works are: *Natural Law and Natural Rights* (1980); *Fundamentals of Ethics* (1983); *Nuclear Deterrence, Morality, and Realism* (1987); *Natural Law* (1991); *Moral Absolutes: Tradition, Revision and Truth* (1991); *Aquinas: Moral, Political and Legal Theory* (1998); *The Collected Essays of John Finnis* (2011).

Lon Luvois Fuller (Hereford, 1902 – Munich, 1978) was an American professor of law and a legal philosopher, who criticized legal positivism and defended a secular and procedural form of natural law theory. He taught at Harvard University for several years, and his academic contributions mainly covered jurisprudence and contract law.
His debate with H.L.A. Hart in 1958, addressed more in depth in *The Morality of Law* (1964), aimed to explain the reasons for rejecting traditional religious forms of natural law theory, and to promote an idea according to which in some cases, unjust laws or legal systems are not law. In other words, Fuller did not see human law as bound to a higher, rationally knowable law that directly stems from God, but argued that legal systems themselves contained an 'internal morality' that imposed on individuals a presumptive obligation of obedience; therefore, unjust norms simply are not to be considered as norms, and individuals thus do not have to comply with them. Opposed to legal positivism, Fuller argued that there was a necessary connection between law and morality. *The Morality of Law* was criticized by Hart, who claimed that Fuller's so-called principles of legality were not bound to morality, since an individual could have a socially unacceptable inner morality as an inner morality of law, which is absurd according to Hart.
His main works are: *Law in Quest of Itself* (1940); *Basic Contract Law* (1947); *Problems of Jurisprudence* (1949); *The Morality of Law* (1964); *Legal Fictions* (1967); *Anatomy of Law* (1968).

Herbert Lionel Adolphus Hart (Harrogate, 1907 – Oxford, 1992) was one of the most prominent English legal and political philosophers of the twentieth century. After serving in the British army during World War II, he became Professor of Philosophy at the University of Oxford, where he graduated in 1929. In 1952 Hart took over the Chair of Jurisprudence, from which he retired in 1969, and was succeeded by Ronald Dworkin.
Hart is remembered for his ability to reconcile the different legal traditions and, especially, for his masterpiece, *The Concept of Law*, first published in 1961. The work, considered a remarkable contribution to legal philosophy, enshrines the positivist thought of the author, according to which law and morality are not necessarily connected, as well as rules and social habits. Furthermore, Hart detected two essential parts of the law: primary rules and secondary rules. The former, also known as 'rules of conduct', govern general social behavior, while the latter, generally named 'empowering rules', confer sovereignty and deal with three of the most disconcerting qualities of the law: its uncertainty, its inefficiency, and its static character.

His main works are: 'The Ascription of Responsibility and Rights' (1949) 49 Proceedings of the Aristotelian Society 171; *Definition and Theory in Jurisprudence* (1953); *Causation in the Law* (1959); *The Concept of Law* (1961); *Law, Liberty and Morality* (1963); *The Morality of the Criminal Law* (1964); *Punishment and Responsibility* (1968); *Essays on Bentham: Studies in jurisprudence and political theory* (1982); *Essays in Jurisprudence and Philosophy* (1983).

David Hume (Edinburgh, 1711 – Edinburgh, 1776) was a Scottish historian, economist, and one of the most celebrated empiricist philosophers of the Enlightenment era.
Hume lost his father when he was only 3 years old and was admitted to the University of Edinburgh at the young age of 12. In 1734, after recovering from a nervous breakdown, he lived in France for three years. During this period he devoted himself to his studies and the writing of his masterpiece, *A Treatise of Human Nature* (1739), in which he examined the psychological fundament of human nature by applying a scientific approach and realized that, as opposed to the previous rationalists' theories, human acts are primarily driven by passions, rather than reason. Furthermore, Hume investigated the mental process of human beings and developed the theory that knowledge is intrinsically related to experience. Therefore, individuals are able to know the only things that they can directly experience. In his words, the science of man is the 'only solid foundation for the other sciences' and it is based on experience as the foundations of a logical argument. In 1763, Hume was appointed secretary of the British embassy in Paris, where he remained until 1766. Then he moved back to Edinburgh, where he lived the rest of his life.
His main works are: *A Kind of History of My Life* (1734); *A Treatise of Human Nature: Being an Attempt to introduce the experimental Method of Reasoning into Moral Subjects* (1739-1740); *An Abstract of a Book lately Published: Entitled A Treatise of Human Nature etc.* (1740); *Essays, Moral, Political, and Literary* (1741); *An Enquiry Concerning Human Understanding* (1748); *An Enquiry Concerning the Principles of Morals* (1751); *The Natural History of Religion* (1757); *Dialogues Concerning Natural Religion* (1779).

Immanuel Kant (Königsberg, 1724 – Königsberg, 1804) was one of the leading figures in the Age of Enlightenment and a remarkable contributor to contemporary philosophy.
In 1740 he began his studies at the University of Königsberg where he attended classes of philosophy, mathematics, and physics. Despite his lectures and works, Kant only took over the Chair of Logic and Metaphysics in 1770. From that moment, he pursued an academic career and developed religious opinions based on the rationalistic doctrine that were revolutionary for the time and gave rise to real opposition by the Prussian government against his works. Indeed, Kant was subject to censorship that precluded him from lecturing and publishing.
His name is especially remembered for the development of the doctrine of transcendental idealism, by which Kant described the limits of human knowledge of things. Indeed, he outlined an essential difference between how things are

perceived and appear to humans' eyes, ie the 'phenomenon', and how they really are in themselves, ie the 'noumenon' (thing-in-itself). Kant's claim that human understanding cannot extend beyond experience is enshrined in his masterpiece, the *Critique of Pure Reason* (*Kritik der reinen Vernunft*) (1781).
His main works are: *Gedanken von der wahren Schätzung der lebendigen Kräften und Beurteilung der Beweise, deren sich Herr von Leibniz und andere Mechaniker in diese Streitsache bedient haben, nebst einigen vorhergehenden Betrachtungen, welche die Kraft der Körper überhaupt betreffen* (1749); *Allgemeine Naturgeschichte und Theorie des Himmels oder Versuch von der Verfassung und dem mechanischen Ursprunge des ganzen Weltgebäudes, nach Newtonischen Grundsätzen abgehandelt* (1755); *Meditationum quarundam de igne succinta delineatio* (1755); *Die falsche Spitzfindigkeit der vier syllogistischen Figuren erwiesen* (1762); *Der einzig mögliche Beweisgrund zu einer Demonstration des Daseins Gottes* (1763); *Versuch den Begriff der negativen Größen in die Weltweisheiten einzuführen* (1763); *Beobachtungen über das Gefühl des Schönen und Erhabenen* (1764); *Kritik der reinen Vernunft* (1781); *Prolegomena zu einer jeden künftigen Metaphysik* (1783); *Beantwortung der Frage: Was ist Aufklärung?* (1784); *Grundlegung zur Metaphysik der Sitten* (1786); *Kritik der praktischen Vernunft* (1788); *Kritik der Urteilskraft* (1790); *Die Religion innerhalb der Grenzen der bloßen Vernunft* (1793); *Die Metaphysik der Sitten* (1797).

Hans Kelsen (Prague, 1881 – Berkeley, 1973) was an Austrian-American legal philosopher and jurist.
Kelsen studied in Vienna, where he became Professor of Public Law. He contributed to the drafting of the Austrian Constitution (which to a large extent is still in force).
In 1929 he moved to Cologne, but in 1933 the rise of the Nazi regime forced him to resign. After some years spent in Geneva and in Prague, he fled from Europe and reached America, where he taught at Harvard and then at Berkeley.
Kelsen has dedicated his life to building a pure doctrine of law, that is, free from any political or ethical contamination.
According to Kelsen, law differs from sociology and represents a scheme of qualifications of facts. It consists of norms, ie primary commands whose disobedience leads to the application of secondary sanctions.
According to Kelsen, the validity of norms does not depend on their content but only on the formal approval procedure. At the basis of the system there is a fundamental norm, which is called *Grundnorm*.
Kelsen's vision is positivistic and is based on a strictly pyramidal theory of sources (*Stufenbautheorie*). Although strongly criticized, it exerted a very strong influence on the philosophy of law throughout the twentieth century.
His main works are: *Reine Rechtslehre. Einleitung in die rechtswissenschaftliche Problematik* (1934); *General Theory of Law and State* (1945); *The Law of the United Nations. A Critical Analysis of its Fundamental Problems* (1950); *Reine Rechtslehre. Einleitung in die rechtswissenschaftliche Problematik* (2nd edn, 1960); *Was ist Gerechtigkeit?* (1953); *Principles of International Law* (1952); *Allgemeine Theorie der Normen* (1979).

Julius von Kirchmann (Schafstädt, 1802 – Berlin, 1884) was a German jurist and philosopher. He began his legal studies at the University of Leipzig and completed them at the University of Halle in 1829, where he became a judge. Later, in 1846, he was appointed state's attorney in the criminal court of Berlin and became friend to the philosopher Adolf Lasson and Eduard von Hartmann, the politician Franz Wilhelm Ziegler, and the composer Richard Wagner. In 1848, he became a member of the Prussian national Assembly. Therefore, he was also politically active and was a member of the Progressive Party and, later, of the Reichstag. Kirchmann contributed to the development of a common criminal code for the North German Confederation.
In the philosophical field, Kirchmann tried to find a balanced compromise between the realism and idealism doctrines and translated parts of Aristotle, Grotius, Bacon, Hume, and Spinoza works.
His main works are: *Die Wertlosigkeit der Jurisprudenz als Wissenschaft* (1848); *Ueber Unsterblichkeit* (1865); *Aesthetik auf realistischer Grundlage* (1868).

Gustav Radbruch (Lübeck, 1878 – Heidelberg, 1949) was a German legal scholar and politician, considered one of the most influential legal philosophers of the twentieth century.
He studied law in Munich, Leipzig, Berlin, where he also passed his bar exam in 1901. His career rose rapidly: in 1902 he received his doctorate with a dissertation on the theory of adequate causation, in 1903 he qualified to teach criminal law in Heidelberg, where he was appointed Professor of Criminal and Trial Law and Legal Philosophy in 1904. Ten years later, he moved to Königsberg and assumed a professorship, then he taught in Kiel.
He was also a member of the Social Democratic Party of Germany and held a seat in the Parliament (*Reichstag*) from 1920 to 1924, covering the role of Minister of Justice, from 1921 to 1922, in the cabinet of the Chancellor Joseph Wirth, and in 1923, in the cabinet of the Chancellor Gustav Stresemann. Important laws were approved when Radbruch was in office, such as the law that gave women the right to access to the justice system, and the law for the protection of the republic.
Due to his political beliefs, after the Nazi seizure of power in 1933, Radbruch was compelled to quit his position at university, but was able to teach at University College in Oxford in 1935-1936. During the Nazi period, his academic contribution mainly focused on history, but during his professorship in England he was able to write *Der Geist des englischen Rechts* (*The Spirit of the English Law*), although it was published only in 1945.
Radbruch's legal philosophy stemmed from Neokantianism; he used to distinguish the concept of law, being a given fact meant to serve the idea of law, defined, instead, as a combination of justice, utility, and certainty. His philosophical thoughts may be – roughly – summarized into the famous 'Radbruch formula', according to which if statutory law is incompatible with the requirements of justice 'to an intolerable degree', or if statutory law was obviously designed in a way that deliberately negates 'the equality that is the core of all justice', statutory law must be disregarded by a judge in favor of the justice principle.

His main works are: *Einführung in die Rechtswissenschaft* (1910); *Paul Johann Anselm Feuerbach. Ein Juristenleben* (1934); *Der Geist des englischen Rechts* (1945); *Gesetzliches Unrecht und übergesetzliches Recht* (1946).

Joseph Raz (Mandate Palestine, 1939) is an Israeli legal and moral philosopher. He studied at the Hebrew University of Jerusalem and then he became Doctor at the University of Oxford under the supervision of H.L.A. Hart. He worked as a professor at the Hebrew University and later at the University of Oxford. Now he teaches at Columbia University Law School and King's College London.
Raz is a positivist (like Hart) and, more precisely, an exclusive positivist. His theory tends to distinguish law and morality and to explain what legitimate authority is. The central idea in Raz's theses is the distinction between first-order and second-order reasons. First-order reasons are reasons to perform an act; second-order reasons are those which argue against acting (the latter are called exclusionary reasons). According to the philosopher, rules are exclusionary reasons, or both first-order reasons and exclusionary reasons.
Raz states that law is a legitimate authority, because it provides exclusionary reasons which in turn represent a better balance of first-order reasons than those otherwise autonomously accomplished by individuals. Therefore, it is more convenient for individuals to respect the legitimate authority.
His main works are: *The Concept of a Legal System* (1970); *Practical Reason and Norms* (1975); *The Authority of Law* (1979); *The Morality of Freedom* (1986); *Ethics in the Public Domain* (2nd edn, 1995); *The Practice of Value* (2003).

Baruch Spinoza (Amsterdam, 1632 – The Hague, 1677) was a Dutch philosopher and a prominent exponent of rationalism. Born into a Jewish family who was forced to leave Portugal due to the religious intolerance of the time, he studied within the Israeli community of Amsterdam. However, in 1656 he was excommunicated, primarily because he socialized with businessmen from different cultures and religions. He then moved to The Hague where he worked as a craftsman and devoted his life to a humble existence.
Despite his lack of reputation as a philosopher while alive, Spinoza is still remembered as a brave author who strongly believed in the freedom of men. One of his most celebrated works, the *Tractatus Theologico-Politicus* (1670), in which he combined political philosophy and philosophy of religion, was strongly condemned by the Catholic Church, since it was clear evidence of the author's skepticism toward the Bible and the superstition that comes from the religion. The real essence of this work lays in the defense of the freedom of thought, which is identified as the most important right within a political organization. Such a standpoint was further confirmed with the publication, in 1677, of *Ethics*. Indeed, in this work, Spinoza starts from the concept of metaphysics that he identifies in the 'substance' and that does reconcile with God. Nevertheless, such a God is identified in nature itself, to which every individual is subject. Furthermore, Spinoza believed that the civil state is the outcome of a common agreement between individuals and developed the idea that the state itself is subject to the same rational laws that citizens must respect, in order to guarantee peace and security.

His main works are: *Principia Philosophiae Cartesianae* (1663); *Tractatus Theologico-Politicus* (1670); *Tractatus Politicus* (1677); *Tractatus de Intellectus Emendatione* (1677); *Ethica Ordine Geometrico Demonstrata* (1677).

Leo Strauss (Kirchhain, 1899 – Annapolis, 1973) was a German-American political philosopher and classicist.
He was born in Kirchhain, Germany, and was raised as an Orthodox Jew. He enrolled at the *Gymnasium Philippinum*, affiliated with the University of Marburg, and graduated in 1917, at the age of eighteen; in 1921 he received his doctorate at the University of Hamburg. Subsequently, he attended Freiburg University in order to follow Heidegger's lectures, which have strongly influenced Strauss' philosophical thoughts.
In 1932 he received the Rockefeller Fellowship and left his position at the Higher Institute for Jewish Studies in Berlin in order to move to Paris; afterwards, also due to the spread of racial issues over continental Europe, he moved to England in 1935 where he temporarily worked at the University of Cambridge. In 1937, Strauss crossed the Atlantic and settled in the United States, where he was helped by Harold Laski to obtain a lecturing position. After working at Columbia University, The New School for Social Research and Hamilton College, he became an American citizen in 1944, and in 1949, he was appointed Professor of Political Science at the University of Chicago, where he stayed until 1969.
In Strauss' view, opposed to historicism, politics and philosophy are strongly connected and based on universal principles and moral norms: in his *Natural Right and History* (1965), he criticizes Max Weber's epistemology, engages the relativism of Heidegger and discusses the evolution of natural rights by analyzing the thought of Thomas Hobbes and John Locke; he finally criticizes Jean-Jacques Rousseau and Edmund Burke. In his texts, he also refers to classical philosophers such as Plato, Socrates, Aristoteles.
His main works are: *Die Religionskritik Spinozas als Grundlage seiner Bibelwissenschaft* (1930); *Philosophie und Gesetz. Beiträge zum Verständnis Maimunis und seine Vorläufer* (1935); *Hobbes' politische Wissenschaft in ihrer Genesis* (1936); *On Tyranny* (1948); *Persecution and the Art of Writing* (1952); *Natural Right and History* (1953); *What is Political Philosophy?* (1955); *Thoughts on Machiavelli* (1958); *The City and Man* (1964); *Liberalism: Ancient and modern* (1968).

CHAPTER 6

Legal rules, principles, systems

- The structure and scope of rules
- The division of mandatory and default rules
- The legal system: gap-filler devices and settlement of antinomies
- The principles of law

According to the doctrine of normativism, law is a set of rules, each of them characterized by a conditional structure following the 'IF-THEN' approach: IF a 'state of affairs' occurs, THEN a 'sanction' is applied. A staple of legal rules is their generality and abstractness. A rule is 'general' insofar as it applies to anyone finding herself in the state of affairs envisaged by the IF-clause. A rule is 'abstract' insofar as it is applicable to whatever event or conduct matches the state of affairs envisaged by the IF-clause. Exceptional rules may contravene the principle of equal treatment.

Most private law rules may be set aside via an agreement between their addressees (default rules), whereas most public law rules apply irrespective of any agreement between their addressees (mandatory rules).

Primary rules are aimed at sanctioning some human actions and steering others. A legal system also requires secondary rules, which provide dynamism, certainty, and efficiency of the law.

A legal system is dynamic thanks to the sources of law, which over time create new rules, or change or repeal those already existing.

A legal system is certain and efficient thanks to gap-filler devices (analogy, judge-made law) and the criteria for solving antinomies.

Principles can be defined as guidelines that express and guarantee the overall rationality of a legal system. They carry out an interpretative function, a supplementary function and, to a minor extent, a corrective function as well.

1. THE LEGAL RULES

1.1. The conditional structure of rules

According to the tenets of legal positivism (see *supra*, ch 3, para 1; ch 5, paras 1 and 3), law consists essentially of rules. This description of law, which is known as **normativism**, can be qualified as idealistic, in that it conceives of law as an objectively existing reality that can be ascertained in itself, beyond practical cases or concrete judicial decisions.

> This view of law has been radically challenged by the **Scandinavian legal realism**.[1]
> According to Alf Ross (1899-1979), law must be conceived as a set of beliefs, psychological suggestions, and social conditioning, which leads the judge to make one decision instead of another.
> In this way, law is substantially reduced to a fact and its application consists merely of its imposition by the judge (or by another officer), as claimed by Karl Olivecrona (1897-1980).

During the first historical stage of normativism, legal rules were conceived as commands issued by a sovereign and backed up by threats of a harm, to be inflicted upon those who disobey (**imperativism**) (see *supra*, ch 5, paras 3-4). This concept of law was theoretically framed by **John L. Austin** (1911-1960) (see *supra*, ch 5, para 3).[2]
During the twentieth century, however, the imperativist conception of law advocated by Austin was severely criticized,[3] not least because it was argued to still contain several traces of subjectivism and because it did not adequately explain the distinction between a norm and an arbitrary imposition made through a threat. Furthermore, it implied that sovereign power was exempted from abiding by law (*legibus solutus*), and did not explain how, in the modern ***Rechtsstaat*** (see *supra*, ch 1, para 2), law is also binding for the legitimate authority that issued it (see *supra*, ch 5, paras 3-4).
In one of the most famous legal works of the twentieth century, named *Reine Rechtslehre*,[4] **Hans Kelsen** (1881-1973) (see *supra*, ch 5, para 3) stated that, contrary to what a layman might sense, a norm may not properly be embedded in a commandment such as: 'Thou shalt not kill'. This kind of absolute imperative may be appropriate for religion or morality but not for law.
The reason is that law conveys a coercive social order, whereas religion binds only those who believe in it and morality only those who accept it. According to Kelsen's doctrine, therefore, a norm is such not because it stipulates a

[1] Jes Bjarup, *Skandinavischer Realismus: Hägerstrom, Lundstedt, Olivecrona, Ross* (Alber 1978).
[2] John Austin, *The Province of Jurisprudence Determined* (John Murray 1832) 5ff.
[3] Herbert LA Hart, *The Concept of Law* (2nd edn, Clarendon Press, 1994) 18ff.
[4] Hans Kelsen, *Pure Theory of Law* (Max Knight tr, 2nd edn, University of California Press 1967).

command, but because it stipulates the **(secondary) sanction** to be applied in case the (primary) command is disobeyed by someone.

> This is a theory of law that the author depicts as **pure** (*reine*), because it makes possible to keep law clearly severed from other prescriptive social phenomena (first of all from morality) (see *supra*, ch 5, paras 3-4).
> Moral rules have in fact the structure of categorical imperatives (according to Kant's model), which are devoid of any (legal) sanction.

A legal rule is therefore to be brought back to the following logical scheme: IF a 'state of affairs' occurs (ie an act is carried out, an event takes place, and so on), THEN someone will be burdened with a 'sanction' (ie conviction, fine, and so on). Adopting linguistic terminology, a legal rule is therefore shaped as a hypothetical independent period, the protasis of which (ie the IF-clause) consists of a **state of affairs** and the apodosis of which (ie the THEN-clause) consists of a sanction.
Since this conception of normativism is based on the logical structure of legal rules and on their definition in linguistic terms, it can be termed as 'formalistic'. 'State of affairs' means any occurrence of the same sort, consisting either in a natural event or in a human act (see *infra*, ch 9, para 1). By '**sanction**', reference is made to a punishment meted out by an official acting within her authority, be it a judge, a policeman, a major, etc.

> The term (and the concept of) 'sanction', utilized by Kelsen, shows that his theory is mostly moulded on public law, rather than on private law (see also *infra*, ch 7, para 1). More generally, it would be preferable to talk of '**legal effects**', ie a change in someone's rights or duties (see also *infra*, ch 10).

The 'sanction' is triggered by the 'state of affairs' envisaged by the norm. To put it differently, it is the norm that attaches a (negative) reaction of the state to a possible event or conduct.

> IF a contract is breached by one of the parties that have entered into it, THEN that party will be deprived of her rights towards the other. IF a good is stolen, THEN the thief will be convicted or condemned to give it back and to compensate the owner for the damages suffered.

In order to refer to such an IF-clause, German jurisprudence of the nineteenth century coined a specific term, deriving it from the expression of *facti species*, which frequently appears in the sources of Roman law. In Latin, the expression *facti species* meant 'appearance of the fact', 'phenomenon', or 'hypothetical fact', or 'model fact situation'. It was rendered in German as *Tatbestand*, a word that has a similar meaning, ie the state (*Bestand*) of the fact (*Tat*). From German, the term was introduced into Italian, where it was easily transposed as *fattispecie*, drawing this term back from the Latin.

By contrast, common lawyers do not base their legal reasoning on 'model fact situations', so that their terminology is here at a loss. Nevertheless, the term 'state of affairs' can be adopted in this context, also drawing on Anglo-American studies in jurisprudence developed since the mid-nineteenth century on the topic of rights (see *infra*, ch 10).

A norm regards a state of affairs by describing a natural event that might take place (an earthquake, someone's death, etc.) or by human conduct which someone might carry out (ie entering into a contract, committing a tort, etc.).

1.2. The scope of rules: their generality and abstractness

Legal rules are characterized by two elements, ie generality and abstractness, which may eventually be brought back to a common root. Although not necessarily coincident, in fact, both may be held to be underpinned by the same precept, ie that of equal treatment ('treating like cases alike').

A rule is **general** insofar as it applies to anybody who finds herself in the state of affairs envisaged by the IF-clause contained therein.

One could take the following example: IF a good is stolen, THEN the thief shall be convicted or condemned to give it back and to compensate the owner for the damages suffered.

This norm does not provide for the fact that a good is stolen by a given Titius or Caia but for the fact that a good is stolen by anybody. It is therefore applicable to anybody stealing a good, provided that her conduct matches the state of affairs envisaged by the IF-clause.

In other words, a norm is a rule that is addressed not to specific subjects identified as such but rather to a class of subjects, ie all who happen to find themselves in the state of affairs envisaged by the IF-clause.

Therefore, a **norm *ad personam***, ie identifying one or more specific subjects as addressees, is exceptional and likely to contravene the principle of equal treatment, which generally commands a constitutional status. At any rate, this kind of norms risks being unreasonable.

Conversely, a rule is **abstract** insofar as it applies to whatever event or conduct matches with the state of affairs envisaged by the relevant IF-clause contained therein.

The above-mentioned norm, for example, does not provide for the fact that this or that specific good is stolen but for the fact that any good is stolen.

In other words, a state of affairs provided for by a norm encompasses any possible events or actions of the kind. Any given case at issue which meets that model fact situation (for example, each theft of a book which historically takes place as a concrete fact) must be distinguished from the abstract state of affairs envisaged by a norm.

Of course, the scope of a norm might be broader or narrower without affecting its essential abstractness.

IF a book is stolen, THEN the thief shall be convicted or condemned to give it back and to compensate the owner for the damages suffered.
The state of affairs envisaged by this potential norm is not the theft of any good but solely of a book. Nonetheless, law takes into consideration not the theft of this or that book but of any book, so that the norm is no less abstract.

There are, however, **exceptional norms**, which by definition cannot be applied analogically (see *infra*, ch 6, para 2.2), as was already pointed out about norms *ad personam*.

1.3. Mandatory and default rules

Since public law pertains to the state's authoritative power, most of it consists of **mandatory rules**, which may not be set aside via an agreement between their addressees. In fact, it is not private autonomy that is paramount for public law but rather the supremacy of public interest over the interests of the individual (see *infra*, ch 7, para 1).

For example (most) rules belonging to criminal law are notably mandatory, since they punish each crime by stipulating a sanction which is not subject to negotiation with the culprit. Also mandatory are (most of) those administrative rules that regulate the exercise of authoritative and discretionary powers by the state.

Nonetheless, it shall be noted that both the administrative and the judiciary process have been more recently redesigned in order to leave room for the possibility of certain modules of negotiation with the private parties concerned.

For example, codes of criminal procedure may authorize plea bargaining between the prosecutor and the defendant. Another example: administrative authorizations are sometimes given on the basis of a binding agreement between the administration and the applicant(s).

Conversely, nearly the entirety of private law consists of **default rules**, which may be set aside via agreement between their addressees. With particular reference to contract law, a major role is played by default rules that supplement agreements concluded by the parties. In this sense, they amount to rules of thumb.
This does not mean that private law does not provide for mandatory norms, but that they constitute a small minority (see *infra*, ch 7, para 1).
For example, under Italian law, a loan cannot be subject to interest rates above a certain threshold, since usurious interests are forbidden by article 1805(2) cc. It follows that a clause setting an interest rate above said threshold is void and the loan thus becomes free of charge (see *infra*, ch 9, para 5).

2. THE LEGAL SYSTEMS

2.1. The sources of law

Herbert L.A. Hart (1907-1992) (see *supra*, ch 5, para 3) pointed out that a legal system is comprised not only of **'primary' rules** but also of **'secondary' rules**, which aim at identifying, changing, and enforcing the primary ones.
The 'basic norm', or 'rule of recognition', is typically a secondary rule, which aims to identify primary rules, thus ensuring the **certainty of a legal system**. Almost equally important are two types of secondary rules. Firstly, those that regulate the possible change of primary rules, thus ensuring the **dynamism of a legal system**, and, secondly, those that deal with the enforcement of primary rules, thus ensuring the **efficiency of a legal system**.
In other words, a legal system is an order of norms which proves certain, dynamic, and efficient.
In particular, the secondary rules that govern possible changes of the primary rules are commonly known as **sources of law** and play a major role in the historical development of any legal order. They stipulate what facts or acts are capable of creating new rules and of changing or repealing pre-existing rules. Each legal system is based on its own sources of law, which are not effective as such in any other legal system.
Just as a door 'is' closed does not imply that it 'ought to' be closed,[5] the fact that a certain conduct is regularly carried out by an overwhelming majority of people does not imply that it corresponds to a legally binding rule (see *supra*, ch 5, para 3).[6]
Consequently, the very foundation of legal positivism requires acknowledgement of some kind to distinguish legally binding rules (ie the norms) from other rules that, however rooted in societal mentality and intercourse, are not legally binding.
According to Kelsen's theory, this test could rest solely on the origin of a norm, ie the process that political institutions must go through to adopt it. On the contrary, the content of a norm, particularly the degree of inner justice which it entails, would fail as a criterion of its **validity**, ie its existence as a legally binding rule.
By way of example, a text is legally binding as a judgment if, and only if, it has been rendered by a court pursuant to the civil procedure norms of a state (the plaintiff must be summoned in a certain way, the judge must be competent for that kind of dispute, etc.). In turn, civil procedure norms are legally binding if, and only if, they have been enacted by parliament pursuant

[5] On the distinction between law as it is and law as it ought to be, see Herbert LA Hart, 'Positivism and the Separation of Law and Morals' (1958) 71 Harvard L Rev 593. A famous debate on the point was ignited between Hart and Fuller; for an account of it, see Lon L Fuller, 'Positivism and Fidelity to Law: A Reply to Professor Hart' (1958) 71 Harvard L Rev 630 (see *supra*, ch 5, para 5).
[6] Kelsen (n 4) 10ff.

to the constitutional norms that establish and govern the process of enactment of statutes (for example, majority rule, promulgation by the president of the state, publication in an official gazette, etc.).
Therefore, each norm owes its validity to another norm, which governs and regulates the procedure through which the former is enacted.
In other words, norms are stacked in a hierarchical order (*Stufenbau*), where each of them depends on the ones positioned above it. A norm is valid if, and only if, it pertains to such a hierarchical order, termed as **legal order** (or **legal system**).

> Significantly, however, Kelsen himself admitted that: 'A norm that is not obeyed by anybody anywhere, in other words, a norm that is not effective at least to some degree, is not regarded as a valid norm. A minimum of effectiveness is a condition of validity'.[7]

The most difficult aspect of such a theory of law is identifying the norm sitting at the top of the pyramid, ie the starting point from which this line of norms hangs and begins to descend downwards. Kelsen calls such a norm a '**basic norm**' (*Grundnorm*). Its peculiarity is that it is not essentially positive, but that, it embodies a general acknowledgement of the binding force of rules by the members of a society. The Kantian foundation of Kelsen's theory is evident, since the *Grundnorm* is essentially a categorical imperative, which requires one 'obey the authority who has power on you' (see also *supra*, ch 5, para 3).
In the version of normativism proposed by Hart, the **rule of recognition** is conceived as 'a form of judicial customary rule existing only if it is accepted and practiced in the law-identifying and law-applying operations of the courts'.[8] It consists therefore of a set of social practices, which enjoy common acceptance by members of a group (**conventionalism**).

> In his postscript replying to **Dworkin's criticism** (see *supra*, ch 5, para 3, and *infra*, ch 6, para 3), Hart introduced a major amendment to this merely conventional version of legal positivism. In fact, he admitted and even emphasized that, besides its pedigree, the conventional rule of recognition for a norm may well also incorporate principles of justice or substantive moral values.[9] Therefore, Hart's theory of law has been defined as 'soft positivism' (and Hart himself ultimately accepted this definition),[10] or 'inclusive'.[11]
> Hart's correction was decisively rejected by **Joseph Raz** (see *supra*, ch 5, para 3), who operated from the conception of authority as a service to its subjects.[12] It implies that the addressees of the rule must be able to apply it

[7] Kelsen (n 4) 11.
[8] Hart, *The Concept of Law* (n 3) 256ff.
[9] ibid 72, and, emphasizing the point as a reply to Dworkin's criticism, 247, 250, 258. See also Hart, 'Positivism and the Separation of Law and Morals' (n 5).
[10] Hart, *The Concept of Law* (n 3) 250.
[11] Kenneth E Himma, 'Inclusive Legal Positivism' in Jules L Coleman, Kenneth E Himma and Scott J Shapiro, *The Oxford Handbook of Jurisprudence and Philosophy of Law* (OUP 2004) 125ff.
[12] Joseph Raz, *Practical Reasons and Norms* (2nd edn, Princeton Press 1990) 21.

without the need to renew those fundamental evaluations, something that rests on the authority to do in their place.[13] It follows that any moral assessment cannot, and should not, be relevant for identifying the rule applicable to a case, since it is a matter of competence for the authority and not for the legal interpreter.[14]

According to a traditional claim of positivism, a legal system is both complete and consistent. It is **complete**, in the sense that no gaps (lacunae) can be encountered in its primary rules, since they regulate any relevant case. It is **consistent**, in the sense that no contradictions can be encountered in its primary rules, since each relevant case leads to just a single legal outcome.
It is, however, undeniable that, if taken statically and synchronically into consideration, any legal system is incomplete (ie with gaps existing in its primary rules) and inconsistent (ie with contradictions existing in its primary rules). The point is, however, that every legal system comprises some secondary rules that are designed to fill in such gaps (see *infra*, ch 6, para 2.2) and others that are designed to solve such contradictions (see *infra* ch 6, para 2.3). A legal system is therefore only both complete and consistent from a dynamic and diachronic viewpoint.

2.2. The gaps (lacunae) and the devices to fill them

Gaps in primary norms (lacunae) may be filled by secondary rules authorizing judges either to create new rules of law or to extend the scope of the ones already in place.
According to a well-established view, the first option has been adopted by Anglo-American jurisdictions, given that the declaration theory of common law has been set aside over time as unsound and fictitious (see *supra*, ch 4, para 4; *infra*, ch 7, para 3.2). Hart's claim that gaps in law are filled by **judges' discretion** has proved particularly influential in this line of reasoning. Under this argument, the judges exercise a genuine law-making power, though interstitial.[15]

This assumption has been sharply contended by **Ronald Dworkin** (1931-2013) (see *supra*, ch 5, para 3), who considers it unrealistic (because lawyers' and judges' discourses deal with the application of law, not judiciary law-making), undemocratic (because judges, or at least some of them, are not elected by the people and are not held accountable towards them), and unjust (because judge-made law would apply retrospectively to a case existing prior to such law being made). Dworkin's point is that no gaps in law really exist, but that there are '**hard cases**', ie cases which cannot be adjudicated on the basis of 'explicit' law. Judges should decide them by resorting to 'implicit' law, ie to principles,

[13] Joseph Raz, *Ethics in the Public Domain* (Clarendon Press 1994) 219.
[14] ibid 199ff. See also Andrei Marmor, 'Exclusive Legal Positivism' in Coleman, Himma and Shapiro (eds) (n 11) 104ff.
[15] Hart, *The Concept of Law* (n 3) 259, 272.

which would constitute the **'preinterpretive' basis of adjudication** (see *supra*, ch 5, para 3; *infra*, ch 6, para 3).[16]

By contrast, civil law jurisdictions have adopted normative devices to extend already existing law to unregulated cases. They are gathered under the institution of **analogy**.[17]
At the first level of analogy, gaps are to be filled by applying legal rules that govern similar cases or similar matters (***analogia legis***). Criminal law and exceptional norms are, however, not to be applied analogically. As a matter of fact, the exceptional character of a norm implies that it provides for cases not similar to any other or that it contravenes the general principles of law (see *supra*, ch 6, para 1.2). Therefore, such a norm does not even fulfill the very basic requirement of analogy.
If no rules that govern similar cases or similar matters are found, general principles of law (see *infra*, ch 6, para 3) are applied directly to the unregulated case (***analogia iuris***).[18]

The first to resort to this approach was the **Austrian Civil Code** (*Allgemeines Bürgerliches Gesetzbuch*, ABGB) of 1811, which in § 7 explicitly mentions natural law principles as the final criterion to decide a case not taken into account by specific legal provisions ('If a case cannot be decided on the basis either of the words or of the natural sense of a statute, consideration must be given to similar cases, which are decided precisely in the statutes, and to the grounds of other related statutes. If the case appears still doubtful, it must be decided according to natural principles of law with regard to carefully collected and meticulously considered circumstances').[19]
That model was followed by the Civil Code of the States of His Majesty the King of Sardinia of 1838 (article 15 of the Introductory Chapter), then by the first **Italian Civil Code** of 1865 (article 3 of the Preliminary Provisions) and finally by the current Italian Civil Code of 1942, where article 12(2) of the Preliminary Provisions stipulates that: 'If a dispute cannot be decided by a specific provision, the provisions governing similar cases or similar matters are to be taken into account; if the case still remains doubtful, it is decided according to the general principles of the legal system of the State'.[20] In a

[16] Ronald Dworkin, *Taking Rights Seriously* (1st edn, Harvard UP 1977) 81ff. Hart's replied in *The Concept of Law* (n 3) 272ff.
[17] Analogy, however, is not unknown to common law courts as well. For a classical instance, see the judgment passed by the Court of Appeal of the State of New York in *Adams v New Jersey Steamboat Co* (1896) 151 NY 163.
[18] Angelo Falzea, 'Relazione introduttiva' in *Convegno sul tema: I principi generali del diritto (Roma, 27-29 maggio 1991)* (Accademia Nazionale dei Lincei 1992) 11, 18.
[19] '*Läßt sich ein Rechtsfall weder aus den Worten, noch aus dem natürlichen Sinne eines Gesetzes entscheiden, so muß auf ähnliche, in den Gesetzen bestimmt entschiedene Fälle, und auf die Gründe anderer damit verwandten Gesetze Rücksicht genommen werden. Bleibt der Rechtsfall noch zweifelhaft; so muß solcher mit Hinsicht auf die sorgfältig gesammelten und reiflich erwogenen Umstände nach den natürlichen Rechtsgrundsätzen entschieden werden*'. See Franz Bydlinski and Peter Bydlinski, *Grundzüge der juristischen Methodenlehre* (3nd edn, Facultas 2018) 93ff.
[20] '*Se una controversia non può essere decisa con una precisa disposizione, si ha riguardo alle disposizioni che regolano casi simili o materie analoghe; se il caso rimane ancora dubbio, si*

much more explicit manner, the **Spanish Civil Code** (*Codigo civil español*) of 1889 regulated the matter in article 1 of its Introductory Chapter (*Título preliminar*), which did not hesitate to include general principles among the sources of Spanish law (paragraph 1: 'The sources of the Spanish legal system are the statutes, custom and the general principles of law'),[21] although it immediately adds that they are applicable only when there is no specific rule in a statute and no appropriate custom (paragraph 4: 'General principles of law may be applied in the absence of statutory law or custom, without prejudice to the informing nature of the legal system').[22]

Some national jurisdictions resort to a combination of analogy and discretion by judges.

A prominent example is article 1(2-3) of the **Swiss Civil Code** (*Zivilgesetzbuch*), which stipulates: 'In the absence of a provision, the court shall decide in accordance with customary law and, in the absence of customary law, in accordance with the rule that it would make as legislator'.[23]

2.3. The conflicts of norms (antinomies) and the criteria to settle them

Inconsistencies in primary norms, traditionally termed **antinomies**, may be solved by secondary rules authorizing judges to apply only one of the colliding primary norms, which is to be identified on the basis of criteria given by law.
The first possible criterion stipulates that, if a norm, which is subordinated according to the hierarchical order of a legal system (see *supra*, ch 6, para 2.1), collides with another, which is superordinate, the latter prevails over the former (*lex superior derogat inferiori*) (**hierarchical criterion**).
In case the first criterion fails, because both colliding norms are set at the same level of the hierarchical order, then a second possible criterion, based on the content of the norm, can come into play. This criterion stipulates that, if a norm, which has a broader scope, collides with another, which has a narrower scope, the latter prevails over the former (**content-based criterion**).
If the second criterion also fails, due to the fact that both colliding norms are set at the same level of the hierarchical order and their scope has the same width, then a third possible criterion is deployed. This criterion is based on

decide secondo i principi generali dell'ordinamento giuridico dello Stato'. See Rodolfo Sacco, 'I principi generali nei sistemi giuridici europei' in *Convegno* (n 18) 163; Gino Gorla, 'I principi generali comuni alle nazioni civili e l'art. 12 delle disposizioni preliminari del Codice civile italiano del 1942' in *Convegno* (n 18) 177.

21 '*Las fuentes del ordenamiento jurídico español son la ley, la costumbre y los principios generales del derecho*'.

22 '*Los principios generales del derecho se aplicarán en defecto de ley o costumbre, sin perjuicio de su carácter informador del ordenamiento jurídico*'.

23 '*2. Kann dem Gesetz keine Vorschrift entnommen werden, so soll das Gericht nach Gewohnheitsrecht und, wo auch ein solches fehlt, nach der Regel entscheiden, die es als Gesetzgeber aufstellen würde. 3. Es folgt dabei bewährter Lehre und Überlieferung*'.

time and stipulates that, if a norm which was enacted earlier collides with another, which has been enacted later, the latter prevails over the former (**time-based criterion**).

To some extent, the content-based criterion and the time-based criterion are to be coordinated.

If a norm enacted later has a scope that is narrower than that of another norm enacted earlier, the former is seen as a special norm that derogates from the latter, which nonetheless is still in force as a general norm (*lex posterior specialis derogat priori generali*). In other words, the enactment of a special norm shrinks the scope of a pre-existing general norm.

If a norm enacted later has the same or a large scope than that of another norm enacted earlier, by contrast, the latter is repealed by the former.

3. THE PRINCIPLES OF LAW

Developments in general theory of law have shown that, in order to exhaustively describe a legal system, rules as a concept must be accompanied by **principles**, which are the guidelines that express and guarantee rationality in law. According to the conception outlined by **Josef Esser** (1910-1999), principles do not provide for an instant fact and therefore, unlike norms, they do not directly apply to practical cases.[24] Nevertheless, it is now generally recognized that principles have an actual preceptive content.[25]

On that basis, it is still debated whether principles are a particular species of rules or whether they differ radically from the latter and constitute a category of their own. More generally, it is disputed whether the recognition of principles can take place within the conceptual framework of legal positivism, even if broadened and mitigated, or whether that recognition must be overcome (see *supra*, ch 5, para 3; ch 6, para 2.1).[26]

From a functional point of view, principles are the most reliable tools not only to systematically reconstruct but also to critically examine the reasons justifying the remaining legal norms, which are usually characterized by a lower degree of generality. In particular, principles are relevant in the interpretation of statutory law, since they represent a systematic basis and substantial explanation of the legal rules set out by the legislator (**interpretative function**).[27] At least under certain conditions, legal principles

[24] In this regard, a fundamental contribution was given by Josef Esser, *Grundsatz und Norm in der richterlichen Fortbildung des Privatrechts* (Mohr Siebeck 1956) 132ff, followed in particular by Claus-Wilhelm Canaris, *Systemdenken und Systembegriff in der Jurisprudenz. Entwickelt am Beispiel des deutschen Privatrechts* (2nd edn, Duncker & Humblot 1987) 57.

[25] See in this sense Mario Libertini, 'Clausole generali, norme di principio, norme a contenuto indeterminato. Una proposta di distinzione' [2011] Riv crit dir priv 345, 367.

[26] See Gustavo Zagrebelsky, 'Ronald Dworkin's Principle Based Constitutionalism: An Italian Point of View' (2003) 4 IJCL 621, 621-25.

[27] Among others, see Joseph Raz, 'Legal Principles and the Limits of Law' (1972) 81 Yale LJ 823, 839f.

are also utilized by judges and other officials to fill gaps in a legal system (**supplementary function**) (see *supra*, ch 6, para 2.2).[28] Finally, when they are mandatory, principles can even call into question the validity or effectiveness of another legal norm; or, at least, limit its application in a restrictive manner (**corrective function**).[29]

In civil law jurisdictions, one of the most characteristic principles of private law is undoubtedly the one of **good faith**, especially in the domain of contracts and obligations (see *supra*, ch 4, para 1; *infra*, ch 8, para 1.2.1).

According to the definition given in article I.-103 (*Good faith and fair dealing*) of the **Draft Common Frame of Reference** (see *infra*, ch 8, para 3), '(1) The expression "good faith and fair dealing" refers to a standard of conduct characterized by honesty, openness and consideration for the interests of the other party to the transaction or relationship in question. (2) It is, in particular, contrary to good faith and fair dealing for a party to act inconsistently with that party's prior statements or conduct when the other party has reasonably relied on them to that other party's detriment'.

According to the traditional conception, the principle of good faith, which is historically derived from the *iudicia bonae fidei* of Roman law, is alien to common law jurisdictions.

In the US, however, paragraph 1-304 of the **Uniform Commercial Code** (see *supra*, ch 3, para 5) states that '[e]very contract and duty within the Uniform Commercial Code imposes an obligation of good faith in its performance and enforcement'. According to paragraph 205 of the Restatement (Second) of Contracts (*Duty of Good Faith and Fair Dealing*), furthermore, '[e]very contract imposes upon each party a duty of good faith and fair dealing in its performance and its enforcement'.

In **England**, a particular concretization of the principle of good faith has traditionally been recognized in relation to insurance contracts, qualified by common law as *uberrimae fidei*, which literally means 'of utmost good faith'.[30] More recently, a more general openness to the application of such principles to long-term relational contracts has been observed, such as joint venture agreements, franchise agreements, and long-term distributorship agreements.[31]

[28] ibid 840ff. With regard to European law, see Takis Tridimas, *The General Principles of EC Law* (2nd edn, OUP 2006) 1. The link between the lack of completeness of a legal system and the application of its general principles is already clear in nineteenth century civil codes, which endeavor to ascribe it to the mechanism of analogy.

[29] Among others, see Raz, 'Legal Principles' (n 27) 840. In the well-known American case *Riggs v Palmer* [1889] 115 NY 506, the principle according to which no man should take profit from its unlawful conduct led the Court of Appeals of New York to exclude the application of a legal rule which in the abstract was relevant to the case, but in practice would have given rise to a manifestly unfair decision. In *Klemer v Guy* CA 986/93 [1996] 50(l) IsrSC 185 the Supreme Court of Israel used the principle of good faith to affirm the validity of a real estate sale contract which had been stipulated in oral form, although statutory law considered contracts concluded without a written form null and void.

[30] In the leading case *Carter v Boehm* (1766) 3 Burr 1905, 97 ER 1162, Lord Mansfield stated that in insurance contracts there are particular duties of disclosure, derived from the good faith.

[31] *Yam Seng PTE Ltd v International Trade Corp Ltd* [2013] EWHC 111 (QB), [2013] 1 All ER (Comm) 1321.

This trend seems to be supported by subsequent case law concerning other long-term contracts.[32] Nevertheless, there is no shortage of rulings to the contrary,[33] which find that the principle of good faith cannot be generally applied to all commercial contracts.[34]

Although principles can be directly formulated by **constitutional norms** (see *infra*, ch 7, paras 3.1 and 3.2), there is no exhaustive catalogue in the legislation that encapsulates and enumerates them.

During the preparatory work for the Italian Civil Code of 1942, Mussolini's government tried to shape private law to the political dictates of fascism, advocating in favor of listing general principles of law in the preliminary chapter (and interpreting them as a salient expression of the predominant ideology).
In the Pisa Congress of 1940, entitled 'I principi generali dell'ordinamento giuridico fascista',[35] the young Francesco Santoro-Passarelli (1902-1995) successfully argued against this approach,[36] and went on to become one of the most important Italian private law scholars of the twentieth century.

In fact, as far as private law is concerned, principles are generally enunciated by doctrine and jurisprudence, which derive them via the systematic interpretation of a multiplicity of single norms or homogeneous disciplines:[37] accordingly, principles are the systematic reasons that unite and represent the logical-juridical reason for these norms and disciplines (*ratio legis*).
Principles are often expressed with reference to the Romanistic *brocarda*,[38] elaborated by medieval scholars on the basis of the *Corpus iuris civilis* (see *supra*, ch 2, para 2).[39] This explains why, in English common law, principles were formulated above all with regard to equity, the original historical formation of which was affected by Romanistic and canonistic influence; for

[32] *Bristol Groundschool Ltd v Intelligent Data Capture Ltd & Ors* [2014] EWHC 2145 (Ch).
[33] *Mid Essex Hospital Services NHS Trust v Compass Group UK and Ireland Ltd (trading as Medirest)* [2013] EWCA Civ 200, [2013] BLR 265.
[34] *MSC Mediterranean Shipping Company SA v Cottonex Anstalt* [2016] EWCA Civ 789.
[35] *Convegno nazionale universitario sui principi generali dell'ordinamento giuridico fascista tenuto in Pisa nei giorni 18 e 19 maggio 1940 – XVII* (Arti grafiche Pacini Mariotti 1940).
[36] See Francesco Santoro-Passarelli, 'Riflessioni sulla formulazione legislativa dei principi generali del diritto (dopo il Convegno di Pisa)' [1940] Riv dir civ 270; Pietro Rescigno, 'Conclusioni' in *Convegno* (n 18) 331.
[37] Bruno de Witte, 'Institutional Principles: A Special Category of General Principles of EC Law' in Ulf Bernitz and Joakim Nergelius (eds), *General Principles of European Community Law: Reports from a Conference in Malmö. 27-28 August 1999* (Kluwer Law International 2000) 143; Tridimas (n 28) 1. See also Gerald Fitzmaurice, 'The General Principles of International Law Considered from the Standpoint of the Rule of Law' in *Collected Courses of the Hague Academy of International Law* (The Hague Academy of International Law 1957) 1, 92.
[38] Legal aphorisms.
[39] Peter Stein, Regulae iuris. *From juristic rules to legal maxims* (Edinburgh University Press 1966).

example, 'equity will not assist a volunteer', 'he who comes into equity must have clean hands', 'between equal equities the first in order of time shall prevail', etc. (see *supra*, ch 2, para 4.2).

Although it is almost impossible to provide a definition of principles that is unambiguous and likely to command general consensus,[40] there is no doubt that there is a certain agreement on a number of elements that are considered to characterize principles in a particular way and that can be used to identify them in the legal system.

From a structural (or formal) point of view, it is commonly perceived that principles are characterized by the indeterminacy or vagueness of their preceptive content, which therefore is to a certain extent non-exhaustive, and always exceeds any of its specific concretizations.[41] Rules, on the contrary, entail particular precepts, subject to well-defined conditions of application.[42]

According to the conceptual approach outlined by **Luigi Mengoni** (1922-2001), principles prescribe an attitude, which may materialize in countless specific precepts, whereas rules prescribe a specific conduct. It follows that principles do not provide for an instant fact, since they are not contingent upon any certain event.

However, it is increasingly frequent for rules to envisage an 'open' or 'indeterminate' fact model,[43] which therefore makes more difficult distinguishing them from principles. Anglo-American doctrine refers to them as **legal standards**.

For example, in contemporary legal systems, tort and compensatory damages are based on the violation of a general duty of negligence, or care.[44] This is, indeed, a concept that makes the fact situation provided for by tort 'open' or 'indeterminate', so the typical (ie restricted to cases that are abstractly already predetermined by the legislator) becomes atypical.

The analysis is different in the case of a rule, which, however precise and specific, uses an **elastic concept**, which requires an assessment or, in any case, a factual evaluation by the judge.[45] For example, articles 49(1)(a) and 64(1) CISG state that the contract may be terminated only when its breach is 'fundamental'. The qualification of the breach of contract as 'fundamental' (or 'material', as

[40] On the ambiguity of this concept, see, among others, Norberto Bobbio, 'Principi generali di diritto', *Novissimo Digesto italiano*, vol 30 (UTET 1966), 887.

[41] Arthur S Hartkamp, 'The General Principles of EU Law and Private Law' (2011) 75 RabelsZ 241, 242; Jean Boulanger, 'Principes généraux du droit et droit positif' in *Le droit privé français au milieu du XXe siècle – Études offertes à Georges Ripert* vol 1, *Études générales – droit de la famille* (LGDJ 1950) 51, 56. In the Italian doctrine, see above all Emilio Betti, *Interpretazione della legge e degli atti giuridici* (Giuffrè 1949) 209ff.

[42] See above all Raz, 'Legal Principles' (n 27) 838, who also points out that the distinction based on the elements of generality and specificity is not dichotomous but gradual.

[43] In the sense that the determinacy of preceptive content is not an essential constitutive element of rules, see Frederick Schauer, *Playing by the Rules: A Philosophical Examination of Rule-Based Decision-Making in Law and in Life* (Clarendon Press 1991) 14.

[44] With regard to English law, see *Donoghue v Stevenson* [1932] UKHL 100, [1932] AC 562.

[45] On the definition of elastic concepts, see Francesco Gazzoni, *Manuale di diritto privato* (19th edn, ESI 2019) 48.

often stated in analogous national legislative provisions) is a perfect example of an elastic concept, defined in article 25 CISG with reference to other elastic concepts such as the one of substantial detriment.

Furthermore, a norm may incorporate a principle within its structure,[46] so that judges are entrusted with the power to provide a discretionary solution to the specific case that falls within their scope of application. In particular, under these circumstances, the judge has the power to establish which are the prevailing interests among many that emerge whilst carrying out an activity or within a legal relationship. These interests, despite deserving legal protection in abstract terms, in practical and concrete terms are structurally and, so to speak, inevitably in conflict with each other. The best examples come from the numerous rules that specifically apply **good faith** to the discipline of obligations and contracts: eg the one who behaves in violation of the principle of good faith during the negotiation phase and in the formation of the contract has to pay compensation.

The terminology introduced by German doctrine[47] refers to **general clauses** (*Generalklauseln*),[48] which, above all, raise the problem of whether their concretization by the judge can be regarded as a question of law rather than a question of fact and whether it can, therefore, be reviewed from the point of view of its legality.[49] In the context of European law, a similar problem,

[46] With reference to this conception of general clauses, see Libertini (n 25) 370, according to which the envisaged state of affairs is undoubtedly very wide, but not indeterminate, whereas the criterion of response that the legal system intends to give in the presence of such conflicts is indeterminate (the author defines these conflicts as 'modals', on the basis of Mario Barcellona, 'Struttura della responsabilità e "ingiustizia" del danno' [2000] Eur dir priv 401). In other words, the peculiarity of general clauses is ultimately the attribution to the judge of discretionary power (of course different from the administrative power, because it is characterized by the neutrality, but still a power) to comparatively evaluate conflicting interests. This implies that general clauses are logically and legally conceived as complete juridical norms (in this sense, see Angelo Falzea, 'Gli standards valutativi e la loro applicazione' [1987] Riv dir civ I 1). According to the well-known thesis of Luigi Mengoni, 'Spunti per una teoria delle clausole generali' [1986] Riv crit dir priv 5, reiterated in Id, 'Autonomia privata e Costituzione' [1997] Banca borsa tit cred I 1, and followed by Carlo Castronovo, 'L'avventura delle clausole generali' [1986] Riv crit dir priv 21; general clauses instead are techniques of juridical formation of the rule to be applied to the case, which do not describe a state of affairs and do not operate directly, being instead destined to operate in the area of application of other norms and in the function of the legal relationships which are constituted in them.

[47] The related German-language literature is immense; for a brief report, see Peter Schlechtriem, 'The Functions of General Clauses, Exemplified in Regarding German Law and Dutch Law' in Stefan Grundmann and Denis Mazeaud (eds), *General Clauses and Standards in European Contract Law: Comparative Law, EC Law and Contract Law Codification* (Kluwer Law International 2005) 41. On the other hand, the concept of general clauses has been less important for the development of French law; in this respect, see Camille Jauffret-Spinosi, 'Théorie et pratique de la clause générale en droit Français et dans les autres systèmes juridiques Romanistes' ibid 23.

[48] For an update and in-depth overview, see Salvatore Patti, 'L'interpretazione delle clausole generali' [2013] Riv dir civ 263.

[49] See Ernesto Fabiani, *Clausole generali e sindacato della Cassazione* (UTET 2003); Federico Roselli, 'Le clausole generali, oggi' (2003) 10 Dir rom attuale 37; Angelo Falzea, 'Il controllo di legittimità sull'impiego degli standards valutativi' in *Studi in onore di Nicolò Lipari*, vol 1 (Giuffrè 2008) 893.

which has been the subject of lively debate for some time (in particular in German-language literature), is the possibility of the ECJ having jurisdiction to interpret and to apply the general clauses prescribed in EU directives and regulations.[50]

> According to the most consolidated thesis, general clauses constitute a 'full delegation with unrestricted powers' to the judge, which can determine their preceptive content through the use of extra-legal criteria, ie technical or evaluation standards taken from social morality (so-called **hetero-integration**).[51] According to a different line of thought, the preceptive content of general clauses has to be determined by the judge through the application of legal principles (so-called **self-integration**).[52]

In reality, it is to be considered that the characteristics of **generality, vagueness, and indeterminacy of preceptive content** do not represent indefectible constitutive elements of legal principles but only characteristics that they have in a normal and, so to speak, regular way.

This depends on their nature as objectively rational and axiologically neutral categorical imperatives. In fact, it is clear that the more a precept takes on a precise and determinate content, the more it departs from this reference model and it is aimed at achieving a particular purpose, to realize the interests of a party, and so on.

On the contrary, it is only appropriate for a rule to have a vague or indeterminate content in case there are particular reasons of law-making policy:[53] since they are laid down by the legislator for the achievement of a purpose that has been deliberately set, any specific and determinate precepts imposed by the rules usually serve the achievement of this purpose.

[50] For an in-depth analysis of this issue, and for the criticism of the thesis according to which the national courts have jurisdiction, see Patti (n 48) 290ff.

[51] See Pietro Rescigno, 'Appunti sulle clausole generali' [1998] Riv dir comm I 1; Id, 'Le clausole generali dalle codificazioni moderne alla prassi giurisprudenziale' in Luciana Cabella Pisu and Luca Nanni (eds), *Clausole generali e principi generali nell'argomentazione giurisprudenziale degli anni Novanta* (Cedam 1998) 29, 30; Giovanni D'Amico, 'Clausole generali e ragionevolezza' in Pietro Perlingieri and Michele Sesta (eds), *I rapporti civilistici nell'interpretazione della Corte Costituzionale*, vol 1 (ESI 2007) 429; Pietro Rescigno, 'Una nuova stagione per le clausole generali' [2011] Giur it 1689.

[52] See Stefano Rodotà, *Le fonti di integrazione del contratto* (Giuffrè 1969); Id, 'Il tempo delle clausole generali' [1987] Riv crit dir priv 709; Id, 'Le clausole generali nel tempo del diritto flessibile' in Andrea Orestano (ed), *Lezioni sul contratto* (Giappichelli 2009) 97. Rodotà's opinion is followed by Mario Libertini, 'Le fonti private del diritto commerciale. Appunti per una discussione' [2008] Riv dir comm I 599, and Libertini, 'Clausole generali' (n 23) 354. Critically, see Patti (n 48) 272ff.

[53] In this case, the problem of their relationship with legal principles clearly arises. This issue has been scrutinized in depth above all with regard to general clauses: in general, see Attilio Guarneri, 'Clausole generali', *Digesto discipline privatistiche – Sezione civile*, vol 2 (UTET 1988) 403; Id, 'Le clausole generali' in Rodolfo Sacco (ed), *Trattato di diritto privato. Le fonti del diritto italiano*, vol 2, *Le fonti non scritte e l'interpretazione* (UTET 1999) 131; Mario Barcellona, *Clausole generali e giustizia contrattuale* (Giappichelli 2006); Vito Velluzzi, *Le clausole generali. Semantica e politica del diritto* (Giuffrè 2010); Ernesto Fabiani, 'Clausola generale', *Enciclopedia del diritto – Annali* (Giuffrè 2012) V, 183; Giovanni Sala and others, 'Le clausole generali nel diritto amministrativo' [2012] Giur it 1191.

From a substantive point of view, it is commonly believed that principles derive from the **moral values** positioned at the foundations of a society; therefore, they are acknowledged to have an ethical content.[54]
Based on these premises, it was noted that, when a judge applies a legal principle, she intends to justify her decision on the basis of a moral value which already exists in the society concerned (**deontological reasoning**), rather than on the basis of some practical or political consequence that might result from the decision itself, such as, for example, prevention of illegal conduct or economic growth (**teleological, or consequentialist, reasoning**).[55]

This clearly raised the problem of how to identify the values of **social morality**. It has been argued that such values (could and) should be objectively ascertained and recognized by the judge regardless of any personal beliefs.[56] This stance is not easily reconcilable with the positivistic view of law, which tends to suggest that, since law does not impose its own conception of justice and of the common good, judges should ultimately refer to their own values.[57]

On the basis of such considerations, Dworkin (see *supra*, ch 5, para 3) has described the distinction between principles and legal rules as the one between two kinds of concepts that are not only distinct but also radically incompatible.[58]

From a philosophical point of view, a similar result can be observed in the refoundation of (legal) hermeneutics carried out by **Hans-Georg Gadamer** (1900-2002). His main work, *Wahrheit und Methode* (1960),[59] interprets hermeneutics from the point of view of existentialist phenomenology developed in Heidegger's *Sein und Zeit* (1927).[60]

Moving from this conceptual approach, it has been pointed out that rules are based on a **mechanical subsumption of the case** into a state of affairs, so that either they are applicable in all respects, or they are not applicable at all. On the contrary, principles are susceptible to a **discreet application** (or, so to speak, milder application), as they must always be balanced with each

[54] With regard to European law, see in this sense Hartkamp (n 41) 241f. Generally see the classical work of Franz Bydlinski, *Fundamentale Rechtsgrundsätze. Zur rechtsethischen Verfassung der Gesellschaft* (Springer 1988) 128.
[55] Harry H Wellington, 'Common Law Rules and Constitutional Double Standards: Some Notes on Adjudication' (1973) 83 Yale LJ 221, who admits that a certain rule or a certain judicial decision may be justified both through a deontological reasoning and through a teleological, or consequentialistic, reasoning.
[56] Among others, see Wellington (n 55) 244ff.
[57] Among others, see Raz, 'Legal Principles' (n 27) 847.
[58] Dworkin (n 16). This conceptual approach has been criticized in particular by Raz, 'Legal Principles' (n 27) 842ff.
[59] Hans-Georg Gadamer, *Truth and Method* (Joel Weinsheimer and Donald G Marshall trs, 2nd edn, 2004).
[60] Martin Heidegger, *Being and Time* (John Macquarrie and Edward Robinson trs, Blackwell 1962).

other and in any case, they do not tend to exclude each other according to an 'all-or-nothing' paradigm (see *supra*, ch 5, paras 1 and 3).[61]

In reality, principles are not meant to achieve a purpose (social, political, or even moral) that is stipulated by the legislator, but they establish themselves on the ground of intrinsic objective rationality.

In this sense, legal principles have to be distinguished from **policies**, which instead identify social or political purposes that the legislator aims to achieve and, for this reason, are constitutively characterized by a teleological or consequentialist structure (*stat pro ratione voluntas*, the will takes the place of reason).[62]

It must be considered that legal principles cannot be identified, nor criticized, from a strictly axiological point of view. Therefore, they apply regardless of the social morality professed in a certain historical, cultural, or environmental context.

In other words, the debate on legal principles can only be based on the objective **rationality** of which they are a manifestation. This does not mean, however, that they are eternal and unmutable, because in all areas of human knowledge, experience shows that reason is not self-evident; it is, rather, historically revealed through a continuous search for the truth.[63]

[61] Dworkin (n 16) 22ff. This conception has been further elaborated and integrated by German scholarship into a constitutional theory of law. See in particular Robert Alexy, 'Zum Begriff des Rechtsprinzips' in Werner Krawietz and others (eds), *Argumentation und Hermeneutik in der Jurisprudenz* (1979) 1 RT Beihefte 59; Id, 'Rechtsregeln und Rechtsprinzipien' in Neil MacCormick, Stavros Panou and Luigi Lombardi Vallauri (eds), *Geltungs- und Erkenntnisbedingungen im modernen Rechtsdenken* (1985) 25 ARSP Beihefte 13; Id, 'Zur Kritik des Rechtspositivismus' in Ralf Dreier (ed), *Rechtspositivismus und Wertbezug des Rechts* (1990) 37 ARSP Beihefte 9. In the Italian literature, see above all Gustavo Zagrebelsky, *Il diritto mite* (Einaudi 1992); Id, *Principî e voti. La Corte costituzionale e la politica* (Einaudi 2005).

[62] Dworkin (n 16) 22. A rigid distinction between principles and policies has, however, been deemed inappropriate by Wellington (n 55), 222f, who opines that a certain rule or a certain judicial decision could be based on both.

[63] Gadamer (n 59) 562ff.

GLOSSARY

Abstractness (1.2): characteristic of those rules that can be applied not only to specific events but to all the events that match the state of affairs envisaged by the norm. Abstractness is strictly connected to generality (see *ad vocem*), although it is possible that a rule is abstract but not general (or general, but not abstract). Through this abstractness, the legal system affords uniformity of treatment.

Analogy (2.2): normative device used in the event of legal gaps, ie when a specific case is not governed by any legal norm. In particular, it is aimed at extending the scope of the existing rule to unregulated cases. In the Italian legal system, recourse to analogy is provided for and regulated by article 12(2) of the Preliminary Disposition to the Italian Civil Code. A distinction is usually made between *analogia legis* and *analogia iuris*. For the former, the legal gap is filled with the application of another rule that governs a similar case, while for the latter, since there is no similar rule that can govern the specific case, it is necessary to directly apply the general principles of the legal system. Exceptional norms are not to be applied analogically; moreover, analogy *in malam partem* is excluded with regard to criminal law rules, by virtue of the principle of *favor rei* and the principle of legality.

Antinomy (2.3): inconsistency between two or more norms that compete to regulate the same case. It means that the application of one of the norms in competition excludes the application of the others, even if they abstractly govern the factual situation. Any legal system based on a plurality of sources of law naturally entails contradictions between the various legal provisions. The (only apparent) conflict between the various rules in competition is resolved by the use of certain criteria, which identify, on a case-by-case basis, the only rule which is applicable in the practical case.

Content-based criterion (2.3): criterion used in event of antinomies, when there is an incompatibility between two rules set at the same level. According to this criterion, the special rule, ie the one with the narrower scope, should be preferred to the general rule, ie the one with the broader scope. In this case, the general rule is not invalid: it is simply derogated by the more specific rule and, for this reason, it remains valid and effective.

Default rules [*Règles dispositives*; *Dispositives Recht*; *Norme dispositive*] (1.3): rules that can be derogated via an agreement between their addressees. Default rules are the opposite of mandatory rules (see *ad vocem*). Most of private law consists of default rules: above all in the field of private autonomy, legal rules are normally intended to supplement agreements concluded by the parties.

Effectiveness [*Effectivité*; *Effektivität*; *Effettività*] (2.1): character of a legal rule, connoted by a sufficient degree of compliance by individuals or a sufficient degree of punishment by officials. From a positivistic point of view, effectiveness has to be distinguished from validity (see *ad vocem*), since effectiveness identifies the degree of obedience or punishment, while validity corresponds to the fact that a rule belongs to the legal system. According to legal realism, the validity of a rule is essentially conditional on its effectiveness, since law is seen only as a social fact, which has no reality if it is not effective.

Elastic concept (3): concept, used in a precise and specific rule, that requires a factual evaluation by the judge. For example, the qualification of the breach of contract as 'fundamental', under articles 49(1)(a) and 64(1) CISG is an elastic concept.

General clause [*Generalklausel*; *Clausola generale*] (3): norm that incorporates a principle within its structure. In this case, the judge can give a discretionary solution and can establish which are the prevailing interests among many that emerge whilst carrying out an activity or within a legal relationship. The best-known example of a general clause is good faith (see *ad vocem*) in contract law.

Generality (1.2): characteristic of those rules that can be applied not only to a specific person, but to anybody who finds themselves in the state of affairs envisaged by the norm. Generality is strictly connected to abstractness (see *ad vocem*), although it is possible that a rule is general but not abstract (or abstract but not general). The generality of the legal system affords uniformity of treatment.

Good faith [*Bonne foi*; *Treu und Glauben*; *Buona fede*] (3): general clause in Roman law and in civil law systems. It refers to a standard of conduct, based on honesty and fairness. According to the DCFR, good faith is characterized by consideration for the interests of the other party to the transaction or relationship in question. Good faith, for example, imposes limits on the exercise of a right (abuse of right) and pre-contractual information duties (duty of disclosure), prohibits acting inconsistently with the reliance induced (reliance protection), guides the interpretation of the contract, and implies the terms of the contract (or the content of the obligation).

***Grundnorm* [Basic norm] (2.1)**: concept elaborated by Hans Kelsen in his *Pure Theory of Law*. According to Kelsen, each legal system has a pyramidal structure (*Stufenbau*), and at its top there is a basic norm, which is the basis for the validity of any other norm. Validity of the *Grundnorm* depends on its effectiveness, since the basic norm can be replaced by another because of a revolution or a constitutional change.

Hierarchical criterion (2.3): first criterion used in event of antinomies. On the basis of this criterion, in such cases, preference must be given to the norm which emanates from the source of law which is superordinate according to the hierarchy of sources proper to each legal system.

Lacuna [*Lacune*; *Lücke*; *Lacuna*] (2.2): gap in primary norms that has to be filled by the judge. If there is a lacuna, there is no legal rule applicable to the case (technical gap) or there is no legal rule which is axiologically applicable to the case (axiological gap). Common law systems normally authorize judges to create a new legal rule in order to fill the gap, while civil law jurisdictions normally ask the judge to apply norms that govern similar cases or to directly apply general principles of the legal system.

Legal Effect [*Effet juridique*; *Rechtswirkung*; *Effetto giuridico*] (1.1): legal consequence produced by the occurrence of an event or behavior legally relevant.

Legal order (or legal system) [*Ordre juridique, or système juridique*; *Rechtsordnung, or Rechtssystem*; *Ordinamento giuridico, or sistema giuridico*] (2.1): according to the normative theory of Hans Kelsen, the set of all legal rules that derive from a *Grundnorm*; vice versa, according to the Santi Romano's theory, it is an institution, ie a system not only of rules but also of people. Following Santi Romano's thesis of the plurality of legal systems, it has to be admitted that the state legal order, albeit the most important, is not the only legal system that is effective within the same territory or for the same people. In comparative law, it is common to group national legal systems into families, which share some common characteristics (eg civil law systems and common law systems).

Legal standards (3): general legal criteria, whose characteristic is to be flexible. While a rule such as 'maximum legally allowed speed is 100 km/h' is precise, a standard, such as 'drivers must drive carefully', is a fuzzy norm. In other words, standards are norms that envisage an 'open' or 'indeterminate' fact situation and which require a difficult operation by the judge to specify the preceptive content. The most famous example of legal standard is the duty of negligence, or care, in modern tort laws.

Mandatory rules [*Règles imperatives*; *Zwingendes Recht*; *Norme imperative*] (1.3): rules that cannot be derogated via an agreement between their addressees. Mandatory rules are the opposite of default rules (see *ad vocem*). Most of public law consists of mandatory rules: nonetheless, in recent times the number of default rules in administrative and procedural law has increased.

Normativism (1.1): theory of law according to that the legal system consists essentially of rules; more precisely, of legal rules, which must be distinguished from the rules of religion or morality. It states that norms exist objectively, that is before their interpretation, and can be ascertained by jurists through the interpretation of the sources of law. The most famous example of normativism is the 'pure theory of law' of Hans Kelsen.

Precedent (1.1): judgment passed by a court that can have a binding or a persuasive force on the decision of new similar cases. In common law systems, judges are normally bound to their precedents or to the precedents of superior courts, according to the principles of *stare decisis*. In civil law jurisdictions, precedents do not have a binding character but only a persuasive one: even if there is not a duty for the judges to respect precedents, the latter normally influence their decision. Nonetheless, the importance of case law in civil law systems has increased in the last decades, just as has happened in common law jurisdictions with regard to statutory law.

Primary rules (2.1): according to H.L.A. Hart, rules that directly regulate the conduct of the members of the state. The philosopher distinguished primary and secondary rules (see *ad vocem*) in his major work *The Concept of Law*.

Principles (3): general tenets, requirements of justice or fairness that represent the best framework of and justification for legal practices and paradigms of law, commanding lawyers' general consensus of a given legal system. They also serve as interpretative criteria of law.

(Legal) realism (1.1): theory of law, according to which validity of a law is to be based on its effectiveness. It is common to distinguish between Scandinavian and American realism: the first claims that rights and duties are not metaphysic entities but simply modes of expression; the second underlines that law is not the set of norms established by the authority but, in reality, the set of norms applied in the courts (law in action).

Sanction [*Sanction*; *Strafe*; *Sanzione*] (1.1): punishment that is inflicted by the law (directly or indirectly, ie through an officer) on one who disobeys law. According to strict positivism, legal norms are those for which a sanction is provided. Nowadays it is recognized that not every norm is coercive: nonetheless, the legal system as a whole is coercive.

Secondary rules (2.1): according to H.L.A. Hart, rules that govern the entire legal system, conferring sovereignty and the power to change and to enforce primary rules (see *ad vocem*). In his major work, *The Concept of Law*, the philosopher distinguished primary and secondary rules and, among the latter, the rule of recognition (ie a social rule which provides for a test for validity of a norm), the rule of change (which allows to change primary rules) and the rule of adjudication (which regulates remedies and judicial procedures).

Sources of law [*Sources de droit*; *Rechtsquellen*; *Fonti del diritto*] (2.1): facts or acts capable of creating new norms, or changing or repealing existing norms. Rules on the sources of law are intended to regulate who can adopt the sources of law and how they can be adopted. These rules are also called, following H.L.A. Hart, secondary rules, because they are rules about the rules. Each legal system has its own sources of law, and does not recognize the sources of law of another legal system.

State of affairs [*État des faits*; *Tatbestand*; *Fattispecie*] (1.1): particular factual situation (a 'model fact situation') taken into account and governed by a legal provision. A distinction is to be made between an abstract and concrete state of affairs: the first consists of the legislative description of a natural event or a human act, to which legal effects are connected; the second refers, instead, to the specific event or a human act, which can be subsumed into the abstract state of affairs. The state of affairs can consist of one or more legally relevant facts: in the first case, reference is made to a simple state of affairs; in the second case, to a complex state of affairs.

Time-based criterion (2.3): criterion used when there is incompatibility between two norms, which are set at the same level and whose scope of application has the same width. In particular, it commands that, if a norm has been enacted after another, the most recent provision should apply, with the result that the previous provision is repealed and ceases to have effect from the entry into force of the later provision.

Validity [*Validité*; *Gültigkeit*; *Validità*] (2.1): connotation of the norm that belongs to a legal system and, for this reason, exists as a legally binding rule. According to the strict positivism of Hans Kelsen, the only criterion for validity is a formal one, ie the compliance with the procedure through which a norm can be adopted. Conversely, legal realism claims that validity of a norm depends on its degree of effectiveness (see *ad vocem*). A contract and an administrative act can be invalid, if they infringe a mandatory rule (see *infra*, ch 9, para 5).

BIOGRAPHIES

Josef Esser (Schwanheim am Main, 1910 – Tübingen, 1999) was a German jurist. He studied in Frankfurt am Main, and received his *Habilitation* in 1939 with an essay entitled *Grundlagen und Entwicklung der Gefährdungshaftung*. He taught at the University of Greifswald, Innsbruck, Mainz, and Tübingen.
Esser's fields of research were, on one hand, the theory of law and, on the other hand, the general law of obligations (*allgemeines Schuldrecht*).
With reference to legal theory, Esser stressed the importance of principles in the identification by the judge of the rule provided for the specific case. In his masterpiece *Vorverständnis und Methodenwahl in der Rechtsfindung*, which is highly influenced by Gadamer's hermeneutic, he demonstrated the strong influence of the preconceptions underlying the judges understanding, ie their anticipated hypothesis about the legal solution to be provided to the case.
Esser's matters of interest in the field of obligation law reflect his methodological investigation. He examined in depth, above all, good faith (§ 242 BGB, *Treu und Glauben*) and its *Konkretisierung* (concretization), and the structure of the obligatory relationship (*Schuldverhältnis*). His textbook has been for years the reference point for German legal literature; after the fourth edition, it was continued by other important German scholars until the end of the twentieth century.
His main works are: *Wert und Bedeutung der Rechtsfiktionen* (1940); *Lehrbuch des Schuldrechts* (1949); *Grundsatz und Norm in der richterlichen Rechtsfortbildung* (1956); *Schuldrecht* (2nd edn, 1960); *Vorverständnis und Methodenwahl in der Rechtsfindung* (1970).

Hans-Georg Gadamer (Marburg, 1900 – Heidelberg, 2002) was a German philosopher.
Born in Marburg, he studied at the University of Breslau and the University of Marburg, where he came into contact with the Neo-Kantian School of Natorp and Hartmann. Then, he moved to the University of Freiburg, where he found a young Heidegger, whom he followed later to Marburg. After having lectured for some years there, he became professor in Leipzig. It is disputed whether or not Gadamer supported the Third *Reich*: he probably preferred to remain in a neutral position.
After the war, he left East Germany, moving to the University of Frankfurt and then to the University of Heidelberg, where he was held to be a successor to Karl Jaspers. In his last year of teaching an important debate between him and Habermas took place. Gadamer died, at the age of 102, in Heidelberg, where he is buried.

Gadamer's masterpiece and most famous work is the book *Truth and Method* (*Wahrheit und Methode*, 1960). According to Gadamer, when we approach a text, our interpretation is affected by our prejudices, which represent our horizon (our historical tradition). Prejudices are normally considered obstacles in the process of interpretation, but, in reality, they are the conditions for understanding a text. In order to interpret, we create a fusion of horizon, a hermeneutical experience, through the so-called hermeneutic circle.
His main works are: *Wahrheit und Methode. Grundzüge einer philosophischen Hermeneutik* (1st edn, 1960; 3rd edn, 1975); *Lob der Theorie* (1983); *Das Erbe Europas* (1989); *Hermeneutische Entwürfe. Vorträge und Aufsätze* (2000).

Luigi Mengoni (Villazzano, 1922 – Milan, 2001) was an Italian legal scholar. He worked as a professor at the University of Trieste and then in the Catholic University of Milan, where he taught civil law, commercial law, and labor law. From 1987 to 1996 he was judge in the Italian Constitutional Court.
Mengoni's work is marked by constant methodological attention. The author's concern, which is evident both in his writings on the general theory of law and in those on positive law, derives from the need to combine systematic thinking and modernity, legal categories and the fragmentation of pluralist societies, in the conviction that only dogmatics – an updated dogmatics – can guarantee the rationality and controllability of legal decisions.
Among the various research topics dealt with by Mengoni, his writings in matters related to obligations must feature in the first place. In these writings, he criticized the distinction between obligations of care and skill and obligations to achieve a result and examined in depth the object of obligation and the liability for default. Equally important are the works on intestate succession and forced heirship (characterized by an unrivalled technical precision, combined with an uncommon attention to the history of law), on real estate recordings (also from the point of view of the *sistema tavolare*), and on *a non domino* purchases.
Mengoni was also one of the first scholars, together with Santoro-Passarelli, to devote himself with methodological rigor to the study of labor law, of which he can be defined as one of the founding fathers.
His main works are: *Gli acquisti* a non domino (1st edn, 1948; 3rd edn, 1975); 'Obbligazioni "di risultato" e obbligazioni "di mezzi"' [1954] Riv dir comm 185; 280; 366; 'Sulla natura della responsabilità precontrattuale' [1956] Riv dir comm 360; 'Problema e sistema nella controversia sul metodo giuridico' [1976] Jus 3; *Ermeneutica e dogmatica giuridica. Saggi* (1996); *Successioni per causa di morte. Parte speciale. Successione legittima* (6th edn, 1999); *Successioni per causa di morte. Parte speciale. Successione necessaria* (4th edn, 2000).

Karl Olivecrona (Uppsala, 1897 – Lund, 1980) was a Swedish legal philosopher. He studied in Uppsala, as a pupil of Vilhelm Lundstedt, and then he became Professor of Civil Law and Roman Law. From 1933 to 1964 he was Professor of Procedural Law in Lund.
Olivecrona's conception of law was strongly influenced by Axel Hägeström's

theories. The first edition of *Law as Fact* (1939) is one of the most emblematic examples of Scandinavian legal realism.
For Olivecrona, norms are not general commands issued by a sovereign, whose validity or invalidity can be preached. On the contrary, norms must be understood as an instrument through which the state can influence the conduct of its affiliates; moreover, they must be considered in their effectiveness.
Olivecrona's realism devalues the role of traditional juridical concepts, considered as devoid of any scientific value and, indeed, as the result of a mystical vision of law. Duties and rights do not have a metaphysical reality of their own; their only function is to arouse emotions.
The Swedish philosopher's reflection also developed on another, more purely political, side. In particular, during World War II, Olivecrona considered it necessary that Germany exercised its coercive power in order to guarantee peace in Europe.
His main work is: *Law as Fact* (1939; 2nd edn, 1971).

Alf Ross (Copenhagen, 1899 – Virum, 1979) was a Danish legal philosopher.
Born in 1899, he graduated in Copenhagen. After a short period of work as a barrister, he moved to France and to Austria, and then obtained his doctorate in Uppsala. He was professor at the University of Copenhagen and contributed to the drafting of the Danish Constitution.
While at an early stage of his work, Ross was strongly influenced by Hans Kelsen's theories, he soon turned his attention to the Scandinavian legal realism and its founder Axel Hägerström. Nowadays, he is recognized as the most famous exponent of this School.
Ross strongly criticized the way of thinking that finds realities in the concepts of right and duty: in fact, according to the philosopher, these qualifications simply constitute modes of expression.
The rules, according to Ross, are valid if effective; they are directives which affect the decision of the judges. If the rules of positive law serve as a framework for reading legal reality, the task of the philosophy of law is to examine legal notions in depth, to increase jurists' awareness of the reality that they study.
The importance of Ross in legal realism is due, among other things, to the attention he paid to the analysis of language, probably because of Kelsen's early influence.
His main works are: *Kritik der sogennanten praktischen Erkenntnis. Zugleich Prolegomena zu einer Kritik der Rechtswissenschaft* (1933); *Why Democracy?* (1952); *On Law and Justice* (1958); *Directives and Norms* (1968); *On Guilt, Responsibility and Punishment* (1974).

Francesco Santoro-Passarelli (Altamura, 1902 – Rome, 1995) was an Italian jurist.
He graduated from Rome University La Sapienza with Vittorio Polacco, and began his career in Urbino, before continuing to Catania, Padua, Naples and Rome.
The book, *Dottrine generali del diritto civile*, the last edition of which (the ninth) was published in 1966, is central to his academic work.
The academic work of Santoro-Passarelli developed over a period of more than sixty years and is obviously composite: however, in the scholar's work, legal

categories and private autonomy, understood as the centrepiece of private law, always play a fundamental role.
At first, this concept of law was declined by the author in a more formalistic way: at this stage, we clearly see Santoro-Passarelli's opposition to the introduction of provisions containing general principles in the new *Codice civile*. It was however also thanks to this intervention the Code could maintain a certain detachment from the fascist political ideology and was thus able to survive the fall of the regime.
In the following years, Santoro-Passarelli elaborated his most famous work, *Dottrine generali*, in which the author paid attention, on the one hand, to the interests of private individuals and, on the other hand, to the search for a rigorous and rational systematic construction.
His main works are: *La surrogazione reale* (1926); *Nozioni di diritto del lavoro* (first published, 1945; 35th edn, 1995); *Saggi di diritto civile* (1961); *Dottrine generali del diritto civile* (first published, 1954; 9th edn, 1966); *Libertà e autorità nel diritto civile. Altri saggi* (1977); *La transazione* (2nd edn, 1986).

CHAPTER 7

Private law and its sources

- **The divide of private law and public law**
- **The sources of private law in civil law and common law jurisdictions**
- **The historical formation of commercial law and its codification**
- **The unification of private law**
- **The role of legal scholarship as a formant of law**
- **The dialectics between formalistic legal reasoning and realistic legal reasoning**
- **The advent of critical legal studies**

Albeit rooted in Roman law, the divide between private and public law was introduced into French law in the first decade of the nineteenth century and, by imitation of that model, soon became a staple of civilian jurisdictions. This division affected the judiciary, since administrative tribunals were established aside from ordinary courts, but it impinged on substantive law as well, insofar as the state's authoritative powers were exempted from abiding by the ordinary rules on civil liability and contracts. Private law governs (horizontal) relationships between peers and is grounded on freedom as its overarching principle; public law governs (vertical) relationships between the state and individuals, or entities and is grounded on the resort to authoritative power as its overarching principle.

Conversely, private law is traditionally subdivided into civil law *stricto sensu* and commercial law (ie special private law addressing particularly businesses and other professionals in order to uphold their economic activities). The Italian *Codice civile* of 1939-1942 was the first case of a unique code, embracing both civil law *stricto sensu* and commercial law (particularly, company law). This 'unified' model of private law was later followed by other codifications, both in continental Europe and in Latin-American countries.

In civil law jurisdictions the Constitution is at the top of the hierarchy of the sources of law

and, in the systems where it is 'rigid', it overrides the civil code, which is on the same footing as other legislative acts. Statutory laws are therefore subject to a constitutional test and, if they do not meet it, they can be struck down, generally by a specialized court or tribunal. Regulations issued by the government, other bodies belonging to the administration, or independent authorities, may also have a normative content, thus amounting to sources of law. Customary law can operate solely in the interstices of legislative and regulatory acts, thus playing a very marginal role among the sources of law. Aids for the interpretation of statutory (or regulatory) provisions include the following: literal rule (or grammatical interpretation); systematic interpretation; historical interpretation; and teleological interpretation.

Anglo-American common law has traditionally been developing on the basis of leading cases decided by the superior courts (precedents), which, due to the doctrine of 'stare decisis', are binding. Therefore, it is characterized by a casuistic approach and underpinned by a tendency to develop legal reasoning bottom-up, ie upwards from the facts of single cases. Attempts to codify the common law remained completely unsuccessful in the UK; instead, they bore some fruit in the US. Since World War II, at any rate, statutory law has been increasingly gaining ground, and it has now become predominant. In this respect, the impact of the European Union's legal system on the UK's legal system proved particularly strong. In the US private law remains overall between the preserves of each State's legislature (except for some matters, like interstate commerce); the most significant initiative to achieve a certain uniformity among the different US judicatures was undertaken through the drafting of the Uniform Commercial Code (UCC). Accordingly, the rules of interpretation of statutes evolved over time. The literal rule is still paramount but was supplemented by the mischief rule (ie corrective interpretation) and the so-called golden rule (ie antiliteral interpretation, when the wording of a provision is not clear). No judicial review of legislative acts enacted by Parliament is allowed in the UK, whilst this power was entrusted to the US Supreme Court since 1803. Administrative regulations are also a source of law in the Anglo-American systems; in the US they gained a material momentum, since they govern federal agencies' activities. Usages are acknowledged to be a source of law of last resort.

1. THE DIVIDE OF PRIVATE LAW AND PUBLIC LAW

Jurisdictions of continental Europe are generally acquainted with the fundamental divide between private and public law.[1] Private and public law can be understood as two complementary branches of each national legal system.

[1] Paolo Alvazzi Del Frate, Sylvain Bloquet and Arnaud Vergne (eds), *La* summa divisio *droit public/droit privé dans l'histoire des systèmes juridiques en Europe (XIXe-XXIe siècles)* (Institut Universitaire Varenne 2018).

Historically rooted in Roman law sources,[2] their distinction was elaborated over time by German and French scholars.[3] It eventually gained a positive statutory foundation in 1811, when Napoleon created **administrative tribunals** as special courts, separated from the ordinary ones; this jurisdictional duality was soon imitated by other states,[4] which adopted the French system of **administrative law**.[5]

While the distinction between private and public law has become established, although somewhat recently, also in Anglo-American jurisdictions,[6] the **solid absolutism** and the **state centrality**, which characterize the French model of administrative law,[7] have been considered incompatible with (or even repugnant to) English liberalism.[8]

> According to a famous analysis by **Albert Venn Dicey** (1835-1922): 'The "rule of law" in this sense excludes the idea of any exception of officials or others from the duty of obedience to the law which governs other citizens or from the jurisdiction of the ordinary tribunals; there can be with us nothing really corresponding to the "administrative law" ("*droit administratif*") or the "administrative tribunals" ("*tribunaux administratifs*") of France. The notion which lies at the bottom of the "administrative law" known to foreign countries is, that affairs or disputes in which the government or its servants are concerned are beyond the sphere of the civil courts and must be dealt with by special and more or less official bodies. This idea is utterly unknown to the law of England, and indeed is fundamentally inconsistent with our traditions and customs'.[9]

Indeed, continental public law had been historically driven by the aim of exempting the state from abiding by private law, particularly in order to exonerate it from civil liability towards citizens and from the binding force

[2] As Ulpianus put it: '*publicum ius est quod ad statum rei romanae spectat, privatum quod ad singulorum utilitatem*' (D 1,1,1,2).

[3] Sabino Cassese, 'The Administrative State in Europe' in *The Max Planck Handbooks in European Public Law*, vol 1, Armin von Bogdandy, Peter M Huber and Sabino Cassese (eds), *The Administrative State* (OUP 2017) 57ff; Luca Mannori and Bernardo Sordi, *Storia del diritto amministrativo* (Laterza 2001) 343ff.

[4] Giulio Napolitano, *Introduzione al diritto amministrativo comparato* (Il Mulino 2020) 39ff. See also the national reports in *The Max Planck Handbooks in European Public Law*, vol 1 (n 3), particularly: Bernardo Giorgio Mattarella, 'Evolution and *Gestalt* of the Italian State' ibid 329ff; Armin von Bogdandy and Peter M Huber, 'Evolution and *Gestalt* of the German State' ibid 196ff.

[5] Hanns Peter Nehl, 'Administrative law' in Jan M Smits (ed), *Elgar Encyclopedia of Comparative Law* (2nd edn, Elgar 2012) 21; Jacques Ziller, 'Public Law' ibid 744.

[6] Uwe Kischel, *Comparative Law* (Andrew Hammer tr, OUP 2019) 345ff; William J Novack, 'The Administrative State in Europe' in *The Max Planck Handbooks in European Public Law*, vol 1 (n 3) 98ff; Martin Loughlin, 'Evolution and *Gestalt* of the State in the United Kingdom' ibid 451ff. For the traditional opinion, according to which Anglo-American law was unaware of a clear division of private law and public law, see Eibe Riedel, *Kontrolle der Verwaltung im englishen Rechtssystem* (Duncker & Humblot 1976) 174.

[7] Jean-B Aubry and Marcel Morabito, 'Evolution and *Gestalt* of the French State' in *The Max Planck Handbooks in European Public Law*, vol 1 (n 3) 165ff.

[8] Cassese (n 3) 60ff. See also Jason NE Varuhas, *Damages and Human Rights* (Hart 2016) 167ff.

[9] Albert V Dicey, *Introduction to the Study of the Law of the Constitution* (first published 1885, 8th edn 1915, reprint Liberty Fund 1982) 120ff.

of contracts entered into with them. Public law has therefore been styled as a special body of rules, aimed at conferring an **authoritative power** (*puissance publique*) to the state, thus running contrary to the principle of equal treatment that is underpinned by private law. The reason alleged for such exemption from private law is basically that the state is seen to pursue the general interest, thus having to command a higher standing and to be treated differently than individuals and private entities, who pursue instead their own private interests. The criteria upon which **the distinction between public and private law** should be based are often not neat.[10]

However, it is safe to say that private law provides a legal framework for (horizontal) relationships between peers and its overarching principle is that of liberty. At the core of private law lies the assumption that individuals are free and entitled to decide on the regulatory regime that will govern their interests, without prejudice to the freedom of others (**private autonomy**) (see *infra*, ch 9, paras 2 and 5). Conversely, public law governs the (vertical) relationship between the state and the citizens; it is enshrined in the 'command and control' logic.

Therefore, private law autonomy, grounded on liberty, is opposed to public law **heteronomy**, grounded on power.

> **Friedrich August von Hayek** (1899-1992) argued that private law provides a set of rules of conduct (*nomoi*) that govern the behavior of individuals, but do not interfere with the natural balance of society and, thus, the marketplace (*catallaxy*). On the contrary, public law is driven by specific purposes (*thesis*), all of which steer the behavior of individuals towards achieving a special interest set out by authorities.
>
> **Herbert L.A. Hart** (1907-1992) focused on the perspective of those who are subject to the legal authority of a government and argued that private law consists of a set of guidelines governing free choices of individuals and entities as to their own life and assets. Public law, instead, amounts to a cluster of tolls and sanctions.

Elaborating on labor and family law, **Cesare Massimo Bianca** (1932-2020) takes the view that any form of private power infringes the principle of equal treatment, unless regulated for the sake of a constitutionally overarching interest.[11]

Yet, the state does not necessarily act through the exercise of its authoritative powers. It may instead decide to resort to its private autonomy and act like any other legal entity to pursue its interests. Any such act performed by the

[10] Salvatore Pugliatti, 'Diritto pubblico e diritto privato' in *Enciclopedia del diritto*, vol 12 (Giuffrè 1964) 696. See also Andrea Zoppini, 'Diritto privato vs diritto amministrativo (ovvero alla ricerca dei confini tra Stato e mercato)' in Vincenzo Roppo and Pietro Sirena (eds), *Il diritto civile e gli altri. Atti del convegno dell'Associazione civilisti italiani, Roma, 2-3 dicembre 2011* (Giuffrè 2013) 371.

[11] Cesare M Bianca, *Le autorità private* (first published 1977), in Id, *Realtà sociale ed effettività della norma. Scritti giuridici, I, Teoria generale e fonti – persone e famiglia – garanzie e diritti reali*, vol 1 (Giuffrè 2002) 47ff.

state will be governed by private law, and the state is then said to **act *iure privatorum*.**

The border between private law and public law is historically contingent on political choices.[12] These are, in turn, affected by external circumstances, especially financial ones, and, as a result, the balance between private and public law can change over time.[13] Particularly, the expansion of public law is usually driven by the pressing social need to exercise the authority to control, restrict, and limit social unrest and unrestrained self-interest on the part of companies and owners. On the contrary, private law is expanded and developed when freedom of individuals and enterprise is preferred. Therefore, during wars or social uprising '*tout devient droit public*'.[14]

In general terms, legal scholars have suggested that during the twentieth century and especially after World War I, private law has dramatically changed,[15] becoming more 'public' or 'social':[16] the radical **tendency to centralize and bureaucratize the economic life** was able to transform 'what was originally considered to be governed by private law'.[17] A fundamental step of this transformation of legal systems was marked through the **constitutionalization of private law**, as well as through the introduction of collective bargaining and government intervention in the economy (see *infra*, ch 7, para 3.1).[18]

In the 1980s, however, private law ideology became dominant by far and – seemingly – gave rise to a 'wayout' or 'escape' from public law,[19] eg through

[12] Michael Stolleis, 'Öffentliches Recht und Privatrecht im Prozeß der Entstehung des modernen Staates' in Wolfgang Hoffman-Riem and Eberhard Schmidt-Aßmann (eds), *Öffentliches Recht und Privatrecht als wechselseitige Auffangordnungen* (Nomos 1996) 41ff.

[13] Sabino Cassese, 'Diritto privato/diritto pubblico: tradizione, mito o realtà?' in Giuseppe Conte, Andrea Fusaro, Alessandro Somma and Vincenzo Zeno-Zencovich (eds), *Dialoghi con Guido Alpa* (RomaTre P 2018) 51.

[14] This phrase was coined by Jean-Étienne-Marie Portalis (see *supra*, ch 4, para 3.1.1) during the nineteenth century and in the mid-twentieth century was used by Georges Ripert, *Le déclin du droit: Études sur la législation contemporaine* (LGDJ 1949) 37ff. On this topic, see also René Savatier, *Du droit civil au droit public* (2nd edn, LGDJ 1950); Id, 'Droit privé et droit public' [1946] DC 25; Jean Rivero, 'Droit public et droit privé: conquête, ou statu quo?' [1947] DC 69ff.

[15] See the three-volume series of René Savatier, *Les métamorphoses économiques et sociales du droit privé d'aujourd'hui*, the first published in 1948 (2nd edn, Dalloz Tours 1952) the second and the third in 1959.

[16] For a critical analysis of these conceptual formulas, see Michele Giorgianni, 'Il diritto privato ed i suoi attuali confini' in Id, *Scritti minori* (Jovene 1988) 441ff.

[17] Harold J Berman, *Law and Revolution: The Formation of the Western Legal Tradition* (Harvard UP 1985) 65ff.

[18] Umberto Breccia, 'L'immagine che i privatisti hanno del diritto pubblico' in Id, *Immagini del diritto privato*, vol 1 (Giappichelli 2013) 105ff.

[19] For an overview, see Eberhard Schmidt-Aßmann, 'Öffentliches Recht und Privatrecht: ihre Funktionen als wechselseitige Auffangordnungen. Einleitende Problemskizze' in Hoffman-Riem and Schmidt-Aßmann (eds) (n 12) 41ff. In Spanish literature see Sebastián Ricardo Martín-Retortillo, 'Reflexiones sobra la "huida" del derecho administrativo' [1996] RAP 25ff; Ignacio Borrajo Iniesta, 'El intento de huir del derecho administrativo' [1993] RAP 233ff.

a **gradual decriminalization of business law** (financial law, tax law, company law, etc.). The monopoly of the state itself in the process of lawmaking ended up being severely challenged,[20] giving leeway to new forms of 'law beyond the state' (see also *infra*, ch 8, para 2.1).

Subsequently, public law gained new momentum from the financial crisis which started in 2007-2008,[21] and again more recently with the outbreak of the COVID-19.

It is often argued that the distinction between private and public law was weakened – or even surpassed – by the creation of the EU (see *infra*, ch 8, para 1).[22]

While it is true that European law has introduced far-reaching liberalization policies across many industries, it is also true that such political and financial processes did not reduce the role of administrative law, but rather expanded its remit.[23]

In becoming European,[24] on the other hand, administrative law has experienced a tremendous change in many of its most characteristic traits. **European administrative law** is no longer characterized solely by the public functionalization of private action, particularly in the field of economics.[25] It is instead aimed at pursuing primary interests protected by individual freedoms. Discretionary powers of public administration are now more limited than in traditional administrative law (see also *infra*, ch 10, para 3), and administrative proceedings are now based on the principle of legal due process.[26]

[20] Nils Jansen and Ralf Michaels, 'Private Law and the State. Comparative Perceptions and Historical Observations' (2007) 71 RabelsZ 345ff. Even within the framework of more traditional concepts of the state, it was also possible to argue that the state was not the creator of the law, instead holding only a monopoly on its application; see Carl Schmitt, *Der Wert des Staates und die Bedeutung des Einzelnen* (Mohr Siebek 1914) 54ff. This point of view could easily be agreed upon by ordo-liberal thought, even within the framework of a radically different political approach; see Karl-Heinz Ladeur, *Der Staat gegen die Gesellschaft. Zur Verteidigung der Rationalität der 'Privatrechtsgesellschaft'* (Mohr Siebeck 2006).

[21] Giulio Napolitano (ed), *Uscire dalla crisi. Politiche pubbliche e trasformazioni istituzionali* (Il Mulino 2012); Id, 'From the Financial to the Sovereign Debt Crisis: New Trends in Public Law' [2012] Riv trim dir pubbl 81ff; Id, 'Il nuovo Stato salvatore: strumenti di intervento e assetti istituzionali' [2008] Giornale dir amm 1083ff; Id, 'Miti e funzioni del diritto privato nella sfera del diritto amministrativo' in Roppo and Sirena (eds) (n 10) 393ff.

[22] Jürgen Basedow, 'EU Private Law' in *The Max Planck Encyclopedia of European Private Law*, vol 1 (OUP 2012) 541.

[23] See Sabino Cassese, 'Quattro paradossi sui rapporti tra poteri pubblici e autonomia privata' [2000] Riv trim dir pubbl 389ff; Mario Libertini, 'Autonomia privata e concorrenza nel diritto italiano' [2002] Riv dir comm I 433ff.

[24] Carol Harlow, Leino Päivi and Giacinto Della Cananea (eds), *Research Handbook on EU Administrative Law* (Edward Elgar 2017).

[25] Jean-Bernard Auby, 'The Transformation of the Administrative State and Administrative Law' in *The Max Planck Handbooks in European Public Law* (n 3) 601ff.

[26] Giacinto Della Cananea, *Due Process of Law Beyond the State: Requirements of administrative procedure* (OUP 2016).

2. COMMERCIAL LAW AND ITS RELATIONSHIP WITH THE REST OF PRIVATE LAW

Historically, commercial law consisted of a body of trading principles used by merchants and applied by their corporations (***lex mercatoria***).The importance of **maritime law** gained more and more ground, and this led to a higher need to regulate risks like ship breakdown, insurance, and bottomry. Italian municipalities as well as maritime republics played a vital role in shaping such legal concepts, particularly in the banking industry.

Benvenuto Stracca (1509-1578) is historically regarded as the founding father of commercial law. In his work *De mercatura seu mercatore tractatus* (1553), he was the first to systematically analyze commercial law and separate it from civil and canon law.

Merchants' trade associations had their own **special courts**. These applied commercial and maritime law to settle disputes among their members and were free from any influence by local judges.

Established in 1258, the *Consolat de mar of Barcelona* was particularly important, because it contributed to the creation of a body of customary laws and ordinances in Catalan, which was later published in Valencia in 1494. Similar courts had already been established in Messina (in the early decades of the thirteenth century) and Genoa (in 1250).

In continental Europe, the **codification of commercial law** progressed throughout the nineteenth century, in parallel with the codification of civil law. In 1807, France enacted its first *Code de commerce*,[27] which accompanied the *Code civil* of 1804 (see *supra*, ch 4, para 3.1.1); at the same time, special jurisdictions were created for commercial matters, as separated from civil courts. Similarly, the German Code of Commerce – *Handelsgesetzbuch* (HGB) – was introduced in 1897 and came into force on 1 January 1900, along with the German Civil Code (BGB) (see *supra*, ch 4, para 3.1.2); commercial courts were also introduced into the judicial system.

In 1673, Louis XIV, the then King of **France**, in the context of his nationalist and statesman policy, had codified French commercial law by means of an *ordonnance pour le commerce*. Jacques Savary (1622-1690) played a pivotal role in drafting it, which is why the document is also known as *ordonnance Savary* (or *Code Savary*). With some minor amendments, it was to become the *Code de commerce* of 1807.[28]
Similar advancements were achieved a decade later in **German-speaking countries** united under the German confederation (*Deutscher Bund*) after the

[27] Gebhard Rehm, 'Code de commerce' in *The Max Planck Encyclopedia of European Private Law*, vol 1 (n 22) 205.
[28] Gebhard Rehm, 'Ordonnances' in *The Max Planck Encyclopedia of European Private Law*, vol 2 (OUP 2012) 51.

Restoration (1815). The *Allgemeines Deutsches Handelsgesetzbuch* (ADHGB) in 1861 codified the commercial legislation of the Confederate States into a code of commerce.[29] In 1868, the *Reichsoberhandelsgericht* (ROHG) was established to settle commercial disputes, having exclusive jurisdiction in German countries that were part of the *Norddeutscher Bund* by 1866.[30]

Italy followed the French model, which was based on the duplication of the code of commerce and commercial courts as distinct from civil courts.

The Code of Commerce of the Reign of Sardinia was temporarily extended to the rest of the territory (1865) until the introduction of a new code of commerce in 1882.

During the twentieth century, however, some Italian legal scholars advanced a highly influential theory that commercial and civil law should be unified to combat merchants' privileges and ensure equal treatment among citizens, thus providing a single legal framework for contracts and obligations.

This theory was strongly supported by one of Italy's most renowned commercial law scholars, Cesare Vivante (1855-1944). He established a journal called *Rivista del diritto commerciale e del diritto generale delle obbligazioni* (1903). His ideas were followed by Tullio Ascarelli (see *supra*, ch 5, para 4) and, for some time, by Angelo Sraffa (1865-1937). Vivante eventually had a radical shift in thought and re-embraced the doctrine of autonomy of commercial law. The ideal of a **unique code of private law** was also advocated by Mario Rotondi (1900-1926).

A few decades later, the project of a single code of private law was (unexpectedly) supported by the fascist regime, while the reform of the 1865 Civil Code was underway. Italian fascism sought to prevent class conflict and was averse to the merchant bourgeoisie. At the same time, the issue of a unique code of private law was aimed at enhancing the efficiency of civil law, furthering the generalization already underway such that most commercial law rules included all citizens irrespective of their profession (**commercialization of civil law**).[31] The Italian *Codice civile* of 1939-1942 eventually led to the **unification of private law** (see *supra*, ch 4, para 3.1.3). Not only did it govern civil law, but it also regulated commercial law, including company law.

The Swiss *Obligationenrecht* (OR) of 1881,[32] which later became the fifth

[29] Andreas M Fleckner, 'Allgemeines Deutsches Handelsgesetzbuch (ADHGB)' in *The Max Planck Encyclopedia of European Private Law*, vol 1 (n 22) 51.
[30] Andreas M Fleckner, 'Reichsoberhandelsgericht (with Reichsgericht)' in *The Max Planck Encyclopedia of European Private Law*, vol 2 (n 28) 1438.
[31] Jan Peter Schmidt, 'Code Unique' in *The Max Planck Encyclopedia of European Private Law*, vol 1 (n 22) 210.
[32] Ulrich Ernst, 'Polish Civil Code' in *The Max Planck Encyclopedia of European Private Law*, vol 2 (n 28) 1288; Michael Gondek, 'Poland' in *Elgar Encyclopedia of Comparative Law* (n 5) 681.

book of the *Zivilgesetzbuch* (ZGB) in 1907,[33] had already provided a single legal framework for obligations, where it did not distinguish between civil and commercial law.

The model of a unified private law was later implemented in the Polish Civil Code of 1964;[34] more recently, in the new (and third) Dutch Civil Code (*Burgerlijk Woetboek*) of 1992,[35] as well as in the Russian Civil Code of 1994.[36] A similar process took place also in some Latin American countries: a unique code of private law was issued by Paraguay (1985) and Brazil (2002). More recently, ie in 2014, Argentina issued a combined Civil and Commercial Code (*Código civil y commercial*), which clearly draws on the model of the Italian *Codice civile*.

In **common law jurisdictions**, commercial law was heavily influenced by continental civil law in two material ways. It exerted influence on that branch of commercial law that was historically administered by special jurisdictions like the Court of Admiralty (see *supra*, ch 4, para 1), which adjudicated on the basis of Roman law, as well as on that part of commercial law that was developed by Lord Mansfield (see *supra*, ch 4, para 1) throughout the seventeenth century. In the United States, the push for a uniform commercial law resulted in the adoption of the **Uniform Commercial Code** (UCC) (see *supra*, ch 3, para 5). Established in Paris in 1919, the **International Commercial Chamber** (ICC) was instrumental in developing and applying uniform commercial law globally.[37] One of its objectives is to collect and publish the **International Commercial Terms** (INCOTERMS),[38] ie commercial best practices and standard contract clauses, most notably in the context of international sales and trade of goods. They were first published in 1936 and have, since then, been revised from time to time.[39] Commercial law has expanded to include antitrust law, intellectual and industrial property law, business-to-business contract law, company law (see *infra*, ch 11, para 1.2.1), bankruptcy law, and debt instruments (such as promissory notes and bank cheques). Most of these fields have been significantly unified by the European Union (see *infra* ch 8, paras 1.5.1 and 1.5.2).

[33] Kurt Siehr, 'Swiss Code of Obligations (OR)' in *The Max Planck Encyclopedia of European Private Law*, vol 2 (n 28) 1646; Pascal Pichonnaz, 'Switzerland' in *Elgar Encyclopedia of Comparative Law* (n 5) 852.
[34] Kurt Siehr, 'Swiss Civil Code (ZGB)' in *The Max Planck Encyclopedia of European Private Law*, vol 2 (n 28) 1644; Pichonnaz (n 33) 852.
[35] Liane Schmiedel, 'Burgerlijk Wetboek (BW)' in *The Max Planck Encyclopedia of European Private Law*, vol 1 (n 22) 125; Jan M Smits, 'The Netherlands' in *Elgar Encyclopedia of Comparative Law* (n 5) 620.
[36] Eugenia Kurzynsky-Singer, 'Russian Civil Code' in *The Max Planck Encyclopedia of European Private Law*, vol 2 (n 28) 1491.
[37] Klaus J Hopt, 'International Chamber of Commerce (ICC)' in *The Max Planck Encyclopedia of European Private Law*, vol 1 (n 22) 958.
[38] Ulrich Magnus, 'Incoterms' in *The Max Planck Encyclopedia of European Private Law*, vol 1 (n 22) 855.
[39] For an article-by-article commentary, see Peter Mankowski, *Commercial Law* (Nomos 2019) 828ff.

3. THE LEGISLATURE AND THE JUDICIARY

3.1. Civil law jurisdictions

In civil law countries, the prevailing source of law is the statutory legislation, ie a set of written legal statutes issued in accordance with constitutional forms and procedures; national **civil codes** are to be found among those legal statutes and serve to draw up general principles and rules of private law (see *supra*, ch 4, para 3). By contrast, **case law (or judge-made law)** is not considered a formal source of law,[40] but, rather, a measuring rod for how laws are actually interpreted, as well for their level of effectiveness; namely, how laws are applied and enforced within society.

> The fact that a legal rule is valid, ie it is formally in force and created by way of a legislative act, does not necessarily mean that it is also effective, ie it is actually applied and followed in practice. The **validity** of legal provisions must be therefore distinguished from their **effectiveness** (see *supra*, ch 6, para 2.1). This may lead to a dissociation between the law written in statutes and that applied (or eventually made) by judges (see *supra*, ch 3, para 3.2).

At any rate, it must be taken into consideration that the precedents of the higher courts may be held to be highly persuasive in civil law jurisdictions and, therefore, they may tend to be followed by other courts.[41]

The **Constitution** is ranked at the top of the hierarchy of the sources of law (see *supra*, ch 6, para 2.1). Although usually enshrined in a charter, it tends to be considered as 'pre-existing' the state, rather than 'stipulated' by the latter. In this vein, it coincides with the *Grundnorm*, ie the rule of recognition of the entire legal system (see *supra*, ch 6, para 2.1), which incorporates material values that may be conceived of as a positivization of natural law (see *supra*, ch 5, paras 1 and 3).

In most jurisdictions of civil law, the **Constitution is 'rigid'**. It means that the Constitution cannot be amended through ordinary legislative acts; it can only be modified through a specific procedure of constitutional review. Such special procedures generally include a complex system of Parliamentary voting that is sometimes followed up by a popular referendum. In addition, a constitutional court or tribunal may be designed to ensure the supremacy of the Constitution over other sources of law, namely acts of Parliament or other legislative acts.

The Constitution usually governs how legislative acts should be voted on and issued by the Parliament. Scholars have raised the question of whether constitutional laws should not only apply to vertical relationships between the state and its citizens but also to horizontal relationships between individuals or entities (see also *supra*, ch 7, para 1). The horizontal application of

[40] Stefan Vogenauer, 'Precedent, Rule of' in *The Max Planck Encyclopedia of European Private Law*, vol 2 (n 28) 1305.
[41] ibid 1305.

constitutional laws is also known by the German term ***Drittwirkung*** and is still highly debated, as it may restrict the freedom of individuals (for example, when entering into a contract).
Conversely, it is a widely accepted fact that private law is now in the process of being 'constitutionalized', particularly when it comes to its interpretation and application by courts. Every provision of private law must be construed and applied in accordance with the Constitution, especially regarding the protection of fundamental human rights.

> Important methodological and dogmatic considerations came from **Claus-Wilhelm Canaris** and, in the area of labor law, from Hans Carl Nipperdey (1895-1975).
> In Italy, the Constitution-theory advanced by **Pietro Rescigno** is primarily based on the valorization of intermediate communities and pluralism. In turn, **Pietro Perlingieri** offered a systematic reinterpretation of private law that is founded on the constitutional protection of individuals and the supremacy of their fundamental rights over property rights.

As far as private law is concerned, sources of law tend to attribute primacy to **civil codes**. This perceived primacy, however, concerns only the systematic centrality of civil codes, not their formal force as sources of law: in this respect, they are on the same footing with other legislative acts. The same holds true for other codes across continental European jurisdictions, most notably those concerning commercial law and civil procedure.
The central role of the civil code within continental European jurisdictions did, however, come into question in the 1970s. During that time, there was a great number of legislative acts of Parliament (known as 'special statutes') governing special or exceptional regimes outside the remit of the civil code to protect certain social or political interests, leading to a substantial limitation of the scope of application of the civil code.

> **Natalino Irti** coined the term '**decodification**', which became popular during the 1970s and afterwards. The term conveyed the concept that the civil code was becoming less and less important and being replaced by a number of legislative acts, each having its own independent legal force. There was indeed a shift from the systematic analysis of private law to a new critical interpretation of the sources of law based on special laws.

Also **administrative regulations** issued by the government, other bodies belonging to the administration, or independent authorities may have a normative content. Should this be the case, however, they must be authorized by a statutory provision and cannot overstep the limits of that authorization, nor override any other statutory provision. In the hierarchical order of the sources of law (see *supra*, ch 6, para 2.1), regulations are therefore subordinate to legislative acts.

Legislative and regulatory acts fundamentally consist of documents, the terms of which need to be interpreted to determine their legal significance. Case law plays a pivotal role in the interpretation process.

Despite attempts by lawmakers to regulate the **interpretation of statutes** (and regulations), it is legal scholars who have guided it from a scientific and doctrinal perspective.[42] The civilian canon of aids to interpretation was elaborated upon by Friedrich Carl von Savigny (see *supra*, ch 4, para 3.1.2) and entails the following arguments: 1. **Grammatical (or literal) interpretation**: the interpreter sticks to the wording of the relevant provision and accords their own interpretation to the plain text of it; 2. **Systematic interpretation**: the interpreter derives the meaning of the provision so that it is consistent with the rest of the legal system, including its own rules and principles; 3. **Historical interpretation**: the interpreter draws on the objective intention of the lawmaker (*mens legis*), as it is laid down in preparatory works, 'whereas' clauses, explanations of vote, etc.; 4. **Teleological interpretation**: the interpreter construes the policy underpinning the rule and may even disregard the declarations of lawmakers; this aid to interpretation allows the interpreter to carefully narrow (reductive interpretation) or broaden (expansive interpretation) the scope of a statutory provision.[43]

> In Germany, courts and legal scholars do not only contribute to the interpretation of law (*Auslegung*) but also to the **development (or supplementation) of law** according to renovation of social values (*Rechtsfortbildung*). This serves as a solution to practical issues that are not addressed by lawmakers. This is traditionally the core tenet of legal methodology (*juristische Methodenlehre*).[44]

Statutory laws are subject to the **constitutional test**. If an act of legislation can be interpreted both in accordance with and in contrast to the Constitution, the interpreter has to choose the former interpretation. If an act of legislation has no meaning that is in accordance with the Constitution, in almost the entirety of civil law jurisdictions it may be struck down (**judicial review**), generally by a specialized court or tribunal.

Across the Member States, the criteria of interpretation of national laws and the constitutional test, however, are overridden by the principle of compliance with the European Union's law. This reflects the supremacy of European law over national laws (see *infra*, ch 8, para 1.3).

Customary law plays a marginal role (see also *supra*, ch 2, para 2), and it is considered as a source of law solely in those areas where its authority is recognized by law (**usages *secondum legem***). Furthermore, customary law is tacitly applicable in those areas which are not governed by law (**usages *praeter***

42 Stefan Vogenauer, 'Statutory interpretation' in *Elgar Encyclopedia of Comparative Law* (n 5) 826.

43 Manfred Wolf and Jörg Neuner, *Allgemeiner Teil des Bürgerlichen Rechts* (11th edn, CH Beck 2016) § 4, RdNr 32ff.

44 Karl Larenz and Claus-Wilhelm Canaris, *Methodenlehre der Rechtswissenschaft* (3rd edn, Springer 1995).

legem). By contrast, customary laws that are in contrast with existing laws (**usages *contra legem***) are illegitimate and, thus, unenforceable.
Customary law is defined as a body of legal facts. Although it is not constituted by legislative acts passed by the state, customary law is recognized by the state as binding. Official gazettes collecting customary law, which are sometimes kept, represent legal repositories rather than sources of binding law.
Traditionally, **two essential requirements** must be met for a usage to be acknowledged as a source of law.
The first requirement – material or objective in nature – is that a number of individuals must observe a certain pattern of behavior on a recurrent basis. The second one, with a psychological or subjective nature, is that the relevant actors consider such conduct to be legitimate or at least in accordance with law (*opinio iuris ac necessitatis*).
As was mentioned earlier, customary law lies at the bottom of the hierarchy of sources, and cannot modify or repeal any laws derived from other sources. Most importantly, customary laws cannot repeal or modify a legislative act (**desuetude**).

3.2. Common law jurisdictions

Anglo-American jurisdictions are largely based upon **case law (or judge-made law)**.
The traditional explanation of the role thus played by common law courts in the process of lawmaking was fathered by William Blackstone (1723-1780) (see *supra*, ch 2, para 5), according to whom the judge 'is not delegated to pronounce new law, but to maintain and expound the old one':[45] the judgments of common law courts would actually do nothing more than ascertain and declare the already pre-existing law, thus bringing it into the light (**declaration theory of the common law**).[46] However, this doctrine has been discredited over time by modern lawyers, most prominently by John L. Austin (1911-1960) (see *supra*, ch 5, para 3; ch 6, para 1.1),[47] and it has eventually come to be considered unsound and fictitious ('we do not believe in fairy tales any more').[48]
Therefore, it is nowadays widely assumed that, in Anglo-American jurisdictions, judicial decisions amount to a proper source of law. The question of **the**

[45] William Blackstone, *Commentaries of the Law of England*, vol 1 (first published 1765, Chicago UP 1979) 69.
[46] Allan Beever, 'The Declaratory Theory of Law' (2013) 33 OJLS 421ff. See also Stefan Vogenauer, 'Judge-made Law' in *The Max Planck Encyclopedia of European Private Law*, vol 2 (n 28) 1015; John Baker, *Introduction to English Legal History* (5th edn, OUP 2019) 206ff.
[47] John L Austin, *Lectures on Jurisprudence or the Philosophy of Positive Law* (first published 1869, 5th edn, Murray 1885) 634: 'The childish fiction employed by our judges, that [...] common law is not made by them, but is a miraculous something made by nobody, existing, I suppose, from eternity and merely declared from time to time by the judges'.
[48] Lord James Reid, 'The Judge as Law Maker' (1972/1973) 12 Journal of the Society of Public Teachers of Law 22.

nature of common law, however, cannot be considered as a remnant of the past: particularly, it is still discussed with regard to the nature of the courts' power, when it comes to gap-filling devices (see *supra*, ch 6, para 2.2) and to adjudicating 'hard cases' (see *supra*, ch 6, para 3).

It has been convincingly claimed that, in Anglo-American jurisdictions, judicial decisions consist of **provisional statements of general (or fundamental) principles**, which have to be reviewed and developed on a case-by-case basis;[49] by contrast, provisions of civil law codifications are styled as large and abstract generalizations, endowed with a would-be eternity. In other terms, common lawyers 'tend to reason *upwards* from the facts of the cases' brought to a court, whereas civil lawyers 'tend to reason *downwards* from abstract principles embodied in a code'.[50]

The supremacy of judge-made law and its casuistic approach inevitably led common law jurisdictions to risks of inconsistencies and inequalities, due also to a piecemeal attitude of judges and interpreters. Therefore, it was necessary to seek devices that could remedy – or at least alleviate – this serious inconvenience.

> Between the sixteenth and the seventeenth centuries, the decisions rendered by the Exchequer Chamber, which gathered judges belonging to all the three central courts of common law (ie the Court of Exchequer, the King's Bench and the Court of Common Pleas), began to be considered binding. By the end of the seventeenth century, this attitude became a principle. Similarly, the judgment of the Equity Court began to have binding force at that time.[51]

During the nineteenth century, it was eventually considered a rule that a single precedent has an absolute binding force for a lower judge (**vertical precedent**). It was also established that it also has an absolute binding force for the same judge who rendered it, or for another court at a similar level (**horizontal precedent**);[52] this rule, however, is looser than that on vertical precedent and, at any rate, is observed by US courts less than by UK courts[53]. The **doctrine of *stare decisis*** was thus established and is nowadays regarded as a staple of common law (including equity).[54]

The binding force of a precedent properly regards its **holding** (or ***ratio decidendi***), ie the point or the points of law on which the court rested – or, in a

[49] John Bell, 'Sources of Law' in Andrew Burrows (ed), *English Private Law* (3rd edn, OUP 2013) para 1.23.

[50] Lord Robert Goff of Chieveley, 'The Future of the Common Law' (1997) 46 ICQL 745, 753.

[51] Antonio Padoa Schioppa, *A History of Law in Europe: From the Early Middle Ages to the Twentieth Century* (Caterina Fitzgerald tr, CUP 2017) 398.

[52] *London Street Tramways Co Ltd v London County Council* [1898] AC 375 (HL). See Kischel (n 6) 258; Vogenauer 'Precedent, Rule of' (n 40) 1304; Arthur T von Mehren and Peter L Murray, *Law in the United States* (2nd ed, CUP 2007) 9ff.

[53] von Mehren and Murray (n 52) 9ff.

[54] The formula of *stare decisis* was used for the first time in the seventeenth century by the judge – and first great historian of English law – Matthew Hale (1609-1676).

stricter version, had to rest – the disposition of the case. The remaining part of what is said in a judicial decision is called ***obiter dictum*** and does not fall within the scope of the doctrine of *stare decisis*.[55]

A precedent ceases to be binding if and when a higher judge assesses it as unsound and wrong (**overruling**).[56]

Furthermore, a court is not bound by a precedent insofar as it acknowledges that it is hearing a case which is substantially different from that previously adjudicated (**distinguishing**).[57]

Between eighteenth and nineteenth century, some endeavors were undertaken to attend to a **codification of common law**. One of the first individuals that actively promoted the necessity of such an enterprise was **Jeremy Bentham** (1748-1832) (see *supra*, ch 5, para 3), moved by his dissatisfaction with the then present state of common law.[58]

> After hearing Blackstone's lectures at the age of only sixteen, Bentham was disgusted by the former's proclivity to praise unreservedly the English common law and by his unwillingness to notice any defect in it; this aversion led Bentham to prompt his first published work,[59] where he fiercely attacked one part of the Introduction to Blackstone's *Commentaries* (which were drawn from the latter's lectures). In Bentham's view, existing law was not only cumbersome and illogical, but it advanced only the interests of the lawyers, instead of pursuing 'the greatest happiness of the greatest number'. Therefore, he advocated for its replacement with a complete code of laws, which he termed 'pannomion'; each law had to be 'rationalized', ie accompanied by a set of reasons aimed at justifying it in the eyes of its addressees.[60]

If Bentham's efforts failed in the UK, they eventually bore fruit in the US,[61] where a wide and long-lasting movement for codification was tirelessly promoted by David Dudley Field (1805-1894). Thanks to his engagement, a **code of civil procedure of the state of New York** was enacted in 1848-1849 (also known as Field Code) (see also *supra*, ch 4, para 4), which is nowadays adopted by some thirty States of America;[62] it was followed by a **code of criminal procedure of the state of New York**, enacted in 1850 and nowadays

[55] Bell (n 49) paras 1-74ff; von Mehren and Murray (n 52) 11.
[56] The possibility for the UK Supreme Court (formerly known as the House of Lords) to disregard its own precedents has been settled by the Practice Statement (Judicial Precedent) [1966] 1 WLR 1234 (HL) 1234. On the point, see Bell (n 49) paras 1.83ff.
[57] Bell (n 49) paras 1.78f.
[58] Dean Alfange Jr, *Jeremy Bentham and the Codification of Law* (1969) 55 Cornell LR 58.
[59] Jeremy Bentham, *A Fragment on Government* (first published 1776) in *The Works of Jeremy Bentham*, vol 1 (John Bowring ed, William Tait 1843) 221ff.
[60] Jeremy Bentham, *Papers relative to Codification and Public Instruction* (first published 1817) in *The Works of Jeremy Bentham*, vol 4 (John Bowring ed, William Tait 1843) 451ff; Id, *Codification Proposals, addressed by Jeremy Bentham to all Nations Professing Liberal Opinions* (first published 1822) ibid 535ff; Id., *First Lines of a proposed Code of Law for any Nation compleat and rationalized*, in Philip Scholfield and Jonathan Harris (eds), *'Legislator of the World': Writings on Codification, Law, and Education* (Clarendon Press 1998).
[61] Andrew P Morriss, 'Codification and Right Answers' (1999) 74 Chicago-Kent LR 355.
[62] von Mehren and Murray (n 52) 16.

adopted in sixteen States,[63] as well as by a **code of penal law**. On the contrary, Field's resoluteness to codifying substantive private law was less successful: although his civil code was passed in 1879, the bar of the City of New York successfully instigated the governor of the state to veto it.[64] Subsequently, five States, including California, adopted their **civil codes on the basis of Field's blueprint**;[65] they are still in force, but they are looked upon just as a revised and improved compilation and systematization of common law rules and principles, far from attaining the degree of completeness and consistency that are a staple of civil law codifications.[66]

> The main opponent to Field's ideas was James C. Carter (1827-1905), whose paper 'The Proposed Codification of Our Common Law' has been defined as 'perhaps an American analogue to Savigny's *Vom Beruf unserer Zeit für Gesetzgebung und Rechtswissenschaft*',[67] because it decidedly gainsays the advantages of codification. This paper was read on 13 December 1883 at a meeting of the Committee of the Association of the Bar of the City of New York and unanimously approved;[68] it was thus put an end to any hope that Field's civil code could finally enter into force.

Traditionally, **statutes** have been seen as 'either declaratory of common law, or remedial of some defects therein'.[69] However, this account of the sources of English common law has been facing increasing challenges from the growing number of statutes after World War II, as well as by the binding force of the sources of the EU's law (see also *supra*, ch 4, para 2). It means that statutes are now acknowledged as the primary source of English law,[70] and a similar approach applies even more strongly to US law.[71]

With regard to the US, particularly, it must be pointed out that the Constitution confers to the Congress the power to enact statutes of private law solely for certain limited purposes, like regulating interstate commerce. Although during the twentieth century the relevant clauses of the Constitution have been interpreted more and more broadly, it holds still good that private law as such falls out of the scope of **federal statutes**, being instead stipulated by each American State. Federal statutes are collected in the US Code and those of each State in similar **codes**, which, however, have little to do with civil law codifications: for the most part, they are merely convenient, sometimes unofficial, groupings of legislation according to subject matter.[72]

[63] ibid 17.
[64] ibid.
[65] ibid.
[66] ibid 18.
[67] ibid 17.
[68] ibid.
[69] Blackstone (n 45) 86.
[70] Geoffrey Samuel, *A Short Introduction to the Common Law* (Elgar 2013) 88.
[71] James R Mexeiner, *Failures of American Methods of Lawmaking in Historical and Comparative Perspectives* (CUP 2018).
[72] von Mehren and Murray (n 52) 18.

Therefore, private law of each American state may be considerably different from that of another. The most effective attempt to attain a certain degree of uniformity between them was achieved through the **Uniform Commercial Code** (UCC) of 1952 (see *supra*, ch 3, para 5).

In Anglo-American jurisdictions, the rules governing **interpretation of statutes** have significantly evolved over time.[73]

The starting point is that, being considered a kind of exception to or amendment of common law precedents,[74] statutes have been traditionally interpreted in their 'plain, literal, ordinary meaning'.[75] No heed has been traditionally paid to the Parliamentary debates or to the purpose of the legislator (**no historical interpretation**).[76]

Since the nineteenth century, however, this 'shallow' hermeneutical methodology has been significantly broadened and enriched,[77] in the sense that courts have shown a growing willingness to interpret statutes beyond the words of their provisions.[78] This trajectory marks a progressive convergence of the interpretation of statutes in common law and civil law jurisdictions.[79]

The **literal rule**, which is still paramount,[80] stipulates that: '1. The judge must give effect to the grammatical and ordinary or, where appropriate, the technical meaning of words in the general context of the statute; he must also determine the extent of general words with reference to the context. 2. If the judge considers that the application of the words in their grammatical and ordinary sense would produce a result which is contrary to the purpose of the statute, he may apply them in any secondary meaning they are capable of bearing'.

The literal rule has been over time supplemented by the mischief rule and the so-called golden rule.

Using the **mischief rule**, the interpreter can assess a statutory provision on the basis of the 'mischief' or 'defect' it intended to cure within the pre-existing common law.[81] The historical development of this hermeneutical rule showed

[73] Konrad Zweigert and Hein Kötz, *An Introduction to Comparative Law* (Tony Weir tr, 3rd edn, OUP 1998) 259.

[74] ibid.

[75] Sussex Perage case [1844] ER 1034 (HL) 1057.

[76] Bell (n 49) paras 1.31ff; Kischel (n 6) 326f.

[77] Bell (n 49) paras 1.34f.

[78] Stefan Vogenauer, *Die Auslegung von Gesetzen in England und auf dem Kontinent: eine vergleichende Untersuchung der Rechtsprechung und ihrer historischen Grundlagen*, 2 vols (Mohr Siebeck 2001).

[79] Stefan Vogenauer, 'Interpretation of statutes, History of' in *The Max Planck Encyclopedia of European Private Law*, vol 2 (n 28) 986.

[80] Bell (n 49) paras 1-40ff.

[81] Heydon's case [1584] 76 ER 637 (KB) 639. 'The so-called mischief rule [...] was propounded by the judges in an age when statutes were drafted in a form very different from that which they assume today. Those who composed the Parliament of those days were chary of creating exceptions to common law; and, when they did so, thought it as necessary to incorporate in the statute the reasons which justified the changes in the common law that the statute made. Statutes in the sixteenth century and for long thereafter in addition to the enacting words contained lengthy preambles reciting the particular mischief or defect in the common law that the enacting words were designed to remedy. So,

a (limited) willingness on the part of the courts to take the purpose of the legislator into consideration.[82]

The so-called **golden rule** enables the interpreter to depart from the literal meaning of the provisions, but only provided their wording is unclear (otherwise, 'you must follow them,[83] even though they lead to a manifest absurdity. The Court has nothing to do with the question of whether the legislature has committed an absurdity').[84]

In principle, statutes must comply with the **Constitution**, which is said to be the highest source of domestic law.

> The **English Constitution** is not written but draws on sources of different nature, namely (constitutional) statutes, common law, and parliamentary conventions.[85] The latter can be defined as understandings and practice that regulate the conduct of the sovereign power of the state but are not enforced directly by courts.[86] Some scholarly publications are recognized as works of authority, the most prominent among them being the *Introduction to the Study of the Law of the Constitution* by Albert Venn Dicey (1835-1922) (see *supra*, ch 7, para 1).
> By contrast, the **Constitution of the United States** is enshrined in a written document (1789), which followed the Declaration of Independence (1776). It consists of only seven articles, which, albeit preserved untouched over time, have been supplemented by twenty-seven amendments. It co-exists with the constitutions of the different states,[87] being the US a federal system.

However, a major distinction can be drawn between jurisdictions of common law as to their attitude towards statutes that do not comply with the Constitution.

In the **UK**, unlike many European countries, no constitutional court is settled,[88] nor courts explicitly do have the power to strike down any statute as

when it was so laid down, the "mischief" rule did not require the court to travel beyond the actual words of the statute itself to identify "the mischief and defect for which the common law did not provide", for this would have been stated in the preamble. It was a rule of construction of the actual words appearing in the statute and nothing else' (Lord Diplock in *Black-Clawson Ltd v Papierwerke AG* [1975] AC 591, 637). Nevertheless: 'In constructing modern statutes which contain no preambles to serve as aids of construction of enacting words the "mischief" rule must be used with caution to justify any reference to extraneous documents for this purpose. If the enacting words are plain and unambiguous in themselves there is no need to have recourse to any "mischief" rule' (Lord Diplock in *Black-Clawson Ltd v Papierwerke AG* [1975] AC 591, 637).

82 Lord Nicholls in *R v Secretary of State for the Environment, Transport and the Regions, Ex p Spath Holme Ltd* [2001] 2 AC 349, 397.

83 *River Wear Commission v Adamson* [1876-77] 2 App Cas 743 (HL) 764.

84 Lord Esher in *R v City of London Court Judge* [1892] 1 QB 273 (CA) 290. 'We must [...] in this case have recourse to what is called the golden rule of construction [...] viz., to give the words used by the legislature their plain and natural meaning unless it is manifest from the general scope and intention of the statute injustice and absurdity would result' (Jervis CJ in *Mattison v Hart* (1854) 14 CB 357, 385).

85 Bell (n 49) para 1.15ff.

86 Dicey (n 9) 277ff.

87 von Mehren and Murray (n 52) 5.

88 Bell (n 49) para 1.18.

unconstitutional,[89] even after the Human Rights Act 1998 came into force.[90] This conclusion draws on the doctrine of parliamentary sovereignty, which traditionally commands an absolute abidance in England: along the words of Dicey, '[t]here is no person or body of persons who can, under the English constitution, make rules which override or derogate from an Act of Parliament'.[91] By contrast, the principle of **judicial review** of primary legislation contravening the constitution has been established in the US since the case *Marbury v Madison* of 1803,[92] whereby this power was acknowledged to the **US Supreme Court**.[93]
In the hierarchy of sources of law of Anglo-American jurisdictions, **administrative regulations** are ranked lower than statutes.
In the US, federal agencies are often conferred through a statute enacted by the Congress the power to issue administrative regulations with rulemaking authority, thus amounting to sources of law.[94] These regulations are published in the Federal Register and codified into the Code of Federal Regulations.
In Anglo-American jurisdictions, like in civil law countries (see *supra*, ch 7, para 3.1), **custom** (or **usage**) is acknowledged to be a source of law of last resort (see also *supra*, ch 2, para 2), provided that it is reasonable, certain, and considered by those involved as binding.[95] It has relatively little importance in the US,[96] more in the UK.

> English law distinguishes between customs existing from time immemorial (ie since 3 September 1189) and those of more recent date. The former have equal authority to common law, whilst the latter do not prevail over it.[97]

4. LEGAL EDUCATION AND LEGAL SCHOLARSHIP

Along the tenets of legal positivism (see *supra*, ch 5), **legal scholarship** cannot be classified as a source of law. However, it has been convincingly contended that: 'The positivist view that law is created and enforced by the state creates a dangerous optical illusion. The organs of the state may choose, conscientiously or unconsciously, to enforce rules created elsewhere, for example, the rules found in scholarly writing, in manuals, and in teaching in the universities. The positivist view leads one to neglect these sources.'[98] It must be therefore acknowledged that legal scholarship is a formant of law (see *supra*, ch 3, para 3.2).

[89] Samuel (n 71) 88ff.
[90] *In re K (A Child)* [2001] 2 WLR 1141, 119.
[91] Dicey (n 9) 40.
[92] *Marbury v Madison*, 5 U.S. (1 Cranch) 137 (1803).
[93] von Mehren and Murray (n 52) 134ff, 142ff.
[94] Bernard Schwartz, *American Constitutional Law* (CUP 2013) 283ff.
[95] Bell (n 49) para 1.24.
[96] von Mehren and Murray (n 52) 7.
[97] *Plumer v Leicester* (1329) 97 Selden Society 45, 46.
[98] Rodolfo Sacco, 'Legal Formants: A Dynamic Approach To Comparative Law (Installment II of II)' (1991) 39 Am J Comp L 344.

Since the medieval renaissance of Roman law (see *supra*, ch 2, para 3), the role played by legal scholars proved to be of the utmost importance for the application and the development of **civil law** (see *supra*, ch 2, para 4.1). In the civilian tradition, scholars have been resorted to by sovereigns, courts, and private parties to apprehend the right interpretation of the books containing the law (from the Justinian compilation to national codifications). No less importantly, legal scholars were teachers of law at universities, where they not only transmitted knowledge and information but molded in depth their students' mentality.

Still nowadays in civil law jurisdictions, university professors of law often practice as barristers or serve on the panel of courts; their treatises and commentaries may be extremely influential on practice and thus provide a reliable guidance for the interpretation of national laws.

By contrast, till recent times legal scholarship has been much less influential in common law jurisdictions,[99] particularly in that of **England**.[100]

One of the reasons for this fact is that it was only towards the mid-eighteenth century that English law began to be studied in a systematic way and taught at universities (see *supra*, ch 2, para 4.2). Indeed, for several centuries legal education was not provided by English universities, nor was common law taught by their professors. In fact, English barristers were trained at the Inns of Court, and solicitors at the Inns of Chancery.[101]

> The four Inns of Court based in London are Lincoln's, Inner Temple, Middle Temple, and Gray's, and they still play a significant (although minor) role in the education of future English barristers.
> Since 1903, solicitors have been trained at the Law Society of England and Wales.

However, nine **books of antiquity** are considered binding, one of them being Blackstone's *Commentaries* (1765-1769) (see *supra*, ch 2, para 5; ch 4, para 5).[102]

In the **US**, legal scholarship is deemed to play a greater role than in England, probably due to the need of overcoming the parochialism of each state's private law and of rationalizing it.[103]

As a matter of fact, the outset of American law was decidedly forged by the grand treatises of some nineteenth-century lawyers, like the *Commentaries on American Law* by James Kent (1763-1847) and the *Commentaries on the Constitution of the United States* by Joseph Story (1779-1845) (see *supra*, ch 3, para 4).[104]

[99] Stefan Vogenauer, 'Common law' in *The Max Planck Encyclopedia of European Private Law*, vol 1 (n 22) 266.
[100] Bell (n 49) paras 1.103f.
[101] Baker (n 46) 168ff.
[102] Kischel (n 6) 262.
[103] Von Mehren and Murray (n 52) 22.
[104] John B Cassoday, 'James Kent and Joseph Story' (1903) 12 Yale LJ 146.

Nonetheless, professional schools of law were settled outside universities at least until 1817, when Harvard Law School was founded.

It was **Christopher Columbus Langdell** (1826-1906) that paved the way for modern legal education in the US. When appointed in the 1870s at Harvard Law School (afterwards becoming its dean until 1895, when he resigned), Langdell was the first of a new generation of professors of law who believed, firstly, that law was not practice (which professors did not undertake or only minimally) but 'a science'; and, secondly, 'that all the available materials of that science are contained in printed books'.[105]

Langdell claimed that American law was a complete and coherent conceptual system, endowed with an inner logic and capable of generating the right answer to any practical problem through deductive syllogism (**classicism**).[106] Since Langdell was a pragmatist, however, his claim was based on a methodology of discussion of cases, which he first adopted in teaching.[107] Furthermore, he invented 'casebooks' as a genre of legal literature.[108]

Although in a different vein, a recent resurgence of formalism has been identified in the textualism (or originalism) advocated for and applied by **Antonin Scalia** (1936-2016) as a member of the Supreme Court of the US.

> 'Of all the criticisms levelled against textualism, the most mindless is that it is "formalistic". The answer to that is, *of course it's formalistic!* The rule of law is *about* form. [...] Long live formalism. It is what makes a government of laws and not of men'.[109]

According to **textualism (or originalism)**, the Constitution is to be interpreted in accord with its original meaning, and statutes are to be read in accord with their plain meaning.

According to Justice Scalia,[110] one should agree with Holmes's remark which reads: 'We do not inquire what the legislature meant; we ask only what the statute means'.[111]

Justice Scalia conceded that, contrary to the doctrine of strict constructionism, 'a text should not be construed strictly, and it should not be construed leni-

[105] This observation was contained in the inspired speech delivered by Langdell on 5 November 1886 at the Meeting of the Harvard Law School Association on the Law School Day Commemoration of the 250th Anniversary of the Founding of Harvard College: cf Charles Warren, *History of the Harvard Law School and of the Early Legal Conditions in America*, vol 2 (Lewis 1908, reprint The Lawbook Exchange 1999) 374.

[106] Cf Gary Minda, *Postmodern Legal Movements: Law and Jurisprudence at Century's End* (New York UP 1995) 13ff.

[107] See Bernard Schwartz, *Main Currents in American Legal Thought* (Carolina Academic Press 1993) 346ff.

[108] Cristopher Columbus Langdell, *A Selection of Cases on the Law of Contracts* (Little, Brown & Co 1871).

[109] Antonin Scalia, *A Matter of Interpretation: Federal Courts and the Law* (Princeton UP 1997) 25.

[110] ibid 23.

[111] Oliver Wendell Holmes, 'The Theory of Legal Interpretation' in Id, *Collected Legal Papers* (Harcourt, Brace and Howe 1920) 207.

ently; it should be construed reasonably, to contain all that it fairly means'.[112] He could not, however, resist to add: 'Though better that [ie being a strict constructionist], I suppose, than a nontextualist'.[113]
In the first decades of the twentieth century, American culture was affected by a valuable current of **legal realism**, which, however, never carved out a unitary doctrine nor established one school of thought; rather, it remained a scattered assortment of different views on law and varying trains of thought, advocated for by scholars that had different ideas, styles, and temperaments.[114] A first relevant stream of this cultural environment may be identified in the so-called **sociological jurisprudence**.

> It was **Roscoe Pound** (1870-1964) the first to claim that the 'law in books', as purported by the classicism of Langdell and his followers, had to be replaced with a 'law in action'.[115]

A radical change of paradigm was advocated for, since law was no longer to be conceptualized as an autonomous order of logical concepts but as 'social control through the systematic application of the force of politically organized society'.[116] In this vein, the method of finding the law was sought in a strong interaction with other social sciences.
After World War I, the 'realistic credo' was embraced by a group of irreverent and iconoclastic scholars, who imposed the notion as a strand of the debate on the nature and the goals of law.

> The birth of the movement was announced by its recognized chief, namely **Karl N. Llewellyn** (1893-1962), with an article published in 1930,[117] which also read as an attack on Dean Roscoe Pound of Harvard Law School.[118] The latter replied,[119] thus engendering a further reaction by Llewellyn.[120]

Legal realists were committed to challenging scholars and courts to behave responsibly, by abandoning any mechanical solutions attributable to a conservative formalism and resorting instead to the methods of empirical social sciences. Particularly, they intended to challenge courts not only to achieve

[112] Scalia (n 110) 23.
[113] ibid.
[114] Brian Leiter, 'American Legal Realism' in Martin P Golding and William A Edmundson (eds), *The Blackwell Guide to Philosophy of Law and Legal Theory* (Blackwell 2005) 50ff.
[115] Roscoe Pound, 'Law in Books and Law in Action' (1910) 44 Am LR 12.
[116] Roscoe Pound, 'The Scope and Purpose of Sociological Jurisprudence' (Pts 1-3) (1911) 24 Harvard LR 591; (1912) 25 Harvard LR 140ff, 489; Benjamin N Cardozo, *The Nature of the Judicial Process* (Yale UP 1941).
[117] Karl N Llewellyn, 'A Realistic Jurisprudence – The Next Step' (1930) 30 Col LR 431.
[118] Something of the kind happened as well with Jerome Frank, *Law and the Modern Mind* (reprint Routledge 2009) 207ff, 295ff.
[119] Roscoe Pound, 'The Call for a Realistic Jurisprudence' (1931) 44 Harvard LR 697.
[120] Karl N Llewellyn, 'Some Realism about Realism – Responding to Dean Pound' (1931) 44 Harvard LR 1222.

justice but also to advance public policy, as courts had traditionally done before the American Civil War.

The polemic attitude of legal realists was also flavored by the fact that, being centered in the law faculties of Columbia and Yale Law Schools, they were pitted against Harvard Law School, which had been the realm of Langdell. Furthermore, despite what he had advocated in the first period of his activity, Pound was by far considered an over-arching conservative, while the new realists were all committed to political progressivism.

The representatives of American legal realism acknowledge as their forerunner **Oliver Wendell Holmes**, Jr. (1841-1955),[121] whom they considered as the (first) 'completely adult jurist'.[122]

Holmes was Justice of the Supreme Court of the United States. His successor, **Benjamin N. Cardozo** (1870-1938), drew on his teachings and is considered one of the main followers of legal realism.

The basic assumption shared by legal realists is that: 'The life of the law has not been logic: it has been experience'.[123] Accordingly, the claim of classic legal thought, namely to derive law from a conceptual order, implies an omniscient and overall knowledge of things; thus, it was derided as childish or pretentious. Instead, legal realists claimed that judicial decisions were largely based on '**hunches**', relying on an intuitive sense of what is right or wrong, an understanding that thus attributed a major role to a judge's personality and experience. Some of these authors stressed the systemic and social determinants of such 'biases' and 'prejudices'. Secondly, legal realists advocated for the '**bad-man theory of law**', based on the assumption that such a man 'does not care two straws for the axioms or deductions, but that he does want to know what the Massachusetts or English courts are likely to do in fact'.[124] Therefore, 'the prophecies of what the courts will do in fact, and nothing more pretentious, are what I mean by law'.[125]
Thirdly, although anti-formalist, legal realists considered legal terminology as a key-question, thus viewing as essential the task of fixing properly the meaning of the words used in legal discourse.
Wesley Newcomb Hohfeld (1879-1918) authored a seminal essay on the taxonomy of rights and duties, where he defined the relevant terminology (see *infra*, ch 10, para 1).[126]

[121] Cf the essays collected to celebrate the ninetieth birthday of Holmes, in Felix Frankfurter (ed), *Mr. Justice Holmes* (Coward-McCann 1931), and particularly the introduction by Benjamin N. Cardozo, 1-20.
[122] Jerome Frank, *Law and the Modern Mind* (6th edn, Stevens & Sons 1949) 253ff.
[123] Oliver Wendell Holmes, *The Common Law* (Little, Brown & Co 1881) 1.
[124] Oliver Wendell Holmes, 'The Path of the Law' (1897) 10 Harvard LR 497 and in Id, *Collected Legal Papers* (n 17) 167, 173.
[125] Holmes (n 125) 173.
[126] Wesley N Hohfeld, 'Fundamental Legal Conceptions as Applied in Judicial Reasoning' (1913) 23 Yale LJ 16; (1917) 26 Yale LJ 710.

5. LAW AND ECONOMICS (AND OTHER INTERDISCIPLINARY LEGAL STUDIES)

The developments of the American twentieth century legal culture have been qualified as '**postmodern**', having abandoned the search for foundational truths based either on transcendent values or on the myth of the neutrality of the law. These modern movements have instead turned to a multiplicity of interpretative methods aimed at 'unmasking' the great theoretical or axiological narratives of the law, unveiling the stereotypes and social prejudices that used to dwell beneath them. Five major cultural movements have been subsequently identified:[127] law and economics, critical legal studies,[128] feminist legal theory,[129] law and literature, and critical race theory.
There is no doubt that a major diffusion and success, not only in the US but also in Europe, has been achieved by the law and economics movement, which is characterized by subjecting the law to an analysis based on economic methods,[130] in particular those of **microeconomics** and of **institutional economics**. In what is known as its normative version, this analysis is ultimately aimed at suggesting modifications to current legislation or to established jurisprudence.

The expression 'law and economics' was coined in 1925 by the economist John R. Commons (1862-1945).

At its early stage of development, the law and economics movement dealt exclusively with competition law, and in particular **antitrust law**. It was only later on (since the 1960s) that it spread to other areas of private (and even public) law, moving forward to encompass patrimonial sectors such as contracts, tort liability, and company law, but finally also reaching topics such as personal liberties and family law. This cultural trend of the law and economics movement, referred to as the **economic analysis of law** (EAL), developed at the University of Chicago. A fundamental premise for its development was represented by the acclaimed essay written by **Ronald Coase** (1910-2013) and published under the title of 'The Problem of Social Cost' in 1960.[131]

After having taught a course on the organization and financing of the UK radio industry at the London School of Economics, Coase, who was English, moved to the US (University of Virginia) in 1951. In 1959, he published an article on legal and economic problems associated with the allocation of legal

[127] See Minda (n 107).
[128] Mark V Tushnet, 'Critical Legal Studies' in Golding and Edmundson (eds) (n 114) 80ff.
[129] Patricia Smith, 'Four Themes in Feminist Legal Theory: Difference, Dominance, Domesticity, and Denial' in Golding and Edmundson (eds) (n 114) 90ff.
[130] Lewis A Kornhauser, 'Economic Rationality in the Analysis of Legal Rules and Institutions' in Golding and Edmundson (eds) (n 114) 67ff.
[131] Ronald Harry Coase, 'The Problem of Social Cost' (1960) 3 J L&Econ 1.

entitlements for radio frequencies in the Journal of Law and Economics. As this article prompted a vivid debate among the economists at Stanford, Coase was invited to clarify his theses. To this end, he wrote and published 'The Problem of Social Cost': the article that became one of his most famous works.

Discussing the questions posed by industrial pollution and its harmful effects on third parties (**negative externalities**), Coase surmised that, if rights over resources are clearly specified and transferable and individuals have all the information necessary to reach an agreement without wasting time or incurring significant expenses, they are always in the position, through negotiations, to reach a Pareto-efficient allocation of resources, regardless of their original distribution. Subsequently, the basic idea supporting this argument was formalized as the '**Coase theorem**', which has been re-elaborated in many variations.

As Coase himself stated, the central core of his thesis departed from the insights of an article published by Leo Herzel in 1951 in the University of Chicago Law Review.[132]

As for the social role of law, the Coase theorem implies some consequences of great significance. Firstly, it implies that, where its hypothetical condition is satisfied (ie that **transaction costs** are zero or irrelevant), the law would have a neutral effect with respect to the achievement of Pareto-efficiency. As an example, regardless of the illicit polluting activity of a company, the latter could always continue to carry out its business activity after having reached an agreement with the injured parties, compensating their losses by paying damages.

It must nonetheless be observed that Coase himself considered the assumption of the absence of transaction costs as a 'very unrealistic' one. Using his words, 'in order to carry out a market transaction, it is necessary to discover who it is that one wishes to deal with, to inform people that one wishes to deal and on what terms, to conduct negotiation leading up to a bargain, to draw up the contract, to undertake the inspection needed to make sure that the terms of the contract are being observed, and so on'.

From this, it follows that the law is not irrelevant from the point of view of the achievement of a Pareto-optimum, because the original allocation of a right can imply a significant social cost, given the inability of private parties to negotiate 'in the shadow of the law'. As a corollary, a specific task of the economic analysis of law is that of assessing the social costs of legal rules or of the solutions given to individual cases by judges (**descriptive law and economics**).

Hence, it can further be deduced that the task of the law is precisely that of lowering and possibly eliminating transaction costs, thus allowing private in-

[132] Leo Herzel, 'Facing Facts about the Broadcast Business: Rejoinder' (1952) 20 U Chi L Rev 106.

dividuals to negotiate efficiently, allocating resources to those who value them the most. To this end, the economic analysis of the law proposes to indicate to a legislator or to a judge how the law should be reformed or interpreted in order to achieve efficient results (**normative law and economics**).
From a policy point of view, the Coase theorem suggests that, under certain conditions, private negotiations would be preferable to public law interventions (eg higher taxation of polluting industrial activities) as a legal device for the regulation of the market. More generally, this theory is underpinned by a liberal approach to the economy and, consequently, by a rather radical liberalism both in politics and in legal theory. This approach has a relevant corollary in legal theory: Coase's analysis paved the way for a markedly anti-positivistic attitude, a perspective shared by **Richard Posner** and all the scholars that, at the University of Chicago, subsequently carried out law and economics studies.

After the publication of 'The Problem of Social Cost', Coase was appointed in 1964 by the University of Chicago as Professor of Law and Economics, and later as Director of the Journal of Law and Economics. As early as the 1950s, the same university, although not the faculty of economics, hosted **Friedrich von Hayek** (1899-1992), another leading actor in European liberalism. Thanks to the intervention of Aaron Director, the University of Chicago Press had published von Hayek's *The Road to Serfdom* (1944), which can be considered one of the manifestos of liberalism. Although not formally associated with the law and economics movement, he crucially contributed to the development of its more general liberal approach. Other members of the University of Chicago (such as Frank Knight and George Stigler) co-operated with von Hayek in the Mont Pelerin Society, an international classical liberal organization (see *supra*, ch 7, para 1).

A different strand of the law and economics movement originated in the research and teaching of **Guido Calabresi** and still has its center at Yale University. In 1961, in parallel with the work of Coase, Calabresi published the essay 'Some Thoughts on Risk Distribution and the Law of Torts',[133] which, together with his subsequent book *The Costs of Accidents* (1970),[134] represents a cornerstone of law and economics literature. On the same topic, again in 1961, **Pietro Trimarchi** published another important monographic work in Italy, entitled *Rischio e responsabilità oggettiva*.
While the Chicago school focuses on allocative efficiency and is characterized by a clearly liberalist ideological orientation, the approach that evolved at Yale also considers the **distributional efficiency** of legal rules, and it is more sensitive to democratic and reformist issues.
This renewed approach is perfectly illustrated by an important revision proposed by Calabresi to the efficiency definition elaborated by Pareto, originally

133 Guido Calabresi, 'Some Thoughts on Risk Distribution and the Law of Torts' (1961) 70 Yale LJ 499.
134 Guido Calabresi, *The Costs of Accidents* (Yale UP 1970).

illustrated in an unreleased part of Calabresi's article 'Some Thoughts on Risk Distribution and the Law of Torts',[135] a text that was formally published only in 1991.[136]

Contrary to what Coase had suggested, Calabresi observed that it is not always the case that those who suffer from the negative effects of someone else's activity can enforce their rights, forcing the externality to stop. This is possible only when the entitlement is protected by the legal system through a '**property rule**'. Conversely, when the entitlement is protected via a mere '**liability rule**', the right-holders can file claim solely for financial compensation of the damages they suffer.[137]

In terms of policy options, Calabresi has thus shown that the **Pareto criterion**, adopted by Coase when comparing the *status quo* with a merely hypothetical change, can end up favoring conservatism.

> The Pareto criterion states that, for society, moving from Status A to Status B is efficient if, after the change, no one is worse off and at least one individual is better off. In other words, Social Situation B is preferable to Social Situation A only if no one prefers A over B and at least one member of society prefers B over A. According to this criterion, therefore, social or legal reform is justified only on the basis of unanimous consensus.

At the same time, the **Kaldor-Hicks criterion**, which allows the situation of one individual to be worsened simply based on an abstract possibility of compensation, unambiguously results in optimal outcomes only if transaction costs are always irrelevant, because only under such an assumption would compensation actually be paid. However, since these costs are often positive, the afore-mentioned criterion demonstrates the risk of ensuring that those who are advantaged become even richer, while those who are disadvantaged become increasingly poorer. The problem of distributive justice becomes thus crucial.

> The Kaldor-Hicks criterion states that, for society, moving from Status A to Status B is efficient only if, after the change, those who are better off are in the position to fully compensate those who are worse off. Compared to the Pareto criterion, the Kaldor-Hicks criterion is based on a purely hypothetical assessment, as it does not presuppose that the compensation is later actually paid to those who have been disadvantaged.

Moreover, Calabresi's teaching is based on the assumption that the law is not wholly linked to the economy and that therefore economic criteria cannot always be a reason to criticize or modify the law.

[135] See Guido Calabresi, 'Commentary on Some Thoughts on Risk Distribution and the Law of Torts (1991)' (2013) Faculty Scholarship Series 1ff.

[136] Guido Calabresi, 'The Pointlessness of Pareto: Carrying Coase Further' (1991) 100 Yale LJ 1121.

[137] Guido Calabresi and Douglas Melamed, 'Property Rules, Liability Rules, and Inalienability: One View of the Cathedral' (1972) 85 Harvard LR 1089.

> 'In this sense, while in Economic Analysis of Law economics dominates and law is its subject of analysis and criticism, in Law and Economics the relationship is bilateral. Economic theory examines law, but not infrequently this examination leads to changes in economic theory rather than to changes in law or in the way legal reality is described'.[138]

A further strand of the law and economics movement is linked to the developments of **institutional economics**, which have found their academic seat especially at Michigan State University. Also in this case, a crucial role has been played by another path-breaking article written by Coase, 'The Nature of the Firm' (1937),[139] which compared the costs of an enterprise as a hierarchical organization with those of horizontal relationships based on market negotiations.

This approach was subsequently taken up and decisively developed by **Oliver Williamson**, who pointed out that within the extreme poles of a vertically integrated firm, on one hand, and autonomous market transactions, on the other, there lies a discrete series of hybrid forms of organization (eg franchising networks, long-term contracts, supply and distribution chains). Williamson's theory has helped to extend the analysis of governance theory, originally applied only to corporate structures but more recently developed also with regard to complex contractual relationships.[140]

This method of investigation has been profitably applied in particular to the analysis of **relational contracts**, which, according to a study carried out by **Ian R. Macneil** (1929-2010), are characterized by a condition of reciprocal dependence that links the contractual parties. This dependence develops over time and requires continuous adjustments and renegotiation within the 'frame of reference' traced by the terms of the original agreement.

[138] Guido Calabresi, *The Future of Law & Economics* (Yale UP 2016).
[139] Ronald Harry Coase, 'The Nature of the Firm' (1937) 4 Economica 368.
[140] See Stefan Grundmann, Florian Möslein and Karl Riesenhuber (eds), *Contract Governance: Dimensions in Law & Interdisciplinary Research* (OUP 2015); Walter Doralt, *Langzeitverträge* (Mohr Siebeck 2018).

GLOSSARY

Administrative law [*Droit administratif*; *Verwaltungsrecht*; *Diritto amministrativo*] (1): branch of public law that regulates the structure and aims of public bodies belonging to the administration, primarily the government. Administrative law rules the activity of the administrations that pursue the public interest and the relationship between public powers and the citizens subject to them.

Authoritative power [*Puissance publique*] (1): power granted to public bodies belonging to the administration, primarily the government, to take an authoritative decision to pursue the public interest.

Case law (or judge-made law) (3.1): law as it is applied by courts.

Civil codes (3.1): statutory acts that, in civil law jurisdictions, collect the general rules and principles of civil law and, in some countries, of commercial law as well. Historically, the first civil code was enacted by France in 1804 (and entered into force in 1806). Its cultural archetype was the *Corpus iuris civilis* that, during the Middle Ages, grew from the Justinian compilation.

Codification of commercial law (2): process of codifying the customary law that merchants had spontaneously developed in trading (*lex mercatoria*). Traditionally, the codification of commercial law progressed in parallel with that of civil law, thus resulting in the enactment of two distinct codes. In the middle of the twentieth century, however, Italian *Codice civile* absorbed the commercial code (see 'Unification of private law'); later on, this unified model was adopted by other civil codes.

Commercialization of civil law (2): policy of generalizing (some of) the rules of commercial law to apply to all citizens irrespective of their profession, in order to enhance the efficiency of civil law. It may be one of the goals aimed at by the unification of private law.

Commercial law [*Droit commercial*; *Handelsrecht*; *Diritto commerciale*] (2): special branch of private law that dictates businesses law, ie the body of rules applicable to businesses and other professionals. Company law is a prominent part of commercial law, which furthermore regulates competition (including antitrust regulation), bankruptcy, financial services.

Constitution [*Constitution*; *Verfassung*; *Costituzione*] (2.1): preeminent source of law, which lays down the foundations of the state and provides protection of human rights. It is often posited in a written document of provisions (charter), but may also consist in a collection of other acts and practices acknowledged to exist from immemorial time. In most countries, the constitution cannot be amended or even repealed by means of ordinary laws (it is then said to be 'rigid'). If laws do not meet a constitutional test, ordinary laws can be struck down by courts (judicial review), except in the UK.

Constitutionalization of private law [*Constitutionalisation du droit privé*; *Materialisierung des Privatrechts*; *Costituzionalizzazione del diritto privato*] (1): impact of fundamental rights and other constitutional principles on private law.

Customary law [*Coutumes*; *Gewohnheitsrecht*; *Usi normativi*] (2.1): law created by usage, accompanied by the belief that it is legally binding. It holds the lowest position in the hierarchy of the sources of law (see also 'Desuetude'). It may be put into writing and published in official journals, which however only constitute repositories of said law.

Declaration theory of common law (3.2): traditional explanation of the role played by common law courts, which would ascertain and declare already existing legal rules and would not have the power to change or amend them.

Decriminalization [Depenalizzazione] (1): policy of shrinking criminal law and abolishing criminal sanctions previously provided for certain issues (of business law, of family law, and so on).

Desuetude (3.1): repeal or amendment of statutory acts by means of customary law, which is not permitted (see also 'Customary law').

Development (or supplementation) of law [*Rechtsfortbildung*] (3.1): 'creative interpretation' by courts and legal scholars directed to adapt the law and to extend it to new cases not envisaged by the lawmaker. The aids and the limits of this interpretative practice are set out by the core tenets of legal methodology (*juristische Methodenlehre*).

Distinguishing (3.2): technique used by common law courts to adjudicate a case differently from a binding precedent, assuming that the latter did not deal with the same facts or legal issue.

***Drittwirkung* (3.1)**: application of constitutional principles by courts adjudicating private law cases. In its milder version, it consists of shaping the interpretation of the ordinary laws to constitutional principles (*mittelbare Drittwirkung*); in its more direct version, it consists of grounding rights and duties between the parties directly from constitutional principles (*unmittelbare Drittwirkung*).

Golden rule (3.2): in common law jurisdictions, the aid to statutory interpretation that allows the interpreter to depart from the literal meaning of a provision, but only provided that its wording is unclear.

Grammatical (or literal) interpretation (3.1): aid to statutory interpretation binding the interpreter to adhere to the wording of a provision and shaping the interpretation to its plain text.

***Handelsgesetzbuch* (HGB) (2)**: German code that regulates commercial law. It was introduced in 1897 and came into force on 1 January 1900 along with the German Civil Code (*Bürgerliches Gesetzbuch*, BGB).

Historical interpretation (3.1): aid to interpretation according to which the interpreter draws on the objective intention of the lawmaker (*mens legis*), as it is laid down in preparatory works, 'whereas' clauses, explanations of vote, and so on. In civil law jurisdictions, it is allowed, although its role is decidedly less than other aids for interpreting the law; in common law jurisdictions, it is not allowed.

Horizontal precedent (3.2): case adjudicated by a common law court, which has an absolute binding force for the same court who rendered it or for another court at a similar level (see also 'Vertical precedent' and 'Leading case').

INCOTERMS (2): International Commercial Terms, first published by the International Chamber of Commerce in 1936 and periodically revised. They are standard contract terms relating to international commercial law, largely used in international business transactions or procurements. The latest version is Incoterms 2020.

Inns of Court (3.2): London professional associations for barristers. There are four inns of court: Lincoln's Inn, Inner Temple, Middle Temple, Gray's Inn. Barristers must belong to one of these inns, which provide all the necessary facilities and by which they are supervised.

International Commercial Chamber (ICC) (2): international organization playing a prominent role in developing and applying a uniform commercial law. One of its objectives is to collect and publish commercial best practices and standard contract clauses.

Interpretation of law [*Interprétation du droit*; *Auslegung*; *Interpretazione del diritto*] (3.1): practice by which lawmakers determine the legal significance of the legislative acts. The interpretation of law is usually subdivided into four categories: the grammatical interpretation (see *ad vocem*), which matches the wording of the relevant provision; the historical interpretation (see *ad vocem*), which focuses on the intention of lawmakers; the teleological interpretation (see *ad vocem*), according to which the interpreter construes the purpose of the rule and may even disregard the declarations of lawmakers; the systematic interpretation (see *ad vocem*), which is centered on consistency with the rest of the legal system, including the latter's own roles and priciples.

***Iure privatorum* (1):** the state acts *iure privatorum* when it decides to pursue the public interest by means of private law (for example entering into a contract to buy a plot of land), instead of public law (for example expropriating a plot of land).

Judicial review (3.1): process that allows a court to assess whether a legislative act is constitutionally legitimate and, if it is not so, to strike it down.

Leading case (3.2): binding precedent at common law courts (see also 'Horizontal precedent' and 'Vertical precedent').

***Lex mercatoria* (2)**: body of customary law developed in international trade to rule business transactions beyond national borders.

Maritime law [*Droit maritime*; *Seerecht*; *Diritto della navigazione*] (2): law regulating maritime activities and aviation, whether commercial or non-commercial. Although more rooted in private law, it entails also elements of public law.

Mischief rule (3.2): aid to interpretation directed to cure the 'mischief' or 'defect' of pre-existing common law.

***Obligationenrecht* (OR) (2)**: Swiss legislation, passed in 1881, which provided a single legal framework for obligations, not distinguishing between civil and commercial law. In 1907, it became the fifth book of the *Zivilgesetzbuch* (ZGB) (see *ad vocem*).

Overruling (3.2): technique used by common law courts to depart from a leading case, repealing it.

Private law [*Droit privé*; *Privatrecht*; *Diritto privato*] (1): branch of the legal system that regulates (horizontal) relationships between peers. It is underpinned by the principle of private autonomy, according to which individuals are free to decide which regulatory regime should govern their interest, without prejudice to the freedom of others. It is opposed to public law (see *ad vocem*).

Public law [*Droit public*; *öffentliches Recht*; *Diritto pubblico*] (1): branch of the legal system that regulates (vertical) relationships between the state and private individuals, or entities. It is underpinned by the principle of authoritative power, which is based on the 'command and control' logic. It is opposed to private law (see *ad vocem*).

Regulations (2.1): within civil law jurisdictions, general acts of the administration that amount to sources of law, hierarchically inferior to legislative acts. Not to be confused with the regulations of the EU (see *infra*, ch 8, para 1.2.2).

Separation of powers (or Tria Politica principle) [*Principe de séparation des pouvoirs*; *Grundsatz der Gewaltenteilung*; *Principio della separazione dei poteri*] (2.1): tenet of political philosophy and constitutional law forged by the late eighteenth century Enlightenment, according to which the state should maintain the three powers separated from one another and should entrust each of them to a different body: the legislative (entrusted to the Parliament), the executive (entrusted to the government and the rest of the administration), and the judiciary (entrusted to courts).

***Stare decisis* (doctrine of) (2.2)**: doctrine according to which a single precedent has an absolute binding force for a lower-court judge (although it is still uncertain whether it might have the same binding force for the same judge who rendered it), who must align his following decisions.

Statutes [*Lois*; *Gesetze*; *Leggi*] (2.2): legislative acts approved by the Parliament. They represent the cornerstone of civil law system of the sources of law.

Systematic interpretation (2.1): aid to interpretation according to which the interpreter must derive the meaning of the provision so that it is consistent with the rest of the legal system, including the latter's own rules and principles.

Teleological interpretation (2.1): aid to interpretation according to which the interpreter must construe the policy underpinning the rule and may even disregard the declarations of lawmakers; this aid to interpretation allows the interpreter to carefully narrow (reductive interpretation) or broaden (expansive interpretation) the scope of a statutory provision.

Unification of private law (3): process of merging civil law (ie general private law) and commercial law (ie special private law for businesses and professionals) into one single code.

Vertical precedent (2.2): case adjudicated by a common law court, having an absolute binding force for a court lower than that the one which rendered it (see also 'Horizontal precedent' and 'Leading case').

***Zivilgesetzbuch* (ZGB) (3)**: Swiss Civil Code adopted in 1907. It was influenced by French and German Civil Codes.

BIOGRAPHIES

Cesare Massimo Bianca (Catania, 1932 – Roma, 2020) was an eminent Italian jurist and professor, known especially for his remarkable academic life, which has been mainly focused on the study of private law.
Bianca lectured Civil Law at the University La Sapienza of Rome and Family Law at LUISS Guido Carli. His interest in these two legal fields is further confirmed by numerous roles in heterogeneous bodies. Indeed, he was member of the *Accademia dei Giusprivatisti Europei*, and he is one of the founding fathers of the SECOLA (Society of European Contract Law). Furthermore, Bianca has been co-director of the Italian prestigious journal *Rivista di diritto civile*, President of the CeTM (*Centro di Ricerca per la Tutela della Persona del Minore*) based at the University La Sapienza of Rome and has been named Professor *honoris causa* of the Universidad Nacional Mayor de San Marcos in Lima.
His main works are: *Il debitore e i mutamenti del destinatario del pagamento* (1963); *La vendita e la permuta*, 2 vols (first published, 1972; 2nd edn, 1993); *Dell'inadempimento delle obbligazioni* (first published, 1967; 2nd edn, 1979); *Diritto civile*, 7 vols (1978-2020).

Claus-Wilhelm Canaris (Liegnitz, 1937) is a German jurist best known for his contributions to the theory of legitimate expectation's protection (*Vertrauenshaftung*) and of legal lacunae.
After completing his legal and philosophical studies between the cities of Paris, Geneva and Munich, he started his academic career at the University of Munich as assistant. There, he first revealed his theory of legal gap in the dissertation *Die Feststellung von Lücken im Gesetz* (*How to Ascertain Lacunae in the Law*) in 1964.
In 1968, he became professor at the University of Graz and, one year later, at the University of Hamburg. In 1972, he returned to the University of Munich, where he was Professor of Private Law, Commercial Law, and Labor Law until his retirement in 2005.
Canaris holds five honorary doctorates from the Universities of Lisbon, Madrid, Athens, Verona, and Rio. His numerous memberships further confirm his wide legal engagement. Indeed, he was appointed member of the philosophical-historical class of the Bavarian Academy of Sciences in 1990, the European Academy of Sciences and Arts in 1991, the *Accademia dei Giusprivatisti Europei* in 1994 and the *Istituto Lombardo Accademia di Scienze e Lettere* in 2008.
His main works are: *Die Feststellung von Lücken im Gesetz* (1964); *Die Vertrauenshaftung im deutschen Privatrecht* (1971); *Bankvertragsrecht* (1975); *Grundrechte und Privatrecht* (1999); *Schuldrechtsmodernisierung 2002* (2002).

Albert Venn Dicey (Lutterworth, 1835 – Oxford, 1922) was a British Whig jurist and a constitutional theorist. He attended the King's College School in London and Balliol College in Oxford, where he graduated in Classical Moderations in 1856 and in *Literae humaniores* in 1858. His career included diverse positions: he won a fellowship at Trinity College in Oxford in 1860, was called to the bar

by the Inner Temple in 1863, subscribed to the Jamaica Committee in 1865, was appointed Vinerian Professor of English Law at Oxford in 1882 and became King's Counsel in 1890. Subsequently, he left Oxford and became one of the first professors of law at the London School of Economics, newly created at that time. Dicey was politically affiliated with the group 'University Liberals' and was often labelled as a radical; in his view, outlined in his first major work *Introduction to the Study of the Law of the Constitution* (1885), personal freedom was 'the basis of national welfare' and depended on the sovereignty of parliament, the impartiality of the courts, and the supremacy of the common law.
He was strongly opposed to home rule for Ireland, women's suffrage, proportional representation, and to the idea according to which citizens are entitled to ignore unjust laws: he believed that the need to set a stable legal system was more important than the potential injustice that would occur from applying unjust laws. However, he did admit that in some rare cases it would be appropriate to invoke an armed rebellion.
He was the most important theorist of the 'rule of law', ie the principle whereby all members of a society are deemed equally subject to legal provisions and processes. His main works are: *The Privy Council* (1860); *Introduction to the Study of the Law of the Constitution* (1885); *A Digest of the Law of England with Reference to the Conflict of Laws* (1896); *Lectures on Relation between Law and Public Opinion in England during the Nineteenth Century* (1905).

David Dudley Field (Haddam, 1805 – New York, 1894) was an American lawyer. After his family moved to Stockbridge (Massachusetts) because of work commitments of his father, Field opted for the nearby Williams College, which was founded by Colonel Ephraim Williams. The decision was motivated by the leaving of Connecticut, where Field was born in 1805.
Field did not graduate because of a falling out with the president of the college. Therefore, he decided to abandon his academic track in 1826.
This circumstance did not, however, prevent him from being admitted to the bar in 1828, practicing in New York City.
One of his main interests was in the structure of the judicial system. This penchant led him to advocate a campaign in order to reform the New York judicial system (1837). Years later (1847), the New York legislature appointed him as chief draftsman of a pleading and practice commission. The work of this commission culminated in the drafting of a code of civil procedure and then a code of criminal procedure. This new code-based pleading represented indeed the great purpose of Field. At a later time, he was appointed chairman of a commission for the codification of the whole body of New York law, both substantive and procedural. Thereafter, he was appointed to draft the so-called 'Field Codes', which were adopted entirely by California and partly by New York.
On the whole, he strongly contributed to the reform of American civil procedural law. His greatest achievement was devising a parting from the pleading of common law towards the above-mentioned code-based pleading.
Field submitted his codes for review to the Lord Chancellors in England as well. Particularly, Codes of Procedure, drafted by Field, were analysed by five Lord

Chancellors (Lords Cairns, Cranworth, Hatherley, Westbury, and Wood). The Field's Codes were deeply treasured on this occasion, thus swaying the English Judicature Acts of 1873 and 1875, which were later embraced by several British colonies across the world (ie India).
Moreover, Field became one of the founders of the Institute of International Law (1873). Its primary purpose was the formulation and promotion of international law as mandatory tool to guarantee world peace. He also prepared the draft of an international code (1876).
Apart from the above-mentioned professional achievements, it is generally noteworthy that he was a highly appreciated lawyer and law scholar; at the same time, his intellectual standing has fascinated some of the most prominent America's authors. On a truly celebrated occasion, which traces back at 1850, Field hosted a picnic at Monument Mountain where he introduced Nathaniel Hawthorne to Herman Melville, who was trying to elaborate a novel about a whale hunt. This allowed Hawthorne and Melville to establish a strong bond of friendship that induced Melville to transmute his work from an adventure novel into the great Moby-Dick.
His main works are: *Book of forms adapted to the Code of procedure* (1861); *Outlines of an International Code* (1876); *The Electoral Votes of 1876: Who Should Count Them, What Should be Counted, and the Remedy for a Wrong Count* (1876); *The Vote That Made the President* (1876); *Projet d'un code international proposé aux diplomates, aux hommes d'état, et aux jurisconsultes du droit international. Contenant en outre l'exposé du droit international actuel sur les matières les plus importantes* (Albéric Rolin tr, 1881).

Friedrich August von Hayek (Vienna, 1899 – Freiburg im Breisgau, 1992) was an Austrian-British economist and philosopher. He won the 1974 Nobel Memorial Prize in Economic Sciences, together with Gunnar Myrdal, for his 'pioneering work in the theory of money and economic fluctuations and penetrating analysis of the interdependence of economic, social and institutional phenomena'. Hayek served in World War I and said that his experience in the war and his desire to help avoid the mistakes that had led to the war drew him into economics. He attended the University of Vienna, earning doctorates in Law and Political Economics in 1921 and 1923 respectively. In 1929, Hayek joined the University of Vienna as a lecturer, while in 1931, he moved to the London School of Economics and Political Science as a professor, becoming a good friend of Karl Popper and achieving academic exposition thanks to his criticisms of the Keynesian welfare state and the totalitarian socialism. In 1944, Hayek rose to fame for his book *The Road to Serfdom*, in which he accused socialism of having impracticable ideas and for having been the root of Nazism. In 1950, he left the London School of Economics to join the Chicago University. He remained in Chicago until 1962, producing many valuable papers. Among them, *The Constitution of Liberty*, published in 1960, is considered to be a cornerstone of twentieth-century liberalism. In 1962, Hayek left Chicago for the University of Freiburg im Breisgau in West Germany. He remained there until his retirement, in 1968, when he accepted an honorary professorship at the University of Salzburg in Austria. In 1977, he returned to

Freiburg permanently and finished the work on what would become the three-part *Law, Legislation and Liberty* (1973-1979), a critique of efforts to redistribute incomes in the name of social justice. He was also one of the founders of The Mont Pelerin Society (MPS). Hayek's philosophy is entirely built on the ideal of individual freedom and on the close connection between economic freedom and individual freedom in general. He strongly advocated for free market economics, conceiving trade as a spontaneous order established thanks to the self-regulation of the economy and society.
His main works are: *Monetary Theory and the Trade Cycle* (1933); *Monetary Nationalism and International Stability* (1937); *Profits, Interest & Investment* (1939); *The Pure Theory of Capital* (1941); *The Road to Serfdom* (1944); *Individualism and Economic Order* (1948); *The Counter-Revolution of Science: Studies on the Abuse of Reason* (1952); *The Sensory Order: An Inquiry into the Foundations of Theoretical Psychology* (1952); *The Constitution of Liberty* (1960); *Law, Legislation and Liberty* (1973-1979).

Natalino Irti (Avezzano, 1936) is an Italian lawyer and professor. He became ordinary professor in 1968 and taught at the Universities of Sassari, Parma, Perugia, Turin; in 1977, he moved to Rome, to teach Private Law, Civil Law, and General Theory of Law at the University La Sapienza. He is the President of the Italian Istituto per gli Studi Storici, a member of the State Bar and of the *Accademia dei Lincei*, and he has directed several prominent Italian legal journals.
His legal thought analyses legal rules from a conceptual and a formal point of view; he claims that legal norms are the expression of the will of economic, political, technological power groups, and their rationality may be found in their functionality related to given purposes.
Irti also argues that a phenomenon of 'decodification' is affecting the law, especially private law, leading both to the creation of legal subsystems ('legislative polycentrism'), governed by specific principles, and to the loss of the certainty of law, which can only be filled by strongly authoritative scholars.
His main works are: *Proprietà e impresa* (1965); *La ripetizione del negozio giuridico* (1970); *L'età della decodificazione* (1978); *La cultura del diritto civile* (1990); *L'ordine giuridico del mercato* (2004); *La tenaglia. In difesa dell'ideologia politica* (2008); *Diritto senza verità* (2011); *Un diritto incalcolabile* (2016).

James Kent (Fredericksburg, Dutchess County, New York, 1763 – New York City, 1847) was an American jurist and the author of the *Commentaries on American Law*.
He studied at Yale College, where he graduated in 1781, although the Revolutionary War required him to suspend his studies periodically. In that period of time, he strongly contributed to the institution of the 'Phi Beta Kappa Society'. He started to practice law at the bar in 1787.
Kent was a member from Dutchess County of the New York State Assembly in 1791 and 1792-1793.
He became the first Professor of Law at Columbia College in 1793 and, at a later time, again served in the Assembly in 1796-1797.

He received several designations: Recorder of New York City (1797), Justice of the New York Supreme Court (1798), Chief Justice (1804), and Chancellor of the New York Court of Chancery (1814). In the role of chancellor, Kent was entitled to do justice related to the specific facts of each case, taking into consideration the equitable principles which had been previously elaborated in England. In a broader perspective, the Kent's thought was crucial in progressively adapting the common law of England to the common law of the Unites States.
Kent was also elected member of the American Antiquarian Society in 1814.
According to his view, the predictability of justice represented a mandatory condition for accomplishing the commercial progress and durable social order searched for by the Federalists. This theory was combined with the emphasis given to judicial precedent, which was fundamental in reaching the above-mentioned predictability. Where a precedent was deficient, he used to resort to civil law, conceived as a derivation of Roman law.
The *Commentaries on American Law* (first published 1826) represent the great work of Kent. Their conceptual core is rooted in some of Kent's lectures at Columbia University after his retirement in 1823. The treatise is divided into four volumes dealing with international law, the Constitution and government of the United States, the municipal laws of the states, personal rights (including real and personal property).
His main work is: *Commentaries on American Law* (first published 1826).

Baron de Montesquieu (La Brède, 1689 – Paris, 1755) was a French philosopher, jurist, historian and political thinker of the early French Enlightenment.
Born into an eminent family of jurists, his life was deeply affected by the significant historical period of his time, a profound political and social transformation which considerably shaped his studies and writings. In 1721, he published his immediate success *Lettres persanes* (*Persian Letters*), a satire that, through the eyes of two fictional Persians, describes French society and institutions from the perspective of two non-European visitors. The outcome was a disenchanted overview of French absolutism, of the crisis in civil society at the time, and even of the religion, which, according to Montesquieu, increases the conflicts and divisions between people.
In 1748, Montesquieu published his most important work *De l'esprit des lois* (*The Spirit of the Laws*), which is a real political and judicial encyclopedia, especially famous for the development of the theory of separation of powers between legislative, executive, and judiciary. This distribution is set as an essential guarantee for the freedom of the citizen, which must be protected from absolutism. Therefore, the outlined three powers must be exercised by three different subjects, able to limit one another in order to prevent any abuse or tyranny. However, Montesquieu clarified that the freedom of the citizen shall not be confused with independence: the freedom is the right to act within the limits set by the law. Therefore, Montesquieu defined the right balance between the three powers, a separation many countries throughout the world have used when creating their national Constitutions.
His main works are: *Système des idées* (1716); *Lettres persanes* (1721); *Le Temple*

de Gnide (1725); *Considérations sur les causes de la grandeur des Romains et de leur décadence* (1734); *Arsace et Isménie* (1742); *De l'esprit des lois* (1748); *La défense de 'L'Esprit des lois'* (1750); *Mes Pensées* (1720-1755); *Essai sur le goût* (1757).

Hans Carl Nipperdey (Bad Berka, 1895 – Cologne, 1968) was a German jurist specialized in the study of labor law. He is a controversial figure, mainly due to his cooperation with the Nazi Reich and his contribution to the Academy for German Law (*Akademie für Deutsches Recht*) founded in 1933.
He firstly became Professor of Labor Law at the University of Cologne, where he firmly supported the conservative orientation of this legal branch.
Afterwards, during his membership of the Academy for German Law he worked in conjunction with Alfred Hueck on drafting Nazi labor law.
During the post-World War II, Nipperdey continued his academic life, became President of the Federal Labor Court and considerably restricted the right to take strike action.
His main works are: *Lehrbuch des Arbeitsrechts* (1927-1930); *Gesetz zur Ordnung der nationalen Arbeit. Kommentar* (1943); *Tarifvertragsgesetz mit Durchführungs- und Nebenvorschriften*, in collaboration with A. Huech (1950), *Soziale Marktwirtschaft und Grundgesetz* (1961); *Grundrechte und Privatrecht* (1961).

Pietro Perlingieri (Naples, 1937) is an eminent Italian jurist, politician and professor.
Perlingieri graduated in Law from the University of Naples in 1959. Shortly afterwards, he was named assistant professor and, at the young age of 28, became the youngest Italian dean at the University of Camerino. During his academic life, he taught Civil Law and Philosophy of Law at the University of Benevento, being also its dean. Afterwards, he lectured in the most prestigious Italian Universities of Rome (La Sapienza and LUISS Guido Carli), Turin, Naples (Federico II), and Salerno.
Beyond his noteworthy academical roles, Perlingeri is also a lawyer and supporter of the personalism philosophical school of thought, which is mainly founded on the centrality of individual persons in a realistic vision of the human being.
His numerous publications (more than 600) are mainly focused on the discussion of civil law and constitutional law issues.
His main works are: *Diritto comunitario e legalità costituzionale. Per un sistema italo-comunitario delle fonti* (1992); *Arbitrato e Costituzione* (2002); *Le cessioni dei crediti ordinari e 'd'impresa'* (1993); *Il diritto dei contratti fra persona e mercato. Problemi del diritto civile* (2003); *L'ordinamento vigente e i suoi valori* (2006); *La persona e i suoi diritti* (2005); *Leale collaborazione tra Corte costituzionale e Corti europee. Per un unitario sistema ordinamentale* (2008); *Funzione giurisdizionale e Costituzione italiana* (2010); *Sulle tecniche di redazione normativa nel sistema democratico* (2010).

Pietro Rescigno (Salerno, 1928) is an Italian jurist and professor especially known for his work on civil law, and has been teaching at the University La Sapienza of Rome from 1970.
In 1954, he started lecturing Civil Law in Macerata and then in Pavia, Bologna,

and Rome. He also lectured at the Universities of Luxembourg and Heidelberg. Rescigno is member of numerous cultural institutes, such as the *Accademia dei Lincei*, *Accademia Pontiana*, *Accademia Plerotiana*, *Accademia delle Scienze di Bologna*. Furthermore, he is co-director of several Italian law reviews, among which *Rivista di diritto civile*, *Giurisprudenza italiana*, *Rivista di diritto commerciale*, *Rivista critica di diritto privato*, *Il diritto dell'informazione e dell'informatica* must be remembered.

In his *Introduzione al Codice civile* (1991), Rescigno made a critical assessment of the application of the Italian Civil Code and outlined the most important stages that led to its drafting. Thanks to the continuous updates of his private law handbook to the evolutions of the law, his work is now a real point of reference for students and scholars.

In 2001, Rescigno received the *honoris causa* graduation in law from the University of Bologna in 2001 and was named *honoris causa* Professor at the San Marcos University of Lima and the Externado University of Bogota.

His main works are: *Incapacità naturale e adempimento* (1950); *Interpretazione del testamento* (1952); *Studi sull'accollo* (1958); *I sindacati nello Stato moderno* (1965); *Persona e comunità* (1966); *Manuale del diritto privato italiano* (1973); *Persona e comunità*, 2 vols (1998).

Georges Ripert (La Ciotat, 1880 – Paris, 1958) was a French lawyer, politician and committed conservative.

From 1906 to 1918, he was Professor of Law at the Aix-en-Provence University and, afterwards, at the University of Paris, where he taught Civil Law, Trade Law, and Maritime Law.

With World War II fast approaching, Ripert encouraged his students to welcome those who were expelled because of their religious faith or their ethnic origin. Nevertheless, in 1930, Ripert was appointed Secretary of State for Public Instruction and Youth in the Vichy Regime, ie the French state under German occupation, and he actively contributed to the exclusion of Jewish students and teachers from the university, by applying the Jewish Statute. For this reason, he was arrested for a brief period of time during the early post-World War II period.

His main works are: *De l'exercice du droit de propriété dans ses rapports avec les propriétés voisines* (thesis) (1902); *Traité général théorique et pratique de droit commercial* (1914); *Le droit maritime* (1922); *La règle morale dans les opérations civiles* (1926); *Le régime démocratique et le droit civil moderne* (1936); *Précis de droit maritime* (1939); *Cours de droit commercial* (1944); *Législation maritime et aérienne comparée* (1944); *Aspects juridiques du capitalisme moderne* (1946); *Le déclin du droit: études sur la législation contemporaine* (1949); *Les forces créatrices du droit* (1955).

Angelo Sraffa (Pisa, 1865 – Rapallo, 1937) was an Italian jurist and academic, also considered one of the founders of modern Italian commercial law.

He was Professor of Commercial Law at the Universities of Macerata, Pisa, Parma, Turin, Milan, and took on the rectorship of Bocconi University from 1919 to 1926,

when he decided to resign due to his antifascist beliefs; he is the author of several treatises and monographies on economic and commercial matters.
Sraffa's significant academic commitment includes the founding of the journal *Rivista di diritto commerciale e del diritto generale delle obbligazioni* (1903) with Cesare Vivante, the direction of the 'Private Law' section of the Italian Encyclopaedia *Treccani*, the membership of the Lincean Academy and of the commission for the reform of the Italian Commercial Code; he was also a representative of the Italian government in The Hague for the unification of Exchange Law.
Although little information is available on his initiation into Masons, it is well-known that in 1893 he was a Master Mason in Pisa's lodge 'Charles Darwin'.
His main works are: *Il fallimento delle società commerciali* (1897); *La liquidazione delle società commerciali* (1899); *Il mandato commerciale e la commissione* (1900).

Cesare Vivante (Venice, 1855 – Siena, 1944) was an Italian jurist, co-founder of the journal *Rivista di diritto commerciale e del diritto generale delle obbligazioni* (1903), together with Angelo Sraffa. He earned a law degree at the University of Padua and subsequently taught at various universities in Rome, Parma, and Bologna, and also practiced as a lawyer.
He was a great reformer of commercial studies, by coordinating the dogmatic construction of legal rules, general principles and the whole private law system. In his view, the Italian legal system would benefit from the unification of the civil and commercial codes. Vivante did believe however that the unification of the two matters would have updated Italian law and also improved Italy's international relationships. Yet, this unification only took place later, in 1942, when Vivante's position on the matter had changed.
He also leaned towards legal socialism, claiming that the legislator should intervene in social matters in order to defend workers' rights, whose protection was exclusively left to the employer at that time.
His main works are: *Trattato di diritto commerciale* (1893-1901); *Istituzioni di diritto commerciale* (1891); *La polizza di carico* (1881); *Il contratto di assicurazione* (1885-1890).

CHAPTER 8

European law

- **The European Union and its law**
- **The sources of European Union law**
- **The supremacy (or primacy) of the European Union law over national laws**
- **State liability for infringement of European Union law**
- **European private law in force (*acquis communautaire*)**
- **The European common core of national private laws (*acquis commune*)**
- **European restatements and model laws regarding contracts and other areas of private law**
- **The projects calling for a European codification of private law**

The cataclysmic experience of two world wars induced European countries to promote the achievement of a kind of supranational unity, aimed at the promotion of peace among them. Thus, in 1957-1958, six European countries signed the Treaty of Rome, creating the European Economic Community (EEC), which was later accompanied by and eventually absorbed into the European Union (EU).
The aim of establishing and running a single market of the EU is pursued through a European law that is instrumental to an economic constitution based upon a system decision in favor of a 'social market economy'
EU law not only operates at the level of international relations between the Member States, but also confers individual rights and liberties on citizens and ensures that they are entitled to petition both domestic and European courts for the enforcement of such legal positions.
The sources of EU primary law are the founding Treaties, in which the Charter of Fundamental Rights of the European Union, as well as the general principles derived from the European Convention on Human Rights have been embedded. Furthermore, the European Court of Justice resorted to some 'general principles of civil law', which would represent part of the rules 'common to the legal systems of the Member States'.

The sources of EU secondary law are the regulations and the directives. The overall body of the principles and rules they provide is called *acquis communautaire*.

The principle of the EU law's supremacy over national law has been progressively elaborated and applied by the ECJ. An implication of this principle may be detected in the rule according to which a private citizen has to be compensated in case of damage caused by the infringement of the law by a Member State.

EU private law is based on a vertical approach and has been mostly enacted by means of directives, which, pursuant to article 288 TFEU, are 'binding as to the result to be achieved', but 'shall leave to the national authorities the choice of form and methods', EU law and national laws are, therefore, to coexist and to interact in a multi-levelled system.

This is all the more true if one considers that the directives initially enacted are aimed at a 'minimum harmonization' of the Member States' private law, whereas only those subsequently issued pursue a 'maximum harmonization' of it. At the primary level, EU private law covers the fundamental economic freedoms (including the prohibition of discrimination) and competition law (above all, antitrust law).

At the secondary level, the EU has regulated labor (or employment) law, company law, intellectual and industrial property law. From the mid-1980s onwards, an EU contract law has been growing as well, mostly directed at business-to-consumer transactions. It consists of a general part (whose rules apply to any type of contract) and of a special part (whose rules apply solely to single types of contracts).

In recent decades, the idea emerged that national laws share a 'common core' that can be depicted as European (so-called *acquis commune*). This 'common core' is presented as rooted in the legacy of Roman law and its historical development during the Middle Ages; a European 'law beyond the state' has also surfaced in merchants' practices and standard contracts of international trade (*lex mercatoria*). This understanding led some groups of scholars to draft collections of model rules, which proved influential on national and EU legislatures; they can also be elected by the contracting parties as the substantive law to be applied to their contract, at least by arbitration tribunals.

Despite the efforts of the European institutions, attempts to merge the *acquis communautaire* and the *acquis commune* into a European civil code have failed thus far.

1. EUROPEAN UNION LAW (*ACQUIS COMMUNAUTAIRE*)

1.1. History and concept

The cataclysmic experience of two world wars unleashed by European countries in the first half of the twentieth century led some of the latter to seek to mitigate the economic and political nationalism that had previously characterized their states. They thus promoted the idea of a supranational unity, aimed at achieving peace and freedom for their citizens.

Through the Paris Treaty of 1951-1952, six European countries ('the inner Six') came to set up the **European Coal and Steel Community** (ECSC) in order to create a supranational control over the areas of production of these raw materials, located between France and Germany.

> The main proponents of the initiative were Jean Monnet (1888-1979) and Robert Schuman (1886-1963).
> The areas of production of coal and steel that had caused bloody conflicts between France and Germany were the Ruhr, the Alsace, and the Lorraine.

Whereas endeavors to establish similar entities with political and defense tasks failed, the aim of economic cooperation was further pursued, particularly after the Messina Conference of 1955. In 1957, the 'inner Six' came to sign the **Treaties of Rome**, thus creating the **European Economic Community** (EEC), as well as the **European Atomic Energy Community** (EURATOM).[1]

> The 'inner Six' were Belgium, France, Italy, Luxembourg, the Netherlands, and Germany.
> Seven countries that were unable or unwilling to become Member States of the EEC ('the outer Seven'), namely Austria, Denmark, Norway, Portugal, Sweden, Switzerland, the UK, established the **European Free Trade Association** (EFTA in 1960). Most of these countries, however, subsequently joined the EEC (or its further evolutions) and, therefore, left the EFTA. Current members of the latter are Iceland, Liechtenstein, Norway, and Switzerland.

The EEC was established with the main purpose of creating a **European common market** (ECM) among the Member States, which could provide not merely a customs union but a free trade area. From its outset, the EEC was endowed with legal personality and with some **sovereign powers**, held by its own institutions (above all, the Council and the Commission for the legislature and the executive, and the Court of Justice for the judiciary; to a much lesser extent, the Assembly, which initially was purported solely to monitor the Commission).
The first major revision of the Treaty of Rome was accomplished through the Single European Act of 1986-1987, after which the fundamental aim of the EEC was shifted from the establishment and functioning of a common market to those of a **single (or internal) market**, ie a trade bloc characterized by a fully-fledged freedom of movement of capital and persons as well as of goods and services. Importantly, this also provided that the adoption of legislative measures pursuing that aim was no longer based on unanimity within the Council but on a qualified majority.

[1] Ninon Colneric, 'European Community' in Jürgen Basedow, Klaus J Hopt, Reinhard Zimmermann and Andreas Stier (eds), *Max Planck Encyclopedia of European Private Law*, vol 1 (OUP 2012) 565.

Through the **Maastricht Treaty** of 1992-1993, the competences entrusted to the EEC were extended to sectors of social and political importance,[2] so that it was no longer referred to as 'economic' and became the **European Community** (EC). At the same time, the latter became the bulk of a new entity, the **European Union** (EU), which was characterized by a 'three-pillar structure', because it entailed, beside the EC itself, two forms of intergovernmental cooperation, namely in the fields of foreign and security policy, and of criminal justice.[3]

> The second and third pillars were officially termed, respectively, the Common Foreign and Security Policy (CFSP) and the Police and Judicial Cooperation in Criminal Matters (PJCC), which was initially known as Justice and Home Affairs (JHA).
> Moreover, the Treaty of Maastricht created an Economic and Monetary Union (EMU), whose currency is the euro, as well as Union citizenship.[4] Through the establishment of the 'procedure of co-decision', the European Parliament finally gained some effective power in law-making, shared with the Council upon initiative of the Commission.[5]
> Subsequently, through the Treaty of Amsterdam from 1997, most of the topics covered by the second and third pillars of the EU were shifted from the 'intergovernmental method' to the 'community method';[6] the focus on fundamental rights protection and social policy was considerably strengthened.[7] The legislative procedure of co-decision was simplified, and its scope broadened.[8]
> The Treaty of Nice from 2001 largely revised the composition and functioning of the European institutions, in preparation for the forthcoming enlargement of the Union to the countries of Eastern Europe. The legislative procedure of co-decision was extended to further topics.[9]

Through the **Treaty of Lisbon** of 2007-2009, the two still existing European Communities (namely the EC and the EURATOM) were absorbed into the EU.[10] The three pillars that had characterized the structure of the latter were abolished, and the community method was extended to all its competences. The legislative 'procedure of co-decision' eventually became the 'ordinary legislative procedure'.

The number of Member States has gradually grown over time, up to the level of 28 until end of January 2020. The new accessions to the EEC/EC/EU occurred in stages, known as 'enlargements' (or 'European integration'). First to step in

[2] Ninon Colneric, 'EU Treaty' in *The Max Planck Encyclopedia of European Private Law*, vol 1 (n 1) 542.
[3] ibid 541.
[4] ibid 542; Norbert Reich, 'Union Citizenship' in *The Max Planck Encyclopedia of European Private Law*, vol 2 (OUP 2012) 1739.
[5] Colneric (n 2) 542.
[6] ibid 543.
[7] ibid.
[8] ibid.
[9] ibid.
[10] The ECSC Treaty had expired on 23 July 2002 and the functions of that had been taken on by the EC.

(after an initial veto from France) was the UK (together with some countries whose economies are linked to it, like Ireland); secondly, the Mediterranean countries that had not yet applied; thirdly, those of Eastern Europe.

Historical enlargements of the EEC/EC/EU were as follows:
1973: UK, Ireland, Denmark;
1981: Greece;
1986: Spain and Portugal;
1995: Austria, Sweden, Finland;
2004: Cyprus, Estonia, Latvia, Lithuania, Poland, Czech Republic, Slovakia, Slovenia, Hungary;
2007: Bulgaria, Romania;
2013: Croatia.

Following a referendum held on 23 June 2016,[11] however, the UK initiated in 2017 the procedure set out in article 50 TEU to exit the EU ('**Brexit**').[12] The date of this departure had to be repeatedly postponed by the UK,[13] due to long negotiations with the EU and also to a deep turmoil between the UK Parliament and the government. While the UK Parliament had refused to approve a first withdrawal agreement between the UK and the EU in December 2018, an amended withdrawal agreement between the UK and the EU was eventually signed on 24 January 2020.[14] The UK therefore ceased to be a Member State of the EU on 31 January 2020 at 11 PM GMT, and the withdrawal agreement with the EU thus came into force.
Since its foundation, the EEC has developed and depicted itself as 'a Community based on the rule of law'.[15] The path of promoting the economic and social integration between Member States is pursued through law (**integration through law**). Although the EU is an organization of international law, created through the traditional instrument of the interstate agreement, it has peculiar characteristics. According to the formula coined by the German Constitutional Court (*Bundesverfassungsgericht*) in the so-called **Maastricht ruling** of 1993,[16] the EU, on the one hand, has sovereign rights and therefore is not a pure confederation of states, but on the other hand, is not founded on a unified constitutional state population and thus cannot be considered as a federal state.

[11] The referendum resulted in a narrow majority of 51.9% in favor of leaving the EU; see <www.bbc.com/news/politics/eu_referendum/results> accessed 27 August 2020.
[12] European Union (Notification of Withdrawal) Act 2017.
[13] European Union (Withdrawal) Act 2019; European Union (Withdrawal) (No 2) Act 2019.
[14] Agreement on the withdrawal of the United Kingdom of Great Britain and Northern Ireland from the European Union and the European Atomic Energy Community, signed on 24 January 2020, approved by UK Parliament through the European Union (Withdrawal Agreement) Act 2020 and ratified by EU Council on 30 January 2020 upon approval by EU Parliament on 29 January 2020.
[15] Case C-294/83 *Parti écologiste 'Les Verts' v European Parliament* [1986] ECR 1339, para 23.
[16] *Bundesverfassungsgericht* 12 October 1993, Az. 2 BvR 2134, 2159/92, BVerfGE 89, 155.

In matters that are attributed to its competence, the EU exercises both legislative power (through the **Parliament**,[17] the **Commission**,[18] the **Council** and the **European Council**),[19] and judiciary power (through the **Court of Justice**).[20] It follows that, by implying a renunciation of national sovereignty, the accession of a Member State to the EU at times required an *ad hoc* constitutional justification, which has been sometimes adopted through a specific revision of the respective fundamental charter and/or through a referendum.

In **Germany**, for example, article 23 GG was rewritten and transformed into a veritable *Europa-Klausel*.

On becoming a member of the EU, the **UK** Parliament enacted the European Communities Act 1972,[21] which made provision in particular for the incorporation of EU law into UK law and also for the interpretation of both directly applicable EU law and relevant UK law in accordance with the principles laid down by the European Court.[22] While the 1972 Act was repealed on the UK's leaving the EU (on 'exit day', as eventually set at 31 January 2020),[23] most of its effect was 'saved' by the European Union (Withdrawal Agreement) Act 2020 so as to give effect to the transitional provisions in the UK's agreement with the EU for a period termed the 'implementation period'.[24] For most purposes, therefore, while the UK left the EU on 31 January 2020, EU law will still apply in the UK until 31 December 2020 (termed by the legislation 'IP completion day'). Moreover, even after the end of the 'implementation period', most EU-law as already existing is to be retained as part of UK law. This includes: (1) EU-derived domestic law, so far as in force immediately before IP completion day;[25] (2) direct EU legislation, so far as operative immediately before IP completion day;[26] and (3) any rights, powers, liabilities, obligations, restrictions, remedies, and procedures, which, immediately before IP completion day, were created or arose by or under the EU Treaties;[27] if they arose under an EU directive (not implemented in the UK's law), however, they are to be retained only if they are 'of a kind recognised by the ECJ or any court or tribunal in the UK in a case decided before exit day'.[28]

When interpreting such 'retained EU law', UK courts and tribunals (bar the

[17] Jörn Axel Kämmerer, 'European Parliament' in *The Max Planck Encyclopedia of European Private Law*, vol 1 (n 1) 621.
[18] Colneric, 'European Community' (n 1) 561.
[19] Despite bearing very similar names, the two institutions are not coincident; on this point, see Jörn Axel Kämmerer, 'Council and the European Council' in *The Max Planck Encyclopedia of European Private Law*, vol 1 (n 1) 419.
[20] Jürg Pirrung, 'European Court of Justice (ECJ)' in *The Max Planck Encyclopedia of European Private Law*, vol 1 (n 1) 561.
[21] John Bell, 'Sources of Law' in Andrew Burrows (ed), *English Private Law* (3rd edn, OUP 2013) para 1.05.
[22] European Communities Act 1972, ss 2-3.
[23] European Union (Withdrawal) Act 2018, s 1.
[24] ibid ss 1A-1B. The 'implementation period' is due to expire on 31 December 2020. The text and accompanying notes refer to the provisions of the European Union (Withdrawal) Act 2018 as amended (or to be amended) by the European Union (Withdrawal Agreement) Act 2020.
[25] European Union (Withdrawal) Act 2018, s 2.
[26] ibid s 3.
[27] ibid s 4.
[28] ibid s 4(2)(b).

Supreme Court)[29] are bound by any retained case law and any retained general principles laid down by the European Court before IP completion day;[30] furthermore, they must have regard for the limits of EU competence existing immediately before the completion day of the 'implementation period'.[31] By contrast, while UK courts may have regard to anything done by the ECJ, another EU entity, or the EU on or after IP completion day, they are under no obligation to do so.[32]

The status of such 'retained EU law' is that of UK domestic law,[33] and so it can be modified by the UK Parliament;[34] it may also be amended by government regulation so as to deal with 'deficiencies arising from withdrawal' from the EU. [35]

The creation and expansion of EU law was strongly influenced by the doctrine of German ordo-liberalism (*Ordoliberalismus*), which clearly advocated a **society based on private law** (*Privatrechtsgesellschaft*),[36] where the constitutional principle of protecting individual freedoms was to be incorporated into strong economic regulation. The foundation of the EU was therefore laid through its **economic constitution** (*Wirtschaftsverfassung*).[37]

The EU economic constitution is based on economic freedoms, particularly the right to undertake private initiatives, while also addressing the fact that, if not duly regulated, such freedoms endanger the existence and the functioning of the market itself and, in the long run, compel it to fail (**market failure**). A paramount case is that of cartels between businesses aimed, for example, at imposing certain prices, or at boycotting a competitor. A selected few thus gain the **private power** to act to the detriment of other businesses, and possibly

[29] The European Union (Withdrawal Agreement) Act 2020 provides for a second category of exceptions to the general position by providing that a minister may determine by regulation that other UK courts or tribunals are not bound by any retained EU case law so far as is provided for by regulations; see European Union (Withdrawal) Act 2018, s 6(4)(ba); ss 6(5A)-6(5D), as inserted by the European Union (Withdrawal Agreement) Act 2020, s 26(1)(d). This power exists only until IP completion day; see European Union (Withdrawal Agreement) 2018, s 6(5D), as inserted by the European Union (Withdrawal Agreement) 2020, s 26(1)(d).

[30] European Union (Withdrawal) Act 2018, ss 6(3)(a)-6(4).

[31] ibid s 6(3)(b).

[32] ibid s 6(2).

[33] ibid s 7(1).

[34] ibid s 7(2).

[35] ibid s 8.

[36] The complete elaboration of this model is due above all to Franz Böhm, 'Privatrechtsgesellschaft und Marktwirtschaft' [1966] ORDO 75ff. In this regard see Claus-Wilhelm Canaris, 'Verfassungs- und europarechtliche Aspekte der Vertragsfreiheit in der Privatrechtsgesellschaft' in Peter Badura and Rupert Scholz (eds), *Wege und Verfahren des Verfassungslebens. Festschrift für Peter Lerche zum 65. Geburtstag* (CH Beck 1993) 85ff, as well as the essays collected in Karl Riesenhuber, *Privatrechtsgesellschaft: Entwicklung, Stand und Verfassung des Privatrechts* (Mohr Siebeck 2007). For the importance of this concept in the establishment and evolution of European private law see Stefan Grundmann, 'The Concept of the Private Law Society: After 50 Years of European and European Business Law' (2008) 16 ERPL 553ff, and previously Klaus Mayer and Jörg Scheinpflug, *Privatrechtsgesellschaft und die Europäische Union* (Mohr Siebeck 1996) 11ff, 75ff.

[37] Ernst-Joachim Mestmäcker, 'European Economic Constitution' in *The Max Planck Encyclopedia of European Private Law*, vol 1 (n 1) 588.

of consumers as well. Ordo-liberalism urges the holders of the public power to ban and sanction such conduct,[38] and it has taken a fundamental **system decision** (*Systementscheidung*) in favor of a **social market economy**,[39] that is now enshrined in article 3(3)(1) TEU.

> Ordo-liberalistic doctrines were historically strong critics of the dictatorial view of society and economy that the *Drittes Reich* led by Adolf Hitler had embraced in Germany.
> Nonetheless, after World War II, ordo-liberalism was sometimes accused of promoting a form of authoritarianism, however liberal it may be,[40] or even resembling the form of totalitarianism it was supposed to combat.[41]

Consequently, EU law was first articulated in a *pars destruens*, properly designed to carry out a liberalistic function. It was created by removing from national legal systems those legislative and administrative provisions that constituted potential obstacles to the exercise of economic freedoms guaranteed by the founding Treaties (**negative integration**).
On the other hand, the *pars costruens* of EU law acts as a re-regulation of the market and society, creating a legislative framework that unifies the legal systems of the Member States (**positive integration**).
One of the milestones of EU law was the ECJ judgment of the **van Gend en Loos case** (1963),[42] according to which not only do the founding Treaties operate on the level of international relations between the Member States, they also confer individual rights and liberties on citizens and ensure that they are entitled to petition both domestic and European courts for the enforcement of such legal positions.

> 'The European Economic Community constitutes a new legal order of international Law for the benefit of which the States have limited their sovereign rights, albeit within limited fields, and the subjects of which comprise not only the Member States but also their Nationals'.[43]

This turning point in European law must be ascribed to the merit of a great Italian jurist who was then a judge of the ECJ, namely Alberto Trabucchi (1907-1998). He managed to convince the other members of the judging

[38] Franz Böhm, *Die Ordnung der Wirtschaft als geschichtliche Aufgabe und rechtsschöpferische Leistung* (W Kohlhammer 1937) 54ff.
[39] Wilhelm Röpke, *Die Gesellschaftskrise der Gegenwart* (5th edn, Erlenbach 1948) 259ff.
[40] Dieter Haselbach, *Autoritärer Liberalismus und Soziale Marktwirtschaft: Gesellschaft und Politik im Ordoliberalismus* (Nomos 1991) 77ff.
[41] Alessandro Somma, *Temi e problemi di diritto comparato: Diritto comunitario* vs. *diritto comune europeo*, vol 4 (Giappichelli 2002) 21ff; Id, 'Tutte le strade portano a Fiume. L'involuzione liberista del diritto comunitario' [2002] Rivista critica di diritto privato 263ff; Id, 'Il diritto privato liberista. A proposito di un recente contributo in tema di autonomia contrattuale' [2001] Riv trim dir proc civ 263ff.
[42] Case C-26/62 *NV Algemene Transport- en Expeditie Onderneming van Gend & Loos v Netherlands Inland Revenue Administration* [1963] ECR 3.
[43] ibid 3.

panel to abandon the previous conception of European law, which was merely internationalist.[44]

The overall corpus of EU law has traditionally taken the name of ***acquis communautaire***.

In 2011, the **European Law Institute (ELI)** was established and entrusted with the quest for better law-making in Europe, the enhancement of European legal integration, and the building up of a European legal culture.[45]

1.2. The sources of European Union law

The sources of EU law are divided into primary (or original) and secondary sources.

1.2.1. At the primary level

EU primary law is not posited by the EU itself, but constitutes its own foundation, laid down by the Member States. Its main sources are the founding Treaties and their subsequent revisions over time.

The **Treaty on the European Union** (TEU) and the **Treaty on the Functioning of the European Union** (TFEU) have been in force since 2009. They are the final resolution of a gradual revision of the Rome Treaties, along with major substantial changes and institutional reforms (see *supra*, ch 8, para 1.1).

The founding Treaties have framed the powers and organized the structure of European institutions,[46] setting out their constitutional basis.[47]

Since the judgment in **van Gend en Loos case** (1963), the ECJ clarified that the founding Treaties are directly applicable not only to Member States but also to their citizens, thus creating rights and obligations for the latter that are likely to be protected both by national and European courts (see *supra*, ch 8, para 1.1).

The last version of article 6(1) TEU expressly embedded the **Charter of Fundamental Rights of the European Union** (CFR) of 7 December 2000 into the primary law of the EU, binding the latter to recognize the rights, freedoms and principles set out in the former.[48] However, article 6(2) TEU specified that: '[t]he provisions of the Charter shall not extend in any way the competences

---

[44] The events are told in Alberto Trabucchi, 'Un nuovo diritto' [1963] Riv dir civ I 259.

[45] Christiane Wendehorst, 'European Law Institute (ELI)' in *The Max Planck Encyclopedia of European Private Law*, vol 1 (n 1) 615.

[46] Ninon Colneric, 'European Constitution' in *The Max Planck Encyclopedia of European Private Law*, vol 1 (n 1) 573.

[47] *'Les Verts' v European Parliament* (n 15) para 23.

[48] Article 6(1) TEU stipulates that: 'The Union recognises the rights, freedoms and principles set out in the Charter of Fundamental Rights of the European Union of 7 December 2000, as adapted at Strasbourg, on 12 December 2007, which shall have the same legal value as the Treaties'.

of the Union as defined in the Treaties'. It means that Member States are not bound by the Charter or forced by the EU to apply it according to the same terms and conditions, except in those areas in which the EU has competence provided by the founding Treaties.

> After Brexit comes into full effect on 'IP completion day' (see *supra*, ch 8, para 1.1), the CFR will not form part of UK domestic law.[49] This will not affect, however, the retention of any fundamental rights or principles which existed in UK domestic law irrespective of the CFR.[50]

The primary sources of EU law also include its **general principles** (see also *supra*, ch 6, para 3).[51]
At the outset, such principles were drawn by the ECJ from the founding Treaties and were directed at conceptualizing some of the inner characteristics of EC law, like its supremacy (priority) over national laws (see *infra*, ch 8, para 1.3), its effectiveness,[52] subsidiarity, proportionality,[53] and certainty;[54] in a number of cases the ECJ affirmed as well a **prohibition of abuse of EEC/EC/EU law**,[55] which has gone on to become a general tenet of its jurisprudence.[56] These principles may be depicted as 'institutional',[57] since they are rooted

[49] European Union (Withdrawal) Act 2018, s 5(4).
[50] ibid s 5(5).
[51] See Guido Alpa, 'CESL, Fundamental Rights, General Principles of Contract Law' [2012] Diritto commerciale internazionale 837ff, as well as the papers collected in Stefan Grundmann and Denis Mazeaud (eds), *General Clauses and Standards in European Contract Law: Comparative Law, EC Law and Contract Law Codification* (The Hague 2006). See also Reiner Schulze, 'Allgemeine Rechtsgrundsätze und europäisches Privatrecht' [1993] ZeuP 442; Fabio Toriello, *I principi generali del diritto comunitario. Il ruolo della comparazione* (Giuffrè 2000); Jürgen Basedow, 'The Court of Justice and Private Law: Vacillations, General Principles and the Architecture of the European Judiciary' (2010) 18 ERPL 462; Matthias Storme, 'Une question de principe(s)?' in Angelika Fuchs (ed), *European Contract Law – ERA Forum Special Issue* 2008, in *ERA Forum* scripta iuris europaei (Heidelberg 2008) 72ff; Arthur S Hartkamp, 'The General Principles of EU Law and Private Law' (2011) 75 RabelsZ 241. Furthermore, the second issue of the European Review of Private Law of 2012 collected most of the essays presented at the conference 'Principles and the Law', organised by the University of Utrecht on 25 May 2011; on this point, see the editorial of Ewoud Hondius, 'Principles and the Law' (2012) 20 ERPL 289.
[52] Case C-78/98 *Shirley Preston and Othes v Wolverhampton Healthcare NHS Trust and Others and Dorothy Fletcher and Others v Midland Bank plc* [2000] ECR I-3201, para 31, and Joined Cases C-392/04 and 422/04 *i-21 Germany GmbH and Arcor AG & Co. KG v Bundesrepublik Deutschland* [2006] ECR I-8559, para 57. See Christian Heinze, 'Principle of Effectiveness' in *The Max Planck Encyclopedia of European Private Law*, vol 1 (n 1) 1316.
[53] Case C-25/70 *Einfuhr- und Vorratsstelle für Getreide und Futtermittel* v *Köster, Berodt & Co* [1970] ECR 1161. See Olivier Remien, 'Principle of Proportionality' in *The Max Planck Encyclopedia of European Private Law*, vol 1 (n 1) 1321.
[54] Case C-13/61 *Kledingverkoopbedrijf de Geus en Uitdenbogerd v Robert Bosch GmbH, Maatschppij tot vvortzetting van de zaken der Firma Willem van Rijn* [1962] ECR 89.
[55] Filippo Ranieri, 'Abuse of Law' in *The Max Planck Encyclopedia of European Private Law*, vol 1 (n 1) 7.
[56] Rita de la Feria and Stefan Vogenauer (eds), *Prohibition of Abuse of Law. A New General Principle of EU Law?* (Hart 2011).
[57] Bruno de Witte, *Institutional Principles: A Special Category of General Principles of EC Law* in Ulf Bernitz and Joakim Nergelius (eds), *General Principles of European Community Law* (The Hague 2000) 143.

in constitutional and – at least partially – administrative law;[58] it is therefore consequential that some of them, initially enshrined in the jurisprudence of the ECJ, were afterwards laid down in the founding Treaties.

For example, the principle of subsidiarity was eventually posited by article 5(3) TEU; that of proportionality by article 5(4) TEU.[59]

A similar development took place with regard to the **protection of human (or fundamental) rights**,[60] which, although remaining the preserve of the Member States, has been provided for by the ECJ since the 1970s and is based on 'the constitutional traditions common to the Member States'[61].
Later,[62] the jurisprudence of the ECJ on the protection of human (or fundamental) rights was based also on an express reference to international treaties obliging Member States to respect the above-mentioned rights, and in particular the **European Convention on Human Rights** (ECHR). The latest version of article 6(3) TEU stipulates that: 'Fundamental rights, as guaranteed by the European Convention for the Protection of Human Rights and Fundamental Freedoms and as they result from the constitutional traditions common to the Member States, shall constitute general principles of the Union's law'.

The ECHR, formally the Convention for the Protection of Human Rights and Fundamental Freedoms, was drafted and adopted in 1950 by the Council of Europe (not to be confused with either the Council or the European Council of the EEC/EC/EU)[63]. It is applied by the European Court of Human Rights (ECtHR)[64], whose seat is in Luxembourg.

More recently, the ECJ resorted to '**general principles of civil law**' (for example, compensation for loss, good faith, and restitution of unjust enrichment),[65] in

[58] John Usher, *General Principles of European Community Law* (Pearson Education Limit 1998) 52, 72, 199ff.
[59] Colneric, 'EU Treaty' (n 2) 542.
[60] About the difference between 'human' and 'fundamental rights' see Patrick Kinsch, 'Human Rights and Fundamental Rights (ChFR and ECHR)' in *The Max Planck Encyclopedia of European Private Law*, vol 1 (n 1) 839.
[61] Case C-11/70, *Internationale Handelsgesellschaft mbH v Einfuhr- und Vorratsstelle für Getreide und Futtermittel* [1970] ECR I-1125, para 4.
[62] Case C-4/73 *J Nold, Kohlen- und Baustoffgroßhandlung v Commission of the European Communities* [1975] ECR 491; Case C-36/75 *Roland Rutili v Ministre de l'interiéur* [1975] ECR 1219; Case C-44/79 *Hauer v Land Rheinland-Pfalz* [1979] ECR 3727. For a general overview, see Henricus G Schermers, *Human Rights as General Principles of Law* in Bernitz and Nergelius (n 25) 61; Xavier Groussot, *General Principles of Community Law* (Hardback 2006) 56ff.
[63] Jörn Axel Kämmerer, 'Council of Europe (Institutional Aspects)' in *The Max Planck Encyclopedia of European Private Law*, vol 1 (n 1) 621.
[64] Patrick Kinsch, 'European Court of Human Rights (ECtHR)' in *The Max Planck Encyclopedia of European Private Law*, vol 1 (n 1) 579.
[65] Case C-277/05 *Société thermale d'Eugénie-les-Bains v Ministère de l'Économie, des Finances et de l'Industrie* [2007] ECR I-6415, para 24; Case C-412/06 *Annelore Hamilton v Volksbank Filder eG* [2008] ECR I-2383ff, para 24; Case C-47/07 *Masdar (UK) Ltd v*

order to fill in the gaps of EU law. Such principles represent part of the rules 'common to the legal systems of the Member States'.[66] Some of the values that traditionally underpin private law have been thus recognized as principles of EU law.[67]

1.2.2. At the secondary level

Pursuant to article 288(1) TFEU, the secondary sources of EU law are regulations, directives, and decisions. The latter also include **recommendations and opinions**, which however are not legally binding and, as a result, cannot be considered sources of law.

More specifically, article 288(2) TFEU provides that 'a **regulation** shall have general application. It shall be binding in its entirety and directly applicable in all Member States'.[68] EU regulations are applicable generally because they consist of abstract and general provisions, regulating an unlimited number of cases;[69] they are applicable directly because they do not require that Member States adopt any national measure to transpose or implement them, but they take immediate effect in both vertical (between Member States and citizens) and horizontal relationships (between citizens). Due to their direct effect, they achieve a **unification** of the Member States' legal systems.

EU regulations are capable of creating individual rights that national courts must protect (**Leonesio case** of 1972).[70]

According to article 288(3) TFEU, 'a **directive** shall be binding, as to the result to be achieved, upon each Member State to which it is addressed, but shall leave to the national authorities the choice of form and methods.'

As a result, directives are clearly binding on the Member States; nevertheless, a national (legislative or regulatory) measure from each Member State is required for their application to citizens, if necessary to determine the forms and methods of achieving the aim pursued by the EU legislator. Directives are, thus, applied or implemented into national law through the specific tools

Commissione delle Comunità Europee [2008] ECR I-9761, para 50; Case C-489/07 *Pia Messner v Firma Stefan Krüger* [2009] ECR I-7315, para 29; Case C-215/08 *E Friz GmbH v Carsten von der Heyden* [2010] ECR I-2947, paras 48-49.

66 *Masdar (UK) Ltd* (n 65), para 50.

67 Martijn W Hesselink, 'The General Principles of Civil Law: their Nature, Roles and Legitimacy' in *Centre for Study of European Contract Law Working Paper Series*, n. 2011-14' <http://ssm.com/abstract=1932146> accessed 12 October 2018; Chantal Mak, 'Hedgehogs in Luxembourg? A Dworkinian Reading of the CJEU's Case Law on Principles of Private Law and Some Doubts of the Fox' (2012) 20 ERPL 323; Kai P Purnhagen, 'Principles of European Private or Civil Law? A Reminder of the Symbiotic Relationship Between the ECJ and the DCFR in a Pluralistic European Private Law' in *Centre for Study of European Contract Law Working Paper Series*, n. 2011-04 <http://ssm.com/abstract=1652039> accessed 12 October 2018.

68 Karl Riesenhuber, 'Regulation' in *The Max Planck Encyclopedia of European Private Law*, vol 2 (n 4) 1433.

69 Case C-101/76 *Koninklijke Scholten Honig NV v Council and Commission of the European Communities* [1977] ECR 797, paras 8-11, 20-22.

70 Case C-93/71 *Orsolina Leonesio v Ministero dell'agricoltura e foreste della repubblica italiana* [1972] ECR 287, para 22.

provided for by national legislation. They are therefore said to carry out a **harmonization** (or **approximation**) of the Member States' legal system.
The interpretation of this national legislation must be undertaken in harmony with the directive, so that the objective set by European lawmakers can be achieved (**von Colson and Kamann case** of 1984).[71]
In even broader terms, all national legislative acts, whether adopted before or after a directive, must be construed in accordance with the directive, having regard to its wording and ultimate purpose (**Marleasing case** of 1990).[72]
The harmonization of national legislation imposes a strict standard in cases where a state's decision not to implement legislative or administrative measures rests on the discretional assumption that national legislation is already in line with the directive (**Wagner Miret case** of 1993).[73]
If a directive not implemented by a Member State contains a provision 'which is not subject to any exception or condition and which, by its very nature, does not require the intervention of any act on the part either of the institutions of the community or of Member States', then this provision must apply regardless of any incompatible national laws (**van Duyn case** of 1974).[74]
It was later clarified that this is true only in cases where the non-implemented directive requires a State to comply with an obligation that is – not only unconditioned, but also – 'sufficiently precise' (**Ratti case** of 1979).[75]
This solution will help prevent any defaulting States from taking advantage of their violation of the founding Treaties as a basis for resolving disputes with individuals. It follows that the rule of direct applicability of the so-called self-executing directives applies only to the state (vertical relations), even if the latter acts *iure privatorum* (**Marshall case** of 1986).[76]
To this end, the state is not identified on the basis of the legal nature of the person acting, but on the basis of the public nature of the functions or of the activity it performs (**Foster case** of 1990).[77]
Non-executing directives are not directly applicable to individuals (horizontal relationships), but national laws must be interpreted in accordance with the directive (**Faccini Dori case** of 1994).[78]
If a State fails to implement a directive, or implements a directive inaccurately, that State is in breach of EU law and, consequently, is obliged to pay damages to its citizens who could have benefited from the rights granted by it. Three conditions, however, must first be met (**Francovich case** of 1990; see also *infra*,

[71] Case C-14/83 *Sabine von Colson and Elisabeth Kamann v Land Nordrhein-Westfalen* [1984] ECR I-1891, para 26.
[72] Case C-106/89 *Marleasing SA v La Comercial Internacional de Alimentación SA* [1990] ECR I-4135, para 8.
[73] Case C-334/92 *Teodoro Wagner Miret v Fondo de Garantía Salarial* [1993] ECR I-6911.
[74] Case C-41/74 *Yvonne Van Duyn v Home Office* [1974] ECR 1337, paras 12-13.
[75] Case C-148/78 *Criminal proceedings v Tullio Ratti* [1979] ECR 1629, paras 21-24.
[76] Case C-152/84 *M H Marshall v Southampton and South-West Hampshire Area Health Authority (Teaching)* [1986] ECR 723, paras 48-49.
[77] Case C-188/89 *A Foster and others v British Gas plc.* [1990] ECR I-3313, para 20.
[78] Case C-91/92 *Paola Faccini Dori v Recreb Srl* [1994] ECR I-3325, para 30.

ch 8, para 1.4):[79] 'Firstly, the purpose of the directive must be to grant rights to individuals. Secondly, it must be possible to identify the content of the rights on the basis of the provisions of the directive. Finally, there must be a causal link between the breach of the state's obligation and the damage suffered'.

1.3. The supremacy (priority) of European Union law over the Member States' laws

The competence to interpret and apply EU law lies not only with the judges of the ECJ but above all with the national courts, who can resolve doubts about the interpretation of supranational law by issuing the so-called **preliminary ruling**, ie suspending the judgment and referring the interpretative question to the ECJ (article 267 TFEU). If the doubt about the interpretation of EU law arises in a superior national court 'against whose decisions there is no judicial remedy under national law', then the latter court has not only the opportunity but the duty to refer the case for a preliminary ruling.
It therefore falls primarily to national courts to solve issues related to the relationships between EU law and national law. In this regard, the ECJ has progressively elaborated on and declared the principle of the EU law's supremacy over national law.

> After the UK's leaving the EU comes into full effect on 'IP completion day' (see *supra*, ch 8, para 1.1), '[t]he principle of the supremacy of EU law does not apply to any enactment or rule of law passed or made on or after IP completion day' in the UK;[80] on the other hand, that principle 'continues to apply on or after IP completion day so far as relevant to the interpretation, disapplication or quashing of any enactment or rule of law passed or made before IP completion day' in the UK.[81]
> Before the completion day of the implementation period (see *supra*, ch 8, para 1.1), however, a UK court is bound by principles and decisions made by the ECJ,[82] to which it can still refer a matter.[83]

An outspoken declaration of that principle appeared for the first time in the judgment concerning the **Costa v Enel case** (1964), whereby the Court of Justice stated that an EU legislative act prevails over a national one even if the second piece of legislation is enacted after the first. Thus, the relationship between the two legal systems cannot be solved using the classic canon *lex posterior derogat priori* (see also ch 6, para 2.3).[84]

[79] Joined Cases C-6/90 and C-9/90 *Andrea Francovich and Danila Bonifaci and others v Italian Republic* [1991] ECR I-5357, para 39.
[80] European Union (Withdrawal) Act 2018, s 5(1).
[81] ibid s 5(2).
[82] ibid s 6(1)(a).
[83] ibid s 6(1)(b).
[84] Case C-6/64, *Flaminio Costa v ENEL* [1964] ECR 585, paras 3ff.

In the subsequent **Simmenthal case** (1978), the ECJ further clarified that the EU law's primacy implies that it must be directly applied by the national judge. The latter does not need to suspend the proceeding in order to refer such a task to a different authority of the state.[85]
In conclusion, the principle of EU law's primacy was affirmed in the seventeenth annexed declaration of the final act of the intergovernmental conference which adopted the Lisbon Treaty (see *supra*, ch 8, para 1.1). There, it is written as follows: 'The Conference recalls that, in accordance with well settled case law of the Court of Justice of the European Union, the Treaties and the law adopted by the Union on the basis of the Treaties have primacy over the law of Member States, under the conditions laid down by the said case law'.

This decision, and more generally, the new European Union's institutional framework, were put under the scrutiny of the German Constitutional Court (*Bundesverfassungsgericht*), which considered them legitimate according to the German Fundamental law (*Grundgesetz*) (**Lissabon Urteil** of 2009).[86]

1.4. State liability for infringement of European Union law

One result of the principle of EU law supremacy is found in the rule according to which a private citizen has to be compensated for damage arising from an infringement of the law by a Member State. In reality, with respect to the application and the observance to EU law, Member States are considered as private entities, because they have accepted limitations to their sovereignty. Ultimately, this solution corresponds to more recent developments in contemporary constitutionalism.[87]
A typical hypothesis of such an infringement was envisaged in the absent or incomplete implementation of EU directives by a Member State (**Francovich case** of 1990; see also *supra*, ch 8, para 1.2). In this case, the Member State who has infringed EU law is obliged to compensate the victim under three conditions: 'The first of those conditions is that the result prescribed by the directive should entail the grant of rights to individuals. The second condition is that it should be possible to identify the content of those rights on the basis of the provisions of the directive. Finally, the third condition is the existence of a causal link between the breach of the State's obligation and the loss and damage suffered by the injured parties'.[88]
The ECJ has further clarified that the State is obliged to pay damages regardless of which government body was responsible, by act or omission, for the violation of European Union law (**joined cases Brasserie du Pêcheur**

[85] Case C-106/77, *Amministrazione delle Finanze dello Stato v Simmenthal SpA* [1978] ECR 629, paras 17-23.
[86] BVerfGE 123, 267.
[87] Luigi Buonanno, 'Rilievi civilistici in tema di responsabilità del legislatore da atto normativo' [2016] Jus civile 369.
[88] *Francovich* (n 79) para 40.

and Factortame III of 1996).[89] Moreover, it affirmed that, where a Member State acts in a field where it has a wide discretion, comparable to that of the European institutions, it can incur liability solely for manifestly and gravely disregarding Union law (joined cases Brasserie du Pêcheur e Factortame III of 1996).[90]

Subsequently, the ECJ declared that the liability of the State also exists when EU law has been infringed by a national judge of last instance (**Köbler case** of 2003),[91] in particular when a manifest breach of the ECJ jurisprudence has been committed.[92] A Member State cannot therefore exclude or limit its liability for damages in cases in which the infringement of EU law arises from an interpretation of the provisions of law made by national judges or from the assessment of the facts and evidence, insofar as these have been made in the context of applying specific provisions relating to the burden of proof or the weight or admissibility of evidence (**Traghetti del Mediterraneo case** of 2006).[93]

1.5. Existing private law of the European Union

From the outset, European institutions mainly pursued the approximation of Member States' public law, first of all in the field of taxation.

However, during the grand speech delivered in 1963 at the Max Planck Institute of Hamburg, Walter Hallstein (1901-1982), the first President of the EEC, made clear that the pursuit of the Community's aims, in particular with regard to the establishment and functioning of the common market, necessarily required an extension of the legislative action of European institutions to also encompass private law, particularly in matters of society and employment.[94]

As a matter of fact, the number of private law rules posited by the European institutions has increased tremendously over time, thus gaining considerable momentum within the *acquis communautaire*. A turning point was definitely marked by the SEA of 1986-1987 (see *supra*, ch 8, para 1.1), flanked by the *White Paper on the Completion of Internal Market* of 1985:[95] the newly envisaged aim of the establishment and functioning of a single (or internal) market called for (not only a negative integration which would serve to merely liberalize the market but also) a positive integration that would implement market regulation (see *supra*, ch 8, para 1.1). Furthermore, the abandonment of the

[89] Joined Cases C-46/93 and C-48/93, *Brasserie du Pêcheur SA v Federal Republic of Germany and The Queen v Secretary of State for Transport, ex parte Factortame Ltd and Others* [1996] ECR I-1029, para 32.
[90] ibid paras 45-49.
[91] Case C-224/01, *Gerhard Köbler v Republik Österreich* [2003] ECR I-10239, paras 33ff.
[92] ibid para 56.
[93] Case C-173/03, *Traghetti del Mediterraneo s.p.a. (in liquidation) v. Repubblica italiana* [2006] ECR I-5204, para 24ff.
[94] Walter Hallstein, 'Angleichung des Privat- und Prozessrechts in der Europäischen Wirtschaftsgemeinschaft' (1964) 28 RabelsZ 211.
[95] COM (85) 310 final.

unanimity requirement within the Council obviously removed the possibility that the veto of a single Member State could hamper the EEC legislature, as had previously occurred (see *supra*, ch 8, para 1.1).

At least from mid-1980s, therefore, (German) scholarship conceptualized the existence of an **EU private law**, which would entail binding rules of private law with an identical content across the Member States.[96] This definition may be spurious, particularly as almost all sources of EU private law do not exist in regulations but in directives, which, by definition, do not strive for unification but the approximation of the Member States' laws (see *supra*, ch 8, para 1.2.2). Until the beginning of the 2000s, moreover, the directives that stipulated EU private law were aimed at **minimum harmonization**, to leave the Member States the option to provide for a stricter protection of consumers and, therefore, to maintain (or even to introduce) national differences; it is only in recent years that the EU legislature has turned to a **maximum (or full) harmonization**, which sets out a European **level playing field**.

Due to the principles of conferral, subsidiarity, and proportionality (see *supra*, ch 8, para 1.2.1), therefore, EU private law traverses solely the single sectors of the common market where the call for regulatory intervention of the EU is more stringent (**vertical approach, or piecemeal approach**)[97]. In contrast to the national tradition of private law, as a consequence, its scope is more fragmented, and its content is not organized as a complete or consistent system,[98] but it proves rather pointillist. EU private law regulations have been therefore depicted as 'islands' in the ocean of national private law.[99]

Substantially, EU private law may be depicted as **market law**, since it deals with organizational issues of undertakings (businesses and other professionals) and with the transactions they enter into, either with other undertakings or with consumers. This does mean that EU private law may be understood as commercial law, or business law.

Since EU private law has been enacted over time and is drawn from a significant number of sources, a group of European scholars, called Research Group on the Existing EC Private Law (*Acquis* Group, for short), envisaged collecting and rationalizing it. To date, however, the resulting Principles of the Existing EC Private Law, or ***Acquis* Principles** (ACQP), have been solely published with regard to contract law.[100]

[96] Peter-Christian Müller Graff, 'Privatrecht und europäisches Gemeinschaftsrecht' in Peter-Christian Müller Graff and Manfred Zuleeg (eds), *Staat und Wirtschaft in der EG* (Nomos 1987) 17. It was however questioned whether all the rules belonging to EU private law do actually have an identical content (arguing against, see Jürgen Basedow, 'EU Private Law' in *The Max Planck Encyclopedia of European Private Law*, vol 1 (n 1) 539).

[97] Basedow, 'EU Private Law' (n 96) 539; Norbert Reich, 'European Legal Policy' in *The Max Planck Encyclopedia of European Private Law*, vol 1 (n 1) 617.

[98] Nils Jansen, 'European Private Law' in *The Max Planck Encyclopedia of European Private Law*, vol 1 (n 1) 639.

[99] Basedow, 'EU Private Law' (n 96) 540.

[100] Research Group on the Existing EC Private Law (Acquis Group), *Principles of the Existing EC Contract Law (Acquis Principles), Contract I. Pre-contractual Obligations.*

Pursuant to article 1:101(2) ACQP, they are purported to 'serve as a source for the drafting, the transposition and the interpretation of European Community law'. To achieve this goal, the ACQP strive not only to provide a systematic analysis of existing EC contract law but also to generalize large parts of it, thus overcoming its inherent fragmentation; moreover, they are accompanied by a critical evaluation of EU legislation, directed at identifying its deficiencies and improve its quality.[101]

1.5.1. At the primary level

Historically, two key domains of EU private law have been addressed and ruled by the sources of primary EU law, namely (fundamental) economic freedoms and competition.

The **(fundamental) economic freedoms** enshrined in the TFEU aim to safeguard and enhance:[102] 1) the free movement of goods; 2) the free movement of persons (including the free movement of workers and the freedom of establishment); 3) the free movement of services; 4) the free movement of capital and payments.[103] Save for the free movement of goods, the (fundamental) economic freedoms are deemed by the ECJ to be directly applicable not only to protect interests of private citizens against a State (vertical relationships), but also between citizens (horizontal relationships).[104]

Since the (fundamental) economic freedoms cover (solely) cross-border transactions, they necessarily imply a **prohibition of discrimination** on grounds of nationality, which in general terms is laid down through article 18(1) TFEU and moreover specified with regard to single policy areas through various provisions of the same Treaty.[105] Similarly, the principle of equal pay for men and women was established at the very outset of the EEC and is now stipulated through article 157 TFEU. Furthermore, article 10 TFEU clearly proclaims anti-discrimination as an overarching principle of EU law, and article 19 TFEU confers to the EU a special competence for combatting contraventions of that principle. To this effect, a number of directives have been issued over

Conclusion of Contract. Unfair Terms, 2008; *Contract II. General Provisions. Delivery of Goods. Package Travel and Payment Services*, 2009.

[101] Nils Jansen and Reinhard Zimmermann, 'Grundregeln des bestehenden Gemeinschaftsrechts' [2007] JZ 1113; Nils Jansen and Reinhard Zimmermann, 'Restating the Acquis Communautaire? A Critical Examination of the Principles of the Existing EC Contract Law' (2008) 71 MLR 505; Thomas Wilhelmsson, 'The Contract Law Acquis: Towards More Coherence Through Generalization?' [2008] Proceedings to the 4th European Jurists' Forum 111ff; Hans Schulte-Nölke, 'From the Acquis Communautaire to the Common Frame of Reference – The Contribution of the Acquis Group to the DCFR' (2008) XIV Tartu L Rev 27; Hans Cristoph Grigoleit and Lovro Tomasic, 'Acquis Principles' in *The Max Planck Encyclopedia of European Private Law*, vol 1 (n 1) 10.

[102] Thorsten Kingreen, 'Fundamental Freedoms' in Armin von Bogdandy and Jürgen Bast (eds), *Principles of European Constitutional Law* (2nd edn, Hart-CH Beck 2009) 315ff.

[103] Olivier Remien, 'Fundamental Freedoms (General Principles)' in *The Max Planck Encyclopedia of European Private Law*, vol 1 (n 1) 763.

[104] Pietro Sirena, 'Il diritto dei contratti nello spazio giuridico europeo' in Francesco Mezzanotte (ed), *Le 'libertà fondamentali' dell'Unione europea e il diritto privato* (RomaTre P 2016) 121ff.

[105] Jürgen Basedow, 'Discrimination (General)' in *The Max Planck Encyclopedia of European Private Law*, vol 1 (n 1) 483.

time,[106] particularly with regard to employment,[107] and subsequently to the supply of goods and services.[108]

> Even beyond the legislative measures taken by the EU, the ECJ derives a **general principle of equal treatment** from the international law and constitutional traditions that are common to the Member States, which it tentatively applies to labor and company law.[109]
> In the field of labor law, the ECJ proclaimed the unlawfulness of unequal treatment on the grounds of the worker's age (**Mangold case** of 2005).[110] The Court seemed to take a different stance with regard to the principle of equal treatment for minority shareholders in a capital company (**Audiolux case** of 2009).[111]
> More recently, the Court of Justice also derived the non-discrimination principle from the CFR in a case of unfair treatment based on the employee's age (**Kücükdeveci case** of 2010).[112]

The purpose of protecting economic freedoms is not only to prevent preferential treatment of professionals who are citizens of the nation in question (or professionals only working across national markets) over professionals from other Member States (or professionals also working in other States) but to promote as well the effective liberalization of the economy and the law in each Member State.[113] Moreover, the ECJ acknowledged that these fundamental freedoms give legal subjects the possibility to choose between the various State laws, for example, to elect where the seat of a company is to be registered (**Centros case** of 1999;[114] on this case, see *infra*, ch 11, para 1.2.1.1); particularly, the ECJ ruled that the choice of a national legal system that may better

106 Council Directive 2000/43/EC of 29 June 2000 implementing the principle of equal treatment between persons irrespective of racial or ethnic origin [2000] OJ L180/22.
107 Directive (EC) 2006/54/EC of the European Parliament and of the Council of 5 July 2006 on the implementation of the principle of equal opportunities and equal treatment of men and women in matters of employment and occupation [2006] OJ L204/23; Council Directive 2000/78/EC of 27 November 2000 establishing a general framework for equal treatment in employment and occupation [2000] OJ L303/16. See Gregor Thüsing and Sally Horter, 'Discrimination (Employment Law)' in *The Max Planck Encyclopedia of European Private Law*, vol 1 (n 1) 478.
108 Council Directive 2004/113/EC of 13 December 2004 implementing the principle of equal treatment between men and women in the access to and supply of goods and services [2004] OJ L303/37. See Jan D Lüttringhaus, 'Discrimination (Contract Law)' in *The Max Planck Encyclopedia of European Private Law*, vol 1 (n 1) 474.
109 Axel Metzger, Extra legem, intra ius: *Allgemeine Rechtsgrundsätze im Europäischen Privatrecht* (Mohr Siebeck 2009).
110 Case C-144/04 *Werner Mangold v Rüdiger Helm* [2005] ECR I-9981, paras 74-76.
111 Case C101/08 *Audiolux SA ea v Groupe Bruxelles Lambert SA (GBL) and Others and Bertelsmann AG and Others* [2009] ECR I-9823.
112 Case C-555/07 *Seda Kücükdeveci v Swedex GmbH & Co KG* [2010] ECR I-365, paras 21-23.
113 For a different opinion, cf Stefan Perner, *Grundfreiheiten, Grundrechte-Charta und Privatrecht* (Mohr Siebeck 2013) 70ff, as well as Andrea Zoppini, 'Il diritto privato e le "libertà fondamentali" dell'Unione europea (Principî e problemi della Drittwirkung nel mercato unico)' in Mezzanotte (n 104) 9ff.
114 Case C-212/97 *Centros Ltd v Erhverws- og Selskabsstyr* [1999] ECR I-01459. See Olivier Remien, 'Freedom of Establishment' in *The Max Planck Encyclopedia of European Private Law*, vol 1 (n 1) 755.

satisfy the interests of the parties involved (**forum shopping**), does not *per se* amount to an abusive practice (see *supra*, ch 10, para 4.3). **Competition between the Member States' legal systems** has been thus decidedly enhanced.[115]

The bulk of European **competition law** was already regulated by the Rome Treaty on the EEC as part of the 'Community policy',[116] being an essential component of the legal framework of the market.[117] At the EU level,[118] competition law is primarily constituted by **antitrust law**, embedding the prohibition of restrictive agreements, stipulated through article 101(1) TFEU,[119] and that of the abuse of a dominant position, stipulated through article 102(1) TFEU.[120]

These principled provisions of the founding Treaties are supplemented by regulations and directives, for whose issue a special competence is conferred to the EU through article 103 TFEU; particularly of note are the directive on private enforcement of antitrust law,[121] which regulates actions for damages,[122] and the regulations on block exemptions from the prohibition of restrictive agreements.[123]

[115] Eva-Maria Kieninger, 'Competition between Legal Systems' in *The Max Planck Encyclopedia of European Private Law*, vol 1 (n 1) 301.
[116] Matthias Leistner, 'Unfair Competition and Freedoms of Movement' in *The Max Planck Encyclopedia of European Private Law*, vol 2 (n 4) 1718. For competition law at the international level, see Dietmar Baetge, 'Competition Law (International)' in *The Max Planck Encyclopedia of European Private Law*, vol 1 (n 1) 309.
[117] Jürgen Basedow, 'Competition (Internal Market)' in *The Max Planck Encyclopedia of European Private Law*, vol 1 (n 1) 304; Ansgar Ohly, 'Unfair Competition (Basic Principles)' in *The Max Planck Encyclopedia of European Private Law*, vol 2 (n 4) 1712.
[118] Reinhard Ellger, 'Competition Law (Relationship between European and National Law)' in *The Max Planck Encyclopedia of European Private Law*, vol 1 (n 1) 320.
[119] It deals with 'all agreements between undertakings, decisions by associations of undertakings and concerted practices which may affect trade between Member States and which have as their object or effect the prevention, restriction or distortion of competition within the internal market'. See Reinhard Ellger, 'Prohibition of Restrictive Agreements and Exemptions' in *The Max Planck Encyclopedia of European Private Law*, vol 2 (n 4) 1361.
[120] It deals with '[a]ny abuse by one or more undertakings of a dominant position within the internal market or in a substantial part of it'. See Wolfgang Wurmnest, 'Abuse of a Dominant Position' in *The Max Planck Encyclopedia of European Private Law*, vol 1 (n 1) 1.
[121] Directive 2014/104/EU of the European Parliament and of the Council of 26 November 2014 on certain rules governing actions for damages under national law for infringements of the competition law provisions of the Member States and of the European Union [2014] OJ L349. By contrast, the public enforcement of antitrust prohibitions is in the hands of the Commission: see Friedrich Wenzel Bulst, 'Competition Law (Sanctions)' in *The Max Planck Encyclopedia of European Private Law*, vol 1 (n 1) 324; Friedrich Wenzel Bulst, 'Competition Law (Procedure)' ibid 315.
[122] Friedrich Wenzel Bulst, 'Competition Law (Private Enforcement)' in *The Max Planck Encyclopedia of European Private Law*, vol 1 (n 1) 1; Olaf Sosnitza, 'Unfair Competition (Consequences)' in *The Max Planck Encyclopedia of European Private Law*, vol 2 (n 4) 1715.
[123] Reinhard Ellger, 'Block Exemptions Regulations' in *The Max Planck Encyclopedia of European Private Law*, vol 1 (n 1) 109.

1.5.2. At the secondary level

At the secondary level, organizational issues for businesses (and other professionals) are addressed by labor law (or employment law),[124] company law (see *infra*, ch 11, para 1.2.1),[125] as well as by intellectual property law (including industrial design).[126]

The EU competence on **labor law (or employment law)** is based on articles 151-164 TFEU. Legislative measures issued by the EU deal with; 1) the free movement of workers; 2) equal treatment (non-discrimination); 3) individual employment rights; and 4) collective labor relations.[127]

The EU thirteen directives on **company law** revolve around: 1) setting up a company, including capital and disclosure requirements; 2) company operations involving more than one country; 3) restructuring of a company (domestic mergers and division, transfer of seat); 4) guarantees concerning the financial situation of companies; and 5) the cross-border exercise of shareholders' rights. Furthermore, the EU enacted a number of regulations aimed at creating and governing some EU legal entities that coexist with national rules. Thus far, the following EU legal entities have been introduced: 1) the European Company, or *Societas Europaea* (SE);[128] 2) the European Cooperative Society, or *Societas cooperativa Europaea* (SCE);[129] 3) the European Economic Interest Grouping (EEIG).[130] Additionally, the following entities have been proposed and are still underway: 1) the Sole Proprietorship, or *Societas unius personae* (SUP);[131] 2) the European Foundation, or *Fundatio Europaea* (FE).[132]

The main provision on **intellectual property** is embodied in the directive ruling its private enforcement,[133] and the directive on industrial design is also worthy of mention.[134]

[124] Karl Riesenhuber, *European Employment Law* (Intersentia 2012).

[125] Stefan Grundmann, *European Company Law* (2nd edn, Intersentia 2011).

[126] Alexander Peukert, 'Intellectual Property' in *The Max Planck Encyclopedia of European Private Law*, vol 1 (n 1) 926; Axel Metzger, 'Copyright' in *The Max Planck Encyclopedia of European Private Law*, vol 1 (n 1) 403.

[127] Martin Henssler, 'European Labour Law' in *The Max Planck Encyclopedia of European Private Law*, vol 1 (n 1) 612.

[128] Council Regulation (EC) No 2157/2001 of 8 October 2001 on the Statute for a European company [2001] OJ L295/1. See Dirk Van Gerven and Paul Storm (eds), *The European Company*, 2 vols (CUP 2006); Karl Riesenhuber 'European Company (*Societas Europaea*)' in *The Max Planck Encyclopedia of European Private Law*, vol 1 (n 1) 569.

[129] Council Regulation (EC) No 1435/2003 of 22 July 2003 on the Statute for a European Cooperative Society (SCE) [2003] OJ L207/1. See Thomas von Hippel 'European Cooperative (*Societas Cooperativa Europaea*)' in *The Max Planck Encyclopedia of European Private Law*, vol 1 (n 1) 577.

[130] Council Regulation (EEC) No 2137/85 of 25 July 1985 on the European Economic Interest Grouping (EEIG) [1985] OJ L199/1. See Rainer Kulms, 'European Economic Interest Grouping (EEIG)' in *The Max Planck Encyclopedia of European Private Law*, vol 1 (n 1) 592.

[131] Commission, 'Proposal for a Directive of the European Parliament and of the Council on single-member private limited liability companies' COM (2014) 212 final.

[132] Commission, 'Proposal for a Council Regulation on the Statute for a European Foundation' COM 2012/35. See Thomas von Hippel, 'European Foundation' in *The Max Planck Encyclopedia of European Private Law*, vol 1 (n 1) 592.

[133] Directive 2004/48/EC of the European Parliament and of the Council of 29 April 2004 on the enforcement of intellectual property rights [2004] OJ L195/16. See Christian Heinze, 'Intellectual Property (Enforcement)' in *The Max Planck Encyclopedia of European Private Law*, vol 1 (n 1) 930.

[134] Directive 98/71/EC of the European Parliament and of the Council of 13 October

From the mid-1980s onwards, a **contract law** was progressively enacted by the EU in order to rule transactions entered into by businesses, mostly with consumers. Therefore, it is commonly assumed that EU contract law should be conceptualized as consumer law. Widespread though this assumption may be, it does not fully grasp the inner rationality of EU contract law, nor account for its overall structure. In fact, the attention of the EU legislature is mostly drawn to **business-to-consumer (or B-to-C) transactions**, because they are characterized by a structural asymmetry between the contracting parties that calls for legislative protection for the weaker of the two, ie the consumer. In contrast, in **business-to-business (or B-to-B) transactions**, the contracting parties are generally on the same footing, and, therefore, their private autonomy is paramount and must not be controlled or limited by the legislature (with the exception of competition law). The fact that EU contract law is concentrated on transactions between businesses and consumers, however, does not mean it does not deal with transactions between businesses as well. Although less frequent, there is still some engagement, particularly when one of such businesses is weaker than the other (**B-to-b transactions**).
In this vein, it should be pointed out that almost all the directives on European contract law were adopted on the basis of article 114 TFEU, which allows an ordinary legislative procedure for measures contributing to the approximation of law required to achieve the internal market as set out through article 26 TFEU.

After the Treaty of Amsterdam (see *supra*, ch 8, para 1.1), consumer protection was set out in the founding Treaties as an autonomous competence of the EC/EU. Nevertheless, EU measures aimed at attaining that goal must be 'adopted pursuant to article 114 in the context of the completion of the internal market' (article 169(2)(a) TFEU), unless they merely 'support, supplement and monitor the policy pursued by the Member States' (article 169(2)(b) TFEU).

As a consequence, **consumer protection** as such may not be deemed to constitute the underpinning or the rationale of EU contract law but only to describe the scope of most of it; like the rest of EU private law, EU contract law may be better understood as market law (see *supra*, ch 8, para 1.5).

Article 114(3) TFEU mandates the Commission submit proposals that provide for a 'high level' of consumer protection.
In order to determine the scope of EU contract law, the ECJ referred to the 'average consumer',[135] defined as a consumer that is 'reasonably well-informed

1998 on the legal protection of designs [1998] OJ L298/28. See Annette Kur, 'Industrial Design Law' in *The Max Planck Encyclopedia of European Private Law*, vol 1 (n 1) 865.
135 Stephen Weatherhill, 'Who is the average consumer?' in Stephen Weatherhill and Ulf Bernitz (eds), *The Regulation of Unfair Commercial Practices under EC Directive 2005/29* (Hart 2007) 115ff; Vanessa Mak, 'The "average consumer" of EU law in domestic litigation: Examples from consumer credit and investment cases' [2012] Tilburg Law School Legal Studies Research Paper Series, issue n 4, 5.

and reasonably observant and circumspect'.[136] This definition was subsequently crystallized in the directive enacted by the European Union in the field of contract law. European legislation only sporadically addressed to particular groups of consumers that may be vulnerable due to their mental or physical infirmity, age or credulity.[137]

EU contract law may be subdivided into a general part and a special part. The **general part of EU contract law** entails sets of rules that apply to a contract irrespective of its type (whether a sale or a loan, etc.); they address marketing techniques or commercial practices that may impair the informed and genuine consent of consumers (or, although rarely, undertakings) to enter into a contract.

The **Unfair Trading Directive** of 2015 regulates the pre-contractual stage of the offer, or the invitation to treat, issued to consumers, banning commercial practices that may be deemed misleading or aggressive to the consumers' detriment.[138]
The **Consumer Rights Directive** of 2011 poses extensive duties of the contracting businesses to disclose information, both during pre-contractual negotiations and the execution of the contract. A more stringent regime is provided for off-premises and distance contracts, where a right of withdrawal is also granted to the consumer (albeit within a restricted period of time).
The **Unfair Terms Directive** of 1993 strikes out the terms of standard contracts that 'contrary to the requirement of good faith, [cause] a significant imbalance in the parties' rights and obligations [...], to the detriment of the consumer' (article 3(1)).[139]. The **Late Payment Directive** of 2011 addresses

[136] Case 210/96 *Gut Springenheide GmbH and Rudolf Tusky v Oberkreisdirektor des Kreises Steinfurt – Amt für Lebensmittelüberwachtung* [1988] ECR I-4657; Case 385/01 *Commission v Spain* [2003] ECR I-13143, para 53. Already earlier, the ECJ had clearly mentioned the 'reasonably circumspect consumers' as a point of reference for applying European private law: Case 470/93 *Verein gegen Unwesen in Handel und Gewerbe Köln eV v Mars GmbH* [1995] ECR I-1923, para 24.
[137] The most important case of this kind is that of the Directive 2005/29/EC of the European Parliament and of the Council of 11 May 2005 concerning unfair business-to-consumer commercial practices in the internal market and amending Council Directive 84/450/EEC, Directives 97/7/EC, 98/27/EC and 2002/65/EC of the European Parliament and of the Council and Regulation (EC) No 2006/2004 of the European Parliament and of the Council (Unfair Commercial Practices Directive) [2005] OJ L149/22. Pursuant to article 5(2)(b) UCPD, the assessment of unfairness of commercial practices is treated differently when it is targeted at 'a particular group of consumers', instead of the 'average consumer'. Moreover, article 5(3), UCPD acknowledges that commercial practices may be 'likely to distort the economic behavior only of a clearly identifiable group of consumers who are particularly vulnerable to the practice or the underlying product because of their mental or physical infirmity, age or credulity.' The paradigm of the 'vulnerable consumer', which had already been used by the European legislature in directives governing universal service with regard to the supply of energy and telecommunication, was thus introduced into European private law.
[138] Council Directive 84/450/EEC of 10 September 1984 relating to the approximation of the laws, regulations and administrative provisions of the Member States concerning misleading advertising, OJ L250/17, as amended by Directive 97/55/EC of the European Parliament and of the Council of 6 October 1997 amending Directive 84/450/EEC concerning misleading advertising to include comparative advertising, OJ L290/18.
[139] Council Directive 93/13/EEC of 5 April 1993 on unfair terms in consumer contracts [1993] OJ L95/29.

the remuneration of B-to-B transactions and rules damages owed for its late payment.[140]

Under the **Sales of Goods Directive** of 2019,[141] the seller must guarantee for a minimum period of two years that the goods (which may entail digital elements) delivered to the consumer that purchased them conform with the contract between the parties. In this, the burden of proof is reversed in favor of the consumer. A similar provision is included in the **Supply of Digital Content Directive** of 2019.[142]

The **special part of EU contract law** comprises sets of rules addressing contracts relating to goods or services that, due to the difficulty and technicality of information needed to evaluate them, are purchased on the basis of credence given to the supplier. In most cases, the structural information asymmetry thus resulting between the contracting parties affects the purchaser irrespective of her being a consumer or another business (except if trading the same goods or services). This is the case for most contracts concluded for the trade of financial services, particularly banking, investment, and insurance contracts.

In the **banking sector**, the Consumer Credit Directive of 2008 covers credit agreements directed at the purchase of consumer goods;[143] the Mortgage Directive of 2014 those for the purchase of residential immovable property.[144] The Payment Services Directive of 2015 (PSD 2) is also worth mention,[145] which applies to any client, be it a consumer or (with exceptions) a business.

An overall regulatory framework of **investment market and contracts** is set out by the directive of 2014, commonly known as MiFID 2,[146] complemented

[140] Directive 2011/17/EU of the European Parliament and of the Council of 16 February 2011 on combating late payment in commercial transactions [2011] OJ L48/1.

[141] Directive (EU) 2019/771 of the European Parliament and of the Council of 20 May 2019 on certain aspects concerning contracts for the sale of goods, amending Regulation (EU) 2017/2394 and Directive 2009/22/EC, and repealing Directive 1999/44/EC [2019] OJ L136/28.

[142] Directive 2019/770/EU of the European Parliament and of the Council of 20 May 2019 on certain aspects concerning contracts for the supply of digital content and digital services [2019] OJ L136/1.

[143] European Parliament and Council Directive 2008/48/EC of 23 April 2008 on credit agreements for consumers and repealing Council Directive 87/102/EEC Directive 2008/48/EC [2008] OJ L133/66. See Norbert Reich and Peter Rott, 'EU Consumer Credit Law' in *The Max Planck Encyclopedia of European Private Law*, vol 1 (n 1) 532.

[144] European Parliament and Council Directive 2014/17/EU of 4 February 2014 on credit agreements for consumers relating to residential immovable property and amending Directives 2008/48/EC and 2013/36/EU and Regulation (EU) No 1093/2010 [2014] OJ L 60/34.

[145] Directive 2015/2366/EU of the European Parliament and of the Council of 25 November 2015 on payment services in the internal market, amending Directives 2002/65/EC, 2009/110/EC and 2013/36/EU and Regulation (EU) No 1093/2010, and repealing Directive 2007/64/EC [2015] OJ L337/35.

[146] European Parliament and Council Directive 2014/65/ of 15 May 2014 on markets in financial instruments and amending Directive 2002/92/EC and Directive 2011/1/EU [2014] OJ L173/349.

by an *ad hoc* regulation (MiFIR).[147] A special provision addresses the distance marketing of consumer financial services.[148]

In the **insurance sector**,[149] the main EU provision is that of the Directive on Insurance Distribution (IDD) of 2016.[150]

EU legislature took on some types of **tourist arrangements**, which provide complex combinations of goods and services and therefore require information that is too complex for the consumers purchasing them. Timeshare contracts were thus regulated,[151] as well as those selling package tours.[152]

A very specialized sector of EU contract law (and largely embedded in public law) is that of **public procurements**.[153]

Finally, the **private international law** of the Member States has been largely unified through EU regulations (see also *supra*, ch 3, para 4).

PIL regulations were enacted by the EU on the basis of article 81 TFEU, which confers the competence on 'judicial cooperation in civil matters'.

With regard to the law applicable to contractual obligations, the **Rome I Regulation** of 2008[154] eventually took the place of the **Convention of Rome** of 1980, which, however, is still in force for dealings with countries outside the EU. Obligations arising from sources other than contracts (mainly, torts and unjustified enrichment) are covered by the **Rome II Regulation** of 2007.[155] The **Rome III Regulation** of 2010 deals with the law applicable to divorce and legal separation.[156]

For the conflicts of law on civil proceedings and the recognition and enforcement of foreign judgments in civil and commercial matters, the main source is the **Brussels I Regulation** of 2001.[157] The **Brussels II *bis* Regulation** of 2002

[147] Commission delegated Regulation (EU) 2017/565 of 25 April 2016 supplementing Directive 2014/65/EU of the European Parliament and of the Council as regards organizational requirements and operating conditions for investment firms and defined terms for the purposes of the Directive [2017] OJ L87/1.

[148] Directive 2002/65/EC of the European Parliament and of the Council of 23 September 2002 concerning the distance marketing of consumer financial services and amending Council Directive 90/619/EEC and Directives 97/7/EC and 98/27/EC [2002] OJ L271/16.

[149] Jürgen Basedow, 'Internal Market (Insurance)' in *The Max Planck Encyclopedia of European Private Law*, vol 1 (n 1) 955.

[150] European Parliament and Council Directive (EU) 2016/97 of 20 April 2016 on insurance distribution [2016] OJ L26/19.

[151] Directive 2008/122/EC of the European Parliament and of the Council of 14 January 2009 on the protection of consumers in respect of certain aspects of timeshare, long-term holiday product, resale and exchange contracts [2009] OJ L33/10.

[152] Directive (EU) 2015/2302 of the European Parliament and of the Council of 25 November 2015 on package travel and linked travel arrangements, amending Regulation (EC) No 2006/2004 and Directive 2011/83/EU of the European Parliament and of the Council and repealing Council Directive 90/314/EEC [2015] OJ L326/1.

[153] Heike Schweitzer, 'Public Procurement Law' in *The Max Planck Encyclopedia of European Private Law*, vol 2 (n 4) 1399.

[154] Regulation (EC) 593/2008 of the European Parliament and of the Council of 17 June 2008 on the law applicable to contractual obligations (Rome I) [2008] OJ L177/6.

[155] Regulation (EC) 864/2007 of the European Parliament and of the Council of 11 July 2007 on the law applicable to non-contractual obligations (Rome II) [2007] OJ L199/40.

[156] Council Regulation (EU) No 1259/2010 of 20 December 2010 implementing enhanced cooperation in the area of the law applicable to divorce and legal separation [2010] OJ L343/10.

[157] Council Regulation (EC) No 44/2001 of 22 December 2000 on jurisdiction and the

provides for the same aspects of matrimonial matters and the matters of civil responsibility.[158]

The general rule of European private international law grants the parties the **freedom of choice** of the law applicable to their relationship (article 3 Rome I Regulation; article 14 Rome II Regulation; article 5 Rome III Regulation).[159] It thus engendered a proper **market of rules**, which is based on the **competition between the Member States' legal systems** (see *supra*, ch 8, para 1.5.1). However, several exceptions to that general rule of freedom of choice are set forth. In contract law, for example, **consumers** cannot be deprived of the protection afforded to them by the law of the country where they have their habitual residence (article 6(2) Rome I Regulation), provided that the professional either (a) pursues commercial or professional activities in the country of habitual residence, or (b) by any means directs such activities to that country or to several countries including that country (article 6(1) Rome I Regulation).

When a trader presents her activity on her website, or on that of an intermediary, the question arises whether she 'directs' such activity to other countries, since consumers of the latter can log on the website and through it enter into a contract with the trader. If the question is answered in the affirmative, then the trader must possibly draft 27 forms of contract, one for each Member State whose consumers could not be deprived of the legal protection afforded.

In the **Pammer and Hotel Alpenhof joined cases** of 2010,[160] the ECJ answered that question by ruling 'it should be ascertained whether, before the conclusion of any contract with the consumer, it is apparent from those websites and the trader's overall activity that the trader was envisaging doing business with consumers domiciled in one or more Member States'. Furthermore, the ECJ laid down a (not exhaustive) list of circumstances that are conductive for such an ascertainment: 'the international nature of the activity, mention of itineraries from other Member States for going to the place where the trader is established, use of a language or a currency other than the language or currency generally used in the Member State in which the trader is established with the possibility of making and confirming the reservation in that other language, mention of telephone numbers with an international code, outlay of expenditure on an internet referencing service in order to facilitate access to the trader's site or that of its intermediary by consumers domiciled in other Member States, use of a top-level domain name other than that of the Member State in which the

recognition and enforcement of judgments in civil and commercial matters [2000] OJ L12/1.

[158] Council Regulation (EC) No 2201/2003 of 27 November 2003 concerning jurisdiction and the recognition and enforcement of judgments in matrimonial matters and the matters of parental responsibility, repealing Regulation (EC) No 1347/2000 [2003] OJ L338/1.

[159] Giesela Rühl, 'Choice of Law by the Parties' in *The Max Planck Encyclopedia of European Private Law*, vol 1 (n 1) 190.

[160] Joined Cases C-585/08 and 144/09 *Peter Pammer v Reederei Karl Schlüter GmbH & Co. KG (C-585/08) and Hotel Alpenhof GesmbH v Oliver Heller* [2010] ECR I-12527.

> trader is established, and mention of an international clientele composed of customers domiciled in various Member States', On the other hand, 'the mere accessibility of the trader's or the intermediary's website in the Member State in which the consumer is domiciled is insufficient. The same is true of mention of an email address and of other contact details, or of use of a language or a currency which are the language and/or currency generally used in the Member State in which the trader is established'.

In tort law, one of the most important cases where the freedom of choice is barred is that of the acts of **unfair competition** (article 6(4) Rome II Regulation).

Furthermore, it must be pointed out that even when the parties are free to choose the law applicable to their relationship, they cannot derogate from the **overriding mandatory provisions** of the law that would otherwise apply according to the rules of private international law (article 9 Rome I Regulation; article 16 Rome II Regulation; article 10 Rome III Regulation).[161]

> Overriding mandatory rules are those provisions of national law 'with which has been deemed to be so crucial for the protection of the political, social or economic order in the Member State concerned as to require compliance therewith by all persons present on the national territory of that Member State and on all legal relationships within that State' (**Arblade case** of 1999).[162]

In addition, the application of single provisions of the law chosen by the parties may be refused if it is manifestly incompatible with the **public policy (*ordre public*)** of the forum (article 21 Rome I Regulation; article 26 Rome II Regulation; article 12 Rome III Regulation).[163]

> The public policy (*ordre public*) of the Member States *inter alia* entails the competition rules set forth in the founding Treaties (**Swiss case** of 1999),[164] as well as consumer protection granted by EU law (**Mostaza Claro case** of 2006).[165]

[161] Reinhard Ellger, 'Overriding mandatory provisions' in *The Max Planck Encyclopedia of European Private Law*, vol 2 (n 4) 1228.

[162] Joined cases C-369 and 376/96 *Criminal proceedings against Jean-Claude Arblade and Arblade & Fils SARL (C-369/96) and Bernard Leloup, Serge Leloup and Sofrage SARL (C-376/96)* [1996] ECR I-8454, paras 30-31.

[163] Dieter Martiny, 'Public Policy' in *The Max Planck Encyclopedia of European Private Law*, vol 2 (n 4) 1395.

[164] Case C-126/97 *Eco Swiss China Time Ltd v Benetton International NV* [1999] ECR I-3055.

[165] Case C-168/05 *Elisa María Mostaza Claro v Centro Móvil Milenium SL* [2006] ECR I-10421.

2. THE EUROPEAN COMMON CORE OF NATIONAL PRIVATE LAWS (*ACQUIS COMMUNE*)

2.1. Concept and history

In recent decades, the idea that national laws share a common core that may be deemed European has gained a growing consensus and has been developed in different ways.
One of them is to be found in the **Common Core Project**, started in 1995 at the University of Trento by Ugo Mattei and Mauro Bussani.[166] In general terms, this project follows the Cornell Studies' methodological approach, developed by Rudolf B. Schlesinger (without referring to the European context) during the 1960s (see *supra*, ch 3, para 2).[167]

> Schlesinger's research method entailed questionnaires that every participant had to fill out to provide a very detailed case law of her own jurisdiction. This great number of cases was published together with some introductory contributions in a book series devoted to monographs.[168]

A similar methodological approach also characterizes works with a dominant didactical function, like the ***Ius commune Casebooks*** *for the Common Law of Europe* series,[169] which were initiated by Walter van Gerven, following the

[166] Mauro Bussani and Ugo Mattei, 'The Common Core Approach to European Private Law' (1997) 3 Colum J Eur L 339, 349-351.
[167] Ulrich Drobnig, 'A Memorial Address for Rudolf Schlesinger', in Ugo Mattei and Mauro Bussani (eds), *The Common Core of European Private Law* (Kluwer Law International 2002) 29, 31ff. The paradigmatic result can be found in Rudolf B Schlesinger (ed), *Formation of Contract: A Study of the Common Core of the Legal Systems*, 2 vols (Oceana 1968).
[168] Reinhard Zimmermann and Simon Whittaker (eds), *Good Faith in European Contract Law* (CUP 2000); James Gordley (ed), *The Enforceability of Promises in European Contract Law* (CUP 2001); Mauro Bussani and Vernon V Palmer (eds), *Pure Economic Loss in Europe* (CUP 2003); Eva-Maria Kieninger (ed), *Security Rights in Movable. Property in European Private Law* (CUP 2004 und 2009); Franz Werro and Vernon V Palmer (eds), *The Boundaries of Strict Liability in European Tort Law* (Bern 2004); Ruth Sefton-Green (ed), *Mistake, Fraud and Duties to Inform in European Contract Law* (CUP 2005); Michele Graziadei, Ugo Mattei and Lionel Smith (eds), *Commercial Trusts in European Private Law* (CUP 2005); Barbara Pozzo (ed), *Property and Environment* (Bern 2007); Thomas Möllers and Andreas Heinemann (eds), *The Enforcement of Competition Law in Europe* (CUP 2008); Monika Hinteregger (ed), *Environmental Liability and Ecological Damage in European Law* (CUP 2008); Gert Brüggemeier, Aurelia Colombi Ciacchi and Patrick O'Callaghan (eds), *Personality Rights in European Tort Law* (CUP 2010); John Cartwright and Martijn Hesselink (eds), *Precontractual Liability in European Private Law* (CUP 2011); Ewoud Hondius and Hans-Cristoph Grigoleit (eds), *Unexpected Circumstances in European Law* (CUP 2011); Cornelius van der Merwe and Alain-Laurent Verbeke (eds), *Time Limited Interests in Land* (CUP 2012); Vernon V Palmer (ed), *The Recovery of Non-Pecuniary Loss in European Contract Law* (CUP 2015); Cornelius G van der Merwe (ed), *European Condominium Law* (CUP 2015); Sonia Martín Santisteban and Peter Sparkes (eds), *The Protection of Immovables in European Legal System* (CUP 2015); Marta Infantino and Eleni Zervogianni (eds), *Causation in European Tort Law* (CUP 2017); Luz M Martínez Velencoso, Saki Bailey and Andrea Pradi (eds), *Transfer of Immovables in European Private Law* (CUP 2017).
[169] Walter MML van Gerven, Jeremy Lever, Pierre Larouche, Christian von Bar and Geneviève Viney (eds), *Cases, Materials and Text on Tort Law. Scope of Protection* (Hart 1998);

North American model of *Text, Cases and Materials*. In German, it is worth mentioning the monumental handbook of Filippo Ranieri on *Europäisches Obligationenrecht*.[170]

A further step was taken, starting from the 1980s, when the prospect of a European codification launched by the Parliament (see *infra*, ch 8, para 3) induced some study groups, composed of private law scholars from different countries, to draft projects on European private law. The latter are hence the result of purely private initiatives, even if some of them were supported, sometimes financially, by European institutions.

These works, which to a certain extent demonstrate similarities with the model of the restatements drafted by the American Law Institute (see *supra*, ch 3, para 5),[171] have been drawn up on the basis of comparative research, aimed at finding the 'best solutions', namely the solutions that are better suited to achieving the harmonization of the law. In this regard, the solutions could also be made up of rules that are unknown in the majority of the legal systems, or that are unknown at all in the legal systems.[172]

Therefore, this constitutes a **law beyond the state**,[173] which may be defined as European and scientific.[174]

It may be defined as **European law**,[175] because it represents the common core of the national legal systems of the Member States and mirrors their historical core resting on the tradition of Roman law.[176] However, it may also

Walter MML van Gerven, Jeremy Lever and Pierre Larouche (eds), *Cases, Materials and Text on Tort Law* (Hart 2000); Jack Beatson and Eltjo JH Schrage (eds), *Cases, Materials and Text on Unjustified Enrichment* (Hart 2003); Hans-W Micklitz, Jules Stuyck and Evelyn Terryn (eds), *Cases, Materials and Text on Consumer Law* (Hart 2010); Dagmar Schiek, Lisa B Waddigton and Mark Bell (eds), *Cases, Materials and Text on National, Supranational and International Non-Discrimination* (Hart 2007); Hugh Beale, Bénédicte Fauvarque-Cosson, Jacobien W Rutgers, Denis Tallon and Stefan Vogenauer (eds), *Cases, Materials and Text on Contract Law* (2nd edn, Hart 2007); Sjef van Erp and Bram Akkermans (eds), *Cases, Materials and Text on Property Law* (Hart 2012); Arthur Hartkamp, Carla Sieburgh and Wouter Devroe (eds), *Cases, Materials and Text on European Law and Private Law* (Hart 2017).

170 Filippo Ranieri, *Europäisches Obligationenrecht. Ein Handbuch mit Texten und Materialen* (3rd edn, Springer 2009). In his introduction, where the aims and the methods of the contribution are explained, the author describes his work as a 'casuistic, inductive and case oriented presentation of the materials' ('*kasuistische, induktiv am konkreten Fall orientierte Stoffpräsentation*').

171 Joakim Zekoll, 'Das *American Law Institute* – ein Vorbild für Europa?' in Reinhard Zimmermann (ed), *Globalisierung und Entstaatlichung des Rechts*, vol 2, *Nichtstaatliches Privatrecht: Geltung und Genese* (Mohr Siebeck 2008) 101ff.

172 Ole Lando, 'Principles of European Contract Law. An Alternative or a Precursor of European Legislation' (1992) 40 RabelsZ 267.

173 See the contributions of the Symposium 'Beyond the State? Rethinking Private Law' held at the MPI Hamburg, the twelfth and thirteenth of July 2007 (2008) 56 Am J Comp L 527-539.

174 Reinhard Zimmermann, '*Ius Commune* and the Principles of European Contract Law: Contemporary Renewal of an Old Idea' in Hector L Mac Queen and Reinhard Zimmermann (eds), *European Contract Law: Scots and South African Perspectives* (EUP 2006) 6ff.

175 Nils Jansen, 'Europäisches Privatrecht' in Jürgen Basedow, Klaus J Hopt and Reinhard Zimmermann (eds), *Handwörterbuch des Europäischen Privatrechts*, vol 1 (Mohr Siebeck 2009) 548, 549ff; Reinhard Zimmermann, *Die Europäisierung des Privatrechts und die Rechtsvergleichung* (De Gruyter 2006) 15.

176 Jansen 'European Private Law' (n 98) 638.

be defined as **scientific law**,[177] given the fact that it was made by private law scholars (and not by the holder of sovereign power) through the application of doctrinal methodology (and not dependent on legislative needs of policy). This does not detract from the projects dealt with here: they were drafted according to the usual standards of the legislature,[178] and resemble a true civil code (or part of it) in nature.[179] They are referred to as principles solely because they are not binding in a positivistic sense (see *supra*, ch 6, para 3), not belonging to an individual legal system; yet, they consist of black-letter rules, which are precise in their content and germane to a would-be enforcement.[180]

In fact, the projects addressed here not only represent academic endeavors of great significance, but also proved to be effective as **model laws**, which influenced the existing and the forthcoming law, both at the national and at the EU level. Therefore, they indicate a path for the creation of uniform law, which is an alternative to legislation,[181] especially with respect to a European civil code.[182]

Furthermore, private parties may agree to elect these projects with as the law to be applied to their legal relationships, insofar as it is allowed by private international law (see *infra*, ch 8, para 2.2).

Far from merely being a gigantic patchwork of preliminary drafting of a would-be European civil code, they may be therefore deemed to represent sources of **soft law**,[183] ie law that operates in the framework of interpretation as supplementary to national law and as an alternative to it, insofar as such a choice is permitted for the involved parties.

177 Reinhard Zimmermann, '"Wissenschaftliches Recht" am Beispiel (vor allem) des europäischen Vertragsrechts' in Christian Bumke and Anne Röthel (eds), *Privates Recht* (Mohr Siebeck 2012) 21ff.

178 Nils Jansen and Reinhard Zimmermann, 'Im Labyrinth der Regelwerke' [2017] ZEuP 761.

179 Reinhard Zimmermann, 'Principles of European Contract Law (PECL)' in *The Max Planck Encyclopedia of European Private Law*, vol 1 (n 1) 1325.

180 Reinhard Zimmermann, 'The Present State of European Private Law' (2009) 57 Am J Comp L 479.

181 On the alternatives to a legislative unification of the law, see the contributions of the Symposium held at the MPI Hamburg, the 3-4 May 1991, published in the second issue of (1992) 52 RabelsZ.

182 For sharp criticism against this possibility, see Ugo Mattei, 'Hard Code Now! A Critique of "Softness" and a Plea for Responsibility in the European Debate over Codification' in Id, *The European Codification Process. Cut and Paste*, The Hague 2003, 107, 118ff (also in Stefan Grundmann and Jules Stuyck (eds), *An Academic Green Paper on European Contract Law* (Kluwer Law Int'l 2002) 215; Ugo Mattei and Anna di Robilant, 'The Art and Science of Critical Scholarship. Post-Modernism and International Style in the Legal Architecture of Europe' (2001) 75 Tulane L Rev 1054; Anna di Robilant, 'Genealogies of Soft Law' (2006) 54 Am J Comp L 499.

183 Nils Jansen, *The Making of Legal Authority: Non-Legislative Codifications in Historical and Comparative Perspective* (OUP 2010). Cf Karl Riesenhuber, 'Privates Rechts, wissenschaftliches Recht, Systembildung. Systembildung im Europäischen Vertragsrecht', in Bumke and Röthel (eds) (n 177) 49ff.

2.2. European restatements and model laws regarding contracts

Given the possible contents of a future European codification of private law, and more generally, of the competences conferred to the EEC/EC/EU, it is natural that, at least at the outset, such scientific projects were focused quite exclusively on contract law.

In addition, contract law is the field of private law that more naturally fits internationalization and harmonization, as demonstrated by the CISG and its predecessors (see *supra*, ch 3, para 5).

The CISG has to be considered the point of reference for the most successful project of a European and scientific private law, namely the **Principles of European Contract Law** (PECL), or the Lando (commission's) principles.

The PECL were prepared and discussed at the beginning of the eighties and published in three volumes between 1995 and 2002.[184]

Colloquially, they are also known as Lando Principles, as they are often identified with Ole Lando, who acted as the initiator of the whole project and subsequently as chair of the Commission,[185] which elaborated the rules and whose members came from different European States. The individual provisions and comments were presented by rapporteurs, subsequently discussed in plenary meetings and then adopted (with the necessary amendments).[186]

Part I, which encompasses 59 articles, concerns performance, non-performance and undue performance (as well as remedies for such), was drafted between 1981 and 1982, and published in 1995.[187] The German version was published in 1995,[188] the French in 1997.[189]

In 2000, a revised version of Part I was published, together with the new Part II, which contains 73 articles and concerns conclusion, validity, interpretation,

[184] Ole Lando, 'Principles of European Contract Law: An Alternative to or a Precursor of European Legislation' (1992) 40 Am J Comp L 573; Reinhard Zimmermann, Die *Principles of European Contract Law als Ausdruck und Gegenstand europäischer Rechtswissenschaft* (Zentrum für Europäisches Wirtschaftsrecht 2003); Carlo Castronovo, 'I Principi di diritto europeo dei contratti e l'idea di codice' [1995] Riv dir comm I, 21; Guido Alpa, 'La seconda versione dei *Principles of European Contract Law*' [2000] NGCC II, 121.

[185] On Lando's academic profile and intellectual undertaking, see the articles published in the third issue of (2020) 28 ERPL 465ff.

[186] Ole Lando, 'European Contract Law' (1983) 31 Am J Comp L 653; Reinhard Zimmermann, '*Ius Commune* and the Principles of European Contract Law: Contemporary Renewal of an Old Idea', in Hector L Mac Queen and Reinhard Zimmermann, *European Contract Law: Scots and South African Perspectives* (Edinburgh Studies in Law 2006) 1, 4ff.

[187] Ole Lando and Hugh Beale (eds), *Principles of European Contract Law*, Part I, *Performance, Non-Performance and Remedies*, prepared by the Commission of European Contract Law (Kluwer Law International 1995).

[188] Ulrich Drobnig and Reinhard Zimmermann, 'Grundregeln des europäischen Vertragsrechts' [1995] ZEuP 864.

[189] Georges Rouhette, Isabelle de Lamberterie, Denis Tallon and Claude Witz (eds), *Principes du droit européen du contrat* (Société de législation comparée 2003).

contents and effects of contract, and authority of agents.[190] The Italian version was published in 2001,[191] the German in 2002.[192]
Part III, which has 69 articles and concerns plurality of parties, assignment of claim, substitution of new debtor and transfer of contract, set-off, prescription, illegality, conditions, capitalization of interest, was published in 2002.[193] The French Version was released in 2003,[194] the German in 2003 and 2005.[195]

PECL's analogous features are shared by the **Principles of International Commercial Contracts** (PICC),[196] which, however, being prepared by the UNIDROIT (see *supra*, ch 3, para 5), go beyond a pure European dimension and constitute instead a project of **global law**.[197]

The working group that drafted the PICC was set up in 1980 by the UNIDROIT Directorate and led by Michael Joachim Bonell.[198]
The 1994 version consisted of 120 articles dealing with the conclusion of contract, validity of contracts (including defects of will), the interpretation and content of contracts, performance, and (remedies for) non-performance.[199]

[190] Ole Lando and Hugh Beale (eds), *Principles of European Contract Law*, Parts I and II (Combined and Revised), prepared by the Commission of European Contract Law (Kluwer Law International 2000).
[191] Carlo Castronovo (ed), *Principi di diritto europeo dei contratti*, Parte I e II (Giuffrè 2001).
[192] Reinhard Zimmermann and Christian von Bar (eds), *Grundregeln des Europäischen Vertragsrechts*, Teile I und II, *Kommission für Europäisches Vertragsrecht* (Sellier 2002).
[193] Ole Lando, Eric Clive, André Prüm and Reinhard Zimmermann (eds), *Principles of European Contract Law*, Part III, prepared by the Commission of European Contract Law (Kluwer Law International 2003).
[194] Georges Rouhette, Isabelle de Lamberterie, Denis Tallon and Claude Witz (eds) (n 189).
[195] Ulrich Drobnig, Reinhard Zimmermann and Jan Kleinheisterkamp, 'Grundregeln der Kommission für Europäisches Vertragsrecht' [2003] ZEuP 895 and Reinhard Zimmermann and Christian von Bar (eds), *Grundregeln des Europäischen Vertragsrechts*, Teil III, *Kommission für Europäisches Vertragsrecht* (Sellier 2005).
[196] Michael J Bonell, 'The CISG, European Contract Law and the Development of a World Contract Law' (2008) 56 Am J Comp L 1; Ole Lando, 'CISG and its Followers: A Proposal to Adopt Some International Principles of Contract Law' (2005) 53 Am J Comp L 379; Harry M Fletchner, 'The CISG's Impact on International Unification Efforts: The UNIDROIT Principles of International Commercial Contracts and the Principles of European Contract Law' in Franco Ferrari (ed), *The 1980 Uniform Sales Law: Old Issues Revisited in the Light of Recent Experience* (Giuffrè-Sellier 2003) 169ff. For an article-by-article commentary, see Eckart J Brödermann, *UNIDROIT Principles of International Commercial Contracts* (Nomos 2018); Stefan Vogenauer (ed), *Commentary on UNIDROIT Principles of International Commercial Contracts (PICC)* (2nd edn, OUP 2015); Peter Mankowski, *Commercial Law* (Nomos 2019) 462ff.
[197] Ralf Michaels, 'The Unidroit Principles as Global Background Law' (2014) 19 Unif L Rev 643; Id, 'Umdenken fur die UNIDROIT Prinzipien: Vom Rechtswahlstatut zum Allgemeinen Teil des transnationalen Vertragsrechts' (2009) 73 RabelsZ 866; Jan Kleinheisterkamp, 'UNIDROIT Principles of International Commercial Contracts (PICC)' in *The Max Planck Encyclopedia of European Private Law*, vol 2 (n 4) 1727.
[198] With respect to the members of the group and their working methods, see Michael J Bonell, 'Unification of Law by Non-Legislative Means: The UNIDROIT Draft Principles for International Commercial Contracts' (1992) 40 Am J Comp L 617; Id, 'Das UNIDROIT-Projekt für die Ausarbeitung von Regeln für internationale Handelsverträge' (1992) 56 RabelsZ 274.
[199] UNIDROIT, *Principles of International Commercial Contracts*, 1994, available at https://www.unidroit.org/instruments/commercial-contracts/unidroit-principles-1994.

The 2004 version consisted of 185 articles,[200] which represented an extension and improvement of the preceding version.[201]
The 2010 version consisted of 2010 articles,[202] as does the 2016 version,[203] which was extended particularly to issues related to long-term contracts.[204]
Every version was translated into a plurality of languages by the UNIDROIT.

The PICC may be understood as a modern rationalization of the ***lex mercatoria***,[205] namely as a collection of commercial customs that concern international transactions (see also *supra*, ch 7, para 3). As a consequence, the PICC exclusively address **commercial contracts**, as suggested by their title, and therefore do not apply to consumer contracts; by contrast, the PECL do not provide for a similar restriction of their scope, so that they may be deemed to be applicable to **consumer contracts** as well, it being understood that, as implied by article 1:103(2) PECL, consumer protection rules provided for by EU law are mandatory and overriding in the sense of article 7 Rome I Regulation (see *supra*, ch 8, para 1.5.2). This difference in the subjective scope of the PECL and the PICC does not detract them from being quite comparable and, to a certain extent, similar.[206] This is due to the fact that, albeit addressing exclusively commercial contracts, the PICC do not provide for a commercial law *stricto sensu* but for a market law that amounts to general contract law.
Over time, the PECL and the PICC proved quite influential on national as well as on uniform and EU law.
This **influence on national legal systems** was enabled by the fact that the PECL (as the PICC) have been referred to in some civil codifications.[207] Moreover,

[200] UNIDROIT, *Principles of International Commercial Contracts* 2004 available at https://www.unidroit.org/instruments/commercial-contracts/unidroit-principles-2004 accessed 15 August 2019.
[201] Michael J Bonell, 'UNIDROIT Principles 2004 – The New Edition of the Principles of International Commercial Contracts Adopted by the International Institute for the Unification of Private Law' (2004) 9 Unif L Rev 6; Reinhard Zimmermann, 'Die Unidroit-Grundregeln der internationalen Handelsverträge 2004 in vergleichender Perspektive' [2005] ZEuP 264.
[202] UNIDROIT, *Principles of International Commercial Contracts* 2010 available at https://www.unidroit.org/instruments/commercial-contracts/unidroit-principles-2010 accessed 15 August 2019. See on the latter Stefan Vogenauer, 'Die UNIDROIT Grundregeln der internationalen Handelverträge 2010' [2013] ZEuP 7.
[203] UNIDROIT, *Principles of International Commercial Contracts* 2016 available at https://www.unidroit.org/instruments/commercial-contracts/unidroit-principles-2016 accessed 15 August 2019.
[204] Walter Doralt, *Langzeitverträge* (Mohr Siebeck 2018) 86ff, 440ff.
[205] Michael J Bonell, 'The Law Governing International Commercial Contracts and the Actual Role of the Unidroit Principles' (2018) 23 Unif L Rev 15; Ole Lando, 'The Principles of European Contract Law and the Lex Mercatoria' in FS Siehr (Asser Press 2000) 391. A different opinion is expressed by Cécile Legros, 'Common Core, PECL and DCFR: Could They be Used to Interpret Shipping Law?' in Wouter Verheyen, Frank GM Smeele and Marian AIH Hoeks (eds), *Common core, PECL and DCFR: Could they change shipping and transport law?* (Intersentia 2015) 1, 13. See also Philip Hellwege, 'Lex Mercatoria' in *The Max Planck Encyclopedia of European Private Law*, vol 2 (n 4) 1086.
[206] Michael J Bonell, 'The UNIDROIT Principles of International Commercial Contracts and the Principles of European Contract Law: Similar Rules for the Same Purposes?' (1996) 1 Unif L Rev 229; Reinhard Zimmermann, 'Konturen eines Europäischen Vertragsrechts' [1995] JZ 477.
[207] For example, for the Netherlands, see Danny Busch, Ewoud Hondius, Hugo van

they served also a model for the codification of private law in countries of middle and eastern Europe, which recently entered the EU.[208]
Moreover, national courts referred to PECL[209] and PICC[210] in order to check new solutions and suggestions of national private law on a European level.[211] This development seems particularly remarkable if one considers that this has involved both common law legal systems and some characteristic constructions of continental private law, such as the principle of good faith[212] and *culpa in contrahendo.*[213]

Kooten and Harriet Schelhaas (eds), *The Principles of European Contract Law and Dutch Law: A Commentary* (Kluwer Law International 2002); Id (eds), *The Principles of European Contract Law and Dutch Law: A Commentary* II (Kluwer Law International 2006). For Italy, see Luisa Antoniolli and Anna Veneziano (eds), *Principles of European Contract Law and Italian Law. A Commentary* (Kluwer Law International 2005).

208 For a set of national reports, see the works of the international conference for the 375th jubilee of the University of Tartu, 15th-16th November 2007: *European Initiatives (CFR) and Reform of Civil Law in New Member States* (2008) XIV Tartu L Rev (<http://www.juridicainternational.eu/index.php?id=10521> accessed 11 September 2019). In addition, see Monika Józon, 'The Influence of European Private Law on the New Romanian Civil Code' [2012] ZEuP 568, 571ff; Monika Pauknerová, 'The Unidroit Principles and Czech Law' in *Eppur si muove: The age of uniform law: Essays in honour of Michael Joachim Bonell to celebrate his 70th birthday*, vol 2 (Unidroit 2016), 1583ff; Tadas Zukas, *Einfluss der 'Unidroit Principles of International Commercial Contracts' und der 'Principles of European Contract Law' auf die Transformation des Vertragsrechts in Litauenien: eine rechtsvergleichende Studie unter besonderer Berücksichtigung der Schweizer Lehre und Praxis zur Auslegung des rezipierten Rechts* (Stämpfli 2011).

209 For example, in Spain: Encarna Roca Trías, 'The Modernisation of the Law of Obligations Using the Principles of European Contract Law', in Francisco de Elizalde (ed), *Uniform Rules for European Contract Law? A Critical Assessment* (Hart 2018) 83ff; Encarnación Roca Trías and Beatriz Fernández Gregoraci, 'The Modern Law of Obligations in the Spanish High Court' (2009) 5 ERCL 45; Carles Vendrell Cervantes, 'The Application of the Principles of European Contract Law by Spanish Courts' [2008] ZeuP 533; María del Pilar Perales Viscasillas, 'La aplicación jurisprudencial en España de la Convención de Viena de 1980 sobre compraventa internacional, los Principios de UNIDROIT y los Principios del Decrecho contractual europeo: de la mera referencia a la integración de lagunas' [2007] La Ley: Revista juridica española de doctrina, jurisprudencia y bibliografía 1750.

210 For Spain, see Núria Bouza Vidal, 'The Unidroit Principles as Legal Background in Spanish Case Law' in *Eppur si muove* (n 208) 1266ff; Pilar Perales Viscasillas, 'Los Principios de Unidroit en la jurisprudencia del Tribunal Supremo español' ibid 1619ff. For countries outside Europe, see notably Alfredo M Rabello and Pablo Lerner, 'The UNIDROIT Principles of International Commercial Contracts and Israeli Contract Law' (2003) 8 Unif L Rev 601; Pablo Lerner, 'The Principles of International Commercial Contracts as model law: An Israeli perspective' (2019) 24 Unif L Rev 1.

211 On the other hand, the German courts have given less consideration to the PECL, in particular the German Federal Court, which so far has cited them only in two rulings (see Thomas Ackermann, 'Uniform Rules as Guidelines for National Courts and Legislatures: The German Experience', in de Elizalde (n 209) 91, 98-102).

212 *Yam Seng Pte Ltd v International Trade Corporation Ltd* [2013] EWHC 111, [2013] Bus LR D53, para 124: 'In refusing, however, if indeed it does refuse, to recognise any such general obligation of good faith, this jurisdiction would appear to be swimming against the tide. [...] Attempts to harmonise the contract law of EU Member States, such as the Principles of European Contract Law proposed by the Lando Commission and the European Commission's proposed Regulation for a Common European Sales Law on which consultation is currently taking place, also embody a general duty to act in accordance with good faith and fair dealing. There can be little doubt that the penetration of this principle into English law and the pressures towards a more unified European law of contract in which the principle plays a significant role will continue to increase'.

213 *Chartbrook Ltd v Persimmon Homes Ltd and Others* [2009] UKHL 38, [2009] Bus LR 1200, para 39, where Lord Hoffmann affirms: 'Both the Unidroit Principles of Inter-

The PICC more than the PECL have been applied as general principles of law (or *lex mercatoria*) in **arbitration**,[214] also to interpret and meet the shortcomings of national legislations and instruments of international law. Particularly, they have been referred to by arbitration tribunals to interpret and fill the internal gaps of the CISG, ie issues covered but not explicitly regulated by it.[215]

On the level of EU Law, PECL and DCFR were quoted several times by the Advocate General of ECJ, in order to promote determinate (harmonized) solutions.[216]

Where contracting parties have agreed upon an **arbitration clause**, their right to also choose the PECL or the PICC as the law to be applied to their contract is undisputed and implicitly allowed by article 28(1) UNCITRAL Model Law on International Commercial Arbitration.[217] In case such a choice is lacking, the PECL or the PICC could be nonetheless applied by the arbitral tribunal, since most national and international rules on arbitration allow arbitration tribunals to apply the most suitable 'law', or 'rules of law', and that could be identified precisely in the PECL or the PICC; article 28(2) UNCITRAL Model Law on International Commercial Arbitration, however, seems to support the opposite view,[218] since it mandates the arbitration tribunal to apply 'the conflict of laws rules'.[219]

Should the contracting parties not have agreed upon an arbitration clause, it is disputed whether they can make the **choice of the PECL or the PICC**

national Commercial Contracts (1994 and 2004 revision) and the Principles of European Contract Law (1999) provide that in ascertaining the "common intention of the parties", regard shall be had to prior negotiations: Articles 4.3 and 5.102 respectively. [...] One cannot in my opinion simply transpose rules based on one philosophy of contractual interpretation to another, or assume that the practical effect of admitting such evidence under the English system of civil procedure will be the same as that under a Continental system'.

214 Zeynep Derya Tarman, 'Non-national Rules in the Arbitration of Commercial Contracts' in de Elizalde (n 209) 71. In the framework of the twentieth conference of the *Académie International de Droit Comparé* (AIDC), which has been held in Fukuoka, the following subject was discussed: 'The UNIDROIT Principles as a common frame of reference for the uniform interpretation of national law'. Some national contributions are already available: For Germany, see Katharina Erler and Martin Schmidt-Kessel, 'The Use of the UPICC in Order to Interpret or Supplement German Contract Law' in Martin Schmidt-Kessel (ed), *German National Reports on the 20th International Congress of Comparative Law* (Mohr Siebeck 2018) 39; for Italy, see Anna Veneziano and Eleonora Finazzi Agrò, 'The Use of the UNIDROIT Principles in Order to Interpret or Supplement National Contract Law' in *Annuario di diritto comparato e di studi legislativi, special edition*, vol 1 (Edizioni Scientifiche Italiane 2018) 39. In addition, see Klaus P Berger, 'International Arbitral Practice and the UNIDROIT Principles of International Commercial Contracts' (1998) 46 Am J Comp L 129.

215 Derya Tarman (n 214) 71.

216 Case C-445/06, *Danske Slagterier v Bundesrepublik Deutschland* [2009] ECR I-2119, para 94 (DCFR); case C-404/06, *Quelle AG v Bundesverband der Verbraucherzentralen und Verbraucherverbände* [2008] ECR I-02685, para 44 (PECL); case C-227/08, *Martín Martín v EDP Editores SL* [2009] ECR I-11939, para 51 (DCFR); case C-618/10 *Banco Español de Crédito SA/Calderón Camino* ECLI:EU:C:2012:74, para 4 (DCFR).

217 'The arbitral tribunal shall decide the dispute in accordance with such rules of law as are chosen by the parties as applicable to the substance of the dispute. Any designation of the law or legal system of a given State shall be construed, unless otherwise expressed, as directly referring to the substantive law of that State and not to its conflict of laws rules'.

218 Hellwege (n 205) 1277.

219 'Failing any designation by the parties, the arbitral tribunal shall apply the law determined by the conflict of laws rules which it considers applicable'.

as the law to be applied to their contract.[220] The positive answer is possibly suggested by recital 13 of the Rome I Regulation, but is not provided for by its articles (even more significantly, it was struck out of the initial proposal).

Recital 13 of the Rome I Regulation refers explicitly to 'non-state body of law' and sets forth that the parties can incorporate it by reference into their contract.

Under the traditional conception of private international law, this question should be answered in the negative,[221] because, absent any conflict of law, the will of the contracting parties cannot stand as a connecting factor. If private international law is understood as enabling the private autonomy of the contracting parties beyond national borders, however, its function is not necessarily that of solving conflicts of law, and the will of the contracting parties is not necessarily confined to the role of connecting factor, thus becoming the source itself of the contract law. Article 3 (Rules of law) of the Principles of Choice of Law in International Commercial Contracts of 2015 supports this view,[222] in that it states: 'The law chosen by the party may be rules of law that are generally accepted on an international, supranational or regional level as a neutral and balanced set of rules, unless the law of the forum provides otherwise'.[223]

On the other hand, the ***Code européen des contrats***,[224] drafted by the *Accademia dei Giusprivatisti Europei*,[225] must be acknowledged as having its own particular character.

The proposal was first presented by the initiator of the whole project, Giuseppe Gandolfi, in the framework of the conference organized by the Italian private

[220] Against this view, Claus-Wilhelm Canaris, 'Die Stellung der *UNIDROIT Principles* und der *Principles of European Contract Law* im System der Rechtsquellen' in Jürgen Basedow (ed), *Europäische Vertragsvereinheitlichung und deutsches Recht* (Mohr Siebeck 2000) 5ff. A different opinion is expressed by Stefan Grundmann, 'Law Merchant als lex lata Communitatis' in *Festschrift für Walter Rolland zum 70. Geburtstag* (Bundesanzeiger 1999) 145ff.

[221] For an overall analysis of the question, see Peter Mankowski, sub article 3, in Peter Magnus and Peter Mankowski (eds), *European Commentaries on Private International Law*, vol 2 (Otto Schmidt 2017) 185ff.

[222] Principles on Choice of Law in International Commercial Contracts <https://www.hcch.net/en/instruments/conventions/full-text/?cid=135> accessed 11 September 2019.

[223] Brooke Marshall, 'The Hague Choice of Law Principles, CISG, and PICC: A Hard Look at a Choice of Soft Law' (2018) 66 Am J Comp L 175.

[224] Giuseppe Gandolfi (ed), *Code européen des contrats. Avant-projet, Livre premier* (2nd edn, Giuffrè 2004); Id (ed), *Code européen des contrats. Avant-projet, Livre deuxième*, vol 1 (Giuffrè 2007), vol 2 (Giuffrè 2008). See Kurt Siehr, 'Code Européen des Contrats (Avant-Projet)' in *The Max Planck Encyclopedia of European Private Law*, vol 1 (n 1) 207.

[225] The *Accademia* was grounded in 1992 in Pavia and directed by André Tunc until his death (18 April 1998), afterwards by Alberto Trabucchi. The grounding of the *Accademia* was decided during the conference *Incontro di studio sul futuro codice europeo dei contratti*, Pavia, 20 and 21 October 1990. For in-depth information on the *Accademia*'s work, see Peter Stein (ed), *Convegni di studio per la redazione del progetto di un Codice europeo dei contratti* (Pavia, 1992-1994) (Giuffrè 1996).

law scholars' association in June 1989.[226] It was not until 1995 that the *Accademia* decided to elaborate model rules.
The *Code* has followed two different models.[227]
On the one hand (and at the beginning), it took inspiration from the fourth book of the Italian civil code. This decision was based on two reasons. First, the Italian civil code represented a synthesis between the two great codifications of France and Germany. Due to the comprehensive approach which encompasses both civil law and commercial law, the Italian civil code is more modern and closer to English law than the French or the German Civil Code.
On the other hand, the project under analysis followed the Contract Code drafted by Harvey McGregor. The only existing edition of this work was presented to the public during a conference in Pavia in 1990.[228]
In the 1960s, McGregor was appointed by the English Law Commission to draft the first version of a codification of English contract law, which had to be discussed by the members of the Commission. During the works, the Scottish Law Commission, which in the meantime had stepped into the project, was disappointed by McGregor's work, even though the latter followed their suggestions with specific regard to the elimination of the doctrine of consideration and the recognition of contracts in favor of third parties. The project was ultimately abandoned.
The *Code européen des contrats* was originally discussed and drafted in French and afterwards translated in English (and in other European languages). This contrasts with the PECL, which were drafted in part in English and in French.

2.3. European restatements and model laws regarding other areas of private law

Notwithstanding the position of prominence gained by contract law in the framework of the Europeanization of private law, one has to also consider attempts to harmonize the law of obligations in different (European) States, as it is witnessed by the *Progetto italo-francese delle obbligazioni - Projet franco-italien du code des obligations*, published in 1927.[229] In addition, it must

[226] Giuseppe Gandolfi, 'Una proposta di rilettura del IV libro del codice civile nella prospettiva di una codificazione europea' in *La civilistica italiana dagli anni '50 ad oggi tra crisi dogmatica e riforme legislative. Congresso dei civilisti italiani, Venezia, 23-26 giugno 1989* (CEDAM 1991) 1037ff.

[227] Salvatore Patti, 'Kritische Anmerkungen zum Entwurf eines europäischen Vertragsgesetzbuches' [2004] ZEuP 118; Id, *Diritto privato e codificazioni europee* (2nd edn, Giuffrè 2007) 59ff; Reinhard Zimmermann, 'Der "Codice Gandolfi" als Modell eines einheitlichen Vertragsrechts für Europa? Überlegungen zur Regelung der Aufrechnung (Art. 132)' in *Festschrift für Erik Jayme*, vol 2 (Sellier 2004) 1401ff.

[228] Due to the great interest that was demonstrated on this occasion, McGregor's text has been published: Harvey McGregor, *Contract Code: Drawn up on behalf of the English Law Commission* (Giuffrè 1993). In his presentation to the volume, Giuseppe Gandolfi, ibid V, observes: 'This project can, to some extent, be compared to the landing of the Apollo 11 team on the moon [...] or the fall of the Berlin wall'.

[229] Guido Alpa and Giovanni Chiodi (eds), *Il progetto italo francese delle obbligazioni (1927). Un modello di armonizzazione nell'epoca della ricodificazione* (Giuffrè 2007). See in detail Mario Rotondi (ed), *Le projet franco-italien du code des obligations* (CEDAM 1980).

be particularly pointed out that PECL's third part, even if primarily devoted to contract law, contains rules for a general part of the law of obligations.[230] Moreover, the **Principles of European Tort Law** (PETL) cover one of the most important fields of extracontractual law of obligations,[231] that of liability for unlawful damages inflicted on someone else.

They were drafted by the European Group on Tort Law (colloquially also called 'Tilburg Group'), which worked in Vienna together with the European Centre of Tort and Insurance Law (ECTIL) and the Institute for European Tort Law (ETL) of the *Österreichische Akademie der Wissenschaften*.
Helmut Koziol was the initiator of the whole project and long-standing director of ECTIL and ETL.[232]

The law of **unjustified enrichment** was addressed by the seventh book of the DCFR.
With respect to **ownership and the other property rights**, the DCFR has encompassed the transfer of ownership of chattels, security property rights, and trusts. Since 1996, some Principles of European Trust Law have been drafted by the Business and Law Research Centre of the Radboud University and were published in 1999.[233]
In the field of **family law**, one has to mention the Principles of European Family Law,[234] which were drafted by the Commission on European Family Law (CEFL).[235] To date, the Commission has published three parts of these Principles, namely the Principles regarding divorce and maintenance between former

230 For the subsequent observation that the connection with contract law appears not to be precise, see Zimmermann, 'Principles of European Contract Law (PECL)' (n 179) 1325.
231 European Group on Tort Law, *Principles of European Tort Law. Text and Commentary* (Springer 2005).
232 Ulrich Magnus, 'Principles of European Tort Law (PETL)' in *The Max Planck Encyclopedia of European Private Law*, vol 1 (n 1) 1189; Helmut Koziol, 'Die Principles of European Tort Law der European Group on Tort Law' [2004] ZEuP 427; Reinhard Zimmermann, 'Principles of European Contract Law and Principles of European Tort Law: Comparison and Points of Contact', in Helmut Koziol and Barbara C Steininger (eds), *European Tort Law 2003* (Springer 2003) 2ff; Bernhard A Koch, 'The European Group on Tort Law and Its Principles of European Tort Law' (2005) 53 Am J Comp L 189; Jaap Spier and Olav A Maazen, 'The European Group on Tort Law ("Tilburg Group") and the European Principles of Tort Law' [1999] ZEuP 469.
233 David J Hayton, SCJJ Kortmann and HLE Verhagen (eds), *Principles of European Trust Law* (Kluwer law international 1999).
234 Katharina Boele-Woelki and Dieter Martiny, 'Prinzipien zum Europäischen Familienrecht betreffend Ehescheidung und nachehelicher Unterhalt' [2016] ZEuP 6; Susanne Ferrari, 'Principles of European Family Law Regarding Property Relations Between Spouses' [2014] ZEuP 902; Walter Pintens, 'Principles of European Family Law (PEFL)' in *The Max Planck Encyclopedia of European Private Law*, vol 1 (n 1) 1329; Walter Pintens, 'Die Commission on European Family Law. Hintergrund, Gründung, Arbeitsmethode und erste Ergebnisse' [2004] ZEuP 548; Jens M Scherpe, 'European Family Law in Action' [2004] ZEuP 1088; Gerard-René de Groot, 'Auf dem Wege zu einem europäischen (internationalen) Familienrecht' [2001] ZEuP 617.
235 The Commission was grounded in September 2001 in Utrecht, and its President is Katharina Boele-Woelki.

spouses in 2004,[236] the Principles regarding parental responsibility in 2007 [237] and the Principles regarding property relations between spouses in 2011.[238] A Feasibility Study of **Principles for a Data Economy** was recently published,[239] as the result of a common project run by the European Law Institute and the American Law Institute.[240]

3. THE PERSPECTIVE OF A EUROPEAN CODIFICATION OF PRIVATE LAW

The EU Parliament has repeatedly urged the adoption of a European civil code.[241] The Commission has also suggested that this proposal should be evaluated as a desirable option of EU legislative policy, specifically as part of the critical review of European contract law that has been undertaken.[242]
Nevertheless, in the public consultation launched on this issue, most of the opinions of the institutions and stakeholders involved were negative. This fact led the Commission to proceed more cautiously than originally planned. In the so-called Action Plan that was included in a 2003 communication to ensure higher consistency within European contract law,[243] the Commission concluded that the idea of a European civil code was not realistically feasible. Moreover, it suggested that as well as improving the quality of *acquis communautaire*, a **Common Frame of Reference** should be set in order to establish common principles and language in the realm of contract law.[244]

[236] Katharina Boele-Woelki and others (eds), *Principles of European Family Law Regarding Divorce and Maintenance Between Former Spouses* (Intersentia 2004).
[237] Katharina Boele-Woelki and others (eds), *Principles of European Family Law Regarding Parental Responsibility* (Intersentia 2007).
[238] Katharina Boele-Woelki and others (eds), *Principles of European Family Law Regarding Property Relations Between Spouses* (Intersentia 2013).
[239] Feasibility Study ALI-ELI Principles for a Data Economy <https://www.europeanlaw-institute.eu/projects-publications/current-projects-feasibility-studies-and-other-activities/current-projects/data-economy/> accessed 11 September 2019.
[240] Christiane Wendehorst, 'Of Elephants in the Room and Paper Tigers: How to Reconcile Data Protection and the Data Economy' in Sebastian Lohsse, Reiner Schulze and Dirk Staudenmayer (eds), *Trading Data in the Digital Economy: Legal Concepts and Tools* (Hart-Nomos 2017) 327.
[241] EP Resolution of 26 May 1989 on action to bring into line the private law of the Member States [1989] OJ C158/400; EP Resolution of 26 May 1994 on the harmonization of certain sectors of the private law of the Member States [1994] OJ C205/518; EP Resolution of 15 November 2001 on the approximation of the civil and commercial law of the Member States [2001] OJ C140E/538.
[242] Commission, 'Communication from the Commission to the European Parliament and the Council – A more coherent European contract law – An action plan' COM (2003) 398 final.
[243] Commission (n 215).
[244] Commission, 'Communication from the Commission to the European Parliament and the Council – European Contract Law and the revision of the *acquis*: the way forward' COM (2004), 651 final. See also EP Resolution of 23 March 2006 on European contract law and the revision of the acquis: the way forward [2006] OJ C292E/109; EP Resolution of 14 December 2006 on European contract law [2006] OJ C305E/247; EP Resolution of 12 December 2007 on European contract law [2007] P6-TA-PROV(2007)0615; EP Resolution of 3 September 2008 on the common frame of reference for European contract

In the meantime, such a project has been fulfilled by some international groups of academic jurists and published under the title of **Draft Common Frame of Reference** (DCFR), first in the so-called *interim edition* of 2008,[245] and then in the final version of 2009.[246] The project was initiated by Christian von Bar. In reality, the DCFR was conceived from the outset as the precursor of a proper civil code according to the traditional model established in the nineteenth century.[247] The Commission's political caution, however, and the unfavorable reaction of most European civil law scholars led its editors to present it more modestly as a 'toolbox', ie as a repertoire of possible reference models, or as a shared vocabulary to be used by the European legislator and by each Member State.

To this effect, the DCFR envisaged merging the two tiers of European contract law that had developed separately from one another until then, ie the *acquis communautaire* (as collected in the ACQP) and the *acquis commune* (as collected in the PECL,[248] whose terminology and conceptual framework, however, were considerably altered,[249] not always with good reasons) (see also *supra*, ch 8, para 2.2). The outline edition also considered the *Principes directeurs du droit européen du contrat*, which were the result of an initiative of the *Association Henri Capitant des Amis de la Culture Juridique Française* and the *Société de Législation Comparée* and published in 2008.[250]

The drafters of the DCFR envisaged traversing not only contract law in general but also individual types of contracts (like that of sale, etc.); moreover, they intended to take the project a step further in covering patrimonial law as a whole.[251] Materials for the provisions on special contracts and other

law [2009] OJ C295E/31. Within the doctrine, see Carlo Castronovo, 'Quadro comune di riferimento e acquis comunitario: conciliazione o incompatibilità?' [2007] Eur dir priv 275; Carlo Marchetti, *Il DCFR: lessici, concetti e categorie nella prospettiva del giurista italiano* (Giappichelli 2012), as well as the papers collected in Reiner Schulze (ed), *The Common Frame of Reference and Existing EC Contract Law* (Sellier 2008).

245 Christian von Bar and others (eds), *Principles, Definitions and Model Rules of European Private Law: Draft Common Frame of Reference (DCFR): Interim outline edition* (Sellier 2008).

246 Christian von Bar and others (eds), *Principles, Definitions and Model Rules of European Private Law: Draft Common Frame of Reference (DCFR). Outline edition* (Sellier 2009).

247 Nils Jansen and Reinhard Zimmermann, 'A European Civil Code in All But Name: Discussing the Nature and Purposes of the Draft Common Frame of Reference' (2010) 69 Cambridge LJ 98.

248 Thomas Pfeiffer, 'Von den Principles of European Contract Law zum Draft Common Frame of Reference' [2008] ZeuP 679.

249 The reasons of these deviations of the DCFR from the text of the PECL are explained in Outline edition, paras 49ff.

250 Bénédicte Fauvarque Cosson and Henri Mazeaud, *Principes contractuels communs* (Société de législation comparée 2008). Regarding the mentioned issue, see Alpa, 'CESL, Fundamental Rights, General Principles, Rules of Contract Law' (n 51); for a radical critique of that solution, cf Martijn W Hesselink, 'If you don't like our principles we have others. On core values and underlying principles in European private law: a critical discussion of the new "principles" section in the draft CFR' in Roger Brownsword and others (eds), *The Foundations of European Private Law* (Hart 2011) 59ff.

251 Guido Alpa and Giovanni Iudica (eds), *Draft Common Frame of Reference (DCFR), What for?* (Giuffrè 2013); Marchetti (n 244); Karl Riesenhuber, 'Wettbewerb für das europäische Vertragsrecht' [2011] JZ 537; Maria Rosaria Maugeri, 'Alcune perplessità in

branches of private law (like unjustified enrichment, trusts, etc.) were drawn from the Principles of European Law (PEL), drafted by the Study Group on a European civil code and published in 2006-2010.[252] In addition, one must mention the Principles of European Insurance Contract Law (PEICL),[253] which were prepared as a contribution to the DCFR, but further pursue the goal of creating an autonomous Draft Optional Instrument of European Insurance Contract Law.[254]

> The PEICL were drafted by the Project Group Restatement of European Insurance Contract Law, founded in September 1999. Its founder and chair was Fritz Reichert-Facilides.
> Their first edition was published in 1999,[255] the second edition followed in 2016.[256]

After the abandonment of the goal to enact a European civil code, the Commission drew on the provisions of the DCFR addressing sale contracts and wrapped them into a proposed regulation on a **Common European Sales Law** (CESL),[257] published in 2011 and approved, albeit with significant changes,

merito alla possibilità di adottare il DCFR come strumento opzionale (o facoltativo)' [2011] NGCC II 253; Luisa Antoniolli and Francesca Fiorentini (eds), *A Factual Assessment of the Draft Common Frame of Reference* (Sellier 2011); Umberto Breccia, 'Principles, definitions e modes rules nel "comune quadro di riferimento europeo" (Draft Common Frame of Reference)' [2010] I Contratti 95; Gerhard Wagner (ed), *The Common Frame of Reference: A View from Law & Economics* (Sellier 2010); Luisa Antoniolli, Francesca Fiorentini and James Gordley, 'A Case-Based Assessment of the Draft Common Frame of Reference' (2010) 58 Am J Comp L 343; Horst Eidenmüller and others, 'The Common Frame of Reference for European Private Law-Policy Choices and Codification Problems' (2008) 28 Oxford J Leg Stud 659; Reiner Schulze, 'Der DCFR – Funktionen, Methoden und Strukturen' in Hans Schulte-Nölke and others (eds), *Der akademische Entwurf für einen Gemeinsamen Refernzrahmen, Kontroversen und Perspektiven* (Mohr Siebeck 2008); Stefan Grundmann, 'The Structure of the DCFR – Which Approach for Today's Contract Law?' (2008) 4 ERCL 225.

[252] Ewoud Hondius and others, Sales (Sellier 2009); Kåre Lilleholt and others, *Lease of Goods* (OUP 2009); Ulrich Drobnig, *Personal Securities* (OUP 2009); Maurits Barendrecht and others, *Service Contracts* (OUP 2009); Martjin W Hesselink and others, *Commercial Agency, Franchise and Distribution Contracts* (OUP 2009); Christian von Bar, *Benevolent Intervention in Another's Affairs* (OUP 2009); Stephen Swann and Christian von Bar, *Unjustified Enrichment* (OUP 2010); Wolfgang Faber and Brigitta Lurger, *Acquisition and Loss of Ownership of Goods* (OUP 2011); Odavia Bueno Díaz and Marco B.M. Loos, *Mandate Contracts* (OUP 2012); Ulrich Drobnig and Ole Böger, *Proprietary Security in Movable Assets* (OUP 2015).

[253] Christian Armbrüster, 'The Principles of European Insurance Contract Law' [2010] Dir econ assic 1029; Helmut Heiss, 'Principles of European Insurance Contract Law (PEICL)' in *The Max Planck Encyclopedia of European Private Law*, vol 1 (n 1) 1331.

[254] Helmut Heiss and Mandeep Lakhan, *Principles of European Insurance Contract Law. A Model Optional Instrument* (Sellier 2009).

[255] Jürgen Basedow and others, *Principles of European Insurance Contract Law* (Sellier 2009).

[256] Jürgen Basedow and others, *Principles of European Insurance Contract Law* (2nd edn, Sellier 2016).

[257] Commission, 'Proposal for a regulation of the European Parliament and of the Council on a Common European Sales Law' (COM) 2011 635 final. For a general review of the issue, see Carlo Castronovo, 'Sulla proposta di regolamento relativo a un diritto comune europeo della vendita' [2012] Eur dir priv 289; Pasquale Stanzione, 'Il regolamento di diritto comune europeo della vendita' [2012] I Contratti 624; Giovanni D'Amico, 'Diret-

by a large majority of the European Parliament on 26 February 2014.[258] In the accompanying report, it was expressly held that the CESL was designed to create a second, parallel system of contract law within the legal order of each Member State of the EU. This system would have been in addition and alternative to national rules.[259]

Despite the Commission's efforts, the adoption of that regulation would have led to an unprecedented crisis in European private law, irreversibly transforming not only its basic structure but also its very constitutional legitimacy. It is, therefore, not surprising that the proposal for a CESL sparked vigorous debate among civil law scholars.[260] Most importantly, however, it was subject to hostile response from some of the leading Member States. These States indeed officially held that the proposal was in breach of the principle of subsidiarity enshrined in article 5 TEU, and, in any case, excessive in connection with the institutional objectives of the legislative procedure established by article 114 TFEU. This view was especially backed by the German *Bundesrat* and the House of Lords, as well as the Austrian and Belgian Parliaments.

Consequently, the CESL legislative proposal was withdrawn by the Commission on 16 December 2014.[261] This event marked a turn in the making of private law at the European level, which faced the risk of an unparalleled failure as a whole.

tiva sui diritti dei consumatori e Regolamento sul diritto comune europeo della vendita: quale strategia dell'Unione Europea in materia di armonizzazione?' [2012] I Contratti 611, as well as the numerous papers collected in the special issue of Contratto e impresa/ Europa, 2012, titled 'Trenta giuristi europei sull'idea di codice europeo dei contratti'. Within foreign literature, prominently, see Reiner Schulze (ed), *Common European Sales Law (CESL). Commentary* (CH Beck-Hart-Nomos 2012).

258 Carlo Castronovo, 'L'utopia della codificazione europea e l'oscura Realpolitik di Bruxelles dal DCFR alla proposta di regolamento di un diritto comune europeo della vendita' [2011] Europa e diritto privato 837; Simon Whittaker, 'The Proposed "Common European Sales Law": Legal Framework and the Agreement of the Parties' (2012) 75 MLR 578; Alpa, 'CESL, Fundamental Rights, General Principles of Contract Law' (n 30) 837; Jan M Smits, 'The Common European Sales Law (CESL) Beyond Party Choice' [2012] ZeuP 904; Hugh Beale, 'A Common European Sales Law (CESL) for Business-to-Business Contracts' in Luigi Moccia (ed), *The Making of European Contract Law* (Sellier 2013) 65; Gehard Dannemann and Stefan Vogenauer (eds), *The Common European Sales Law in Context. Interactions with English and German Law* (OUP 2013); Martin Schmidt-Kessel (ed), *Der Entwurf für ein Gemeinsames Europäisches Kaufrecht. Kommentar* (Sellier 2014); Javier Plaza Penadés and Luz M. Martínez Velencoso (eds), *European Perspective on the Common European Sales Law* (Springer 2015).

259 Commission, 'Communication from the Commission to the European Parliament, the Council, the European Economic and Social Committee and the Committee of the Regions: A Common European Sales Law to facilitate cross-border transactions in the single market' (Communication) COM (2011) 636 final.

260 For the view that this proposal was incompatible with the principle of subsidiarity, see Michael Educate, 'The Common European Sales Law's Compliance with the Subsidiarity Principle of the European Union' (2013) 14 Chicago J Int Law 317.

261 This point emerges from an annex to the 'Commission Work Programme 2015. A new start' COM (2014) 910 final. The justification provided in the document is as follows: 'Modified proposal in order to fully unleash the potential of e-commerce in the Digital Single Market' (available at http://ec.europa.eu/atwork/pdf/cwp_2015_withdrawals_it.pdf). In this regard, see the Communication of Commission of 6 May 2015, which is titled 'A Digital Single Market Strategy for Europe' COM (2015) 192 final.

In summation, the political, social, and cultural conditions that constituted fertile ground for the major codifications crowning the formation of the national state,[262] do not exist at a European level.[263]

First, the EU never gained a general **competence**; neither for private law, nor any of its main branches (like contract law); due to the constitutional principle of conferral, the feasibility of a European civil code is, therefore, seriously challenged.[264] It is true that the EU nevertheless passed pieces of legislation on crucial sectors of private law (and especially of contract law), but they were based on article 114 TFEU, that entrusts the EU with the power to 'adopt the measures for the approximation of the provisions laid down by law, regulation or administrative action in Member States'. This legal basis, by contrast, would be unfit for a unification of private law like that envisaged through a prospective European civil code, which would override (and not harmonize) the Member States' private law. Nor are other legal bases for such a piece of European legislation otherwise provided for by the founding Treaties.

Moreover, the **principle of subsidiarity** binds the EU legislature to give priority to the legislative power of Member States (vertical subsidiarity), as well as to the freedom of individuals (horizontal subsidiarity) to choose which law should govern their contracts and, more generally, their obligations. Therefore, it thus erected a major constitutional barrier to the enactment of a European civil code,[265] at least if such code is designed according to the canons that historically have underpinned civil codes since the introduction of the *Code Napoléon* paradigm (see *supra*, ch 4, para 3.1.1).[266]

Although EU private law overrides national private law (see *supra*, ch 8, para 1.3), the latter still plays a crucial role in the interpretation and supplementation of the former, starting with its general principles. It is, in a way, a peculiar manifestation of the 'paradox of Böckenförde', according to which the liberal state (*Rechtsstaat*) rests on preconditions that it cannot constitutionally guarantee itself.[267] Moreover, domestic jurisdictions are still paramount in

[262] Jan P Schmidt, 'Codification' in *The Max Planck Encyclopedia of European Private Law*, vol 1 (n 1) 222.

[263] See Luigi Mengoni, 'L'Europa dei codici o un codice per l'Europa?', in Id, *Scritti*, I, in Carlo Castronovo, Andrea Albanese and Antonio Nicolussi (eds), *Metodo e teoria giuridica*, vol 1 (Giuffrè 2011) 329, as well as Pietro Perlingieri, 'Quella di Hugh Collins sul "codice civile europeo" non è la via da seguire' [2014] Rassegna di diritto civile 1205, according to which the Constitution, and not a code, would be the instrument for achieving greater European integration of the Member States. In the same vein, see Pietro Perlingieri, *Diritto comunitario e legalità costituzionale. Per un sistema italo-comunitario delle fonti* (ESI 1992) 10; Id, 'Normativa comunitaria e ordinamento interno' in Luigi Moccia (ed), *I giuristi e l'Europa* (Laterza 1997) 111. See also Pietro Sirena, 'Il Discorso di Portalis e il futuro del diritto privato europeo' [2016] Riv dir civ 652ff.

[264] Martin Schmidt-Kessel, 'European Civil Code' in *The Max Planck Encyclopedia of European Private Law*, vol 1 (n 1) 556ff.

[265] Mengoni 'L'Europa dei codici o un codice per l'Europa?' (n 263) 330; Perlingieri 'Quella di Hugh Collins sul "codice civile europeo" non è la via da seguire' (n 263) 1206.

[266] For a different perspective, cf Hugh Collins, *The European Civil Code: The Way Forward* (CUP 2008) 141ff.

[267] The famous paradox has been formulated as follows: *'Der freiheitliche, säkularisierte Staat lebt von Voraussetzungen, die er selbst nicht garantieren kann'*. The author also adds:

all the domains of private law that fall outside the institutional aims and the legislative competence of the EU, a competence that is rather limited when compared to the Member States' sovereignty.

The constitutional principles of conferral and subsidiarity bind the EU legislature to coexist and to interact mutually with the national laws of the Member States,[268] thus creating a **multi-levelled system**,[269] where both the legal system of the EU and those of the Member States have to coexist and to interact. More than creating a private law of its own, the EU may therefore be said to have accomplished a **Europeanization of private law**.

Legal pluralism – namely the coexistence and competition of different jurisdictions and legal systems within the same community – has historically marked the beginning of the Western legal tradition,[270] and it has also represented an extraordinary driver of political and economic development for Europe.[271]

A Union of twenty-seven nation States, where twenty-four different languages are spoken and where numerous civil codes – issued between the nineteenth and twentieth centuries – are in force does not really resemble a single state,[272]

'Als freiheitlicher Staat kann er einerseits nur bestehen, wenn sich die Freiheit, die er seinen Bürgern gewährt, von innen her, aus der moralischen Substanz des einzelnen und der Homogenität der Gesellschaft, reguliert. Anderseits kann er diese inneren Regulierungskräfte nicht von sich aus, das heißt, mit den Mitteln des Rechtszwanges und autoritativen Gebots zu garantieren versuchen, ohne seine Freiheitlichkeit aufzugeben und – auf säkularisierter Ebene – in jenen Totalitätsanspruch zurückzufallen, aus dem er in den konfessionellen Bürgerkriegen herausgeführt hat'. For both quotations, see Ernst-Wolfgang Böckenförde, *Staat, Gesellschaft, Freiheit. Studien zur Staatstheorie und zum Verfassungsrecht* (Suhrkamp 1976) 60.

268 Metzger, Extra legem, intra ius: *Allgemeine Rechtsgrundsätze im Europäischen Privatrecht* (n 109) (who makes an interesting comparison with the federal legal system of the United States of America); Stefan Grundmann, 'General Standards and Principles, Clauses Générales and Generalklauseln' in Id and Denis Mazeaud (eds), *European Contract Law – A Survey*, in *General Clauses and Standards in European Contract Law: Comparative Law, EC Law and Contract Law Codification* (Kluwer Law Int'l 2006) 4; Martijn W Hesselink, 'The Structure of the New European Private Law' (2002) 6.4 Electronic J Com Law 2; Id, 'How many systems of Private law are there in Europe? On plural legal sources, multiple identities and the unity of law' in Leone Niglia (ed), *Pluralism and European Private Law* (Hart 2013) 199ff. For the methodological implications of the constitutional architecture of the Union, also with regard to the system of sources of European law, see prominently Sebastian AE Martens, *Methodenlehre des Unionsrechts* (Mohr Siebeck 2013) 123ff; Stefan Grundmann, 'System (Systemdenken) and System Building' in Karl Riesenhuber (ed), *European Legal Methodology* (Intersentia 2017) (2nd edn, De Gruyter 2015) 201ff.

269 Collins (n 266) 205ff; Beate Gsell, 'Zivilrechtsanwendung im Mehrebenensystem' (2014) 214 AcP 100ff. In the Italian literature, prominently see Zoppini (n 113) 9ff.

270 In this regard, see the classical pages of Harold J Berman, *Law and Revolution: The Formation of the Western Legal Tradition* (Harvard UP 1985) 28ff. Focusing the attention on the dualism between 'secular forum' and 'ecclesiastical forum' as the origin of the pluralism of legal orders and, moreover, of the secularity of law, see Paolo Prodi, *Una storia della giustizia. Dal pluralismo dei fori al moderno dualismo tra coscienza e giustizia* (Il Mulino 2000).

271 Schmidt-Kessel 'European Civil Code' (n 264) 554.

272 For the concept of the state as a political unit, based on the 'sovereign decision', see Carl Schmitt, 'Der Staat als konkreter, an geschichtliche Epoche gebundener Begriff' in Id, *Verfassungsrechtliche Aufsätze aus den Jahren 1924 - 1954* (first published 1958, Duncker & Humblot 1985) 103ff, and also Id, *Der Wert des Staates und die Bedeutung des Einzelnen* (first published 1914, Duncker & Humblot 2014) 49ff. As is well known, the author

not even a federal one. Rather, it resembles a multinational empire,[273] for which the motto *'In varietate concordia'*[274] is well suited.
The lasting worth of the endeavors to forge a European private law remain of course untouched, since it laid the foundations of a European scholarship of private law. This achievement may be acknowledged in monumental works like the ***Commentaries on European Contract Law***, edited by Nils Jansen and Reinhard Zimmermann.[275]

adopted this thesis to develop his conception of the *ius publicum europaeum*, for which prominently see Id, *Der Nomos der Erde im Völkerrecht des Jus Publicum Europaeum* (first published 1950, Duncker & Humblot 2011). Conversely, for the view that the state has historically developed on the basis of a political pact (covenant), constituting the basis of the civil body, see Paolo Prodi, *Homo europaeus* (Il Mulino 2015) 19ff and prior to this, Id, *Il sacramento del potere. Il giuramento politico nella storia dell'Occidente* (Il Mulino 1992). Prominent in the italian literature on the topic, see Pierangelo Schiera, *Lo Stato moderno. Origini e degenerazioni* (CLUEB 2004), as well as the papers collected in Raffaella Gherardi and Maurizio Ricciardi (eds), *Lo Stato globale* (CLUEB 2009) and within Giorgio Chittolini, Anthony Molho and Pierangelo Schiera (eds), *Origini dello Stato. Processi di formazione statale in Italia fra medioevo ed età moderna* (Il Mulino 1994) (particularly see that of Paolo Prodi, 'Il patto politico come fondamento del costituzionalismo europeo' (2005) 32 Scienza e Politica 19).

[273] For the thesis that the European Union cannot be understood in the so-called Westphalian paradigm but in that of a 'neo-medieval empire', see Jan Zielonka, *Europe as Empire. The Nature of the Enlarged European Union* (OUP 2006) 140ff. For the theory that the cosmopolitan empire of Europe constituted a nova res publica, cf Ulrich Beck and Edgar Grande, *Das kosmopolitische Europa* (Suhrkamp 2004) 71ff.

[274] This motto was first adopted by the European Union in 2000. In his speech 'Why we need a United States of Europe now' at the European Law Centre at the University of Passau on 8 November 2012 (<http://europa.eu/rapid/press-release_SPEECH-12-796_en.htm> accessed 11 September 2019), Vice-President of the European Commission and Commissioner for Justice, Fundamental Rights and Citizenship, Viviane Reding, recalled that this motto was already reflected in the lecture that Victor Hugo gave at the Paris Peace Conference in 1849. In the Preamble to the Treaty establishing a Constitution for Europe, signed in Rome on 29 October 2004, ratified by most of the Member States and then abandoned in 2009, due to the negative outcome of the referendum of France and the Netherlands, Europe is defined as 'united in diversity' (this can be read in the OJ of 16 December 2004, C 310).

[275] Nils Jansen and Reinhard Zimmermann (eds), *Commentaries on European Contract Law* (OUP 2018).

GLOSSARY

***Acquis communautaire* (1.1)**: set of rights, legal obligations, and policy objectives set out by the EU. Candidate countries for accession to the EU must abide by the *acquis* in order to join the EU and for full integration must incorporate it into their national laws, adapting and reforming them according to it.

***Acquis commune* (2)**: common core of general principles and rules shared among the national laws of European countries, as the legacy of their belonging to the same legal tradition, stemming from Roman law.

Acquis Principles (ACQP) (1.5): compilation of model rules and principles belonging to the EU private law. The relevant drafting was performed by a group of European scholars (Research Group on the Existing EC Private Law, so-called Acquis Group). The objective of these principles is enshrined in article 1:101(2), which clarifies that ACQP serve as a source for the drafting, transposition, and interpretation of the European Community law.

Antitrust law (1.5.1): field of law that provides general protection for competition by preventing companies, either individually or jointly, from impairing regular economic competition by means of restrictive practices, abuses of a dominant position, or concentrations capable of creating or strengthening a monopoly position (see also 'Competition law').

Arbitration (2.2): alternative method of dispute resolution (ie without recourse to judicial proceedings), consisting of entrusting one or more third parties (the arbitrators) with the task of resolving a dispute, by means of a decision (the award) which will be binding on the parties and capable of being enforced (see also 'Arbitration clause').

Arbitration clause (2.2): specific agreement, contained within a contract or in a separate act, by which the parties settle that any dispute relating to the interpretation or execution of the same contract shall be decided by arbitrators (see also 'Arbitration').

Arblade Case (1.5.2): ECJ judgment delivered on 23 November 1999. The Court established that the most favorable social legislation of a given Member State applies to protect all employees working in its territory. On the other hand, the additional social and administrative obligations imposed on undertakings by the legislation of the host Member State are justified only if the workers temporarily employed in that Member State enjoy equivalent social protection in their home Member State.

Audiolux Case (1.5.1): ECJ judgment delivered on 15 October 2009. The Court had to decide about the existence of a general principle of equal treatment of minority shareholders upon a transfer of control. The Court denied the existence of a principle according to which the person who purchases the control of a company should then offer all other shareholders the same opportunity to sell their shares, inasmuch it cannot be inferred from specific provisions of derivative EU law beyond their scope of application. Furthermore, the Court clarified that, imposing a duty to purchase all outstanding shares on the acquirer of corporate control would require a specific legislative decision, with the aim of weighing all involved interests.

Brasserie du Pêcheur and Factortame III joined cases (1.4): ECL judgment delivered on 5 March 1996. It enabled a better delineation of the content of the previous ECJ decision about Francovich case (see *ad vocem*). It clarified that the obligation of Member States to compensate victims constitutes a general remedy, regardless of whether the rule infringed could have direct effect or not. Furthermore, the Court ruled that the infringement giving rise to compensation for damage may relate not only to a specific legal provision but also to a principle, a fundamental right, or a judgment of the ECJ. For the first time, this judgment assimilated the system of liability of Member States to that of the EC (now EU), by stating that the conditions of the two remedies must not be different in the absence of a specific justification.

Brexit (1.1): portmanteau of 'British' and 'exit' that describes the process of withdrawal of the United Kingdom from the EU. The UK's decision to leave the EU was established through a referendum held on 23 June 2016. The relevant result was 51.9% of people who voted in favor of the idea to leave the EU. Article

50 TEU was invoked by the UK Government in order to start and conclude the process of withdrawal, which eventually became effective on 31 January 2020.

Brussels I Regulation (1.5.2): EU regulation (EC) 44/2001, dealing with international jurisdiction and with the recognition and enforcement of judgments in civil and commercial matters.

Brussels II bis Regulation (1.5.2): EU regulation (EC) 2201/2003, concerning jurisdiction and the recognition and enforcement of judgments in matrimonial matters and matters of parental responsibility. Such regulation, aimed at ensuring equality for all children, covers all decisions on parental responsibility, encompassing measures for the protection of the child, irrespectively of eventual links with a matrimonial proceeding.

Business-to-business (or B-to-B) transactions (1.5.2): transactions that are bilaterally commercial, performed between businesses, generally on the same footing. They are distinguished from transactions between businesses and other counterparts, such as those between businesses and consumers/individual customers (B2C), or between businesses and government (B2G).

Business-to-consumer (or B-to-C) transactions (1.5.2): transactions that are unilaterally commercial, where the business is generally the provider of a good or a service and the consumer is the client of the former. The contractual relationship is then characterized by a structural asymmetry between the parties, which calls for legislative protection of the weaker one.

Centros Case (1.5.1): ECJ judgment delivered on 9 March 1999. The Court clarified that, if a company exercises its freedom of establishment under the EC Treaty, the Member States cannot discriminate against said company on the ground that it was established in accordance with the law of another Member State, in which it has its registered office but does not perform any business. Moreover, the Court maintained that a State is not entitled to diminish freedom of establishment on the ground of protecting creditors or preventing fraud, when there are other ways of countering fraud or protecting creditors.

Charter of Fundamental Rights of the European Union (CFR) (1.2.1): supranational legal text that was solemnly proclaimed for the first time on 7 December 2000 in Nice and for the second time, in an adapted version, on 12 December 2007 in Strasbourg by the Parliament, the Council, and the Commission. With the entry into force of the Lisbon Treaty, the Charter acquired the same legal value as the Treaties, in accordance with Article 6 TEU. It is therefore fully binding on the European institutions and the Member States; it is virtually at the apex of the European Union legal system.

***Code Européen des Contrats* (2.2)**: set of model rules on contract law drafted by the *Accademia dei Giusprivatisti Europei* (European Academy of Private Law Scholars), under the guidance of the Italian law Professor Giuseppe Gandolfi and upon the proposal of the Italian private law scholars' association, in 1989. The project followed two different models. On the one hand, it relied on the Italian civil code, regarded as a synthesis of the two most relevant European codifications (the German and the French). On the other hand, it followed the draft of the contract code drawn up in the UK by Harvey McGregor on behalf of the English Law Commission.

Common European Sales Law (CESL) (3): proposal for a regulation published in 2011 and approved by a large majority of the European Parliament on 26 February 2014. This proposal aimed to create a second, additional system of contract law within the legal order of each Member State of the European Union, intended to serve as an alternative to national rules. However, this vigorously debated proposal was withdrawn by the Commission on 16 December 2014.

Common Frame of Reference (3): set of principles and definitions of European private law directed at improving the quality of the *acquis communautaire* (see *ad vocem*). The drafting of a Common Frame of Reference was envisaged by the Commission in a 2003 Communication to ensure greater consistency within European contract law.

Common Market (1.1): trade area within which typically there is free movement of capital and services. It normally provides common external tariffs on imports from non-member States. The common market is often identified within a specific geographical area. The creation of a European Common Market (ECM) represented the goal pursued by the EEC/EC from 1957 (Treaty of Rome) to 1992-1993 (Treaty of Maastricht).

(European) Commission (1.1): EU's politically independent executive institution. Political leadership is guaranteed by a team of 27 Commissioners, one from each EU country. This group's activity is guided by the Commission President, who is empowered to establish who is responsible for which policy area. The Commission is the sole body empowered to propose new EU legislation; moreover, it can enforce existing legislation and implement the decisions of the European Parliament and the Council of the EU. It sets EU spending priorities, together with the Council and Parliament and formulates annual budgets for approval by the Parliament and Council. Furthermore, it supervises how the money is spent, under the scrutiny of the Court of Auditors. Significantly, together with the Court of Justice, it ensures that EU law is properly applied in all the member countries.

Common core project (2.1): commenced in 1994 at the University of Trento by Ugo Mattei and Mauro Bussani, under the auspices of the late Professor Rudolf B. Schlesinger, the aim of this collective scholarly enterprise is to unearth what is already common to the legal systems of EU Member States. Case studies widely circulated and discussed between lawyers of different traditions are employed to draw at least the main lines of a reliable map of the law of Europe. The idea underlying such a project pushes in the direction of uniformity that is the most relevant cultural difference between the Common Core project and other enterprises. In the long run, this project contributes to build a common European legal culture.

Company law (1.5.2): branch of commercial law that traverses corporate life and legal relationships intra-firm, particularly between the company and its members. Inter alia, it regulates the formation, management, and dissolution of corporate structures formed by the union of a number of natural persons or legal entities such as public or corporate entities, with the aim of achieving a common goal with the collaboration of all members and the pooling of assets (see *infra*, ch 11, para 1.2.1).

Competition between the Member States' legal systems (1.5.1): opportunity for European citizens to choose to subject certain legal relationships to the rules of the law which they consider most favorable (see also 'Market of rules').

Competition law (1.5.1): branch of the law that promotes market competitiveness and regulates anti-competitive agreements made by companies. Competition law is an essential pillar of European integration, as it must enable businesses to compete on a level playing field in the EU single market; it ensures the global competitiveness of their products and services; at the same time, it provides the best possible protection for European consumers (see also 'Antitrust law').

Consumer Rights Directive (1.5.2): directive 2011/83/EU, which imposes extensive duties on the contracting businesses to disclose information, both during pre-contractual negotiations and the execution of the contract. A stringent regime is provided for off-premises and distance contracts, where a right of withdrawal is also granted to the consumer (albeit within a restricted period of time).

Consumers (1.5.2): natural persons who are acting outside their trade, business, craft, or profession. In the case of dual-purpose contracts, if the contract is stipulated for purposes partly within and partly outside the person's trade and the trade purpose is so limited as not to be predominant in the overall context of the contract, that person should also be considered a consumer. European law ensures pervasive legislation to protect these subjects, who are considered to be the weaker party in the commercial relationship. Historically, the directives issued by the EEC/EC/EU since 1973 have established important concepts such as corporate liability for damage caused by defective products, misleading advertising, consumer protection of price indications, consumer guarantees, and product safety.

Contract law (1.5.2): field of private law that deals with all aspects of the contract. In addition to the traditional national contract laws, a supranational contract law was progressively enacted by the EU in order to rule transactions entered into by businesses, mostly with consumers. Therefore, it is commonly assumed that EU contract law is to be conceptualized as 'consumer law' (see also 'Consumers').

Convention of Rome of 1980 on international private law (1.5.2): replaced by Rome I Regulation (see *ad vocem*) on the applicable law to contractual relationship, it is still in force in all the countries of the EU towards third countries.

Costa v Enel case (1.3): ECJ judgment delivered on 15 July 1964, which clarified that, contrary to what had been ruled by the Italian Constitutional Court, an EU legislative act prevails over a national law even if the second was enacted after the first. Thus, the relationship between the two legal systems cannot be solved by applying the classic canon *lex posterior derogat priori*.

(European) Council (1.1): EU institution composed of the ministers of the governments of each EU country (no permanent members), who meet to discuss, amend and adopt supranational legislation and coordinate policies. They are hereby authorized to commit their respective governments to pursue the actions agreed upon therein. Together with the European Parliament, the Council is the main decision-making body of the EU. Specifically, the Council negotiates and adopts EU laws, together with the European Parliament, on the basis of proposals formulated by the European Commission. It coordinates the policies of EU countries, as well as draws up the EU's foreign and security policy on the basis of guidelines from the European Council. It also signs agreements between the EU and other countries or international organizations and issues the final approval for the annual EU budget together with the European Parliament.

Directive [*Directive*; *Richtlinie*; *Direttiva*] (1.2.2): one of the secondary sources of European Union law. In contrast to regulations (see *ad vocem*), which are directly applicable in Member States' legal systems, directives need to be ratified within a given deadline. They bind Member States with reference to the result they aim to achieve, leaving them the choice as for the form and methods by which the objective is actually to be achieved.

Draft Common Frame of Reference (DCFR) (3): academic text, subtitled *Principles, Definitions and Model Rules of European Private Law*, produced by a large number of scholars as the result of a joint project of the Study Group on a European civil code and the Acquis Group, funded by the European Commission. The model rules it contains are based on a comparative research, on the *acquis communautaire* (see *ad vocem*) and on the relevant international instruments. The outline edition was published in 2008, while the integral edition, containing comments and notes, was published in 2009. The DCFR is composed by 10 books, which cover contract law, tort law, unjustified enrichment, acquisition and loss of ownership, proprietary security rights in movable assets, and trusts.

EU law (2.1): legal system laid down by the EU. The sources of EU law are divided into primary and secondary. The Treaties, which represent the primary law, are the normative basis for all EU actions. Secondary legislation, embracing regulations, directives, and decisions, which mainly stems from the principles and objectives laid down in the Treaties.

European Atomic Energy Community (EURATOM) (1.1): international organization created by the Treaties of Rome in 1957, which comprises the States that are part of the European Union. EURATOM is legally distinguished from the EU. Its purpose was to coordinate the research projects about nuclear energy, the dissemination of technical information, and regular supply of nuclear materials. Later, it also embraced numerous areas intertwined with the aforementioned purposes, such as radiation shielding or the building of the International Thermonuclear Experimental Reactor.

European Coal and Steel Community (ECSC) (1.1): organization established with the Treaties of Paris dating back to 1951 on the initiative of a French politician, Robert Schuman (inspired by Jean Monnet). ECSC membership was taken up by Belgium, Italy, France, Luxembourg, the Netherlands, and West Germany (currently Germany). It could be considered the first international organization driven by the goal of overcoming a rigid concept of nationalism. Although the objective provided for in article 2 seemed to be general (economic expansion, employment growth, raising leaving standard of Member States), its specific outcomes included a more efficient combination of the production of coal and steel within Europe. Moreover, it imposed the prohibition of customs duties and the elimination of quantitative restrictions on coal and steel products. The ECSC expired on 23 July 2002.

European (Economic) Community (EEC/EC) (1.1): community established in 1957, which consisted of three international organizations (the European Coal and Steel Community, the European Atomic Energy Community, and the European Economic Community), governed by an identical set of institutions. The six states that formed the EC in 1957 were Belgium, Germany, France, Italy, Luxembourg, and the Netherlands.

European Convention on Human Rights (ECHR) (1.2.1): international convention drafted by the Council of Europe and signed in 1950 in Rome. Forty-seven Council of Europe Member States are parties to this Convention, which aims to protect human rights and political freedoms in Europe. Its provisions are protected and enforced by the European Court of Human Rights (ECtHR).

European Council (1.1): collective body that defines the EU's overall policy priorities and orientations. It has no legislative power. However, it sets the Union's political agenda, generally by adopting conclusions at its meetings identifying problematic issues and actions to be taken. The members of the European Council are the Heads of State or Government of the 27 EU Member States, the President of the European Council, and the President of the European Commission. The High Representative of the Union for Foreign Affairs and Security Policy also attends European Council meetings when foreign policy issues are discussed.

European Court of Justice (ECJ) (1.1): jurisdictional entity of the EU, located in Luxembourg and set up in 1952. The main task of the Court of Justice is to ensure compliance with the whole EU law in the process of its interpretation and application. To this end, it is possible to bring different kinds of actions. Its composition provides for one judge, assisted by General-Advocates, per EU Member State.

European economic constitution (1.1): it is enshrined in the Founding Treaties and historically marked the foundation of the overall EU law. It clearly draws on the tenets of German ordo-liberalism (*Ordoliberalismus*), according to which the protection of economic freedoms is to be incorporated into a strong regulation of the market, to prevent firms and any individuals from gaining private power over the others.

European Union (EU) (1.1): political and economic union between 27 countries, which are subject to the obligations and the privileges of the membership. Every Member State is part of the founding Treaties of the Union and is subject to binding laws within the common legislative and judicial institutions. The EU has developed an internal single market through a standardized system of laws that apply to all Member States in those matters, and only those matters, where members have agreed to act as one. EU policies ensure the free movement of people, goods, services, and capital within the internal market, enact legislation in justice and home affairs and maintain common policies on trade, agriculture, fisheries and regional development. A monetary union was established in 1999 and came into full force in 2002. It is composed of 19 EU Member States that use the euro currency.

European Law Institute (ELI) (1): independent organization founded in 2011 under Belgian law. Its aim is to initiate, conduct and facilitate research, make recommendations, and provide practical guidance in the field of European legal development. Currently, its Secretariat is hosted by the University of Vienna.

Europeanization of private law (3): legislative, jurisprudential, and doctrinal process of progressively reducing divergences between the national laws of Member States.

Faccini Dori case (1.2.2): ECJ judgment delivered on 14 July 1994, where the Court excluded that non-executing directives are directly applicable to horizontal relationships (individuals), but national laws must be interpreted in accordance with such directives.

Family law (2.3): sector of private law which governs family relationships in their broadest sense, dealing with issues relating to marriage, filiation, adoption, and even kinship and affinity. The notion of family rights not only takes into account the interests of the individual but of the whole family group. Family law contains numerous public policy rules, which cannot be derogated from, duly limiting the principle of the autonomy of individuals.

Forum shopping (1.5.1): opportunity granted to a party to elect the national jurisdiction that best suits her own interests, also in terms of taxation.

Foster case (1.2.2): ECJ judgment delivered on 12 July 1990, which clarified the issue of the so-called self-executing directives. The Court stated that, as far as the direct application of self-executing directives is concerned, the state is not identified on the basis of the legal nature of the person acting but on the basis of the public nature of the functions or of the activity it performs.

Francovich case (1.2.2): ECJ judgment delivered on 19 November 1991, with which the Court of Justice stated the obligation of each Member State to compensate the victims caused by an infringement of European Union law, if some specific criteria are met. This legal claim has to be proposed to national courts whose competence is established by their own provisions of civil procedural law, and who may directly order the State to compensate for damages. The case giving rise to this decision was Italy's failure to implement the directive 80/987/EEC on the protection of employees in the event of insolvency of their employer.

Freedom of choice (1.5.2): principle according to which the parties of a contract are free to choose the law applicable to it. This freedom of choice of law governing the contract is in turn an expression of the prominent principle of the parties' autonomy, which is widely recognized both by the laws and codes of the main countries of civil law, and by those of common law. The above-mentioned freedom has some specific limitations (see 'Public policy' and 'Overriding mandatory provisions').

(Fundamental) economic freedoms (1.5.1): set of freedoms enshrined in the TFEU that are directed at safeguarding and enhancing the free movement of goods, the free movement of persons (including the free movement of workers and the freedom of establishment), the free movement of services, and the free movement of capital and payments. It is now seen as a separate body of law, which is teleologically designed to pursue the constitutional model.

General part of EU contract law (1.5.2): set of EU law rules that apply to a contract irrespectively of its type (whether a sale or a loan, etc.); they address marketing techniques or commercial practices that may impair the informed and genuine consent of consumers (or, although rarely, undertakings) to enter into a contract.

General principles of civil law (1.2.1): principles underpinning the national or supranational legal system with regard to civil law. They are required, both at national and European level, to ensure that the specific disciplines governing several areas of civil law are uniform, by performing different functions (ie filling gaps or helping to interpret legal texts) according to the needs of a given circumstance. Such principles represent part of the rules 'common to the legal systems of the Member States'.

Harmonization (or approximation) of laws (1.2.1): process aimed at establishing a standardized set of law, regulations, and practices across the internal market, thus allowing the application of such instruments to businesses operating in more than one Member State. The aim is to prevent one such business taking economic advantage of the divergent instruments operating in the Member States.

Intellectual property (1.5.2): field of law that gives creators and inventors a legal monopoly in the exploitation of their creations or inventions, placing in their hands the legal instruments required to protect themselves from any use for profit by unauthorized parties.

Köbler case (1.4): ECJ judgment delivered on 30 September 2003. In this decision, the Court specified that the principles delineated in the Francovich case (see *ad vocem*), and further clarified in Brasserie de Pêcheur (see *ad vocem*), apply to all public organs, including the judiciary, the acts of which can trigger the liability of the State. In this case, however, the Court held that liability arises only when the domestic court 'has *manifestly* infringed the applicable law'.

Kücükdeveci case (1.5.1): ECJ judgment delivered on 19 January 2010, in which the ECJ discussed a case of unfair treatment based on an employee's age and claimed that the principle of non-discrimination derived also from the CFR (see *ad vocem*) of 7 December 2000.

Labor law (or employment law) (1.5.2.): branch of law that is focused on the aspects and problems related to the discipline of work, the employment relationship, and all issues intertwined with it. It concerns the regulation of employer-employee relations, labor relations (which are properly covered by trade union law), and social security.

Late Payment Directive (1.5.2): directive 2011/7/EU, designed to achieve a decisive shift towards a culture of prompt payment and require debtors to pay interest and reasonable recovery costs to the creditor in the case they do not pay for the goods or services on time. The limits are within 60 days for companies and within 30 days for public authorities.

Legal pluralism (3): coexistence and competition of different jurisdictions and legal systems within the same community. It has historically marked the beginning of the Western legal tradition and has also represented an extraordinary driver of political and economic development for Europe.

Leonesio case (1.2.1): ECJ judgment delivered on 17 May 1972. The Court established that a EEC/EC/EU regulation has direct effect and is, as such, capable of creating individual rights that national courts must protect.

Level playing field (1.5): hallmark of market regulation pursued by EU private law, which is directed to lay down a unique regulatory framework for the trade of goods and services within the single market, in order to grant and foster fair competition among the businesses and professionals of the Member States.

Lisbon Treaty (1.1): international agreement through which the two still existing European Communities (namely, the EC and the EURATOM) were absorbed into the EU. The three pillars that had characterized the structure of the latter were abolished and the community method was extended to all its competences. The legislative 'procedure of co-decision' eventually became the 'ordinary legislative procedure'. The Treaty of Lisbon was signed by EU Member States on 13 December 2007 and entered into force on 1 December 2009. Significantly, it amends the Maastricht Treaty (1992), the update of which is the Treaty on European Union (2007), and the Treaty of Rome (1957), known in updated form as the Treaty on the Functioning of the European Union (2007). The relevant attached treaty protocols and the Treaty establishing the European Atomic Energy Community (EURATOM) were amended by the Lisbon Treaty as well.

Lissabon Urteil **(1.2.1)**: judgment of 30 June 2009 delivered by the German Constitutional Court (*Bundesverfassungsgericht*), which established that the German 'Act Approving the Treaty of Lisbon' is compatible with the German Constitution (*Grundgesetz*). In contrast, the German judges claimed that the German 'Act Extending and Strengthening the Rights of the Bundestag and the Bundesrat in European Union Matters' infringed article 38(1) GG, in conjunction with article 23(1) GG, insofar as the *Bundestag* and the *Bundesrat* have not been accorded sufficient rights of participation in European lawmaking procedures and treaty amendment procedures (see also 'Lisbon Treaty').

Maastricht ruling (1.1.): judgment of 12 October 1993 delivered by the German Constitutional Court (*Bundesverfassungsgericht*). It clarified that the obligations entered into by Germany with its signing of the Maastricht Treaty (see *ad vocem*) could not be deemed in violation of the German Constitution (*Grundgesetz*), thus erasing the last relevant obstacle for the ratification of the above-mentioned Treaty. At the same time, the German Constitutional Court claimed that the right of final review must be assigned to national courts.

Maastricht Treaty (1.1): international agreement that contributed to the creation of the EU. It was signed on 7 February 1992 and entered into force on 1 November 1993. Primarily, the Maastricht Treaty established that some competences attributed to the EEC were extended to sectors of social and political importance, so that it was no longer referred to as 'economic' and turned into the EC. At the same time, the latter became the bulk of a new entity, the EU, which was characterized by a 'three-pillar structure'. Furthermore, the Treaty of Maastricht created an Economic and Monetary Union (EMU), whose currency is the euro, as well as a Union citizenship. Through the establishment of the 'procedure of co-decision', the European Parliament finally gained some effective power in law-making, shared with the Council upon the initiative of the Commission.

Market failures (1.1): occurrences of inefficient distribution of goods and services within the free market. In a typical market failure, the individual incentives for rational behavior do not lead to rational outcomes for the group. Therefore, market failure can occur if individuals, deciding to act in rational self-interest, generate a less than optimal or economically inefficient result.

Market of rules (1.5.2): opportunity granted to European citizens to freely choose among different rules offered by each Member State, thus generating competition (see *ad vocem*) between them.

Mangold case (1.5.1): ECJ judgment delivered on 22 November 2005, in which the Court stated and specified that the principle of non-discrimination applies to labor law, in order to establish the unlawfulness of unequal treatment on the grounds of a worker's age.

Marleasing case (1.2.2): ECJ judgment delivered on 13 November 1990, which broadened the scope of the principle already stated in 1984 in Von Colson and Kamann case (see *ad vocem*). In particular, this time the Court claimed that all national legislative acts, whether adopted before or after a directive, must be construed in accordance with the directive, having regard to its wording and ultimate purpose.

Marshall case (1.2.2): ECJ judgment delivered on 26 February 1986. The Court argued that the direct applicability of a directive that requires Member States to comply with an unconditioned and sufficiently precise obligation is a helpful solution to prevent any defaulting States from violating the founding Treaties as a basis for resolving the disputes with individuals. The Court also clarified that this rule applies only to the state (vertical relations), even if acting *iure privatorum*.

Maximum harmonization (1.5): approximation of the national laws of Member States pursued by directives that do not empower the Member States to exceed the level of consumer protection they provide (see also 'Minimum harmonization').

Minimum harmonization (1.5): approximation of the national laws of Member States pursued by directives that set a threshold which must be met by Member States, but the latter are, to some extent, entitled to exceed the level of consumer protection thus provided by EU legislation (see also 'Maximum harmonization').

Mostaza Claro case (1.5.2): ECJ judgment delivered on 26 October 2006. The Court held that directive 93/13/EEC on unfair terms in consumer contracts (see also 'Unfair terms directive') should be interpreted as meaning that a national court that is called upon to rule on an appeal against an arbitration award must find that the arbitration agreement is void and set aside the award, if it considers that that agreement contains an unfair term, even if the consumer only relied on that invalidity for the appeal of the award and not in the arbitration proceeding.

Multi-levelled system (3): staple of European law, which rests on both a supranational level of legislature and judiciary (devised by the EU) and a national one (devised by each Member State).

Negative integration (1.1): function carried out by EU private law insofar as it aims at erasing national barriers or obstacles that restrict and compress the movement of goods, services, and key elements for production, and, from a wider perspective, the exercise of economic freedoms guaranteed by the founding Treaties. To this extent, EU private law 'purges' rules impeding trading within the EU from the national laws of Member States. It may be thus spoken of as a 'confrontational part' (*pars destruens*) of EU private law (see also 'Positive integration').

Overriding mandatory provisions (1.5.2): provisions of each Member State that must be observed to safeguard its public interests, such as its political, social, or economic organization. Under EU private international law, such provisions apply to any situation falling within their scope, irrespective of the law otherwise applicable to the contract.

Pammer and Hotel Alpenhof joined cases (1.5.2): ECJ judgment delivered on 7 December 2010. The main issue of the cases was whether the special consumer protection regulation is applicable to contracts that have been concluded through online activities. The Court had to clarify the concept of the crucial prerequisite of 'directing activities', and eventually stated that, in order to 'determine whether a trader whose activity is presented on its website or on that of an intermediary can be considered to be "directing" its activity to the Member State of the consumer's domicile', it must be ascertained whether it is apparent that the trader was envisaging doing business with the consumer in question. The ECJ also provided a non-exhaustive list of matters to be considered for such an ascertainment.

(European) Parliament (1.1): one of the seven institutions of the EU. It is endowed with legislative power (but not legislative initiative), which is exercised together with the European Commission and the Council of the EU. The EU Parliament embraces 705 members, who are elected every five years by EU citizens through universal suffrage. The relevant headquarters are located in Brussels, Luxembourg City, and Strasbourg.

Positive integration (1.1): function carried out by EU private law, insofar as it aims to provide a re-regulation of market and society. To this extent, EU private law creates a legislative framework that unifies the legal systems of the Member States. It may be thus spoken of as a 'constructive part' (*pars costruens*) of EU private law (see also 'Negative integration').

Preliminary ruling (1.3): ECJ decision about the interpretation of EU law, adopted in response to a request from a court or tribunal operating in EU Member State, as set out by article 267 TFEU. A preliminary ruling has no scope for appeal. The referring court is then obliged to implement the ruling.

Principle of proportionality (3): one of the general principles of the European Union, which has a legal, political, and administrative dimension. As set out in article 5 TEU, it determines that any action by the EU should not go beyond what is necessary to achieve the objectives of the treaties. It is tightly connected to the principle of subsidiarity (see *ad vocem*),

Principle of subsidiarity (3): one of the general principles of the European Union, which has a legal, political, and administrative dimension. As set out in article 5 TEU, it determines that decisions should be taken as closely as possible to the citizen while determining the most relevant level of intervention. It is tightly connected to the principle of proportionality (see *ad vocem*).

Principles of European Contract Law (PECL) (2.2): set of model rules on contracts elaborated by a group of European academics reunited in a working commission chaired by Ole Lando, and published between 1995 and 2002. The Principles aim at building a uniform framework of European contract law, by detecting the common core of the rules proper of the systems of the different Member States. They are considered an instrument of soft law and are generally seen as part of the European *lex mercatoria*. The PECL are divided into two different parts, and their drafting was carried out following a strict procedure that entailed the presentation of the single provisions by rapporteurs, their discussion in a plenary meeting and, then, the adoption of the provision by the plenary, with amendments where necessary.

Principles of European Tort Law (PETL) (2.3): compilation of guidelines drafted by the European Group on Tort Law, aimed at harmonizing European tort law. The principles serve as a common framework of reference for the development of tort law both at a domestic and at a European level, in order to avoid a further drifting apart of the legislation proper of the different national systems. Although their wording may resemble a statutory text, the PETL are not meant to serve as a model code: they rather have the form, the structure, and the aims typical of the American model of the restatement of law.

Principles of International Commercial Contract (PICC) (2.2): set of model rules on commercial contracts drawn up by UNIDROIT (Institute for the Unification of Private Law).

In contrast to the PECL, the UNIDROIT principles go beyond the European dimension and constitute a project aimed at helping to harmonize commercial contract law at a global level. Although not binding (the UNIDROIT principles are an instrument of soft law), they have been very successful in international contractual practice, and they are often called upon by agreements concluded in international trade. Together with the PECL, also the PICC can be considered as part of the *lex mercatoria*. Their latest version (published in 2016) consists of 2010 articles and is available in a plurality of languages.

Prohibition of discrimination (1.5.1): principle expressly mentioned by article 18(1) TFEU (the reference is made to nationality) and moreover specified with regard to special policy areas through various provisions of the same Treaty. It also entitles the Council to perform appropriate actions to contrast discrimination based on sex, racial or ethnic origin, religion or belief, disability, age, or sexual orientation.

Protection of human (or fundamental) rights (1.2.1): cardinal need underlying the current idea of EU. The case law of the ECJ was particularly relevant in assigning increased significance to the above-mentioned concept, by establishing that fundamental rights are enshrined in the general principles of Community law protected by the Court. These rights are inspired by the constitutional traditions common to the Member States and by international treaties – to which Member States are parties – for the protection of human rights.

Public procurements (1.5.2): contracts concluded by public authorities in order to guarantee the provision of works and services. They obviously play a significant and prominent role in the economies of Member States.

Public policy [*Ordre public*] (1.5.2): bundle of principles and rules of a political entity that explicitly state and safeguard the basic options adopted by that entity with regard to its political, economic, social order. It can take on a variety of content in relation to the different branches of the law. Public order, if understood as a value of social order, can also be conceived as a guarantee of peace and collective security.

Ratti case (1.2.2): ECJ judgment delivered on 5 April 1979, in which the Court clarified that a non-implemented directive may be directly applied only when it requires a Member State to comply with an obligation that is unconditioned and sufficiently precise.

Recommendations and opinions [*Recommandations et avis*; *Empfehlungen und Stellungnahmen*; *Raccomandazioni e pareri*] (1.2.2): secondary sources of EU law, that are not legally binding for Member States.

Regulation [*Règlement*; *Verordnung*; *Regolamento*] (1.2.2): secondary source of EU law, according to article 288(2) TFEU. Regulations have a general application and are legally binding for and directly applicable in Member States: therefore, they can be enforced by individuals, notwithstanding the provisions of national law.

Restatements (of the Law) (2.2): in the US, legal treatises published by the American Law Institute, which systematize common-law principles according to specific subjects. They generally take the form of compilations of case-law. The restatements are not formally binding and they serve to inform the case-law developed for a certain area (for example, property, contract, and so on): they thus do not substitute the law, neither they can repeal it. Although they only bear a secondary authority (as opposed to the primary and binding authority proper of statutes and case-law), the restatements reflect the consensus of the American legal community on what the law is, and therefore, they are highly persuasive as courts often rely on them to solve their cases.

Rome I Regulation (2.2): regulation (EC) No 593/2008 on international private law. It governs the choice of law for contractual obligations and applies within the Member States of the EU when the applicable law to an international contract is to be determined.

Rome II Regulation (1.5.2): regulation (EC) No 864/2007 on international private law. It governs the identification of the law applicable in the event of a conflict of laws regarding a non-contractual obligation in civil or commercial matters.

Rome III Regulation (1.5.2): regulation (EU) No 1259/2010 on international private law. It aims to establish a clear and comprehensive legal framework in matters of the law applicable to divorce and legal separation in the participating Member States, providing citizens with adequate solutions as regards legal certainty, predictability, and flexibility. It also prevents situations where one spouse applies for divorce before the other, in order to ensure that the proceedings are governed by a law she considers more favorable to her own interests.

Sales of Goods Directive (1.5.2): directive (EU) 2019/771, which applies to all goods, embracing the products distinguished by digital element, and provides that the seller is obliged to guarantee, for a minimum period of two years, that the goods (which may entail digital elements) delivered to the consumer that purchased them conform with the contract between the parties. It is worth noting that the burden of proof is reversed in favour of the consumer.

Simmenthal case (1.3): ECJ judgment delivered on 9 March 1978. Challenging the rooted opinion of the Italian Constitutional Court, the ECJ emphasized the need for a general judiciary review, whereby each national court, when applying Community legislation, shall ensure its highest effectiveness. Each court should cease the application of national law that is contrary to Community law, without the need for a judgment of unconstitutionality issued by the Constitutional Court.

Single (or internal) Market (1.1): trade bloc, embracing EU Member States, characterized by a fully-fledged freedom of movement of capital and persons, as well as of goods and services (the so-called 'four freedoms') (see also '(Fundamental) economic freedoms'). Importantly, the adoption of legislative measures pursuing that aim is not based on the unanimity within the Council but on a qualified majority. One of the most important features of the European Single Market is represented by the absence of internal borders and regulatory prohibitions.

Social market economy (1.1): socioeconomic model merging a free market capitalist economic system with social policies that establish both fair competition within the market and a welfare state. It was highly inspired by ordo-liberalism, social democratic reformism, and the political ideology of Christian democracy (see also 'European economic constitution'). Oftentimes, the social market economy has been designed to represent an alternative to laissez-faire economic liberalism and socialist economics.

Society based on private law [*Privatrechtsgesellschaft*] (1.1): doctrinal conception – forged by Franz Böhm and, from a wider perspective, by the doctrine of German ordo-liberalism – that significantly contributed to the creation and expansion of the EU. According to this doctrine, the constitutional principle of individual freedoms protection is to be incorporated into a strong regulation of economy (see also '(Fundamental) economic freedoms' and 'European economic constitution').

Soft law (2.1): wide range of quasi-legal instruments that do not bear an actual legally binding force (or the binding force of which is somewhat weaker than the one of traditional law). This classification is generally used in opposition to hard law, which refers to ordinary binding legal provisions. Albeit not binding, soft law instruments usually bear a strong persuasive power and are often used by judges both as a guideline and as an integrative criterion for the interpretation of ordinary legal provisions.

Special part of EU contract law (1.5.2): part of EU contract law that entails sets of rules about contracts relating to goods or services that, due to the difficulty and technicality of information needed to evaluate them, are purchased on the basis of credence given to the supplier. The relationship between the general and special parts of contract law has often been discussed in the doctrine, investigating whether or not there is complementarity between the two parties.

Supply of Digital Content Directive (1.5.2): directive (EU) 2019/770, which intends to harmonize a set of rules on the conformity of the digital content, remedies available to consumers where digital content does not conform with the contract, and certain modalities for the exercise of those remedies. Moreover, the Directive is designed to harmonize certain aspects concerning the right to terminate a long-term contract, as well as certain aspects concerning the modification of the digital content.

Swiss Case (1.5.2): ECJ judgment delivered on 1 June 1999. The Court was asked whether article 81 EC Treaty could be deemed part of the public policy serving as a ground for the annulment of arbitration awards within domestic law. The ECJ clarified that, if the law of a Member State requires a national court to grant an application for annulment of an arbitration award where such an application is founded on a failure to observe national rules of public policy, an application founded on failure to comply with the prohibition laid down in article 85 of the Treaty (then article 81 TEC) must also be granted. The judges pointed out that such a provision is crucial for the accomplishment of the tasks entrusted to the Community and, specifically, for the functioning of the internal market.

Traghetti del Mediterraneo case (1.4): ECJ judgment delivered on 13 June 2006. In this case, the Court further refined the principles set forth in Köbler case (see *ad vocem*). At stake, there was an Italian law that provided for the exclusion of the liability of the State for the infringement of Community (now EU) law committed by a national court adjudicating at last instance, unless the infringement was caused by intentional fault and serious misconduct of the court in the interpretation of the law or in the assessment of the facts and evidence. The ECJ held that a law as such should be considered contrary to EU law, in so that it narrows down the liability of a Member State to the point of excluding cases where a manifest infringement of the applicable law has occurred. In other words, Traghetti del Mediterraneo set forth the principle according to which Member States cannot enact laws that provide for criteria less favorable to individuals than the ones stated in Köbler case.

Treaties of Rome (1.1): international treaties establishing the European Economic Community (EEC) and the European Atomic Energy Community (Euratom). They were both signed on 25 March 1957.

Treaty on the European Union (TEU) (1.2.1): one of the fundamental treaties of the European Union, setting general principles of European law, its purposes, and the governance of EU's central institutions. The former version of this Treaty is the Treaty of Maastricht (1992) (see *ad vocem*), while this version entered into force in 2009, following the Treaty of Lisbon (2007) (see *ad vocem*).

Treaty on the functioning of the European Union (TFEU) (1.2.1): one of the fundamental treaties of the EU, setting out the scope of the EU authority to legislate and the principles of law in those fields where European law operates. It originated from the Treaty of Rome (1957) (see *ad vocem*); the current version entered into force in 2009, following the Treaty of Lisbon of 2007 (see *ad vocem*).

Unfair competition (1.5.2): any fraudulent, deceptive, or dishonest trade practice that causes economic harm to either consumers or business entities. The use of names or trademarks reminiscent of those of other companies (up to and including counterfeiting), or the dissemination of information that discredits the activities of competitors constitute examples of unfair competition.

Unfair Terms Directive (1.5.2): directive 93/13/EEC safeguarding consumers against unfair standard contract terms imposed by traders. This directive's provisions apply to all kinds of contracts for the purchase of goods and services.

Unfair Trading Directive (1.5.2): directive 2015/29/EC, which regulates the pre-contractual stage of the offer, or the invitation to treat, towards consumers, banning commercial practices that may be deemed misleading or aggressive to their detriment.

Unification (1.2.1): process pointing to assimilate divergent legal systems into a single order that, to some extent and depending on the level of unification, reduces the fragmentation of the existing laws and case laws. The instruments for achieving this objective may vary accordingly to the different strategies needed.

Unjustified enrichment (2.3): advantage of economic nature gained by one person to the detriment of another, without the former being entitled to obtain it at the expense of the latter by virtue of a legal transaction or other sources of obligations. This case may also arise without the activity of the enriched person, who may even be unaware of the fact that she is in such a situation. It entails an obligation on the part of the enriched person to return to the damaged person that she has obtained without cause.

Van Duyn case (1.2.2): ECJ judgment delivered on 4 December 1974, where the Court stated that if a directive not implemented by a Member State contains provisions not subject to exceptions or conditions and that do not require the intervention of any act by the institutions of the community or of Member States, then that directive must be applicable regardless of any incompatible national laws.

Van Gend en Loos case (1.1): ECJ judgment delivered on 5 February 1963. It primarily established that the EU legal order must be qualified as new and distinct from others in the field of international law. Consequently, the ECJ formulated the principle of direct effect, according to which the provisions of the EEC's Treaties not only operate on the dimension of international relations among Member States, but they directly bind the latter. Therefore, the ECJ acknowledgment has recognized an individuals' right to directly protect their subjective legal situations in court, without the need of any intervention of the European Commission in opposition to the State that does not comply with its international obligations.

Vertical approach, or piecemeal approach (1.5): approach according to which, in light of the principles of conferral, of subsidiarity, and of proportionality, EU private law traverses solely the single sectors of the common market where the call for a regulatory intervention of the EU is more stringent.

Von Colson and Kamann case (1.2.2): ECJ judgment delivered on 10 April 1984, in which the ECJ claimed that national legislation must be interpreted in harmony with directives, so that the objectives set at European level can be evenly achieved.

Wagner Miret case (1.2.2): ECJ judgment delivered on 16 December 1993. The Court stated that European harmonization imposes a strict standard in cases where a state's decision not to take legislative or administrative ratifying measures is based on the discretional assumption that national legislation is already in line with the directive.

BIOGRAPHIES

Rudolf Berthold Schlesinger (Munich, 1909 – San Francisco, 1996) was a German-American jurist, whose academic work was particularly relevant in comparative law.

He studied law in Geneva, Berlin, and Munich, and subsequently earned a second degree at the Columbia Law School; following *Kristallnacht* in Berlin in 1938, he escaped from Germany and settled in the United States. There, after graduating from Columbia, he started working as an assistant to a New York Supreme Court Judge, before working at Milbank, Tweed, Hadley & McCloy's law firm, finally focusing his career on academia. He first taught Comparative Law at the Cornell Law School and then at the University of California's Hastings College of the Law until his retirement in 1995. The following year he reportedly committed suicide, together with his wife.

Schlesinger had a considerable impact on the comparative legal studies; in 1955, while he was working on behalf of the New York Law Revision Commission, he examined the question of whether to codify commercial law: his study, *Problems of Codification of Commercial Law* (1955), was parallel to the development of the Uniform Commercial Code. In the 1960s, he launched the Cornell project on the formation of contract, which deployed the original methodology of the 'factual approach' in comparative legal scholarship.

His main works are: *Comparative Law: Cases-Texts-Materials* (1950); *Problems of Codification of Commercial Law* (1955); *Formation of Contracts – A Study of the Common Core of Legal Systems* (1968).

Alberto Trabucchi (Verona, 1907 – Padua, 1988) was an Italian jurist, as well as judge of the European Court of Justice. He graduated in law from the University of Padua in 1928 and, one year later, was appointed as Assistant Professor of Philosophy of Law with the supervision of Adolfo Ravà. He was the pupil of Francesco Carnelutti, a foremost Italian scholar in the field of civil law and civil procedural law. At some point, Trabucchi's scientific research began to relate to civil law issues; therefore, a few years later (1935), he was appointed Extraordinary Professor of Civil Law at the Universities of Ferrara and of Venice. He actively collaborated in the preliminary draft of the second book of the Italian Civil code currently in force. He became full Professor at the University of Padua in 1942. Moreover, he played an active role in politics, being the mayor of Illasi, a small town located in Veneto, from 1952 up until 1993. He was also Head of the Department of Comparative Private Law at the University of Padua from 1953-1954.
Trabucchi became a judge of the European Court of Justice in 1962, and his way of legal thinking took on special relevance, because it influenced his colleagues' thinking in relation to the renowned Van Gend en Loos Case. This case could be considered the most important judgment in the history of Europe, inasmuch it attributes a new role to the founding Treaties and gives each citizen the right to directly protect its individual liberties – conceived as a subjective legal situation – in court. After this experience, he had the chance to change his job, becoming General-Advocate of the ECJ.
Trabucchi received numerous awards for his brilliant career and, especially, for the high quality of his research. He founded and directed the following legal journals: *Rivista di diritto civile* and *Giurisprudenza italiana*. He was member of the *Accademia Nazionale dei Lincei*.
His main works are: *Istituzioni di diritto civile* (48th edn, 2017); *Il matrimonio putativo* (1936); *Il dolo nella teoria dei vizi del volere* (1937); *Il trasferimento dei diritti sul credito ceduto* pro solvendo (1937); *Il rispetto del testo nell'interpretazione degli atti di ultima volontà* (1950); *La stima dei beni e criteri legali di valutazione* (1952); *Codice delle comunità europee* (1962); *Per una visione sistematica del diritto comunitario. Comunità europee e sovranità degli stati* (1967).

CHAPTER 9

Legal facts and legal acts

- **The legal relevance of natural events and human actions**
- **Taxonomies of legal facts and legal acts**
- **The centrality of (autonomous) legal acts in private law**

All events and actions that are legally relevant are classified as legal facts.
Material facts are natural events that are of legal effect. They may also be human actions that carry legal effect irrespective of any judgment or discernment by the author/-s.
Heteronomous legal acts are human actions whose legal effects are not elected by the author/-s but are stipulated by the law irrespective of her/their intention. Such acts are ineffective (or subject to avoidance), where there has been no judgment or discernment by their author/-s.
Autonomous legal acts consist in one or more declarations of will (be it through language or by conduct) that are intended to achieve a change in the rights and duties of the author/-s (or – albeit rarely, if not exceptionally – those of a third party). The most notable legal acts are contracts, last wills (or testaments), and marriage.
Legal acts may be unilateral, bilateral, or multilateral; patrimonial or non-patrimonial; *inter vivos* or *mortis causa*.
Legal acts are subject to invalidity when they either: *a)* infringe or circumvent a mandatory prohibition, be it provided for by a statutory provision or embedded in public policy; or *b)* one of their authors' will is flawed by a deficiency of judgment or discernment. This may happen either: *a)* because one of the parties was incompetent, ie she had no capacity to act; or *b)* because one of the parties' consent was affected by a vitiating factor such as mistake, fraud and misrepresentation, duress and undue influence.
Invalidity may result in voidness (or nullity) or in voidability.
In the event of voidness (or nullity), a legal act is wholly ineffective from the outset (*ab initio*), whether or not any of the parties has disaffirmed it. A legal act may be void

because it is illegal, or because it is affected by indefiniteness or vagueness, or it lacks some formal requirements (like when a statutory provision requires a contract to be in writing). Any of the parties or a third person can invoke a legal act's voidness, which can be also raised by a court on its own motion. The non-performance of any party is excused. In the event of performance, each party can claim restitution for it, even from any sub-purchaser (with certain exceptions). Voidness cannot be remedied, unless differently provided for by the law.

By contrast, a voidable juridical act is effective, until its avoidance (or rescission, or annulment) occurs at the election of the innocent party (eg the minor). If it is avoided, it is retrospectively (*ab initio*) reversed.

The innocent party (eg the minor) has the power-right to avoid a voidable legal act, either: *a)* by bringing an action before a court against the other party (in some jurisdictions); or *b)* by serving notice on the other party (in other jurisdictions). Non-performance of the innocent party is excused solely if it occurs after avoidance, in which case each of the parties can claim restitution for any previous performance. Affirmation (or confirmation, or ratification) of a voidable legal act is generally allowed but conditionally on the fact that the ground of avoidance has terminated. It may happen through the innocent party's waiver of her claim to avoidance (express affirmation, or confirmation, or ratification). It may also take place through voluntary performance of the voidable contract (implied affirmation, or confirmation, or ratification).

1. THE LEGAL RELEVANCE OF NATURAL EVENTS AND HUMAN ACTIONS

Not any event that may take place or any action that may be undertaken triggers legal effects. In fact, some of them do not have any impact on social intercourse and, therefore, need not be scrutinized or regulated by the law. Others may involve some sort of societal compulsion but nonetheless are clearly outside the realm of the law, as they do not involve any proceedings in front of the state (eg they pertain to **etiquette**). If one violates a rule of etiquette, she may incur social disapproval, consisting of some negative reaction by other members of society. However, there is no room for a **sanction** (see *supra*, ch 6, para 1.1), unless a norm can be found mirroring such a rule of etiquette. In the latter case, however, the sanction is stipulated by the norm, not by the rule of etiquette that it mirrors.

Moreover, events or actions that are originally of no **legal effect** can begin to produce it starting from a certain point of time on, insofar as a norm enters into force providing for such model fact situations. Conversely, events or actions that originally carry some legal effects may cease to produce them from a certain point of time on, insofar as a norm enters into force reversing or repealing pre-existing law.

For example:
a) Same-sex partnerships, which until recently were not allowed or not in any event recognized under the law, have over time been allowed and in some way recognized as (akin to) marriage by most jurisdictions.
b) In some European jurisdictions in the 1930s, people of Jewish origin were expelled from public schools and universities, and also disqualified as officials. Being of Jewish origin was therefore a factual situation that produced such legal consequences. After World War II, these norms were repealed.

In the light of the above, one may wonder: 1) How it is possible to identify events or actions that carry legal effects; 2) How it is possible to verify whether such events or action subsequently cease to be of legal effect.
There is solely a tautological answer to these questions: an event or action carries legal effects if, and in so far as, a norm attaches legal effects to that event or action.
In other words, it is not possible to set out any criterion to distinguish what is *per se* legal from what is not. The same event or action may carry legal effects or not: it depends solely on what the norms actually in force provide for.
If a certain **state of affairs** is provided for by a norm (see *supra*, ch 6, para 1.1), we are confronted with an event or an action that carries legal effects. If such a state of affairs is not provided for by a norm, the correlative event or action does not exist for the law, regardless of how material for society it may be. Therefore, events and actions that carry legal effects can be identified only by a recognition of all norms existing at a given time and by ascertaining which states of affairs such norms provide for.
A state of affairs provided for by a norm may consist of a single event or action whose occurrence will trigger the attached legal consequence. In this case, the **IF-clause** of the norm (see *supra*, ch 6, para 1.1) is simple.

If a chattel is delivered by the seller to the buyer, for example, the bare fact of the delivery makes the latter acquire its possession (eg material control).

However, this is not the most frequent scenario. Innumerable states of affairs instead consist of a whole chain of events and/or actions, and the correlative sanction is triggered only by the occurrence of the entirety of them. The **complexity of the IF-clause** is particularly remarkable when it consists of events and/or actions that are not supposed to happen simultaneously but rather in a consequential way.

In most jurisdictions, in order to transfer the property of a chattel to the buyer, not only the formation of a contract (of sale) is required, but also the fact that said chattel is delivered by the seller to the buyer. Therefore, the transfer of property is performed through a combination of the conclusion of the contract and the delivery of the chattel. Although it is not necessarily the case, delivery may well be performed not simultaneously but subsequent to the conclusion of the contract.

Any event or action that is included in the state of affairs provided for by a norm, whether it is simple or complex, is said to be of **legal relevance**. Even if the sanction is triggered only by a whole chain of events and/or actions, each of them may produce **(partial or preliminary) legal effects** (see *supra*, ch 6, para 1.1).

> Although in most jurisdictions the conclusion of a contract (of sale) does not suffice to transfer the property to the buyer, it nevertheless obliges the seller to convey the sold thing to the former. This obligation serves the ultimate purpose of transferring the property.

By the same token, each of the natural events and/or human actions comprised in the factual chain of a norm may be regarded by another norm as a state of affairs on its own (**relativity of legal qualifications**). This helps to explain the reason why any given case or practical issue is generally regulated by many norms, which are, therefore, to be coordinated and applied simultaneously.

> For example, the conveyance of real estate (see *infra*, ch 10, para 4.2.2) that is subsequent to a contract of sale may be regulated by the law of contract as well as by the law of property, to speak nothing of tax law, administrative law, etc. A bank loan whereby the borrower promises to pay interests at a usury rate to the lender is a contract entered into the two parties and regulated by private law. At the same time, the bank's entering into a contract whereby her client promises to pay interests at a usury rate may be punished as a crime by penal law. The same action by the bank is therefore regarded as contractual consent under private law and as a crime under penal law.

All events and actions that are legally relevant are classified as **legal (or juridical, or juristic) facts**. This concept is, therefore, the result of an analytical judgment, ie an assessment *a posteriori* (or *ex post*) that ascertains which model fact situations (or state of affairs) are provided for by norms.

Like other legal concepts (see *infra*, ch 10, para 1), that of legal facts is aimed at achieving a reduction and simplification of legal discourse, by summarizing the contents of a large number of norms and effectively conveying their meaning. In a sense, therefore, concepts like that of legal facts represent a metaphor for a norm, or for a number of norms, or for their single elements.

Legal facts form a vast, highly heterogeneous mass, for they comprise events and actions of the most diverse nature: contracts and torts, someone's birth or someone's death, and so on. Intuitively, it would be unreasonable if they were treated in the same way by the law. For example, contracts and torts are both legally relevant, but, in a sense, they are so for quite opposite reasons: contracts are promoted, whereas torts are redressed by the law.

Therefore, within the same category of legal facts, which stands as a genus, a number of sub-categories are to be identified in order to distinguish and categorize the different kinds. Each of these sub-categories stands as a species of legal facts, in the sense that each sub-category gathers those legal facts that are legally relevant in the same way and, therefore, sets them apart from the other legal facts that, pertaining to a different sub-category, are legally relevant in another way.

2. THE GERMAN TRIPARTITE TAXONOMY OF LEGAL FACTS, HETERONOMOUS LEGAL ACTS, AND AUTONOMOUS LEGAL ACTS

In the late nineteenth century, Pandectists (see *supra*, ch 4, para 3.1.2) started developing an overall classification of legal facts on a group-by-group basis, which was further developed by German scholarship.[1]

A major role in that classification is played by the concept of ***Rechtsgeschäft***, a term which has no precise translation in English but that may be referred to as a **legal (or juridical, or juristic) act**, or as a **legal transaction** (cf *infra*, ch 9, para 5).

The concept of *Rechtsgeschäft* was employed in the German Civil Code (BGB), which devotes a set of rules to it (§§ 104-185 BGB) in the context of its 'General Part' (*Allgemeiner Teil*) (see *supra*, ch 4, para 3.1.2).[2] Nonetheless, the BGB does not provide any specific definition of this concept.[3]

According to its usual understanding, such a legal act consists in someone's **declaration of will** (be it through language or by conduct) that is intended to achieve a change (legal effect) in the rights and duties of its author (or – albeit rarely, if not exceptionally – even those of a third party) (see also *infra*, ch 10, para 4).[4]

To put it differently, every legal subject is conferred by the law the power to produce a legal effect on her own property or her own personality (see *infra*, ch 10, para 3), to the extent to which the law does not impose any mandatory prohibition against doing so (see also *supra*, ch 6, para 1.3; *infra*, ch 10, para 5). Such power is directed to and underpinned by **private autonomy**, the latter word stemming from ancient Greek which literally means a stipulation of rules (νωμία, *nomìa*) by oneself (αὐτός, *autòs*), ie by the addressees of the rules. Therefore, a legal act in the German sense of *Rechtsgeschäft* is an **act**

[1] Alfred Manigk, *Das rechtswirksame Verhalten* (de Gruyter 1939).

[2] Manfred Wolf and Jürg Neuner, *Allgemeiner Teil des Bürgerlichen Rechts* (11th edn, CH Beck 2016) 327ff; Dieter Medicus and Jen Petersen, *Allgemeiner Teil des BGB* (11th edn, CF Müller 2016) 83ff.

[3] The *Sächsisches Bürgerliches Gesetzbuch* of 1865, by contrast, stipulated the following definition of *Rechtsgeschäft*: '*Geht bei einer Handlung der Wille darauf, in Übereinstimmung mit den Gesetzen ein Rechtsverhältnis zu begründen, aufzuheben oder zu ändern, so ist die Handlung ein Rechtsgeschäft*' ('A *Rechtsgeschäft* consists in a declaration of will that, in accordance with the law, is directed to establish, terminate, or change a legal relation')

[4] Jan P Schmidt, 'Juridical Act' in Jürgen Basedow, Klaus J Hopt, Reinhard Zimmermann and Andreas Stier (eds), *The Max Planck Encyclopedia of European Private Law*, vol 2 (OUP 2012) 1016.

of private autonomy (or an **autonomous legal act**) (see *supra*, ch 7, para 1; *infra*, ch 10, para 5).[5]

> According to article II-1:102 DCFR (*Party autonomy*), '(1) Parties are free to make a contract or other juridical act and to determine its contents, subject to any applicable mandatory rules. (2) Parties may exclude the application of any of the following rules relating to contracts or other juridical acts, or the rights and obligations arising from them, or derogate from or vary their effects, except as otherwise provided. (3) A provision to the effect that parties may not exclude the application of a rule or derogate from or vary its effects does not prevent a party from waiving a right which has already arisen and of which that party is aware'.

The legal effects attached to an autonomous legal act are, therefore, those that are intended by the party/-ies performing such transaction, provided that her/their will is genuine and not affected by any factor of irrationality, like lack of judgment or discernment, mistakes, etc. (see also *infra*, ch 10, para 5). In other words, an autonomous legal act means that anyone can freely decide not only to undertake or not to undertake a certain action that is legally relevant, but also to elect the legal effects attached to it. The archetype of legal transactions are **contracts** and, to a lesser extent, **last wills (testaments)**, and **marriage**.

> By entering into a contract, the parties intend to make some changes to their own rights and duties, and thus these changes are effected by the law. In the case of sale contract, a party acquires the ownership of a thing from the other party, and the latter receives the monetary payment of the consideration as envisaged in the contract. In principle, something similar can be held true for testaments, whereby the testator devises and bequeaths her property to a beneficiary or acknowledges a child born outside her marriage, whose family status will be therefore changed.

Hence, the legal effects of an autonomous legal act are not mainly set out by the law as such, but are rather elected by the party/-ies who entered into such transaction. When and where a property is to be transferred to a purchaser, when and where the price is to be paid, what its amount is to be, and so on: (almost) the entirety of the legal effects produced by a contract of sale, for instance, depends on the parties' mutual consent, ie on their agreement. To put it differently, norms pertaining to contracts allow the parties to produce the very legal effects that they envisage, as far as their agreement is lawful (see *supra*, ch 6, para 1.3; *infra* ch 9, para 5).

> Since the legal effects of a contract are envisaged and purported to exist by the contracting parties, they cannot be ascertained as a matter that is mandated by the law once and for all (*quaestio iuris*) but only with reference to each single

[5] ibid.

contract: it is, above all, a matter of interpretation of the parties' mutual will, which may vary from one contract to another (*quaestio facti*).

By contrast, norms may attach legal effects to some action irrespective of any would-be intention of its author to have or not have some legal effects produced. In other words, a legal subject (see *infra*, ch 11) can freely decide whether or not to undertake certain action, but she cannot elect the legal effects attached thereto, which are stipulated by the relevant norms. In opposition to autonomous legal acts, such actions may be called **heteronomous legal (or juridical, or juristic) acts**.[6]

Nonetheless, legal acts of this kind produce their own legal effects only on the condition that they have been done by their author with sufficient judgment and discernment of her own action. If this is not the case, such action does not produce the legal effects stipulated by the relevant norms, or these effects are subject to avoidance.

In most jurisdictions, for example, the author of a tort is not liable if she is a child in her 'tender years' or is mentally impaired in a most severe way, and other circumstances concur (see *infra*, ch 11, para 2).
However, the legal consequences of a tort are not conditional upon its author's would-be intention to produce or not produce some legal effects.
Therefore, a tort is to be regarded as a heteronomous legal act.

Finally, some legal facts are addressed by a norm irrespective of the particular judgment or discernment of their authors, or they simply consist in natural events. They may be termed **material facts**.

For example, when a person dies, title to her property vests in the heirs, subject to administration. That is, the right to possession of an intestate's property and the right to take through intestate succession accrue on the death of the ancestor, whatever event or action may have caused it – be it a murder, a heart attack, etc. In this respect, death is regarded by the law as a material fact.
As another example. In some jurisdictions (eg article 1191 *Codice civile*), a person cannot ask for the return of payment by invoking her lack of capacity to have made it (see also *infra*, ch 11, para 2). In other terms, the obligation is discharged even if the paying debtor was underage, mentally impaired, etc. In this respect, a payment is regarded as a material fact.

Given that any occurrence may be regarded as a legal fact or as a legal act by a norm, one should point out that, despite the common parlance of lawyers, an event or action may not be properly said to be a legal fact or a legal act *per se*. It may be either the former or the latter, always and only depending on how a given norm has regard to it.

Therefore, any event or action which is regarded as an autonomous legal act by one norm may be simultaneously regarded as a heteronomous legal act

[6] ibid 1017.

by another norm, due to the relativity of legal qualifications (see *supra*, ch 9, para 1).

> For example, a contract as such is an autonomous legal act. Therefore, if one of the contracting parties is underage, for example, she may elect to avoid the contract (see *infra*, ch 9, para 5).
> Nonetheless, when a contract is concluded in order to fulfil a previous obligation to enter into it, it is a material act as well. This means that, even when it is concluded by an underaged party, the contract discharges such an obligation (to the extent it is not avoided).

3. THE FRENCH BIPARTITE TAXONOMY OF LEGAL FACTS AND LEGAL ACTS

The concept of autonomous legal acts and its distinction from other legal acts has not been acknowledged by all civil law jurisdictions. This lack of uniformity gives rise to considerable uncertainty within the legal terminology adopted across Europe.
The French Civil Code, in part because it was enacted in 1804 and therefore prior to the 'invention' of the *Rechtsgeschäfte* in German scholarship (see *supra*, ch 9, para 2), does not contain any norm mentioning autonomous legal acts as such, ie as opposed to heteronomous legal acts. Any fact that is legally relevant is, therefore, qualified as either an *acte juridique* or as a *fait juridique*.
Following the 2016 reform of the *Code civil* (see *supra*, ch 4, para 3.1.1), the **division between *actes juridiques* and *faits juridiques*** has been sketched by the new article 1100(1) *Code civil*, though with particular regard to the sources of obligations. That provision stipulates that: '*Les obligations naissent d'actes juridiques, de faits juridiques ou de l'autorité seule de la loi*'.
However, one should note that, within the *Code civil*, the category of *actes juridiques*, though it could potentially encompass all legal acts, has been *de facto* used with the meaning of autonomous legal acts. After the above-mentioned 2016 reform, this issue has been plainly acknowledged by the French legislature, particularly in laying down the new article 1100-1: '*Les actes juridiques sont des manifestations de volonté destinées à produire des effets de droit. Ils peuvent être conventionnels ou unilatéraux. Ils obéissent, en tant que de raison, pour leur validité et leurs effets, aux règles qui gouvernent les contrats*'.

> In a similar way, article II.-1:101(2) DCFR gives the following definition of a juridical act: '[a]ny statement or agreement, whether express or implied from action, which is intended to have legal effect as such. It may be unilateral, bilateral or multilateral'.

Conversely, pursuant to the new article 1100-2 *Code civil*, '[l]*es faits juridiques sont des agissements ou des événements auxquels la loi attache des effets de droit. Les obligations qui naissent d'un fait juridique sont régies, selon le cas, par le sous-titre relatif à la responsabilité extracontractuelle ou le sous-titre relatif aux autres sources d'obligations*'. In other words, juridically significant facts (*faits juridiques*) not only comprise material facts (*des événements*) but also heteronomous legal acts (*des agissements*), because in both cases the legal effect is stipulated by the applicable norms, irrespective of any will by the author to produce it.

It is therefore not surprising that, within the French *Code civil*, torts are classified as *faits*, not as *actes juridiques*. Particularly, the very famous general rule about liability arising from torts, provided for by article 1240 (former article 1382) *Code civil*, reads: 'Tout fait *quelconque de l'homme, qui cause à autrui un dommage, oblige celui par la faute duquel il est arrivé, à le réparer*'.[7]

4. THE ECLECTIC ITALIAN TAXONOMY OF LEGAL FACTS AND LEGAL ACTS

In the provisions of the Italian *Codice civile*, the distinction between *fatti giuridici* and *atti giuridici* mirrors that between *faits juridiques* and *actes juridiques* in the French *Code civil.* Yet, as far as Italian scholarship is concerned, this is not an accurate account.

The *Codice civile* is French-oriented, whereas Italian scholarship is German-oriented (see also *supra*, ch 4, para 3.1.3), and it predominantly (although not unanimously) acknowledges the category of *negozi giuridici* (ie autonomous legal acts) as opposed to that of *atti giuridici in senso stretto* (ie heteronomous legal acts).

Therefore, Italian law is in this respect characterized by a mismatch between the categories acknowledged by the *Codice civile* and those acknowledged by legal scholars.

For instance, article 2043 *Codice civile* follows the French model, reading that '*Qualunque fatto doloso o colposo che cagiona ad altri un danno ingiusto, obbliga colui che ha commesso il fatto a risarcire il danno*'. According to some legal scholars, however, the tort is an *atto giuridico in senso stretto* and not a *fatto giuridico*.

5. THE EUROPEAN TAXONOMY AND THE CENTRALITY OF LEGAL ACTS IN PRIVATE LAW

Autonomous legal acts play a major role in private law. Undeniably, they constitute the most important category of legal facts, whose domain tends to expand also to other areas of legal systems (eg criminal and administrative law).

[7] Emphasis added.

From the point of view of their structure, legal acts may be unilateral, bilateral, or multilateral. Legal acts are **unilateral** when they are performed by the declaration of will of one single party (eg the withdrawal from a contract); apart from some exceptions (like testaments or last wills), that declaration of will is directed to a specific addressee and carries legal effects only if and when its notice is served on the latter. Legal acts are **bilateral** when the manifestation of mutual consent of two parties is required, ie an agreement (as is the case with the majority of contracts). Legal acts may well also be **multilateral** (eg the establishment of most companies or other legal entities) (see *infra*, ch 11, para 1.2).

The subject-matter of legal acts can be **patrimonial**, thus when the interest pursued by the party or the parties may be lawfully haggled over by them, as is the case for contracts. In some legal acts, the interest can even be **non-patrimonial**, as is the case with testaments (or last wills) and marriage.

Traditionally, private autonomy is broadened as far as its exercise impinges upon the **parties' patrimony**, while it is shrunk by the law when its exercise impinges upon the **parties' personality**. In the latter case, it is not infrequent that the law provides for mandatory prohibitions (see *supra*, ch 6, para 1.3), since personal integrity is deemed to be worth protection even against the consent of the party concerned (for sake of her dignity as a human being).

For example, pursuant to article 5 *Codice civile*, any decision about one's own body is prohibited if it undermines her physical integrity permanently or is in any way contrary to law, to public order, or to morality.[8]

Therefore, the physical integrity of persons is protected even against their own will. No decision about it is allowed beyond the limits posed by law.

Furthermore, a legal act is usually aimed at regulating the interests of the parties while they are still alive (***inter vivos***). However, some (few) legal acts are carried out in order to make a disposition of the author's property that is to take effect after her death (***mortis causa***). The most paradigmatic among *mortis causa* acts is the testament (or last will), but within some jurisdictions it is also possible to enter into contracts aimed at devising or bequeathing property.[9]

In the case of **illegality** of a legal act, ie when it violates or circumvents a mandatory prohibition (be it set out by a statutory provision or embedded in public policy), the act is generally affected by **invalidity**,[10] ie by a legal pathology. A legal act may be invalid also when the will of one of the parties

[8] 'Gli atti di disposizione del proprio corpo sono vietati quando cagionino una diminuzione permanente della integrità fisica, o quando siano altrimenti contrari alla legge, all'ordine pubblico o al buon costume'.

[9] For German law, see §§ 1941, 2274ff BGB (*Erbvertrag*). For US law, see 'Wills', 79 *Am Jur 2d*, §§ 300ff.

[10] Phillip Hellwege, 'Invalidity' in *The Max Planck Encyclopedia of European Private Law*, vol 2 (n 4) 990.

is somehow tainted with a deficiency of judgment or discernment. This may happen either:

a) because one of the parties was incompetent, ie she had **no capacity to act** (see *infra*, ch 11, para 2);

b) because one of the parties' consent was affected by a factor of irrationality (**vitiating factors**). Such vitiating factors traditionally include mistake, fraud and misrepresentation, duress and undue influence.

The invalidity of a legal act may result in its voidness (or nullity) or voidability. In the event of **voidness (or nullity)**, a legal act is wholly or partially ineffective from the outset (*ab initio*, or *ex tunc*), regardless of whether or not any of the parties has disaffirmed it. A legal act may be void because it is illegal, or because it is affected by indefiniteness or vagueness, or because it lacks some formal requirements (like when a statutory provision requires a contract to be in writing).

A legal act's voidness can be invoked not only by any of the parties but also by a third person, whose rights might be affected by that act; it can even be raised by a court on its own motion. These actions and defences are not subject to any statutes of repose or of limitation (see *infra*, ch 10, para 5), and a legal act's voidness cannot be validated unless differently provided for by the law. The non-performance of any party is excused. In the event of performance, each party can claim restitution for it, even from a sub-purchaser (with certain exceptions).

By contrast, a voidable legal act is effective until its **avoidance (or rescission, or annulment)** occurs at the election of the aggrieved party (eg the minor), who thus holds the power-right (see *infra*, ch 10, para 4.2.1) to disaffirm such act. This power-right is time-barred, being subject to statutes of repose or to statutes of limitation (see *infra*, ch 10, para 5). In most jurisdictions, however, the aggrieved party of a voidable legal act can excuse her non-performance even where that legal act has not previously been avoided, and this defence is not time-barred.

The aggrieved party can repudiate a voidable legal act either by bringing an action before a court against the other party (in some jurisdictions) or by serving notice on the other party (in other jurisdictions).

If a voidable legal act is avoided, it is retrospectively (*ab initio*, or *ex tunc*) reversed, and any performance is to be returned to the party who rendered it, be it the aggrieved party or another.

> A voidable conveyance can vest the seller's ownership in the buyer. However, if such conveyance is avoided, the ownership is re-vested in the seller as though it had not passed to the buyer. If the seller has in the meantime transferred the possession to the buyer, the latter is furthermore obliged to return the sold thing to the former; if the buyer has paid the price to the seller, conversely, restitution of it is owed.

Affirmation (or confirmation, or ratification) of a voidable legal act is generally allowed, but conditionally on the fact that the ground of avoidance has ceased to exist. It may happen through the aggrieved party's waiver of her claim to avoidance (express affirmation, or confirmation, or ratification). It may also happen through voluntary performance of the voidable contract (implied affirmation, or confirmation, or ratification).

GLOSSARY

Avoidance (or rescission, or annulment) [*Nullité relative; Anfechtung; Annullamento*] (5): if avoided, an act is retrospectively reversed. Non-performance of the innocent party is excused only after avoidance, in which case each of the parties can claim restitution for any previous performance. Affirmation (or confirmation, or ratification) of a voidable legal act may be express or implied, but it is conditional on the fact the ground of avoidance has ceased in the meanwhile.

Contract [*Contrat*; *Vertrag*; *Contratto*] (2, 5): bi- or multilateral, patrimonial legal act that creates obligations (see *infra*, ch 10, para 4.2.1) between two or more parties. In some jurisdictions a contract is necessarily *inter vivos*; in others (like Germany and the US) it may also be *mortis causa*. Under French and Italian law, a contract can have also a real effect, ie it can directly produce the transfer of property (see *infra*, ch 10, para 4.2.2) from one of the contracting parties to another, as well as the assignment of a real right in someone else's property (see *infra*, ch 10, para 4.2.2).

Duress [*Violence*; *Drohung*; *Violenza*] (5): one of the vitiating factors (see *ad vocem*), consisting in violence or a threat towards one of a legal act's parties.

Fraud [*Dol*; *arglistige Täuschung*; *Dolo*] (5): one of the vitiating factors (see *ad vocem*), consisting in a knowing misrepresentation or knowing concealment of a material fact that has been done to induce another to perform a legal act to her detriment.

Heteronomous legal act [*Acte juridique au sens strict*; *Rechtshandlung im engeren Sinne*; *Atto giuridico in senso stretto*] (2): conduct whose legal effects are not elected by the party/-ies but stipulated by the law irrespective of her/their intention. However, such an act is ineffective (or subject to avoidance) in the event of an absence of judgment or discernment by its author/-s.

Invalidity (of legal acts) [*Invalidité*; *Ungültigkeit*; *Invalidità*] (5): pathology of a legal act that may result either in the act's voidness (see *ad vocem*) or voidability (see *ad vocem*).

Legal fact [*Fait juridique*; *Fatto giuridico*] (1): any event or action which is legally relevant and included in the state of affairs provided for by a norm, and the occurrence of which has legal consequences.

(Autonomous) legal act [*Acte juridique*; *Rechtsgeschäft*; *Negozio giuridico*] (2): one or more declarations of will (be it through language or by action) that are intended to achieve a change (legal effect) in the rights and duties of their author/-s (or – albeit rarely, if not exceptionally – in those of a third party). The most notable legal acts are contracts (see *ad vocem*), wills (or testament) (see *ad vocem*) and marriage (see *ad vocem*).

Marriage [*Mariage*; *Ehe*; *Matrimonio*] (2, 5): bilateral, mostly non-patrimonial legal act which establishes the legal union of a couple as spouses.

Material fact [*Fait matériel*; *Realakt*; *Fatto materiale*] (2): natural event that carries legal effects, or human action that has legal effects irrespective of any judgment or discernment by its author/-s.

Mistake [*Erreur*; *Irrtum*; *Errore*] (5): one of the vitiating factors (see *ad vocem*), consisting in an erroneous belief by one of a legal act's parties.

Private autonomy (2): power of private subjects (be they individuals or entities) (see *infra*, ch 11) to freely regulate their own interests and to change their legal positions (see *infra*, ch 10) accordingly.

Undue influence [*Timore*] (5): one of the vitiating factors (see *ad vocem*), consisting in the improper use of power or trust vis-à-vis one of a legal act's parties.

Vitiating factors [*Vices du consentement*; *Willensmängel*; *Vizi del consenso*] (5): factors affecting the validity of a legal act by impairing the freedom of consent of one of the contracting parties. Factors traditionally vitiating a legal act are mistake, fraud, duress and undue influence.

Voidability [*Nullité relative*; *Anfechtbarkeit*; *Annullabilità*] (5): kind of invalidity (see *ad vocem*) that may affect a legal act. A voidable legal act is effective until its avoidance (or rescission, or annulment) (see *ad vocem*) at the election of the innocent party.

Voidness (or nullity) [*Nullité absolue*; *Nichtigkeit*; *Nullità*] (5): kind of invalidity (see *ad vocem*) that may affect a legal act. When a legal act is void (or null), it is wholly ineffective from the outset (*ab initio*), whether or not any of the parties has disaffirmed it. A legal act may be void because it is illegal, because it is affected by indefiniteness or vagueness, or because it lacks some formal requirements (like when a statutory provision requires a contract to be in writing). Any of the parties or a third person can invoke a legal act's voidness, which also can be raised by a court on its own motion. The non-performance of any party is excused. In the event of performance, each party can claim restitution for this, even from a sub-purchaser (with certain exceptions). Voidness cannot be remedied, unless differently provided for by the law.

(Last) will (or testament) [*Testament*; *Testament, or letzter Wille*; *Testamento*] (2, 5): unilateral, mostly patrimonial legal act whereby the author makes a disposition of her property to be effective upon death.

CHAPTER 10

Rights and duties

- **Legal positions and legal relations**
- **Freedoms (or liberties, or privileges) and licenses**
- **Powers (and power-rights)**
- **(Subjective) rights and their classification**
- **Relative rights (or rights *in personam*) and absolute rights (or rights *in rem*)**
- **Abuse of rights doctrine in civil law jurisdictions and its 'functional equivalents' in common law jurisdictions**
- **Prescription and statutes of limitations**
- **Statutes of repose and nonclaim statutes**

Legal positions are concepts used to map what legal subjects can/may do or not do, and, conversely, what they shall/must do or not do.

A legal relation is established between the holder of a position of advantage (mostly a right) and the holder of the correlative position of disadvantage (mostly a duty).

A freedom (or privilege, or liberty) is a simple position of 'may do' that allows a certain person, or group of certain persons, to do something or to abstain from doing something. It may amount to a liberty-right.

A power is a simple position of 'can do' that enables a specific person, or group of specific persons, to change either her/their own entitlements or those of someone else. If a power is granted in the holder's own interest, it amounts to a power-right.

(Subjective) rights are characterized by the power to seek enforcement. They may be patrimonial or non-patrimonial (or extra-patrimonial), relative (*in personam*) or absolute (*in rem*). They are relative (like credits and power-rights) when they can be enforced only against a specific person or group of specific persons; they are absolute (like real rights and rights of personality) when they can be enforced against anyone else who interferes with the possession of an entitlement.

The civilian tradition historically acknowledged a general principle that forbids abuse of rights, which has eventually settled in EU law as well. Although that general principle is traditionally strange to common law jurisdictions, the latter are acquainted with a number of (mostly equitable) remedies that work as 'functional equivalents' to the civilian prohibition.
With the possible exception of property, patrimonial rights are time-barred. If these rights are infringed, their holder must seek a timely redress, unless they become unenforceable (prescription, or statutes of limitations).
Some statutory provisions put a time bar on rights irrespectively of any possible infringement of them, or they put a time bar on any prospective litigation (statutes of response and nonclaim statutes).

1. LEGAL POSITIONS AND LEGAL RELATIONS

As is the case with legal facts and acts (see *supra*, ch 9, para 1), legal positions are concepts deployed in legal discourse to epitomize unitary bodies of principles and rules. The main legal positions (like property or obligations) thus amount to **legal institutes**, which streamline the boundaries and the content of entire branches of the legal system (like the law of property, or that of obligations).
In the parlance of **civil lawyers**, legal positions are usually qualified as 'subjective', because they are to be predicated on a specific person or group of specific persons (see also *infra*, ch 10, para 4). While the scope of legal facts and legal acts clings to natural events and human actions, in fact, the scope of legal positions clings to relations between legal subjects. Instead of dealing with legal positions as such, therefore, part of civil law scholarship, particularly in Germany, prefers to focus primarily on **legal relations**, each of them being conceptualized as a complex and unitary whole of legal positions (see also *infra*, ch 10, para 4.2.1).[1] Nevertheless, the analysis of the different kinds of rights, ie the most significant legal positions (see *infra*, ch 10, para 4), was developed already by the Pandectists of the late nineteenth century (see *supra*, ch 4, para 3.1.2).
In Anglo-American legal systems, it may be said that '**remedies precede rights**'.[2] Due to the origins of the English legal system (see *supra*, ch 2, para 4.2), the discourse of **common lawyers** has been traditionally centered on actions, ie suits brought in a court, more than on rights; therefore, it is the

[1] Manfred Wolf and Jörge Neuner, *Allgemeiner Teil des Bürgerlichen Rechts* (11th edn, CH Beck 2016) § 19; Dieter Medicus and Jens Petersen, *Allgemeiner Teil des BGB* (11th edn, CF Müller 2016) paras 54ff.
[2] See the essays collected in Franz Hofmann and Franziska Kurz (eds), *Law of Remedies. A European Perspective* (Intersentia 2019); particularly, see Paul S Davies, 'Remedies in English Private Law. A "Stand-Alone" Research Area?' ibid 27ff.

procedural, not the substantive, layer of the common law that has come to the forefront of Anglo-American jurisprudence.

> A (judicial) **remedy** is a response to a 'cause of action' (like breach of contract, tort, etc.).[3]

A path-breaking article published in the 1910s by **Wesley Newcomb Hohfeld** (1879-1918), however, proved seminal and paved the way for a thriving body of literature on legal positions,[4] which straddles jurisprudence and legal philosophy. Hohfeld's analytical scheme is the upshot of a definitional, or stipulative, approach, which is aimed at introducing more precise and rigorous patterns of legal discourse, particularly with regard to judicial litigation; this feature may explain why his teachings gained a considerable consensus among the representatives of legal realism (see *supra*, ch 7, para 4).[5]

Any legal relation is based on the **entitlement** of a specific person or group of specific persons, which is therefore in a legal position of 'can/may do' or 'not do' something, against another specific person or group of persons, which is therefore in a position of 'shall/must do' or 'not do' something; for example, the creditor can claim the sum of money that is owed to her by the debtor, and a proprietor can keep a trespasser off her plot of land. The **substance (or the content) of the legal relation** between the two counterparts consists in a given action or state of affairs;[6] for example, the payment that is owed by the debtor, or the enjoyment of the plot of land that is owned by the proprietor. Within each legal relation, a position of **advantage** entails a matching position of **disadvantage**. In other terms, a legal relation is structured as a pair (or dyad) of **correlative legal positions**, one of 'can/may do' or 'not do', and the other of 'shall/must do' or 'not do' something. Mostly, a right of someone relates to the conduct of another, who thus bears a correlative duty (see *infra*, ch 10, para 4).

> For example, a right of credit is a legal position of 'can do', which entitles its holder to claim performance from someone else. Conversely, this very 'someone else' holds a correlative legal position of 'shall do', ie the debt, which obliges her to render that performance in the interest of the creditor (see *infra*, ch 10, para 4.2.1).
>
> Therefore, credit and debt are counterparts, and the legal relation between the holder of the former (ie the creditor) and that of the latter (ie the debtor) is termed an **obligation** (see *infra*, ch 10, para 4.2.1).

[3] Andrew Burrows, 'Remedies' in Id (ed), *English Private Law* (OUP 2013) 1253.

[4] Wesley N Hohfeld, 'Some fundamental legal conceptions as applied in judicial reasoning' (1913) 23 Yale LJ 16.

[5] William Twining, *General Jurisprudence. Understanding Law from a Global Perspective* (CUP 2009) 49; Nigel E Simmonds, 'Rights at the Cutting Edge' in Matthew H Kramer, Nigel E Simmonds and Hillel Steiner, *A Debate over Rights. Philosophical Enquiries* (OUP 1998, rist 2002) 177.

[6] Carl Wellman, *A Theory of Rights* (Rowman & Allanheld 1985) 15; Matthew H Kramer, 'Rights without Trimmings' in Id, Simmonds and Steiner (n 5) 8.

Following the conceptual framework set out by Hohfeld, it is commonly argued that two legal positions may be not only correlatives (when they entail each other) but also **contradictories or opposites** (when they negate each other).[7] For example, 'power' negates 'disability' and, albeit only to a certain extent, 'duty' does so with 'liberty' (see *infra*, ch 10, paras 2-3). Logically admissible as it may be, however, the simultaneous holding of contradictory legal positions is usually not tolerated by legal systems.

Furthermore, a distinction may be drawn between **first-order relations**, which apply directly to people's conduct and social intercourse, and **second-order relations**, which apply directly to people's entitlements and only indirectly (but crucially) to people's conduct and social intercourse.[8] Most typically, a right is an entitlement establishing a first-order relation (since it demands that someone else does something or abstains from interfering with something),[9] whereas a power pertains to a second-order relation (since its exertion effects a transfer of entitlement to someone else).

To put it differently, the conceptualization of legal positions is finally centered on rights, since they represent the entitlements that prompt any legal relation (see *infra*, ch 10, para 4). The other legal positions that are usually conceptualized by legal theory are either counterparts or components of rights, but they hardly attain a considerable degree of self-being. In that sense, they can be qualified as **ancillary** to rights.

2. SIMPLE POSITIONS OF 'MAY DO': FREEDOMS (OR PRIVILEGES OR LIBERTIES)

A **freedom (or privilege or liberty)** is a position of 'may do' that allows a certain person, or group of certain persons, to do something or to abstain from doing something.[10] More precisely, having a liberty to engage in a certain action means to be free from any duty to eschew that action, and having a liberty to abstain from a certain action means to be free from any duty to undertake that action.[11] The counterperson or group of counterpersons is said to have a **no-right** of halting the activity or state of affairs to which the freedom itself pertains.[12]

> The owner of a plot of land holds the freedom to enter on it (she may do that), no matter how insistently her neighbor demands that she stays away. A trespasser does not enjoy such privilege (she has no right to enter on someone else's plot of land and, if she does so, she commits a wrong).

[7] On terminology, see Kramer (n 6) 8 fn 1.
[8] ibid 20.
[9] Ludwig Raiser, 'Der Stand der Lehre vom subjektiven Recht im Deutschen Zivilrecht' [1961] JZ 465.
[10] Glanville Williams, 'The Concept of Legal Liberty' (1956) 56 Columbia LR 1129.
[11] Kramer (n 6) 10, 13.
[12] ibid.

If considered on its own, a freedom does not entail any right or power.[13] In principle, therefore, the person or group of persons that has a correlative no-right may well have the **liberty to interfere** with the actions or the states of affairs concerned by the liberty of her/its counterpart, by making recourse (not to mechanisms of public governance but) to her/its own devices.[14]

> For example, freedom of speech as such does not confer the power as well to seek enforcement, not being a right (see *infra*, ch 10, para 4). Therefore, people can permissibly do their utmost to interfere with someone else's voicing of opinions (eg by making so much noise that the former's words are drowned out).[15]

However, it must be pointed out that (human) rights in most cases shield the halting of the action or state of affairs concerned by a liberty, albeit sometimes imperfectly.[16]

> For example, one who seeks to interfere with someone else's freedom to speech cannot do so by physically assaulting the latter while talking, since she is protected by her right to be free from physical assaults.[17]

Even more importantly, freedoms are generally accompanied by a corona of cognate rights that are purported to protect their exercise,[18] so that they are eventually reducible to those very rights (**liberty-rights**).[19]

> For example, in most legal systems fundamental economic freedoms are flanked by some duties of the competitors to refrain from distortion of fair competition.[20]

Be it as it may, it is safe to say that most freedoms end up being ancillary to rights and sometimes are not even acknowledged as autonomous legal positions.

Although embodied in a right, however, specific freedoms can be restricted under the force of an agreement entered into by the rightsholder.

> For example, if a plot of land is sold under a condition of its inalienability (no-sell term), the buyer may not convey it to another (she may not do so) (see also *infra*, ch 10, para 3).

A specific privilege may be voluntarily vested in someone else through a **license (leave, permission)**.

[13] ibid 14f; Wellman (n 6) 9.
[14] Kramer (n 6) 10.
[15] ibid 11.
[16] ibid.
[17] ibid.
[18] For an account of the discussion on that point, see Kramer (n 6) 12 fn 3.
[19] Wellman (n 6) 63ff.
[20] Kramer (n 6) 12 fn 3.

The owner of a plot of land can grant someone else the leave or license to enter on it. Both the owner and the licensee may do that (unless the former voluntary obliges herself not to do it).

3. SIMPLE POSITIONS OF 'CAN DO': POWERS (AND POWER-RIGHTS)

A **power** enables a specific person, or group of specific persons, to expand or reduce or otherwise modify, in particular ways, her/its own entitlements or those of another.[21] In other terms, a power consists of an ability to effect changes in legal relations, either by means of a legal act intending those changes, or (but less frequently) by means of a lawsuit (see *supra*, ch 9, paras 2-5).[22]
In some cases, the entitlement susceptible to being thus changed is held by the powerholder herself.[23]

For example, the power of assigning a credit or conveying a plot of land is generally held by, respectively, the holders of the credit and of the property, who, for example, can sell or donate their own rights.

In other cases, the entitlement susceptible to being changed by a powerholder is held by someone else, who is then said to bear a **liability**, ie an exposure to the imposition of such changes. In fact, a liability-bearer is unshielded from the bringing about of changes in her entitlements by the exertion of someone else's power.
The power to change someone else's entitlements may arise either from the command of the law or from a previous legal act of the liability-bearer herself, which is termed **authorization**.
In most cases, a power to change someone else's entitlements is directed at preserving an interest of the liability-bearer.

For example, **agency** is the power (of the agent) to act on behalf of someone else (the principal) and to perform some legal acts in the latter's name (bar those acts which are strictly personal, like marriage and testament).[24]

In some other cases, a power is directed at preserving an interest of the powerholder herself; if that is the case, it amounts to a right, which is termed a **power-right** (see *infra*, ch 10, para 4.2.1).

For example, 'the consumer shall have a period of 14 days to withdraw from a distance or off-premises contract, without giving any reason', and without

[21] Andrew Halpin, 'The Concept of a Legal Power' (1996) 16 OJLS 129.
[22] Wellman (n 6) 42; Kramer (n 6) 20.
[23] Wellman (n 6) 24, 42.
[24] Francis Reynolds, 'Agency' in Andrew Burrows (ed), *English Private Law* (OUP 2013) 613ff.

incurring any costs other than those necessary to return the merchandise.[25] If, before the expiry of the **withdrawal** period, the consumer notifies the trader of her decision to withdraw from the contract, the rights and duties of both contracting parties are terminated. Particularly, the consumer's unilateral choice of withdrawal will terminate not only her own contractual rights and duties but also those of the trader (like that of claiming the price agreed).

Notably, a power is not always accompanied by the liberty to exercise it. The holder can exercise her power while being under a duty not to do so; the breach of this duty can incur a penalty without nullifying the exercise of the power.[26]

For example, the no-sell term of a contract of tenancy (see *infra*, ch 10, para 4.2.2) obliges the proprietor of a plot of land not to sell it (unless to the tenant) (see *supra*, ch 10, para 2). While bearing this contractual obligation, the proprietor is not deprived of the power to convey her property to someone else. Therefore, if she happens to convey her plot of land to a third person, the latter acquires the propriety despite the breach of that contractual obligation; conversely, she may be held liable for damages towards the tenant.

In turn, a duty can bind a powerholder to exercise her power.

For example, a legal monopolist or an enterprise operating in a regulated market may be required by a statutory provision to enter into a contract for the supply of the goods or services it provides to the public.

Yet, it is nowadays generally acknowledged that any private power has to be exercised according to the **general principle of good faith** (see *supra*, ch 4, para 1; ch 6, para 3; ch 8, para 1.2); conversely, one who is exposed to the exercise of a power is deemed to be vested with a **legitimate interest** in being protected against an abusive imposition by the powerholder (**abuse of power**).

The legal position which negates a liability is termed **immunity**.[27] The holder of an immunity is not exposed to the exercise of a power by someone, with respect to any entitlements covered by the immunity. Correlatively, one who is devoid of that power is said to bear a **disability**, ie the absence of a power.[28]

[25] Directive 2011/83/EU of the European Parliament and of the Council of 25 October 2011 on consumer rights, amending Council Directive 93/13/EEC and Directive 1999/44/EC of the European Parliament and of the Council and repealing Council Directive 85/577/EEC and Directive 97/7/EC of the European Parliament and of the Council, art 9 (1). See *supra*, ch 8, para 1.5.2.

[26] Kramer (n 6) 63.

[27] Wellman (n 6) 75ff.

[28] Kramer (n 6) 21.

4. (SUBJECTIVE) RIGHTS

A (subjective) right is a complex legal position that consists of **an aggregate of freedoms, claims, powers, and immunities**,[29] whose backbone is the **power to seek enforcement** through mobilization of the state's coercion, if necessary.[30]

The qualification of rights as 'subjective' (see also *supra*, ch 10, para 1) is characteristic of civil lawyers' parlance and is due to the fact that Romance as well as Germanic languages use one single term (*droit, diritto, derecho, direito, Recht*) to denote both a right, ie a kind of legal position, and the law, ie the system of legal principles and rules (see *supra*, ch 6, para 2). Therefore, it is rather customary to indicate in context whether it is talked of *droit, diritto, derecho, direito, Recht* in a **subjective sense** (ie a right) or in an **objective sense** (ie the law).[31] In English language, by contrast, the term 'right' does not coincide with that of 'law', so that there is no risk of confusion between the two concepts thus denoted (see *supra*, ch 2, para 1).
Since embryos and fetuses are not recognized as legal persons (see *infra*, ch 11, para 1.1), the rights they are nevertheless vested in by the law are sometimes depicted as (temporarily) **'non-subjective' rights**.[32]

The perimeter of this complex of positions of 'may do' and 'can do' changes from one kind of right to another: some rights (that of property, above all) encompass a large number of freedoms, powers, and immunities, whereas some others encompass only very few of them. Despite their variability, rights share a minimum commonality: they are **enforceable** through the legal system.

For example, if a debtor fails to perform her obligation, the creditor can mobilize a state's officials, who will seize and auction off the debtor's property, so that the proceeds may be handed over to the creditor. On the basis of the various sets of norms, of both a substantive and procedural nature, that govern this proceeding, it can be safely said that the creditor has a power to seek enforcement of her credit and, therefore, the latter amounts to a right.

Most rights are centered on **a claim**, which affords to a specific person, or a group of specific persons, legal protection against someone else's interference or against someone else's withholding of assistance or remuneration, in regard to a certain action or a certain state of affairs.[33] The specific person or group of specific persons that is required to abstain from interference or to render assistance or remuneration is under a **duty** to do so.[34]

[29] Wellman (n 6) 59f, who follows Herbert LA Hart, 'Bentham on Legal Rights' in Id, *Oxford Essays in Jurisprudence* (2nd edn, Clarendon Press 1973) 171ff.
[30] Kramer (n 6) 21.
[31] Wolf and Neuner (n 1) § 20 para 1; Dieter Medicus and Jens Petersen (n 1) para 61.
[32] Wolf and Neuner (n 1) § 20 para 13.
[33] Donal Nolan and Andrew Robertson (eds), *Rights and Private Law* (Hart 2012).
[34] Kramer (n 6) 9.

A duty to do something does not perforce involve a liberty to do that thing, particularly since a person may be under **contrary duties**. In fact, it may happen that a duty to do something coexists with a duty to refrain from doing the same thing.[35]

> For example, a restrictive covenant can bind the covenantor not to convey her plot of land to others. If the covenantor enters into a contract of sale in spite of the covenant, however, she is obliged to convey her property to the buyer (assuming that she is a person different than the covenantee). The duty arising from the restrictive covenant thus collides with that arising from the subsequent contract of sale. As a result, the covenant owes the conveyance of her property to the buyer, but at the same time she is not allowed by the law to do so. If the covenant performs his duty towards the buyer, she breaches the restrictive covenant, and vice versa.

Furthermore, **conflicting rights** are possible, ie rights to inconsistent states of affairs.[36]

> For example, in some civil law jurisdictions the proprietor of a chattel or of a plot of land can vest her property in several buyers or promisees, thus engendering a conflict between their rights. The conflict is generally solved by the law in favor of the first who gains the possession of the chattel or who provides for land registration, respectively.

4.1. Will theory (or choice theory) vs interest theory (or benefit theory)

The relationship between the holding of a right and that of the power to seek its enforcement has historically represented a bone of contention among scholars. The seeds of this theoretical dispute, which is still bubbling in contemporary Anglo-American literature, may be traced back to the German Pandectistic School of the late nineteenth century (see *supra*, ch 4, para 3.1.2).[37]
The first fully fledged theoretical conception of rights was fathered by **Friedrich Carl von Savigny** (see *supra*, ch 4, para 3.1.2), and it was instrumental in securing a territory where the individual could enjoy her freedom of self-determination. Being tightly hinged on the procedural backbone of Roman law, Savigny's theory depicted a right as an action (*Klage*), which was to be brought against someone else in court.[38]

[35] Kramer (n 6) 18 (with a different terminology). However, it must be emphasized that a contradiction lies not between the duty to do something and the liberty to do that thing but between a duty to do something and the liberty to abstain from doing that thing; on this point, see ibid 4.
[36] ibid 19f (with a different terminology).
[37] Wolf and Neuner (n 1) § 20 paras 3ff.
[38] Friedrich Carl von Savigny, *System des heutigen römischen Rechts*, vol 1 (Veit 1840) para 4.

It was contended by **Bernhard Windscheid** (see *supra*, ch 4, para 3.1.2), however, that such doctrine was appropriate for Roman law but not for modern law.[39] In fact, he argued, the former was 'not a law of rights, but a law of actions to be brought about at courts';[40] for Roman lawyers, in fact, 'actions were not a derivative, but a primary and autonomous concept'.[41] Under modern law, by contrast, this understanding would prove untenable, since procedural law would now be 'the servant of private law'.[42] In order to shift the discourse from substantive to procedural law, Windscheid centered the definition of rights on the concept of a claim (*Anspruch*),[43] which he initially described as 'the device guaranteeing the will of individuals as legal subjects';[44] later on, after falling under the influence of **August Thon**'s teachings (1839-1912),[45] Windscheid depicted a right as 'the will-power granted by the legal system to an individual'.[46] This doctrine may be termed the **will theory (or choice theory) of rights**.

Although such a view was followed by the majority of Pandectists,[47] it was opposed by **Rudolf von Jhering** (see *supra*, ch 4, para 3.1.2), who advocated for a functionalistic rather than a voluntarist conception of rights. He therefore defined a right as an 'interest enforceable at law'.[48] This doctrine may be termed the **interest theory (or benefit theory) of rights**.

Both theories agree on the point that any right must be enforceable, ie accompanied by the power to seek enforcement.[49] They are divergent, however, insofar as they touch upon the precise location of that power, which actually may not always be held by the claimholder but also by someone else.

If the power to seek enforcement does not lie within the discretion of the person who has the claim, the will theory (or choice theory) opines that that claim does not amount to a proper right. In other terms, this doctrine contends that what is sufficient and necessary for someone's holding of a right is that she is competent and authorized to demand or waive the enforcement of that right.[50]

[39] Götz Schulze, 'Subjektives Recht und Klage – Axiome im deutschen und französischen Zivilrechtssystem' in Id (ed), *Europäisches Privatrecht in Vielfalt geeint. Der modernisierte Zivilprozess in Europa* (Sellier 2013).

[40] Bernhard Windscheid, *Die* Actio *des römischen Civilrechts, vom Standpunkte des heutigen Rechts* (Buddeus 1856) 3: '*nicht die Ordnung der Rechte, sondern die Ordnung der gerichtlich verfolgbaren Ansprüche*'.

[41] ibid: '*Die* Actio *ist nichts Abgeleitetes, sie ist etwas Ursprüngliches und Selbständiges*'.

[42] ibid: '*die Magd des Privatrechts*'.

[43] Windscheid (n 40) 5.

[44] Bernhard Windscheid, *Pandektenrecht*, vol 3 (Buddeus 1873) para 3: '*rechtliche Garantie der Willensmacht des Individuums als Willenssubjekt*'.

[45] August Thon, *Rechtsnorm und subjektives Recht* (Scientia 1864) 147.

[46] '*von der Rechtsordnung dem Einzelnen verliehene Willensmacht*'.

[47] *Inter alia*, see Georg Friedrich Puchta, *Kursus der Institutionen*, vol 1 (Breitkopf & Härtel 1841) para 6.

[48] Rudolf von Jhering, *Geist des römischen Rechts*, vol 3 (Breitkopf & Härtel 1865) para 60: '*rechtlich geschütztes Interesse*'. See Gerhard Wagner, 'Rudolph von Jherings Theorie des subjektiven Rechts und der berechtigenden Reflexwirkung' (1993) 193 AcP 319.

[49] See also Wolf and Neuner (n 1) § 20 para 7.

[50] For this stance, see Hillel Steiner, 'Working Rights' in Kramer, Simmonds and Steiner (n 5) 233ff. For a marked criticism, see Kramer (n 6) 66ff.

By contrast, the interest theory (or benefit theory) argues that a right is unaffected by the precise location of the power to seek enforcement.
To a certain extent, however, the two theories prove to be complementary. Particularly, will theory (or choice theory) accounts for the structural component of rights (which is hinged on the power of enforcement of the rightsholder), and interest theory (or benefit theory) accounts for their functional component (which consists in preserving the vested interest of the rightsholder).
To sum up, a right may be depicted as the power of a person or group of persons to seek enforcement for the preserve of her/its vested interest.

4.2. Classifications of rights

Some rights are **patrimonial**, some others are **non-patrimonial (or extra-patrimonial)**, depending on whether or not they purport to preserve an interest that the rightsholder may lawfully haggle over.

For example, property is a patrimonial right, the right to life is non-patrimonial. The right to receive alimonies or spousal support, despite appearances, is non-patrimonial, because it is awarded for the needs and future maintenance of the recipient spouse.

Patrimonial rights can generally be assigned or waived by their holder (whether in exchange for a consideration or gratuitously); by contrast, the **assignment or waiver** of a non-patrimonial right is generally not permitted by the law.

For example, the right to receive alimony or spousal support is non assignable, at least with regard to alimony not yet accrued.[51]

However, one can consent to the use of some personality rights (like that of image) to someone else, albeit either temporarily or with the right of withdrawal from that consent;[52] therefore, some specific aspects of personality can be licensed (and merchandized) as though they were intangibles.
Patrimonial rights that are alienable are generally also inheritable: at the death of their holder, therefore, they descend to the latter's heirs. **Alienability and inheritability**, however, are distinct characteristics of rights, which, though commonly concomitant, are not necessarily coexistent.

For example, the right of usufruct (see *infra*, ch 10, para 4.2-2), though assignable under certain conditions, terminates at the holder's death.

[51] For US law, see 'Divorce and Separation', 24A *Am Jur 2d*, § 572.
[52] For German law, see Wolf and Neuner (n 1) § 20 para 15. For US law, see 'Privacy', 62A *Am Jur 2d*, § 182.

Non-patrimonial rights, by their nature, do not pass but rather terminate at their holder's death; the same applies to those patrimonial rights that are not alienable.

> For example, human rights are neither assignable nor inheritable.
> The same applies to the right to receive alimony or spousal support, at least with regard to alimony not yet accrued.

On the basis of Roman law, rights have been traditionally divided into two categories: **relative rights (*in personam*)** and **absolute rights (*in rem*)**. The former can be enforced only against a particular person or group of particular persons (see *infra*, ch 10, para 4.2.1); the latter can be enforced against whoever interfere with the rightsholder's possession of an entitlement (see *infra*, ch 10, para 4.2.2). The distinction is well settled also in common law systems, where, however, it does not regard substantive rights as such but the actions that can be brought to enforce them (see also *supra*, ch 10, para 1).[53]

4.2.1. Relative rights (or rights *in personam*)

A right is qualified as relative (or *in personam*) when the action to enforce it can be brought only against one who holds the correlative position of disadvantage, be it a specific person or a group of specific persons.

> The **credit** is typically a relative right. If A holds a credit for a sum of money, it means that B, or C, or both of them owe(s) her that money, and nobody else. Obviously, A can claim her money only from B, or C, or either of them, but not from D or anybody else.

Patrimonial rights *in personam* are credits and power-rights. In common law legal systems, the actions for the recovery of personal property are personal as well.

Someone who holds a **credit** (the creditor) is entitled to claim that another person or group of persons (the debtor/-s), which owe/-s the correlative **debt**, perform/-s an action or an abstention in her interest. The performance owed by the debtor must be of economic nature and, according to a classification stemming from Roman law, can consist in giving something (*dare*), doing something (*facere*), or abstaining from doing something (*non facere*). The legal relation between the creditor and the debtor is called an **obligation**.

An obligation may arise from a contract, from a tort, or from an instance of unjustified enrichment (**sources of obligations**). Actions on contract (*ex contractu*), ie for the enforcement of a contract or to redress its breach, and actions in tort (*ex delicto*), ie for the recovery of damages caused by an injury to person or property, are therefore relative; consequently, judgments on

[53] See 'Actions', 1 *Am Jur 2d*, §§ 287ff.

them will impose solely a personal liability or obligation and do not affect the parties' interest in property (see also *infra*, ch 10, para 4.2.2).

Credits are legal positions that are not final, but which are instrumental to the debtor's performance. Once the debtor has discharged her duty, or the creditor's interest has been otherwise somehow achieved, the correlative credit terminates. For this reason, the assumption that credits are rights has been challenged by some scholars.

Be that as it may, it can be safely assumed that the law applicable to credits is purported to facilitate and accelerate the achievement of the creditor's interest and therefore the termination of her right, particularly through the performance of the debtor's duty.

Following the teachings of Claus-Wilhelm Canaris, which conversely rest on the earlier theories of the latter's mentor Karl Larenz (1903-1993), German scholarship has conceptualized obligations as complex legal relations, in which the correlative positions of credit and debt are surrounded by a vast **bundle of complementary and supplementary duties** imposed upon both parties. These duties are to be drawn from the general principle of good faith.

A **power-right** enables its holder to change someone else's entitlements.[54] The peculiarity of this sort of rights is that the other party's correlative position is (not a duty but) a **liability** (see *supra*, ch 10, para 3).

> The category of power-rights was created by German scholars. Particularly, Ernst Zitelmann (1852-1923), taking as his starting point the right to withdraw from a contract, identified the '*Rechte des rechtlichen Könnens*'.[55] Later on, Konrad Hellwig (1853-1916) redefined the concept as *Gestaltungsrechte*,[56] and finally Hemil Seckel (1864-1924) once again and definitively forged the notion of power-rights.[57] Italian scholarship – especially that of Giuseppe Messina (1877-1946) – also played a crucial role in streamlining the concept of power-rights.[58]

Most power-rights can be used by their holder through a unilateral legal act (see *supra*, ch 9, para 5), whose notice has to be served on the liability-bearer and which, once served, cannot be withdrawn.[59] Some other power-rights, however, can be used only insofar as the rightsholder files a lawsuit.[60]

> For example, under certain conditions, one who has entered a contract by mistake holds a power-right to avoid it. In some jurisdictions, that contract is avoided by the innocent party's serving notice on the other party of a declaration;

[54] See Wolf and Neuner (n 1) § 20 paras 28ff.
[55] Ernst Zitelmann, *Internationales Privatrecht* (Duncker & Humblot 1912) 32.
[56] Konrad Hellwig, *Anspruch und Klagrecht* (Scientia 1967) 2.
[57] Emil Seckel, *Die Gestaltungsrechte des bürgerlichen Rechts* (Deutsche Buchgemeinschaft 1954).
[58] Giuseppe Messina, 'Sui cosiddetti diritti potestativi' in Id, *Scritti giuridici*, vol 5 (Giuffrè 1948).
[59] See Wolf and Neuner (n 1) § 20 para 39.
[60] ibid § 20 para 41 (*Gestaltungsklage*).

in some other jurisdictions, by the innocent party's bringing an action before a court against the other party (see *supra*, ch 9, para 5).

Power-rights as such cannot be generally assigned to someone else.[61]
In common law legal systems, property in everything movable (like goods, chattels and money, as well as notes, bonds and stocks) can be recovered by the owner only by bringing a relative action (*in personam*):[62] in this sense, it is called **personal property** (see also *infra*, ch 10, para 4.2.2).[63]
Non-patrimonial rights *in personam* are mostly established between the members of a family. Of particular importance are the rights and the duties between spouses, as well as between parents and (minor) children.

4.2.2. Absolute rights (or rights *in rem*)

A right is qualified as absolute (or *in rem*) when the action to enforce it can be brought against whoever interferes with the rightsholder's possession of an entitlement. In other terms, an absolute right is accompanied by the **power of its holder to exclude everyone else from interfering** with its use (*ius excludendi alios*).
In this sense, an absolute right may be said to be held **'against the world', or 'against all the others'** (*erga omnes*), since anyone (with the exception of the rightsholder) can be brought within the sway of the duty of non-interference that is correlative to that right.
This definition seems to challenge, however, the very concept of rights as engendering legal relations between two particular persons or groups of particular persons (see *supra*, ch 10, para 1). In order to square absolute rights with legal relations between two specific persons or groups of specific persons, therefore, it has been suggested that an absolute right really consists of **a set of indefinitely numerous rights**, each of which would be held against a specific person. Insofar, they have been defined as **multital rights**, opposed to **paucital rights** like those that are relative.
In the event of interference with the entitlement of the rightsholder, the latter can institute a real action to **determine the status of things and the rights of individuals with respect thereto**.
In **civil law systems**, property in everything tangible, be it movable or immovable, is a right that is absolute and that may be described as an exclusive and potentially unrestricted right to a thing, implying the power to dispose of it in any way and the liberty to use it: it therefore encompasses the complete array of 'can do' positions that can be privately owned. Given that the Latin for 'thing' was *res*, property is therefore classified as a **real right**, in the sense of a right having a thing as its object.

61 ibid § 20 para 43.
62 See 'Actions', 1 *Am Jur 2d*, § 23.
63 See 'Property', 63C *Am Jur 2d*, § 21.

Furthermore, civil law systems traditionally acknowledge a limited number (*numerus clausus*) of real rights other than property:[64] they share the characteristic of being absolute rights encumbering a tangible whose property is owned by someone else (ie the proprietor). Therefore, they are traditionally called **real rights in someone else's property**, a name stemming from Latin ***iura in re aliena***. In most cases, it is the proprietor herself that conveys those rights to one other, who thus acquires their ownership; sometimes, however, they are imposed by statutory provisions, be it automatically or through a judicial decision.

Real rights in someone else's property run with the latter (*ius sequendi*), ie they encumber property also against any successor of the proprietor (whether a purchaser or an heir); if they are in immovables, however, they must be generally recorded, or registered, at that end.

> The real rights in someone else's property are usually subdivided into two subsets: possession rights and security rights.
> Possession rights in someone else's property are those of usufruct and of servitude.
> **Usufruct** is a real right to use a thing belonging to someone else and to enjoy its fruits, the usufructuary being conversely obliged to preserve the substance of that thing for the property owner of it.
> **Servitudes** are real rights that are held by the proprietor of a land (called the 'dominant estate') and encumber another's adjacent land (called the 'servient estate'). These rights may consist in a liberty, privilege, or advantage that the owner of the dominant estate can use on the servient estate: for example, a right of way (ie of passage on a strip of the servient estate).
> Security rights in someone else's property are those of pledge and of hypothec.
> A **pledge** is a lien on movables that are delivered as security for the payment of the debt owed either by the pledgor or by a third person; the pledgee acquires a right of possession on the pledged chattel and, in the event the debt owed to her is not payed, she can sell it without the aid of a court.
> A **hypothec** is a lien on immovables that are conveyed (and recorded or registered) as security for the payment of a debt owed either by the mortgagor or by a third person; the mortgagee acquires no right of possession or control on the hypothecated immovable, but, in the event the debt owed to her remains unpaid, she can sell it on foreclosure.

In **civil law systems**, therefore, property and the other real rights, be they in movables or in immovables, can be recovered against anyone who unlawfully detains the thing or otherwise interferes unlawfully with its possession, since they are absolute rights. Something similar applies to **intellectual property** (in copyright) and **industrial property** (in trademarks, patents, and the like).

In **common law systems**, by contrast, property in movables is personal (see *supra* ch 10, para 4.2.1): therefore, it can be recovered only by bringing a relative action (*in personam*), ie only from one who committed a tort against its

[64] See Francesco Mezzanotte, *La conformazione negoziale delle situazioni di appartenenza.* Numerus clausus, *autonomia privata e diritti sui beni* (Jovene 2015).

owner or who has privity of contract with the latter. Property in immovables ('lands, entitlements, hereditaments'), by contrast, is treated as **real property**, which the owner can recover by bringing an absolute action (*in rem*) against whoever else.[65] The interest in immovable comparable to civil law property is called a **fee simple, or absolute fee**, which is the broadest **freehold estate**. However, it may be encumbered through someone else's interests in real property, which can be recovered by bringing an absolute action as well.

Interests in someone else's immovables are those of **usufruct, easements** (as well as **profits, or profits à prendre**) and **mortgage**. They all present traits comparable to those of their civil law equivalents.
A **leasehold estate** is an interest in full possession of real property, which the landlord conveys to the tenant for a consideration, usually the payment of rent. It is thus created privity of property, as well as privity of contract between the lessor and the lessee.

Absolute non-patrimonial rights *in rem* are the **rights of personality** (see also *supra*, ch 10, para 4.2),[66] which can be classified in the broader genus of **human rights**. Among the rights of personality, particularly noteworthy are those to privacy, image, likeness, and name.

4.3. The doctrine of abuse of rights

In civil law jurisdictions, a **prohibition of abuse of rights** is acknowledged as a general principle,[67] whether or not enshrined in constitutional charters or civil codes. Not rarely, statutory provisions cover just some specific instances of abuse of rights, but courts are inclined to apply a broader prohibition, be it styled as an autonomous principle or as an offshoot of the principle of good faith.[68]

Article 2 (*Acting in Good Faith*) of the **Swiss Civil Code** stipulates that: (1) 'Every person must act in good faith in the exercise of her rights and in the performance of her obligations';[69] (2) 'The manifest abuse of a right is not protected by law'.[70]
Under the heading of 'abuse of rights' (Κατάχρηση δικαιώματος) article 281 of the **Greek Civil Code** (Αστικός Κώδικας) stipulates that: 'The exercise of a right shall be prohibited if such exercise obviously exceeds the limits imposed by

[65] ibid.
[66] Johann Neethling, 'Personality Rights' in Jan M Smits (ed), *Elgar Encyclopedia of Comparative Law* (2nd edn, Elgar 2012) 661.
[67] Mario Rotondi (ed), *L'abus de droit, l'abuso del diritto, the abuse of rights, el abuso del derecho, der Rechtsmissbrauch* (CEDAM 1979).
[68] Filippo Ranieri, 'Bonne foi et exercise du droit dans la tradition de droit civil' (1998) 4 Revue international du droit comparé 1055.
[69] '*Chacun est tenu d'exercer ses droits et d'exécuter ses obligations selon les règles de la bonne foi*'.
[70] '*L'abus manifeste d'un droit n'est pas protégé par la loi*'.

good faith or by morality or by the social or economic purpose of the right'.[71] Similarly, art. 334 (*Abuso do direito*) of the **Portuguese Código Civil** stipulates that: 'The exercise of a right is unlawful insofar as the rightsholder evidently infringes the limits set out by good faith, by morality or by the social or economic purpose of her right'.[72]

Since 1974, also the **Spanish Código Civil** stipulates that: '1. Rights shall be exercised accordingly to the requirements of good faith. 2. The law will not protect the abuse of a right or its bringing against the societal interest. Any action or abstention that, having regard to their author's intention, to their object and to the circumstances surrounding them, evidently exceed the normal limits of a right's exercise, thus harming a third person, will be remedied through the award of the resulting damages and the application of the judicial and administrative sanctions aimed at their forbearance' (art. 7).[73]

Even if a general principle prohibiting abuse of rights is unknown to common law jurisdictions, the latter deploy a number of endogenous doctrines to afford similar legal responses to relevant cases, which, therefore, are treated not so differently as done in civil law jurisdictions. It may ultimately be said that, although the legal discourse on the cases here concerned is couched in markedly different terms within the two legal traditions, they eventually show a rather similar attitude towards them.

The civilian prohibition traditionally applies when a right is maliciously exercised with the sole purpose of harming or bothering someone else (**chicane**); the latter can then seek from a court damages and/or an injunction compelling the rightsholder to refrain from such misconduct. Historically, this prohibition was introduced in Roman law to redress malevolent actions undertaken by the proprietor of a land in spite of her neighbors (so-called *aemulatio*).[74] This explains why, in some civil codifications (like in the Italian *Codice civile*), it is still encapsulated in a provision specifically pertaining to property as such;[75] in others (like in the German BGB), it is couched in more general terms. At any rate, its requirements remain extremely strict, and therefore, it finds application only seldom.

[71] Ἄρθρο 281 Αστικός Κώδικας (Κατάχρηση δικαιώματος): 'Η άσκηση του δικαιώματος απαγορεύεται αν υπερβαίνει προφανώς τα όρια που επιβάλλουν η καλή πίστη ή τα χρηστά ήθη ή ο κοινωνικός ή οικονομικός σκοπός του δικαιώματος'. See Penelope Agallopoulou, *Basic Concepts of Greek Civil Law* (Youlika Kotsovolou Masry tr and ed, Sakkoulas-Stämpfli-Bruylant 2005) 83ff.

[72] '*É ilegítimo o exercício de um direito, quando o titular exceda manifestamente os limites impostos pela boa fé, pelos bons costumes ou pelo fim social ou económico desse direito*'.

[73] '*1. Los derechos deberán ejercitarse conforme a las exigencias de la buena fe. 2. La Ley no ampara el abuso del derecho o el ejercicio antisocial del mismo. Todo acto u omisión que por la intención de su autor, por su objeto o por las circunstancias en que se realice sobrepase manifiestamente los límites normales del ejercicio de un derecho, con daño para tercero, dará lugar a la correspondiente indemnización y a la adopción de las medidas judiciales o administrativas que impidan la persistencia en el abuso*'.

[74] James Gordley, 'The Abuse of Rights in the Civil Law Tradition' in Rita de la Feria and Stefan Vogenauer (eds), *Prohibition of Abuses of Law: A New General Principle of EU Law?* (Hart 2011) 33f.

[75] Mario Rotondi, *L'abuso del diritto:* Aemulatio (CEDAM 1979).

Under **Italian law**, article 833 cc ('Prohibition of chicane') stipulates that: 'The proprietor is prohibited from undertaking actions that are exclusively aimed at harming or bothering someone else'.[76]
Although **French law** does not provide for a similar prohibition, a judgment passed by the Court of Appeal of Colmar in 1855 held that a house owner could not build a false chimney for the sole purpose of blocking his neighbor.[77] This ruling sparked a most vivid debate among French jurists of the time.[78] It was saluted by René Demogue and Louis Josserand as paving the way (together with other contemporary decisions by French courts) for a theory of abuse of rights, which was allegedly in line with an anti-formalistic conception of rights.[79] Albeit gainsaid by other notable French jurists like Marcel Planiol (see *supra*, ch 4, para 3.1.1) and Georges Ripert (see *supra*, ch 7, para 1),[80] this account of French judge-made law passed into **German law** in the 1930s, particularly via a book authored by Wolfgang Siebert.[81] It eventually prompted the provision of § 226 BGB (Prohibition of chicane), stipulating that '[t]he use of a right is not permitted when it can only have the purpose to cause harm to another'.[82]

Although common law jurisdictions do not provide for a similar doctrine, they are acquainted with a variety of **malice rules** and **reasonableness tests**, which can work as 'functional equivalents' of the abuse of rights doctrine (at least in fields like water law, nuisance, tortious interference with contractual relations, labor law), as it has been thoroughly demonstrated with regard to American law.[83]
In a different set of cases, the civilian prohibition of abuse of rights serves primarily to ground a defense against the rightsholder's claim, to the extent that its bringing is tainted with **immorality** (in a broad sense),[84] or otherwise it proves to be **inequitable**. These doctrines are rooted in Roman law, too,[85] and were heralded by the institution of *exceptio doli generalis* that was coined by medieval jurists of continental Europe.[86]

After its reception by the vast majority of the Pandectists, the *exceptio doli generalis* was legitimized under **German law** by § 242 BGB ('Performance

[76] 'Il proprietario non può fare atti i quali non abbiano altro scopo che quello di nuocere o recare molestia ad altri'.
[77] Colmar, 2 May 1855, Recueil Dalloz 1856.II.9, 10.
[78] For further references, see Gordley (n 74) 36ff.
[79] René Demogue, *Traité des obligations en général*, vol 4 (Rousseau 1924) 679; Louis Josserand, *De l'esprit des droits et de leur relativité: théorie dite de l'abus des droits* (2nd edn, Dalloz 1939) 245.
[80] Marcel Planiol and Georges Ripert, *Traité pratique de droit civil français*, vol 6 (LGDJ 1930) 573; Georges Ripert, *La règle morale dans les obligations civiles* (3rd edn, LGDJ 1935) 90.
[81] Wolfgang Siebert, *Verwirkung und Unzulässigkeit der Rechtsausübung* (Elwert 1934).
[82] *'Die Ausübung eines Rechts ist unzulässig, wenn sie nur den Zweck haben kann, einem anderen Schaden zuzufügen'*.
[83] Anna di Robilant, 'Abuse of Rights: The continental drug and the common law' (2010) 61 Hastings LJ 687.
[84] See Wolf and Neuner (n 1) § 20 para 82ff.
[85] Gordley (n 74) 34ff.
[86] Filippo Ranieri, *Europäisches Obligationenrecht. Ein Handbuch mit Texten und Materialien* (3rd edn, Springer 2009) 1801ff.

according to good faith'), pursuant to which: 'The debtor is bound to perform accordingly to the requirements of good faith regarding legal intercourse'.[87] Furthermore, § 826 BGB ('Intentional harming contravening morality') stipulates that: 'Who intentionally harms someone else through an action that is contrary to morality, is liable for damages'.[88]

In common law jurisdictions, the coverage of such cases may be afforded by the **doctrine of clean hands**,[89] which provides a defense against the bringing of a claim by someone who had previously behaved in a way that, albeit not illegal, may be deemed to be tricky, iniquitous or unconscionable.[90] Due to its historical origins, this defense can bar only equitable actions, like those pertaining to fiduciary law,[91] as well as to intellectual property law;[92] however, American courts seem increasingly prone to permit its being pleaded also against legal actions.[93] Furthermore, the doctrine of clean hands is settled in international law as well.[94]

The UKSC held that in 'some cases of artificial tax avoidance the court might think it right to refuse relief [...] on ground of public policy [because] artificial tax avoidance is a social evil which put an unfair burden on the shoulders of those who do not adopt such measures'.[95]

In civil law jurisdictions, furthermore, the exercise of a right is deemed to be abusive when it appears to be inconsistent with, or contradictory to, the rightsholder's previous behavior. A defense is then granted insofar as the rightsholder's previous behavior has been conducive to the defendant's reasonable reliance that is now frustrated or disregarded by the rightsholder herself. Not rarely, courts ground their ruling on this sort of cases by making reference to the infringement of the rightsholder's duty of ***venire contra factum proprium***.[96]

[87] *'Der Schuldner ist verpflichtet, die Leistung so zu bewirken, wie Treu und Glauben mit Rücksicht auf die Verkehrssitte es erfordern'*.
[88] *'Wer in einer gegen die guten Sitten verstoßenden Weise einem anderen vorsätzlich Schaden zufügt, ist dem anderen zum Ersatz des Schadens verpflichtet'*. See Wolf and Neuner (n 1) § 20 para 79f.
[89] The terminology derives from the maxim of equity according to which 'he who comes to equity must have clean hands'. See also *supra*, ch 2, para 4.2; ch 6, para 3.
[90] *Dering v Earl of Winchelsea* (1787) 1 Cox 318, 319; 29 ER 1184 (Eyre LCB). See Nicholas J McBride, 'The Future of Clean Hands' in Paul S Davies, Simon Douglas and James Goudkamp, *Defences in Equity* (Hart 2008) 267ff.
[91] Samuel L Bray, 'Fiduciary Remedies' in Evan J Criddle, Paul B Miller and Robert H Sitkoff (eds), *The Oxford Handbook of Fiduciary Law* (OUP 2019) 465.
[92] T Leigh Anenson, *Judging Equity. The Fusion of Unclean Hands in US Law* (CUP 2018) 12ff; Terence P Ross, 'Remedies' in Rochelle Dreyfus and Justine Pila (eds), *The Oxford Handbook of Intellectual Property Law* (OUP 2017-2018) 680f.
[93] Anenson (n 92) ibid.
[94] Stephen M Schwebel, 'Clean hands, principle' in Id, *Justice in International Law: Further Selected Writings* (CUP 2011) 297ff.
[95] *Pitt v Holt* [2013] UKSC 26, [2013] 2 AC 108.
[96] For German law, see Wolf and Neuner (n 1) § 20 paras 75, 88.

> For example, a seller, whose false statements induce the buyer to believe that what she is purchasing has a business use, is prevented from pleading protection under consumer law.[97]
> Another example: after having benefitted from an insurance for many years, a policyholder is prevented from filing a claim that the contract is void.[98]
> Under German law, some rulings on cases of *venire contra factum proprium* are conceptualized through the doctrine of ***Verwirkung***,[99] ie when the rightsholder's bringing of a claim is so long delayed that the defendant believed (or could have believed) that the right has terminated in the meanwhile or was not going to be asserted any longer.[100]
> For example, consider a case where the facilities of a hotel have been rented for twenty years in consideration of a proportion of the revenues of the business but with a minimum floor of € 1.250,00 per month. For many years, the tenant had paid the proportionate fee, though it amounted to less than € 1.2500; the landlord had never raised any objection. Later on, however, the landlord suddenly maintained that the tenant should have been paying the minimum fee of € 1.250,00 per month and claimed for the balance. The claim for arrears accrued until then was dismissed by the BGH.[101]
> Conversely, the affirmative behavior of one party that lasts or recurs over time can generate the other party's reasonable reliance upon a (in fact non-existing) right (***Erwirkung***).[102]
> For example, the payment of a rent or a salary higher than that due to the recipient, provided that it is regularly performed over a considerable span of time, cannot be subsequently recovered by the employer or the lessee, respectively.[103]
> This does not mean that they are obliged to make such payment in the future.

In Anglo-American jurisdictions, such cases may be covered by the **doctrine of estoppel**, which, albeit of equitable origin, has been developed by common law courts.[104] According to a concise description, this doctrine commands that 'when a man, by his words or conduct, has led another to believe in a particular state of affairs, he will not be allowed to go back on it when it would be unjust or inequitable for him to do so'.[105] Provided that someone else has been induced by the rightsholder to trust in some of her statements or actions, the latter is prevented from insisting on her right, insofar as by doing so she

[97] BGH NJW 2005, 1045ff.
[98] BGH NJW 2014, 2723ff.
[99] For German law, see Wolf and Neuner (n 1) § 20 para 89ff. For a comparative analysis, see Filippo Ranieri, *Rinuncia tacita e* Verwirkung (CEDAM 1971); Salvatore Patti, *Profili della tolleranza nel diritto privato* (Jovene 1978); Id, 'Verwirkung', *Digesto delle discipline privatistiche, Sezione civile*, vol 19 (Utet 1999) 722ff; Antoni Vaquer, '*Verwirkung* versus Laches: A Tale of Two Legal Transplants' (2006) 21 Tulane European & Civil Law Forum 61ff; Salvatore Patti, *Tempo, prescrizione e* Verwirkung (Mucchi 2020).
[100] BGH NJW 2006, 219; BGH NJW 2008, 2254; BGH NJW 2016, 473.
[101] BGH JZ 1965, 682.
[102] Medicus and Petersen (n 1) paras 144f.
[103] BGH DB 1986, 1118.
[104] Elizabeth Cooke, *The Modern Law of Estoppel* (OUP 2000) 16ff. For US law, 'Estoppel and Waiver', 28 *Am Jur 2d*; 'Estoppel and Waiver', 31 *CJS*.
[105] Denning MR in *Moorgate Mercantile Co. Ltd v Twitchings* [1976] 1 QB 225, CA, at 241.

would deny or go back on what she said or did, and the defendant would thus suffer detriment in reliance.

For example, if a bank pays money into one of its clients' account by mistake, and reassures her that that money was hers, thus inducing her to spend it, that bank can be estopped from seeking restitution of the mistaken payment.[106]
If the parties to a commercial deal agree that a certain document will be treated in a certain way and they go ahead with the deal on that basis, they may have to abide by that agreement if the construction of the document is disputed later.[107]
If a landlord reassured her tenant that 'I will not insist that you pay for the roof repairs, even though your lease obliges you to do so', the former can then be estopped from demanding payment.[108]
Specific instances of estoppel (by so-called acquiescence) may be absorbed in the equitable defense of **laches**,[109] ie when a rightsholder's standing by is so unreasonably long that it induces the other party to believe that that right will not be asserted any more (the wrong will be consented to, etc.).[110]

The prohibition of abuse of rights has played a major role in the application of **EU law**, eventually amounting to one of its general principles. Since 1974,[111] the ECJ has been dealing with abuse of rights (or, alternatively, with abuse of law) in order to tackle two different kinds of issues:[112] 1) preventing nationals from attempting, under cover of the fundamental freedoms granted by the Treaties, to circumvent their national legislation fraudulently (abusive rule avoidance); 2) preventing individuals from improperly taking advantage of provisions of EU law (abusive rule appropriation).[113] Cases of both kinds most frequently involve **U-turn transactions**, whereby persons or goods based in one Member State (home state) cross the border to another Member State (host state) and then immediately return to the home state or carry out activities there;[114] when these initiatives prove to be **artificial arrangements**,[115]

[106] *Lloyd's Bank Ltd v Brooks* (1950) 6 Legal Decisions Affecting Bankers 161; contrast *United Overseas Bank Ltd v Jiwani* [1977] 1 All ER 733. On this issue, see Paul Key, 'Excising Estoppel by Representation as a Defence to Restitution' (1995) 54 Cambridge LJ 525.
[107] *Amalgamated Investments & Property Co Ltd (In Liquidation) v Texas Commerce International Bank Ltd* [1982] 1 QB 84.
[108] *Birkom Investments Ltd v Carr* [1979] 1 QB 467, CA. See also *Central London Property Trust Ltd v High Trees House Ltd* [1947] KB 130.
[109] This French legal word ('*lachesse*') stands for 'remissness', 'slackness'; see 'Laches', *Black's Law Dictionary* (11th edn 2019). For a comparative analysis, see Vaquer (n 99) 51ff.
[110] Cooke (n 104) 66. For intellectual property law, see Ross (n 92) 680f.
[111] Case 33/74 *Van Binsbergen v Bestuur van de Bedrijfsvereniging voor de Metaalnijverheid* [1974] ECR 1299.
[112] Case C-212/97 *Centros Ltd v Erhvervs- og Selskabsstyr* [1999] ECR I-01459 (on this case, see also *supra*, ch 8, para 1.5.1; *infra*, ch 11, para 1.2.1.1).
[113] For an in-depth account of ECJ-made law and its conceptualization, see the essays collected in de la Feria and Vogenauer (eds) (n 74). For an overall discussion of abuse of rights under EC law, see Stefan Vogenauer, 'The Prohibition of Abuse of Law: An Emerging General Principle of EU Law' in de la Feria and Vogenauer (eds) (n 74) 521ff.
[114] Vogenauer (n 113) 527.
[115] Case C-110/99 *Emsland-Stärke GmbH v Hauptzollamt Hamburg-Jonas* [2000] ECR I-11569.

ie aimed at the sole purpose of creating the right claimed, they can amount to abusive practices.

For example, a television broadcaster is entirely owned by Dutch nationals, its employees come mostly from the Netherlands, its programs are made in the Netherlands and transmitted in the same country. However, the entity is established in Luxembourg for the sole purpose of escaping Dutch legislation that, in order to maintain the pluralistic and public service content of television programs, imposes certain restrictions on domestic broadcasters.[116]
A German company exported several consignments of a potato-based product to Switzerland and thus received an export refund. However, the German customs authorities, after inquiries, revealed that immediately after their release for home use in Switzerland the exported consignments in question were transported – unaltered and by the same means of transport – back to Germany. Hence, an export refund had been gained abusively by the German company.[117]

One of the fields where the prohibition of abuse of rights found application most frequently in ECJ-made law is that of **tax law**, both in cases of abusive rule avoidance and abusive rule appropriation.[118] Also in other areas of law, the prohibition of abuse of rights has been applied by the ECJ almost exclusively to vertical relationships of a private person with a Member State or the EU itself; only very rarely did it find application in horizontal relationships between private persons.[119] It is therefore contended that the concept of abuse of rights is here completely different than that developed in national jurisdictions, particularly of civil law.[120]

In the cases of abusive rule avoidance, the talk should perhaps be more of **abuse of law** than of abuse of rights. In fact, fraudulent circumvention of national law has to do not so much with the abusive exercise of subjective rights but with what the civilian tradition has depicted as a *fraus legi facta*, ie a 'fraud against statutory provisions' (*fraude à la loi*, *frode alla legge*).[121]

From 1990 onwards, prohibitions of specific kinds of abuse began to be enacted in particular areas of EU law.[122] Eventually, a general prohibition of abuse of rights was provided for by **article 54 CFR**, which stipulates that:

[116] Case C-23/93 *TV10 SA v Commissariaat voor de Media* [1994] ECR I-4795.
[117] Case C-110/99 *Emsland-Stärke GmbH v Hauptzollamt Hamburg-Jonas* [2000] ECR I-11569.
[118] Case C-255/02 *Halifax PLC, Leeds Permanent Development Services Ltd, County Wide Property Investments Ltd v Commissioners of Customs & Excise* [2006] ECR I-1609.
[119] One of the most important cases is C-367/96 *Alexandros Kefalas* et alii *v Elliniko Dimosio and Organismos Oikonomikis Anasygkrotisis Epicheiriseon* [1998] ECR I-2843, where a number of shareholders successfully challenged the application of a Greek statute empowering a public authority to order an increase in the capital of an undertaking in difficulties. In doing so, they relied on a European directive which conferred to them the right to decide upon any capital increase in a general meeting. They were not considered to have undertaken an abusive practice.
[120] Gordley (n 74) 34ff.
[121] Vogenauer (n 113) 555f.
[122] ibid 522f.

'Nothing in this Charter shall be interpreted as implying any right to engage in any activity or to perform any act aimed at the destruction of any of the rights and freedoms recognized in this Charter or at their limitation to a greater extent than is provided for herein'. A similar provision had been already laid down in **article 17 ECHR**.

5. DELAYED EXERCISE OF RIGHTS

For a number of reasons, the law subjects the exercise of rights to several constraints of time, both on the substantive level (ie the legal relations with the holder of the correlative position of 'shall/must do' or 'not do') and on the procedural level (ie the lawsuits and the proceedings thus taken).
In the field of private law, the most important time constraints on the exercise of rights are: first, prescription and statutes of limitations (see *infra*, ch 10, para 5.1); secondly, statutes of repose and nonclaim statutes (see *infra*, ch 10, para 5.2).
Other time constraints are overwhelmingly of procedural character and, also for this reason, will not be expanded upon in this book.

5.1. Prescription and statutes of limitations

In **civil law systems**, most patrimonial rights (safe property) have to be enforced within certain time periods, which are set out by the law: when those time periods run out, the rights that have not been pursued become unenforceable (prescription). In **common law systems** such time-based limitations of enforcement of rights do not belong to the common law, but are set out through apposite statutory provisions (statutes of limitations);[123] they do not affect substantial rights as such, be they absolute or relative, but the actions to enforce them, and they are therefore considered a procedural mechanism.[124]

In civil law systems, the bulk of the provisions on prescription is set out by civil codes, although special provisions are not rarely contained in other pieces of legislation. Remarkably, at the outset of the new millennium, first the BGB and then the *Code civile* have been intensively reformed as to prescription and brought in line with European law, particularly as provided for by the PECL (see *supra*, ch 8, para 2.2).[125]

[123] For a comparative perspective, see the essays collected in Patrick Jourdain and Patrick Wéry (eds), *La prescription extinctive: études de droit comparé* (Bruylant 2010); Harry Dondorp, David Ibbetson and Elio JH Schrage (eds), *Limitation and Prescription. A Comparative Legal History* (Duncker&Humblot 2019); Israel Gilead and Bjarte Askeland (eds), *Prescription in Tort Law. Analytical and Comparative Perspectives* (Intersentia 2020).
[124] 'Limitation of actions', 51 *Am J 2nd*, §§ 11, 20.
[125] Reinhard Zimmermann, *Comparative Foundations of a European Law of Set-Off and Prescription* (CUP 2002) 62ff; Id, *The New German Law of Obligations: Historical and comparative perspectives* (OUP 2005) 122ff; Oliver Remien (ed), *Verjährungsrecht in Eu-*

In **Germany**, the provisions on prescription set forth by the BGB were rewritten on occasion of the grand reform of the law of obligation enacted in 2001 (*Modernisierung des Schuldrechts*),[126] and they were subsequently adjusted through a piece of legislation enacted in 2004 (*Gesetz zur Anpassung von Verjährungsvorschriften an das Gesetz zur Modernisierung des Schuldrechts*) (see *supra*, ch 4, para 3.1.2). Moreover, they were amended again in 2008 with regard to the contract of insurance (*Versicherungsvertragsgesetz*).
In **France**, the *Code civil*'s provisions on prescription were amended in 2008,[127] and rewritten again in the framework of the overall reform of the law of contract and obligations that was passed between 2016 and 2018 (see *supra*, ch 4, para 3.1.1).
In **Italy**, the civil code provisions have thus far not been reformed as a whole;[128] however, some proposals have recently begun to be discussed.[129]
In common law systems, the **UK** enacted the Limitation Act 1964, which was subsequently amended and eventually replaced by the Limitation Act 1980.[130]
In the **US**, statutes of limitations may be set out both in federal and in state legislation.[131]

The **objective of prescription** may be acknowledged in finality, certainty, and predictability of legal positions of disadvantage, above all of duties.[132] Lawsuits are time-barred, particularly, because such limitation ensures that the search for the truth is not impaired by stale evidence or loss of evidence.[133] **Non-patrimonial rights** are generally not subject to prescription, be they absolute (personality rights) (see *supra*, ch 10, para 4.2.2) or relative (like the right to receive alimony or spousal support, until they are accrued) (see *supra*, ch 10, para 4.2.1).[134] In civil law systems, **property** is not time-limited

ropa – zwischen Bewährung und Reform (Mohr Siebeck 2011); Reinhard Zimmermann, 'Prescription' in Niels Jansen and Reinhard Zimmermann (eds), *Commentaries on European Contract Laws* (OUP 2018) 1823ff.

126 Reinhard Zimmermann, '*Ut sit finis litium*. Grundlinien eines modernen Verjährungsrechts auf rechtsvergleichender Grundlage' [2000] JZ 853ff; Id, 'Das neue deutsche Verjährungsrecht – ein Vorbild für Europa?' in Peter Schlechtriem (ed), *Wandlungen des Schuldrechts* (Nomos 2002) 53ff; Heinz-P Mansel, 'Die Reform des Verjährungsrechts' in Wolfgang Ernst and Reinhard Zimmermann (eds), *Zivilrechtswissenschaft und Schuldrechtsreform* (Mohr Siebeck 2001) 351ff; Dirk Looschelders, 'Verjährungsbeginn und -frist im subjektiv-objektiven System sowie die Wirkung von Treu und Glauben' in Remien (ed) (n 125) 181ff.

127 Loi 17 juin 2008, n 2008-131. See David Deroussin, 'Le droit français de la prescription depuis 1804, ou l'impossible simplicité' in Dondorp, Ibbetson and Schrage (eds) (n 123) 459ff; François-X Licari, 'Le nouveau droit français de la prescription extinctive à la lumière d'expériences étrangères récentes ou en gestation (Louisiane, Allemagne, Israël)' [2009] RID comp 740ff; Philippe Pierre e Philippe Casson (eds), *La réforme de la prescription en matière civile* (Dalloz 2010).

128 Salvatore Patti, *Possesso e prescrizione* (CEDAM 2010).

129 Geo Magri, *La prescrizione. Ricodificazione degli ordinamenti giuridici europei e prospettive di modernizzazione del diritto italiano* (ESI 2019).

130 See Andrew Mc Gee, *Limitation Periods* (8th ed, Sweet&Maxwell 2018; first supplement, 2020).

131 'Limitations of Actions', 54 *CJS*, § 10; 'Limitation of actions', 51 *Am J 2nd*, §§ 26ff.

132 For German law, see Wolf and Neuner (n 1) § 22 para 1.

133 For German law, see Wolf and Neuner (n 1) § 22 para 1. For US law, see 'Limitation of actions', 51 *Am J 2nd*, §§ 7, 9.

134 For German law, see § 194(2) BGB. For Italian law, see art 2934(2) cc.

as well;[135] however, if someone else takes possession that is adverse to the proprietor and, without interruption by the latter, that possession continues for the time period set out by the law, the former proprietor's ownership is subject to forfeiture, and the former possessor may thus become the new owner of property or of a real right of possession, like that of usufruct or of servitude (**acquisitive prescription**).[136]

> Under **German law**, it is explicitly set forth that it is claims (*Ansprüche*) that are subject to time limitation (§ 194(2) BGB),[137] according to Windscheid's theory on rights (see *supra*, ch 10, para 4.1). Differently than under French law and Italian law,[138] this provision implies that, on one hand, not only property but also real rights in someone else's property are not time-barred; on the other hand, that all claims for the recovery of property (and of other real rights) are subject to time limitations (§ 197(1)(3) BGB).[139]

Prescription cannot be raised by courts on their own motion but is to be pleaded as an **affirmative defense** by one who is sued by the rightsholder;[140] if she does not assert it promptly, in most legal systems prescription is subject to forfeiture.[141] Furthermore, the defendant is prevented from invoking prescription when she has misrepresented the truth or otherwise behaved dishonestly towards the rightsholder, particularly by unduly delaying the latter's commencement of an action.

> In **civil law jurisdictions**, such conduct or misrepresentation detrimental to the rightsholder may be considered abusive (see *supra*, ch 10, para 4.3), insofar as it infringes the principle of good faith.[142] This is the case when the rightsholder is induced in error as to the length of prescription,[143] or she is otherwise prevented from a timely lawsuit.[144]
> In **common law jurisdictions**, similar responses are construed on the basis of the doctrine of estoppel (see *supra*, ch 10, para 4.3).[145] In these sort of cases, UK law extends the limitation period through statutory provisions (see also *infra*, ch 10, para 5.1).[146]

[135] For French law, see art 2227 *Code civil*. For Italian law, see art. 948(3) cc, pursuant to which the action for the recovery of property is not time limited.
[136] For French law, see arts 2255ff *Code civil*. For German law, see §§ 937ff BGB. For Italian law, see arts 1158ff cc. For UK law, see *JA Pye (Oxford) Ltd and Another v Graham and Another* [2003] 1AC 419.
[137] See § 194(1) BGB.
[138] Magri (n 129) 52ff.
[139] See Wolf and Neuner (n 1) § 22 para 3.
[140] For French law, see art 2247 *Code civil*. For German law, see § 214(1) BGB. For Italian law, see art. 2938 cc. For US law, see 'Limitation of actions', 51 *Am J 2nd*, § 16.
[141] Cf however art 2248 *Code civil*.
[142] For German law, see Wolf and Neuner (n 1) § 22 para 12; Medicus and Petersen (n 132) para 125.
[143] BGH NJW 2008, 2776ff.
[144] BGH NJW 2002, 3110ff.
[145] For US law, see 'Limitation of Actions', 51 *Am Jur 2d*, § 283ff.
[146] Limitation Act 1980, ss 32-32A.

Prescription can be **waived** but not for the future.[147] At any rate, the debtor who, despite prescription of the creditor's right, freely discharges her obligation, cannot subsequently seek restitution of such payment.[148]

The **length of the limitation period** is specifically set out though the relevant statutory provisions and may vary for each type of right. By and large, time limits set out for real rights (or actions to enforce them) are considerably longer than those set out for obligations.

Civil codes generally set forth an **'ordinary' time limit**,[149] which is to apply to any right, unless otherwise settled in specific provisions of the codes themselves or in other pieces of legislations.

Albeit with some restrictions (for example, for purposes of consumer protection), in most legal systems the parties to a legal relation can **agree to shorten or to lengthen the limitation period** in a reasonable manner, as well as to derogate from the norms on its suspension and interruption as set out in statutory provisions.[150]

The limitation period begins to run from the day when (***dies a quo***) an issue of enforcement of the relevant right arises,[151] because either the correlative duty is infringed by the counterparty (eg breach of contract) or someone else interferes with the enjoyment of that right (eg adverse possession).

In common law jurisdictions, it is held that the limitation period begins to run only when a plaintiff knows, or should know through the exercise of due diligence, that a cause of action might exist; in other terms, the start of that period is postponed until the plaintiff discovers, or has reason to discover, the cause of action (**discovery rule**).[152] By contrast, the civilian tradition has traditionally held that, even if excusable, the **ignorance of the rightsholder** that a cause of action had accrued cannot generally delay the running of prescription; this rule, however, has been increasingly challenged by courts, particularly with regard to litigation for malpractice by doctors or, to a lesser extent, by other professionals (like notaries public). Since 2000, furthermore, an increasing number of civil code provisions began to stipulate that, at least when the time period set out by the law is short, the running of prescription is conditional upon the awareness of the rightsholder that her right was breached or she was the victim of a tort. In

147 For French law, see arts 2250ff *Code civil*. For German law, see § 214(1) BGB. For Italian law, see art 2937 cc. For US law, see 'Limitation of Actions', 51 *Am Jur 2d*, §§ 345ff.

148 For French law, see art 2249 *Code civil*. For German law, see § 214(2) BGB. For Italian law, see art 2940 cc.

149 For German law, see § 199 BGB. For Italian law, see art 2946 cc.

150 For French law, see art 2254 *Code civil*. For German law, see § 202 BGB. For US law, see 'Limitation of actions', 51 *Am J 2nd*, §§ 79ff. For Italian law, however, cf art 2936 cc, according to which, since all norms governing prescription are mandatory, any agreement aimed at derogating from them is void.

151 For Italian law, see art 2935 cc.

152 For US law, see 'Limitation of Actions', 51 *Am Jur 2d*, §§ 158ff. For UK law, see Limitation Act 1980, ss 11ff.

case such awareness is lacking, prescription runs all the same, but a longer time period is set out by the law.[153]

Prescription is subject to **tolling** when a statutory provision stipulates that, for some reason, its start is delayed until some event takes place or that its running is suspended (**extension of period**).[154] When prescription undergoes **interruption**, instead, the time period starts running anew (**renewal of period**).

For example, prescription is generally **tolled** in a case of minority or mental illness of the rightsholder, until she attains (again) her capacity to act,[155] or a legal representative is appointed to act on her behalf (see *infra*, ch 11, para 2.1);[156] similarly, it does not run against a decedent until the appointment of her administrator or the acceptance of the succession by the heirs;[157] neither does it run where the existence of a right has been fraudulently concealed.[158] Prescription is tolled also between spouses or between parents and children;[159] the same applies insofar as negotiations or mediation are ongoing between the parties,[160] or during the litigation or arbitration proceeding taken by the rightsholders.[161]

Prescription is **interrupted** when the rightsholder claims for enforcement of her right,[162] or when the counterparty acknowledges that right.[163]

Under French law, the reforms of 2008 and 2016 set forth that, despite any suspension or interruption, prescription cannot generally exceed twenty years from the birth of a right (so-called **délai butoir**),[164] unless differently settled.

[153] For German law, see § 199 BGB. For UK law, see also Limitation Act 1980, s 14.

[154] In common law systems, tolling can be not only statutory but also equitable, ie allowed by a court beyond the statute of limitations. Equitable tolling is treated, however, as a narrow doctrine which must be applied sparingly; see 'Limitation of Actions', 51 *Am Jur 2d*, §§ 153ff.

[155] For UK law, see Limitation Act 1980, s 28. For US law, see 'Limitation of Actions', 51 *Am Jur 2d*, §§ 202ff.

[156] For German law, see § 210 BGB. For French law, see art 2235 *Code civil*. For Italian law, see art 2942(1) cc.

[157] For German law, see § 211 BGB. For French law, art 2237 *Code civil*. For UK law, see Limitation Act 1980, s 11(5). For US law, see 'Limitation of Actions', 51 *Am Jur 2d*, §§ 129, 219.

[158] For Italian law, see art 2941(8) cc. For US law, see 'Limitation of Actions', 51 *Am Jur 2d*, §§ 162ff.

[159] For German law, see § 207 BGB. For French law, see art 2236 *Code civil*. For Italian law, see art 2941 cc.

[160] For German law, see § 203 BGB. For UK law, see Limitation Act 1980, ss 33A-33B.

[161] For French law, see art 2242 *Code civil*. For German law, see § 204 BGB. For Italian law, see art 2945 (2) cc.

[162] For German law, see § 212(1)(2) BGB. For French law, see art 2241 *Code civil*. For Italian law, see art 2943 cc.

[163] For German law, see § 212(1)(1) BGB. For French law, see art 2240 *Code civil*. For Italian law, see art 2944 cc. For UK law, see Limitation Act 1980, s 29ff. For US law, see 'Limitation of Actions', 51 *Am Jur 2d*, § 282ff.

[164] See art 2232 *Code civil*.

5.2. Statutes of repose and nonclaim statutes

Statutes of repose **extinguish** a right because of its prolonged non-use, whether or not an issue of enforcement has arisen in the meanwhile.[165] Unlike prescription (or statutes of limitations),[166] therefore, statutes of repose run irrespectively of any wrong sustained by its holder.[167] This explains the reason why statutes of repose may apply not only to claims but also to other sorts of rights, particularly power-rights (see *supra*, ch 10, para 4.2.1).

> For example, the period of 14 days within which a consumer can withdraw from a distance or off-premises contract under EU law (see *supra*, ch 10, para 3) is a statute of repose.

Nevertheless, like prescription (or statutes of limitations) (see *supra*, ch 10, para 5.1), in most legal systems statutes of repose are **affirmative defenses** subject to forfeiture if not asserted promptly.[168]
Time periods of statutes of repose tend to be significantly shorter than those of statutes of limitations.
Parties are generally allowed not only to **derogate** from statutes of repose,[169] but also to subject by agreement their mutual rights to a period of repose not provided for by any statutory provision, on the condition that it does not make their exercise unreasonably difficult.[170]
Statutes of repose cannot be **tolled**, nor can they be **interrupted**.[171] The only way for the rightsholder to eschew the forfeiture of her right, in case the latter is not acknowledged by the counterpart,[172] is bringing it before the period of repose has expired. Statutes of repose cannot be waived either.[173]
In most cases, statutes of repose are aimed at immunizing the wrongdoer from long-term liability, putting a time bar on potential litigation (**nonclaim statutes**);[174] in doing so, they are frequently combined with prescription of any claim arisen in the meanwhile.[175] This statutory combination is frequently pro-

[165] 'Limitations of Actions', 54 *CJS*, §§ 27-28; 'Limitation of actions', 51 *Am J 2nd*, §§ 24, 87.
[166] Heinz-P Mansel and Christine Budzikiewicz, *Das neue Verjährungsrecht* (Deutscher Anwaltverlag 2002) 38f.
[167] 'Limitations of Actions', 54 *CJS*, § 10; 'Limitation of actions', 51 *Am J 2nd*, § 4.
[168] For US law, see 'Limitations of Actions', 54 *CJS*, § 10. For Italian law, see art 2969 cc. For German law, however, cf Wolf and Neuner (n 1) § 22 para 6: statutes of repose can be raised by courts on their own motion.
[169] For Italian law, cf art 2968 cc: safe with regard to unwaivable rights.
[170] For German law, see Wolf and Neuner (n 1) § 20 paras 6ff. For Italian law, see art 2965 cc.
[171] For Italian law, see art 2964 cc.
[172] For Italian law, see art 2966 cc.
[173] 'Limitation of Actions', 51 *Am Jur 2nd*, § 345.
[174] 'Limitations of Actions', 54 *CJS*, § 27; 'Limitation of Actions', 51 *Am Jur 2nd*, §§ 3, 23, 86.
[175] 'Limitation of actions', 51 *Am J 2nd*, § 78.

vided for with regard to seller liability for defects in property sold, constructor liability for construction defects, and producer liability for defective products.

For example, article 39 CISG stipulates that: '(1) The buyer loses the right to rely on a lack of conformity of the goods if he does not give notice to the seller specifying the nature of the lack of conformity within a reasonable time after he has discovered it or ought to have discovered it. (2) In any event, the buyer loses the right to rely on a lack of conformity of the goods if he does not give the seller notice thereof at the latest within a period of two years from the date on which the goods were actually handed over to the buyer, unless this time-limit is inconsistent with a contractual period of guarantee'. Paragraph 1 provides for a statute of limitations, whereas paragraph 2 provides for a statute of nonclaim, combined with the former.

GLOSSARY

Abuse of power (3): exercise of a power (see *ad vocem*) beyond the reason it was granted, so that its exercise constitutes an unlawful (albeit valid) act of the powerholder.

Abuse of rights (in civil law systems) (4.3): doctrine according to which a rightsholder is prevented from bringing her right in a way that contravenes the general principle of good faith.

Acquisitive prescription [*Prescription acquisitive*; *Ersitzung*; *Usucapione*] (5.1): adverse possession lasting for the time period set out by the law, after the completion of which the former proprietor's ownership is subject to forfeiture and the possessor may thus become the new owner of property (see *ad vocem*) or of a real right of usufruct (see *ad vocem*) or servitude (see *ad vocem*).

Agency [*Représentation*; *Vertretung*; *Rappresentanza*] (3): power (of the agent) (see *ad vocem*) to act on behalf of someone else (the principal).

Assignment (3, 4): voluntary transfer of rights or property (see also 'Conveyance').

Authorization [*Autorisation*; *Einwillung*; *Autorizzazione*] (3): legal act by which a power (see *ad vocem*) is granted to someone else.

Chicane (prohibition of) (4.3): kind of abuse of rights (see *ad vocem*) where the rightsholder pursues the sole purpose of harming or bothering someone else (particularly with regard to relations between neighbors).

Claim [*Revendication*; *Anspruch*; *Pretesa*] (4): simple legal position (see *ad vocem*) that affords protection against someone else's interference or against someone else's withholding of assistance or remuneration, in regard to a certain action or a certain state of affairs.

Clean hands (in common law systems) (4.3): equitable defense against the bringing of a claim by one who had previously behaved in a way that, albeit not illegal, may be deemed to be tricky, iniquitous, or unconscionable.

Conveyance (3, 4): voluntary transfer of rights or property (see also 'Assignment').

Credit [*Créance*; *Forderung/Glaube*; *Credito*] (4.2.1): patrimonial right *in personam* that entitles its holder (the creditor, *le créancier*, *der Gläubiger*, *il creditore*) to claim that someone else (the debtor, *le débiteur*, *der Schuldner*, *il debitore*) render an economic performance.

Debt [*Dette*; *Schuld*; *Debito*] (4.2.1): duty (of the debtor) to render the patrimonial performance owed to someone else (the creditor).

***Erwirkung* (in civil law systems) (4.3)**: one party's affirmative behavior that, since it lasts or recurs over time, can generate the other party's reasonable reliance upon an (in fact non-existing) right.

Estate (in common law systems) (4.2.2): real property (see *ad vocem*) that is or may become possessory. An estate may be a freehold (see *ad vocem*) or a leasehold (see *ad vocem*).

Estoppel (in common law systems) (4.3): defense against someone who, by her words or conduct, induced the defendant to believe in a particular state of affairs, which would be denied by the bringing of an action.

Fee simple, or absolute fee (in common law systems) (4.2.2): the broadest freehold (see *ad vocem*) allowed by the law.

Foreclosure [*Execution forcée/saisie*; *Zwangsvollstreckung*; *Esecuzione forzata*] (4.2.2): legal proceeding to terminate an insolvent debtor's interest in property, instituted by the creditor either to gain title or to force a sale in order to satisfy an unpaid debt.

Freedom, or privilege, or liberty [*Liberté*; *Freiheit*; *Libertà*] (2): simple legal position (see *ad vocem*) that allows the doing of something or the abstaining from something.

Freehold (in common law systems) (4.2.2): estate (see *ad vocem*) of indeterminate duration (in fee, or for life).

Industrial property (4.2.2): body of legal principles and rules that governs property in such intangibles as patents, trademarks, technological and design innovations, and industrial designs.

Intellectual property (4.2.2): body of legal principles and rules that governs property in such intangibles as copyright on artistic and literary works, architectural design, and models.

Interruption of limitation/Renewal of period [*Interruption; Unterbrechung/Neubeginn; Interruzione*] (5.1): an event that makes the time period of limitation start running anew.

Laches (in common law systems) (4.3): equitable defense that can be pleaded when a rightsholder's standing by has been so unreasonably long that it has induced the defendant to believe that that right will not be raised any more (the wrong will be consented to, etc.).

Leasehold (in common law systems) (4.2.2): a tenant's estate (see *ad vocem*) in land or premises that are owned by a landlord.

Legal positions (1): legal concepts used to map what legal subjects can/may do or not do, and, conversely, what they shall/must do or not do.

Legal relation (1): the relationship between one who holds a legal position of advantage (eg the creditor) and one who holds the correlative legal position of disadvantage (eg the debtor).

Legitimate interest (3): legal position (see *ad vocem*) of a liability-bearer against any abuse by the holder of the correlative power.

Liability [*Assujettissement*; *Gebundenheit*; *Soggezione*] (3): exposure to the exercise of someone else's powers (see *ad vocem*) or power-right.

Lien (4.2.2): right or interest that a creditor has in another's property, lasting until a debt or duty that it secures is satisfied.

License (or leave, permission) [*Concession*; *Zustimmung*; *Concessione*] (2): legal act that confers a privilege (see 'Freedom') to someone else.

Mortgage (or hypothec) [*Hypothèque*; *Hypothek/Grundschuld*; *Ipoteca*] (4.2.2): real right in someone else's immovables, which are recorded or registered as security for the payment of a debt owed either by the mortgagor or by a third person; the mortgagee acquires no right of possession or control on the hypothecated immovable, but, in the event the debt owed to her remains unpaid, she can sell it on foreclosure (see *ad vocem*).

Obligation [*Obligation*; *Schuldverhältnis*; *Obbligazione*] (1, 4.2.1): legal relation between a creditor and a debtor.

Pledge [*Gage*; *Pfandrecht*; *Pegno*] (4.2.2): real right on someone else's movables that are delivered as security for the payment of the debt owed either by the pledgor or by a third person; the pledgee acquires a right of possession on the pledged chattel and, in the event the debt owed to her is not payed, she can sell it without the aid of a court.

Power [*Pouvoir*; *Macht*; *Potere*] (3): simple legal position (see *ad vocem*) that entitles one to change an entitlement either of the powerholder or of someone else.

Power-right [*Droit potestatif*; *Gestaltungsrecht*; *Diritto potestativo*] (3): right (see *ad vocem*) to change someone else's entitlement through either a legal act (whose notice has to be served on the counterparty) or a lawsuit filed with a court.

Prescription (or limitation) [*Prescription*; *Verjährung*; *Prescrizione*] (5.1): lapse of a certain time period, within which most patrimonial rights (safe property) have to be enforced; otherwise they become unenforceable.

Profit (or profit à prendre) (in common law systems) (4.2.2): right or privilege to go on another's land and take away something of value from its soil or from the products of its soil (as by mining, logging, or hunting).

Property (4.2.2): in civil law systems, patrimonial, absolute, and non-time-limited right in tangibles, be they movables or immovables, which entails an exclusive and potentially unrestricted power to dispose of a thing and a liberty to use it. In common law systems, only property in immovables is real (and therefore absolute), whereas property in movables is personal (and therefore relative).

Real rights (in civil law systems) [*Droits réels*; *Dingliche Rechte*; *Diritti reali*] (4.2.2): patrimonial and absolute rights in tangibles, be they movables or immovables. Either they are property (see *ad vocem*) or real rights in someone else's property (see *ad vocem*).

Real rights in someone else's property (in civil law systems) [*Droits réels sur le bien d'autrui*; *Beschränkte dingliche Rechte*; *Diritti reali su cosa altrui*] (4.2.2): they are acknowledged in a limited number (*numerus clausus*) and are subdivided into two subsets: possession rights (usufruct and servitudes) and security rights (pledge and hypothec). They run with property (*ius sequendi*), provided that, if they are in immovables, they have been recorded or registered.

Remedy (1): a response to a 'cause of action' (like breach of contract, tort, etc.).

Rights [*Droits* (*subjectifs*); (*subjektive*) *Rechte*; *Diritti* (*soggettivi*)] (4-4.3): complex legal positions that consist of an aggregate of freedoms, claims, powers, and immunities, whose backbone is the power to seek enforcement through the mobilizing of the state's coercion, if necessary.

Rights of personality [*Droits de la personnalité*; *Persönlichkeitsrechte*; *Diritti della personalità*] (4.2.2): non-patrimonial and absolute rights (see *ad vocem*) to the single aspects of individuals' personality. Some of them (like those to image and name) may be granted to entities as well.

Servitudes (or easements/profits or profits à prendre) [*Servitudes*; (*Grund-*)*Dienstbarkeiten*; *Servitù (prediali)*] (4.2.2): rights that are held by the proprietor of a 'dominant estate' and encumbers another's adjacent 'servient estate'. They may consist in a liberty, privilege, or advantage that the former can use on the servient estate. See also 'Profit (or profit à prendre)'.

Statutes of repose (or nonclaim statutes) [*Déchéance/Forclusion*; *Ausschlussfrist/Verfall*; *Decadenza*] (5.2): they extinguish a right because of its prolonged non-use, whether or not an issue of enforcement has arisen in the meanwhile. They may be particularly aimed at putting a time bar on potential litigation.

Tolling of limitation/Extension or Postponement of period [*Suspension/Report du point de départ*; *Hemmung/Ablaufshemmung*; *Sospensione*] (5.1, 5.2): when statutes of limitations stipulate that, for some reason, the start of the time period is delayed until some event takes place or that its running is suspended.

Usufruct [*Usufruit*; *Nießbrauch*; *Usufrutto*] (4.2.2): right to use a thing belonging to someone else and to enjoy its fruits, the usufructuary being conversely obliged to preserve the substance of that thing for the property owner of it.

U-turn transactions (4.3): transactions that are fictitiously performed across borders only, but in fact they originate and terminate in the same country so as to circumvent a mandatory norm that applies to domestic transactions.

***Venire contra factum proprium* (in civil law systems) (prohibition of) (4.3)**: kind of abuse of rights (see *ad vocem*), when they are used in a way that appears inconsistent with, or contradictory to, the rightsholder's previous behavior. A defense is then granted, insofar as the rightsholder's previous behavior has been conducive to the defendant's reasonable reliance that is now frustrated or disregarded by the rightsholder herself.

***Verwirkung* (4.3)**: kind of abuse of rights (see *ad vocem*), which entails rights asserted with so long a delay that the defendant believed (or could have believed) that they had terminated in the meanwhile or were not going to be asserted any longer.

Waiver (of a right) [*Renonciation*; *Verzicht*; *Rinuncia*] (4.2): voluntary relinquishment of one's own right.

Withdrawal [*Résiliation*; *Rucktritt/Kündigung*; *Recesso*] (3): power-right to terminate a contract through a unilateral legal act, which has to be served on the counterparty.

BIOGRAPHIES

Étienne Louis Josserand (Lyon, 1868 – La Sauvetat, 1941) was a French jurist. Together with Raymond Saleilles (see *supra*, ch 3), he is considered a prominent exponent of so-called risk theory, which can be identified as one of the cornerstones of the French system of civil liability. He was co-author of the Lebanese Civil Code project on obligations and contracts.
Josserand studied at the School of Law of Lyon University between 1886 and 1895 and wrote a thesis on civil law entitled *Les successions entre époux*. After a short period of time during which he practiced law at the bar in Lyon, he began to teach Roman law (as a *suppléant*) at the *Ecole de droit* in Algiers.
After three attempts (1892, 1895, and 1896), he obtained the *agrégation* in 1898, being immediately appointed as *agrégé* at the School of Law of Lyon University. He became full professor in 1902; at a later time, Josserand was appointed *assesseur du doyen* (1908) and Dean in 1913. He held this role until 14 June 1935, the date on which he was named *conseiller* at the *Cour de Cassation* (*chambre civil*). Moreover, he was elected President of the *Société de législation comparée* in 1938. The academic work of Josserand is characterized by a pervasive criticism of the notion of quasi-contract, as well as an extensive interpretation of the prohibition of abuse of law, which, according to his theory, amounts to a right not exercised in a manner consistent with its socially relevant purpose. In particular, he examines various hypotheses attesting that the right can unfold effects not consistent with its scope, evaluating, to this end, the interests affected by the exercise of that right. Josserand also condemned the developments of French private law after World War I, arguing that they were prone to create a class law – a legal display of class struggle – that could potentially lead to 'civil war'.
His main works are: *De la responsabilité du fait des choses inanimées* (1897); *Essai sur la propriété collective* (1904); *De l'esprit des droits et de leur relativité : Théorie dite de l'abus des droits* (1905; 2nd edn, 1939); *Les mobiles dans les actes juridiques du droit privé* (1928).

Karl Larenz (Wesel, 1903 – Olching, 1993) was a German jurist and professor best known for being a convinced supporter of neo-Hegelianism thought.
He lived in Berlin, Munich, and Göttingen before passing the law exam in Celle and obtaining his doctorate in 1926. Larenz was professor at two of the most important German universities, the University of Kiel and that of Munich, where he was also the teacher of some influential jurists of our time, such as Claus-Wilhelm Canaris, Uwe Diederichsen, Helmut Köhler, Detlef Leenen, and Manfred Wolf. Larenz became known especially after 1945 thanks to his works on the methodology of jurisprudence and on the law of obligations. Among his remarkable output, one of the most significant and remembered contributions is the theory that every person must be respected by any law as a human being and must not be harmed in her existence and intimacy, with the consequence that every individual is obliged to behave consistently with these principles toward any other subject.
His main works are: *Hegels Zurechnungslehre und der Begriff der objektiven Zurechnung* (1929); *Hegelianismus und preußische Staatsidee* (1940); *Methodenlehre*

der Rechtswissenschaft (1960); *Lehrbuch des Schuldrechts*, vol 1 (first published 1953) and vol 2 (first published 1956).

Giuseppe Messina (Naro, 1877 – Rome, 1946) was an eminent Italian jurist. He studied law at the University of Sassari, where he graduated in 1898. His dissertation was published after one year and proved the incredible maturity of Messina's legal thought and research activity. In 1902, he was awarded the chair of Civil Law at the University of Perugia, and in 1911, he started his lectures on Civil Procedure at the University of Palermo, where he also became a lawyer. Afterwards, he was assigned the chair of Civil Law at the University of Rome. Messina's works on civil law and civil procedural law are a remarkable contribution to these legal fields, especially regarding the interpretation of contracts. Moreover, Messina was the first Italian author who acknowledged the contractual power asymmetry between the parties in the context of labor relations; consequently, he strongly supported the development of mandatory law within collective labor agreements. Beyond his judicial work, Messina is also remembered for his active participation in political life.
His main works are: *La promessa di ricompensa al pubblico nel diritto privato* (1899); *Contributo alla dottrina della confessione* (1902); *L'interpretazione dei contratti* (1906); *Sui così detti diritti potestativi* (1906); *La simulazione assoluta* (1907-1908); *Negozi fiduciari: introduzione e parte prima* (1910); *Teoria generale del contratto* (1940).

August Thon (Weimar, 1839 – Jena, 1912) was a German jurist. Born to a family of civil servants, he enrolled at the University of Heidelberg in 1857 to study law; in 1861 he became *Doktor der Rechte* at the University of Jena and was appointed *Privatdozent* at the University of Heidelberg in 1863. Later, from 1873, he taught the Pandects as an ordinary professor at the University of Rostock. Besides his academic engagements, Thon's career also involved his holding the offices of court assessor (*Kreisgerichtsassessor*) in Eisenach (1867), and state's attorney in Eisenach (1870) and in Weimar (1872).
His main work is: *Rechtsnorm und subjektives Recht* (1878).

Ernst Zitelmann (Szczecin, 1852 – Bonn, 1923) was a German jurist best known for his studies and works in the area of civil law. Moreover, his publications dealt with international law issues and focused, especially, on the founding of private international law.
Zitelmann studied law in Leipzig, Heidelberg, and Bonn and completed his doctoral studies in 1873. After the publication of his monograph *Irrtum und Rechtsgeschäft*, he was appointed in 1879 as associate professor at the University of Göttingen. Zitelmann lectured in numerous prestigious universities, among which are those of Rostock, Halle, and Bonn, where he taught German civil law and Roman law.
His main works on private law are: *Begriff und Wesen der sogenannten juristischen Personen* (1873); 'Die juristische Willenserklärung' (1878) 16, in Jherings Jahrbücher für die Dogmatik des bürgerlichen Rechts 357; *Irrtum und Rechtsgeschäft* (1879).

His main works on international law are: *Internationales Privatrecht* (1897-1912); *Sondergut nach deutschem Internationalprivatrecht* (1911); *Haben wir ein Völkerrecht?* (1914); *Der Krieg und das Völkerrecht* (1915).
His main works on legal education are: *Zum Grenzstreit zwischen Reichs- und Landesrecht* (1902); *Die Vorbildung der Juristen* (1909).

CHAPTER 11

Legal subjects

- **Legal personhood and capacity to act**
- **Natural persons and legal persons**
- **Incorporated and unincorporated legal persons: the corporate veil**
- **For-profit and non-profit legal persons**
- **Companies, partnerships and cooperative societies**
- **Foundations and associations**
- **Emerging legal subjects (animals, 'Mother Earth', e-persons)**

Natural persons are granted legal personhood from birth. Embryos and fetuses can solely hold a number of specific rights (and duties), conferred *ad hoc* to them, and conditionally on their subsequent birth.

Natural persons attain the general capacity to act when they come of age. Minors enjoy (after a certain threshold of infancy) the capacity to enter into some lesser and daily bargains, as well as contracts for labor and services, and for sports or entertainment services. They may gain a wider (albeit still limited) capacity in cases of emancipation (obtaining the authorization to contract marriage or other special circumstances). Conversely, adults may be incapacitated, if they are affected by mental illness or by another pathological factor (like habitual abuse of alcohol or drugs, excessive prodigality, and so on).

In civil law jurisdictions, minors and incapacitated adults are legally represented by their parents or by a guardian, who holds a general (albeit not unlimited) power to act on behalf of the child or ward. Under common law, parents and guardians (or conservators) do not hold such a general and statutory power to act, unless they are specifically authorized by a court to enter into individual contracts on behalf of the child or ward.

Legal persons can be non-profit (foundations, or corporations sole; associations, or corporations aggregate) or for profit (companies and cooperative societies), acting solely through the agency of their legal representatives (eg managing directors).

Companies may be incorporated (corporations) or unincorporated (partnerships). Corporations are legal persons that are completely autonomous and whose assets are fully separated from those of their owners; the latter are not liable for the debts owed by the former (corporate veil), with due exceptions (so-called lifting, or piercing, of the corporate veil). Corporations may be either joint-stock/public limited companies (PLC), whose shares can be traded on exchanges (listed companies), or private limited (liability) companies (LLC, or Ltd).
In partnerships, the capacity to manage the business may be held by any of the partners (general partnerships, GP) or solely by some of them (limited partnership, LP). The managing partners are personally and jointly liable for the debts owed by the partnership. Limited liability partnerships (LLP) are a hybrid of partnership and corporation, since partners, albeit responsible for management, enjoy a limited liability.

1. LEGAL PERSONHOOD

Legal personhood is defined as the capacity to hold rights and duties protected by the law (see *supra*, ch 10). It consists, therefore, in a **legal standing (or *status*)**, which is granted by the law to those who are thus recognized as legal subjects. Such subjects are traditionally subdivided into natural persons and legal persons.

1.1. Natural persons

All **people** have legal personhood and, therefore, are recognized as legal subjects, simply by virtue of their being human. Particularly, they are categorized as natural persons.
In contrast to the past, when, for example, human beings were divided between 'masters' and 'slaves', contemporary law has widely acknowledged the constitutional principle of anti-discrimination, which *inter alia* prevents national legislators from depriving some categories of human beings of their legal personhood[1] or from limiting it in any way.[2]

Slavery was advocated for by Aristotle as being part of natural law (see *supra*, ch 5, para 4).

[1] With particular regard to the pivotal role played by French law in that direction, see Jean Carbonnier, 'Scolie sur le non-sujet de droit. L'esclavage sous le régime du Code civil' in Id, *Flexible droit. Pour une sociologie du droit sans rigueur* (LGDJ 2014) 247ff.
[2] The UN Committee on the Rights of Persons with Disabilities stated that: 'Legal capacity is an inherent right accorded to all people, including persons with disabilities'. See the Committee's General Comment No. 1 (2014) on the UN Convention on the Rights of Persons with Disabilities, n. 14 <https://documents-dds-ny.un.org/doc/UNDOC/GEN/G14/031/20/PDF/G1403120.pdf?OpenElement> accessed 7 March 2020.

> Persisting in the nineteenth century, slaves were denied having legal personhood in some countries, like the US. See *Lenoir vs Sylvester* (North Carolina, 1830): 'a legacy cannot be given to a slave; for he can have no right, whatsoever which does so, the instant it is transferred to him, passes to his master. Everything which belongs to him, belongs to his master. In other words, he is in law himself chattels personal; and it would be absurd to say that property can own property'. Litigation over slavery led in early 1861 to the outbreak of the American Civil War,[3] which resulted in some of the amendments to the US Constitution (see *supra*, ch 7, para 3.2). The Thirteenth Amendment (1865), in particular, provides that slavery shall not exist within the US or in any place subject to its jurisdiction.

Yet, nationality is generally deemed as grounds for some restrictions of legal personhood, in the sense that **foreign nationals or stateless persons** (**aliens**) may be not granted the capacity to hold some rights. This happens above all in the domain of public law (see *supra*, ch 7, para 1), particularly with regard to political rights (like the right to vote), which may typically be reserved for **citizens**. Albeit less frequently, this may occur in the domain of private law as well, when aliens may be, for example, denied the capacity to set up a corporation or to acquire ownership of real estate situated within the national territory; however, in contrast, human rights under constitutional command must be granted equally to foreigners (or stateless persons) and to citizens. In the vast majority of Western legal systems, legal personhood is attained by a human being at **birth**.[4] Therefore, **embryos** and **fetuses**, protected and safeguarded as they may be by the law,[5] are not considered natural persons by definition, since they are not (yet) born.[6]

> Some legal systems of Latin America explicitly set forth that '[t]he existence of a human person begins with her conception' (article 19(2) *Código civil y commercial de la Nación Argentina*). If so, embryos and fetuses are to be classified as legal subjects (article 1(2) *Código civil* of Perú), albeit devoid of the capacity to act (see *infra*, ch 11, para 2).

Equating birth and the start human personhood provides the basis of the constitutional legitimacy of abortion:[7] when embryos and fetuses are put on the same footing with those who have already been born, abortion amounts to homicide and, therefore, cannot be legalized without infringing the principle of equal treatment.

[3] Arthur T von Mehren and Peter L Murray, *Law in the United States* (2nd ed, CUP 2007) 135ff.

[4] For German law, see § 1 BGB. For Italian law, see art 1(1) cc. For US law, see 'Infants' 43 *CJS*, § 3.

[5] Timothy Stoltzfus Jost, 'Rights of Embryo and Foetus in Private Law' (2002) 50 Am J Comp L 633.

[6] In French law, this point is made by courts confronted with cases of homicide (see Cour de Cassation, Assemblée plénière, 29 juin 2001, 99-85.973). For US law, see 43 'Infants', 43 *CJS*, § 3.

[7] Cf Carl Wellman, *A Theory of Rights* (Rowman & Allanheld 1985) 2.

In order to legalize abortion as a private right of a pregnant woman, conversely, a famous sentence of the Supreme Courts of the United States stated that: 'the word "person" as used in the Fourteenth Amendment of the United States Constitution does not include the unborn' (**Roe v Wade case** of 1973).[8]
More generally, a **woman is under no duty** to guarantee the mental and physical health of a child at birth and thus cannot be compelled to do or not do anything merely for the benefit of an unborn child.[9]

Although not being natural persons, embryos and fetuses are nonetheless conferred *ad hoc* a number of rights (and duties), particularly some personality rights (like that to health), as well as heirship and rights conferred through donations (or contracts for their benefit)[10] (see *supra*, ch 10, para 4). However, these rights may be dependent on the subsequent birth of the child.[11]

Medical practices that harm an embryo or a fetus oblige the negligent doctors to compensate the resulting damages. If during gestation doctors fail to inform the parents that their embryo or fetus is congenitally abnormal, the negligent doctors may be held liable for the higher expenses that the parents will have to cover to rear their child, as well as for their moral damages (**wrongful birth**).[12]
In most jurisdictions, on the contrary, no moral damages are awarded to a new-born because of her congenital abnormality (**wrongful life**), since it was not caused by the doctor's negligence.[13]

When natural persons die, their legal personhood is extinguished. Most of their (patrimonial) rights (eg property) and duties (eg debts) pass, except some which terminate (eg alimonies, rights of personality) (see *supra*, ch 10, para 4).

1.2. Legal persons

Legal persons are **organizations** set up to undertake an activity either for profit or for non-profit.[14] They may be established and ruled under public law (eg the state) or under private law (eg a club).[15]

[8] *Roe v Wade*, 410 U.S. 113 at 159 (1973). See 'Abortion and Birth Control' 1 Am Jur 2d, § 3.
[9] For US law, see 'Infants', 43 *CJS*, § 3.
[10] For German law, see §§ 331(2) and 1923(2) BGB. For Italian law, see arts 462 and 783 cc.
[11] For a general statement of this rule, see art 1(2) cc.
[12] *Parkinson v St James and Seacroft University Hospital NHS Trust* [2001] EWCA Civ 530; [2002] QB 266. For US law, see 'Prenatal Injuries', 62A Am Jur 2d, §§ 1ff.
[13] John K Mason, 'Wrongful Pregnancy, Wrongful Birth and Wrongful Terminology' (2002) 6 Edin LR 46; Id, *The Troubled Pregnancy: Legal Wrongs and Rights in Reproduction* (CUP 2007).
[14] Ngaire Naffine, 'Who are Law's Persons? From Cheshire Cats to Responsible Subjects' (2003) 66 MLR 346.
[15] For an in-depth historical account of how the doctrine of legal persons was forged and developed in civil law jurisdictions, see Filippo Ranieri, 'Die Rechtskategorie "Juristische Person" als Schöpfung von Doktrin und Gesetzgebung im 19.-20. Jahrhundert. Zugleich ein Kapitel aus der neueren Geschichte des kontinentalen Zivil- und Handelsrecht' in

For-profit legal persons aim to earn a profit and to distribute it to their owners (dividends); by contrast, **non-profit** legal persons are established to pursue a common purpose of a different nature, be it the pursuit of personal pleasure or advantage of their owners or founders (eg in the field of sport, culture, leisure, etc) or some outside purpose (charitable or not).[16] Consequently, non-profit legal persons are prohibited from distributing any gain to their owners or founders, and they enjoy some exemption from taxation.
Both for-profit and non-profit legal persons under private law may be incorporated or unincorporated legal entities.
Corporations are legal entities that are completely separated from the persons who established them and have property and organizations on their own. This eventually led most jurisdictions worldwide (including those of the US, EU, and UK) to allow them to be set up even by one individual.
Perfect **asset partitioning** between a corporation and its owner(s) creates a shield (**veil**) in favor of the latter and against third-party claims towards the former, and vice versa. Be it one or many, consequently, the owners of a corporation are personally not liable for the debts owed by the latter.

> In a cornerstone case of English common law, the sole proprietor of a boot-making business, named Salomon, transferred the business to a company, named Salomon Ltd, which he himself had established together with six other members of his family; instead of being paid with money in consideration of this transfer of his property, he was conferred with shares and debentures having a floating charge on the assets of the company. When the company's business failed and it went into liquidation, Salomon's right of recovery, although being secured on the assets of the company, was not honored by the liquidator, who alleged that the other six signatories of the memorandum were mere 'dummies' and that the company was just Salomon in another form, an alias, or at most his agent. He therefore contended that Salomon himself should have been made responsible for the company's debts. Having Salomon sued, his claim was dismissed both by the High Court and the Court of Appeal; the latter's ruling, however, was reversed by the House of Lords, which unanimously proclaimed that '[t]he company is at law a different person altogether from the subscribers to the memorandum; and, though it may be that after incorporation the business is precisely the same as it was before, and the same persons are managers, and the same hands receive the profits, the company is not in law the agent of the subscribers or trustee for them. Nor are the subscribers as members liable, in any shape or form, except to the extent and in the manner provided by the Act' (***Salomon v A Salomon & Co Ltd*** [1896] UKHL 1, [1897] AC 22).

Under exceptional circumstances, however, that shield is disregarded by the law, and the shareholders are personally and unlimitedly liable for the debts owed by the corporation (so-called **lifting, or piercing, of the corporate veil**).

Herbert Kronke, Heinz-P Mansel and Marc-Philippe Weller (eds), *Liber amicorum Giuseppe B. Portale* (Nomos 2019) 109ff.
[16] John Armour, 'Companies and other associations' in Andrew Burrows (ed), *English Private Law* (3rd edn, OUP 2013) para 3.115.

This may happen, for example, where the corporate entity is a fraud or a sham (façade), or because the shareholders' actions have deleterious effects on the survival of the corporation.[17]
Corporations are mostly registered and regulated at least by one (**board of directors**) or even two legal bodies (**management board** and **supervisory board**) (see *infra*, ch 11, para 1.2.1). Therefore, they are encumbered with start-up and annual costs of a certain amount, as well as with administrative burdens that are rather invasive.
By contrast, **unincorporated legal entities** consist of a collection of individuals that, to some extent, share property and organization. Consequently, all or some of the owners of an unincorporated legal entity are personally and unlimitedly liable for the debts owed by the latter. In contrast to corporations, unincorporated legal entities are not registered and not necessarily regulated by a legal body. Therefore, start-up and annual costs sustained by their owner(s) are relatively low, and they do not incur administrative burdens.
It has been traditionally held that acts undertaken on behalf of a legal person but outside the objects spelled out in its memorandum of association (or an akin constitutive document) (so-called ***ultra vires* acts**) are void and cannot be ratified by the directors or the members of that legal person, not even unanimously. As far as corporations are concerned, however, that doctrine has been generally abandoned, or at least mitigated, since it proved excessively harsh towards third parties and thus discouraged them from entering into negotiations with a corporation: in the EU, UK and US, acts undertaken *ultra vires* by corporations are generally not affected by invalidity on that ground; yet, if the authority to undertake such acts is lacking on the part of the person that purports to act on behalf of a corporation, they may be devoid of legal effects, particularly if the third party has acted in bad faith (see *infra*, ch 11, para 2.2).
Furthermore, different jurisdictions are prone to restrict variously the legal personhood of legal entities with regard to their **capacity to take under a will**.[18]

1.2.1. For-profit organizations

Legal persons for profit are called companies, if they are incorporated, and partnerships, if they are unincorporated. They are regulated by **company and partnership law** (or **corporate law** in the US), which is a special branch of commercial law (see *supra*, ch 7, para 2).

> Within the **EU**, the key issues of Member States' company law have been intensively harmonized by thirteen directives (see *supra*, ch 8, para 1.5.2), some of them having over time been repealed, replaced, or amended. Furthermore, the EU enacted a number of regulations aimed at creating and governing some EU companies that coexist with national rules (see *supra*, ch 8, para 1.5.2).

[17] Felix Steffek, 'Piercing the Corporate Veil' in Jürgen Basedow, Klaus J Hopt, Reinhard Zimmermann and Andreas Stier (eds), *The Max Planck Encyclopedia of European Private Law*, vol 2 (OUP 2012) 1276.
[18] For US law, see 'Wills', 79 Am Jur 2d, §§ 153ff.

In the **UK**, company law is overall regulated by the Companies Act 2006. In the **US**, federal law provides solely for some minimum standards for trade in company shares and governance rights, whereas the rest of company law is stipulated by each state and territory, which has its own corporate code.[19] It is the State of Delaware that has by far succeeded in the regulatory competition thus raised, having been able to attract the majority of the largest US corporations; its judge-made law is therefore particularly influential and may be said to be paramount also for scholars of company law.

1.2.1.1. Companies

Companies are either joint-stock companies/public limited companies (PLC) or private limited liability companies (LLC, or Ltd).[20]
The **memorandum (of association)** (if required) and the **articles of association** form the key constitutional documents of a company; *inter alia*, they spell out the name, the purpose, and the capital of the entity. The **bylaws** generally define the internal structure of a company and regulate the functions and decision-making processes of its legal bodies.
Joint-stock companies/public limited companies (PLC) generally suit the needs of mid-size or large enterprises.[21] Their ownership is subdivided into shares that are fully transferable and freely tradable on stock exchanges,[22] subject to corporate charter or statutory restrictions.

> Despite some traces of PLCs dating back to antiquity, their prototype is generally acknowledged in two large trading companies founded in the early modern period, ie the English East India Company (Charter of 31 December 1600) and the Dutch *Vereenigde Oost-Indische Compagnie* (Octroy of 20 March 1602).

PLCs whose shares are quoted on a stock exchange, and therefore publicly traded, are called **listed companies**.

> Listed companies are regulated not only by company law, which falls under private law, but also by **capital markets law**, which is cross-sectional, encompassing public as well as private law (see *supra*, ch 7, para 1).[23] The building blocks of capital markets law include stock exchanges law, regulation of insider trading (or insider dealing) and market manipulation, and takeover law. **Insider trading (or insider dealing)** is the buying and selling of financial instruments

[19] See also the *ALI Principles of Corporate Governance: Analysis & Recommendations.*
[20] Confusing though it may read, the term 'company' is not infrequently used in a broader sense, ie to encompass any association of individuals formed for a common purpose, be it incorporated or not; see Armour (n 16) para 3.34.
[21] Andreas M Fleckner, 'Stock Corporations' in *The Max Planck Encyclopedia of European Private Law*, vol 2 (n 17) 1602.
[22] Andreas M Fleckner, 'Exchanges' in Jürgen Basedow, Klaus J Hopt, Reinhard Zimmermann and Andreas Stier (eds), *The Max Planck Encyclopedia of European Private Law*, vol 1 (OUP 2012) 658.
[23] Klaus J Hopt, 'Capital Markets Law' in *The Max Planck Encyclopedia of European Private Law*, vol 1 (n 22) 141.

by board members (and other persons) who make use of their privileged access to information relating to the company.[24] **Takeovers** are the transfer of control of a company.[25]

The continental model (also followed by the EU) traditionally requires a **statutory minimum capital**, even if more recent developments of national company law of most countries tend to mitigate that requirement. By contrast, the English system does not require a statutory minimum capital but relies on **solvency tests** and enforcement mechanisms for wrongful trading when facing insolvency.[26]

Under EU law, a Member State is not allowed 'to refuse to register a branch of a company formed in accordance with the law of another Member State in which it has its registered office but in which it conducts no business where the branch is intended to enable the company in question to carry on its entire business in the State in which that branch is to be created, while avoiding the need to form a company there, thus evading application of the rules governing the formation of companies which, in that State, are more restrictive as regards the paying up of a minimum share capital' (**case Centros** of 1999;[27] on this case, see also *supra*, ch 8, para 1.5.1; ch 10, para 4.3).

The structure of PLCs is regulated through mandatory rules that leave little room for intrafirm contractual freedom and is based on a rigid separation between ownership (the **shareholders**) and management/control (the **directors**).
This feature engenders the so-called **principal-agent conflict**, since the shareholders (principals) may lose control of the corporation to its management and the directors (agents) may aim to maximize their own gain instead of acting in the best interest of the shareholders. The potential shortcomings of this model must be remedied through proper rules of **corporate governance**.

A pivotal (and illustrious) contribution with regard to the role played by the separation between ownership and management of corporations for the development and the governance of big corporations is that by Berle and Means, *The Modern Corporation and Private Property*, whose first edition dates to 1932.[28] The core of the principal-agent conflict had already been well described by Adam Smith in 1776: 'The directors of such companies [...], being the managers rather of other people's money than of their own, it cannot well be expected,

[24] Harald Baum, 'Insider Dealing' in *The Max Planck Encyclopedia of European Private Law*, vol 1 (n 22) 895.
[25] Harald Baum, 'Takeover Law' in *The Max Planck Encyclopedia of European Private Law*, vol 2 (n 17) 1649.
[26] Rainer Kulms, 'Legal Capital' in *The Max Planck Encyclopedia of European Private Law*, vol 2 (n 17) 1057. For the UK rules on capital maintenance, see Paul Davies, *Introduction to Company Law* (2nd edn, OUP 2010) 74ff.
[27] Case C-212/97 *Centros Ltd v Erhvervs- og Selskabsstyrelsen* [1999] ECR I-1459.
[28] Adolf A Berle and Gardiner C Means, *The Modern Corporation and Private Property* (2nd edn, Harcourt, Brace and World 1967).

> that they should watch over it with the same anxious vigilance with which the partners in a private copartnery frequently watch over their own [...]. Negligence and profusion, therefore, must always prevail, more or less, in the management of the affairs of such a company'.[29]

There are two basic models of internal governance for corporations in legal systems. The **dualistic (or two-tier board system)** is based upon the co-existence of a management board, which is responsible for the management of the corporation, and a supervisory board, which is responsible for its control. This system originated in Germany, but it is widespread in other countries of continental Europe: in some of them, the shareholders' meeting appoints the supervisory board, which in turn appoints the management board; in others, like in Italy, it is also possible to opt for a so-called **'traditional' system**, where both the supervisory board and the management board are appointed by the shareholders' meeting. By contrast, the **monistic (or one-tier board system)** is dominant in Anglo-American jurisdictions: both management and control are placed in the hands of the board of directors, inside which, however, there is a distinction between executive and non-executive (often independent) directors.[30]

Private limited (liability) companies (LLC, or Ltd) generally suit the needs of family-owned enterprises, or at any rate closely held firms that have only a handful of shareholders.[31] Although transferable, in fact, shares of LLCs are not tradable on stock exchanges; importantly as well, the implementation of direct shareholder management is allowed, and the form provides for broad intrafirm contractual freedom.[32]

1.2.1.2. Partnerships

Partnerships are either general partnerships (GP), limited partnerships (LP), or limited liability partnerships (LLP).[33]

Unless otherwise agreed in the partnership agreement, each member of a **general partnership (GP)** has the capacity to manage the partnership business; for the very same reason, each partner has joint and several liability for the debts owed by the partnership. Some legal systems impose a duty not to compete on each partner; however, the soft regulatory approach adopted by most legal systems means the majority of duties owed by the partners have been shaped through judge-made law or private contracting and practitioners' expertise.[34]

[29] Adam Smith, *An Inquiry into the Nature and Causes of the Wealth of Nations* (5th edn, Methuen & Co Ltd 1904).

[30] Klaus J Hopt, 'Board' in *The Max Planck Encyclopedia of European Private Law*, vol 1 (n 22) 116.

[31] Daniel Annoff, 'Gesellschaft mit beschränkter Haftung (GmbH)' in *The Max Planck Encyclopedia of European Private Law*, vol 1 (n 22) 783.

[32] Herbert Hirte, 'Private Limited Company (England and Wales)' in *The Max Planck Encyclopedia of European Private Law*, vol 2 (n 17) 1344.

[33] Rainer Kulms, 'Partnership' in *The Max Planck Encyclopedia of European Private Law*, vol 2 (n 17) 1252.

[34] ibid 1253.

The peculiarity of **limited partnerships (LP)** is that some of the partners are general, others are limited. General partners have exclusive decision-making power and are the sole representative of an LLP; for the very same reason, they are personally and unlimitedly liable for the debts of that legal person. By contrast, the liability of limited partners, who are devoid of any power to make decisions or represent the LLP, is restricted to the amount contributed under the limited partnership agreement.[35] The LP is the vehicle of choice for private equity, hedge funds and investment funds.[36]

By contrast, the partners of a **limited liability partnership (LLP)** are not personally and jointly liable for the debts owed by the partnership, although they are involved in the management. The LLP is the vehicle of choice for professional services firms (eg law or accounting firms).[37]

1.2.1.3. Cooperative societies and other self-help organizations

From the end of the eighteenth century, various forms of self-help organizations began to be developed, which were meant to meet the needs of the working class through the mechanisms of mutuality. The goods and services they provide to (some of) their members are funded primarily (if not exclusively) out of the pool of their members' subscriptions. Noteworthy among them are: 1. **friendly societies**, ie mutual insurance associations providing their members with benefits in the event of sickness, death or bereavement; 2. **building societies**, which raise money in order to allow their borrowing members build or buy a house; 3. **industrial and provident societies**, which engage in commercial and industrial activity for their members' mutual benefit or for that of the wider community.

All these entities were generally established as unincorporated associations, but over time they were entitled to register and thus incorporate.

1.2.2. Non-profit organizations

Non-profit organizations are either foundations or associations.

Foundations are corporations sole. They consist of a single incorporated office (eg the Crown in the UK).

Associations are corporations aggregate. They consist of a group of members, or **civil partnership** (eg a scientific society).

In some legal systems, associations may also be unincorporated entities, and this applies (albeit rarely) to foundations as well. If that is the case, such entities remain generally unregistered and are not always regarded by national laws as holding the status of legal persons. Hence, they may lack the capacity to hold property; furthermore, some of their founders or members may be held personally liable for the debts owed by the entity.

[35] ibid 1253.

[36] Davies (n 26) 3 fn 4.

[37] ibid 3; Armour (n 16) paras 3-81ff.

The members of an unincorporated association enjoy a wider freedom than those of an incorporated one, since statutes only minimally regulate their mutual rights, which are governed almost exclusively by the terms of each association; conversely, artificial personality may be perceived as limitation on the associates' freedom, since it involves more regulation and supervision by the public administration (see *supra*, ch 10, para 1.2). This reason explains why **trade unions** and **political parties** historically refrained from seeking any artificial personality, which could prospectively endanger their autonomy as social and political actors; nonetheless, special pieces of legislation may provide for a registration of trade unions, which may thus gain the status of quasi-corporations.[38]

1.3. Emerging legal subjects

The traditional understanding of legal personhood has been increasingly challenged by new demands for protection of the environment (animals, wildness), as well as by liability issues raised by the advancement of technology (robots, systems of artificial intelligence). Tremendously affected is thus the societal view of (1) what is a being, which has her own rights, and (2) what is an object, which, be it inert or somehow animated, is possibly owned by someone. Hence, under law the division between subjects and non-subjects tends to be less neat than in the past and is styled more like a continuum between the extremes of men, on one side, and things, on the other.[39]

According to the tradition of Roman law, in most legal systems, including those of common law,[40] **animals** are considered as things that can be objects of property rights (eg ownership), rather than subjects able to hold rights. However, modern laws seek to provide a special protection for animals,[41] and these laws, albeit to a lesser extent, differentiate them from inanimate natural objects; it has been even urged to grant human rights to great apes.[42]

> Under **German law** since 1990, '[a]nimals are not things. They are protected by special statutes. They are governed by the provisions which apply to things, with the necessary modifications, except insofar as otherwise provided' (§ 90a BGB).[43]

[38] For English law, see Armour (n 16) paras 3.58ff.

[39] Jean Carbonnier, 'Être ou ne pas: être sur les traces du non-sujet de droit' in Id, *Flexible droit* (n 1) 231-246.

[40] For US law, see 'Animals', 4 Am Jur 2d §§ 2ff.

[41] Simon Brooman and Debbie Legge, *Law Relating to Animals* (Cavendish 1997); Charlotte E Blattner, *Mapping the Territory of Animal Law within and across Borders: Extraterritorial Jurisdiction and the Challenges of Globalization* (OUP 2019); S Marek Muller, *Impersonating Animals: Rhetoric, Ecofeminism, and Animal Rights Law* (Michigan State UP 2020); Anne Peters (ed), *Studies in Global Animal Law* (SpringerOpen 2020) < https://link.springer.com/content/pdf/10.1007%2F978-3-662-60756-5.pdf> accessed 4 August 2020.

[42] Paola Cavalieri and Peter Singer (eds), *The Great Ape Project. Equality beyond Humanity* (St Martin's Press 1993).

[43] § 90a BGB: '*Tiere sind keine Sachen. Sie werden durch besondere Gesetze geschützt. Auf sie sind die für Sachen geltenden Vorschriften entsprechend anzuwenden, soweit nicht etwas anderes bestimmt ist*'.

Under **French law** since 2015, '[a]nimals are living beings that are endowed with sensitivity. Unless differently set forth by the statutes aimed at animals' protection, the law of things applies to them'.[44]
Peter Singer, moving from a utilitarian (not moral) understanding of rights, claims that their entitlement should be based on the principle of minimizing suffering. Assuming that some animals prove capable of feeling pain and, conversely, some human beings do not, he condemns discrimination grounded on the belonging to human or animal species (**speciesism**). Notwithstanding some important differences, animals capable of feeling pain should be vested with rights like the human beings (and consequently a vegetarian or vegan diet should be followed, vivisection should be banned, and so on).[45]

In an increasing number of legal systems worldwide, particularly (but not exclusively) in Latin America,[46] some constitutional charters, statutory provisions, and court rulings acknowledge the rights of '**Mother Earth**', a development that was eventually supported by the United Nations.[47]

Most notable is the pathbreaking article 10 of the 2008 Constitution of Ecuador,[48] pursuant to which 'nature is to be held as a legal subject holding the rights bestowed on it through this Charter'.[49]

On a different note, the development of new technologies, particularly in the field of artificial intelligence, poses the question of whether **robots and other autonomous systems** (like unmanned cars) (see *supra*, ch 1, para 4) should be prospectively granted legal personhood, as they are potentially going to take autonomous decisions that can imply also a liability towards others.[50]

[44] Article 515-14 *Code civil*: '*Les animaux sont des êtres vivants doués de sensibilité. Sous réserve des lois qui les protègent, les animaux sont soumis au régime des biens*'.
[45] Peter Singer, *Animal Liberation. A New Ethics for Our Treatment of Animals* (HarperCollins 1975).
[46] Carlos Espinosa Gallego-Anda and Camilo Pèrez Fernández (eds), *Los Derechos de la Naturaleza y la Naturaleza de sus Derechos* (Ministerio de Justicia, Derechos Humanos y Cultos 2011); Alberto Acosta and Esperanza Martínez (eds), *La Naturaleza con Derechos. De la filosofía a la política* (Ediciones Abya-Yala 2011).
[47] For a repository of resources on the topic, see <www.harmonywithnatureun.org> accessed 4 August 2020.
[48] Article 10 Constitución del Ecuador: '*La naturaleza será sujeto de aquellos derechos que le reconozca la Constitución*'.
[49] Livio Perra, 'Naturaleza y Constitución' (2017) 7 Revista Brasileira de Politicas Públicas, 192; Irene Zasimowicz Pinto Calaça, Patrícia Jorge Carneiro de Freitas, Sérgio Augusto da Silva and Fabiano Maluf, 'La naturaleza como sujeto de derechos: análisis bioético de las Constituciones de Ecuador y Bolivia' (2018) 18 Revista Latinoamericana de Bioética, 155.
[50] Lawrence B Solum, 'Legal Personhood for Artificial Intelligences' (1992) 70 North Carolina LR 1231; F Patrick Hubbard, '"Do Androids Dream?": Personhood and Intelligent Artifacts' (2011) 83 Temple LR 405; Robert van den Hoven van Genderen, 'Do we Need Legal Personhood in the Age of Robots and AI?' in Marcelo Corrales, Mark Fenwick and Nikolaus Forgó (eds), *Robotics, AI and the Future of Law* (Kyushu-Springer 2018) 15ff; Florian Möslein, 'Law and Autonomous Systems Series: Regulating Robotic Conduct – On ESMA's New Guidelines and Beyond' <https://www.law.ox.ac.uk/business-law-blog/blog/2018/04/law-and-autonomous-systems-series-regulating-robotic-conduct-esmas> accessed 2 March 2020; Gerhard Wagner, 'Robot, Inc.: Personhood for Autonomous Systems?' (2019) 88 Fordham L Rev 591; Mark Kingwell, 'Are sentient AIs persons' in

Particularly, a resolution issued by the European Parliament in 2017 envisioned creating 'a specific legal status for robots in the long run, so that at least the most sophisticated autonomous robots could be established as having the status of **electronic persons** responsible for making good any damage they may cause, and possibly applying electronic personality to cases where robots make autonomous decisions or otherwise interact with third parties independently' (emphasis added).[51]

2. CAPACITY TO ACT

The capacity to act consists in the power to accomplish legal acts affecting one's own rights and duties (see *supra*, ch 10, para 4; ch 9, para 2).
The capacity to act is required for the accomplishment of **legal transactions** (see *supra*, ch 9, paras 2-5). For **contracts, wills, and marriage**, in particular, the requirements for capacity to act may be different, so that one can talk of a contractual capacity, a testamentary capacity, and a marriage capacity. When a natural person is devoid of legal capacity, statutory provisions or a court's decision can vest a third party with the power to enter into most contracts on behalf and in the best interest of that person (**legal agency**) (see also *supra*, ch 10, para 3; *infra*, ch 11, paras 2.1 and 2.2).
By contrast, **torts** do not require the tortfeasor's capacity to act, as the tortfeasor's duty to compensate the loss sustained by the damaged party does not depend upon a decision taken consciously and voluntarily by her.[52] Nonetheless, legal systems tend to exonerate minors from civil liability, if they have committed a tort before reaching a certain age,[53] and, to a lesser extent, the same applies to mentally incapacitated persons unable to make rational judgments.[54]

> In jurisdictions of **civil law**, parents, or other responsible parties incur a strict or aggravated liability for torts committed by children.
> In the **UK**, by contrast, no specific rule on parental liability is provided for; any claim of the kind must be based upon the tort of negligence.[55] The same applies to the **US** common law, but a limited parental responsibility for some torts of minor children is now imposed by statute in most States.[56]
> Similar considerations apply to the supervisors of adults that are mentally incapacitated.[57]

Markus D Dubber, Frank Pasquale and Sunit Das (eds), *The Oxford Handbook of Ethics of AI* (OUP 2020) 326-341.

[51] European Parliament resolution of 16 February 2017 with recommendations to the Commission on Civil Law Rules on Robotics, n. 59.

[52] For US law, see 'Infants', 42 Am Jur 2d, §§ 42ff.

[53] For German law, see §§ 828-829 BGB. For US law, see 'Infants', 42 Am Jur 2d, § 120 (to be exonerated are children 'of tender years').

[54] For US law, see 'Mentally Impaired Persons', 53 Am Jur 2d, §§ 167ff.

[55] Cees van Dam, *European Tort Law* (2nd edn, OUP 2013) 493ff.

[56] See 'Parent and child', 59 Am Jur 2d, § 88.

[57] van Dam (n 55) 501f.

If a minor gains an unjustified enrichment at someone else's expenses (eg the former is paid by the latter for goods that are subsequently not delivered), she owes restitution for that benefit only to the extent that it has remained in her hands.[58]

Under **English law**, article 3(1)(b) of the 1987 Minors' Contracts Act stipulates that where 'the contract is unenforceable against the defendant (or he repudiates it) because he was a minor when the contract was made, the court may, if it is just and equitable to do so, require the defendant to transfer to the plaintiff any property acquired by the defendant under the contract, or any property representing it'. This order cannot be made once the minor has dissipated the property obtained or its proceeds.[59] Outside the scope of such statutory provision, common law grants restitution in a case of fraud committed by the minor, but under the same condition just set out.[60]

2.1. Natural persons

All people are granted legal personhood when they are born, but they attain their capacity to act only after reaching a certain age (**age of majority**),[61] which legal systems generally set out between 18 and 21 years. The rationale of this rule is that people under this age (**minors**) are deemed by law as lacking the sound judgment needed to take a legally binding decision about their own patrimonial and non-patrimonial interests; accordingly, consent is required of those who hold **parental responsibility** over the minor herself, ie her parents or, if there are none, a guardian appointed by the court (see *infra*, this para).[62] Nonetheless, it is generally allowed that, where minors have achieved sufficient discernment and intelligence to understand fully a **medical treatment**, they can choose to undergo it with or without their parents' consent, this rule being referred to in common law jurisdictions as 'Gillick competence'.

In the Gillick case, a Roman Catholic activist, named Victoria Gillick, who then had four daughters under the age of 16, challenged a Memorandum of Guidance issued in May 1974 by the UK's Department of Health and Social Security, according to which contraceptive advice and treatment might be given to a girl under 16 without her parents' consent, provided that doctors had failed to persuade her to involve her parents (or guardian). The plaintiff's action was eventually dismissed by the House of Lords,[63] which thus spelled out the above-mentioned ruling.

[58] For a comparative analysis, see Birke Häcker, 'Minority and Unjust Enrichment Defences' in Andrew Dyson, James Goudkamp and Frederick Wilmot-Smith (eds), *Defences in Unjust Enrichment* (Hart 2016) 195ff.
[59] Ewan McKendrick, 'Contract: in general' in Andrew Burrows (ed) (n 16) para 8.275.
[60] ibid para 8.277.
[61] Jens M Scherpe, 'Comparative Family Law' in Mathias Reimann and Reinhard Zimmermann (eds), *The Oxford Handbook of Comparative Law* (2nd edn, OUP 2019) 1102ff.
[62] Children Act 1989.
[63] Gillick v West Norfolk and Wisbech Area Health Authority [1986] AC 112.

Conversely, most legal systems set out that a court order may deny adults' capacity to act or diminish it (**incapacitation**), when such adults are affected by an impairment or insufficiency of their personal faculties that endangers their own interests (and possibly those of other members of their own family as well), should they perform an ill-advised legal act. As a general rule, a legal act performed by a minor, as well as by an incapacitated adult is **invalid** (see *supra*, ch 9, para 5), unless otherwise settled by the law.

In civil law jurisdictions, most contracts can be entered into by a **legal representative** of a minor or an incapacitated adult, who acts like a statutory proxy or agent of the latter (see *supra*, ch 10, para 3). The legal representatives of a minor are her **parents**: the consent of one of them suffices for acts of ordinary administration on behalf of the minor, whereas for acts of extraordinary administration the consent of both parents is required (and in some cases it must be supplemented by a judicial authorization). When parents are missing or unable to take on their parental responsibility, the legal representative of the minor is her **guardian**, who is appointed by a court and, in her capacity, can enter into a contract on behalf of her **ward**. The same applies to the guardian that can be appointed by a court to an incapacitated adult.

In common law jurisdictions, by contrast, the parents and the guardians (or **conservators**) cannot act as legal representatives for a person who lacks contractual capacity (or **conservatee**),[64] unless they do so under the direction of a court.[65]

2.1.1. Minors

In the case of contracts, it is generally provided that they are null and void when entered into by an **infant**. The threshold of infancy may be drawn by a legal system either by fixing a certain age (of 7 years, in most cases) (Germany, Austria) or by mandating courts to ascertain that the ability of a contracting party to make a rational judgment is lacking due to her infancy and with respect to that specific contract (Switzerland). Some legal systems, however, refrain from declaring contracts void that, although entered into by an infant, are common for persons of her age (Austria, Poland, and Scotland).

When a minor steps beyond the threshold of infancy, some legal systems set forth special requirements under which contracts entered into by her are deemed valid; to that extent, some legal systems refer to a **limited contractual capacity** (Germany: § 106 BGB; but not in France or Italy). The requirements to be met to that end may vary depending on whether the minor has already reached a certain age (14 years, in most cases), which is considered an intermediate stage between infancy and majority (Austria, Greece, Poland, and Scotland). Some of the most common special requirements of the kind are that: 1. The contract relates to necessities (UK and US);[66] 2. The contract is

[64] For US law, see 'Parent and child', 59 Am Jur 2d, § 3.
[65] For US law, see 'Infants', 42 Am Jur 2d, § 39.
[66] For US law, see ibid §§ 56ff.

with regard to an act of ordinary administration and is reasonable in its terms (France); 3. The contract would be entered into by an adult exercising reasonable prudence; 4. The contract provides the minor with a solely juridical advantage (Germany); 5. The contract serves to protect the minor's estate; 6. The minor will perform her side of the bargain with means that were given to her for her free disposal (Germany).[67]

> **English common law** is reflected in section 3(2) Sales of Goods Act 1979, according to which 'where necessaries are sold and delivered to a minor [...], he must pay a reasonable price for them'.[68]
> Under **German law**, a juridical act of a person that lacks the capacity to act does not need her legal representative's consent, insofar as it brings solely a juridical advantage (§ 107 BGB). Furthermore, a minor's contract is valid, if she can perform her part of it with means provided specially or generally by her legal representative or by some third party with the representative's consent (§ 110 BGB, so-called 'pocket money paragraph').[69]
> Article 1148 ***Code civil*** stipulates that all persons lacking the capacity to act can nonetheless perform the ordinary acts authorized by the law or according to usage, provided that their terms are reasonable.[70] Furthermore, article 1151(1) *Code civil* stipulates that the acts of ordinary administration undertaken by a minor may be avoided if they amount to an economic disadvantage.[71]

If contracts entered into by a minor do not meet these requirements, then they are subject to **invalidity**. In some systems, such contracts are affected by nullity (or being void), either relative (France) or absolute; in others, they are voidable (US,[72] Italy). Under German law, contracts entered into by a minor are 'temporarily ineffective'. Under English law, contracts entered into by a minor are avoidable only in four cases, namely contracts concerning land, subscription for shares in companies, partnerships, and marriage settlements;[73] outside these four cases, contracts entered into by a minor become 'limping' contracts, in the sense that they bind only the other contracting party and not the minor herself,[74] unless the latter ratifies them after becoming of age.[75]

[67] Phillip Hellwege, 'Capacity' in *The Max Planck Encyclopedia of European Private Law*, vol 1 (n 22) 137, 139.
[68] For the common law precedents, see McKendrick (n 59) para 8.269.
[69] § 110 BGB: '*Ein von dem Minderjährigen ohne Zustimmung des gesetzlichen Vertreters geschlossener Vertrag gilt als von Anfang an wirksam, wenn der Minderjährige die vertragsmäßige Leistung mit Mitteln bewirkt, die ihm zu diesem Zweck oder zu freier Verfügung von dem Vertreter oder mit dessen Zustimmung von einem Dritten überlassen worden sind*'.
[70] Art 1148 *Code civil*: '*Toute personne incapable de contracter peut néanmoins accomplir seule les actes courants autorisés par la loi ou l'usage, pourvu qu'ils soient conclus à des conditions normales*'.
[71] Art 1151(1) *Code civil*: '*Les actes courants accomplis par le mineur peuvent être annulés pour simple lésion* [...]'.
[72] See 'Infants', 42 Am Jur 2d, §§ 38, 70ff.
[73] McKendrick (n 59) para 8.271; Edwin Peel, *Treitel on the Law of Contract* (14th edn, Sweet & Maxwell 2015) para 12-017ff.
[74] *Farnham v Atkins* (1670) 1 Sid 446; *Bruce v Warwick* (1815) 6 Taunt 118.
[75] *Williams v Moor* (1843) 11 M & W 256.

§ 108(1) **BGB** provides that, if the contract is concluded by a minor without her legal representative's authorization, then the legal effects of that contract depend upon her legal representative's ratification.
Pursuant to article 1147 ***Code civil***, the lack of capacity to act is grounds for relative nullity.
Article 1425(1) ***Codice civile*** provides that a contract is voidable when one of the parties lacked contractual capacity.[76]

A limited contractual capacity (called **emancipation**) can be obtained by a minor to be judicially authorized to contract marriage (Spain, Poland, Turkey, France, Italy, Greece, and the Netherlands). In some legal systems, other factors may trigger emancipation of a minor as well (like enlistment in military service). Less frequently, emancipation may be declared by a court order on a case-by-case basis.[77]
Furthermore, a **special contractual capacity** may be acknowledged for specific types of contracts, most typically those for labor and services,[78] as well as for sports or entertainment services.[79]

Under **English law**, a minor is bound by a contract of employment that is on the whole beneficial to her, even if it contains some disadvantageous terms (unless harsh and oppressive).[80]

2.1.2. Incapacitated adults

Incapacitation of adults has traditionally been provided for cases of mental illness, as well as for pathological or abnormal behavior (because of habitual abuse of alcohol or drugs, excessive wastefulness, etc.). It must generally be declared through a judicial decree, and may be either **complete or partial**, depending on the seriousness of the pathology (see also *supra*, ch 12, para 2.1).
Complete incapacitation tends to be treated similarly to incapacity of minors, and partial incapacitation like limited capacity of the latter.[81] In general terms, therefore, **contracts** entered into by an incapacitated adult are as invalid as those entered into by a minor. In common law jurisdictions, however, contracts entered into with an adult devoid of mental capacity are generally valid, unless the incapacity was known to the other contracting party: in that case, the contract is voidable.[82] Furthermore, if the property of an adult devoid

[76] Art 1425(1) cc: '*Il contratto è annullabile se una delle parti era legalmente incapace di contrarre*'.
[77] For US law, see 'Infants', 42 Am Jur 2d, §§ 8ff; 'Parent and child' 59 Am Jur 2d, §§ 73ff.
[78] For Italian law, see art 2(2) cc. For US law, see 'Infants', 42 Am Jur 2d, §§ 53, 55.
[79] For US law, see 'Infants', 42 Am Jur 2d, §§ 54, 55.
[80] McKendrick (n 59) para 8.270.
[81] Hellwege (n 67) 140.
[82] For UK law, see *Molton v Camroux* (1849) 4 Ex 17; *Imperial Loan Co v Stone* [1892] 1 QB 599. It is controversial whether the contract is also avoidable when the other party did not know of the incapacity but ought to have known of it (see *Dunhill v Burgin* [2014] 1 WLR 933). For US law, see 'Mentally Impaired Persons', 53 Am Jur 2d, § 162.

of mental capacity is subject to the control of the court and she attempts to dispose of such property, it becomes a 'limping' contract (*negotium claudicans*), in the sense that it binds only the other contracting party and not the incapacitated person herself.[83]
As with contracts entered into by a minor, legal systems also tend to set forth some **special requirements** under which contracts entered into by an incapacitated adult are deemed valid. Some of the most common special requirements of the kind are that: 1. The contract relates to necessaries (UK and US);[84] 2. The contract relates to matters of daily life (Germany); 3. The contract provides the minor with a solely juridical advantage (Germany); 4. The contract deals with an act of ordinary administration and is reasonable in its terms (France).

> Article 1148 ***Code civil*** stipulates that all persons devoid of the capacity to act can nonetheless perform only ordinary acts authorized by the law or according to usage, provided that their terms are reasonable.[85]
> Under **German law**, the contract entered into by an incapacitated adult is valid, insofar as it relates to matters of daily life, and does not involve large amounts (§ 105a BGB).[86]

However, the general trend is that incapacities are becoming an old-fashioned notion, which is disappearing insofar as it eventually points to a gross limitation of private autonomy of those involved, particularly people with disabilities, and may even result in a discrimination against them.[87]

> Pursuant to article 12(3) of the **United Nations Convention on the Rights of Persons with Disabilities**, adopted on 13 December 2006 and ratified by the EU,[88] states must 'take appropriate measures to provide access by persons with

[83] *Re Walker* [1905] 1 Ch 160; *Re Marshall* [1920] 1 Ch 284.
[84] For UK law, see Mental Capacity Act 2005, s 7. For US law, see 'Mentally Impaired Persons', 53 Am Jur 2d, § 165.
[85] 1148 *Code civil*: '*Toute personne incapable de contracter peut néanmoins accomplir seule les actes courants autorisés par la loi ou l'usage, pourvu qu'ils soient conclus à des conditions normales*'.
[86] § 105a BGB: '*Tätigt ein volljähriger Geschäftsunfähiger ein Geschäft des täglichen Lebens, das mit geringwertigen Mitteln bewirkt werden kann, so gilt der von ihm geschlossene Vertrag in Ansehung von Leistung und, soweit vereinbart, Gegenleistung als wirksam, sobald Leistung und Gegenleistung bewirkt sind. Satz 1 gilt nicht bei einer erheblichen Gefahr für die Person oder das Vermögen des Geschäftsunfähigen*'.
[87] Gerard Quin and Eilionóir Flynn, 'Transatlantic Borrowings: The Past and Future of EU Non-Discrimination Law and Policy on the Ground of Disability' (2012) 60 Am J Comp L 23.
[88] See the papers collected in the Special Issue of (2006-2007) 34 Syracuse J Int'l L & Com. Furthermore, see Frédéric Mégret, 'The Disabilities Convention: Human Rights of Persons with Disability or Disability Rights' (2008) 30 Human Rights Quarterly 494; Michael Ashley Stein and Janet E Lord, 'Monitoring the Convention on the Rights of Persons with Disabilities: Innovations, Lost Opportunities, and Future Potentials' (2010) 43 Human Rights Quarterly 689; Eilionóir Flynn, *From Rhetoric to Action: Implementing the UN Convention on the Rights of People with Disabilities*, CUP 2011; Peter Barlett, 'The United Nations Convention on the Rights of Persons with Disabilities and Mental Health Law' (2012) 75 MLR 752; Lisa Waddington and Anna Lawson (eds), *The*

disabilities to the support they may require in exercising their legal capacities'. Pursuant to article 12(4), states must ensure that 'measures relating to the exercise of legal capacity respect the rights, will and preferences of the person, are free of conflict of interests and undue influence, are proportional and tailored to the person's circumstances, apply for the shortest time possible and are subject to regular review by a competent, independent and impartial authority or judicial body'.[89] Even if the matter is not covered by the ECHR, the **jurisprudence of the ECtHR** has on several occasions stressed that safeguarding the personal autonomy and ensuring the social inclusion of adults with disabilities is crucial to the realization of the fundamental rights that the ECHR is meant to protect.[90]

As an alternative, new instruments for **administering a weaker party's affairs** have been provided by most legal systems, such as *Betreuung* in Germany, *sauvegarde de justice* in France, and *amministrazione di sostegno* in Italy. Individuals who are in need of legal aid to look after their interests are thus not deprived of their capacity to act but are supported and counseled by an administrator of their affairs, whose powers may be effectively tailored to the needs of the beneficiary.

The contracts entered into by a *Betreute* are valid insofar as they relate to daily matters (§ 1903(3)(2) BGB) or they bring to her solely a juridical advantage (§ 1903(3)(1) BGB).

In cross-border matters, PIL issues have been addressed by the **2000 Hague Convention on the International Protection of Adults**.[91] *Inter alia*, this instrument deals with questions relating to powers of representation that are granted in advance by adults prior to the onset of their incapacity and designed either to survive such incapacity or to take effect upon it (private mandates). More recently, in March 2020, a set of **Model Rules on the Protection of Adults in International Situations** was approved by the ELI;[92] it calls for the issue of a legislative measure by the EU based upon article 81 TFEU.[93]

UN Convention on the Rights of Persons with Disabilities in Practice. A Comparative Analysis of the Role of Courts (CUP 2018); Ilias Bantekas, Michael Ashley Stein and Dimitris Anastasiou, *The UN Convention on the Rights of Persons with Disabilities. A Commentary* (OUP 2018).

[89] See Anna Arnstein-Kerslake and Eilionóir Flynn, 'The General Comment on Article 12 of the Convention on the Rights of Persons with Disabilities: A roadmap for equality before the law' (2016) 20 International Journal of Human Rights 471. For an overall perspective, see the articles collected in the Special Issue 1 of (2017) 13 International Journal of Law in Context.

[90] *Glor v Switzerland*, 30 April 2009; *Shtukaturov v Russia*, 27 March 2008; *Stanev v Bulgaria*, 17 January 2012; *AN v Lithuania*, 31 May 2016.

[91] Concluded on 13 January 2000, it has until now been ratified by a small amount of states. See David Hill, 'The Hague Convention on the International Protection of Adults' (2009) 58 ICLQ 469; Richard Frimston, Alexander Ruck Keene, Claire van Overdijk and Adrian D Ward (eds), *The International Protection of Adults* (OUP 2015); Pietro Franzina, *La protezione degli adulti nel diritto internazionale privato* (CEDAM 2012).

[92] https://www.europeanlawinstitute.eu/projects-publications/completed-projects-old/protection-of-adults/.

[93] See also the study by the European Parliament Research Service, *Protection of Vul-*

A legal transaction performed by a party that (although not being adjudicated as disable) is temporarily out of her senses due to drunkenness, drugs, insanity, etc. can be avoided or repudiated by that party, provided that some strict conditions are met. In some jurisdictions, it is required (by judge-made law) that the disorder is so serious that it fully negates the ability to form contractual will (Germany, France);[94] others require that the counterparty acted dishonestly, ie she was put on notice or was given reason to suspect the other party's incompetence, such as would indicate to a reasonably prudent person that an inquiry should be made into the party's mental condition (Italy, UK, US).[95]

§ 105(2) **BGB** stipulates that a legal act performed by a person who is out of senses or otherwise disturbed is void.[96]
Pursuant to article 414-1 ***Code civil***, a legal act is valid when the person who performed it was sane; otherwise, it is void, but the burden of the proof lies with the party pleading to have the act avoided.[97]
Article 428 ***Codice civile*** sets forth that the legal acts performed by a person devoid of discernment are voidable, provided that the other party may be deemed to have been acting in bad faith, taking the disadvantage actually or potentially sustained by the incapacitated party into consideration as well as the characteristics of the contract entered into.[98] A similar ruling is settled in **common law**.[99]

Adults may also be hit by **punitive incapacities**. Convictions for committing a serious crime can automatically include a **legal disability** (**disqualification**) for the duration of a sentence (forfeiture of offices, etc.). In those cases, the capacity to get married and to make a will is generally retained by the offenders.

nerable Adults. European Added Value Assessment (2016) <https://www.europarl.europa.eu/RegData/etudes/STUD/2016/581388/EPRS_STU(2016)581388_EN.pdf https://iris.unito.it/retrieve/handle/2318/1593518/214566/EPRS_STU%282016%29581388_EN.pdf> accessed 9 March 2020. Particularly, see Pietro Franzina and Joëlle Long, 'The Protection of Vulnerable Adults in EU Member States. The added value of EU action in the light of The Hague Adults Convention' ibid 106.

94 Jan M Smits, *Contract Law: A Comparative Introduction* (2nd edn, Elgar 2017) 98.

95 McKendrick (n 59) para 8.278.

96 § 105(2) BGB: '*Nichtig ist auch eine Willenserklärung, die im Zustand der Bewusstlosigkeit oder vorübergehender Störung der Geistestätigkeit abgegeben wird*'.

97 Art 414-1 *Code civil*: '*Pour faire un acte valable, il faut être sain d'esprit. C'est à ceux qui agissent en nullité pour cette cause de prouver l'existence d'un trouble mental au moment de l'acte*'.

98 Art 428(1-2) cc: '*Gli atti compiuti da persona che, sebbene non interdetta, si provi essere stata per qualsiasi causa, anche transitoria, incapace d'intendere o di volere al momento in cui gli atti sono stati compiuti, possono essere annullati su istanza della persona medesima o dei suoi eredi o aventi causa, se ne risulta un grave pregiudizio all'autore. L'annullamento dei contratti non può essere pronunziato se non quando, per il pregiudizio che sia derivato o possa derivare alla persona incapace d'intendere o di volere o per la qualità del contratto o altrimenti, risulta la malafede dell'altro contraente*'.

99 For UK law, see *Gore v Gibson* (1843) 13 M. & W. 623 (drunkenness) and, for further detail, see Peel (n 73) 12-062 and 12-063. For US law, see 'Mentally Impaired Persons', 53 Am Jur 2d, §§ 163ff.

Testamentary capacity is generally attained at the age of 18 years. In some systems it is also attained by minors that obtain a judicial authorization to contract marriage.[100]

2.2. Legal persons

By its nature, a legal entity, being fictitious, can only act through the agency of natural persons (**legal representatives**) (see *supra*, ch 10, para 3). Legal representatives of a corporation are its managing director(s), whilst those of a partnership are the partners (all or a selected few) themselves.

Under company law, a third party can rely on the legal representatives' statutory authority, since the latter cannot be affected by any 'internal' limitation (albeit enshrined in the bylaws of the corporation), unless a third party was acting in bad faith, ie knew of the limitation or was unaware of it through carelessness.[101]

[100] Sebastian Herrier, 'Wills' in *The Max Planck Encyclopedia of European Private Law*, vol 2 (n 17) 1775.

[101] Hein Kötz, *European Contract Law* (Gill Mertens & Tony Weir trs, 2nd edn, OUP 2017) 302. For English law, see Armour (n 16) paras 3.57-3.59.

GLOSSARY

Administration of the affairs of a protected person [*Sauvegarde de justice*; *Betreuung*; *Amministrazione di sostegno*] (2.1): when an administrator is appointed by a court to support and counsel an adult with physical or mental limitations.

Building society [*Société coopérative immobilière*; *Baugenossenschaft*; *Cooperativa edilizia*] (1.2.1.3): cooperative society that raises money in order to allow its borrowing members to build or buy a house.

Capacity to act [*Capacité d'exercice*; *Handlungsfähigkeit*; *Capacità d'agire*] (2): power either to create or to enter into a legal relationship.

Company law/Corporation law [*Droit des sociétés*; *Gesellschaftsrecht*; *Diritto societario*] (1.2.1): area of private law governing the rights, relations, and conduct of persons, companies, organizations, and businesses.

Contractual capacity (2, 2.1): capacity to enter into a valid contract. Some legal systems provide for a limited contractual capacity of minors.

Corporation [*Société de capitaux*; *Kapitalgesellschaft*; *Società di capitali*] (1.2.1): legal entity that is completely autonomous and separated from the owners as to its property and organization. Consequently, the owners of a corporation are personally not liable (although with exceptions) for the debts owed by the latter.

Emancipation (2.1.1): freeing of a minor from parental control, triggered by the authorization to contract marriage or by other circumstances provided for by the law. It may imply the attainment of a limited contractual capacity.

Friendly society [*Société d'assurance mutuelle*; *Società di mutua assicurazione*] (1.2.1.3): mutual insurance association providing its members with benefits in the event of sickness, death or bereavement.

General (commercial) partnership (GP) [*Société en nom collectif* (SNC, or SENC); *Offene Handelsgesellschaft* [OHG]; *Società in nome collettivo* (snc)] (1.2.1.2): legal entity in which each partner has the power to manage the partnership business and has the joint and several liability for the debts owed by the legal entity.

Guardian (or conservator) [*Tuteur/Curateur*; *Vormund/Beistand*; *Tutore/Curatore*] (2.1): legal institution in which a guardian (or conservator) is appointed by a court to manage the financial affairs and/or daily life of a minor or of an incapacitated adult (ward, or conservatee).

Industrial and provident society [*Consortium, or Groupement*; *Erwerbs- und Wirtschaftsgenossenschaft*; *Consorzio per il coordinamento della produzione e degli scambi*] (1.2.1.3): cooperative society that engages in commercial and industrial activity for its members' mutual benefit or for that of the wider community.

Joint-stock company/public limited company [PLC] [*Société anonyme* (SA)/*Société en commandite par actions* [SCA]; *Aktiengesellschaft* (AG); *Società per azioni* (spa)/ *Società in accomandita per azioni* (sapa)] (1.2.1.1): corporation in which shares of the company can be bought and sold by shareholders on exchanges. Each shareholder owns a proportion of the company stock, evidenced by their shares (ie certificates of ownership). Shareholders are able to transfer their shares to others without any effects on the continued existence of the company.

Legal personhood [*Capacité de jouissance*; *Rechtsfähigkeit*; *Capacità giuridica*] (1): capacity to hold rights and duties. Those whom the law grants the legal personhood are called legal subjects.

Legal representatives (2.1): persons that hold a statutory and general power to act on behalf of another. A legal entity, being fictitious, can only act through the agency of natural persons.

Limited liability company (LLC, or Ltd.) [*Société à responsabilité limitée* (SARL); *Gesellschaft mit beschränkter Haftung* (GmbH); *Società a responsabilità limitata* (srl)] (1.2.1.1): corporation whose shares, albeit transferable, are not tradable on exchanges. LLCs are known for the flexibility that they provide to business owners.

Limited liability partnership (LLP) (1.2.1.2): legal entity that combines some staples of a partnership (eg each partner has the power to manage the partnership business) and others of a corporation (eg limited liability of partners).

Limited partnership (LP) [*Société en commandite simple* (SCS, or SEC); *Kommanditgesellschaft* (KG); *Società in accomandita semplice* (sas)] (1.2.1.2): partnership in which some of the partners are general, others are limited. General partners have exclusive decision-making power and are the sole representatives of an LLP. By contrast, limited partners, being devoid of any decision-making and representation powers for an LLP, are liable solely for the amount contributed under the limited partnership agreement.

Limping contract [*Negotium claudicans*] (2.1.1, 2.1.2): contract concluded by a minor without the consent of a guardian. The other party is not entitled to invalidate the contract, whereas the guardian can choose to uphold the contract or to repudiate it. The contract can also be ratified by the minor when she becomes of adult age.

Marriage capacity (2, 2.1.1, 2.1.2): capacity to contract marriage. Through emancipation a minor is also judicially authorized to contract marriage.

Partnership [*Société de personnes*; *Personengesellschaft*; *Società di persone*] (1.2.1.2): legal entity that is only partially autonomous and separated from its owners as to its property and organization. Consequently, the owners of a corporation (or a limited selection of them) are personally liable for the debts owed by the latter.

Punitive incapacities [*Interdizione legale*] (2.1.2): sanctions, applicable to persons for committing a serious crime, that determine the loss of the capacity (power) to act.

Testamentary capacity (2, 2.1.2): capacity to make and to modify a valid will. In some systems, testamentary capacity is attained by minors that obtain a judicial authorization to contract marriage (emancipation).

BIOGRAPHIES

Adolf Augustus Berle (Boston, 1895 – New York, 1971) was an American jurist, professor, and US diplomat, known for his groundbreaking works on corporate governance.

In 1916, at age of 21, he became the youngest graduate in the Harvard Law School's history. Upon graduation, Berle joined the US military. Immediately after World War I, Berle became a member of the American delegation to the Paris Peace Conference, advocating for smaller nations' rights of self-determination. In 1919, Berle moved to New York City and became a member of the law firm of Berle, Berle and Brunner. He became a Professor of Corporate Law at Columbia Law School in 1927 and remained on the faculty until retiring in 1964.

Berle served as Ambassador to Brazil from 1945 to 1946 and then returned to his academic career at Columbia. He was a founding member of the Liberal Party of New York, and his main goal was to fight off far-left and Communist influences. Berle briefly returned to government service for the first half of 1961, serving under President John F. Kennedy as head of an interdepartmental task force on Latin American affairs. During that time, he was primarily involved in forming the US response to a newly communist Cuba.

His main works are: *Studies in the Law of Corporation Finance* (1928); *Cases and Materials in the Law of Corporation Finance* (1930); (with Gardiner C Means) *The Modern Corporation and Private Property* (1932); *The Emerging Common*

Law of Free Enterprise: Antidote to the Omnipotent State? (1951); *Legal Problems of Economic Power* (1960); *The American Economic Republic* (1963); *Property, Production and Revolution* (1965); *The Three Faces of Power* (1967).

Gardiner Coit Means (Windham, Connecticut, 1896 – Vienna, Virginia, 1988) was an American economist, who followed the institutionalist tradition of economists. He entered Harvard and while a student there, he enlisted in the Army in 1917. After World War I ended, he went back to Harvard earning a master's degree in 1927 and did economic research at the Columbia Law School for four years, receiving his doctorate in economics from Harvard in the process.
During the New Deal, Means served as an economic adviser to Franklin D. Roosevelt and Henry A. Wallace. In 1934, he coined the term 'administered prices' to refer to prices set by firms in monopoly positions. Means observed that in some industries, such as steel, oil, and automobiles, prices were more inflexible than in other product lines, and he reasoned that large producers in those industries were able to 'administer' prices without regard for the level of demand. Instead of reducing prices when demand fell, they cut production to lower their costs, thereby maintaining profits.
His main works are: (with Adolf A Berle) *The Modern Corporation and Private Property* (1932); *Industrial Prices and their Relative Inflexibility* (1935); *Patterns of Resource Use* (1938); *The Structure of the American Economy* (1939); *Pricing Power and the Public Interest* (1962); *The Corporate Revolution in America* (1962); *Simultaneous Inflation and Unemployment: Challenge to theory and policy* (1975).

Peter Singer (Melbourne, 1946) is an Australian moral philosopher. He is one of the most important contemporary thinkers in the field of ethics and defined as 'the most influential living philosopher' with his theses, always controversial, at the core of the debate. Singer studied law, history, and philosophy at the University of Melbourne, gaining his Bachelor of Arts degree in 1967. In 1969, he entered the University of Oxford, receiving a Bachelor of Philosophy degree in 1971 and serving as Radcliffe Lecturer in Philosophy at University College from 1971 to 1973. Returning to Australia, he lectured at La Trobe University (1975-1976) and was appointed Professor of Philosophy at Monash University in 1977. In 1999, he was appointed Ira W. DeCamp Professor of Bioethics in the University Center for Human Values at Princeton University. He is also professor at the Centre for Applied Philosophy and Public Ethics at the University of Melbourne. Known to the public especially as the 'prophet of animal liberation', his reflection is not limited to animal rights; it also embraces broader issues in the field of ethics and in particular of applied ethics, ranging from the respect for the environment to abortion, from euthanasia to political ethics, from the poor distribution of wealth to the responsibility of rich countries for World War II, representing an articulated system of thought among the most innovative and courageous of the contemporary era (according to him, old morals are to be set aside and, to this end, he proposes to replace them with five new commandments). He is currently the Director of the Centre of Human Bioethics at Monash University in Melbourne. His most famous work is *Animal Liberation* (1975), in which he exposes his theses against speciesism.

His main works are: *Democracy and Disobedience* (1973); *Animal Liberation: A New Ethics for Our Treatment of Animals* (1975); *Practical Ethics* (1979); *The Expanding Circle* (1981); *A Companion to Ethics* (1991); *Rethinking Life and Death: The Collapse of Our Traditional Ethics* (1994); *A Darwinian Left* (1999); *Writings on an Ethical Life* (2000); *One World: Ethics and Globalization* (2002); *The Way we Eat: Why Our Food Choices Matter* (2006); *Living Ethically in the Twenty First Century: Contemporary Society and Practical Ethics* (2008); *The Life You Can Save* (2009); *The Most Good You Can Do. How Effective Altruism is Changing Ideas About Living Ethically* (2015).

Bibliography

Bibliography

CHAPTER 1

Sociology of law (legal sociology)

Roger Cotterell, *The Sociology of Law: An Introduction* (2nd edn, Butterworths 1992); Id, 'Sociology of Law', *Encyclopedia of Law & Society: American and Global Perspectives* (David S Clark 2007) vol 3, 1413; Manfred Rehbinder, *Rechtssoziologie* (8th edn, CH Beck 2014).

Anthropology of law (legal anthropology)

Mark Goodale and Elizabeth Mertz, 'Anthropology of law', *Encyclopedia of Law & Society. American and Global Perspectives* (2007) vol 1, 68; Simon Roberts, *Order and Dispute: An Introduction to Legal Anthropology* (2nd edn, Quid Pro Books 2013); Wolfgang Fikentscher, *Law and Anthropology* (2nd edn, CH Beck-Hart-Nomos 2016); Mark Goodale, *Anthropology of Law: A Critical Introduction* (New York UP 2017); James AR Nafziger (ed), *Comparative Law and Anthropology* (Edward Elgar 2017).

Ethnology of law (legal ethnology)

Leopold J Pospíšil, *The Ethnology of Law* (2nd edn, Cummings 1978).

Digital law

Alberto De Franceschi (ed), *European Contract Law and the Digital Single Market: The Implications of the Digital Revolution* (Intersentia 2016); Francisco X Olleros and Majlinda Zeghu (eds), *Research Handbook on Digital Transformations* (Edward Elgar 2016); David J Harvey, *Collisions in the Digital Paradigm: Law and Rule-making in the Internet Age* (Hart 2017); Stefan Grundmann (ed), *European Contract Law in the Digital Age* (Intersentia 2018); Nikita Aggarwal, Horst Eidenmüller, Luca Enriques, Jennifer Payne and Kristen van Zwieten (eds), *Autonomous Systems and the Law* (CH Beck-Nomos 2019); Alberto De

Franceschi and Reiner Schulze (eds), *Digital Revolution – New Challenges for Law* (CH Beck-Nomos 2019); Adrien van der Branden, *Les robots à l'assaut de la justice. L'intelligence artificielle au service des justiciables* (Bruylant 2019); Martin Fries and Boris P Paal (eds), *Smart Contracts* (Mohr Siebeck 2019); Jean-Benoît Hubin, Hervé Jacquemin and Benoît Michaux (eds), *Le juge et l'algorithme : juges augmentés ou justice diminuée?* (Lefebvre Belgium 2019).

Law and language

Andrei Marmor and Scott Soames (eds), *Philosophical Foundations of Language in the Law* (OUP 2011); Peter M Tiersma and Lawrence M Solan (eds), *Language and Law* (OUP 2012); Michael Freeman and Fiona Smith (eds), *Law and Language* (OUP 2013); Harold J Berman, *Law and Language: Effective Symbols of Community* (CUP 2013).

CHAPTER 2

Western legal tradition

Harold J Berman, *Law and Revolution: The Formation of the Western Legal Tradition* (Harvard UP 1985); Manlio Bellomo, *The Common Legal Past of Europe, 1000-1800* (Lydia G Cochrane tr, Catholic University of America Press 1995); Reinhard Zimmermann, *The Law of Obligations: Roman Foundations of the Civilian Tradition* (OUP 1996); Paolo Grossi, *L'Europa del diritto* (Laterza 2007); Aldo Schiavone, *The Invention of Law in the West* (The Belknap Press of Harvard UP 2012); James Gordley, *The Jurist: A Critical History* (OUP 2013).

History of European codifications

Helmut Coing and Walter Wilhelm (eds), *Wissenschaft und Kodifikation des Privatrechts im 19. Jahrhundert*, 6 vols (Klostermann 1974-1982); Carlo A Cannata and Antonio Gambaro, *Lineamenti di storia della giurisprudenza europea*, vol 2 (Giappichelli 1989); Uwe Wesel, *Geschichte des Rechts in Europa* (CH Beck 2010); Antonio Padoa Schioppa, *A History of Law in Europe: From the Early Middle Ages to the Twentieth Century* (CUP 2017).

CHAPTER 3

Fundamentals of comparative law

Konrad Zweigert and Hein Kötz, *An Introduction to Comparative Law* (Tony Weir tr, 3rd edn, OUP 1998); Giuseppe B Portale, *Lezioni di diritto privato comparato* (2nd edn, Giappichelli 2007); Mauro Bussani and Ugo Mattei (eds), *The Cambridge Companion to Comparative Law* (CUP 2012); Jan M Smits (ed), *Elgar Encyclopedia of Comparative Law* (2nd edn, Edward Elgar 2012); Geoffrey Samuel, *An Introduction to Comparative Law Theory and Method* (Hart 2014); Rodolfo Sacco and Piercarlo Rossi, *Introduzione al diritto comparato* (6th edn,

UTET 2015); Uwe Kischel, *Comparative Law* (Andrew Hammer tr, OUP 2019); Mathias Reimann and Reinhard Zimmermann (eds), *The Oxford Handbook of Comparative Law* (2nd edn, OUP 2019). For a *reference work*, see Konrad Zweigert and Ulrich Drobnig (eds), *International Encyclopedia of Comparative Law*, 17 vols (BRILL, 1971-2018). For *casebooks*, see Ugo A Mattei, Teemu Ruskola and Antonio Gidi, *Schlesinger's Comparative Law: Cases-Text-Materials* (7th edn, Foundation Press 2009); James Gordley, Hao Jiang and Arthur T von Mehren, *An Introduction to the Comparative Study of Private Law: Readings, Cases, Materials* (CUP 2019).

Methods of comparative law

Andrew Harding and Esin Örücü (eds), *Comparative Law in the 21st Century* (Kluwer Academic Publisher 2002); Mark van Hoecke (ed), *Epistemology and Methodology of Comparative Law* (Hart 2004); Pier G Monateri (ed), *Methods of Comparative Law* (Edward Elgar 2012); Jaakko Husa, *A New Introduction to Comparative Law* (Hart 2015); Günter Frankenberg, *Comparative Law as Critique* (Edward Elgar 2016); Maurice Adams, Jaakko Husa and Marieke Oderkerk (eds), *Comparative Law Methodology* (Edward Elgar 2017); Mathias Siems, *Comparative Law* (2nd edn, CUP 2018).

Families of legal systems

H Patrick Glenn, *Legal Traditions of the World* (5th edn, OUP 2014); Gilles Cuniberti, *Grands systèmes de droit contemporains. Introduction au droit comparé* (3rd edn, LGDJ 2015); René David, Camille Jauffret-Spinosi and Marie Goré, *Les grands systèmes de droit contemporains* (12th edn, Dalloz 2016).

International private law

Jürgen Basedow, Giesela Rühl, Franco Ferrari and Pedro de Miguel Asensio (eds), *Encyclopedia of Private International Law*, 4 vols (Edward Elgar 2017). For a *casebook*, see Horatia Muir Watt, Lucia Bíziková, Agatha Brandão de Oliveira and Diego P Fernández Arroyo (eds), *Global Private International Law: Adjudication without Frontiers* (Edward Elgar 2019).

Uniform law

Larry A DiMatteo, André Janssen, Ulrich Magnus and Reiner Schulze (eds), *International Sales Law. Contract, Principles & Practice* (CH Beck-Hart-Nomos 2016); Peter Mankowski, *Commercial Law* (Nomos 2019).

CHAPTER 4

Common law tradition

Geoffrey Samuel, *A Short Introduction to the Common Law* (Edward Elgar 2013); Ugo Mattei and Emanuele Ariano, *Il modello di* common law (5th edn, Giappichelli 2018).

Civil law tradition

John H Merryman, *The Civil Law Tradition: An Introduction to the Legal Systems of Western Europe and Latin America* (2nd edn, Stanford UP 1985).

Scandinavian jurisdictions

Pia Letto-Vanamo, Ditlev Tamm and Bent O Gram Mortensen (eds), *Nordic Law in European Context* (Springer 2019).

Mixed jurisdictions

Reinhard Zimmermann, Daniel Visser and Kenneth Reid, *Mixed Legal Systems in Comparative Perspective: Property and Obligations in Scotland and South Africa* (OUP 1985); Vernon V Palmer (ed), *Mixed Jurisdictions Worldwide: The Third Legal Family* (2nd edn, CUP 2012).

CHAPTER 5

Philosophy of law

Jules L Colemann, Kenneth E Himma and Scott J Shapiro (eds), *The Oxford Handbook of Jurisprudence and Philosophy of Law* (OUP 2004); Martins P Golding and William A Edmundson (eds), *The Blackwell Guide to the Philosophy of Law and Legal Theory* (Blackwell Publishing 2005); Johan Braun, *Einführung in die Rechtsphilosophie: der Gendake des Rechts* (2nd edn, Mohr Siebeck 2011); Joel Feinberg, Julius Coleman and Christopher Kutz (eds), *Philosophy of Law* (9th edn, Wordsworth 2013); Winfried Hassemer, Ulfried Nuemann and Frank Saliger (eds), *Einführung in die Rechtsphilosophie und Rechtstheorie der Gegenwart* (9th edn, CF Müller 2016).

History of philosophy of law

Enrico Pattaro (ed), *A Treatise of Legal Philosophy and General Jurisprudence* (Springer 2005-2016).

CHAPTER 7

Concept of private law

James Gordley, *Foundations of Private Law: Property, Tort, Contract, Unjust Enrichment* (OUP 2007); Ernst J Weinrib, *The Idea of Private Law* (OUP 2015).

General doctrines of private law

Jan M Smits, *Advanced Introduction to Private Law* (Edward Elgar 2017); Jaap Hage, Antonia Waltermann and Bram Akkermans (eds), *Introduction to Law* (2nd edn, Springer 2017).

American legal realism

Wilfrid E Rumble Jr., *American Legal Realism: Scepticism, Reform, and the Judicial*

Process (Cornell UP 1968); William W Fisher III, Morton J Horwitz and Thomas A Reed (eds), *American Legal Realism* (OUP 1993); John H Schlegel, *American Legal Realism and Empirical Social Science* (University of North Carolina Press 1995); William Twining, *Karl Llewellyn and the Realistic Movement* (2nd edn, CUP 2012); Lawrence M Friedman, *A History of American Law* (3rd edn, OUP 2019).

Law and economics

Guido Calabresi, *The Costs of Accident: A Legal and Economic Analysis* (Yale UP 1970); Guido Calabresi and A Douglas Melamed, 'Property Rules, Liability Rules, and Inalienability: One View of the Cathedral' (1972) 85 Harvard LR 1089; Guido Calabresi and Philip Bobbitt, *Tragic Choices: The Conflicts Society Confronts in the Allocation of Tragically Scarce Resources* (WW Norton & Co 1978); Ugo Mattei, *Comparative Law and Economics* (University of Michigan Press 1997); Gerrit de Geest and Roger van der Bergh (eds), *Comparative Law and Economics*, 3 vols (Edward Elgar 2004); Nicholas Mercuro and Steven G Medema, *Economics and the Law. From Posner to Postmodernism and Beyond* (2nd edn, Princeton UP 2006); A Mitchell Polinsky, *An Introduction to Law and Economics* (4th edn, Wolters Kluwer 2011); Richard A Posner, *Economic Analysis of Law* (9th edn, Wolters Kluwer 2014); Robert B Cooter Jr and Thomas Ulen, *Law and Economics* (6th eds, Pearson 2014); Theodore Einsenberg and Giovanni B Ramello (eds), *Comparative Law and Economics* (Edward Elgar 2016); Guido Calabresi, *The Future of Law & Economics: Essays in Reform and Recollection* (Yale UP 2016).

CHAPTER 8

European private law

Mauro Bussani and Franz Werro (eds), *European Private Law: A Handbook*, 2 vols (Stämpfli-Sakkoulas-Carolina Academic Press-Bruylant 2009-2014); Arthur S Hartkamp, Martijn W Hesselink, Ewoud H Hondius, Chantal Mak and C Edgar du Perron (eds), *Towards a European Civil Code* (4th edn, Wolters Kluwer, Ars Aequi Libri 2011); Jürgen Basedow, Klaus J Hopt, Reinhard Zimmermann and Andreas Stier (eds), *The Max Planck Encyclopedia of European Private Law*, 2 vols (OUP 2012).

History of European private law

Helmut Coing, *Europäisches Privatrecht*, 2 vols (CH Beck 1985-1989).

European legal methodology

Karl Riesenhuber (ed), *European Legal Methodology* (Intersentia 2017).

European contract law

Stefan Grundmann, *Europäisches Schuldvertragsrecht. Das Recht der Unternehmensgeschäfte* (2nd edn, de Gruyter 2017); Hein Kötz, *European Contract Law*

(2nd edn, Gill Mertens and Tony Weir trs, OUP 2017); Nils Jansen and Reinhard Zimmermann (eds), *Commentaries on European Contract Laws* (OUP 2018); Reiner Schulze and Fryderyk Zoll, *European Contract Law* (2nd edn, CH Beck-Hart-Nomos 2018). For a *textbook*, see Filippo Ranieri, *Europäisches Obligationenrecht. Ein Handbuch mit Texten und Materialien* (3rd edn, Springer 2009).

CHAPTER 9

Legal facts and their classification

Alfred Manigk, *Das rechtswirksame Verhalten* (de Gruyter 1939).

Legal acts

Manfred Wolf and Jörge Neuner, *Allgemeiner Teil des Bürgerlichen Rechts* (11th edn, CH Beck 2016); Dieter Medicus and Jens Petersen, *Allgemeiner Teil des BGB* (11th edn, CF Müller 2016).

CHAPTER 10

Legal relations and legal positions

Carl Wellman, *A Theory of Rights* (Rowman & Allanheld 1985); Matthew H Kramer, Nigel E Simmonds and Hillel Steiner, *A Debate over Rights: Philosophical Enquiries* (OUP 1998, reprint 2002); Robert Stevens, *Torts and Rights* (OUP 2007); Donal Nolan and Andrew Robertson (eds), *Rights and Private Law* (Hart 2012).

CHAPTER 11

European and comparative company law

Klaus J Hopt and Harald Baum (eds), *Corporate Governance in Context* (OUP 2005); Mads Andenas and Frank Woodridge, *European Comparative Company Law* (CUP 2009); Paul Davies, *Introduction to Company Law* (2nd edn, OUP 2010); Stefan Grundmann, *European Company Law* (2nd edn, Intersentia 2012); Reiner Kraakman, John Armour, Paul Davies, Luca Enriques, Henry Hansmann, Gerard Hertig, Klaus Hopt, Hideki Kanda, Mariana Pargendler, Wolf-Georg Ringe and Edward Rock, *The Anatomy of Corporate Law: A Comparative and Functional Approach* (3rd edn, OUP 2017); Carsten Gerner-Beuerle and Michael Schillig, *Comparative Company Law* (OUP 2019). For casebooks, see Marco Ventoruzzo, Pierre-Henri Conac, Gen Goto, Sebastian Mock, Mario Notari and Arad Reisberg, *Corporations: A Comparative Perspective* (West Academic Publishing 2017); Mathias Siems and David Cabrelli (eds), *Comparative Company Law: A Case-Based Approach* (Hart 2018); Andreas Cahn and David C Donald, *Comparative Company Law: Text and Cases on the Laws Governing Corporations in Germany, the UK and the USA* (2nd edn, CUP 2018).

MISTO
Carta | A sostegno della gestione forestale responsabile
FSC® C001596

Printed by Tipografia Casma, Bologna - Italy -
(September 2025)